GLOBAL BUSINESS NEGOTIATION

GLOBAL BUSINESS NEGOTIATION

Dr. A.N. Sarkar

PENTAGON PRESS

Global Business Negotiation / Dr. A.N. Sarkar

ISBN 978-81-8274-471-4

First Edition 2010

Published by

PENTAGON PRESS
206, Peacock Lane, Shahpur Jat,
New Delhi-110049
Phones: 011-64706243, 26491568
Telefax: 011-26490600
email: rajan@pentagonpress.in
website: www.pentagonpress.in

Printed at
Print Perfect, Noida.

Contents

Preface

Negotiation is conceived to be a process of interactions involving two individuals or groups reaching a joint agreement about differing needs or ideas. Negotiation can also be seen as a kind of social interaction for reaching an agreement for two or more parties with different objectives or interests that they think are important. In cross-cultural negotiation, the situations are more complicated because of different cultures, environments, communication styles, political systems, ideologies, traditions and customs. Negotiation applies knowledge from the fields of communications, sales, marketing, psychology, sociology, politics, economics, trade, and international businesses and even in conflict resolution. Whenever an economic transaction takes place or a dispute is settled, negotiation does occur. The Latin root of the word '*negotiatus*' means to "carry on business". In modern Spanish '*negocios*' means 'business'. A modern definition of negotiation is two or more parties with common and conflicting interests who enter into a process of interaction with the goal of reaching an agreement (preferably of mutual benefit). Negotiation, in practical term, is a decision-making process that provides opportunities for the parties to exchange commitments or promises through which they will resolve their disagreements and reach an amicable settlement.

A business negotiation may be viewed as a formal affair that takes place across the proverbial bargaining table, in which one debates over price and performance or a complex term of partnership ventures. Given the role and significance of negotiations in our personal and professional lives it is increasingly becoming important to improve upon our negotiation skills to expand business horizons. Negotiations in the context of International business lie at the heart of international diplomacy. Parties (viz. governments, businesses, and non-governmental organizations) employ the art and science of negotiation to protect and advance their organizational and constituent interests. The skillful use of negotiation can advance a party's interests and help to avoid a less attractive alternative, e.g., trade wars, litigation, or protracted dispute settlement procedures under the WTO regime. International negotiations in the broad context of trade relations may include negotiations over prices, tariffs, and sales or qualitative negotiations over broad principles related to the environmental, labour, health, safety and environment, or other emerging disputes and impacts of trade related agreements.

Types of Negotiation

Depending upon the situation and time, the way the negotiations are to be conducted differs. The skills of negotiations depend and differ widely from one situation to the other. Basically, the types can be divided into three broad categories, namely Day-to-Day/Managerial Negotiation, Commercial Negotiation, and Legal Negotiation. There are two relatively distinct types of negotiation - namely *distributive negotiations* and *integrative negotiations.* The Negotiation Experts' training courses teach both methods, as both are essential to negotiate successfully in business. The term distributive means there is a giving out; or the scattering of things. By its mere nature, there is a limit or finite amount in the thing being distributed or divided amongst the people involved. Hence, this type of negotiation is often referred to as *'The Fixed Pie'*. There is only so much to go around, but the proportion to be distributed is limited but also variable. *Distributive bargaining,* in essence, implies the old adage 'Play your cards close to your chest - Give little or no information to the other side'. The word *integrative* means to join several parts into a whole. Conceptually, this implies some cooperation, or a joining of forces to achieve something together. Usually this type of negotiation involves a higher degree of trust and a forming of a reliable and sustained relationship. Both parties want to walk away feeling they have achieved something which has value by getting what each wants. Ideally, it is a twofold process. In the real world of business, the results often tilt in favour of one party over the other because it is unlikely that both parties will come to the table at even strength, when they begin the talks. All the same, distributive bargaining should ideally be concluded in a 'win-win' situation

Major Elements of Negotiation

All negotiators have *interests, power* and all negotiators have *strategies to evolve and work through.* For the limited purpose, efforts may be focused on dealing with these three negotiation elements that are conceived to be the 'Core' areas to trigger a *negotiation process.* An understanding of the major elements of negotiation together with its concept is a necessary step to comprehend the negotiation process. But how the negotiation process operates in the cross-cultural context is still a puzzle for most of us and therefore our endeavor should be to use a comprehensive approach. *Negotiation* is the process whereby interested parties resolve disputes, agree upon courses of action, bargain for individual or collective advantage, and/or attempt to craft outcomes which serve their mutual interests. It is usually regarded as a form of *alternative dispute resolution.*

Stages in the Negotiation Process

Stages in the negotiation process are: (i) orientation and fact finding, (ii) resistance, (iii) reformulation of strategies, (iv) hard-bargaining and decision-making, (v) agreement, and (vi) follow-up. Resistance surfaces as pricing and delivery expectations are negotiated. Strategies are reformulated as the parties determine motivation and constraints. Key issues surface as hard bargaining begins. Problems surface, and solutions—such as creative financing or dealer trades—are created to counter pricing and delivery problems. After details are negotiated, the agreement is ratified. Even as different approaches to negotiation across national or international cultures are identified, change is a constant apparent. International business culture tends to privilege Western approaches to negotiation, centered around the pivot of problem-solving and linear communication, as do many settings and formatting to reach a predetermined goal. As Western norms are balanced with Eastern and Southern values, and local traditions are balanced with regional and national approaches, negotiation practices continue their global evolution based on unique corporate as well as institutional experiences over a period of time.

Negotiation Style

Negotiation style varies with the persons, their beliefs and skills, as well as the general context in which hey occur. A number of different negotiation styles may evolve and be considered from different viewpoints and situational perspectives while transacting a business negotiation. These may include: *Belief-based styles* (e.g. collaborative, competitive, balanced negotiation); *Professional styles* (e.g. industrial relation, managing board, international politics & diplomacy, emotional intelligence-based bargaining), *Contextual styles* (e.g. Domestic, everyday, hierarchical). There is a *de facto* Spectrum of Negotiation Styles that may exist- both implicitly and explicitly. Although negotiation styles can be classified as concessional, competitive or collaborative, in practice there are a range of styles, based on the degree to which a person thinks about themselves or thinks about the other person. There is a *de facto* Spectrum of Negotiation Styles that may exist- both implicitly and explicitly. However, the bottom line of all conceivable forms of negotiation should universally unify three approaches of negotiation- *Consideration for self, Consideration for others, a mid-way.*

Two more styles of negotiating, *competitive and cooperative*, are commonly recognized. No negotiation is purely one type or the other; rather, negotiators typically move back and forth between the two styles based on the situation. On one end of the negotiation continuum is the competitive style. *Competitive negotiation*—also called adversarial, non-cooperative, distributive bargaining, positional, or hard bargaining—is used to divide limited resources; the assumption is that the pie to be divided is finite. Competitive strategies assume a "win-lose" situation in which the negotiating parties have opposing interests. Hostile, coercive negotiation tactics are used to force an advantage, and pre-negotiation binding agreements are not allowed. Concessions, distorted communication, confrontational tactics, and emotional ploys are also used. Skilled competitive negotiators give away less information while acquiring more information, ask more questions, create strategies to get information, act firm, offer less generous opening offers, are slower to give concessions, use confident body language, and conceal feelings. They are more interested in the bargaining position and bottom line of the other negotiating party, and they prepare for negotiations by developing strategy, planning answers to weak points, and preparing alternate strategies.

Negotiation Analysis Spectrum

Negotiation is the process of joint decision-making. In international politics, negotiation consists of discussions between officially designated representatives designed to achieve a formal agreement of their governments to the way forward on an issue that is either of shared concern or in dispute between them. Business negotiations, in turn, may be understood as encounters between economic organizations with the goal of reaching agreements to provide economic benefits. Negotiations take place in all domains of life, but the structure and pattern of negotiations are fundamentally the same at a personal level as they are at diplomatic and corporate levels. There seems to be four characteristics common to all international negotiation situations: *First*, there are two or more parties; *Second*, the parties can cooperate to arrive at a joint decision; *Third*, the payoffs to any party depend either on the consequences of the joint decision or alternatives external to the negotiations; *Fourth*, the parties can reciprocally and directly exchange information. Parties may refer to individuals or groups of individuals. However, ultimately it is individuals who interact, for their own purposes or as agents for groups. The concepts of party, individual, decision maker, agent, player, and actor can therefore be considered synonymous in this context: they all refer to a single, unitary decision entity. Groups consist of plural unitary decision makers, but when their interests are shared enough, an abstraction is often made and a group is treated as a unitary decision entity.

Pre-negotiation Preparation and Issues

International marketers are increasingly becoming business negotiators, constantly discussing deals across borders with a variety of people, ranging from consumers to intermediaries and even competitors. The ability to interact effectively with foreign trade partners may well depend on the adjustments made to culturally diverse backgrounds encountered during sales negotiations. In the planning cycle of international management, the negotiation stage is the link between strategic planning and implementation with focus on cross-cultural aspects. The most important aspects of culture for international business negotiations are time, individual versus collective behaviour, pattern of communication and emphasis on personal relations. Stereotypically, many Westerners are heavily focused on time while Latin Americans and Africans find it less important. Another difference across cultures is the degree of *individualism versus collectivism*. In some cultures, the negotiator is more important than the issue at hand or the future relationship between the parties hence is the emphasis on personal relations different. All different aspects of culture have a common consequence and that is that they are aggravating the essential understanding of the counterpart. Another occurring problem is that members of one culture may focus on different aspects of an agreement from members of another culture. When one takes the seemingly simple process of negotiations into a cross-cultural context, it becomes even more complex and complications tend to grow exponentially. A fundamental characteristic of negotiations is the existence of conflict as well as co-operation in the relationship. To some extent, especially in "win-win" negotiation, the two parties have a common interest in finding a solution that is optimal and suitable with regard to the supplier's ability and the user's requirements. Basically, the two parties do need to complement each other.

Best Alternatives to Negotiated Agreement (BATNA)

Parties negotiate in order to better satisfy the complete range of their interests through some jointly determined action than could otherwise be done. In practically all situations, negotiators have outside alternatives that they can turn to, should they fail to reach an agreement in current negotiations. The Best of the Alternatives to a *Negotiated Agreement* is denoted by the acronym BATNA. This is a game theoretic component underlying every negotiation: a party always has the option of taking unilateral action to pursue payoffs outside of the negotiations. Thus a basic test of a proposed agreement is whether it offers a better payoff than that side's best alternative course of action outside of the negotiations. This condition is also known as individual rationality. The payoff of each player's BATNA, therefore, places a lower priority on the payoff that the party must realize from a negotiated settlement. Taken together, these minimum payoffs define the disagreement point, an equivalent of the non-cooperative Nash equilibrium concept. The region of agreements beyond each party's BATNA, in the direction of increasing payoffs, delineates the agreements that are individually rational for both parties Alternatives to negotiated agreement also play a tactical role. The more favourable alternative courses of action negotiators have, the smaller the need for the negotiation and the higher the standard of value that negotiators can expect from any proposed agreement. Research shows that negotiators with more attractive BATNA's capture a greater share of the negotiation zone. Therefore, maneuvering "away from the table" can also strongly affect negotiated outcomes, even more than the strategies employed "at the table." Searching for a better price or an alternative supplier are examples of developing alternatives away from the negotiation table.

Zone of Possible Agreement (ZOPA)

Zopa is an England-based company providing an online money exchange service, allowing people who have money to lend it to those who wish to borrow, instead of using savings accounts and loan applications at traditional banks. The process is sometimes referred to as peer-to-peer lending. Zopa acts as the man in the middle operating the markets. The name, Zopa, stands for Zone of Possible Agreement, a negotiating term identifying the bounds within which agreement can be reached between two parties. A "Zone of Possible

Agreement" (ZOPA) exists if there is a potential agreement that would benefit both sides more than their alternative options do. If both sides know their BATNAs and walk away positions, the parties should be able to communicate, assess proposed agreements, and eventually identify the ZOPA. However, parties often do not know their own BATNAs, and are even less likely to know the other side's BATNA. Shared uncertainties may also affect the parties' abilities to assess potential agreements because the parties may be unrealistically optimistic or pessimistic about the possibility of agreement or the value of alternative options. The nature of the ZOPA depends on the type of negotiation. In case of Integrative negotiation it results in creating value or "enlarging the pie."

International Negotiations between Countries

International negotiation is as it says: inter-national. It is about negotiation between countries. International negotiation occurs all the time between governments. It also happens between individuals and companies, where the traps and tricks of cross-border negotiation can ensnare even the most experienced home-country negotiators. International negotiation is often not just between individual people, but between large delegations, each of which is well organized and where every person has specialized and skilled work. There may be cultural experts, linguists and subject specialists as well as a chief negotiator and support negotiators. In a complex negotiation, there may be multiple and interlined sub-negotiations going on at the same time, for example where a trade negotiation includes deal involving various industries and interests.

Breakthrough Business Negotiations

Negotiating is much more complicated than making an offer and fielding a counter-offer. It's a complex process that can affect the future of individuals and organizations. A "breakthrough negotiator" must analyze, plan, sell, organize and motivate. The best negotiators are also leaders. They bring together a team of players and guide them in all-out battle against the opposition. Top negotiators do not obtain their skills by accident—they learn from experience and studying the art of negotiating. However complicated a negotiation is, it can be understood by breaking it down into its key parts and actions. Every negotiation has a structure: It involves certain people and issues which produce predictable interactions. Thorough analysis of a situation and its structure is an essential negotiating skill and a hallmark of breakthrough negotiators. Breakthrough negotiators never treat the structure of a negotiation as preordained or fixed. In other words, the hand can be played as it is dealt, but it can also be changed. Skilled negotiators can change the structure by inviting additional parties and transforming two-party negotiations into multi-party negotiations. When negotiating stems from clear-eyed analysis, efforts to shape the structure can have a powerful impact on outcomes.

Culture and Negotiation Ethics

Understanding the relationship between culture and *negotiation ethics* is a major challenge for global managers. Today multinational firms consider the task of understanding the cultural and ethical orientations of their global partners a major priority for successfully operating in the global market. Hofstede defines culture as "the collective programming of the mind which distinguishes the members of one group or category of people from another." Christie and associates found that culture has a strong influence on ethical attitudes. Culture is recognized as one of the most important variables influencing ethical decision-making. Bartels defines ethics as a "standard by which business action may be judged 'right or wrong.'" Standards usually differ from one culture to another, and so actions regarded moral by one culture may be in conflict with and judged immoral by another culture. Culture is the standard that determines, in part, the morality of individuals' behaviour in a given society. Studying negotiation ethics of executives from various cultures is vital for companies to capitalize on positive values and safeguard against potentially unethical negotiation tactics.

As international trade and global business opportunities grow, global executives are constantly negotiating with executives from other cultures. The negotiation process is plagued with ethical dilemmas and opportunistic temptations. In a tactical process, as two parties try to reach agreement, each wanting to maximize her/his results, the temptations to use deceptive tactics are certain. Negotiation has been defined as "a process of potentially opportunistic interaction by which two or more parties, with some apparent conflict, seek to do better through jointly decided action than they could otherwise". Despite the potential for opportunistic tendencies, MNC executives continue to regulate their counterparts' behaviour through contractual agreements that have varying capacities to respond effectively to ex post opportunism. Given the considerable resources needed to monitor ex post opportunism and the opportunity costs of deals that will not be executed due to opportunistic behaviour, it is essential that more research focus on *ex ante* opportunism so that global firms can develop the knowledge and expertise necessary to understand how to screen, select and manage exchange partners prior to the establishment of business relationships that may prove ineffective and costly.

Ethical Dilemma in Negotiation

An ethical discernment in the context of international trade must be based upon the principle of the inalienable value of the human person, source of all human rights and every social order. The human being must always be an end and not a means, a subject and not an object, not a commodity of trade. When placed at the service of human development, the international trade system works for people—persons and communities. Trade should benefit people, not just markets and economies. Economic freedom is only one element of human freedom and the economy is only one dimension of the whole of human activity. Trade policy must be organized in such a way as to not be harmful to poor countries but as a contributory factor to their sustainable economic development. The amount and range of concessions should be proportional to the development level of countries, and not the contrary. In trade relations, the good of people cannot be finally achieved against the good of another people.

The changing nature of the workplace is propelling ethics training to institutional priority. Today's work force is composed of people who are more diverse than ever in nationality, culture, religion, age, education, and socioeconomic status. These people enter the work force with differing backgrounds, values, goals, and perceptions of acceptable behaviours. This diverse, multicultural population of workers is being asked to work together in a spirit of cooperation and respect for the good of the organization and the public they serve. However, on the job, workers face decisions that have implications for their job security, their salaries, and the success of their employing organizations—decisions that bring pressures for them to protect their own interests, sometimes at the risk of losing their personal and corporate integrity. There could be more pressure on people in organizations than there ever has been to do more with less and adjust quickly to changes. In response to that pressure, people may cut corners; may engage in expedient but questionable behaviour. Some issues facing society and business include downsizing of staff, pollution control, disposal of toxic waste, depletion and allocation of scarce resources, cost containment, changes in law and technology, employee rights, discrimination against women and minorities, and product safety. Issues such as these are complex and they create ethical dilemmas that are difficult to resolve. In the medical field, for example, new technology has created new problems or dilemmas for which there are no easy solutions.

Negotiation and Conflict Resolution

Resolving conflict can be mentally exhausting and emotionally draining. But it is important to realize that conflict that requires resolution is neither good nor bad. There can be positive and negative outcomes as seen in the box below. It can be destructive but can also play a productive role for you personally and for your relationships-both personal and professional. The important point is to manage the conflict, not to suppress conflict and not to let conflict escalate out of control. Many of us seek to avoid conflict when it arises but there are many times when we should use conflict as a critical aspect of creativity and motivation. Given that organizations are becoming less hierarchical, less based on positional authority, less based on clear boundaries of responsibility and authority; it is likely that conflict will be an even greater component of organizations in the future. Studies have shown that negotiation skills are among the most significant determinants of career success. While negotiation is an art form to some degree, there are specific techniques that anyone can learn. Understanding these techniques and developing your skills will be a critical component of success of any organization.

Understanding Culture

As early as 1952, Kroeber and Kluckhohn listed 164 definitions of culture that they found in the anthropology literature. Many new definitions have appeared since. Geert Hofstede, an expert on management and cross-cultural differences, defined culture as "the collective programming of the mind which distinguishes the members of one human group from another. Culture, in this sense, includes systems of values; and values are among the building blocks of culture." Another definition comes from sociologists Zvi Namenwirth and Robert Weber, who considered culture as "a system of ideas" and argued that these ideas constitute "a design for living." Here one may follow both Hofstede and Namenwirth and Weber by viewing *culture* as a system of values and norms that are shared among a group of people and that when taken together constitute a design for living and negotiating. By *values* it would mean abstract ideas about what a group believes to be good, right, and desirable. In other words, values are shared assumptions about how things ought to be. According to Hofstede, each culture must deal with questions that can be resolved according to a series of dimensions, which results in a unique gestalt for each society, depending on the intensity of its tendency towards one or another end of each culture dimension spectrum.

Characteristics of Culture

In order to better understand culture, it is useful to closely examine its characteristics and their ramifications. Regardless of the differences in defining culture, there is a general agreement on its major characteristics. Exploring these characteristics will help us understand why culture differences exert such a huge impact on international business negotiations, and thus help us adjust our mode of communication to the individual culture in which we are negotiating with our counterparts. Cultures around the world share four common characteristics: culture is shared, it is learned, it is based on symbols, and it is integrated. In order for the culture to be transmitted successfully from one person to the next, and from one generation to the next, a system of symbols needs to be created that translates the ideals of the culture to its members. This is accomplished through language, art, religion, and money. In order to keep the culture functional all aspects of the culture must be integrated. To identify a culture's core values, Walker and Walker outlined eight key cultural dimensions. First of all, each dimension needs to recognize an important aspect of social life. Secondly, each dimension needs to be something to which any socio-cultural environment gives its members a basic orientation as the shared rationale for behaviour. Finally, each dimension has practical value to negotiators who need to reconcile, integrate, or transcend cultural difference in order to obtain a desired outcome. On the line of this core concept, cultural dimensions of negotiation may be categorized into following 8 classes: Individualism, Communication, Time, Action, Power distance, Structure, Thinking, and Environment. Each of these dimensions contains at least one cultural continuum. Such a continuum is the "field of force" between cultural orientations. Each continuum allows us to identify the directionality of hidden values, expectations, and drives of social phenomena and behaviour patterns. These dimensions provide us with a framework for understanding the characteristics of different cultures and for adapting our behaviours. Hendon and Herbig however identified eight situational variables in the negotiating process that will lead to a better understanding of negotiating styles in the context of divergent culture: purpose, issues, protocol, communications, arguments, trust, time, and decision-making.

Ethnocentricity and Cross-cultural Negotiation

Problems in business communication conducted across cultures often arise when participants from one culture are unable to understand culturally determined differences in communication practices, traditions, and thought processing. At the most fundamental level, problems may occur when one or more of the people involved cling to an ethnocentric view of how to conduct business. Ethnocentrism is the belief that one's own cultural group is somehow innately superior to others. It is easy to say that ethnocentrism only affects the bigoted or those ignorant of other cultures, and so is unlikely to be a major factor in one's own business communication. Yet, difficulties due to a misunderstanding of elements in cross-cultural communication may affect even enlightened people. Ethnocentrism is deceptive precisely because members of any culture perceive their own behaviour as logical, since that behaviour works for them. People tend to accept the values of the culture around them as absolute values. Since each culture has its own set of values, often quite divergent from those values held in other cultures, the concept of proper and improper, foolish and wise, and even right and wrong become blurred. In international business, questions arise regarding what is proper by which culture's values, what is wise by which culture's view of the world, and what is right by whose standards. Since no one individual is likely to recognize the subtle forms of ethnocentrism that shape who he or she is, international business practitioners must be especially careful in conducting business communication across cultures. It is necessary to try to rise above culturally imbued ways of viewing the world. To do this, one needs to understand *how* the perception of a given message changes depending on the culturally determined viewpoint of those communicating.

Factors Affecting Cross-cultural Business Communication

Culture directly affects the communication process in an international business setting through seven variables: language, environmental and technological considerations, social organization, contexting and face-saving, authority conception, nonverbal communication behaviour, time conception. These seven items form the acronym LESCANT. Most barriers when communicating across cultures derive from the communicator's misgauge of the LESCANT factors. By assessing in advance the roles these variables play in business communication, one can improve one's ability to convey those messages effectively to an audience from a different culture. The seven LESCANT factors alone do not provide a thorough knowledge of another culture. Moreover, these seven dimensions of culture are not intended to represent the *only* cause of intercultural communication difficulties. Being aware of these factors does, however, provide an underlying foundation on which one can construct a framework for understanding the business people from other cultures. In short, these seven factors represent an approach for asking the right questions needed to see the most significant cultural differences and similarities. The answers to those questions vary according to the individual experiences of those involved.

Interfacing Culture and Negotiation Strategy

A *negotiation strategy* is an integrated set of behaviours chosen because they are thought to be the means of accomplishing the goal of negotiating. All the negotiators have interests, priorities and strategies. These are affected by culture. Culture is the unique character of a social group, including the values and norms shared by members of the group and the group's social, economic, political and other institutions. Cultural values direct the attention of the negotiator to the issues that are more important and influence the negotiators' interests and priorities. Cultural norms define the behaviours that are appropriate and inappropriate in negotiation and influence the negotiators' strategies. Cultural values may reveal the interests of the negotiators. Negotiators from cultures that value Tradition over change may be less enthusiastic about Economic Development. Negotiators from one Culture expecting preferences to be compatible can not understand the rationality of negotiators from another culture. It is generally unwise in negotiation to label the other party as irrational. Cultural differences in preferences may also act as cultural blinders. When people negotiate, their behaviours are strategic and their strategies may be culturally based. Not only are there differences in strategic behaviour between cultures, but also within cultures and overlap between the cultures. With the result, some members of a culture may negotiate less like their own cultural prototype and more like the prototype of another culture. Negotiation Strategies are therefore inextricably linked with culture because cultures evolve norms to facilitate social interaction. Norms are functional because they reduce the number of choices a person has to make, about how to behave and how others in the culture will behave. Culture may also affect the strategies that the negotiators bring to the table – for example, the way they go about negotiating, whether they confront directly or indirectly, their motivations, and the way they use the information and influence.

General Impact of Culture on Business Negotiations

In international business settings, the progress of the negotiation process and the parties' apprehension of their relationship are under the influence of some factors, among which Cultural differences play a crucial role. Culture is a major determinant of strategies and tactics in international business negotiations, because negotiations involve communication, time and power and these variables differ across cultures. Cultural differences create a challenge to the negotiators involved, and demand understanding as well as flexibility. An ability to assess these differences and properly handle the consequences is essential for achieving success in international business negotiations. Culture has influences over all the basic elements of negotiation. It can influence the behavioural predispositions of negotiators. For example, some cultures place group over the individual, some to the contrary. This kind of distinction stemming from their respective cultures will inevitably have different influence on people's attitude toward power distance among social members, people's basis for trust, people's goal orientation, people's way of making decisions and people's tendency to take risks.

According to Hendon *et al.* culture impacts negotiation in four ways: by conditioning one's perception of reality; by blocking out information inconsistent or unfamiliar with culturally grounded assumptions; by projecting meaning onto the other party's words and actions; and by impelling the ethnocentric observer to an incorrect attribution of motive. Negotiators bring to the negotiating table the values, beliefs and background interference of their own culture. These elements influence, without their awareness, their conceptualization of the negotiation process, the objectives they seek in the negotiation, the means they adopt to pursue their goals and the expectations they hold of the behaviours of their partners. Ample evidence exists that negotiation rules and practice differ across cultures. The increasingly global business environment therefore requires managers to approach the negotiation process from the global business person's point of view. This approach includes aspects which are usually unimportant in domestic negotiations. Some of the components of a cross cultural negotiation process are more complex and difficult, but will increase our success in avoiding barriers and failures in the international business arena. When doing business internationally, we therefore need to consider: the negotiating environment, cultural and sub-cultural differences, ideological differences, foreign bureaucracy, foreign laws and governments, financial insecurity due to international monetary factors, political instability and economic changes.

Cultural Intelligence in International Business Negotiation

Cultural intelligence (CQ), defined as one's capability to adapt to new cultural contexts (Earley, 2002) is a new concept in organizational literature. Cultural intelligence is emotional intelligence across contexts, which makes emotional intelligence a prerequisite for cultural intelligence. And while some people can be very emotionally intelligent in their own culture, a shift across boundaries to some place where the norms and assumptions are different can prove to be a step too far. By the same token, higher emotionally-intelligent people are more likely to pick up cultural differences and develop cultural intelligence too. In a global economy, it's a mistake to assume that negotiation strategies are a one-size-fits-all proposition. Understanding the culture of the parties you are negotiating with is vital in order to establish a successful business relationship. With increasing globalization, cultural intelligence becomes only more critical to business success. Livermore points to a study done by 'The Economist' which found that 90% of executives from more than 60 countries said cross-cultural leadership were their top management challenge. "It is important for any business individual from support services all the way up the chain, but especially for a leader who is trying to figure out how we strategize to remain competitive in a global economy. A leader in particular has to be able to adapt on the fly".

International Trade Negotiation Processes

The negotiation process may be distinguished from the structures in which it takes place. *Negotiation* (or *bargaining*) is a sequence of actions in which two or more parties address demands and proposals to each other for the ostensible purposes of reaching an agreement and changing the behaviour of at least one actor. The process includes which strategies negotiators choose, how markets and negotiators influence each other, whether negotiators add tactics to smoke out joint gains, how much they use tactics to guard against their own biases, and how they go about forming and splitting coalitions. The process includes how the negotiators' moves interact with domestic politics. We have however little standardized evidence showing which strategies and tactics international economic regime negotiators use in general, or with what frequencies, or with what effects. International trade agreements can be categorized by different rules. For example, the General Agreement on Trade in Services (GATS) focused primarily on trade in services. The General Agreement on Tariffs and Trade (GATT) focused primarily on trade in goods. World Trade Organization (WTO), an institution for administering multilateral trade agreements, focuses primarily on trade in goods including services and intellectual property rights. Trade in services is different from trade in goods or merchandise. It is difficult for governments to impose limitations as quotas and tariffs to the types of trade in services, because some services are invisible, intangible, and non-storable.

The following are reckoned to be some of the prominent international organizations/Agencies and websites that actively facilitate international negotiation activities by providing appropriate fora for the purpose: World Trade Organization (WTO), North American Free Trade Agreement (NAFTA), Free Trade Area of the Americas and other FTAs, Asia-Pacific Economic Cooperation (APEC) Forum, General Agreement on Tariffs and Trade (GATT), General Agreements of Trade and Services (GATS), Trade- Related Aspects of Intellectual Property Rights (TRIPs), Trade Related Investment Measures (TRIMs), Agreement on Trade Barrier to Trade (TBT), Economic and Social Commission for Asia and Pacific (ESCAP), United Nations Conference on Trade and Development (UNCTAD), Global System of Trade Preferences (GSTP), Asia Pacific Trade Agreement (APTA), Bay of Bengal Initiative for Multi-Sectoral Technical and Economic Cooperation (BIMSTEC), Agency for International Trade Information and Cooperation (AITIC), Centre for Socio-

Economic Development (CSEND), Economic Negotiation Network, Global Trade Negotiations Homepage, Institute for Trade and Commercial Diplomacy (ITCD), International Centre for Trade and Sustainable Development (ICTSD), Processes of International Negotiation Network (PIN), UNCTAD, Trade Negotiations and Commercial Diplomacy Branch (TNCDB), World Trade Law net's Dispute Settlement Commentary (DSC)

Trade Agreements and Inter-business Collaboration

Trade Agreement is any contractual arrangement between states concerning their trade relations. Trade agreements may be bilateral or multilateral, that is, between two states or more than two. Trade agreement is, usually between or among governments that encourages, regulates, and/or restricts elements of trade among the respective countries. For most countries international trade is regulated by unilateral barriers, including tariffs, non-tariff barriers, and government prohibitions. Trade agreements aim to reduce such barriers and thus provide all parties with the benefits of increased trade. Reciprocity is a necessary feature of trade agreements, since neither state will be willing to sign the agreement unless it expects to gain as much as it loses. Another common feature is a most-favoured nation (MFN) clause, which provides against the possibility that one of the parties to the current agreement will later offer lower tariffs to another country. Agreements often include clauses providing for "national treatment of non-tariff restrictions," meaning that both states promise not to duplicate the properties of tariffs with non-tariff restrictions such as discriminatory regulations, selective excise taxes, quotas, and special licensing requirements. Unilateral trade agreement would be any agreement that is imposed on one national by another, and benefits one nation only. Many smaller, developing nations are afraid of trade agreements involving developed nations because the imbalance of power could result in a unilateral benefit to the developed nation. No country would willingly enter a unilateral trade agreement, but fear of such an agreement has stymied many negotiations.

In inter-business collaborative negotiation, the approach should be to treat the relationship as an important and valuable element for effective and result-oriented negotiation. There is also a philosophical dimension to the approach to negotiation pursued by many organizations. Some organizations are renowned for their collaborative approach to doing business whilst others have a reputation for a mercenary approach to conducting business. Some players in the retail sector have reputations of dealing ruthlessly with suppliers—they rationalize the approach by arguing that it is in the interest of the consumer. Whilst one would tend to agree that this approach is short sighted and probably not sustainable in the long run, it would be naïve not to recognize the fact that, at least commercially speaking, a lot of organizations have little interest in collaborative or compromising type negotiations within certain departments

WTO Negotiations for Liberalizing Trade in Services

Service industries are growing in importance as the basic infrastructure for the economic activities of corporations and consumers, not only in developed countries but also in the developing world. These efficient and highly productive service industries help to strengthen the competitiveness of the mining, manufacturing, and agricultural industries, and contribute to improvements in the quality of life. Trade in services has played an important role in the development of efficient and highly productive service industries in every country. In particular, the General Agreement on Trade in Services (GATS), which entered into force in 1995, laid the groundwork for the promotion of trade in services. However, the history of GATS is very brief, and in many countries, there unfortunately remain various barriers to service-related business activities. Based on this situation, we need to strongly support negotiations for the liberalization of trade in services within the WTO. It could be hoped that through such negotiations, trade in services amongst member countries will be further liberalized, and efforts will be made towards strengthening WTO rules.

Need for a Greater Transparency of Regulations

Companies face various hurdles to conducting services-related business in foreign countries, such as incomplete and opaque legal systems, sudden changes, arbitrary operation, and opaque and unreasonable licensing requirements and procedures (licensing criteria and fees, for example). Fundamentally, it is preferable to ensure transparency in all aspects of domestic regulations, including (1) the process of establishing the regulations, (2) the regulations themselves, and (3) actual application of the regulations. However, considering the administrative burden on each country, the realization of greater transparency of the legal system (including the availability of all laws and ministerial ordinances; establishment and announcement of investigation criteria for permits; and documentation of oral guidance) will be a necessary first step. Furthermore, as there have been cases of developing countries with no established legal system governing businesses, such as bankruptcy laws, it is desirable that developed countries provide technical assistance for the establishment of such a legal system. The second step is to create rules to correct the excessive discretion of regulatory authorities regarding permission and approval. Specifically, it is important to establish legal systems and regulations for administrative procedures (such as the obligation to initiate investigations; the establishment and announcement of standard process timeframe; and the disclosure of reasons in cases where permission or approval is denied). Furthermore, if possible, the introduction of so-called "public comment system" related to the establishment, revision, and abolition of regulations through national laws and ministerial ordinances should be considered.

Need for a Crisis Round of Trade Negotiations

Protectionism is steadily mounting. The wide spectrum of new protectionist measures shares two features: They are WTO-legal and largely unaddressed by the ongoing Doha Round. The current solution adopted by the world's leading countries in the G-20 is a restatement of good intentions: not to erect new barriers and to try, yet again, to complete the Doha Round. The former has clearly not worked because seventeen of the G-20 countries have imposed restrictions. And focusing on Doha alone could delay action to head off the protectionist pressures that are emerging. It is time to find an urgent solution to this problem. In some ways, the crisis is an opportunity for the WTO to respond nimbly and effectively in pre-empting protectionism. In a crisis, there can be experimentation that would be difficult in normal times. In the long run, the WTO should take on a wider liberalization agenda. But first, the trading system must survive these potentially perilous times. That survival requires calibrating the agenda and ambition to stem the protectionist tide. Ambition can return when this tide recedes. And it is even possible that an innovative response to the crisis would enhance the WTO's credibility and provide experience and ideas that would facilitate the successful conclusion of Doha or even a more ambitious effort. As Mattoo and Subramanian noted in a 2008 article in *Foreign Affairs*, the Doha agenda has focused on further limited liberalization of bound border barriers on trade in goods. "These barriers are no longer the strategic constraints to international economic integration. The time has come to move on to limiting uncertainty about the way existing rules and disciplines will be applied as well as to address new issues such as food, energy, and economic security. If work on these issues is held hostage progress on old issues, more and more action will shift to the negotiation of discriminatory preferential trading arrangements."

International Trade Barrier—A Barrier to Negotiation Process

When we talk about international trade we mean the exchange of goods and/or services. This exchange usually takes place between two parties from different countries or between two countries located anywhere on the globe. If the international trade takes place between two parties, it is known as bilateral trade and if the trade takes place between more than two parties, it is known as multi-lateral trade. There are basically three barriers to international trade that are used by countries, and they are as follows: (i) *Non-tariff Barrier:* Usually this type of barrier is imposed by a country on imports so that the quantity of imported items is restricted. Due to this, the availability of the imported item or items is restricted in the domestic market and the price too is very high; (ii) *Tariff Barrier:* This is barrier is in the form of duties, taxes, quotas etc. Because of this barrier, imports decrease and price of imported products increase which results in the fall in the demand giving boost to domestic products; (iii) *Voluntary Constraint:* This is a type of international trade barrier wherein a country voluntarily restricts or stops imports from coming in. This is usually used to limit the competition that domestic industries will face with the coming in of imported goods. Whenever a country starts international trade with another country, these three barriers to international trade are always taken into account.

A number of trade barriers have been employed in order to protect industries, to raise revenue, and to counter the barriers erected by other foreign countries. These barriers create a distortion of relative prices across countries and, consequently, distort individual consumption patterns and lower individual welfare.

Challenges before International Trade

The opportunities and challenges of international trade have been an issue of major concern for the economists and policy makers of the contemporary world. As far as the challenges facing the international trade are concerned, they vary with the economic and social scenarios of the countries involved in cross border trade. Be it a developed or developing economy, the primary challenge of global trade is to maximize the gains from trade. The countries involved in international trade always try to focus on the efficient utilization of the opportunities derived from exchange of goods and services with their trading partners. To utilize the benefits of the open market economy is another major challenge before world trade. In this era of globalization, international trade has a crucial role to play so as to bring about economic and social harmony among the developed and developing nations of the world. With openness to trade becoming more popular, the issues of trade solidarity both at the domestic and multilateral level have gained huge importance across the world. Globalization and the resulting economic liberalization have opened up an array of challenges before the developed and less developed economies that are involved in international trade. One of the major challenges that are crucial in the context of relatively backward economies is that the macroeconomic policies of these countries are not always proportionate to utilize the gains from world trade. International trade can be beneficial if the gains derived from it can be distributed evenly across the different layers of the society. Here lies the importance of "trickle-down" effect.

Domestic trade involves exchange of factors of production at the regional level; whereas international trade ensures greater mobility of latest technology and goods and services across the nations. World trade helps the developing countries to have ready access to the modern techniques of production. However, the challenge here is to use these techniques in an efficient manner. The industrial setup and social infrastructure need to be developed as per the global standard to optimize the benefits from international trade. Before opening up the economy, the backward nations need to safeguard the interests of the domestic entrepreneurs. The liberalization policies need to be taken up gradually so as to help the nascent industries face the challenges of the changing economic scenario. So the challenges before international trade may arise from different fronts. The countries involved in world trade need to adopt proportionate policy measures to make use of the gains from trade for the overall development of their economies.

Shaping International Trade, Investment and Regulatory Policies

For many companies and trade associations, global market success depends on the ability to shape international trade, investment and regulatory policies. Formed at the governmental level, these policies shape the business environment in which companies operate throughout the world. For instance, Wilmer Hale's (a Global Consultancy Farm) trade practice works regularly and effectively on behalf of our clients' interests in trade, investment and regulatory policies—whether the result of legislation, administration rulemaking, international negotiation or litigation. The results often make the critical difference that enables a business plan to work in a foreign market. Agreements on international trade and investment negotiations are on the rise, helping to open markets and promote international investment. But these positive effects are sometimes counteracted by new and disguised barriers to investment and trade. Trade negotiations and agreements are vital tools for clients seeking to overcome trade and investment barriers or to offset unfair competition.

Using International Dispute Settlement Mechanisms to Open Markets

It is hardly surprising that international trade and investment agreements and treaties sometimes give rise to disputes—frequently along national lines. But many international trade and investment agreements and treaties include dispute settlement mechanisms to enforce their rules. China's vast size, evolving economic structure and growing economy offer uniquely attractive opportunities for investment and trade. But capitalizing on those opportunities presents formidable challenges—including an intricate array of legal, regulatory, governmental and cultural barriers confronting international companies at the frontiers of Chinese business. Trade negotiations are having more of an impact on national policies. Competition policy is likewise affected by these developments, since in our day it is one of the cornerstones of a properly functioning market economy. It is important to incorporate adequate provisions on competition policy into free trade agreements, to the greatest extent that this is possible. Such provisions are important for establishing measures and national institutions which will ensure that anti-competitive practices will not replace the old tariff and regulatory barriers that have been eliminated through trade negotiations.

Effect of Negotiations on International Trade Agreements

A. Economic and Legal Integration

The globalization phenomenon that is currently reshaping our world and way of life is a multifaceted concept. While it encompasses a wide range of human activities such as employment, technology, finance, business, politics, environment, culture and entertainment, it primarily refers to an economic process related to a world-wide integration of markets. Economic integration is basically the process of eliminating discrimination, through the mechanism of free trade, among the economies of a group a countries. Multilateral economic integration is regulated through the GATT-WTO framework that constitutes the basic set of rules regulating the global trading order, its core principles being non-discrimination, reciprocity and transparency.

B. Harmonization

Harmonization processes are varied and can take many forms, at the domestic, international, or multilateral level. For instance, such a process can be embodied in (a) the revision of a national code (e.g. Mexico modernizing and harmonizing the *Código Comercial* and related statutes, or the National Commissioners on Uniform State Laws and the American Law Institute working on revisions of the *Uniform Commercial Code* (UCC)), (b) the creation of an international code such as the *Convention on the International Sales of Goods* (CISG by UNICTRAL), (c) an international restatement such as the UNIDROIT *Principles of International Commercial Contracts*, (d) the adoption of regional choice of law conventions such as the Rome Convention (1980 *European Convention on the Law Applicable to Contractual Obligations*) or the Mexico City Convention (1994 *Inter-American Convention on the Law Applicable to International Contracts*), (e) the adoption of uniform private rules such as the *Uniform Customs and Practices on Documentary Credits* (UCP), and (f) the universal adoption of arbitral regimes in commercial disputes.

C. Standardization in International Business Law

International business transactions are complex operations that involve identifying and coordinating many issues such as the corporate, antitrust/competition, tax, and regulatory requirements in different countries and multinational jurisdictions. A broad range of legal sub-topics can arise in the course of closing such a transaction. For instance, the determination of the structure of the proposed investment (asset vs. share investment, setting up branches or foreign subsidiary, franchising or joint venturing, mergers and acquisitions, international project financing and cross-border lending), the selection of international representation (international agency and distributorship law), taking into account foreign domestic considerations such as securities regulations, protection of intellectual property rights, regulations applicable to consumer contracts, international technology transfers, etc. Other concerns relate to choosing the applicable law and jurisdiction, and international commercial arbitration.

Business-to-Business (B2B) Negotiation

Conservative advances to business-to-business negotiations for import and export make use of primary terms like order quantity or price analysis without paying due attention to deeper negotiation terms including resource management and corporate culture. Furthermore, B2B negotiation asks for a practical framework whereby past negotiation databank is reused to carry out critical analysis. A historical case study of B2B negotiations facilitates their implementation to current import/export problems with B2B ahead of decision making to simulate various instances of negotiation. A structured approach must be used for evaluating the validity of any purported possibility established on B2B negotiation experts' opinions. Going by statistical tests, the planned framework could be applied to significantly improve the performance of decision in B2B negotiations. Global sourcing customers react to hard B2B negotiations circumstances when confronted by "take-it or leave-it" B2B offers from solitary source providers. So, an automated business to business (B2B) negotiation solution is the pressing need of the hour to overcome B2B monopoly.

Regional Trade Agreements (RTAs): The Rationale for a Multilateral Approach

The multilateral path is a complex and lengthy process. The Kennedy Round took five years, the Tokyo Round went for seven and the Uruguay Round ran for almost eight - double the original target. Negotiations of this duration are a heavy commitment, but testify to the fact that the parties see the rewards as justifying the effort. This is not surprising when one looks at the history. The eight multilateral trade negotiating rounds over the past fifty years have transformed a protectionist post-war environment to a much freer trading world, with tariffs on manufactures alone cut by an average of 90 per cent. Through the development of contractual rules, the trading system is much less vulnerable to economic shocks. Global trade has expanded dramatically, increasing fifteen-fold since 1960. This helped quadruple world economic production and more than double world per capita income over that period. The GATT, now WTO, system has been a fundamental underpinning of post-war economic growth. Of late, however, Regional trade agreements (RTAs) have emerged as an alternative to achieve trade liberalization as multilateral efforts have faced political and economic obstacles. The difficulties of reaching agreements on sensitive issues like agriculture and services have been evident in the Doha Round. The previous rounds were also marked by complex and slow negotiation processes. For one, as the number of participants' increases, it has been more difficult to address each country's demands for special considerations. RTAs convey advantages as well as limitations. By reducing the numbers of participants in the negotiation they can help expand the discussion to include more dimensions of economic integration. Compared with unilateral liberalization, political support for RTAs also seems to be greater given the perception of reciprocity from other member countries. However, since the early work of Viner, these benefits have been weighted against distortions that RTAs can create. By de facto discriminating against nonmembers, RTAs distort resource allocation, favouring regional producers to the potential detriment of local consumers. Recent research also emphasizes the global consequences of multiple and overlapping RTAs in terms of the transaction costs they impose.

South-South Trade and Regional Integration

New trade geography is emerging in international trade with three interlinked determinants, namely the increasing role and importance of developing countries to drive trade and growth, South-South trade and economic cooperation, and the changing context of North-South interdependence. This emerging new trade geography, however, needs to be treated with caution in order to avoid unrealistic expectations in terms of its scope and impact, particularly given that many countries, including African countries, LDCs and SIDS, do not appear to participate significantly in this trend. Developing countries face a considerable challenge in sustaining, maximizing and exploiting the opportunities emerging in the new trade geography, and in particular in mainstreaming into this dynamism the participation of those developing countries that remain marginalized from international trade. Developing country Governments, their regional integration groupings, and their economic operators need to consult, coordinate and cooperate closely and actively on South-South trade, investment and economic cooperation initiatives to devise strategies and actions to advance mutual trade and investment. Such cooperation needs to be conducted on the basis of mutuality of advantage for all parties to maximize the development gains. Approaches that engage countries and their economic operators in mutually advantageous relationships, in which all participants gain, have higher chances of being sustained and strengthened. The challenge is to develop and implement a strategic approach and positive agenda for South-South trade and economic cooperation.

Strategic Aspects of Global negotiation

Global Negotiation is a process of understanding and influencing others in various political, legal, social and cultural environments. If an organization needs to negotiate more effectively in a multicultural context, then negotiation services become essential to help succeed in a diverse and competitive global environment. All organizations are exposed to the negotiation process but few strategically and consciously plan and develop the skills to succeed in a multicultural environment. Learning more about corporate culture and functional style as well as best practices along with that of counterparts during the process can improve the outcome of all of organization's negotiation processes. This includes the ability to illuminate the preparation and strategy analytics, business and emotional intelligence, and the appropriate strategic fit of the corporate style with any given global negotiation situation. Strategic negotiation is about the implementation of the strategic choices already made by the organization, by different people. It is an operational activity which implements the necessary decisions that are made as a result of the plans aiming to take it to the organization's planning horizon. The emergent aspects of negotiations are thus best understood by focusing on how strategies aggregate over time. Strategic intelligence (SI) has mostly been used in military settings, but its worth goes well beyond that limited role. It has become invaluable for improving any organization's strategic decision making process. Rigorous strategic planning can bolster a negotiator's chances of success. However, leadership in negotiation also requires an understanding of, and an ability to practice critical emotional and behavioural skills.

Decision making and the strategic leadership of decision making teams is a process which moves an individual or a group toward common goals. However, people are not alike in their values and beliefs; there are huge differences among people within a single organization, and even greater differences between people in different organizations. Strategic leaders must know how to operate across such boundaries that mark differences in expectations and perspectives, and competing values and goals. It is one thing to influence a group essentially in agreement; it is quite a different thing to influence a group with goals in conflict with those that one wants to pursue.

Some of the common characteristics of effective negotiators are having objective skills, patience tranquil and a good knowledge about party with whom the proposed negotiation is to be made. In the international arena, an effective negotiator would try to have a complete knowledge about the history of the country in which he is going to negotiate. An effective negotiator would be objective in the sense that he would not criticize the system, political structure and form of government of the country in which he is negotiating. He would also keep himself updated with the cultural dimensions of the country in which he proposes to negotiate. It is very important for a negotiator to understand that cultural dimensions play an important role in the process of negotiations. It is often seen that people belonging to 'low context cultures' would have lower negotiation skills than those belonging to 'high context cultures'. Finally an effective negotiator would set apart all aggressions, exertions and emotions during the process of negotiations.

Multinational Corporations in Global Governance

International regimes are a critical element of global governance. Regime theory has been widely criticized for its state centered approach, and increasing attention has been paid to domestic political factors and non-state actors, especially non-governmental organizations (NGOs). Very few, however, have examined regimes from the perspective of multinational corporations (MNCs), despite their critical influence in the international political economy. Drawing on international business and international political economy literatures, this paper outlines an approach to analyzing regimes from the perspective of MNCs. In doing so, we build upon the work of Raymond Vernon, whose Product Life Cycle theory of trade and investment moved the conceptual spotlight from nations to corporate strategy. In this tradition, we seek to understand the formation and content of regimes of international governance in terms of the interests and strategies of MNCs.

Global Business Negotiations: A Sectoral Review

If we happen to scan global business scene, negotiations do take place in most of emerging sectors of the global economy; viz. joint ventures, oil & gas, energy, infrastructure, environment, airlines, defense deal etc. This can also form an integral part of the negotiation processes linked to economic regions, across countries, or companies. In many instances, this can also be a part of the growth as well as competitive strategy. There was a time when business formation was relatively simple but now the law and related regulations, including taxation liabilities, intrude to the point that without legal expertise it is unlikely that the essentially simple decision of two parties agreeing to cooperate for some purpose would be achievable without high-level legal, taxation and accounting advice and guidance. The business plan could envisage that a product is to be taken to a wider market beyond the initial jurisdiction within three years. That strategic decision creates an agenda for future negotiations. New opportunities bring their rewards, but also their burdens. What appears to be a logical development from a strong domestic market for an organization's products, in turn produces a host of questions that complicate what starts out as a straightforward decision. Among these questions is that of how the organization is going to give effect to the decision to market beyond current boundaries. One answer could be to form a joint venture (JV) with another company already located in the target market. This is where strategic negotiators ought to have some exposure to what is involved in a JV and what to look out for. Besides International Joint ventures, Global business negotiations have made their inroads in the shape of International contracts and deals - the prominent pattern of which include: production sharing contracts in oil & natural gas, code-sharing contracts in and strategic alliances in aviation industries, defence and nuclear deals in defence and energy sector, international pipe-line projects for logistics and supply-chain support etc.

WTO and Global Governance

While the WTO is not only the institution in charge of overseeing trade liberalization, it has become the body that is supposed to settle global governance conflicts. The change in issues related to trade liberalization was brought to light in the Doha Round negotiations in November 2001. During this summit, rich countries sought to erase the memory of the Seattle disaster while the southern developing countries, invigorated by China's entrance, for the first time sought to reprogram the WTO to their advantage. They succeeded in exploiting a factor rarely taken into account: at the WTO, there is no Security Council or supreme body—all nations have the right of veto, so all parties must agree in order to launch a negotiating round. Developing countries, despite their diversity, have realized that the WTO'S one-country, one-vote nature represents a considerable political asset. As a result, the Doha Round was launched with a broad agenda designed to take into account the diversity of objectives and expectations among the vastly expanded membership of the original WTO. Indeed, Doha was even baptized the "development round" at the request of southern countries. Its agenda, which debuted in 2001 and remains open, includes no fewer than 21 subjects, ranging from agriculture, industry, services, and intellectual property to rules of origin, anti-dumping regulations, trade facilitation, environmental protections, basic social issues, special and differential treatment for the least-advanced countries, and fisheries—among a host of others. It has become easier to inventory subjects not listed on the WTO agenda than to count all those that appear on it.

This entire complex infrastructure exists within a geopolitical framework of new political coalitions among states and new political demands for trade liberalization. Basically, the geopolitics of the WTO is now built on four major pillars: the United States, the European Union, the G-20 and the G-90. The G-20 bloc encompasses most of the emerging countries in Asia and Latin America that want to break up the EU-U.S. duopoly at the WTO. Most of these G-20 nations export agricultural products and feel disadvantaged either by the closed doors of certain European agricultural markets or by the unfair competition represented by domestic subsidies for American farmers. The G-20 coalesced in 2004 during the Cancun summit. The members derailed the conference to show the United States and the European Union that they could no longer resist the demands of developing countries to change agricultural protections. Brazil and India dominate the G-20. However, these two countries do not necessarily share the same interests: Brazil, for example, has much more defensive positions than India. But both are united by a simple goal—not to yield ground on the protection of domestic industry and agriculture unless they are rewarded by an end to agricultural export subsidies, the opening of European agricultural markets, and the opening of service markets to qualified Indian workers.

Political Dimension of Global Negotiation

The adoption of international norms of antitrust enforcement has so far eluded the international community. With a few exceptions, antitrust harmonization has come, where it has come at all, through the coincidental and unilateral decisions of individual states. Not only key substantive differences, but also important procedural ones characterize the disparate enforcement regimes. And there are at least 80 separate jurisdictions that are active in enforcing competition laws against actions both within and without their borders. Harmonization is arguably desirable for its perceived efficiency effects and the debate over harmonization or internationalization rightly centers on the prospects for adopting a workable worldwide antitrust standard that would reduce the burdensome costs of legal uncertainty occasioned by divergent local standards. But while many states - including particularly the European Union - have advocated in favour of the internationalization of antitrust laws, most notably under the auspices of the WTO, the United States has steadfastly resisted a multilateral solution. Existing efforts to describe or explain the lack of international harmonization have generally focused on the direct economic effects of, and the narrow political difficulties of, the harmonization of competition laws through certain international mechanisms, such as the WTO and the OECD.

Negotiators have a general understanding of their own local political environment. They are raised in a business milieu that clearly distinguishes who the key players are, and who has to be pitched about a proposal. They learn the roles that each level of government may bring to the table, and its impact on the negotiations. When negotiators take their proposals abroad and negotiate with a foreign power, they may not fully realize the impact that different political systems will affect the manner in how the negotiation should be conducted. The scope of the impact by the governments of individual nations will vary in the degree in the amount of influence they may have on international negotiations.

Geopolitics in Global Trade

Since the World Trade Organization (WTO) was first created in 1995, trade issues have ceased to be technical. Instead, they have become highly political, not only because trade issues have changed but also because the geopolitical context in which these exchanges take place has been altered. The creation of the WTO in 1995 in the wake of the General Agreement on Tariff and Trade (GATT), which was set up after World War II, was a direct response to three fundamental changes in the world order. The first was the exponential growth in world trade. Between 1980 and 2005, the volume of trade quadrupled, while during the same period world gross national product (GNP) barely doubled. Trade has thus become the most powerful agent of globalization. This considerable increase was only made possible due to a significant reduction in tariff protection in southern countries, which dropped from an average 30 percent in 1985 to 10 percent some 20 years later.

Geopolitical Consequences of Inadequate Action on Climate Change

There have been a few attempts to describe some of the geopolitical ramifications of the impacts of climate change. These studies suggest that climate change may heighten the risk of violent conflict between countries, and stimulate large scale movements of 'climate refugees' and these effects are seen to be more pronounced in developing countries. The most dramatic of these assessments is a report commissioned by the US Department of Defense that argues that climate change could 'potentially destabilize the geopolitical environment, leading to skirmishes, battles, and even war due to resource constraints'. It identifies shortages of food, water and disrupted access to energy as being key impacts that might trigger war, and talks in terms of 'carrying capacity', 'ancient enmities' and 'struggles for accesses'. This and other geopolitical scenarios are to varying degrees informed by the same neo-Malthusian assumptions about the response of social systems to resource scarcity that inform the larger literature on environmental security. These assumptions are for the most part the product of ideology more than they are of evidence about conflict. They are even more difficult to sustain when applied to the case of climate change given that the outcomes of climate change on biophysical systems are still somewhat uncertain, and the response of social systems to these changes is highly uncertain.

Predictions of international conflicts arising from climate change are premature. More careful analyses suggest that conflict between countries is unlikely, but that the effects of climate change on migration may increase the risk of civil conflicts between groups under certain circumstances. The politics involved in the UNFCCC and the Kyoto Protocol has largely concerned the issue of reducing emissions of greenhouse gases. However, since COP-8 in 2002 negotiations on the ways and means of implementing adaptation have become more intense. There is now a Least Developed Country (LDC) Fund that is beginning to assist the LDCs to plan adaptation activities, a Special Climate Change Fund that can also potentially assist countries in adaptation, and there exists in principle if not yet in practice an Adaptation Fund that is intended to finance adaptation projects in the most vulnerable countries. There are no clear rules about how decisions are to be made under the UNFCCC. Decisions are theoretically not possible without the consent of all Parties. This means that objections to a decision are frequently vetoes. This potentially gives a lot of power to dissenting Parties. However, there are examples where the objections of small groups have been overridden in final agreements. Yet, it remains unclear how many objections make for a veto, and much seems to depend on which Party is making the objection. Parties such as the EU and the USA, which are influential because of the scale of their emissions, the size and capacities of their delegations, and their influence in other arenas of global politics, tend to have considerably more power in negotiations than other countries.

The Geopolitics of Climate Governance

The positions of various countries in the climate regime are nevertheless largely the product of a 'two-level game' in which national leaders seek to maximize the domestic political benefits of action or inaction on the basis of their reading of domestic interests, and seek to minimize the negative effects of international factors on this domestic game. This interlocking internal-external dynamic is important to understand in the case of a given country's position on climate change. For example, most Europeans are supportive of action to address climate change and there is a reinforcing cycle of information through the public, government, media and many industry groups that makes a proactive international position on climate change domestically acceptable. In the USA and Australia, in contrast, media skepticism on climate change's causes, consequences and solutions has been high, and the opposition of fossil fuel and heavy industry groups to the Kyoto Protocol has been strong and influential. The geopolitics of the UNFCCC cannot be explained merely as a matter of the differences between the 'North' and the 'South'. There are vast differences in the positions of countries within both groups. For example, the collective position of the Alliance of Small Island States (AOSIS) group, which is comprised of 44 of the world's small island states, has more in common with that of the collective position of the EU (27 member countries) than it does with the collective position of the 11 Organization of Petroleum Exporting Countries (OPEC), and within the North there are large differences between the EU and the USA—so much so that the EU has been described as a 'protagonist' to the USA on the issue.

Web-based Global Business Negotiation

Access to, and the ability to use computer and communication technologies varies widely between countries. It is often lack of proficiency rather than access that creates the barriers between developed and developing countries. The InterNeg Web site and its online systems INSPIRE and INSS for instance aim at overcoming these barriers by educating people around the world about decision and negotiation analysis and providing them with an opportunity to use decision support techniques. The systems allow one to conduct simulated negotiations with people from different cultures and solve realistic managerial decision problems. Policy makers and managers in developing countries face numerous new challenges in such diverse fields as labour management, international affairs, business relationships, and environmental regulations. Governments, judiciary, business and other organizations, and the public are breaking new grounds in decision processes related to the environment, ecology and policy making. In most cases these decisions can only be made through negotiations which are one of the most common processes for making decisions and resolving conflicts at every organizational level. With an increase of international trade and shifting manufacturing from developed to developing countries there is an increased pressure on managers to engage in negotiations. This leads to growing interest in studying negotiation theory and practice, and cultural similarities and differences in decision making. Studies have revealed that most developing countries lack negotiators capable of translating their own and their organizations principles and general goals into concrete bargaining proposals, and systems for widespread and efficient training of decision makers. To bargain effectively, one must not only have the ability to articulate interests and bargaining positions, but also the skill to interpret and transmit bargaining communications to other negotiators. Similarly, one must now learn the opponent's mindset rooted in their national and organizational cultures internationally. Web-based learning and training can explore and exploit such potential.

A systematic review of the existing literature and their critical analysis as explained above has provided an insight into the possibilities of exploiting the vast galaxy of trade opportunities that can be harnessed with the help of acquiring, developing and applying required skills for international business negotiation. There are a large number of global examples where such negotiation strategies have fetched rich dividends to multi-domestic, transnational as well as Multi-national Corporation; and these examples are worth emulating. There are equally other examples wherein the corporate failure could, among other things, be linked to lack of negotiation skills and appropriate strategies. This can also be linked to a large extent to negotiation styles of individual countries and corporations; including the ability for effective cross-cultural negotiation techniques and skills. A comprehensive understanding of the larger issue related to business ethics, corporate governance, the presence of regulatory framework and favourable geopolitical environment is also fast becoming relevant and critical for successful outcomes of trade negotiations and contracts in regional, inter-regional, international and global context. With a view to capture this perception in a holistic and integrated manner the book on 'Global Business negotiation' is written by the author at a time when negotiation has become an in-thing for successful conduct, transactions and trade-offs from global businesses.

The book is planned to encompass 5 major themes in the forms of following chapters:

Chapter 1: Concept and Principles of Global Business Negotiation
Chapter 2: Impact of Cross-Culture on Global Business Negotiation
Chapter 3: Regulatory Environment in International Trade Negotiation
Chapter 4: Negotiations under International and Regional Trade Agreements with Country-Specific Implications
Chapter 5: Strategic and Geo-Political Dimensions of Global Business Negotiation

Drawing upon the best and updated available literature in the field the author provides a comprehensive treatise on emerging concept of negotiation as are relevant and applicable in modern times to diverse and complex settings of global businesses that are increasingly becoming hyper-competitive. The book not only provides a broad framework on the processes, premises and the various modalities as well as conditionalities in which to conduct negotiations with positive outcomes; this would also guide the reader to have an exposure to practical and live examples of successful negotiations in challenging business environment.

The author feels that the book will be useful to the readers at large, social scientists, policy makers, research scholars, lawyers and dedicated workers in the field of economics, industries and international businesses including foreign trade.

Dr. A.N. Sarkar

CHAPTER 1

Concept and Principles of Global Business Negotiation

Concept of Negotiation

Negotiation is basically conceived to be a process of two individuals or groups reaching joint agreement about differing needs or ideas. Oliver (1996) described negotiation as "negotiators jointly searching a multidimensional space and then agreeing to a single point in the space" (http://www.enotes.com/business-finance-encyclopedia/negotiation). Negotiation applies knowledge from the fields of communications, sales, marketing, psychology, sociology, politics, economics, trading, international businesses and even in conflict resolution. Whenever an economic transaction takes place or a dispute is settled, negotiation occurs. The Latin root of the word '*negotiatus*' means to "carry on business". In modern Spanish '*negocios*' means 'business'.

A business negotiation may be viewed as a formal affair that takes place across the proverbial bargaining table, in which one haggles over price and performance or a complex term of partnership ventures. Given the role and significance of negotiations in our personal and professional lives it is increasing becoming important to improve upon the negotiation skills to expand businesses (HBS, 2003).

Negotiation can also be seen as a kind of social interaction for reaching an agreement for two or more parties with different objectives or interests that they think are important. In cross-cultural negotiation, the situations are more complicated because of different cultures, environments, communication styles, political systems, ideologiės, and customs. In 1997, Kufour indicated that multilateral negotiations are also obviously important. In a business, strategic alliances and the trade negotiation compare WTO to multiple companies, and in 1996, Wiess also reported that studying multilateral negotiation in an international business has become an imperative. According to the School of thinking by the Harvard Business School (HBS, 2003) Negotiation is the means by which people deal with their differences. Negotiation is an ever-present feature of our lives—both at home and at workplace.

A modern definition of negotiation is two or more parties with common and conflicting interests who enter into a process of interaction with the goal of reaching an agreement (preferably of mutual benefit).Negotiation is a decision-making process that provides opportunities for the parties to exchange commitments or promises through which they will resolve their disagreements and reach a settlement. In brief, a negotiation is two or more parties striving to agree when their objectives do not coincide. This definition indicates that negotiations take place within the context of the four Cs: common interest, conflicting interest, compromise, and criteria. Common interest considers the fact that each party in the negotiation shares, has, or wants something that the other party has or does. Without a common goal, there would be no need for negotiation. Conflict occurs when people have separate but conflicting interests. For example, in international business negotiations, conflicting interests could include payment, distribution, profits, contractual responsibilities, and quality. Compromise involves resolving areas of disagreement. Although a win-win negotiated settlement would be best for both parties, the parties cannot avoid making compromises during negotiation. The criteria include the conditions under which the negotiations take place like Business environment, geo-political system etc.

Negotiations in the context of International business lie at the heart of international diplomacy. Parties (governments, businesses, and non-governmental organizations) employ the art and science of negotiation to protect and advance their organizational and constituent interests. The skillful use of negotiation can advance a party's interests and help to avoid a less attractive alternative, e.g., trade wars, litigation, or protracted dispute settlement procedures under the WTO. An effective negotiation process can lead to positive outcomes that can result in the promotion of important international objectives including economic development, business interests, environmental protection, labor rights, and political stability, all of which can minimize the adverse impacts of poverty that can lead to violence and war. Even for practitioners who may not aspire to the role of negotiator in the heavy stakes arenas of international negotiation, most professionals negotiate frequently in the performance of their jobs. Whether negotiating for a raise, a vacation, or a promotion with a supervisor or negotiating with peers and subordinates over work assignments, deadlines, or workplace conflicts, we all negotiate all the time in varying circumstances and the conditionality involved.

As the very first step in approaching the improvement of one's own negotiating technique is to develop an awareness or mindfulness of when you are engaged in a negotiation of small or large consequence. Many people undercut their own self-interest by not paying attention to their own role and participation in day to day negotiating scenarios. Depending on the subject matter of a negotiation, different skills must be employed and options exercised to achieve agreement between or among parties. International negotiations in the broad context of trade relations may include negotiations over prices, tariffs, and sales or qualitative negotiations over broad principles related to the environmental, labor, health & safety, or other impacts of trade related agreements (http://www.commercialdiplomacy.org/manuals/trade_negotiations.htm).

Concept of Negotiation can, in a way, be extrapolated to use as a potent tool for decision-making. It is one of the several options you have when you are attempting to make a decision with another person. It is an exchange of series of offers by two or more people/groups of people. It is a bargaining, deal-making process. Negotiation is the process through which the activity of trading and exchanging tangible or intangible things between negotiators. The process of conferring among two or more interdependent parties to arrive at agreements about some matter over which they are in conflict. It includes the mutual dependence of each negotiator on the other. It usually involves you getting something, tangible or intangible, in return for your consent. But if you have nothing to trade then negotiation is unlikely. One can become competent in negotiation without compromising a sense of ethical conduct. Negotiations do not always end in an agreement. Those making a decision by negotiation usually have the option of choosing some other solution, of saying 'no', of walking away, of minding their own business (http://www.indianmba.com/Faculty_Column/FC178/fc178.html). But most negotiations end-up in win-lose or a win-win situation.

Types of Negotiation

Depending upon the situation and time, the way the negotiations are to be conducted differs. The skills of negotiations depends and differs widely from one situation to the other. Basically the types can be divided into three broad categories, namely Day-to-Day/ Managerial Negotiation, Commercial Negotiation, Legal Negotiation (http://www.laynetworks.com/TYPES-OF-NEGOTIATION-IN-ORGANIZATIONS.html).

A brief description of the various types of negotiation is given below in a nut-shell.

1. *Day-to-day/Managerial Negotiations*

Such types of negotiations are done within the organization and are related to the internal problems in the organization. It is in regards to the working relationship between the groups of employees. Usually, the manager needs to interact with the members at different levels in the organization structure. For conducting the day-to-day business, internally, the superior needs to allot job responsibilities, maintain a flow of information, direct the record keeping and many more activities for smooth functioning. All this requires entering into negotiations with the parties internal to the organization.

2. *Commercial Negotiations*

Such types of negotiations are conducted with external parties. The driving forces behind such negotiations are usually financial gains. They are based

Types	Parties Involved	Examples
Day-to-day/ Managerial Negotiations	1. Different levels of Management 2. In between colleagues 3. Trade unions 4. Legal advisers	1. Negotiation for pay, terms and working conditions. 2. Description of the job and fixation of responsibility. 3. Increasing productivity.
Commercial Negotiations	1. Management 2. Suppliers 3. Government 4. Customers 5. Trade unions 6. Legal advisors 7. Public	1. Striking a contract with the customer. 2. Negotiations for the price and quality of goods to be purchased. 3. Negotiations with financial institutions as regarding the availability of capital.
Legal Negotiations	1. Government 2. Management 3. Customers	1. Adhering to the laws of the local and national government.

on a give-and-take relationship. Commercial negotiations successfully end up into contracts. It relates to foregoing of one resource to get the other.

3. *Legal Negotiations*

These negotiations are usually formal and legally binding. Disputes over precedents can become as significant as the main issue. They are also contractual in nature and relate to gaining legal ground. Like it or not, everybody is a negotiator. Negotiation techniques may almost be used every day. We negotiated when we were kids trading sports cards or toys. We still do it today when we negotiate with the boss for a salary raise, or to buy bigger toys like autos and the latest gimmicks. It doesn't stop there either because we also use negotiation in our personal lives. We all have some combination of family, friends, significant other, or kids. At some level, we negotiate with them all the time without even knowing it. Many people don't like to negotiate because they view it as a hassle. Even though we might consciously think we're avoiding the blatant negotiation process, we end up doing it without realizing that's exactly what's happening. So we may as well learn how to do it well, and decide which of the 2 negotiation types to use. There are two relatively distinct types of negotiation. The 2 types are known as *distributive negotiations*, and *integrative negotiations*. The Negotiation Experts' training courses teach both methods, as both are essential to negotiate successfully in business (http://www.negotiations.com/articles/negotiation-types/).

A. Distributive Negotiations—the Fixed Pie

The term distributive means; there is a giving out; or the scattering of things. By its mere nature, there is a limit or finite amount in the thing being distributed or divided amongst the people involved. Hence, this type of negotiation is often referred to as *'The Fixed Pie'*. There is only so much to go around, but the proportion to be distributed is limited but also variable. How many times has somebody shouted out, *'Who wants the last piece of pizza?'* Everyone looks at each other, then the pizza slice, and two or more hands rush to grab it. In the real world of negotiations, two parties face off with the goal of getting as much as possible. The seller wants to go after the best price they can obtain, while the buyer wants to pay the lowest price to achieve the best bargain. It is really just good old plain haggling, which is not all that much different from playing a tug of war.

A distributive negotiation usually involves people who have never had a previous interactive relationship, nor are they likely to do so again in the near future. Simple everyday examples, would be when we're buying a car or a house. Purchasing products or services are simple business examples where distributive bargaining is often employed. Remember, even friends or business acquaintances can drive a hard bargain just as well as any stranger.

Secondly, when we are dealing with someone unknown to us, and it's a one time only occurrence, we really have no particular interest in forming a relationship with them, except for the purpose of the deal itself. We are generally less concerned with how they perceive us, or how they might regard our reputation. Ours and their interests in that case are usually self serving and mutually inclusive.

Basics of Distributive Bargaining

Distributive Bargaining in essence implies the old adage 'Play your cards close to your chest—Give little or no information to the other side'. The less others know about our interests as to why we want to make the purchase, our preferences, or the point at which we would decline to deal, the better will be our position in the bargain. Expressing eagerness or need, reveals a weakness which could be exploited to our disadvantage.

The opposite could, however, be equally true—Try to pry as much information from the other side. Any additional information that we uncover can be used as leverage to negotiate a better deal. The only thing you should ever tell—The only information we should ever reveal are those alternative options, such as other sellers, which shows we are prepared to walk from the negotiation whenever it suits us. Let them make the first offer—Whatever is used as the first offer will generally act as an anchor upon which the rest of the negotiation will revolve. Try to get the other side to set the stage from which to start. In the end one need to be ground to earth and be pragmatic i.e. being too greedy or too stingy will likely result in no agreement, hence keep it real.

B. Integrative Negotiations to create a 'Win-Win' Situation

The word integrative means to join several parts into a whole.

Conceptually, this implies some cooperation, or a joining of forces to achieve something together. Usually this type of negotiation involves a higher degree of trust and a forming of a reliable and sustained relationship. Both parties want to walk away feeling they have achieved something which has value by getting what each wants. Ideally, it is a twofold process. In the real world of business, the results often tilt in favour of one party over the other because, it is unlikely that both parties will come to the table at even strength, when they begin the talks.

Nonetheless, there are many advantages to be gained by both parties, when they take a cooperative approach to mutual problem solving. The process generally involves some form or combination of making value for value concessions, in conjunction with creative problem solving. Generally, this form of negotiation is looking down the road, to them forming a long term relationship to create mutual gain. It is often described as the *win-win* scenario.

Integrative Negotiation Basics

The following are considered to be the basic elements in an integrative negotiation:

Multiple Issues—Integrative negotiations usually entails a multitude of issues to be negotiated, unlike distributive negotiations which generally revolve around the price, or a single issue. In integrative negotiations, each side wants to get something of value while trading something which has a lesser value.

Sharing—To fully understand each other's situation, both parties must realistically share as much information as they can to understand the other's interests. You can't solve a problem without knowing the parameters. Cooperation is essential.

Problem Solving—Find solutions to each other's problems. If you can offer something of lesser value which gives your counterpart something which they need, and this results in you realizing your objective, then you have integrated your problems into a positive solution.

Bridge Building—More and more businesses are engaging in long term relationships. Relationships offer greater security.

One can use the two types of negotiation described above all the time. Occasionally, these two different forms of negotiation even overlap. By understanding their nature, we will be better prepared when faced with different situations. By learning more, we can improve both our interpersonal and professional relationships, through an increased awareness of the negotiation process utilized in our everyday lives.

Major Motives of Negotiation

All negotiators have *interests, power* and all negotiators have *strategies to evolve and work through.* For the present purpose, efforts may be focused on dealing with these three negotiation elements that are conceived to be the 'Core' areas to trigger a *negotiation process.*

Interests

Interests are defined as the goal each party desires to achieve. It is the motivation that pushes the parties to enter into a negotiation. No party will enter a negotiation without certain interests. Interests are often classified as common, conflicting or complementary. Common interests serve as the impetus for the parties to sit before the negotiating table. A successful transaction is beneficial to both sides. At the same time, their interests may conflict since profit to one can be cost to the other. The parties have complementary interests in cases of many joint ventures: one party is in need of investment or advanced technology and the other wants to enter a particular market and expects to do business with it and possibly the surrounding markets. Common and complementary interests have positive effects on the negotiation process whereas conflicting interests affect the process negatively. When conflicting interests dominate a negotiation, an agreement becomes unlikely; when common and complementary interests dominate, the opportunity for success increases.

Interests may take many forms: economic such as profitability, volume, market share, etc., and they may also be more subtle and even intangible such as principles, saving face or establishing/reinforcing a relationship, defending or promoting an image, a reputation, etc. In a commercial negotiation, price is of course a major issue, but the key point lies in how to connect this topic with negotiator interests (preoccupations, expectations, constraints, etc.) and with other issues (e.g. volume, payment terms, deliveries, quality, guarantees, etc.). Identifying interests is of great importance to forming strategies and conducting behaviors. Interests may be easy to figure out (e.g., profitability or long-term relationships) or difficult to decode (e.g., a desire for dominance or for revenge). They may be an attribute of an individual negotiator or they may represent a collective factor (e.g., a firm's image). In international business negotiations, the interests of the parties are of a similar variety to domestic negotiations, but they are often complicated by cultural factors.

Power (Bargaining Strength)

Generally speaking, the power of a negotiator originates from a number of factors, some of which have links with the negotiation situation; others are either directly or indirectly associated with the negotiator himself. Considerations for the former can be as follows:

The available alternatives: The more choices a party have, the greater bargaining strength it enjoys, that is, the party that is confronted with more competitors will be in a disadvantageous position. For example, if the seller is the sole provider of a certain kind of goods the buyer is in urgent need of, the seller definitely enjoys more power.

The capacity to reward or punish: This capacity is sometimes used in international business negotiations through the channel of regulatory power.

Urgency of the time: If one party is under some deadline pressure, the opponent party benefits from a bargaining strength relative to the other.

The above factors are embedded into the negotiating situation. Also, some other sources of power could be *suo motto* tied to the negotiator. The following are considered to be some of the essential attributes that seem necessary for the acquiring or exerting the necessary bargaining power:

1. *Skill:* Effective negotiating skills, either endowed or acquired through training, help build strength in negotiations. Agile mind, Sound judgment, sensitiveness in communication, and resistance to stress can all be sources of bargaining strength. Skill diversity is complex and one skill that works well in some circumstances may not work as well in some others.
2. *Credibility and reputation:* Both factors are also strengths linked to the negotiation and they can be extended to organizations. This aspect is of particular importance to international business negotiations, for the negotiating parties are generally unfamiliar to each other and have little information about each other's credibility, so then there may exist lots of uncertainties when the two parties begin to do business. Therefore, the credibility and reputation of negotiators exert great impact on the success of international business negotiations.
3. *Information:* In international business negotiations, it is not exaggerated to say "information is power". The collection of valuable information rests on whether or not the negotiator and his organization have an easy access to the relevant data. A good appreciation of your counterparts and their organizations, which involves everything from strength and weakness, to their decision-making mode, to the construction of their team and so forth, is the first step in the initial stage toward the possible forthcoming success.

Exploring the sources of power is very important in planning as well as preparing for a negotiation. It is worth noting that the balance of power between the negotiating parties is subject to changes during the process of negotiation under a given set of circumstance and conditionality. To be an effective negotiator, one needs to be alert to these changes and conditions.

Strategy

Strategy refers to a complete plan regarding problems, the solution available and preferred choices, relative to the other party's choices and preferences. In negotiation, parties try to build up their comparative advantages. They compare the alternatives available, make a checklist and assign arguments for and against these alternatives. Therefore, strategy is both intention and choice. Intention is a matter of will behind objective setting. Choice is the solution of the most effective path to achieve these objectives. In brief, parties apply strategies in negotiation in order to achieve their own goals. The accomplishment of an agreement in international business negotiations is often attributable to the application of *tactics or techniques.* During the negotiation process, negotiators will undoubtedly decide on their own strategic orientations and then implement them in their negotiations with their counterpart. A negotiator's strategic orientation can be predominantly cooperative (integrative, "value creating") or confrontational (distributive, "value claiming", competitive), offensive or defensive. As to his strategic orientation towards time, he may act so as to conclude rapidly or he may prefer to develop a negotiation over a longer time. In respect to the type of agreement sought, a negotiator may want partial, comprehensive or conditional agreement.

Any given generic strategy as described above is associated with a number of different behaviors, initiatives and decisions, which concern techniques as well as tactics to be privileged. Various factors contribute to a negotiator's choices of certain strategic orientation: a negotiator's personality, balance of power, level of trust, etc. An understanding of the major elements of negotiation together with its concept is a necessary step to comprehend the negotiation process. But how the negotiation process operates in the cross-cultural context is still a puzzle for most of us and therefore our endeavor should be made to use a comprehensive and all inclusive/ pervasive approach. This can be effectively achieved if we happen to go through an elaborate negotiation process in a given context.

Phases of Negotiation

Negotiation is the process whereby interested parties resolve disputes, agree upon courses of action, bargain for individual or collective advantage, and/ or attempt to craft outcomes which serve their mutual interests. It is usually regarded as a form of alternative dispute resolution. A negotiation process can be divided into six steps in three phases (http://www.spiritus-temporis.com/negotiation/3-phases-in-negotiation.html) as detailed below:

Phase 1: Before the Negotiation

Step 1: *Preparing and Planning*: In this step, one should gather facts about the other party, learn about the other party's negotiating style and anticipate other sides position and prioritize issues. To ensure smooth negotiation, one should also prepare alternatives proposals and establish BATNA (the Best Alternative To a Negotiated Agreement). The most ideal case is to come out with a win-win plan to both parties.

Phase 2: During the Negotiation

Step 2: *Setting the Tone*: In this step, one should firmly state his position and explain his interest on need base.

Step 3: *Exploring Underlying Needs*: It is also important to actively listen for facts and reasons behind other party's position and explore underlying needs of the other party. If conflict exists, try to develop creative alternatives without losing the win-win focus. Neutralize tactic if necessary.

Step 4: *Selecting, Refining, and Crafting an Agreement*: It is a step in which both parties present the starting proposal. They should listen for new ideas, think creatively to handle conflict and gain power and create cooperative environment.

Step 5: *Reviewing and Recapping the Agreement*: This is the step in which both parties formalize agreement in a written contract or letter of intent.

Phase 3: After the Negotiation

Step 6: *Reviewing the Negotiation*: Reviewing the negotiation helps one to learn the lessons on how to achieve a better outcome. Therefore, one should take the time to review each element and ask oneself, "what went well?" and "what could be improved next time ?"

Four Progressive Sequences in the Negotiation Process

1. Pre-negotiation

Everything we do, if we are to perform the activity properly, requires a certain degree of preparation beforehand. No doubt, there are many occasions we admonish ourselves for not being prepared, when things do not turn out as well as we thought they would be. Preparation is a prerequisite to any successful activity or endeavour. Negotiation is no different (http://www.spiritus-temporis.com/negotiation/3-phases-in-negotiation.html).

The first thing we need to determine is whether there is actually any reason to negotiate at all. Secondly we need to be clear on the specifics we want to negotiate about. We have to get *'our ducks in a row'* before we even contact the person with whom we are to negotiate. We then need to establish some form of agenda before beginning our talks for negotiation. We should identify the correct people who will be involved in the talks and their levels or responsibility and authority.

Wherever possible we should attempt to obtain as much information about these people and their company or organization. Intelligence gathering is crucial in obtaining a picture of the other side so we can assess their needs, motivations, and goals with respect to our own. Next, we need to set up a venue where we are going to meet and have appropriate time to conduct the talks. It is a good idea to begin this process by establishing direct contact with your counterpart. We can begin by building some kind of rapport, and set out the agenda, through a variety of means such as phone calls, faxes, e-mails, and even an informal personal get together beforehand.

2. Conceptualization

This phase is where we develop the foundation of the agreement by framing the issues, without becoming bogged down in the miniscule details. The building blocks need to be put together to understand the basic concept of the agreement we are seeking. It's like two separate parties coming together to consider the blueprint design, or structure of the agreement. We are attempting to formulate principles upon which we can both agree, such as who will provide financing or the licensing aspects for example.

This is the phase where we define each other's goals and objectives through fact finding and by establishing some measure of compatibility. It is not unlike that awkward first date with the opposite sex. We begin to consider creative options and discuss concessions. We advance proposals and counter-proposals, back and forth, until some manner of tentative agreement is reached. The terms of the partnership are also re-framed until they reach the level, where both parties are as satisfied as they can be, within the various parameters of what they bring to the table. This is how we arrive at the basic concept of our agreement.

3. Settling the Stage

Simply put, this phase sees the completion of the agreement. Here, we use our external specialists to complete the details of the venture, that we are about to mutually embark upon. This phase discusses the problems of implementing the partnership realistically, so that it is both viable and workable. We also work out the details as they relate to production, scheduling, handling delays, task responsibility and authority. We need to use our own technical and management people to streamline the process so it works smoothly, and meets both our standards and requirements.

The final portion of this process is then left to the wordsmiths, usually our respective legal experts, to put our agreement into written form documentation, and to describe the contractual obligations to which both parties have agreed. This is not the 'walk in the park' like it sounds. Settling the details correctly and meticulously is extremely important. Many negotiations have collapsed because the parties failed to devote the necessary time and work to address the details efficiently. Until these are properly ironed out, we can't celebrate our success.

4. Follow-up

Just because we have signed on the dotted line doesn't means that it ends there. We cannot toss the contract into our files and forget about it. It seldom ends there as problems always arise. Any aspect of any contract may need to be re-negotiated, or the details altered to counter a broad variety of changing circumstances. Expensive and embittered legal battles can be circumvented simply by keeping the lines of communication open with our counterparts. We should be experienced enough by now to understand, that nothing is ever as simple as it seems. If we properly apply the phases of negotiation effectively and efficiently, positive results will manifest themselves in accordance to our efforts. Anything worth doing is worth doing well, and as negotiation is something we can't hide or run away from, we might as well do it right.

Stages in the Negotiation Process

Stages in the negotiation process are (i) orientation and fact finding, (ii) resistance, (iii) reformulation of strategies, (iv) hard bargaining and decision-making, (v) agreement, and (vi) follow-up (Acuff, 1997). For example, a consumer purchasing an automobile investigates price and performance, then negotiates with an agent regarding price and delivery date. Resistance surfaces as pricing and delivery expectations are negotiated. Strategies are reformulated as the parties deter mine motivation and constraints. Key issues surface as hard bargaining begins. Problems surface, and solutions—such as creative financing or dealer trades—are created to counter pricing and delivery problems. After details are negotiated, the agreement is ratified. After the sale, the agent may follow up with the buyer to build a relationship and set the stage for future purchase and negotiation. The six stages of the process would be approached differently depending on where the negotiators reside on the style continuum.

Basic strategies, both cooperative and competitive, that can be applied in the negotiation process are the following:

- Use simple language.
- Ask many questions.
- Observe and practice nonverbal behavior.
- Build solid relationships.
- Maintain personal integrity.
- Be patient.
- Conserve concessions.
- Be aware of the power of time, information, saying no, and walking away.
- Pay attention to who the real decision maker is, how negotiators are rewarded, and information sources.
- Listen actively.
- Educate the other party.
- Concentrate on the issues.
- Control the written contract.
- Be creative.
- Appeal to personal motivations and negotiating styles.
- Pay attention to power tactics.
- Be wary of such unethical tactics as raising phony issues; extorting; planting information; and making phony demands, unilateral assumptions, or deliberate mistakes.

The following summarizes the strategies that might be used in various stages of negotiations:

Initial Stage

- Plan thoroughly.
- Identify and prioritize issues.

- Establish a settlement range.
- Focus on long-term goals and consequences.
- Focus on mutual principles and concerns.
- Be aware that "no" can be the opening position and the first offer is often above expectations.
- Be aware of the reluctant buyer or seller ploy.

Middle Stage

- Revise strategies.
- Consider many options.
- Increase power by getting the other side to commit first.
- Add credibility by getting agreements in writing.
- Be wary of splitting the difference.
- To handle an impasse, offer to set it aside momentarily.
- To handle a stalemate, alter one of the negotiating points.
- To handle a deadlock, bring in a third party.
- When asked for a concession, ask for a tradeoff.
- Be wary if the other party uses a "higher authority" as a rationale for not meeting negotiating points.
- Be aware of the "vise" tactic ("you'll have to do better than that").

Ending Stage

- Counter the other party's asking for more concessions at the end by addressing all details and communicating the fairness of the deal in closure.
- Counter a persistent negotiator by withdrawing an offer.
- Do not expect the other party to follow through on verbal promises.
- Congratulate the other side.

The Evolution of Negotiation

Even as different approaches to negotiation across national or international cultures are identified, change is a constant apparent. International business culture tends to privilege Western approaches to negotiation, centered around the pivot of problem-solving and linear communication, as do many settings and formatting to reach a predetermined goal. As Western norms are balanced with Eastern and Southern values, and local traditions are balanced with regional and national approaches, negotiation practices continue their global evolution based on unique corporate as well as institutional experiences over a period of time. The following are some of the illustrative landmarks that helped evolve and building-up of the Global Business Negotiation conceptual frameworks:

1. Anonymous. *Negotiating with the Americans*. Disseminated by James T. Felicita, head of contract systems for NASA Systems Division, Hughes Aircraft Co. March 1983.

2. For more explanation of the Western bias of negotiation and conflict resolution research, see Kimmel, Paul. Cultural Perspectives on International Negotiations, *Journal of Social Issues*, 50, (1), 1994, PP. 179-196 and Weldon, Elizabeth and Karen A. Jehn. Examining Cross-Cultural Differences in Conflict Management Behavior: A Strategy for Future Research. *The International Journal of Conflict Management* 1995, 6, (4) October, pp. 387-403.
3. *Intercultural Communication Presentation*, European Career Orientation available at http://eco.ittralee.ie/personal/presentation.php; Internet.
4. Novinger, Tracy. *Intercultural Communication: A Practical Guide*. Austin, TX: University of Texas Press, 2001, p. 121, quoting from Baldrige, Letitia. *Letitia Baldrige's New Complete Guide to Executive Manners*. New York: Macmillan, 1993, p. 121.
5. Lederach, John Paul. *Preparing for Peace*. Syracuse, NY: Syracuse University Press, 1995, p. 43.
6. Adler, Nancy. *International Dimensions of Organizational Behavior (3rd Ed.)* Cincinnati, OH: South-Western College Publishing, 1997, p. 217.
7. Offiong, Daniel A. Conflict Resolution Among the Ibibio of Nigeria. *Journal of Anthropological Research*, 53, 4, Winter 1997, pp. 423-442.
8. Adair *et al*. Negotiating Behavior When Cultures Collide: The United States and Japan. *Journal of Applied Psychology*. Vol 86(3), June 2001.
9. Nakanishi, Masayuki and Kenneth M. Johnson. Implications of Self-Disclosure on Conversational Logics, Perceived Communication, Communication Competence, and Social Attraction. A Comparison of Japanese and American Cultures. In Wiseman, Richard L. and Jolene Koester. *Intercultural Communication Competence*. Newbury Park, CA: Sage Publications, 1993, p. 207.
10. Graham, Sano, and March. Negotiating Behaviors in Ten Foreign Cultures. *Management Science*. Vol. 40(1), January 1994.
11. Nakanishi, Masayuki and Kenneth M. Johnson. Implications of Self-Disclosure on Conversational Logics, Perceived Communication, Communication Competence, and Social Attraction. A Comparison of Japanese and American Cultures. In Wiseman, Richard L. and Jolene Koester. *Intercultural Communication Competence*. Newbury Park, CA: Sage Publications, 1993, p. 207.
12. Brett *et al*. From Adair *et al*. Negotiating Behavior When Cultures Collide: The United States and Japan. *Journal of Applied Psychology*. Vol 86(3), June 2001.

There have been few instances in the history of social science in which a practitioner-oriented book served as the wellspring for cutting-edge academic research for over two decades. *Getting to Yes* by Roger Fisher and William Ury is such a book, a timeless book containing timeless concepts that continue to unravel themselves like a mysterious DNA process (Leigh Thompson and

Geoffrey J. Leonardelli, 2004). The big bang: The evolution of negotiation research'. In writing this article, we toyed with several analogies, such as "great wine" and "DNA material." Neither seemed to capture the sheer enormity of the book and the universality of the concepts. So we opted for big and settled upon the "big bang." The big-bang theory is the dominant scientific theory about the origin of the universe.

In 1927, Belgian priest Georges Lemaitre was first to propose that the universe began with the explosion of a primeval atom. They expressed negotiation in the following words: "We liken the explosion of that atom to the publication of *Getting to Yes,* and we see the current universe of negotiation theory and research to be a result of this big bang. Just like the big-bang theory of the universe, there is no way to ever prove that *Getting to Yes* expanded and facilitated the study of negotiation, but in this article, we are going to try to do so by citing some of the most influential empirical research on negotiation since the book's publication in 1981". The core elements of *Getting to Yes in this perception* are stated simply and succinctly in the Table of Contents as powerful maxims that have served as mantras for countless negotiators:

- People: Separate the people from the problem
- Interests: Focus on interests, not positions
- Options: Invent options for mutual gain
- Criteria: Insist on using objective criteria

The Psychology of Negotiation

Negotiation is the communication between two or more individuals or groups who meet with the intent of producing a cooperative agreement. Each group has conflicting interests and must shift position or change the threshold of acceptance to reach a mutually beneficial agreement. The single most important objective of any honestly negotiated agreement is to ensure each party feels they have won relative to their priority negotiation interest objectives. Achievement of this objective requires that some basic psychological constraints and guidelines are followed during the process. These constraints and guidelines assume that the fundamentals of negotiation are in place, i.e., honesty willingness, shared and conflicting interests, room to maneuver, and authority to maneuver. Quite often we tend to carry out negotiations and achieve agreements with those close to us, with our employers and employees, customers and, of course, also with our contractual partners. We also happen use negotiation techniques in resolving everyday disagreements. In doing so, our preferred style of negotiation is dependent upon our individual characteristics and the overall personality traits. Even experienced negotiators make mistakes when preparing and executing negotiation strategy. After all, even seasoned negotiaters are human, and all human beings are vulnerable to psychological biases–systematic and predictable departures from rationality–that can derail an otherwise sound negotiation strategy (http://www.negotiationgenius.com/4.html).

Negotiation, therefore, is not just the territory of lawyers. Quite the contrary, negotiations have a different meaning and connotation for everyone. Everything also to a large extent depends on the context in which it is examined and seen. Lawyers use negotiations in the context of contracts and dispute resolutions. Negotiations are examined as a process, as a psycho-social phenomenon, a competitive situation, problem resolution and techniques to resolve conflicts. Psychological observations on how individual characteristics affect the style of negotiations are derived from socio-psychological experiments. (Ilona Nurmela-http://www.juridica.ee/juridica_en.php?document=en/articles/2006/2/101530.SUM.php).

The Attitude of Negotiators

When a negotiation fails it is generally attributed to several key issues, but the most common mistake is that people become emotionally involved, take a position and treat the other party as if they are the enemy. The very best negotiators seek a mutually beneficial outcome, thus avoiding taking an unyielding position. They are able to divorce themselves emotionally from the process and focus on what both sides can accomplish together. Successful Negotiations have two parties who understand 'Win – Win' outcomes, and approach the negotiations from an abundance mentality versus a scarcity mentality. That is, both parties see an abundance of opportunity as opposed to a scarcity of opportunity before them. With this in mind they are both willing to approach the table with an earnest desire to satisfy everyone's needs as best as possible, and do not see the solution as scrambling and competing for precious little. So a successful negotiation begins with an attitude and understanding that both parties must win. In the end, who really "won." The inescapable conclusion is that 'BOTH' the parties must feel they achieved a fair outcome given their realistic expectations at the outset.

The negotiation is often times determined by the fundamental philosophy of the parties involved. Is the negotiation a contest which must be won, a contest in which one must squash the "adversary?" Or, is it an opportunity to seek synergy and allow both parties maximum gain? Another way to approach the negotiation is with an objective viewpoint, devoid of the impact of emotion. Each party to a negotiation has a philosophy they bring to the table. It is a fatal mistake to assume the other party shares your philosophy. In fact the only sensible approach is an objective measure based on independent principles. This allows us to successfully negotiate on the merits of the agreement without the influence of emotions or attitudes (http://www.champtrainer.com/content/files/whitepapers/the_psychology_of_negotiation.pdf).

There is a common element universally applicable to all forms of negotiations. The common element which can never be overlooked is that conflict to some degree will be present. One would, whether like or not, see some people's behavioral traits causing them to be aggressive and overpowering, and they become quite active in a conflict situation. Other participants could be quite "people oriented" and quite optimistically seek a peaceful and cooperative solution, placing a greater value on the relationship versus the outcome of the ongoing negotiation process. The most successful negotiators are able to rise above the emotional aspects separating the people from the tasks. They are resolute in their quest for a mutually beneficial agreement but are able to assess and make decisions on the independent merits of the issues. These people are not in the least un-emotional, but they are merely adept at subordinating their emotions to the issues throughout the course of the negotiation to make sure that negotiation process goes uninterrupted all the way through.

The Devil's Advocate Approach

In the advocacy approach, a skilled negotiator usually serves as advocate for one party to the negotiation and attempts to obtain the most favorable outcomes possible for that party. In this process the negotiator attempts to determine the minimum outcome(s) the other party is (or parties are) willing to accept, then adjusts their demands accordingly. A "successful" negotiation in the advocacy approach is when the negotiator is able to obtain all or most of the outcomes their party desires, but without driving the other party to permanently break off negotiations, unless the BATNA is acceptable.

Traditional negotiating is sometimes called *'win-lose'* because of the assumption of a fixed "pie", that one person's gain results in another person's loss. Another view is that in negotiation both parties are equals by definition and that the best possible outcome is reached when both parties agree to it. If the two parties were not equals, the stronger party would dictate the outcome and there would be no negotiation at all.

Hidden 'Blind Spots' in a Negotiation

Many negotiators focus too narrowly on a negotiation problem and fail to adequately consider how the context, the decisions of the other side, and the rules of the negotiation game will affect their strategy and their prospects for success. They also miss out on opportunities for changing the rules of the game to achieve better results. Each one of us has blind spots-gaps in our self-knowledge. less conscious truths about how we operate. A blind spot may involve being unaware of: a particular skill or skill deficit that one exhibits, self-centeredness, aloofness or hostility towards others, an area of emotional sensitivity, or perhaps some dysfunctional family dynamic that gets played out repeatedly with other people. Unidentified blind spots can ruin a career (Mac Hart: http://drmalcolmhart.com/userfiles/254960/file/Your_Blind_Spots_Know_Thyself.doc)

Other impediments to self-knowledge occur when officers exhibit attitudes of arrogance or interpersonal defensiveness. These types of roadblocks to helpful feedback may not involve blind spots, but perhaps rigid interpersonal styles that reduce the likelihood that (i) the person will ask others for help or

(ii) that others around him will be willing to risk offering sincere feedback to this close-minded co-worker.

If people tend to view you as arrogant or defensive, you may have to work harder to get accurate feedback. But, don't give up! Be willing to ask repeatedly. Over time, others may start to experience you as sincere and open to input, and consequently they will become more willing to offer it. At times, you will receive negative feedback from others that you don't agree with and which may not be true at all. Take a deep breath or two, and resist becoming defensive or reactive. Remember, the perceptions of others are hard-core facts to them. Instead, really try to (i) practice the rules of good listening and (ii) initially accept all feedback as accurate-even when you know better. Then, instead of debating the truth of their observations, show them through your future actions and behavior that their perceptions are wrong.

Recognizing and Resolving Ethical Dilemmas

Many people believe that ethics are too personal and idiosyncratic to be discussed broadly or categorically. This is undoubtedly true–to a degree. Yet recent research suggests that people often behave less ethically than they themselves consider appropriate. In other cases, they are not even aware of the damage they are inflicting on others when they pursue certain strategies. And in the shadow of major corporate scandals, there's a renewed emphasis on maintaining integrity while still achieving negotiation success. HBS provides a framework for thinking more carefully and comprehensively about these issues (http://www.negotiationgenius.com/4.html).

Negotiation Style

Negotiation styles vary with the person, their beliefs and skills, as well as the general context in which they occur. Here, we present a number of different styles considered from different viewpoints involved while transacting a business negotiation (http://changingminds.org/disciplines/negotiation/styles/styles.htm).

1. Belief-based styles

There is a common spectrum of negotiation that ranges from collaborative to competitive. The approach taken is generally based on—

- The spectrum of negotiation styles: From concession to competition.
- Collaborative negotiation: Negotiating for win-win.
- Competitive negotiation: Negotiating for win-lose.
- Balanced negotiation: Walking between collaborative and competitive negotiation.

2. Professional styles

Professional styles are those use by people who have a significant element of negotiation in their roles. Here is a selection of different contexts in which such negotiation takes place.

- Industrial relations: Confrontational bargaining.
- Managing board: Together and competing.
- International: Diplomatic dancing.
- Political: Scheming horse-trading.
- Selling and buying: Professional sellers and buyers.
- Hostage: Emotional big-stakes exchanges.

3. *Contextual Styles*

Negotiation often happens within non-professional contexts, where the people either do not know that they are negotiating or they are not skilled at it.

- Domestic: Discussions and arguments at home.
- Everyday: Everybody, every day, negotiates.
- Hierarchical: Parent-child, boss-subordinate, etc.

4. *Spectrum of Negotiation Styles*

Although negotiation styles can be classified as concessional, competitive or collaborative, in practice there are a range of styles, based on the degree to which a person thinks about themselves or thinks about the other person (Fig. 1).

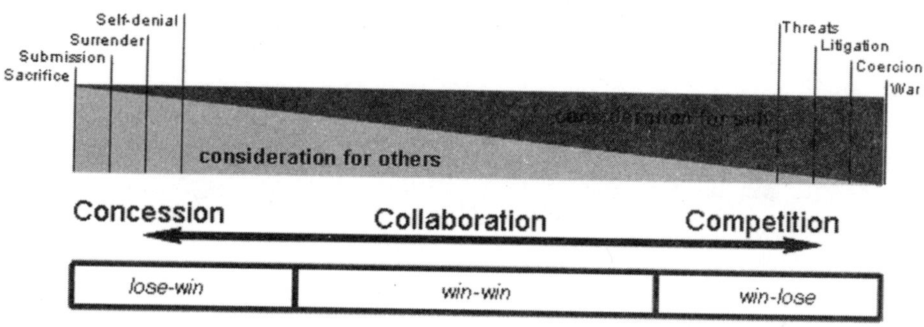

Fig. 1: Three Forms of Negotiation Styles
(http://changingminds.org/disciplines/negotiation/styles/styles.htm)

Consideration for self

Considering yourself in negotiation is natural and reasonable—after all, the main point is to get something that you want. In particular, if you care little about the other person or the relationship, then you will prioritize your needs actions above those of others.

Excessive consideration for self leads to a Machiavellian approach, where the ends justifies the means. Overt aggression, intimidation and coercive deception are considered normal and necessary and destroying the other person in some way may be a symbol of your victory over them.

Consideration for others

Consideration for others will depend on your values, which are often based on your beliefs about people. In particular, if you put yourself down (for example if you have low self-esteem) or you escalate the importance of others too highly, then you will think considerably more about the other person and prioritize their needs well above your own.

Excessive consideration for others leads to relentless concession, where you create a lose-win situation with you as the loser. You may even lose elements of the relationship as giving away too much can just end up in you losing respect. Some people like being the victim, but it is no way to conduct a negotiation.

A Middle path

Between concession and competition lies balance, although in practice this may be more dynamic and variable than may be expected. Thus, what should be a highly collaborative negotiation may become a balanced negotiation, even with competitive elements. Shared values are commonly used, however, to protect the relationship and ensure fair play. At worst, some third person is called in to ensure a reasonable balance.

Two more styles of negotiating, *competitive and cooperative,* are commonly recognized. No negotiation is purely one type or the other; rather, negotiators typically move back and forth between the two styles based on the situation. On one end of the negotiation continuum is the competitive style. *Competitive negotiation*— also called adversarial, non-cooperative, distributive bargaining, positional, or hard bargaining—is used to divide limited resources; the assumption is that the pie to be divided is finite. Competitive strategies assume a "win-lose" situation in which the negotiating parties have opposing interests. Hostile, coercive negotiation tactics are used to force an advantage, and pre-negotiation binding agreements are not allowed. Concessions, distorted communication, confrontational tactics, and emotional ploys are used.

Skilled competitive negotiators give away less information while acquiring more information, ask more questions, create strategies to get information, act firm, offer less generous opening offers, are slower to give concessions, use confident body language, and conceal feelings. They are more interested in the bargaining position and bottom line of the other negotiating party, and they prepare for negotiations by developing strategy, planning answers to weak points, and preparing alternate strategies.

A buyer-seller home purchase transaction illustrates competitive negotiating. The buyer gathers information to determine home value, quality, expenses, and title status. The seller gathers information to ensure that the prospective buyer qualifies for the loan. The parties negotiate concessions regarding home repairs, items to remain in the house, closing dates, and price. The negotiations stall as the buyer and seller disagree on a closing date; the seller retaliates by keeping the buyer out of the home for several days after the closing date. As a consequence of the competitive strategies used, the relationship between the buyer and seller suffers; however, the end result (sale and purchase of a home) satisfies both parties.

On the other end of the negotiating style continuum is cooperative negotiating, also called integrative problem solving or soft bargaining. Cooperative-negotiation is based on a win-win mentality and is designed to increase joint gain; the pie to be divided is perceived as expanding. Attributes include reasonable and open communication; an assumption that common interests, benefits, and needs exist; trust building; thorough and accurate exchange of information; exploration of issues presented as problems and solutions; mediated discussion; emphasis on coalition formation; pre-negotiation binding agreements; and a search for creative alternative solutions that bring benefits to all players. The risk in cooperative negotiating is vulnerability to a competitive opponent.

Cooperative negotiators require skills in patience; listening; and identification and isolation of cooperative issues, goals, problems, and priorities. Additionally, cooperative negotiators need skills in clarifying similarities and differences in goals and priorities and the ability to trade intelligently, propose many alternatives, and select the best alternative based on quality and mutual acceptability. Cooperative negotiating might be used, for example, in a hiring situation. An employer contacts a candidate to encourage the candidate to submit his or her credentials for a job opening. Trust is built and common interests are explored as the employer and candidate exchange information about the company and the candidate's qualifications. Creative solutions are explored to accommodate the candidate's and employer's special circumstances, including work at home, flexible scheduling, salary, and benefits. The two parties successfully culminate the negotiations with a signed job contract.

National Negotiating Styles

Negotiators' culture is expressed in their negotiating style. Generally, negotiating style is defined as the way persons from different cultures behave in negotiations—which in many cases unique to the general cultural pattern of the country in question. This definition implies that:

- There is a strong link between a person's culture and his negotiating style.
- A negotiating style of a certain person can only be evaluated through an analysis of that person's behavior in several negotiation settings.

To identify cross-cultural differences in negotiating styles the scholars typically focus on selected aspects of negotiators' behavior called negotiation factors or traits. These traits are usually selected based on their relevance and potential variability across different cultures. Various traits have been used by various scholars in their research on identifying the influence of culture on negotiation or on measuring negotiating styles. In this document we would like to present the approach pursued by Jeswald Salacuse together with the results of his seminal study on international negotiating styles (Salacuse, 1998). Negotiation is a dialogue intended to resolve disputes, to produce an agreement upon courses of action, to bargain for individual or collective advantage, or to craft outcomes to satisfy various interests. It is the primary method of alternative dispute resolution. (http://en.wikipedia.org/wiki/Negotiation)

Negotiation occurs in business, non-profit organizations government branches, legal proceedings, among nations and in personal situations such as marriage, divorce, parenting, and everyday life. The study of the subject is called *negotiation theory*. Those who work in negotiation professionally are called *negotiators*. Professional negotiators are often specialized, such as *union negotiators, leverage buyout negotiators, peace negotiators, hostage negotiators,* or may work under other titles, such as diplomats, legislators or brokers. It is imperative to understand the various negotiation tactics, negotiation styles, unique regulations, and other cultural issues that influence behaviors during negotiation with Greater China because this will affect the development of world economies over the next ten years.

In 2002, the International Monetary Fund (IMF) International Financial Statistics and World Trade Organization (WTO) World Trade Report indicated Mainland China, Hong Kong and Taiwan account for 10% of global merchandise trade in the world; and, among the three they import 41% of the products in Asian regions. This is 24% more than the Japanese, making China's role as the region's new key market. Presently, the Greater China's economy has an enormous influence in the world.

Even though Taiwan, Hong Kong, and Mainland China have the same ancestors, and the similar cultures (called Chinese culture from Confucianism), they have different ways of doing business and negotiating with other countries. This is because they have different political policies, educational systems, value systems, and different views of acceptance of different world cultures. It is important to understand cross-cultural variations in negotiation if international trade agreements among the three geographic areas (Mainland China, Hong Kong, and Taiwan).

Following the UN recommendations, international merchandise trade is defined as all goods which add to or subtract from the stock of material resources of a country by entering (imports) or leaving (exports) its economic territory (Tsai, 2003). In international trade, however, the situation may be very different from domestic business: lead times can be much longer; transit times in the carriage of goods or documents can be greater; there may be differences in language, time zones, local customs and laws, working week cycles and holiday period, all of which may have an effect on methods of settlement and cash management.

Culture is the unique characteristic of a social group; other social groups can share the values and norms. In 2001, Thompson suggested "culture encompasses many dimensions such as nations, occupational groups, social classes, genders, races, tribes, corporations, clubs, and social movements which should neither be led only in one direction nor be defined to a simple explanation". Culture relates to economic, political, social structure, religion, education, and language, and it plays an important role in determining whether or not negotiators will employ questionable or unethical tactics. Culture alone does not determine attitudes, intentions, and actions. In 1981, Casse indicated that cross-cultural negotiations have different parties, and belongs different cultures, and they have different thinking, feeling, and behaving to negotiate to each other.

Pre-negotiation Preparation and Issues

International marketers are more and more becoming business negotiators, constantly discussing deals across borders with a variety of people, ranging from consumers to intermediaries and even competitors. The ability to interact effectively with foreign trade partners may well depend on the adjustments made to culturally diverse backgrounds encountered during sales negotiations. (Ghauri and Usunier, 1996) In the planning cycle of international management, the negotiation stage is the link between strategic planning and implementation. Deresky, (1996), Ghauri and Usunier (1996) define negotiation as "a voluntary process of give and take where both parties modify their offers and expectations in order to come closer to each other". Every sale or purchase has its negotiation aspect and every negotiation presents opportunities and dangers for both parties. Business negotiation is special due to the fact that it is a voluntary process and that the parties can, at any given moment, quit the process. International negotiations are fast becoming a fact of life for many growing companies and operating across national cultures often magnifies negotiation problems. (Gulbro and Herbig, 1995). The most important aspects of culture for international business negotiations are time, individual versus collective behaviour, pattern of communication and emphasis on personal relations. (Ghauri and Usunier, 1996) Stereotypically many Westerners are heavily focused on time while Latin Americans and Africans find it less important. Another difference between cultures is the degree of individualism versus collectivism. In an individualistic society members tend to be self-actualized, self-motivated and any relationships are defined by self-interest.

There is a high desire for personal time, freedom and challenge. Members of a collectivistic society have a high desire for training, physical conditions and benefits. The United States has a high degree of individualism while several South American countries are typically collectivistic. The third potential and relevant difference is the pattern of communication in consideration of direct/indirect and explicit/implicit communication. Some languages are more contextual than others. Non-verbal communication, personal space, handshakes, ways of greeting each other, communication between males and females and signs of irritation are different aspects of communication patterns. (Ghauri and Usunier, 1996) Non-verbal behaviour may be defined as any behaviour, intentional or unintentional, beyond the words themselves that can be interpreted to have a meaning by a receiver. These behaviours vary between cultures and include facial expressions, eye contact, gestures, body movements, posture, physical appearance, space, touch, and time usage. They either accompany verbal messages or are used independently. They may affirm and emphasize or negate and even contradict spoken messages. (Hendon, Hendon and Herbig, 1996) The fourth and final important difference presented by Ghauri and Usunier (1996) is the personality of the negotiator. In some cultures the negotiator is more important than the issue at hand or the future relationship between the parties, hence is the emphasis on personal relations different.

All different aspects of culture have a common consequence and that is that they are aggravating the essential understanding of the counterpart. (Hendon and Herbig, 1996) Another occurring problem is that members of one culture may focus on different aspects of an agreement (e.g. legal, financial) from members of another culture (e.g. personal relationships). When one takes the seemingly simple process of negotiations into a cross-cultural context, it becomes even more complex and complications tend to grow exponentially.

Ghauri and Usunier (1996) identified two groups of variables in addition to the process and its dimensions that influence international business negotiation; background and atmosphere factors. The background factors influence both the process and the atmosphere. Objectives, the first background factor, are categorized as being common, conflicting or complementary. The environment factor refers to political, social and structural issues, as well as the location of the respective party's market The third background factor includes third parties involvement, such as consultants, agents, and the respective government. The skills and experience of the negotiators is the fourth and final background factor.

The atmosphere variables characterize the relationship that has evolved during the process as a whole. The first factor is the perceived co-operation/ conflict—that the parties have something to negotiate for and something to negotiate about. The distribution of power in the eventual relationship and expectations are the two other presented atmosphere variables. Another issue that also has to be considered and decided before the actual face-to-face meeting is the site for the negotiations. Site selection is an important aspect of protocol because it affects psychological climate, availability and use of communications channels and the presence of time limits. (Hendon and Herbig, 1996)

The strategic dimension involves presentations, strategy, decision-making and need for an agent. These factors will be discussed in the problem discussion. Ghauri and Usunier (1996) further divide the process of international negotiations into three distinct stages. Pre-negotiation refers to both parties attempt to understand each other's needs and demands. Preparation and planning are the most important parts of negotiation. On the surface, the drama and theatrics of face-to-face confrontation can easily create the impression that success lies in persuasiveness, eloquence, clever manoeuvres, and occasional histrionics. While these techniques make the process interesting (and at times even entertaining), the foundations for success are the preparation and planning that take place prior to actual negotiation. (Lewicki and Litterer, 1985)

Because most negotiation problems are caused by differences in culture, language and environment, a distinct advantage can be gained if negotiators familiarise themselves with the entire context and background of their counterparts in addition to the specific subjects to be negotiated. "The importance of careful preparation for international negotiations cannot be overstated." (Deresky, 1996). The dynamism of the process can be observed at this early stage, pre-negotiation, as both parties begin to understand one another's needs and evaluate the benefits of entering into the process of negotiations. "The most important success factor in negotiation is preparation and planning" (Ghauri and Usunier, 1996).

Approaches used in the pre-negotiation Stage

According to Ghauri and Usunier (1996), the process of international negotiation, and consequently pre-negotiation, begins when the first contact between parties in which interest in doing business with each other is shown. The parties involved gather as much relevant information as possible on each other, the operating environment, the involvement of third parties, influences, competitors and the infrastructure. One of the issues is to define the problem to be solved. Some negotiations occur during the pre-negotiation stage and some cautious offers are being made. Informal meetings take place as both parties are examining the other's position. Whether the process will continue to the next stage depends on the perceived level of co-operation or conflict, of power or dependence and the expected benefits of the relationship in this stage. A fundamental characteristic of negotiations is the existence of conflict as well as co-operation in the relationship. To some extent, especially in "win-win" negotiation, the two parties have a common interest in finding a solution that is optimal and suitable with regard to the supplier's ability and the user's requirements. Basically, the two parties complement each other.

Conflict not only has a negative connotation, but also negatively influences the process as a whole. As conflict intensifies, perceptions become distorted and people interpret everything according to their own perspective. As a result, parties get locked into their position and the negotiation process is seriously and negatively affected.

Conflicts in negotiation are almost unavoidable but the important issue is how to handle the conflict and how to understand, and let the other party perceive more co-operation than conflict. The parties should truly see how they are going to co-operate, examine whether it is realistic to expect to achieve the objectives of both sides and to identify the obstacles that have to be overcome to achieve these objectives. The pre-negotiation stage is often more important than the formal negotiations in an international business relationship. Social, informal relationships developed between negotiators during the initial stage can be of great help. Trust and confidence gained from these relationships increase the chances of agreement. One method of establishing that kind of relations is to invite individuals from the counterpart to visit the office or country in order to develop trust. The parties need to understand the interests and fears of the other party. The prime objective with these informal meetings is to get to each other's priorities. It is important to understand the other party's point of view and the power of its arguments.

Strategic Aspect of Negotiation

A strategy is a complete plan regarding problems, the solutions available and preferred choices, relative to the other party's choices and preferences. Parties try to build up their relative power. The initial strategy is dependent on the information gathered so far and the expectations. The parties should list the problems and issues, especially the conflicting issues and form strategies and choices for all possible solutions they or the other party could suggest. These should further be ranked individually as desired, expected and not acceptable. It is important to have several solutions for each problem or issue. Furthermore, Ghauri and Usunier (1996) identify a number of key points to consider while performing preparation and planning.

Identify the Contents of the Deal

The initial points to consider are issues such as implications of the deal, the interests at stake, the "fit" with organizational objectives, and possible economic, political or other restrictions between parties. These issues must be considered in terms of tangible and intangible motives. Comparison of strengths and weaknesses is quite important. In business negotiations are not only the negotiating companies affected but also the competitors who have an interest in the same business. In most cases, a party's arguments or preferences are influenced by the offers competitors have made.

Create alternatives

To negotiate effectively, the marketer must gather information on the strengths and weaknesses not only of the opposite party, but also of the other related parties, such as competitors. By considering the resources and behaviour of competitors, marketers can develop their own alternatives on different issues. One way of creating alternatives is to judge each conflicting issue in the following scale: our ideal position – their ideal position. Here one should look for overlaps. If no overlap exists, one should ask how it could be created.

Put yourself in others' shoes

For negotiations to be successful, one party must understand the other party's position and point of views; including domestic compulsions. This will help each side interpret and anticipate the other side's nature of reactions and quality of responses to arguments. The ability to look at the situation from the other's point of view as well as from a much broader perspective is one of the most important skills required in a successful negotiation.

Gauge the appropriateness of the message

The exchange of information must be adjusted for easier comprehension. Technical specifications and other material should be provided in the local language. Not only does this facilitate effective communication but it also demonstrates respect for the local language and environment. Presence of local representatives can add value and provide more space for democratic options

Build up relative power

Negotiators can determine who has the relative power advantage by gathering information about the other party, considering each party's position and developing different alternatives. They can try to build their own relative power by developing arguments against the elements of power and improving their own position. In the negotiation process, this kind of power may be increased by repeatedly mentioning the weak points of the other party—but all the same, in more subtle way or diplomatically.

Gower's Handbook: Preparation for Negotiation

Gower's Handbook helps the Preparatory stage of Negotiation in the following manner (The Gower handbook of management; Dennis Lock, Gower Publishing Company & P.D.V. Marsh-Gower's Contract Negotiation Handbook (3 rd Edition):

The relationship

Relationships may be independent, where once the business has been completed both parties go their separate ways, or dependent, where negotiation takes place between two parties who are bound together in some way. Important questions to answer about the relationship are:

- What sort of relationship do I need after the negotiation is finished?
- Are we likely to do business again?
- How important are good relations to making what is agreed work in practice?
- How much trust is there between the parties?
- In what context is this negotiation taking place?

Mandate

- What are the things I can negotiate about? What is outside the negotiation, that is, non-negotiable?
- What are the limits to my authority?
- Who sets these limits and what are my options. Should I need to deviate from them?
- Who else has an interest in the outcome of this negotiation and how aware am I of their views?

Assumptions and Expectations

Sometimes negotiations go badly wrong because one or both parties make assumptions about the situation that are not valid or have unrealistic expectations:

- What assumptions am I making about my own position and that of my opponent?
- How clear am I about the difference between what I *know* about the situation and what I *assume*?
- What expectations do I have about my opponent?
- What information do I have or could I get to check the validity of my assumptions?

Reality Check

Once you have done your preparation, you need to subject your plans to a reality check:

- How realistic are my desired outcomes for this negotiation?
- What do I know about similar settlements in the industry or organization?
- What does past history suggest will be a realistic and fair agreement?
- How does what I want match with what either side can reasonably deliver, for example in terms of cost, time and quality?

Assessment of Negotiating Power

Assessment of negotiating power is a particularly important part of the preparation process. How you assess the negotiating power of yourself and your opponent will affect your whole approach to the preparation and conduct of the negotiation. The key to assessing your negotiating power lies in understanding your Best Alternative to a Negotiated Agreement or BATNA. The question to ask yourself is: What is the best outcome I could get if I did not negotiate with this party? What other options do I have if I did not negotiate? The more options you have and the more attractive they are compared with what you can agree through negotiation, then the greater your negotiating power. Working out your BATNA also helps you judge the acceptability of the deal on the table; if the agreement you are heading towards is worse than your BATNA, then it is time to break off negotiations. You also need to make an assessment of your opponent's BATNA to understand their negotiating power. What alternatives do they have to a negotiated deal with you? How attractive do these alternatives look?

Work out your variables

In any negotiation there will be a range of elements or variables that go to make up the issue or problem under discussion.

- What are the different variables that you have to play with?

- Which are negotiable? And which are non-negotiable?
- How important or valuable is each variable to you?
- What is your assessment of the importance or value of each variable to the other side?

Planning

Lewicki and Litterer (1985) states that, in order to plan effectively, a negotiator must observe the following at the planning stage:

Understand the nature of the conflict. Conflicts, like the people who have them, vary in size and seriousness, in their characteristics, and in the parties included. Sometimes, all of these aspects of a conflict are obvious. Sometimes, they are not; and, sometimes, what appears to be a serious conflict is not one at all.

Specify goals and objectives. This includes stating all the goals that are to be achieved in the negotiation, determining their priority, and evaluating the possible trade-offs among them. Goals may also include intangibles, such as maintaining a certain precedent or getting an agreement that is satisfactory to both sides.

Clarify how to manage the negotiation process with the opponent in order to attain goals. This stage involves understanding the conflict, the possible areas of co-operation, ways to establish trust, and the issues to be negotiated. To plan for the negotiation process, negotiators must:

(a) *Identify the issues to negotiate.* Issues are those matters of substance that will be discussed with the opponent. Some issues are simple, such as the price to be paid for a used car. Other issues are more complex, such as the vast array of economic data used to justify a union's wage demands. Some issues are subtle, such as the precise wording of a clause in an agreement—a matter on which both parties are in essential agreement, but which could easily erupt into conflict if care is not taken. For example, both union and management may understand the need for, and agree to, a clause that permits reductions in the workforce in a plant; however, given the sensitivity of the matter, conflict could easily arise if the parties do not agree how it will be accomplished.

(b) *Prioritize the issues.* Which ones are more or less important, more or less critical to achieve at this time?

(c) *Develop a desirable package among the important issues, or better yet develop several alternative packages.* To discuss each issue separately may lead to suboptimal results; it may confuse both parties on what is really important, and it may cause the loss of attractive opportunities for solutions, because of the failure to really understand how the issues fit together.

(d) *Establish an agenda.* Write a procedure for discussing those issues that are important, and the order in which they will be discussed. This is the first step in carrying out any strategy for negotiating with the other party.

Understanding the Opponent

It is necessary to attain information on the opponent's goals –what is most important to them. There are also two other pieces of background information that will be of great importance:

(a) *The opponent's current resources and needs.* A full diagnosis of the opponent might include their financial condition, immediate and pressing problems, and information on the opponent's operating environment (social, political, business or personal). Thus if someone is buying a car, it would help to know it the dealer is overstocked, if it is close to the end of his fiscal year, if he has a quota to meet and is pressed to make a few last quick sales. In negotiating a labour contract, management might want to know if the union leadership is in a weak political position with the rank and file. Conversely, the union might want to know whether the local management is under severe pressure to not experience any interruption of production. Such information provides insight into the other side's unstated goals, and helps to clarify how they will interpret the behaviour.

(b) *The history of the opponent's bargaining behaviour.* How people have acted in the past is usually a good indicator of how they are likely to behave in the future. Therefore, a careful assessment of the opponent's negotiating history will provide valuable information on how to prepare for them.

Considerations in the Negotiation Process

Deresky (1996) lists following 12 variables to consider before a negotiation commences:

Basic conception of negotiation process: Is it a competitive process or a problem-solving approach? There are two opposing approaches to the concept of negotiation: strategic and synergistic. In the strategic model, resources are perceived as limited. The sides are competitive and bargaining is perceived as who will get the larger portion of the pie. In the synergistic model, resources are unlimited. Each party wants to co-operate so that all can have what they want. Counterparts look for alternative ways to obtain the desired results.

Negotiator selection criteria: These criteria include negotiating experience, seniority, political affiliation, gender, ethnic ties, kinship, technical knowledge and personal attributes (e.g., affability, loyalty, and trustworthiness). Each culture has preferences and biases regarding selection.

Significance of type of issues: Is it specific, such as price, or is the focus on relationships or the format of talks? Defining the issues in negotiation is critical. Generally substantive issues focus on control and use of resources (space, power, property). Relationship-based issues center around the ongoing nature of mutual or reciprocal interests. The negotiation should not hinder relationship and future negotiations. For example, Arabic negotiators place much weight on issues such as family and personal interests, while western negotiators emphasize the issues related to the negotiation itself.

Concern with protocol: What is the importance of procedures, social behaviours, and so forth in the negotiation process? Protocol is the accepted practices of social behaviour and interaction. Rules of protocol can be formal or informal; for example, Americans are generally less formal than Germans.

Complexity of Language: What degree of reliance is placed on non-verbal cues to interpret information? Complexity refers to the degree of reliance on non-verbal cues to convey and to interpret intentions and information in dialogue. These cues include distance (space), eye contact, gestures, and silence. There is high- and low-context communication. Cultures that are high context in communication (China) are fast and efficient communicators and information is in the physical context or pre-programmed in the person. Low-context communication, in contrast, is information conveyed by the words without shared meaning implied. The United States is a low-context culture.

Nature of persuasive arguments: One way or another, negotiation involves attempts to influence the other party. Counterparts can use an emotional or logical approach. Do they rely on rational arguments, an accepted tradition, or on emotion?

Role of individuals' aspirations: Are motivations based on individual, company, or community goals? The emphasis negotiators place on their individual goals and needs for recognition may also vary. In some cases, the position of a negotiator may reflect personal goals to a greater extent than corporate goals. In contrast, a negotiator may want to prove that he or she is a hard bargainer and compromise the goals of the corporation.

Bases of trust: Is trust based on past experience, intuition, or rules? Every negotiator at some point must face the critical issues of trust. One must eventually trust one's counterparts; otherwise resolution would be impossible. Trust can be based on the written laws of a particular country or it can be based on friendship and mutual respect and esteem.

Risk-taking propensity: How much do the parties try to avoid uncertainty in trading information or making a contract? Negotiators can be perceived as either "cautious" (low risk takers), or "adventurous" (high risk takers). If a negotiator selects a solution that has lower rewards but higher probability of success, he or she is not a risk taker. If the negotiator chooses higher rewards but a lower probability of success then he or she is "adventurous" and a risk taker.

Value of time: What is each party's attitude toward time? How fast should negotiations proceed, and what degree of flexibility is there? Each culture has a different way of perceiving and acting upon time. Monochronic cultures emphasize making agendas, being on time for appointments and generally seeing time as a quantity to be scheduled. Polychronic cultures stress the involvement of people rather than pre-set schedules. The future cannot be firm, so planning takes on little consequence.

Decision-making system: How does each team reach decisions – by individual determination, by majority opinion, or by group consensus? Broadly understood, decision-making systems can be "authoritative" or "consensual". In authoritative decision-making, an individual makes the decision without consulting with his or her supervisors. However, senior executives may overturn the decision. In consensus decision-making, negotiators do not have the authority to make decisions unless they consult their supervisors.

Form of satisfactory agreement: Is agreement based on trust (perhaps just a handshake), the credibility of the parties, commitment, or a legally binding contract? Generally, there are two broad forms of agreement. One is the written contract that covers possible contingencies. The other is the broad oral agreement that binds the negotiating parties through the quality of their relationship.

Preparing for a Successful Negotiation

Depending on the scale of the disagreement, some preparation may be appropriate for conducting a successful negotiation. For small disagreements, excessive preparation can be counter-productive because it takes time that is better used elsewhere. It can also be seen as manipulative because, just as it strengthens your position, it can weaken the other person's. However, if you need to resolve a major disagreement, then make sure you prepare thoroughly. Effective negotiation is an art—one that requires preparation and practice in order to be successful. Consider these ten tips for preparing for negotiation and improve your odds for a win-win resolution.

- **Goals:** what do you want to get out of the negotiation? What do you think the other person wants?
- **Trades:** What do you and the other person have that you can trade? What do you each have that the other wants? What are you each comfortable giving away?
- **Alternatives:** if you don't reach agreement with the other person, what alternatives do you have? Are these good or bad? How much does it matter if you do not reach agreement? Does failure to reach an agreement cut you out of future opportunities? And what alternatives might the other person have?
- **Relationships:** what is the history of the relationship? Could or should this history impact the negotiation? Will there be any hidden issues that may influence the negotiation? How will you handle these?
- **Expected outcomes:** what outcome will people be expecting from this negotiation? What has the outcome been in the past, and what precedents have been set?
- **The consequences:** what are the consequences for you of winning or losing this negotiation? What are the consequences for the other person?
- **Power:** who has what power in the relationship? Who controls resources? Who stands to lose the most if agreement isn't reached? What power does the other person have to deliver what you hope for?

- **Possible solutions:** based on all of the considerations, what possible compromises might there be?
- **Style is critical**: For a negotiation to be 'win-win', both parties should feel positive about the negotiation once it's over. This helps people keep good working relationships afterwards. This governs the style of the negotiation—histrionics and displays of emotion are clearly inappropriate because they undermine the rational basis of the negotiation and because they bring a manipulative aspect to them.

Despite this, emotion can be an important subject of discussion because people's emotional needs must fairly be met. If emotion is not discussed where it needs to be, then the agreement reached can be unsatisfactory and temporary. Be as detached as possible when discussing your own emotions – perhaps discuss them as if they belong to someone else.

Most negotiations are simple and straightforward and happen without any preparation. This is fine if the issues at stake are not important and the situation really is simple. It is not fine when the issues are important or when negotiations are complex. In fact, the more complex the negotiation the more time and attention we need to invest in preparing. There is, however, some basic preparation we can carry out that will apply to any negotiation and these 10 tips will give you a useful start point (Wolfgang Halliwell: http://ezinearticles.com/?Preparing-to-Negotiate—10-Tips&id=1695005).

1. Carry out any necessary research. For example, if you are negotiating to buy something make sure you know competitors prices and other key terms and conditions before you beginning the negotiation.
2. Identify and list everything that is potentially open to negotiation in this discussion. Try to look beyond the obvious.
3. Prioritize your list in terms of importance to you. Which items are easier for you to compromise and which are you unwilling or unable to move on?
4. Set your negotiating range. What is your opening position going to be? What are you aiming to achieve? What is the least (or most) you are prepared to accept? By setting your range beforehand you are more likely to achieve an acceptable result.
5. Consider what outcome the other negotiator might be looking for or might be prepared to accept.
6. Plan how you will move from your opening position and what you will expect in return.
7. What questions do you need to ask the person you are negotiating with? Think about the information you need to gather from them. This is also about asking questions to check what your opponent needs from the negotiation.
8. What questions might they ask you and how are you going to answer these? In particular, be sure to plan for those questions that might be difficult for you to answer.

9. Find out what you can about the other negotiator. What style of negotiation might they adopt? Are they likely to be competitive or will they be more inclined to take a collaborative approach? This will help you to plan how you will work with them during the negotiation.
10. Consider what you will do instead if your negotiation cannot reach a satisfactory conclusion. This will give you the confidence to walk away or take an alternative approach to negotiation if things are not going well.

This short list cannot possibly cover every aspect of preparing for negotiation. There is also a lot to consider for every one of these ten tips. However, one can use this as a basic checklist when you are preparing for any negotiation. By working through every item on this checklist you are much more likely to have a successful negotiation than if you wade into a discussion without any proper thought.

Negotiating Successfully

The negotiation itself is a careful exploration of your position and the other person's position, with the goal of finding a mutually acceptable compromise that gives you both as much of what you want as possible. People's positions are rarely as fundamentally opposed as they may initially appear—the other person may have very different goals from the ones you expect! In an ideal situation, you will find that the other person wants what you are prepared to trade, and that you are prepared to give what the other person wants. If this is not the case and one person must give way, then it is fair for this person to try to negotiate some form of compensation for doing so – the scale of this compensation will often depend on the many of the factors we discussed above. Ultimately, both sides should feel comfortable with the final solution if the agreement is to be considered win-win.

Only consider win-lose negotiation if you don't need to have an ongoing relationship with the other party as, having lost, they are unlikely to want to work with you again. Equally, you should expect that if they need to fulfill some part of a deal in which you have "won," they may be uncooperative and legalistic about the way they do this.

The Top 10 Keys to Successful Negotiation

Hardly a day passes that we are not involved in some type of negotiation. This negotiation may be as simple as attempting to convince a friend to see the movie we choose or as complicated as negotiating a percentage of a business offering or mediating a labor dispute. At any rate, effective negotiation is an art... one that requires preparation and practice in order to be successful. In the words of Lynne R. Christen (http://www.quazell.com/library/011401.html) consider these ten tips for preparing for negotiation and improve your odds for a win-win resolution.

1. **Know what you really want**
Many people enter negotiation only to find they did not have a clear desired outcome defined in their own mind. Write down your desired outcome as concisely as possible and use this outcome as the center point of your preparation.
2. **Know your opposition**
Learn as much as possible about who you are negotiating with, what they want, their strengths and weaknesses, and their likes and dislikes.
3. **Consider the impact of timing and method of negotiation**
Whenever possible, negotiate face to face. It is easier to say NO over the telephone and in writing. Initiate the negotiation process so that you have the advantage of preparation and timing.
4. **Prepare your presentation... point by point**
Outline your presentation carefully. Place emphasis on benefits to the other party.
5. **Anticipate reactions, objections and responses**
If possible, brainstorm with others who have had similar negotiations to get a jump on what to expect. For each objection or reaction, list positive responses, alternatives and examples that counteract the negatives.
6. **Structure your presentation to ensure agreement on one or two points at the beginning of the negotiation.**
For example, "I think we can agree right away that we have a problem and that we both/all want to resolve it." Initial agreement on minor issues or points early on in the negotiation process sets a positive atmosphere for agreement in later, more significant stages.
7. **Determine paybacks and consequences for each party in the negotiation**
A clear understanding of paybacks and consequences makes it easier to determine when and how to make concessions and when and how to stick to your requirements and requests.
8. **Prepare options rather than ultimatums**
An ultimatum should be used only as a last resort when you are sure you can back it up and the other party knows you can back it up. Even then, in virtually every negotiation there are options and alternatives that reduce defensiveness and lead to positive resolution for all parties.
9. **Get comfortable with silence**
Many negotiators feel compelled to jump in with arguments and comments each time there is a pause in the interaction. Practice holding back on comments and responses. Silence can be a very powerful negotiation tool.
10. **Close all negotiations by clearly outlining agreement**
When agreement or conclusions have been reached and you are ready to end your negotiation, review the agreement that has been reached. Then, end your negotiation on a positive note... commending those involved and emphasizing the progress made.

Bargaining: The Essence of Successful Negotiation

Negotiation is often viewed as a contest between negotiators. A negotiation can have one of three outcomes: no winner, one winner, or two winners.

Negotiation Outcome

(i) One Winner and One Loser

In a successful negotiation, there is always a winner. The negotiation proceeds as follows:

- Two parties become involved in a problem or conflict that interferes with the needs of each party.
- Each party independently recognizes the problems and looks for solutions to the problem.
- Each party independently decides on a solution to the problem that fulfils its own needs.
- The parties meet. Each party tries to force its solution on the other party. The party with the most power wins. The other party loses.

(ii) No Winners

In an unsuccessful negotiation, there is no winner. The negotiation proceeds as follows:

- Two parties become involved in a problem or conflict that interferes with the needs of each party.
- Each party independently recognizes the problems and looks for solutions to the problem.
- Each party independently decides on a solution to the problem that fulfils its own needs.
- One party forces its solution on the other party.
- The "loser" resents the solution and puts up resistance to the solution. This resistance is often concealed, but undermines the solution. Then both parties become losers in the negotiation.

(iii) Two Winners

In a successful negotiation, there is always a winner. In the ideal negotiation, there are two winners. The negotiation proceeds as follows:

- Two parties become involved in a problem or conflict that interferes with the needs of each party.
- The parties meet to discuss the problem.
- Each party creates a list of needs as they relate to the problem. Solutions are not discussed at this point.
- The parties share their lists with each other.
- Parties engage in problem solving to develop solutions that satisfy the needs of both parties.

- Parties make a joint decision on the solution to the problem and take action based on the decision.
- The agreement is monitored and adjusted accordingly, again based on the needs of both parties.

Creating a Negotiation-enabled Climate

A successful negotiation needs a positive climate. Strive for a supportive and trusting climate. If there is a negative climate in the negotiation, the negotiators will be defensive or suspicious and may turn the negotiation into a contest.

Positive Climate

Positive climates are created through what you say and how you say it. Your appearance and demeanor also contributes to the climate of the negotiation. To create and maintain a positive climate:

- Use descriptive terms. This allows your opponents to form their own opinions of your service or product. Don't tell them it's the best, let them learn it.
- Change a negative climate into a positive one by being supportive. Be calm and straightforward, use neutral terms, and avoid value or judgement statements.
- Understand your opponent's body language and your own.
- Use questions to clarify issues, discover objectives, and to create alternatives.
- Listen carefully to your opponents, to understand their concerns and issues.
- Be flexible. Be open to any reasonable alternatives.

In your efforts to create a positive climate, be careful not to create an environment where your opponent feels manipulated.

Strategy and Tactics for Negotiation

A negotiation strategy is used to position the negotiator in the negotiation so that the negotiator's goals and bargaining positions can be achieved or defended. There are several strategies available to negotiators, such as the use of time, disclosure, association, and dealing on amount.

A. Strategies

Timing

The negotiator can use time to set the tempo of events. People are motivated by time. Negotiations often reach their conclusion shortly before the deadline. If a negotiator must have a product by the end of the month, the negotiator is under pressure to reach a settlement. Some timing strategies which the negotiator can use are:

- *Patience*

By waiting out the other party, the negotiator may delay satisfaction with the expectation to gain more in the future. Prolonging the negotiation may also give the negotiating parties time to discover more information about their opponent or the pending deal.

- *Deadline*

By imposing a deadline on the negotiation, the possibility of loss on both parts may force the negotiators to reach a conclusion. It is also important to note that especially quick settlements usually favor one side significantly.

- *Surprise*

If a negotiator is ready to negotiate before the other party, the prepared negotiator has the advantage in the negotiation.

Disclosure

Negotiators can increase their credibility and their opponent's faith in them, if they are open with their opponent. There are varying degrees of openness and different strategies that can be used to disclose information:

- present the information as part of the on-going negotiation,
- provide full freedom to review the books,
- allow controlled access to the information,
- be available to answer questions.

Association

A negotiator's power in negotiation can be enhanced through association with others. Negotiators can align themselves and/or their organizations through:

- alliances or partnerships with well known organizations,
- associates or friends in the other party's organization.

This strategy can also be reversed to disassociate an organization from others. Disassociation can be used to:

- set an organization apart from other similar organizations,
- move an organization away from old methods,
- embrace new methods or technology.

Authority

Strategies dealing with authority allow the negotiators to review the deal prior to approval. Authority can be in degrees:

- limited authority up to a predefined threshold,
- mandatory approval by higher authority,
- deliberate absence of the person with final approval.

Dealing with Amounts

There are several ways to reach a goal with respect to amounts such as price, quantity, and schedule:

- appeal to fairness and reason,
- take it or leave it,
- reduce the total price, small amounts at a time,
- tailor the package (scope) to the overall budget or price,
- bring multiple and different contracts into negotiation,
- openly promote or allow competition in bidding.

A negotiation tactic is used to reach a goal. There are several tactics available to negotiators, such as setting the agenda, asking questions, making concessions, making threats, and listening.

B. Tactics

Agenda

One common tactic used to ensure issues and problems are dealt with during the negotiation is to prepare an agenda. When looking at an opponent's agenda, a negotiator can evaluate the opponent's expectations, attitudes, and values. Use an agenda to highlight or hide motives. An agenda can be developed that keeps negotiations on track or allows for easy digression. An agenda can be developed to coordinate planned strategies and tactics.

When preparing an agenda, put down a large number of issues. It is better to test the goals and intentions of the opponents, than to make assumptions about their objectives. Place the issues that can be solved easily at the beginning, so as to foster a positive environment. Decide where and with whom contentious issues will be discussed. A negative cast may develop on the negotiation in a heated debate, especially in a cooperative mode, if these problems are dealt with at the negotiation table. A better approach is to agree to deal with the issue or problem separately, with specialists from each organization.

Concession and Compromise

Through concession a negotiator can determine:

- What the other party wants.
- How much the other party wants.
- How badly the other party wants something.
- What the other party is willing to sacrifice for an issue.

Successful negotiators set goals higher than what they are willing to accept as a minimum. This gives the negotiator room to compromise. Wherever possible, be prepared to concede something in the course of the negotiation. But the other party should work for every concession made.

It is not necessary to make a concession for every concession the other party makes. ever compromise on an issue without thinking about the consequences of the concession.

Commitment

Commitment is the negotiator's willingness to stand firm on a position or issue. Commitment has two sides. If the other party believes the negotiator is committed then they will agree. If the commitment is not believed, the negotiator's position is weakened. The negotiator must either back down or follow through with the threat. For example, if a negotiator says "This is the bottom line, or I walk", the negotiator must be prepared to walk. To show commitment to a position, the negotiator must create a situation where retreat from the position is difficult. For example, positioning against a recognized standard or principle communicates commitment to the other party.

It may be necessary to allow room for retreat on a commitment. This can be done by deliberately phrasing the commitment such that it sounds firm, but allows room to back out gracefully. This can be done by obscuring the time, content, firmness, or consequences when stating commitment. For example, "I cannot accept this schedule, and will walk if it is not changed." This sounds firm, but does not actually say what the problem with content is nor does it specify when the negotiator will leave the negotiation. It leaves room for retreat. If agreement cannot be reached on an issue, it may be necessary to break the issue down into components, and then deal with each component.

Questions and Answers

The purpose of a question to is find out more about the other party's objectives, assumptions, values, and commitment. Use a supportive style to foster cooperativeness.

When asking questions, let the other party answer. Don't interrupt. Don't interrogate. Use silence. Keep the questions simple. Ask "when," "where," "who," "how," and "why" questions.

When answering questions, it is important to know what to answer, when to answer, and when to be clear. Don't answer questions to please the other party. Some questions cannot be answered. When answering questions, don't give away your bargaining position.

Threat

Threat is part of negotiation. The use of threat needs to be geared to the negotiation strategy. Don't use a threat unless you intend to follow through on it. Threat is effective when the party using it has the power to inflict punishment, without retaliation by their opponent. The other party must believe the threat will be carried out. The "size" of the threat must be consistent with the issue at stake. The overriding question when considering the use of threat is whether the threat will damage the negotiating environment or the long term relationship between the negotiating parties.

Deadlock

Deadlock happens when the negotiation is brought to a "stand still" and cannot move forward. Deadlock can cause the negotiation to be abandoned with no deal reached. Deadlock is a powerful tool which can be used to show commitment and conviction. However, it is not recommended for every negotiation nor every issue in a negotiation.

Negotiation Site

The best place to negotiate is at your place of business. This provides your negotiators with access to their resources (e.g., information, specialists, and authority). It also provides a psychological advantage to your negotiators. If possible, important issues should be discussed on your own premises. Neutral territory is also better than your opponent's place of business. There are several unethical tactics that have been used in negotiations. Negotiators must be able to recognize these tactics, to protect themselves from these tactics.

Negotiation Tricks: Unethical Tactic

These tactics are not recommended. To be a successful negotiator, you must be able to recognize negotiation tricks. Some of these tactics are listed below:

- false or deceiving figures,
- confusion and complication of issues,
- attention drawn away from the real issue,
- low initial price, but many extra charges,
- good guy and bad guy,
- denials and retractions of previous statements.

The best defense against these tricks is to confront your opponent.

Enhance Your Bargaining Power Position

There are many sources of power to enhance a negotiator's position in the negotiation. Understand the sources and know which are available to each negotiator. Negotiators can improve their position in the negotiation by improving their position of power in the negotiation. This is especially true for negotiators with limited skill and experience in negotiation. In order to exercise power in a negotiation, all parties in the negotiation must believe that the dominant party possesses the power and will use it if necessary.

Integrative Bargaining

Integrative bargaining is important because it usually produces more satisfactory outcomes for the parties involved than does positional bargaining. Positional bargaining is based on fixed, opposing viewpoints (positions) and tends to result in compromise or no agreement at all. Oftentimes, compromises do not efficiently satisfy the true interests of the disputants. Instead, compromises simply split the difference between the two positions, giving each side half of what they want. Creative, integrative solutions, on the other hand, can potentially give everyone all of what they want.

There are often many interests behind any one position. If parties focus on identifying those interests, they will increase their ability to develop win-win solutions. The classic example of interest-based bargaining and creating joint value is that of a dispute between two little girls over an orange. Both girls take the position that they want the whole orange. Their mother serves as the moderator of the dispute and based on their positions, cuts the orange in half and gives each girl one half. This outcome represents a compromise. However, if the mother had asked each of the girls why she wanted the orange—what her interests were—there could have been a different, win-win outcome. This is because one girl wanted to eat the meat of the orange, but the other just wanted the peel to use in baking some cookies. If their mother had known their interests, they could have both gotten all of what they wanted, rather than just half.

Integrative solutions are generally more gratifying for all involved in negotiation, as the true needs and concerns of both sides will be met to some degree. It is a collaborative process and therefore the parties actually end up helping each other. This prevents ongoing ill will after the negotiation concludes. Instead, interest-based bargaining facilitates constructive, positive relationships between previous adversaries.

Identifying Interests

The first step in integrative bargaining is identifying each side's interests. This will take some work by the negotiating parties, as interests are often less tangible than positions and are often not publicly revealed. A key approach to determining interests is asking "Why?" Why do you want that? Why do you need that? What are your concerns? Fears? Hopes? If you cannot ask these questions directly, get an intermediary to ask them.

The bottom line is you need to figure out *why* people feel the way they do, *why* they are demanding what they are demanding. Be sure to make it clear that you are asking these questions so you can understand their interests (needs, hopes, fears, or desires) better, not because you are challenging them or trying to figure out how to beat them.

Next one might ask yourself how the other side perceives your demands. What is standing in the way of them agreeing with you? Do they know your underlying interests? Do you know what your own underlying interests are? If you can figure out their interests as well as your own, you will be much more likely to find a solution that benefits both sides. One must also analyze the potential consequences of an agreement you are advocating, as the other side would see them. This is essentially the process of weighing pros and cons, but one should try to do it from the perspective of the other side. Carrying out an empathetic analysis will help you understand your adversary's interests. Then only one will be better equipped to negotiate an agreement that will be acceptable to both of you.

There are a few other points to remember about identifying interests. First, one must realize that each side will probably have multiple interests it is trying to satisfy. Not only will a single person have multiple interests, but if you are negotiating with a group, you must remember that each individual in the group may have differing interests. Also important is the fact that the most powerful interests are basic human needs—security, economic well being, a sense of belonging, recognition, and control over one's life. If you can take care of the basic needs of both sides, then agreement will be easier. You should make a list of each side's interests as they become apparent. This way you will be able to remember them and also to evaluate their relative importance.

Creating Options

After interests are identified, the parties need to work together cooperatively to try to figure out the best ways to meet those interests. Often by "brainstorming"—listing all the options anyone can think of without criticizing or dismissing anything initially, parties can come up with creative new ideas for meeting interests and needs that had not occurred to anyone before. The goal is a win-win outcome, giving each side as much of their interests as possible, and enough, at a minimum that they see the outcome as a win, rather than a loss.

Using Integrative and Distributive Bargaining Together

Although is frequently seen as the opposite of integrative bargaining, the two are not mutually exclusive. Distributive bargaining plays a role in integrative bargaining, because ultimately "the pie" has to be split up. Integrative bargaining is a good way to make the pie (joint value) as large as it possibly can be, but ultimately the parties must distribute the value that was created through negotiation. They must agree on who gets what. The idea behind integrative bargaining is that this last step will not be difficult once the parties reach that stage. This is because the interest-based approach is supposed to help create a cooperative working relationship. Theoretically, the parties should know who wants what by the time they split the pie (Lax & Sebenius, 1986).

Positional Bargaining

Positional bargaining is a negotiation strategy that involves holding on to a fixed idea, or position, of what you want and arguing for it and it alone, regardless of any underlying interests. The classic example of positional bargaining is the haggling that takes place between proprietor and customer over the price of an item. The customer has a maximum amount she will pay and the proprietor will only sell something over a certain minimum amount. Each side starts with an extreme position, which in this case is a monetary value, and proceed from there to negotiate and make concessions. Eventually a compromise may be reached. For example, a man offers a vendor at the flea market $10 for a rug he has for sale. The vendor asks for $30, so the customer offers $15. The merchant then says he will accept $25, but the customer says the highest he will go is $20. The vendor agrees that $20 is acceptable and the sale is made at $20. So the customer pays $10 more than he originally wanted and the vendor receives $10 less.

Importance of Positional Bargaining

Positional bargaining tends to be the first strategy people adopt when entering a negotiation. This is often problematic, because as the negotiation advances, the negotiators become more and more committed to their positions, continually restating and defending them. A strong commitment to defending a position usually leads to a lack of attention to both parties' underlying interests. Therefore, any agreement that is reached will "probably reflect a mechanical splitting of the difference between final positions rather than a solution carefully crafted to meet the legitimate interests of the parties"(Fisher & Urly, 1981). Therefore, positional bargaining is often considered a less constructive and less efficient strategy for negotiation than integrative negotiation (. Positional bargaining is less likely to result in a win-win outcome and may also result in bad feelings between the parties, possibly arising out of the adversarial, "you vs. me" approach or simply a result of one side not being truly satisfied with their end of the outcome. Positional bargaining is inefficient in terms of the number of decisions that must be made. The example above demonstrates the back-and-forth nature of positional bargaining. The more extreme the opening positions are, the longer it will take to reach a compromise.

Merit in Positional Bargaining

Despite criticism of positional bargaining, supporters of this negotiation strategy do exist. It has been argued that consideration of all underlying interests in a negotiation process is unnecessary. In fact it may sometimes be counterproductive. This is because of the distinction and relationship between issues and interests. Issues are universal; they are shared between each party in a conflict. Interests, on the other hand, are specific to each party: what the buyer of the rug in the market wants is a bargain, what the seller wants is profit. This relationship is quite simple. The problem arises when the issue at hand stirs up dramatically opposing interests between the parties, a situation in which it would be very difficult to bring them into agreement. If this is the case, it may sometimes be better to negotiate in terms of positions and go for a compromise. For example, two nations are in a dispute over water rights. However, they also differ on many other issues, including trade, immigration, religion, and politics. Broadening the debate to include these underlying interests will only polarize the sides further. In this case it may be much easier to reach agreement if the two sides focus on the smaller issue of water, and set aside their other concerns. This involves negotiating in terms of positions.

This may help the sides reach a compromise without creating any larger, interest-based conflicts. So, for issues that involve extremely conflicting underlying interests, it may be best to just focus on positions and aim for compromise (Lax and Sebenius, 1991).

Interest-Based Bargaining

Interest-based, or "win-win" bargaining, is receiving serious attention from many negotiators, both union and management. However, although many are discussing it, actual examples of interest-based bargaining are still rather rare. Not surprisingly, both labor and management find it difficult to embrace some of the changes associated with interest-based bargaining in an atmosphere of scarce resources.

The foremost difference between interest-based and traditional approaches to negotiations is the underlying assumption each party brings to the process. Interest-based bargaining is rooted in the idea that the fundamental interests (or concerns) of labor and management typically complement one another. For example, both parties want the employer to excel at what it does. This differs sharply from the traditional view which assumes that the parties' fundamental interests conflict with one another despite their ability to find some common ground.

Traditional collective bargaining is largely based on the premise that the outcome of negotiations creates winners and losers, and both parties use any available leverage to make sure they are the winners. Collective bargaining laws in both the public and private sectors are written to embody this assumption. They regulate the parties' use of power by restricting the use of "weapons" such as strikes, lockouts, and discharges of union activists. Those who explore the unconventional idea of "win-win" negotiations need to understand that the differing interests of labor and management are not easily reconciled to both sides' satisfaction. The resolution of issues may be especially difficult in the public sector in an era of tightening budgets and shrill attacks on AFSCME and public workers. Nonetheless, in spite of such barriers, a small but growing number of parties have successfully implemented interest-based relationships. AFSCME Council 24, the Wisconsin State Employees Union, has recently completed negotiation of their fourth contract using a "consensus-based" process. Council 8 recently negotiated their agreement with the City of Cincinnati, Ohio, using an interest-based process. This followed successful uses of "win-win" by Council 8 at Ohio University and O'Bleness Hospital, both in Athens, Ohio. And, with little fanfare or elaborate process, a number of AFSCME affiliates successfully use labor-management committees to resolve issues on the basis of interests. Health care benefit changes and health and safety issues are among the most common of the difficult issues that labor-management committees have tackled over the past decade.

In redesigning government processes, especially those based on Total Quality Management (TQM) or High Performance Workplace (HPW) theories, it is likely that collective bargaining will become less confrontational and more interest-based. In some cases, interest-based bargaining has led to joint involvement in quality initiatives. In other cases, involvement in quality initiatives has spilled over to the bargaining relationship, leading the parties to use interest-based processes and consensus building techniques with increasing frequency.

Interest-based bargaining goes by a host of names such as "consensus bargaining," "problem-solving negotiations," "win-win," "mutual gains," "collaborative bargaining," "principled negotiations," and others. In Getting to YES, Negotiating Agreement Without Giving In, Roger Fisher and William Ury (1981) defined five characteristics of interest-based negotiations:

1. Bargaining over positions is avoided;
2. People are separated from the problem;
3. Focus is placed on interests, not positions;
4. Options for mutual gain are invented; and
5. Objective criteria are used to select the appropriate resolution to an issue.

Essential to understanding interest-based processes is a thorough grasp of the distinction between a position and an interest. In short, a position, or proposal, is a party's chosen solution to a particular problem, or goal; it may be one of many alternatives that meet a party's needs. An interest is the basic need or concern that is addressed by the proposal.

For example, in 1992, the Connecticut Department of Labor was seeking to reorganize its operations. The reorganization abolished some jobs and created new ones. Because most affected employees did not qualify for the new positions, the reorganization posed a threat to the economic and employment security interests of Council 4 and Local 269 members. Accordingly, the union was tempted to take a position opposed to the reorganization.

Instead, Council 4 agreed to support the reorganization in exchange for a promise of no layoffs and implementation of a "win-win" process to negotiate all aspects of the reorganization. Using the interest-based process, the parties agreed to provide training to affected staff in order to qualify them for the new, higher paying jobs. The result was a pay increase for members who had initially feared layoffs. By not taking a position opposed to the reorganization, Council 4 was able to meet the real interests of its members: employment security and career progression. The employer was able to implement its reorganization without union opposition. The result: both parties "won."

How does interest-based bargaining work?

Some interest-based bargaining techniques are familiar to experienced negotiators. Traditionally, after proposals are presented, union and management negotiators request the other party to justify their position. Good negotiators who carefully listen to this justification can respond to the stated interest of the other party in a manner which also achieves his/her own interest. Often, this is the method by which many issues are resolved.

The identification of interests is also at the center of formal interest-based processes. However, rather than starting from proposals and seeking justification, the interest-based process starts from the justification (the identification of interests) and leads to the joint development of proposals. Once alternative proposals are identified, the parties, often using objective ranking criteria, select the alternative that ranks highest.

In an interest-based process, information is freely exchanged between the parties and, often, joint labor-management subgroups are established to gather information and develop tentative agreements. Communications are open and all participants speak. Internal differences are not concealed because the process requires a consensus decision to which all parties can agree.

In any negotiation some issues are easier to resolve than others. An interest-based process will not lead to quick resolution of a dispute over wages when an employer is in fiscal distress and employees are paid below market rates. Often, when parties cannot resolve such difficult issues, they agree to defer the issue for future discussion, or they negotiate a contingent agreement. For example, wage disputes may be resolved by agreeing that wages will increase at the rate of general fund revenue increases or according to some other formula tied to the employer's ability to pay.

Fisher and Ury (1981) argued that the idea of the BATNA—the Best Alternative To a Negotiated Agreement—should be used in lieu of the resistance point (or "bottom line") approach to determine when parties are at impasse. In their view, bottom lines are often arbitrarily selected and limit a party's flexibility to explore creative settlements. Because parties negotiate to produce something better than what could be obtained without negotiating, the authors argue that final offers should be measured against the best alternative to an agreement, not against a pre-selected resistance point. Typically, as in traditional bargaining, interest-based bargainers set aside seemingly unresolvable issues until all others are settled. At that time, each party can clearly see the disagreement in the context of a full package. If issues remain unresolved, the parties resort to the tradeoffs associated with traditional negotiations. However, it is considered a breach of the interest-based "ethic" for a party to use power, such as a strike or lockout, to resolve issues. Interest arbitration is compatible with an interest-based approach.

Distributive Justice

The Notion of Fair Distribution

Distributive justice is concerned with the fair allocation of resources among diverse members of a community. Fair allocation typically takes into account the total amount of goods to be distributed, the distributing procedure, and the pattern of distribution that results. Because societies have a limited amount of wealth and resources, a question arises as to how those benefits ought to be distributed. The common answer is that public assets should be distributed in a reasonable manner so that each individual receives a "fair share." But this leaves open the question of what constitutes a "fair share."

Various principles might determine of how goods are distributed. Equality, Equity, and Need are among the most common criteria. If equality is regarded as the ultimate criterion determining who gets what, goods will be distributed equally among all persons. (In other words each person will get the same amount.) However, due to differences in levels of need, this will not result in an equal outcome. For example, every incoming freshman to a local college with a grade point above 3.0 might be offered a $500 scholarship. This is a nice reward for students and parents who can afford the remaining tuition, but is of no help to families that cannot afford the additional $6000/year fee to attend the school.

Another possibility is to proceed according to a principle of equity, and distribute benefits in proportion to the individuals' contribution. Thus, those who make a greater productive contribution to their group deserve to receive more benefits. This sort of distribution is typically associated with an economic system where there is equal opportunity to compete. In competitive systems, wealth or goods might also be distributed according to effort or ability. Or, we might distribute goods according to need, so that an equal outcome results. Those who need more of a benefit or resource will receive more, as occurs when colleges offer needs-based scholarships.

Some suggest a system of competition that includes safety nets for those who cannot compete. This sort of system combines the principle of equity with that of need. It attempts to reward people for their productivity at the same time that it ensures their basic needs are met. Finally, we might distribute resources according to social utility, or what is in the best interests of society as a whole.

The Significance of Distribution Procedures and Outcomes

Different sorts of distributions advance different social goals. For a society to function effectively, it must keep its membership, engage in efficient and effective production, and sustain the well-being of its members. The principles of distributive justice arise out of these concerns. Equal distribution is thought to give people a sense of full-fledged membership. Equity fosters the motivation to produce, to be rewarded for one's productivity. Lastly, distribution according to need ensures that everyone's basic and essential needs are met. Because these principles are often in tension with one another, one of them is typically regarded as the central criterion of distribution. Depending on which principle is adopted, an economic system characterized by equality, competition, or social welfare safety nets will arise.

Some believe that what makes a distribution just is the final outcome, while others believe that what matters are the rules followed in determining that distribution. Even in those cases where the outcome is a fair distribution of resources, the procedures used to arrive at that distribution might be unjust. Conversely, a fair procedure might result in an unfair distribution.

In his *Theory of Justice*, John Rawls claims that one's place of birth, social status, and family influences are matters of luck that should not unduly influence the amount of benefits we receive in life. He maintains that the job of distributive justice is to limit the influence of luck so that goods might be distributed more fairly and to everyone's advantage. Robert Nozick, on the other hand, believed that distributive justice is a matter of setting down rules that individuals should follow in acquiring and transferring resources and benefits. The aim of distributive justice is not to achieve any particular outcome of distribution, but rather to ensure a fair process of exchange. Others think that distributive justice must be a matter of both process and outcome. They believe that the processes of distribution must be fair in order for people to feel that they have received a fair outcome. Insofar as it is linked to the notion of fair processes, distributive justice has ties to concerns about procedural justice. In some cases, the thing to be distributed is not a benefit, but a burden. For example, one might be concerned with the fairness of allocation of punishments, which is connected to retributive justice.

Distributive Justice Matters

According to the theory of relative deprivation, a sense of injustice is aroused when individuals come to believe that their outcome is not in balance with the outcomes received by people like them in similar situations.When people have a sense that they are at an unfair disadvantage relative to others, or that they have not received their fair share, they may wish to challenge the system that has given rise to this state of affairs. This is especially likely to happen if a person or groups' fundamental needs are not being met, or if there are large discrepancies between the "haves" and the "have-nots."

Redistribution of benefits, on the other hand, can sometimes help to relieve tensions and allow for a more stable society. Such redistribution can be an important component of social structural changes to remedy injustice. Balancing out gross inequalities of wealth might also be part of compensatory justice after periods of war. During periods of postwar adjustment and peace building efforts, long-term economic policy must aim to achieve equity, or balance in the distribution of income and wealth. Issues of distributive justice are in this way central to any peace building or reconstruction program. Such efforts to ensure a just distribution of benefits following conflict are typically accompanied by democratization efforts to ensure a more balanced distribution of power as well.

Negotiation Analysis Spectrum

Negotiation is the process of joint decision-making. In international politics, negotiation consists of discussions between officially designated representatives designed to achieve a formal agreement of their governments to the way forward on an issue that is either of shared concern or in dispute between them. Business negotiations, in turn, may be understood as encounters between economic organizations with the goal of reaching agreements to provide economic benefits (Dupont, 2002). In fact, the original meaning of the word "negotiation" is simply to carry on business.Negotiations take place in all domains of life, but the structure and pattern of negotiations are fundamentally the same at a personal level as they are at diplomatic and corporate levels (Lewicki *et al.* 1999). There are four characteristics common to all negotiation situations (Lewicki 1992):

- First, there are two or more parties
- Second, the parties can cooperate to arrive at a joint decision
- Third, the payoffs to any party depend either on the consequences of the joint decision or alternatives external to the negotiations
- Fourth, the parties can reciprocally and directly exchange information

Parties may refer to individuals or groups of individuals. However, ultimately it is individuals who interact, for their own purposes or as agents for groups. The concepts of party, individual, decision maker, agent, player, and actor can therefore be considered synonymous in this context: they all refer to a single, unitary decision entity. Groups consist of plural unitary decision makers, but when their interests are shared enough, an abstraction is often made and a group is treated as a unitary decision entity.

The concept of decision has to do with two important aspects: selection and commitment. If there is only one course of action available, no selection can be made, and the concept of decision is inapplicable. On the other hand, if an option has been selected, but a party does not feel committed to it, no decision has been taken. For example in organizations, a plan may have to be ratified by other members before organizational commitment can be said to exist.

In negotiations, the parties must arrive at a joint decision. The word joint means that the parties must select and commit to a common course of action together. A jointly selected, common course of action is called an agreement. Zartman (2002) defines negotiation as a process by which contending parties come to an agreement. An agreement determines a payoff for each party (Sebenius, 1992). The fundamental objective of negotiations is to jointly select and commit to courses of action that are superior to unilateral action for each and every party. Parties are motivated to negotiate by payoffs that they can not achieve without joint behavior. Negotiation is therefore aimed at either creating something that neither party could do on his own, or to resolve a problem or dispute between the parties (Lewicki *et al* 1999).

Finally, the negotiation process is essentially communication, direct or tacit, between individuals who are trying to forge an agreement for mutual benefit (Young, 1991). Also, Kremenyuk (1993) defines negotiation as basically purposeful communication between two or more parties. Communication is a process by which information is exchanged between individuals through a common system of symbols, signs, or behavior (Webster, 2005). Based of the above discussion, negotiation can be defined as "a process of joint decision-making where two or more parties communicate to select and commit to a common course of action that is superior to unilateral alternatives."

At the heart of the subject of negotiation is essentially the insight that unilateral, i.e. separate and independent behavior, even if perfectly intelligent and calculating, often leaves interacting parties with outcomes inferior to what can be achieved through joint behavior. As the classical prisoner's dilemma well illustrates, purely self-serving actions of independent, but interacting parties do not always serve the interests of either of the parties in the best possible way. The key insight is that numerous social contexts are analogous with the prisoner's dilemma, and negotiations can effectively be considered as a process of moving away from less-than optimal outcomes towards increased payoffs, and the distribution of those payoffs. In an era of growing interdependence, negotiation research has experienced a tremendous growth of interest. Key publications in the history of negotiations include: Machiavelli's "The Prince" from the 16th century, and Callières' "On the Manner of Negotiating with Princes" from the 18th century. However, it was only in the late 1900's that research and writings on negotiations became a distinct area of study. Work in this area began with writings on diplomatic negotiation (Iklé, 1987, Zartman & Berman, 1983). The area of study was broadened by those who regarded negotiation as a much more universal type of human activity and an inalienable part of the human decision-making processes (Fisher *et al.*, 1991, Sebenius 1980, Rubin & Brown 1975). More recently, negotiation research has shifted from being exclusively a part of diplomatic or commercial knowledge toward the area of management and business.

Negotiators predominantly rely on implicit knowledge, individual capabilities and situational factors in crafting agreements. Although experience and sound intuition are at least as important to successful negotiation as any amount of analysis, some analysis is necessary to correct people's intuition and to force them to reexamine their assumptions. Analytical reasoning, backed up by empirical evidence, can deepen ones understanding of real world negotiating situations.

Research has shown that the most common mistake in negotiations is that negotiations are perceived as zero-sum games, which demand competitive behavior. In other words, central to negotiations is the belief that there is a limited, controlled amount of resources to be distributed – a "fixed pie" situation (Lewicki *et al.* 1999, Fisher *et al.* 1991). However, most negotiations also present opportunities for solutions, in which one party's gains do not necessarily come at the other parties' expense – the gains need not be mutually exclusive. The fundamental structure of man negotiations is such that it allows for solutions, from which one or all parties only gain –"expanding the pie", or a plus-sum situation (Lewicki *et al.* 1999). The negotiations in which creating joint value is an obvious opportunity are often referred to as integrative, collaborative, win-win or creating negotiations (Lewicki *et al.* 1999, Fisher *et al.* 1991). The negotiations in which the structure presents no or less-obvious opportunities for joint gains are referred to as distributive, competitive, win-lose or claiming negotiations Distributive negotiations are generally concerned with the division of a single resource, i.e. there is only one issue under negotiation, and behaviorally speaking, they tend to be less collaborative than integrative negotiations. Researchers have shown that the failure to reach integrative agreements is often linked to the failure to exchange information to allow the parties to identify efficient contracts. Effective information exchange promotes the development of good integrative solutions (Pruitt 1981, Thompson, 1991). Most negotiations actually present a tension between creating joint value, i.e. increasing the payoffs to all parties, and claiming individual value, i.e. increasing the payoffs to a single party unilaterally, often referred to as the "negotiators dilemma". This is a key distinction central to negotiation research and a prevalent setting in most real-world negotiations.

Theoretical Roots of Negotiation Analysis

Negotiation is a complex process and its eventual outcome could be very speculative at the beginning. This *per se* underlines the desirability of having an analytical approach to negotiation preparation and succeeding processes. Negotiation analysis can therefore be characterized as an approach, which builds on the theory of games, decision analysis and behavioral decision theory, but departs from some of their analytic rigor and formal argumentation in order to pursue a broader scope of application and increased practical value (Sebenius, 1992). Game theory provides a logically consistent framework for analyzing interdependent decision-making. In game theoretic analyses, the parties make their decisions independently of each other, but these separate choices interact to determine a payoff for each side. Game theory proceeds by applying standard utility axioms to abstract the interests of the parties into utility functions. An expected utility criterion is used to rank alternative courses of action. Full descriptions of the courses of action that can be taken by each party are encapsulated into "strategies." Rigorous analysis of the interaction of the strategies leads to search for "equilibria" or complete campaigns of action such that each party, given the choices of the other parties, has no incentive to change its plans.

Decision analysis is the systematic decomposition and clarification of a decision problem. Decision analysis studies independent decision-making, where the payoffs of decisions are not affected by the decisions of other involved parties, anticipating one's actions. It proceeds by structuring and sequencing the party's choices and chance events, then separating and subjectively assessing probabilities and values, as well as risk and time preferences. An expected utility criterion is again used to aggregate these elements in ranking possible courses of action to determine optimal choice Behavioral decision analysis is concerned with describing how and why people think the way they. The field has identified a number of deviations from the rationality ideal. Such deviations are called behavioral errors, biases, heuristics and anomalies. Behavioral decision analysis gives good descriptions of how the other parties might actually behave, and also informs the parties of decision-making fallacies that they are susceptible to.

However, the assumptions required for a game-theoretic analysis are invalid for the majority of real-world situations, decision analysis is not suited to interdependent decision-making and behavioral decision theory lacks prescriptive value. For these limitations, none of the fields of game theory, decision analysis, or behavioral decision analysis alone is sufficient for the prescriptive study of negotiations. In response, negotiation analysis seeks to synthesize contributions from all of these three fields. The negotiation analysis approach uses important aspects from the three fields of theory described above. Thinking game-theoretically about the interaction of separate decisions can help to understand the underlying power structure and the opportunities for leverage in negotiations. An individual decision-making perspective enables comparison of the benefits of a joint agreement with separate or unilateral action and hence the behavioral decision analysis can be correspondingly used in modifying one party's behavior, or for effectively exploiting the behavior of others.

Special Features of Negotiation Analysis

Although negotiation analysis draws heavily from the three fields of theory discussed above in the end of the previous section, the approach has four distinct features (Sebenius, 1992): An asymmetrically descriptive prescriptive orientation, a radically subjective perspective, a sensitivity to "value left on the table", and a focus away from equilibrium analysis and toward perceptions of the zone of possible agreement. Each of these four distinctive features of negotiation analysis are discussed in the following. An asymmetrically prescriptive-descriptive orientation means that negotiation analysis typically seeks to develop prescriptive advice to one party, given a description of how others will behave (Sebenius, 1992). The development of asymmetrical advice to one party is in line with decision analysis; whereas game theory obliges to consider the behavior of other parties; and behavioral decision theory gives descriptions of how the other side might behave. In developing advice, the analysis typically assumes intelligent, but boundedly rational, self-interest seeking behavior by the other parties. Boundedly rational behavior is intended to be rational, in the sense of calculatedly maximizing personal utility, but is constrained by limited cognitive, temporal or computational capabilities.

Self-interest seeking means that a party has goals of its own, which the party actively pursues (c.f. Williamson 1985). When commands or contracts are ambiguous, a party will make choices in ways consonant with his or her self-interests. A radically subjective perspective means that the analysis relies heavily on subjective sources of information in three respects: (i) assessment of probabilities is up to the individuals involved; (ii) all subjective perceptions of basic interests and more operational objectives are considered legitimate. This means that less tangible concerns such as self-image and relationships can have the same analytic importance as economical considerations, such as cost, quality and time (Sebenius, 2003); and (iii) the other sides' expected behavior is assessed subjectively, in light of available evidence. One of the main purposes of negotiation analysis is to help the parties identify and realize potential gains through a systematic study of the negotiation situation.

A focus away from equilibrium analysis and toward perceptions of the zone of possible agreement essentially means that the situation is incompletely determined (Schelling, 1960). In other words, the situation is not fixed and cannot be described objectively in full detail, since the parties themselves construct the situation: the game is simply whatever the parties act as if it is (Sebenius, 2002). For example, the parties can take action to introduce new alternatives, to influence the other parties' preferences, or to change their own conditions for an agreement, thus changing the zone of possible agreement. An equilibrium analysis is impractical if the situation, itself, is subject to modifications.

Basic Elements of Negotiation Analysis

According to Sebenius (1992, 2002), full negotiation analytic accounts generally consider the following basic elements with respect to the actual and potential parties: the parties' perceived interests, negotiated issues and positions, alternatives to negotiated agreement, the linked processes of "creating" and "claiming" value, and efforts to "change the game" itself. Accounts that are not exactly identical, but nevertheless highly similar have been presented by Lewicki *et al.* (1999), and Fisher *et al.* (1991). Sebenius claimed that these basic elements can be found and analyzed in all negotiations, ranging from the simplest bilateral negotiation between monolithic parties to the most complex coalitional interactions; and they must be interpreted for a meaningful negotiation analysis to proceed. In his study, the basic concepts of negotiation analysis are reviewed in a slightly different order, complemented with some other important concepts, yet consistent with the content of the aforementioned list. The idea is to separate concepts that constitute the analytic structure of negotiations from the other concepts that refer to behavior (or flow) within that structure, respectively. Structure is, in a sense, the snapshot of a negotiation situation outside of the time dimension; the flow of negotiations refers to the interaction of the structural elements in time. Concepts, which define the structure, are: parties, interests, issues, options, the best alternatives to negotiated agreements and outcomes. Outcomes can be further broken down to the concepts of contracts, efficiency, fairness and impact. Concepts, which refer to the flow of negotiations – or behavior within the structure – are: the linked processes of "creating" and "claiming" value, efforts to "change the game" itself, and the phase model of negotiations.

Best Alternatives to Negotiated Agreement (BATNA)

Parties negotiate in order to better satisfy the complete range of their interests through some jointly determined action than could otherwise be done (Sebenius, 1992). In practically all situations, negotiators have outside alternatives that they can turn to, should they fail to reach an agreement in current negotiations. The Best of the Alternatives to a *Negotiated Agreement* is denoted by the acronym BATNA (Fisher *et al.*, 1991). This is a game theoretic component underlying every negotiation: a party always has the option of taking unilateral action to pursue payoffs outside of the negotiations. Thus a basic test of a proposed agreement is whether it offers a better payoff than that side's best alternative course of action outside of the negotiations (Sebenius, 1992). This condition is also known as individual rationality (Young, 1991). The payoff of each player's BATNA, therefore, places a lower priority on the payoff that the party must realize from a negotiated settlement. Taken together, these minimum payoffs define the disagreement point, an equivalent of the non-cooperative Nash equilibrium concept. The region of agreements beyond each party's BATNA, in the direction of increasing payoffs, delineates the agreements that are individually rational for both parties Alternatives to negotiated agreement also play a tactical role. The more favorable alternative courses of action negotiators have, the smaller the need for the negotiation and the higher the standard of value that negotiators can expect from any proposed agreement (Sebenius, 1992). Research shows that negotiators with more attractive BATNA's capture a greater share of the negotiation zone. Therefore, maneuvering "away from the table" can also strongly affect negotiated outcomes, even more than the strategies employed "at the table." Searching for a better price or an alternative supplier are examples of developing alternatives away from the negotiation table.

Outcomes

Contract

The ultimate aim of negotiations is to attain favorable outcomes. The fixing of an option for each of the issues is combined to create a contract, which determines the payoff to each party as measured by the degree to which the contract satisfies the interests of the party. The set of all payoff combinations associated with the various possible agreements is called the contract set. The number of possible contracts is the product of the number of resolutions for each issue. Under standard assumptions about the players' payoff, or utility, functions, the contract set is convex, i.e. bowed outward. Important concepts related to a contract include: feasibility, the zone of possible agreement, surplus, potential, domination, and efficiency. A contract is said to be feasible if it is individually rational for each party, that is, it assigns for each party a payoff that is at least as good as that party's BATNA. The set of feasible contracts is called the zone of possible agreement (ZOPA). For any contract, the surplus to a party is the difference between the payoffs associated with that contract and the party's BATNA. The concept of potential refers to the maximum surplus a party can receive, associated with a contract, where the other parties' surpluses are zero, i.e. their payoffs are driven to their BATNA levels. A contract is dominated if there is another contract that leaves none of the parties worse off and is preferred by at least one party. The efficient boundary consists of the complete set of non-dominated contracts. A contract is thus efficient if all potential gains are realized. In other words, the payoffs to any single party cannot be unilaterally improved without worsening the payoffs to some other party.

Fairness

Fairness is an important concept in negotiations, but somewhat more challenging to define than the previous concepts. Fairness is concerned with the problem of selecting an equitable contract that all parties are willing to commit to. Fairness is a concept usually not included in economical analysis; yet, it is present in most real-world settings. For example, people customarily discuss the outcome of labor negotiations, divorce suits and even business deals in terms of fairness or unfairness to the parties concerned. Experienced negotiators often frame their arguments in terms of fair share, such as precedents and principles, customary procedure, splitting the difference, reciprocity and so on.

The set of feasible contracts consists of multiple possible contracts; and even focusing the selection on the set of efficient contracts typically leaves many possible agreements. It is reasonable to assume that negotiators seek to achieve efficient contracts, but it is also realistic to assume that the parties are concerned with a fair distribution of net benefits. For example, a contract, which realizes all the potential for one side, but leaves another party indifferent between his or her BATNA and the proposed contract, is efficient, but hardly fair and may consequently turn out indurable.

In a similar vein, in an exposition of inter-organizational cooperation Ring and Van de Ven (1994) argue that efficiency and equity are essential conditions for cooperative inter-organizational relationships to emerge and be sustained. They define efficiency as a condition, where the parties can achieve better payoffs through cooperation than through unilateral action. Essentially, they refer to what is understood as individual rationality in this study. That is, all feasible contracts are efficient, whereas in this study the concept of efficiency is reserved for feasible, non-dominated contracts. Ring and Van de Ven (1994) defined equity as fair sharing, as perceived by the parties. In their definition, equity does not mean equal amounts; instead, reciprocity and proportional sharing of benefits. In this study the proportional sharing of benefits can be understood with respect to the concept of potential. To review, the concept of potential refers to the maximum surplus a party can receive, associated with a contract, where the other parties' payoffs are driven to their BATNA levels. It is thus possible to examine the proportion of potential a contract assigns to each of the parties. A fair sharing would then refer to a contract that gives each party a similar proportion of their potential. Literature describes many other approaches to fairness in negotiations, but they all refer to the same idea, the problem of picking an equitable contract from multiple alternatives. According to Young (1991), there are two basic approaches to determine a fair outcome: fairness standard and a fair procedure.

The specific fairness standards that are applicable in a given situation vary widely from one class of negotiation to another. In wage negotiations it would be normal to tie wage increase to industry norm; in sharing the profits of joint ventures, it would be natural to allocate rewards in proportion to some measure of contribution, e.g. investment (Young, 1991). In strictly analytic settings, it is possible to employ various fairness concepts, such as the maximum criterion, the mid-mid criterion, the Maimonides solution, or the cooperative Nash equilibrium. As a general remark of these solutions, it is worthwhile to note that they all basically result in an agreement in the "middle" region of the efficient frontier.

The alternative to fairness standards is to rely on a fairness procedure. For example, when two children must share a piece of cake, it is customary for one to divide it in to two pieces and for the other to get first choice; or the children might toss a coin to randomly determine allocation. A fairness procedure may also involve the use of a third party, such as an arbitrator, to whom the negotiating parties turn to for determining a fair outcome. Examples of formalized arbitration procedures include the combined arbitration, the two-stage final offer arbitration and the multi-stage final offer arbitration. There are multiple reasons for involving considerations of fairness in negotiations. They help focus negotiations by narrowing the range of possible agreements. Fairness considerations also enhance the durability of contracts (ibid.). A further benefit is that standards of fairness relieve bargainers of responsibility for having given in. It converts what might otherwise degenerate into a contest of wills into a principled or objective solution that can be justified – both to the negotiators and to their constituents (Fisher *et al.*, 1991).

Impact

Finally, an important distinction related to outcomes is between expected payoffs, i.e. the contract, and actual payoffs, i.e. the impact. The signing of a contract, or in other words the joint selection and commitment to a complete course of action specifies the rights and obligations of each party, with associated payoffs. It is important to note, however, that the payoffs at the time of the signing of the contract are expected payoffs, and are likely to be different from the actual payoffs resulting from implementing the jointly selected course of action. The actual payoffs of a contract can be different for at least four reasons, arising essentially from the inclusion of the time dimension. The first reason is uncertainty regarding the future situation to which an agreement is applied. A considerable amount of uncertainty pertains to, for example, contracts fixing the price and scope of long-term transactions. Although contracts may embody contingencies such as future price fluctuations, most contracts are incomplete in the sense that they do not specify a response to all possible disturbances that may arise in the implementation of the chosen course of action.

Second, parties may adapt their resources in the course of implementation, thus affecting the payoffs. For example, a party may improve its processes required for implementing the contract from the expectations at the time of the signing of the contract, which may result in decreased costs, or conversely, increased payoffs.

Third, in some cases the sheer complexity of the cooperative arrangement, the number of variables and their interdependencies, may be such that no actor can predict the aggregate future impact with great precision and confidence.

Fourth, even when the consequences can be predicted, the evaluation criteria, the interests of the parties themselves may change over time.

Zone of Possible Agreement (ZOPA)

Zopa is an England-based company providing an online money exchange service, allowing people who have money to lend it to those who wish to borrow, instead of using savings accounts and loan applications at traditional banks. The process is sometimes referred to as peer-to-peer lending. Zopa acts as the man in the middle operating the markets. The name, Zopa, stands for Zone of Possible Agreement, a negotiating term identifying the bounds within which agreement can be reached between two parties. The idea for the service was identified following extensive socio-economic research which itself identified a group of individuals, coined Freeformers. Freeformers were identified as displaying different attitudes towards many aspects of life, including their money (http://en.wikipedia.org/wiki/Zopa).

A "Zone of Possible Agreement" (ZOPA) exists if there is a potential agreement that would benefit both sides more than their alternative options do. For example, if Fred wants to buy a used car for $5,000 or less, and Mary wants to sell one for $4,500, those two have a ZOPA. But if Mary will not go below $7,000 and Fred will not go above $5,000, they do not have a zone of possible agreement. The ZOPA is critical to the successful outcome of negotiation, but it may take some time to determine whether a ZOPA exists. It may only become known once the parties explore their various interests and options. If the disputants can identify the ZOPA, there is a good chance that they will come to an agreement.

Foundations of ZOPA: BATNAs

In order for disputing parties to identify the ZOPA, they must first know their alternatives, and thus their "bottom line" or "walk away position (http://www.beyondintractability.org/essay/zopa/)."

Alternatives: Parties must determine what alternatives they have to any agreement. Roger Fisher and William Ury introduced the concept of "BATNA" (Best Alternative To a Negotiated Agreement). This is the *best course of action* that a party can pursue if no agreement is reached (Roger Fisher and William Ury, 1983).

For example, Mary might have two potential buyers. Georgio is willing to pay $6,950. Mary is now negotiating with Fred. If he will pay more than Georgio (Mary's BATNA), she'll sell to him. If he won't pay that much, she'll sell to Georgio. Likewise, if Fred has found another car he likes for $5,500, then he won't pay more for Mary's car than that...maybe even a bit less. Fred's BATNA is $5,500.

Bottom Lines or Walk-Away Positions: BATNAs determine each side's bottom lines. If you have an alternative car available for $5,000, $5,000 is your bottom line. If you can sell your car for $7,000, that is your bottom line. If you don't do better than that in the negotiation, you'll walk away as shown in Fig 2(http://www.beyondintractability.org/essay/zopa/).

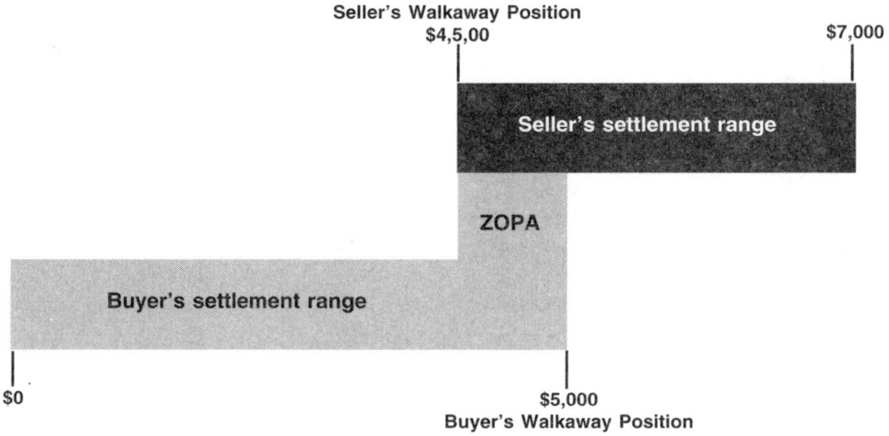

Fig. 2: Batna's Bottom Lines vs. Walk-Away Positions

So, a zone of possible agreement exists if there is an overlap between these walk away positions. If there is not, negotiation is very unlikely to succeed. In fact, it will only succeed if one party either realizes that his or her BATNA is not as good as he or she thought, or she decides for some other reason to accept the agreement, even though an alternative option might have yielded better results. (This often happens when parties do not explore or understand their BATNAs well enough.)

Identifying the ZOPA

If both sides know their BATNAs and walk away positions, the parties should be able to communicate, assess proposed agreements, and eventually identify the ZOPA. However, parties often do not know their own BATNAs, and are even less likely to know the other side's BATNA. Often parties may pretend they have a better alternative than they really do, as good alternatives usually translate into more power in the negotiations. This is explained more in the essay on BATNAs. The result of such deception, however, might be the apparent absence of a ZOPA, when one actually did exist. Shared uncertainties may also affect the parties' abilities to assess potential agreements because the parties may be unrealistically optimistic or pessimistic about the possibility of agreement or the value of alternative options (Michael Watkins and Susan Rosegrant, 2001).

ZOPAs in Distributive and Integrative Negotiations

The nature of the ZOPA depends on the type of negotiation. In a distributive negotiation, in which the participants are trying to divide a "fixed pie," it is more difficult to find mutually acceptable solutions as both sides want to claim as much of the pie as possible. Distributive negotiations over a single issue tend to be zero-sum—there is a winner and a loser. There is no overlap of interests between the parties; therefore, no mutually beneficial agreement is possible. For example, two people may be competing for one job. In the simplest case, there is no ZOPA because both people want the full-time job and are not willing to divide the job responsibilities and salary. One person must "win" and the other must "lose."

On the other hand, integrative negotiations involve creating value or "enlarging the pie." This is possible when parties have shared interests or are dealing with multiple issues. In an integrative negotiation, the parties can combine their interests to create joint value. To achieve integration, negotiators can deal with multiple issues at the same time and make trades between them. This is so that I might get more of something that I value while you get more of something that you value. That way, both parties can "win," even though neither gets all that they originally thought they wanted. In the example above, if rewriting the job description could create an additional job then the distributive negotiation would change into an integrative negotiation between the employer and the two potential employees. If both applicants are qualified, now they may both get jobs. The ZOPA, in this case, exists when two jobs are created and each applicant prefers a different one of the two (Michael Watkins and Susan Rosegrant, 2001).

Barriers to Negotiation and Agreement

We cannot work alone—especially in a negotiation table involving two parties. A business that toils away in isolation, in today's churning and ever evolving global world of dynamic commerce, will likely shrivel and perish with barely a noticeable whimper. We must form alliances if our business is to not only survive, but also prosper and grow. Even then, today, in our negotiations, we still encounter obstacles not so unlike those our ancestors faced. There are many reasons why negotiations may not be carried out successfully. Here, we shall try and examine several of the more such common reasons and offer solutions, to either repudiate or overcome them (HBS, 2003; Max H. Bazerman, Margaret A. Neale, 1992; Leigh Thompson, 2001).

The Hard-nosed Negotiator

The person who views every negotiation as their own personal war where there can be only one winner. Some of their more charming traits include:

- Unreasonable offers.
- Will take concessions, but don't give them, or do so but only with great fanfare and difficulty.
- Will take information and wield it as a weapon against us, while hoarding their own information like a miser guarding their gold.
- Bull-headed and unyielding.

Solution

- Probe your negotiating counterparty first to find out what kind of negotiator you're facing.
- Anticipate unreasonable offers and remember your reservation price, aspiration base, and your BATNA (best alternative)
- Don't give out information that can be used against you.
- Give a little, mostly harmless information to your counterparty and see whether they reciprocate.
- Offer different negotiation solutions and ask which one they prefer.
- Be willing to walk away.

Lack of Trust

It happens. Both of you find yourselves sitting at the negotiation table, eyeball to eyeball, wondering just how much you can really trust the person staring back at you. You've heard unsettling rumours that the negotiator on the other side has a nefarious reputation, making you unsure how to proceed with this individual. The best advice is to proceed by slowly building a bridge, as the situation may yet be salvageable. We simply need to be a little more cautious.

Solutions

- You can begin by being polite and sincere.
- Emphasize that any negotiated agreement hammered out at the table, will be based on the reliability of the information provided by the other side, and will be nullified otherwise.
- Ask them to provide documentation to support the data they present.
- Design the agreement to stipulate fulfilment of the agreed upon terms.
- Use *Compliance Transparency* to verify the terms of the agreement are being fulfilled. This term refers to using some vehicle to monitor the terms of your agreement. For example, you might want to insist on your right to verify their books to guarantee accuracy, by using an accountant to confirm the figures they provide.
- Use enforcement mechanisms, like financial penalties or a security deposit for incidents where they fail to comply with the contractual terms.

Don't Know Anything About Them—The Negotiator's Dilemma

We cannot find it easy to relate to our counterparts when we don't know anything about them, or their goals and objectives. The reverse is equally true. We might need each other without knowing just how much, and that's the dilemma. However, if both parties are hesitant to show their cards and reveal their business purpose, than how can we possibly hope to negotiate a favourable deal in the process? This often transpires when each party fears they will put their side at risk, by opening up first.

Solution

- Nobody can move forward if someone doesn't take the first step. So, don't be afraid to take the first crucial step, but be wise and make it a small one by only revealing something harmless about your goals. Generally, the other side will reciprocate and the beginning of a constructive dialogue can now be initiated. By starting slowly, you will also begin to build up the trust levels as your bridge expands slowly across the chasm, from either side towards the centre.

Spoilers

This often occurs in multi-party negotiations. Occasionally, there's at least one party-pooper who's out to sabotage the negotiations. Their motives may vary, such as wanting to maintain the status quo, or they feel threatened, see themselves as being marginalized and suffer as a result. They may oppose the deal passively by refusing to make a commitment, or actively oppose the deal simply by presenting direct opposition, or using some other form of subterfuge to sabotage the talks.

Solution

- Be prepared for these spoilers, by considering their real fears and anticipating what kind of impact an agreement would have on their objectives. In other words, identify who might have something to lose if a deal were negotiated, or if an agreement was not successful.
- Counter their resistance and explain '*why*' this change will benefit them. Illuminate their gains and explain that they may actually profit from the proposed venture.
- Offer them roles so that they will be able to retain control over their business and be more proactive in the negotiation process. Assure them that they will be active and productive members in a partnership.
- If all else fails, it might best to form a coalition with the other parties, to overwhelm and counter the spoilers.

Culture and Gender Barriers

Area of Differences

Sometimes, companies, people, and cultures simply operate differently from what we usually experience. One company might be conservative and staid in its approach, while another might be more entrepreneurial and dynamic. We might encounter obstacles in negotiating with a person of the opposite gender, or stumble upon culture barriers because of our different perspectives. As a result, we might blame our difficulties solely on these differences as the basis for the obstacles, that block our path to a successful agreement.

It is vital we do not make assumptions in these situations. The solution may lay in stopping ourselves from jumping to a conclusion, and by analyzing the problem thoroughly. We must step outside of any preconceptions or biases that blur our vision. We must view the problem logically to understand what issues are acting as hindrances, or whether there is a pattern that can illuminate our lack of understanding. Go back to the basics. Examine the issues and their positions by learning the motivating reasons that lay behind objections, either theirs or yours. Then, find ways to solve these concerns and revamp the solutions. This process will at least initiate a more positive and productive dialogue (http://www.negotiations.com/articles/negotiator-agreement/). Every barrier to a successful negotiation should be approached as a challenge, not a problem. If you can analyze and isolate the problem, then you can create solutions or options that may possibly resolve whatever is acting as a barrier. The more you can learn to overcome these challenging sticking points, the more you enhance your negotiation skills in the process. If all else fails, and you have truly exhausted all possibilities, then you also have the final option of simply walking away from the deal.

Barrier to Conflict Resolution

Adversaries in negotiation seek "gains of trade". Each must give up something that it values less than their adversary to obtain something they value more than their adversary. Conflicts differ in their "tractability" Tractable conflicts are "win-win" situations on "non-zero-sum" games. Intractable conflicts have no win-win alternatives. The arms race is an example where it would have been mutually beneficial to reduce arms, but the two parties could never agree. This represents an inefficiency in the bargaining process. While some may practice such inefficiencies as a negotiating strategy, strategic and the psychological barriers to negotiation become a major stumbling block to a negotiation process in the following manner (Ross & Stillinger, 1991).

Strategic Barriers

Secrecy and Deception

Parties may conceal interest or feign over-interest in a particular bargaining chip. However, sometimes this causes adversaries to not put forward that which would offer the greatest mutual advantage.

Intransigence

Some adversaries may believe that unwillingness in current negotiations may give them a better position in future negotiations. Maybe it is thought better to "delay gratification" longer than the adversary. They also may believe eagerness in negotiation may be exploited by the other side. However, "standing pat" runs the risk that the other party will do the same and nothing happens. It can actually cause the status quo to deteriorate for both parties.

Psychological Barriers

Comparative Gains and Equity Considerations

A proposed change may be rejected out of a sense of "fairness". Issues of comparative gains are also problematic.

Loss Aversion

Decision makers tend to attach greater weight to prospective losses then prospective gains. This makes them reluctant to trade concessions.

Biases in the Construal Process

Parties may view the concessions they have to make in a way to maximize their importance and value, and view the concessions they will receive as less important or valuable. They will then not agree on the equity of the concessions. They probably also have different construal's of the causes for the conflict as well, and the motives of each party. Each believe they were more grieved in the past and is deserving of more concessions.

Reactive Devaluation of Compromises and Concessions

People also devalue proposals that were made by their adversary. This bias may cause us to view gains as smaller and concessions as larger. People also might devalue what is offered and value more what was not offered in the negotiation. Big concessions may bolster more "hard bargaining". Small concessions will be seen as trivial.

Dissonance about the past, Unrealistic Hopes about the Future

It is dissonant to accept terms today that could have been accepted long ago without the costs of delay. One to reduce this dissonance is to view the past rejection in part because the deal was one-sided, so bigger concessions need to be made by the other this time.

Complexities and added Dimensions

Multiple interest groups and agency problems.

Political and Constituency Considerations

Politicians often have more to lose from a mistake in negotiating than to gain from any breakthrough. Merely continuing negotiations shows dedication and firmness of resolve, protecting one's interests.

Desire for Formal Adjudication and Vindication

Some want court vindication.

Broader Linkages to other conflicts

Problem of Enmity

They might feel that any gain by the adversary is a loss to themselves (and vice versa).

Some Implications for Conflict Resolution

A concession made bilaterally will be seen better than one made unilaterally, especially if it has been proposed by one's adversary. Offering the adversary a menu of small concessions to start the negotiation process may work (with a stipulation of reciprocation).

Managing Attributions

The use of deadlines can help remove attributions to negotiation destroying factors (trust, etc.). The deadline also will use dissonance to its benefit by forcing both sides to confront the realities of not making concessions. The deadlines must be mutually agreed, however.

Role of Third Parties

The drive to maintain the third party's good will can make the adversaries more reasonable. Both sides can been seen as "compromising" rather than conceding. Mediators may help to create a more problem solving environment.

Awareness of Negotiation Process

Simple awareness of the barriers in negotiation can help reduce some of the impact of them. Education about social and psychological processes involved in negotiation can help both sides better use the tool. Finally, both sides must believe a resolution is possible for negotiation to actually work.

Approach to Negotiations

Knowing the key players is just half the battle. As mentioned earlier, negotiations often is the means to influence the entire organization. Knowing whom to influence gives rise to the question of how to influence them? Approach to negotiations means primarily controlling the process of influencing the key players. In international negotiations, one needs to understand the methods and means of influencing people and organizations. Cultural, legal and organizational differences makes it imperative to adapt different negotiation strategies and tactics.

Top-Down Approach

In a typical American (or Anglo-Saxon) negotiation, negotiators would like to deal with the "real boss", an authority figure who makes the final decision. Americans pride themselves on having the full authority to negotiate. As a result most negotiators find a way to interact directly with the "boss" and avoid making deals with relatively powerless agents. While this technique has been proven at home and sometimes abroad, top down approach has serious limitations in international negotiations. And in many cases, it may work to your disadvantage.

For example, a French firm wished to acquire an Indian subsidiary of a Swiss multinational. The two CEOs agreed on the deal and expected the agreement would be accepted by the management in India. The French company even tried to crammed it down on the Indian subsidiary by offering incentives to those who accepted it, and by punishing those who opposed it. This strategy backfired when the subordinates rebelled and the value of the deal soon eroded (Ghoshal, 2001)

In another example, Armand Hammer entered into a joint venture with China National Coal Development Corporation (CNCDC). The deal was negotiated between Hammer and China's supreme leader Deng Xiaoping, who met in person and expressed serious commitment to making the venture a success. Hammer saw this deal as a crowning achievement of his career: the largest foreign investment in Chinese history. The two leaders ordered their subordinates to reach an agreement. Yet the deal failed due to bureaucratic conflicts, escalating demands and misinterpretations. Finally after a decade of negotiations, Armand Hammer pulled out of the deal due to sheer frustration. (MacLeod, 1997). The example of Armand Hammer with CNCDC illustrates the risk with dealing only with omnipotent bosses. The source of real power can be misleading. Organizations have to learn that there are limits of presidential powers which can prevent the deal from transpiring as expected. Even when dealing with authoritarian powers, deals with the top may not translate into action on the ground.

Building Consensus

"Before the Japanese have reached a consensus, they can't negotiate; After consensus is attained on the other side, there is nothing to negotiate" —John Graham & Yoshihiro Sano

Building consensus in another approach to decision-making during a negotiations. The consensus approach is quite common in Japan, China, and India. Consensus building requires agreement among the members of the other side's negotiating team; and at times it requires influences from a higher authority. The need to build consensus among the players on the other side will affect your negotiating strategy in many ways.

For example, when a consortium of U.S. companies submitted a proposal to assist in building a dam in the Three Gorges Area of Yangtze river, the project was debated by the Chinese for more than 70 years! The Chinese needed time to build a consensus before embarking on the project. The American consortium was negotiating with Yangtze Valley Planning Office (YVPO). In China, bureaucratic offices like YVPO are explicitly ranked and no one unit has authority over the other of the same rank; disputes are to be settled by the higher authority. The only practical solution is consensus. (Graham, 2003)

Negotiators have to adjust their strategy to deal with the task of consensus building. Since consensus often focus on relationships rather than the deal itself. People involved in negotiations must take substantial amounts of time to learn about each other and foster a deep relationship before talking about the deal. In consensus approach, the relationship building is more important than the deal itself. *"The path is more important than the ends"*. This means that you should be prepared to provide information readily and must be asking questions continuously to the extent that everyone gets to know everyone before the negotiations can start. It is during this process, the needs and demands of each party has to be included into consensus building. Your objective in consensus building is to get your points of view, your interests and plans incorporated into their consensus process. What happens in the negotiating table is a mere formality of approving the consensus arrived earlier. The negotiating table is not the place to influence others to change their minds. Making new demands or persuasive appeals are ineffective and are inappropriate.

Shaping Expectations

The outcome of a successful negotiation must always match with our expectations. Therefore it is necessary to shape our own organization's expectations from the deal—How long the deal will take? What concessions we have to make? How much we can expect from the deal? What are the possible constraints and possible conflict area that can come in way before making a Deal? etc.

In other words the answer to the question *"What do I want?"* needs to be clarified when new information is revealed during the negotiations. Failure to do so may put one of the parties in a negotiating vice, between your organization demanding you to deliver on their high expectations vis-à-vis the reality on the ground. Similarly, the other party to the negotiation will try hard to influence their expectations from the agreement. The expectations in an International negotiation revolve around the following four key areas:

Underlying opinion of the process: Both sides need to see it as a win-win process, unilateral assumptions about the other side's view is dangerous and misleading.

Building an agreement: Both sides need to agree on how to approach the final agreement. Asian countries seek a broad and wide ranging agreement first with details to be agreed later, while Americans and Europeans want to deal with small specific agreements first.

Level of detail: An extension of the above, firms from countries where legal rules are poorly implemented are content with a broad agreement based on general principles rather than a detailed contract.

Implementation of Agreement: U.S. firms generally expect other to follow the letter of the contract and resorting to legal methods if there were any violations. In many other countries, a contract is a mere starting point of a relationship which will entail several rounds of renegotiation. Both the sides need to understand the expectations of the other side regarding the method of implementation of the contract.

International negotiations are much more complicated than the perceived cultural differences. It is definitely worth noting the cultural differences and learning the do's and don'ts of other cultures. While culture tells a lot about the person with whom you are negotiating with, it tells little about the other hidden players in negotiations, their approach to negotiations and their expectations from the agreement. Due diligence is required to map all the key players, identify factors which influence their decisions and approach the negotiations so as the influence the final outcome.

Coming to an Agreement

Once you have come to a final agreement, it is important that you have it down in writing along with both parties' signature: this is not always possible or practical. Before it is signed, or formally ordered, it is wise not to say anything about the terms agreed because your next sentence could break the agreement: the best sales-people never over sell—well, not until they have to!

If it is a sale/purchase that you are making, then officially, it isn't a sale until you/they have actually ordered the product/service. Usually, this will be an Order Form (we have one in our free business software). In most other negotiations, one party sending a letter and fax to the other in which the agreement is outlined (to a sufficient degree) will form a legal basis.

If the other party then amends the conditions in the agreement in writing to you, those amended terms then become part of the agreement, UNLESS you disagree in writing, and so on (http://www.bizhelp24.com/you-and-work/coming-to-an-agreement-in-negotiation.html)

We use negotiation in everything we do but you have to be sure that it is done in the best way possible to achieve maximum benefit. The most important part is planning: preparing well will give you an advantage when negotiating.

Only use the knowledge and experience you need to achieve your objective: having the business owner negotiating the supply of pencils is over-kill, and leaves you little room to power-bargain with the same supply company when you want them to supply you with, say, colour photo-copiers.

Have confidence and be sure that you can keep control at all times. Aim highly, but don't underestimate the opposition. They too may have just read the same advice. If you're selling something, be persuasive and offer some incentive to keep the customer interested.

Don't close an agreement until you are happy. This could be difficult if you have been put in a 'corner' but this would perhaps be an effect of poor preparation.

Improving Negotiation Skills: Rules for Master Negotiators

A negotiation is an interactive communication process that may take place whenever we want something from someone else or another person wants something from us. The following expressions make it amply clear that mastering negotiation skills could be a critical success factor for an effective negotiation with predictable outcome.

"Take it or leave it!" "This proposal is non-negotiable." "Don't ask me to go back to my client on this. This is all we are going to do." "This is it. If you don't want to accept it at that price, forget it." "Negotiating with you is a waste of time. We'll see you at the courthouse!" How do you feel when you hear statements like this? How do you feel when people are belligerent; when they hang up on you, literally or figuratively; when they let you know that they do not want to have a dialogue with you about such ethereal subjects as your needs, interests, or concerns about a proposal or a transaction?

If you react negatively to ultimatums, inflexibility, and statements like those in the preceding paragraph, you may come to the realization that other people feel the same way. Unless you are in the military, or subject to some similar hierarchical organization, you will conclude that, if you want to have a relationship with the party on the other side of the table or the other end of the phone, you must negotiate. Negotiation is unavoidable.

Most of us negotiate with one another frequently. Once we realize this, theoretically, we have two choices: accept the fact that negotiation is a way of life in our culture and improve our skills so that we can negotiate with confidence; or, do nothing about it. Some may argue that negotiation is an art, that it is intuitive; or, that we all know how to negotiate, learning basic skills on the playgrounds of life(Thomas Noble-http://library.findlaw.com/2001/Jan/1/130785.html.).

We can all improve our skills as negotiators. The Master Negotiator is not someone who works miracles, who can pull off remarkable "swindles" or hypnotize his or her opponents into barking like dogs and doing other things that they would not ordinarily do. The Master Negotiator is simply demonstratively better than the Novice Negotiator. The Master Negotiator's skills are obvious. While he may not walk on water, he will consistently get the best deal possible under the circumstances. On occasion, perhaps even frequently, he will get remarkably good results. Master Negotiators follow certain rules that novices do not understand or that they do not implement (Thomas Noble of Law Offices of Thomas Noble, P.C.: http://library.findlaw.com/2001/Jan/1/130785.html)

Fundamental Elements of the Negotiation Process

One of the interesting aspects to negotiation theory is that even the fundamental elements of the process are subject to varying opinions. However, the Fundamental elements of the negotiation process need to go through the following critical stages in a step-by-step manner:

Phase I: Pre-bargaining Phase

1. Information: Learn as much as you can about the problem. What information do you need from the other side?
2. Leverage Evaluation: Evaluate your leverage and the other party's leverage at the outset. This is important because there may be a number of things you can do to improve your leverage or diminish the leverage of the other side. What will you do to enhance your leverage?
3. Analysis: What are the issues?
4. Rapport: Establish rapport with your opponent(s). You need to determine early on if your opponents are going to be cooperative; if not, consider employing a mediator as soon as practical.
5. Goals and expectations: Goals are one thing; expectations are something else.
6. Type of negotiation: What type of negotiation do you expect? Will this be highly competitive, cooperative, or something unusual? Will you be negotiating face to face, by fax, through a mediator, or in some other manner?
7. Budget: Every negotiation has its costs. Lawyers will avoid conflicts with their clients by discussing budgets sooner rather than later. Many times there are a number of choices for enhancing leverage. For example, you may enhance your leverage by taking several depositions, by adding parties to a law suit, by serving subpoenas on witnesses, or by hiring experts. Unless your client has unlimited resources, you will have to make some hard choices, which should be designed to give you the "most bang for your buck".
8. Plan: What's your negotiation plan?

Phase II: Bargaining Phase

1. Logistics: When, where, and how will you negotiate? This can be especially important in multi-party cases.

2. Opening offers: What is the best offer you can justify? Should you make it, or wait to let another party go first?
3. Subsequent offers: How should you adjust your negotiating plan when responding to unanticipated moves by your opponent?
4. Tactics: What sort of tactics will you employ? What sort of tactics is your opponent using on you?
5. Concessions: What concessions will you make? How will you make them?
6. Resolution: What is the best way to resolve the problem? Is there an elegant solution? Be on constant lookout for compromise and creative solutions.

Phase III: Closure Phase

1. Logistics: How and when will you close? At mediation or later on? Who will prepare the final agreement?
2. Documentation: Prepare a closing checklist.
3. Emotional closure: It's one thing to end a legal dispute; it's another to address the underlying interests and needs of the parties. If you neglect the latter, the agreement will probably not sustain.
4. Implementation: It's not over until it is over.

Some of these elements are self-explanatory and elementary. However, the others may be governed by the following set of rules:

Rule 1: Attitude

Rule 1.1: Everything is negotiable all of the time

Attitude is critical. Novice negotiators do not understand that everything is negotiable all of the time. They give up too easily. If you slam your briefcase and walk out of a negotiation session, they do not understand that this is a tactic; they interpret it as the end of the negotiation.

I had a custody case recently in which I was representing a father who was concerned about his ex-wife's emotional stability. Since their divorce, she had changed jobs several times, changed sexual partners several times, and had problems with her temper and her temperance. On his behalf, I contacted her lawyer and requested that she submit to a psychological evaluation. When that request was ignored, we filed a suit, requesting that the father have primary custody of the children. I then proposed to my opposing counsel that we schedule mediation. She refused because "your client wants custody of the children, and my client will never agree to that". She failed to understand that my client's lawsuit was a negotiating tactic. Had she understood this, she could have saved her client substantial legal fees. This is a common scenario. Many lawsuits wind up in court because lawyers do not understand that "positions" are always negotiable.

- "Many attributes go into making a skillful negotiator, including such things as having a good memory, being 'quick verbally', and handling stress well. But effectiveness is as much a matter of *attitude* as it is of ability. The best negotiators exhibit four key habits of thought that everyone, regardless of their style or IQ, can adopt to improve their negotiation results ...

- A willingness to prepare
- High expectations
- The patience to listen
- A commitment to personal integrity"

Rule 1.2: Compromise is omnipresent

I cannot remember conducting a mediation or being involved in a dispute that could not have been compromised. Master Negotiators are always on the look-out for an acceptable compromise, especially as the gap between the parties narrows.

"Assume that you will end up in the middle, between the two opening negotiation positions. ... In little and in big things, we end up splitting the difference."

Rule 1.3: "Fair" is a range

Many negotiations break down because one person has a number in mind (his "bottom line"), and the other person has a number in mind, and one or both parties adopts a negative attitude about closing the gap. One way that Master Negotiators avoid impasses like this is to understand that reaching agreements with people is rarely such an exact science that we can get things down to decimal points. Whether you are trying to settle a personal injury case, buy or sell real estate, or dickering over a premarital agreement, rare is the book that says what the thing is worth. How much will the jury award? How much would another buyer pay? How much would another future spouse want? And, if the solution to the various problems over which we typically negotiate were so easily found, there would be no reason to negotiate. Thus, by the very nature of the beast, the "fair" resolution in every negotiation, the elegant solution, is a range, not a point in space. By keeping this in mind, Master Negotiators are more flexible than novices.

"... when I negotiate, I look for the *favorable middle ground*—where my client is pleased with the resolution and the other party is satisfied enough to do the deal."

Rule 2: Communication Skills

Rule 2.1: Lines of communication are critical

Without lines of communication there can be no negotiation. Therefore, this rule is essential. Lines of communication are the life-blood of a negotiation.[8] Master Negotiators understand this; novices do not. Novice Negotiators often focus on static elements of the problem, believe that they are "playing a winning hand", and throw down the gauntlet, only to learn later that the dynamic elements of the situation have changed, their leverage has withered, and they have burned their bridges.

This rule suggests that intimidation tactics are ineffective, which, of course, is not true. Master Negotiators understand, however, that persuasion is usually superior to intimidation as a negotiation tactic. If intimidation "works", it only works when the negotiating playing field is skewed for some reason, where one party has so much greater leverage than the other, that the interaction can scarcely be called a "negotiation". And, as every parent who has raised a child to adolescence knows, intimidation almost always results in passive aggressive behavior and resentment.

Rule 2.2: Be cooperative, but don't let your guard down

Statistics show that cooperative negotiators are more effective than competitive negotiators.

"To negotiate well, you do not need to be tricky. But it helps to be alert and prudent. The best negotiators play it straight, ask a lot of questions, listen carefully, and concentrate on what they and the other party are trying to accomplish at the bargaining table."

The Master Negotiator studies the terrain before settling into a negotiation. He understands that some negotiators are cooperative and some are competitive. Being too cooperative with a highly competitive negotiator is a good way to get plucked.

"... pursuing a soft and friendly form of positional bargaining makes you vulnerable to someone who plays a hard game of positional bargaining. In positional bargaining, a hard game dominates a soft one."

Rule 2.3: Listen

"It is hard to overstate the importance of listening skills in bargaining. ... the best negotiators ... ask questions, test for understanding, summarize discussions, and listen, listen, listen. ... You often get more by finding out what the other person wants than you do by clever arguments supporting what you need."

"Perhaps the best strategy to adopt while the other side lets off steam is to listen quietly without responding to their attacks, and occasionally to ask the speaker to continue until he has spoken his last word. In this way, you offer little support to the inflammatory substance, give the speaker every encouragement to speak himself out, and leave little or no residue to fester."

"Listen actively and acknowledge what is being said. ... It has been said that the cheapest concession you can make to the other side is to let them know that they have been heard. ... Standard techniques of good listening are to pay close attention to what is said, to ask the other party to spell out carefully and clearly exactly what they mean, and to request that ideas be repeated if there is any ambiguity or uncertainty. ... Unless you acknowledge what they are saying and demonstrate that you understand them, they may believe you have not heard them."

Rule 2.4: Pare down large groups

Every negotiator confronts situations where each side is a *committee*, rather than an individual. This usually means negotiations within negotiations, as the members of each committee or group have to negotiate an intra-consensus before responding to the other side. If every member of every group has to put in his two cents before you can respond to a proposal, the process is slow and tedious. This problem can often be remedied if each group will appoint a representative. "No matter how many people are involved in a negotiation, important decisions are typically made when no more than two people are in the room."

Rule 3: Planning

Rule 3.1: Develop a flexible negotiation plan

"I am convinced that you need to approach each negotiation with a well conceived game plan."

Master Negotiators develop strategies for each phase of the negotiation process: opening, middle game, and end game. Like master chess players, they come to the table knowing how they are going to open. They understand that, from there, strategies have to be flexible because how their opponents respond to opening offers is unpredictable. Nevertheless, they plan ahead as much as possible.

Freund suggests the follow simple format for developing a negotiating plan:

- *What* do I want?
- *Where* do I start?
- *When* do I move?
- *How* do I close?

While a Novice Negotiator may do some planning, he does not plan thoroughly. For example, a Master Negotiator will always develop a closing strategy. He knows whether he wants to close sooner rather than later and whether he wants extensive documentation or if an outline of the deal will do.

Rule 3.2: Plan your first move carefully

Initial offers define the parameters of the "negotiation zone". The negotiation zone is that range in which negotiators bargain. In every negotiation the parties define the negotiation zone. You get to decide where one end of the zone is located, and your opponent decides the other end. Master Negotiators understand that where leverage is relatively equal, there is always a tendency to meet in the middle. Where the middle is ultimately located depends on where they start. Therefore, they put a lot of time and energy to developing and justifying their initial offers.

Rule 3.3: Goals are more important than bottom lines

"What is the practical effect of having your bottom line become your dominant reference point in a negotiation? Over a lifetime of negotiating, your results will tend to hover at a point just above this minimum acceptable level. ... With experience, you should be able to keep both your goal and your bottom line in view at the same time without losing your goal focus. Research suggests that the best negotiators have this ability."

Rule 3.4: Plan to make concessions

Making concessions triggers the law of reciprocity. When you make a concession, the other party will usually respond with one. Indeed, he will feel compelled to do so. The flip side of this rule is that when you do someone a favor, they will feel indebted to you for it.

Rule 3.5: Understand when and how to mediate

Master Negotiators know when a mediator will facilitate settlement and when a mediator is unnecessary. Master Negotiators know when arbitration is preferable to going to court. Novice Negotiators wait too long before employing a mediator. They let problems fester and parties become too invested in their positions. By the time they get around to mediation, they have wasted considerable resources and the momentum toward trial is formidable. The time to mediate is as soon as the negotiations founder, in cases where the parties employ a mediator out of necessity, or as soon as all parties have enough information to bargain intelligently, in cases where they are mediating by choice (because that is their preferred method of negotiating).

Master Negotiators are usually master manipulators, and mediation is no exception. Novices come to mediation and act combative with the mediator or exclude the mediator from all relevant discussions, relegating the mediator to the function of courier. Master Negotiators understand that the mediator can help them sell their proposals. They arm the mediator with persuasive arguments, legal briefs, or material evidence in support of their proposals. They add a dash of charm and encourage their clients to endear himself or herself to the mediator.

Rule 3.5: Have a theme

Lawyers who argue their cases to juries know the importance of having a simple, unifying theme. Johnnie Cochran's theme in the O.J. Simpson murder trial of "if it doesn't fit, you must acquit" is a sound example. Master Negotiators understand that this same technique works in negotiations.

Rule 4: Evaluation

Rule 4.1: Look beneath the surface

Novice Negotiators focus on facts, or dollar amounts, or legal issues, or personalities. Master Negotiators understand that every negotiation is a combination of these factors, as well as others.

> "... skilled negotiators see more than just opening offers, counteroffers, and closing moves when they look at what happens at the bargaining table. They see psychological and strategic currents that are running just below the surface. They notice where the parties stand in terms of the reciprocity norm. They look for opportunities to use what psychologists call the consistency principle to commit other parties to standards and then hold them to their prior statements and positions, and they know that the timing of a proposal is always as important as its content." "So when you formulate your goals, consider carefully what really matters to you. Sure, money is important. But identify your underlying interests and needs clearly."

Rule 4.2: Break the problem up into issues

Every negotiation involves one or more problems, or "issues", which can be sub-divided when necessary, to make the negotiation more manageable and to allow for partial agreements.

Fisher and Ury discuss methods of negotiating. They argue that their model of "principled negotiation" is superior to the traditional method of "positional bargaining" in which the parties take positions and then make concessions to reach agreements.

> "The method of *principled negotiation* developed by the Harvard Negotiation Project is to decide issues on their merits rather than through the haggling process focused on what each side says it will do and won't do. It suggests that you look for mutual gains wherever possible, and that where your interests conflict, you should insist that the result be based on some fair standards independent of the will of either side. The method of principled negotiation is hard on the merits, soft on the people."

Rule 4.3: Look for multiple solutions

Master Negotiators do not look for the truth or the right answer. They explore options. They know that there are usually a number of workable solutions to the problems that vex us in our social interaction. Finding out what those solutions are may take a little work, and, even though a solution may be workable, it will not necessarily be palatable to everyone. Nevertheless, Master Negotiators know that, once they get an understanding of the whys and wherefores of each party's "positions", more often than not, there will be several options for bridging the gap, solving the problem, or resolving the issue.

Rule 4.4: Evaluate people, interests, options, and criteria

Fisher and Ury summarize their method of principled negotiation as follows:

"**People:** Separate the people from the problem.

Interests: Focus on interests, not positions.

Options: Generate a variety of possibilities before deciding what to do.

Criteria: Insist that the result be based on some objective standard."

"Begin your preparation for negotiation by considering your own underlying needs and interests".

Many people fight over money. But, money usually symbolizes something else. Is "feeling like a winner" what it is really all about? Is it feeling like you are being treated fairly? Look behind the money. You will find a lot of solutions there.

Rule 4.5: Evaluate the leverage

"The first basic skill of smart negotiating is an awareness of the leverage factors at work, plus the ability to apply leverage when it's in your favor and make do when it's not."

Leverage is negotiating power, plain and simple. It is the gas in your tank. If you have no leverage, you are at the mercy of your opponent. Master Negotiators understand leverage. They know how to develop it and use it to maximum advantage. They know that if they do not use it when they have it, it may not be worth as much tomorrow. Leverage has a way of evaporating. Master Negotiators understand that leverage is wonderful, but if you don't use it, you will probably lose it. Because leverage is rarely static, you can usually enhance your leverage, or develop leverage where you had none, through: 1. preparation, 2. information, 3. number-crunching, 4. understanding your opponent, 5. exploring and developing other options, 6. timing, and 7. patience.

Rule 4.5: Consider the "consistency principle"

Master negotiators understand the "consistency principle", which states that we all have a strong psychological need to be consistent with our prior acts and statements. If you are looking for tactics you can use to manipulate your opponent, consider trying to hook him with some small commitment and then following up with a larger request.

> "The goal of the consistency trap is to pre-commit you to a seemingly innocent standard and then confront you with the logical implications of the standard in a particular case—implications that actually turn out to run against your interests. This is a form of intellectual coercion, and you should be ready to defend against it".

This concept may have a material effect on your negotiating strategy. In a fight over money, when they are not getting as much as they want, Novice Negotiators often react by accusing their opponent of being a skinflint or a cheapskate or by threatening him with going to trial if he does not loosen up. Although counter-intuitive, it may be much more effective to remind the skinflint of all of his generous past acts so that he will act consistently with a pattern of generosity. The consistency principle can also be invoked in order to persuade an opponent to act consistently with established standards and norms.

Rule 5: Closure

Rule 5.1: Don't blow the end game

Master Negotiators know how to close. They consider every element of closure: when, where, documentation, pending issues. Novices either rush the end game or delay it interminably, with equally bad results. Rushing the end game usually means slapping a contract together with little time or thought; its ambiguities and deficiencies inevitably result in disputes. Delaying the end game means failing to "strike when the iron is hot"; if you wait long enough, something will happen to prevent closure. Time kills deals.

Rule 5.2: Strive for a "wise agreement"

"Any Method of Negotiation may be fairly judged by three criteria: It should produce a wise agreement. It should be efficient. And it should improve or at least not damage the relationship between the parties. (A wise agreement can be defined as one that meets the legitimate interests of each side to the extent possible, resolves the conflicting interests fairly, is durable, and takes community interests into account). ... Arguing over positions produces unwise agreements. ... As more attention is paid to positions, less attention is devoted to meeting the underlying concerns of the parties."

Rule 5.3: Pay attention to details, but don't sweat the small stuff

Here, again, the middle way is the correct path. You can kill a deal by being too particular just like you can by delaying closure. Master Negotiators are careful about closing, but they do not let petty issues prevent closing.

Rule 5.4: Don't neglect emotional closure

Lawyers are great at analyzing legal issues, negotiating agreements, and closing agreements concerning *legal issues*. But, in situations where people will have a relationship after they sign the agreement, they would be smart to make sure that they have tended to the emotional issues, otherwise the legal agreement may suffer the consequences of any structure with a faulty foundation. Many times, especially in family disputes, agreements addressing emotional issues can be, and should be, intricate and involved. But, as Fisher and Ury advise, "an apology may be one of the least costly and most rewarding investments you can make".

Basic Elements: Checklist

Phase I: Pre-bargaining Phase

- Information
- Leverage
- Issues
- Rapport
- Goals and expectations
- Type of negotiation
- Budget
- Plan

Phase II: Bargaining Phase

- Logistics
- Opening offer
- Subsequent offers
- Tactics
- Concessions
- Resolution

Phase III: Closure Phase

- Logistics
- Closing checklist
- Emotional closure
- Implementation

Negotiation Checklist

- Confirm with other parties (and mediator)
- Confirm logistics with client

Pack

- Files: pleadings, evidence, current matters
- Books
- Checklists
- Laptop/printer/paper/ink cartridge
- Calculator
- Check for mediator?
- Trial notebook
- Calendar
- Notepad/pen/highlighter/post-it notes/file folders/misc.

Analysis

- Review Chronology
- Review prior settlement proposals

- List Issues
- Strengths and weaknesses
- Review and organize docs
- Review discovery responses (incl depos)
- Marshall Evidence re each issue
- Review legal research
- Negotiating Strategy
- Opening offer
- Concessions
- Closing strategy

Document preparation

- Letter to mediator
- Update Inventory?
- Proposed Mediation Agreement/Decree
- Spreadsheets
- Disk (issues/spreadsheets/agreement)
- Questions
- Waiver of Discovery

Negotiation Models

There are several negotiation models that are propounded by various workers predominantly from social sciences. Some of these models are described below:

Janosik's Cross-cultural Negotiation Model

In 1987, Janosik introduced his seminal theory of cross-cultural negotiation research based on his qualitative, phenomenological studies about culture on negotiation (as cited in Osman-Gani & Tan, 2002). This theory identifies four major constructs, and the four approaches are: (1) cultures as a learned behavior, (2) cultures as a system of shared values, (3) cultures as dialectic, and (4) culture in context defined as cross-cultural negotiation research. The major propositions in this theory are no matter which approach is to be used, one of the main issues is how to understand individual variations in negotiation (as cited in Osman-Gani & Tan, 2002). Several empirical studies by Osman-Gani & Tan, led to refinement in the theory. Brett (2001) developed a schematic model depicting these direct and indirect relationships among concepts, which continue to be examined today (Osman-Gani & Tan, 2002). This theory is socially significant addressing essential issues about cross-cultural negotiation in the discipline of negotiation styles, and is useful in explaining, predicting, and discriminating among those with unfamiliar or different cultures demonstrating different negotiation styles. Thus, it is a well-developed guide to cross-cultural negotiation. The theory has a good balance between simplicity and complexity, contributing to its usefulness. Studies by Osman-Gani & Tan verify the propositions of different negotiation styles in different cultures. The theory has been adapted to cross-cultural situations in business negotiation and Asian manager populations. This is the predominant theory used to examine cross-cultural negotiation with well-developed propositions and strong empirical support.

Hofstede's Cultural Dimensions

With the goal of helping individuals distinguish the various cultural differences of individual countries, Hofstede (1980) introduced his seminal theory of four cultural dimensions based on his earlier qualitative, phenomenological studies. This theory identifies four major variables of cultural differences: power, uncertainty/avoidance, individualism/ collectivism, and masculinity/femininity (Hofstede, 1994 & 1980). The major proposition is that cultural differences impact business conduct, decision-making and communication; therefore, an increased cultural awareness is important for international managers. Over the past 20 years, the theory has been revised and adapted to address cross-cultural negotiations by Redpath and Nielson. Several further empirical studies by Chang led to even more refinements. A schematic model was developed to depict these direct and indirect relationships among concepts that continue to be refined.

This theory is socially significant addressing essential issues about cross cultures in the discipline of negotiation, and is useful in explaining, predicting, and discriminating among those people who have conduct international business abroad. Thus it is a well-developed guide to negotiation styles. The theory has a good balance between simplicity and complexity, contributing to its usefulness. Studies by Chang verify the propositions of five cultural dimensions. The theory has been adapted to cross-cultural negotiation situations and American and Chinese populations. This is the predominant theory used to examine different cultures with well-developed propositions and strong empirical support.

Negotiation Process Model

The negotiation process model originated from exchange theory which was created by Rubin and Brown in 1975 (Peterson & Lucas, 2001). The exchange theory is divided into three stages: the antecedent stage, the concurrent stage, and the consequent stage. The exchange theory was revised to the negotiation process model by Graham. In 1987, Graham introduced his seminal theory of the negotiation process model based on his qualitative, phenomenological studies about negotiation (Peterson & Lucas, 2001). This theory identifies three major constructs: negotiator characteristics and situational variables, process variables, and outcome phases. The major propositions in this theory based on the pre-negotiation planning and preparing phase are linked to the negotiators characteristics such as gender, age, experiences in negotiation, and education and situation constraints like competitive or collaborative negotiation. The theory has been adapted to gender differences in negotiation outcome situations in America and Canada populations. This is the predominant theory used to examine differences in gender, age, education, and experiences in negotiation with well-developed propositions and strong empirical support.

Negotiating Styles

Before buyers and sellers become business partners, they need to negotiate the terms of agreements. Because different countries have different cultures, different cultures will affect people who have different approaches in thinking, values, norms and behaviors. Different styles in business negotiation, such as in communication, protocols, persuasion strategy, and personal characteristics like accommodating, determined, flexible and adept (Hung, 1998). Negotiation experts need to understand negotiation styles of other people who live in different countries on the other side of table, and accept their culture beliefs and norms.

Dual Concern Model

The Dual Concern Model originated from the Managerial Grid which was created by Blake and Mouton in 1964 (Chang, 2002). The Managerial Grid is a behavioral theory of management that considers two dimensions of leadership: concern for the task and concern for the relationship (Chang, 2002). In 1964, Blake and Mouton indicated that this model consists of five major styles of leadership: laissez-faire management, country club management style, task management style, team management style, and middle-of-the-road management. In 1995, Pearson indicated that the difference between the Conflict Grid and the Dual Concern Model is that the Dual Concern Model not only concerns our own interest but also concerns other people's interests. In 1964, Blake and Mouton introduced their seminal theory of based on the qualitative, phenomenological studies about the Dual Concern Model. This model consists of five conflict solution styles along with two dimensions. The two dimensions is to concern for own interests and concern for other's interests. These five styles of conflict resolution are: withdrawing, accommodating, demanding, collaborating, and compromising. Gauthier (2002) explained that competitive is a situation of winner and loser; cooperative styles are win-win situation; compromise is win a little—win a little; accommodation is lose now to win later, and withdrawal situation is to negotiate elsewhere where you can win.

A Negotiation Model for Collaborative Decision-Making in Large-Scale Multi-Agent Systems

Modeling agent negotiation is of key importance in building multi-agent system, because negotiation is one of the most important types of agent interaction. Negotiation provides the basis for managing the expectations of the individual negotiating agents, and it enables selecting solutions that satisfy all the agents as much as possible. Thus far, most negotiation models have serious limitation and weakness when employed in large-scale multi-agent systems. Yet, large-scale multi-agent systems find their use in major domains of human development such as space exploration, military technology, disaster response systems, and health technology. Tom Wanyama (http://www.springerlink.com/content/j5763734w5rjj752/) in his book titled 'A Negotiation Model for Collaborative Decision-Making in Large-Scale Multi-Agent Systems', presents an agent negotiation model which extends the capabilities of the model associated with the Agent Negotiation Engine for Collaborative Decision-Making, to address the negotiation issues associated with large-scale multi-agents systems. The model utilizes Qualitative Reasoning and Game Theory algorithms to track the negotiation process, and a similarity criteria algorithm to manage the large amount of negotiation information associated with large-scale multi-agent systems. The book also presents the negotiation models from which the negotiation model for large-scale multi-agent systems evolved, as well as how and why the modifications were made.

Negotiating Tactics

In 1964, Giles indicated that Sun Tzu, a Chinese military strategist, wrote in *The Art of War*, "to fight and conquer in all your battles is not supreme excellence; supreme excellence consists in breaking the enemy's resistance without fighting" (Peterson, Lucas, 2001). In 1985, Wall indicated that negotiators should contrive general strategies that drive the specific tactics they will deploy.

Negotiating tactics can be classified as "competitive or cooperative or as "distributive or integrative". Competitive negotiation tactics is based on the assumption of a zero-sum or a win-lose philosophy like distributive negotiation tactics. Cooperative negotiation tactics are a concept of win-win philosophy like integrative tactics. In 1991, Fisher, and in 1981, Pruitt indicated integrative negotiation concerns for maximizing one's outcomes and the other party's outcomes. In 1994, Lewicki, Litterer, Minton and Saunders indicated that integrative negotiation requires more flexibility, open information to share and a higher concern for each other.

Negotiation Teaching

Traditional Approaches to Negotiation Teaching

The first course entirely devoted to managerial negotiation has been offered at Dartmouth College in 1973 (Lewicki, 1986). In the early 1980s, many business schools started to offer courses on negotiations. Most courses employed an experiential learning methodology (Lewicki 1986). The pedagogical techniques used in experiential learning include: having an actual concrete experience with a phenomenon; reflecting upon that phenomenon to sort out the experience and identify key elements; identifying generalizations and actively experimenting to create the new behavior (Kolb, 1974).

Most negotiation courses implicitly or explicitly follow these steps.

Negotiation teaching concentrates on lectures about theories, discussions of case studies, and conducts and analyses of simple experiments. Case studies describe some elements of negotiations, for example, framing, power strategies, and negotiators' personalities (Shubik, 1971). Their study allows students to evaluate factors that influence the chances that a dispute may be resolved through negotiation. The analysis of the events that occurred in specific instances of a negotiation provides a factual grounding for discussion. This focuses the discourse on gaining insights and practical directions. Furthermore, detailed case studies enable students to see the importance of individuals and organizations involved in the negotiations and also their broader context (Weiss-Wik, 1983).

Negotiation experiments are used in courses as a learning tool (Winham and Bovis, 1979; Carnevale, 1995). They offer an opportunity for students' direct participation and the subsequent rigorous analysis of the dynamic aspects of negotiation and human biases. Some experiments are conducted in the form of pen-and-paper tests involving brief and well contained tasks (Francis, 1991). For practical reasons, these experiments do not extend beyond one or two hours and therefore they are typically narrowly focused. Furthermore, because they are conducted in a classroom, the participants know each other and their interaction is face-to-face.

Many experimental studies are based on classroom experiments. These studies make it possible to analyze, assess and possibly measure specific attributes and mechanisms characterizing the negotiation processes. They are also used to analyze attitudes and perceptions of the subjects. This has usually been achieved at the cost of a highly stylized and unrealistic negotiation process and setting. Experiments have typically dealt with a fairly simplified negotiation problem and a small number of well defined participants.

Discussion of cases and experiments conducted in a classroom are useful in ingraining the principles of the art of negotiation. They also help to illustrate formal techniques of decision and negotiation analysis. However, it is difficult for the students to apply the learned principles and use formal techniques in negotiations that resemble real-life situations. The limitations of these methods that have been discussed in the literature are as follows:

1. Low control and focus: students and trainees often find that they have little control over the negotiation process, and the focus of the negotiation is determined by instructors and trainers. Pruitt (1986), (based on his analysis of six negotiation courses in U.S. universities) observed that most cases fail to anchor the actors, and the locus of control seems to rest with the instructor. Instructors often intervene to complete the game in time, retain students' interest, or cover the various aspects of the negotiation process.
2. No flexibility in scheduling training sessions: given that negotiation experiments are conducted in a classroom and given the restrictions of semesters, instructors find that the lack of flexibility in conducting these

simulations affects the learning process. This problem is acute in courses on International Business, where the instructors should arrange groups of participants from different countries. The problem is not just the time zones, but the sole organization and effort required for such negotiations which typically makes them impossible.

3. Low level of involvement: Short-time and limited focus of negotiation experiments, high level of control, as well as the common lack of real-life complexity in the simulations, contribute to low involvement of the participants (Thompson, 1991).
4. Narrow domain of simulation: Simulations allow one to analyze students' behavior and their interactions and discuss these in a classroom. Hence it is an important vehicle to teach and study negotiations. Traditionally, simulations are restricted to the classroom and did not involve people from outside of the class. Further, the cost of setup, administration, analysis and feedback is high and contributes to limited use of simulations in which only very simple problems are employed.

New Demands and Challenges

Negotiation courses are typically offered for business students and by instructors with a very strong behavioral background. RBS' review of curricula of conflict resolution and negotiation courses offered at the Harvard Business School, Georgetown University, Northeastern University, University of Maryland, University of Washington, University of New Hampshire, Washington University and some of the consulting companies offering negotiation courses (e.g., The Management Concepts, Inc. at: http://www.mgmtconcepts.com/ and The Negotiation Skills Company at:http://negotiationskills.com/) show that the organizational behavior approach to negotiation is predominant. The focus is on types of negotiations and conflicts, parties' behavior, planning and communication, mediation and third party intervention, and the social and organizational context of negotiations.

Negotiations are already being conducted via electronic means and this may require a somewhat different approach to effective communication than in face-to-face negotiations. Data mining and knowledge discovery tools are increasingly being used in situation assessment and process analysis and they may have an important role in the preparation for, and conduct of, negotiations. Decision and negotiation support systems are becoming increasingly popular and used in formulation and evaluation of alternatives, assessment of offers and counter-offers, organization and visualization of the negotiation process. Expert systems were developed to support teaching cross-cultural communication and negotiation. These issues are rarely taught if at all. Another key aspect of negotiation teaching and training involves the use of computer based simulation models. Negotiators dealing with engineering, financial or environmental issues need to be able to construct and assess scenarios to formulate offers and evaluate the opponents' offers.

Negotiation Teaching in Developing Countries: INSPIRE Model

The focus in negotiation training followed curricula prepared in developed countries with the main difference being the emphasis on the cultural factors. That is the focus is on the negotiation process that takes place over time and in space in the context defined by particular economic, political, and cultural environments (Sunshine, 1990).

Educational institutions in developing countries are riddled with many problems. Most business schools offer their courses in the regional language and may suffer due to lack of training materials or poorly translated notes. While obtaining teaching materials from outside sources is not difficult, often the material will not reflect the dominant practices or culture of the country. This not only affects the quality of course delivery, but also the participation of the registrants.

There is a shortage of trained and qualified instructors in these countries and the number of available cases relevant to local conditions. The result is a demand for creating educational programs and systems that allow for an easy development, storage and retrieval of cases and simulation models. It is expected that such systems should also allow to access and use decision and negotiation techniques, and to facilitate communication between instructors and students, from both the developing and developed countries.

There is a growing number of highly educated managers and engineers which are employed in organizations that successfully compete in the global marketplace developing innovative technologies and products. With this success there is an urgent need for these managers and engineers to obtain communication and negotiation skills and this need is being addressed at such educational institutions as the IIMB.

New technologies such as the World Wide Web offer exciting avenues for teaching and training for international negotiation. The technology seems to have the capacity to respond to a variety of negotiation training needs, and to address many of the problems mentioned in the discussion above that developing countries are facing. By offering easy access to materials and computer-based support, the technology can facilitate upgrading the qualifications of instructors. The Web-based negotiation systems can accommodate any number of users, thus many participants, be it instructors or students, can benefit from using it at any given time. Systems such as INSPIRE offer an opportunity for direct participation in a negotiation and thus experiential learning which is deeply rooted in the theory and practice of negotiation training. The level of participants' involvement is considerably higher (comparable to that in real life negotiations) than in the traditional training sessions. This is probably due to the fact that each participant is fully responsible for all the decisions that he/she makes and all the communication that occurs during the negotiation process. Hence, the locus of control is very high.

One of the features of the INSPIRE system that has a promising potential, is the possibility for users to develop their own materials (i.e. case studies) that are relevant to their particular situation and interests. This allows for the development of "custom made" materials. A pool of such materials will grow fast, providing a group of enthusiasts from developing countries interested in preparing such materials to become involved. What the system does not do however, is focus on cultural diversions. The attention of the user who engages in the negotiation is on the procedural aspects and on the analysis of the negotiation process. In other words, while conducting negotiations, the participants rely on procedural rather than regional culture. Thus the experience with negotiations via INSPIRE seem like the first step in "a-cultural training" for international negotiations. All this being said, the authors believe that systems like INSPIRE prepare professionals such as engineers and business people for a negotiation environment that will dominate international negotiations in the very near future.

The following section describes the technological advantages offered by Web based systems such as INSPIRE, a negotiation support system that enables unconstrained inter-cultural negotiations.

The Web and Negotiation Teaching and Training

Technology is a critical resource that can eliminate some of the problems related to teaching and training of communication and negotiation in developing countries. Some of these technologies, being system independent (in terms of operation and maintenance), allow users from remote parts of the world to communicate and to use previously inaccessible resources, Widespread use of computer networks, especially Web-based systems, indicate that the information access barrier between the developing and developed worlds could be overcome.

The principal feature of the World Wide Web is that it provides people at different locations and time zones a communication medium that is rich in functionality, and gives them the ability to use previously inaccessible computational resources. While the Web's greatest use currently is as a powerful source and means for dissemination of information, it is increasingly being used as a means for remote execution and control of complete software systems, thus adding another dimension to the value it delivers. In education, its ability to access and run remote programs and databases allows users to extend classroom and laboratory boundaries across geographical and time zones. It thus allows instructors and students to retrieve and use resources from remote sites. This flexibility can nullify the effects of inequality between developing and developed country managers, policy makers and citizens by enhancing their ability to communicate, negotiate and participate in business and other activities.

These technologies allow rich communication amongst the actors in a negotiation, by virtue of computation-intensive techniques and visualization of data. The users can review the negotiation process and its dynamics. Language and other barriers shrink or disappear since these technologies allow extreme customization. User-specific front ends can be built which can be connected to the common core of the system, thus increasing participation while retaining functionality. The cost of duplicating a technological solution is another major factor that determines whether a particular solution can reach a larger population. Web browsers allow for portability and thus increase the access of the users in remote countries to training and real-life negotiations with minimal computing resources. These tools and systems are accessible to everyone, lay people and experts alike, and enable them to interact more directly with persons from different cultures, thus immensely reducing the effect of distances.

The flexibility of Web based systems enables customization of the case material to reflect regional specifics. It is also easier to bring about a discipline based orientation in teaching and training sessions. The systems can be tailored to reflect, say, behavioral, decision theoretic or any other focus to suit the teaching and training needs. This is very useful for management teaching and training where different modules are combined to reflect a particular focus of the course. Web pages are very good at representing context, and independent Web pages may be assembled by a dispatching system that determines which page to present, based on a given situation.

The InterNeg Web site and its Web-based system INSPIRE have been constructed to exploit these technologies and their use in teaching. They aim to provide people around the world with analytical knowledge and decision support techniques within the domain of negotiations. The INSPIRE system allows to analyze and solve real-like decision problems and conduct negotiations by people from different cultures.

The INSPIRE system is the first Web-based negotiation support system. It is based on analytical models rooted in decision and negotiation analysis (Kersten, 1985; Kersten and Szapiro, 1986; Rangaswamy and Shell, 1994). Developed in the context of a cross-cultural study of decision-making and negotiation, the system has been primarily used to conduct and study negotiation via the World Wide Web as well as in teaching information systems, management science, international management and English as a second language.

Although INSPIRE has been implemented as an application accessible remotely over the Web, it is conceptualized as a client-side software assisting a negotiator, much like a traditional desktop application belonging to the negotiator, and communicating over the Internet with a similar "copy" of the software belonging to the other negotiator. The intention is to convey that INSPIRE does not act autonomously like a third party arbitrator; rather each "copy" acts entirely in support of a given negotiator. INSPIRE supports asynchronous negotiations, thus ameliorating the time zone problem. To facilitate this type of negotiations the system saves the state resulting from each user's actions in a form that can be retrieved when the counterpart logs on some time later (Kersten and Noronha, 1997).

INSPIRE views negotiation as a process involving three stages: pre-negotiation, conduct of negotiation and post-settlement. The first stage involves understanding of the negotiation problem, issues and options and preference elicitation through hybrid conjoint analysis. This allows one to obtain a rating for every possible offer. The second stage involves support for offer construction and counter offer evaluation, and finally, the last stage involves computation of possible offers that dominate the most recent compromise and re-negotiation. Details of the methodology and the system's architecture can be found in Kersten and Noronha, (1998) and at http://interneg.org/.

The system can be used to conduct multiple bilateral negotiations. The most commonly used case involves trade negotiations between two companies: Itex, a producer of bicycle parts and Cypress Cycles, which builds bicycles. To reflect the dynamics of negotiation in developing countries, we have developed cases about negotiations for international technology transfer and for the sustainable development of natural resources.

International Negotiations between Countries

International negotiation is as it says: inter-national. It is about negotiation between countries. International negotiation occurs all the time between governments. It also happens between individuals and companies, where the traps and tricks of cross-border negotiation can ensnare even the most experienced home-country negotiators. International negotiation is often not just between individual people, but between large delegations, each of which is well organized and where every person has specialized and skilled work. There may be cultural experts, linguists and subject specialists as well as a chief negotiator and support negotiators. In a complex negotiation, there may be multiple and interlined sub-negotiations going on at the same time, for example where a trade negotiation includes deal involving various industries and interests.

Cultural confusion

A big trap in negotiation lies in misunderstanding the culture of other countries, especially in the rules that they use to negotiate. Whilst one country may emphasize politeness and integrity, another might use deception and coercive methods as a norm of negotiation, whilst being polite and friendly outside of the negotiation arena.

It is easy also to offend people from other cultures without realizing what you are doing. Body Language, and particularly gestures, can have very different meaning, and what may seem an innocent movement to one person can be extremely rude to another.

Diplomacy and Tact

International negotiation, done well, takes very careful notice of local cultures and customs, and is conducted with remarkable diplomacy and tact. Good international negotiators are very smooth and practiced in their art, and ensure they are extremely well informed not only about national cultures but also about the very individual perceptions of the people on the others side. The complexity and care of international negotiations may mean that the process can take an inordinately long time, quite likely months and possibly even years. Some negotiations never conclude, but the very fact that the two sides are talking is sufficient to distract them from more violent interplay.

Blocs and Alliances

International negotiation often happens between many countries at the same time. These may band together into economic blocs (such as the European Union) or develop shorter-term strategic alliances, such as where smaller countries band together to confront a dominant larger nation. Such collective negotiations are often as much marriages of convenience as the joint action of true friends. Whilst international relationships are essential, each country eventually puts its own needs above the needs of others. Even when countries go to war on behalf of one another, the ultimate goal is still national at root.

War and Destruction

International negotiation can be about life and death, literally, and even survival of the entire planet. In the cold war period, Russia and America engaged in an endless series of Strategic Arms Limitation Talks (SALT) to prevent the horrors of mutually-assured destruction (MAD). More recently, negotiations on limiting global warming have met with limited success that may yet (depending on who you believe) lead to even more damaging outcomes than nuclear war. The madness of not agreeing on matters of global destruction illustrates well the difficulties of international negotiation. It is easy on the international stage to paint yourself into a corner, and for personal posturing and political ambition to morph into extreme and ultimately foolish acts.

Breakthrough Business Negotiations

Negotiating is much more complicated than making an offer and fielding a counter-offer. It's a complex process that can affect the future of individuals and organizations. A "breakthrough negotiator" must analyze, plan, sell, organize and motivate. The best negotiators are also leaders. They bring together a team of players and guide them in all-out battle against the opposition. Top negotiators don't obtain their skills by accident—they learn from experience and studying the art of negotiating. However complicated a negotiation is, it can be understood by breaking it down into its key parts and actions.

Every negotiation has a structure: It involves certain people and issues which produce predictable interactions. More complex negotiation systems can be seen as related sets of negotiations. On face value, these negotiations have nothing in common. But closer examination shows that they all share an underlying structure: All are negotiations that involve more than two parties and no one holds veto power. Thorough analysis of a situation and its structure is an essential negotiating skill and a hallmark of breakthrough negotiators. Breakthrough negotiators never treat the structure of a negotiation as preordained or fixed. In other words, the hand can be played as it is dealt, but it can also be changed. Skilled negotiators can change the structure by inviting additional parties and transforming two-party negotiations into multi-party negotiations. When negotiating stems from clear-eyed analysis, efforts to shape the structure can have a powerful impact on outcomes (Michael Watkins, Breakthrough Business Negotiation (Executive Summary: http://www.google.co.in/search?hl=en&q=Breakthrough+Business+Negotiations&btnG=Search&meta=&aq=f&oq=)

Process Control Is a Source of Power

Control of process is a potent source of power, one that lets you steer the proceedings toward the outcomes you want. This calls for early attention to designing the process and influencing the agenda well before others even realize the game has begun. Skilled negotiators understand the importance of framing arguments and approaching people at the right time to win their support. Great leaders are often great negotiators, and the reverse can also be true. Individual negotiators can make all the difference in the outcome of complex negotiations. This is true when a chief executive officer decides to acquire another company or world leaders negotiate a new international trade regime. The negotiator has to manage negotiations with The opposition, discussions among his or her own team, and interactions between the two. The best negotiators are never passive go-betweens. They shape the perceptions of those they represent and the perceptions of their counterparts across the table.

These are four tasks negotiators embark on at and away from the table:

- **Diagnosing the situation.** Systematically assess the components of the negotiation and identify potential barriers to agreement.
- **Shaping the structure.** Influence who participates, what the issues are, and what the alternatives are, so you don't end up playing someone else's game.
- **Managing the process.** Prepare for and conduct face-to-face interactions to build momentum.
- **Assessing the results.** Set goals and periodically evaluate how you're doing to adjust your plans and manage the process.

Diagnosing the Situation

The first step in preparing to negotiate from strength is to diagnose the particulars of the situation thoroughly. This means taking a hard-headed look at the seven key structural elements of any negotiation: parties, rules, issues, interests, alternatives, agreements and linkages.

Parties

The parties who are participating in the negotiation may seem evident. Sometimes, however, other parties are already involved, or may become involved. Or you may want to bring in other parties yourself. When diagnosing a negotiation, make sure you identify all the players and potential players. Also look for existing and potential coalitions—allies of the parties who may influence the negotiation.

Rules

What are the rules of the game? All negotiations are influenced by formal or informal rules. These include laws and regulations, social conventions and professional codes of conduct.

Issues

Don't take the agenda—the set of issues that the parties decide to negotiate —for granted. Remember that the agenda itself is subject to negotiation. When diagnosing a negotiation be sure to: identify the full set of issues (including issues that are beneath the surface); unbundle the issues (different issues often get intertwined when they should actually be negotiated separately); determine whether relationships are an issue (there's a world of difference between negotiating a deal and negotiating a dispute); and identify and deal with toxic issues.

Interests

What are the goals that you and others are pursuing?

You can create value in the negotiations for everyone if you: seek out shared interests, propose mutually beneficial trades, and secure insecure contracts. This latter step is important. If the parties don't completely trust each other, they must find ways to minimize their vulnerability so that the negotiation is not impeded.

Alternatives

What if you can't reach an agreement? Then look for what is known in negotiation as your BATNA (best alternative to a negotiated agreement). A BATNA needs to be built. For example, if before you start to negotiate for a promotion you've secured an offer from another employer, that offer is a strong BATNA. Developing a BATNA is also key in identifying your walk-away position.

Agreements

Are there agreements that would benefit both sides?

You won't know for sure until you start the negotiations but at this stage you should at least try to discern the bargaining range for both parties. The bargaining range depends on the walk-aways. If you refuse to accept less than a 3 percent raise, and your boss refuses to give you between a 3 percent and a 5 percent raise. However, if you refuse to accept less than 5 percent, and your boss refuses to give you more than 3 percent, then there is no bargaining range, and no possibility of agreement. Keep in mind that not all negotiations are win-lose. The parties may be able to create value. Find ways through mutually beneficial trades to enlarge the pie for everyone.

Linkages

The issue here is to decide whether your current negotiations are linked to other negotiations. Stand-alone negotiations are surprisingly rare. Even the relatively simple negotiation for a raise may involve other negotiations. For example, you may be negotiating for jobs in other companies. Your boss may be negotiating with other employees in other departments who also want a pay hike. These other negotiations will impact the resolution of your negotiation for a raise.

Identifying Barriers and Opportunities

Once you have thoroughly diagnosed the situation, you will be able to put together a table that identifies the barriers and the opportunities with each element. Armed with this information, you are in a much better position to start the negotiation.

Shaping the Structure

A potent way to shape the game is to influence who plays. One method of doing this is to invite other players into the negotiation. Another way is to try to exclude parties. And sometimes it is advantageous to try to prevent parties from participating or to remove them from the game. There are questions to ask about shaping the structure:

- Would it make sense to bring in a mediator?
- Are there parties involved that you might be able to exclude?
- If there are too many parties, can you convince some to allow themselves to be represented by others?

Setting the Agenda

It is crucial to have an impact early, when the agenda for what will and won't be negotiated is being set. This establishes boundaries before momentum builds in the wrong direction, or irreversible commitments are made, or too much time passes. Breakthrough negotiators don't view the agenda as fixed, but as something that can be shaped. Skilled negotiators discuss the agenda early on, trying to define nonnegotiable issues and set preconditions before negotiating the main points. Setting the agenda sometimes involves postponing "toxic" issues or removing them from consideration.

Framing and Reframing

Framing is using argument, analogy and metaphor to define the problem to be solved and the set of potential solutions. Skillful framing reaches the target audience by evoking mental images and emotional reactions that influence their behavior. Efforts to frame (or reframe) often involve coordinated actions at the negotiating table (by means of argument) and away from the table (through use of the media). Negotiators often compete in a "frame game" in which they try to define the dominant frame for the negotiation. Framing tactics work because people's thoughts on what is at stake tend to form clearly only when they are forced to make choices. Reframing is necessary when the existing frame has become a barrier to agreement. It can also give your counterparts ways to back away gracefully from poorly chosen positions.

Controlling Information

Power comes to those who control other parties' access to information. Information-control techniques are especially potent when you have private access to valuable information and when negotiations involve multiple parties and shared decision-making. Information control relies on several techniques:

- Sharing information selectively. Privately held information can be used as a tool to shape the beliefs and attitudes of other parties. This type of information control involves withholding information, releasing information at predetermined times, and communicating information to selected audiences.
- Influencing patterns of communication. Another form of information control involves encouraging or discouraging communication among other parties in the negotiation. Meeting with potential allies can help build a coalition.

Managing the Process

Managing the process is the third major element of the breakthrough negotiation framework. Whoever controls the process can powerfully influence the substance and results of negotiations.

Negotiators are often driven by inner psychological needs or motivations. When assessing your counterparts' motivations (and your own), you should think about these needs in terms of which are dominant and how they will affect your efforts to manage the process:

- Maintaining control. To feel competent, do your counterparts need to feel in control of the process and not controlled by others?
- Exercising power. Do they need to dominate their counterparts, and perhaps show others that they are doing so?
- Preserving reputation. Are they preoccupied with maintaining a reputation as effective or tough negotiators?
- Being consistent. Do they care about staying consistent with prior commitments or statements of principle?

- Maintaining relationships. Do they care about preserving relationships and being liked?

Negotiators approach the table with outcomes in mind. These outcomes typically take two forms: "red lines" that cannot be crossed without creating psychological havoc, and results that would achieve their goals. The opponent's commitment to its goals matters, too. Negotiators who set their sights high tend to do better than those with lower aspirations. But unrealistic expectations can be a barrier to agreement. Emotions, real and feigned, enter into most negotiations. A timely display of anger, for example, can demonstrate resolve as long as it is employed infrequently. By the same token, escalating disagreements and the emotions they provoke can prevent productive interaction.

Planning Strategy

The goal of examining the negotiation process at these three different stages of resolution is to equip you to manage at-the-table interactions more productively. If agreement is your objective, the basic goals at the table are twofold: to learn about your counterpart's interests, alternatives and bottom lines; and to shape your counterpart's perceptions of what is attainable.

Shaping Perceptions

The arsenal that negotiators use to shape their counterparts' perceptions at the table includes the following classic persuasion techniques:

- Anchoring. Your initial stance strongly influences the other side's perception of the bargaining range. An offer that is high (or low) but not so extreme that it triggers dismissal of the offer can give your counterparts a favorable first impression.
- Threats. Threats are promises to do harm that are used to shape others' perceptions of what will happen if no agreement is reached. Threats have to be credible to be effective. Even if credible, they can cause irrational resistance.
- Warnings. Warnings are milder than threats and less likely to trigger resistance. Instead of saying, "If you do that, I will punish you," a warning says, "If you do that, bad things (not caused by me) will happen to you."
- Commitments. Commitments are self-imposed costs. Negotiators commit to a course of action (perhaps by putting their reputations at stake) to convince their counterparts that they have no other option. Over-committed negotiators stand firm long after it is clear that their objectives are unachievable.
- Action-forcing events. Deadlines, meetings and other key events can be established to move the process forward.

Allowing the River to Flow

Managing the flow of negotiations is like influencing the flow of a river. You can try to advance your interests by restricting the flow in places, releasing it in others, and channeling it in desired directions. The flow toward agreement can be dammed by creating impasses on purpose; tensions can be released by proposing a new solution or face-saving compromise. In the process, the patient, creative negotiator might be able to create and claim substantial value.

Assessing the Results

Once a negotiation is under way, you should step back periodically to evaluate how it is going. A natural point to step back is between negotiating sessions, but it can (and should) also be done in the heat of battle. Part of appraising an ongoing negotiation is deciding whether you are meeting the specific goals you set for yourself.

Overcoming Power Imbalances in Breakthrough Negotiation

The following principles provide ways that smaller players can shape the structure and manage the process when facing an opponent of greater size or power in a 'Breakthrough negotiation process:

- **Principle 1: Never do all-or-nothing deals.** The biggest mistake a small player can make is to enter into a single make-or-break negotiation with a larger partner. Doing so just reinforces the larger party's perception of its own strength and inevitably leads to poor deals. This is why it is essential for weaker players to shape the structure so that everything is not riding on a single negotiation. A primary objective is to diversify partner risk so that the larger party cannot exert monopoly power over you.
- **Principal 2: Make them smaller.** Do not treat a larger partner as a single unified entity. The notion of big-company-as-powerful-monolith fails to recognize that large companies are made up of smaller units led by people with their own incentives and interests. This is increasingly true given large companies' tendency to decentralize responsibility and accountability. The smaller player should negotiate with part of the larger organization rather than the whole thing. This means finding individuals and units within the larger company that are interested in what you have to offer.
- **Principle 3: Make yourself bigger.** There is strength in numbers. A smaller player dealing with a larger one should build coalitions to fortify its bargaining power. An effective coalition can be built with one or a few large players or many smaller players. It is essential to diagnose the situation carefully, identify promising allies, and build alliances with them. The larger player must see that you, in conjunction with your allies, are a force to be reckoned with.
- **Principal 4: Build momentum through a sequence of deals.**

Negotiating the right deals early makes it easier to negotiate subsequent deals at better terms. But early deals with the wrong partners can make everything that follows an uphill battle.

- **Principal 5: Harness the power of competition.** Spreading the word that you might do a deal with someone else sets the stage for judicious use of competition in negotiating the terms of deals.
- **Principal 6: Constrain yourself.** By entering into binding prior agreements, smaller negotiators can buttress their bargaining power with larger counterparts.
- **Principal 7: Hold the informational high ground.** The right information, processed and organized for easy access, is a potent source of strength in negotiations with larger counterparts. Negotiation positions are built on supporting arguments: You have to build a solid foundation of fact to support your position while you attempt to knock supporting pillars out from under the other side. It is essential to be better prepared than the larger player and gain and hold the informational high ground.
- **Principal 8: Take control of the process.** Articulating the reasons that both parties came to the table in the first place establishes a sense of momentum. Flesh out the offer thoroughly and work out the basic structure of the deal before raising the subject of money.
- **Principal 9: Negotiate with implementation in mind.** Try not to burn your bridges, and try to preserve the strength of your alternatives in case serious problems arise during implementation.
- **Principle 10: Build superior organizational capabilities.** It is essential to forge relationships with skilled external advisers, such as lawyers and investment bankers. These are the conditions needed for success, but they are not sufficient in and of themselves. You must be organized to learn rapidly as you do more deals with large players. Fast learning is a valuable advantage for small players: If you can learn from past negotiations, capture the resulting insights, and share those insights among yourselves, you will increase your negotiating effectiveness.

Multi-Phase Agreements: Multi-phase agreements follow an important logic: The parties negotiate sets of relatively easy issues first, implement agreement on those, then move on to tougher issues. In one common form of multi-phase agreement, the parties first negotiate the guiding principles for a mutually acceptable settlement. These principles serve as a basis for negotiating more specific agreements and more divisive issues.

Secret Diplomacy: Leaders sometimes choose to craft an agreement using secret or back-channel diplomacy and then present it to their constituencies as a done deal. Secrecy transforms a two-level (internal-external) negotiation into a simpler unified process, delaying internal negotiations and removing opposition. Secrecy also insulates the parties from media attention so they can forget about public appearances and concentrate on substantive issues. The goal of secret diplomacy is to create and sustain a supportive coalition.

Leading Negotiations: When a negotiator represents the interests of others, those who are absent from the table could be principals with decision-making power or constituencies who expect the representative to lead them. Whatever the scenario is, the negotiator functions as a bridge between internal decision-making and external negotiations. When negotiators shape their demands, have a clear vision of what they want to achieve, and work to shape perceptions internally and externally, they can effectively advance their side's interests—and their own.

Orchestrating Teams: Representation is about negotiating on behalf of others; leading teams is about negotiating in concert with others. Teams are valuable because they bring together people with varied expertise. The full cast of participants in an acquisition, including external advisors, can be very large. The goal is to identify and obtain interest from attractive potential partners. The trick is to assemble a critical mass of expertise without creating too large a team: The larger the team, the more difficult and expensive it is to coordinate. To function effectively, a negotiating team needs a clear-cut lead negotiator. You can also assign distinct roles and responsibilities to team members, such as observation of the other side or note-taking. As lead negotiator, you can conserve energy by shifting the burden of talking to another member of your team now and then.

Ethics in Negotiation

Negotiation is all about meeting one's interests. These include explicit goals (*I want to get a 5% raise*) but also less conscious or public interests (*After what he did to me, he deserves to lose. She's got to learn that I am the manager and I make the decisions here.*). When someone else stands in the way, the negotiator faces the core ethical issue of negotiation: when are my needs and wants more important than treating this person in a moral or socially acceptable manner? Whatever choice you make may involve significant costs to yourself, to the other party, to the wider community. Often the "right" thing to do is not clear.

Starting Points

Here are some starting points for thinking about ethical choices you face as a negotiator (http://culture-at-work.com/ethics.html):

1. Ethical judgments are made in social context

The type of work you choose and the type of people you hang out with, will eventually shape your ethical choices as a negotiator. If you care about having honest and forthright relations with others, think carefully about what kind of friends, colleagues, clients you want to have in your life.

2. Even if you choose to lie or be unethical, be honest with yourself

If you are deceptive, you can end up rationalizing your actions to yourself also. Over time, you may get in the habit of lying or using other tactics that are unnecessarily risky or harmful.

3. *There are many unethical negotiation behaviors besides lying.*

For example: harmful or cruel treatment of others, illegal or unethical threats and coercion, bribes, kickbacks, corruption, preventing parties from participating or selling them out if they aren't at the table, demeaning other parties/groups of people, hate-talk, threats or actions of violence, ruining someone's reputation without cause, etc.

4. *Be aware of tradeoffs: Self protection, "bluffing", and distrust also have a cost*

While we worry a lot about the price we might pay for being forthright or for extending a measure of trust the other party, there is also a price to pay for withholding information, lying, or being suspicious of them. In addition to the relationship costs of distrust, and the anger of feeling mistreated, you can incur significant business expenses for protective measures such as fact-finding, inspections, legal discovery processes, drawing up legal contracts, keeping detailed records, certification, etc.

5. *Relationship is almost always a factor*

Transactional negotiations lend themselves to unethical behavior but even in short one-time interactions, relationship matters. You may think you'll never meet someone again but you never know who your company will hire next year, who might become a potential client, a political adversary, a useful connection.... And the way you handle negotiations is noticed by the people around you with whom you may have more significant relationships.

Culture and Negotiation Ethics

Understanding the relationship between culture and negotiation ethics is a major challenge for global managers. Today multinational firms consider the task of understanding the cultural and ethical orientations of their global partners a major priority for successfully operating in the global market (Bagozzi, 1995). Hofstede (1991) defines culture as "the collective programming of the mind which distinguishes the members of one group or category of people from another." Christie et al. (2003) found that culture has a strong influence on ethical attitudes. Culture is recognized as one of the most important variables influencing ethical decision-making (Byrne and Bradley, 2007).

Bartels (1967) defines ethics as a "standard by which business action may be judged 'right or wrong.'" Standards usually differ from one culture to another, and so actions regarded moral by one culture may be in conflict with and judged immoral by another culture (Armstrong and Sweeney, 1994) Culture is the standard that determines, in part, the morality of individuals' behavior in a given society. Studying negotiation ethics of executives from various cultures is vital for companies to capitalize on positive values and safeguard against potentially unethical negotiation tactics.

As international trade and global business opportunities grow, global executives are constantly negotiating with executives from other cultures. The negotiation process is plagued with ethical dilemmas and opportunistic temptations. In a tactical process, as two parties try to reach agreement, each wanting to maximize her/his results, the temptations to use deceptive tactics are certain. Negotiation has been defined as "a process of potentially opportunistic interaction by which two or more parties, with some apparent conflict, seek to do better through jointly decided action than they could otherwise" (Lax and Sebenious, 1986). Despite the potential for opportunistic tendencies, MNC executives continue to regulate their counterparts' behavior through contractual agreements that have varying capacities to respond effectively to ex post opportunism (Williamson, 1985). Given the considerable resources needed to monitor ex post opportunism and the opportunity costs of deals that will not be executed due to opportunistic behavior (Wathne and Heide, 2000), it is essential that more research focus on ex ante opportunism (e.g., opportunism that occurs in early stages of the relationship and during the selection stage of the exchange partner) so that global firms can develop the knowledge and expertise necessary to understand how to screen, select and manage exchange partners prior to the establishment of business relationships that may prove ineffective and costly.

Negotiation is a process by which the negotiating parties interact with one another to reach mutual agreements to provide terms, conditions, and guidelines for future behavior. Negotiation brings two or more parties together to try to accomplish mutually beneficial outcomes, while meeting individual goals that may be at odds with the other parties' goals. "Negotiations involve serial communication between parties to exchange information and attempt to influence or persuade one's counterpart," (Banas and Parks, 2002). The negotiation process is plagued by ethical dilemmas. In a tactical process, as two parties try to reach agreement, each wanting to maximize his or her results, they may be tempted to use deceptive or dishonest tactics. Negotiation behaviors range from the ethical to the unethical. Ethical bargaining in distributive negotiations includes exaggerated demands, hiding one's bottom line, and not being forthcoming about one's negotiation timeline. More questionable tactics include false promises/bluffing where the negotiator shows an intention to perform some act without actually having the intention to follow through. Misrepresenting position occurs when the negotiator distorts her acceptable settlement point in order to convince the opponent to provide more concessions. Attacking the opponent network happens when the negotiator attempts to bring members of the opponent team to join her team. Inappropriate information gathering tactic appears when the negotiator uses bribes to collect sensitive information about opponents (Lewicki and Robinson, 1998).

Several studies have examined the relationship between negotiation tactics and ethics (e.g., Elahee and Brooks, 2004). Lewicki and Robinson (1998) suggest that there are a wide range of negotiation behaviors that vary with respect to perceived ethicality and appropriateness. At the basic level there is traditional competitive bargaining, consisting of tactics which are generally acceptable, such as exaggerating demands and appearing to be in no hurry to come to an agreement. In addition, there are more questionable tactics, such as attacking your opponent's network, making false promises, misrepresenting information, and gathering inappropriate information.

In studying business executives' perceptions of unethical negotiation tactics, Robinson, Lewicki and Donahue (2000) found that respondents are generally more accepting of traditional competitive bargaining tactics and less accepting of the other more serious and potentially illegal tactics. In contrasting U.S. and Mexican samples, Volkema (1998) reported similar results. Elahee and Brooks (2004), in examining the role of trust on Mexican managers' perception of six negotiation tactics, empirically demonstrated that there is a negative relationship between trust and the likelihood of using inappropriate negotiation tactics. Ford *et al.* (1997) compared the cognitive moral development and the percent of time allocated to various negotiation tactics of Chinese businesspeople and their U.S. counterparts. They concluded that U.S. businesspeople negotiating with Chinese executives must be aware of a more collectivist approach to ethics.

Business theories suggest that when individuals are faced with morally questionable situations, they tend to apply rules that are based on different moral philosophies (Hunt and Vitell, 1986). Ferrell, Gresham, and Fraedrich (1989) stated that, "moral philosophies provide standards to judge the act, the actor's intentions, and the consequences of the act." Similarly, in Hunt and Vitell's (1986) general theory of marketing ethics, normative moral philosophy was at the core of their model. These moral philosophies could be deontological or teleological in nature. While the deontological moral philosophy focuses on the specific actions or behavior of the individual, the teleological philosophy stresses the consequences of the action or behavior. When faced with an ethically challenging situation, individuals who subscribe to the deontological philosophy tend to evaluate the inherent rightness or wrongness of a set of possible alternatives that they consider as possible courses of action against predetermined deontological norms or rules that reflect the individual personal value or behavior. As for those individuals who subscribe to the teleological philosophy, their evaluations of actions are based on their perception of the consequences of these actions to various stakeholder groups and relative to the likelihood for the consequences to occur, their desirability, and the importance of the impacted group (Hunt and Vitell, 1986).

Ethical Dilemma in Negotiation

The changing nature of the workplace is propelling ethics training to institutional priority. Today's work force is composed of people who are more diverse than ever in nationality, culture, religion, age, education, and socioeconomic status. These people enter the work force with differing backgrounds, values, goals, and perceptions of acceptable behaviors. Many of them have career expectations that will be difficult, if not impossible, to realize in today's society. This diverse, multicultural population of workers is being asked to work together in a spirit of cooperation and respect for the good of the organization and the public they serve. However, on the job, workers face decisions that have implications for their job security, their salaries, and the success of their employing organizations—decisions that bring pressures for them to protect their own interests, sometimes at the risk of losing their personal and corporate integrity. "There's more pressure on people in organizations than there ever has been to do more with less and adjust quickly to changes. In response to that pressure, people may cut corners...may engage in expedient but questionable behavior" (Kirrane, 1990).

Some issues facing society and business include downsizing of staff, pollution control, disposal of toxic waste, depletion and allocation of scarce resources, cost containment, changes in law and technology, employee rights, discrimination against women and minorities, and product safety. Issues such as these are complex and they create ethical dilemmas that are difficult to resolve. In the medical field, for example, new technology has created new problems or dilemmas for which there are no easy solutions.

The following are examples of these dilemmas:

— The allocation of scarce resources (Who is selected to receive a kidney transplant?)
— The withdrawal of treatment (Under what conditions can treatment be withdrawn from a patient?)
— The use of costly resources (To what extent can expensive life-saving treatment be offered, under what conditions should it be an option, and who should assume responsibility for payment?) (Cassell, 1989; Fisher and Raper, 1990)

Because of the complexity of ethical dilemmas, "corporations are rushing to adopt codes of ethics. Business schools are scrambling to add ethics courses. And hundreds of consultants are being hired to put 'integrity' into corporate cultures" (Byrne 1988, p. 56). Vocational and career development personnel are recognizing the need to prepare students with higher order decision-making and problem-solving skills that will facilitate negotiation and conflict resolution in the workplace.

Resolving Ethical Dilemmas and Value Conflicts

Discussion, analysis, problem solving, and decision-making are critical to the ethical resolution of conflicts. Four competing claims are (i) conflict between two or more personally held values; (ii) conflict between personal values and the values held by another person or the organization; (iii) conflict between basic principles and the need to achieve a desired outcome; and (iv) conflict between two or more individuals or groups to whom one has an obligation (Kirrane, 1990). The resolution of conflict cannot rest in the hands of one or two individuals. All stakeholders in a situation must be involved—for legal as well as ethical reasons. Medical decisions often involve a multidisciplinary team that consists of some or all of the following: patient, family, significant others, nurses, dietitians, social workers, psychologists, physical therapists, clergy, and so forth. In this way, the knowledge, opinions, and expertise of all "stakeholders" in the decisions are considered. The same principle can be applied in business, with decisions based on the expressed viewpoints of all stakeholders in a given situation—even indirect stakeholders. Potential clients should also be recognized as stakeholders because their choice to do business with a firm may be based on the firm's reputation for ethical behavior (Sonnesyn, 1990).

Resolving ethical dilemmas, therefore, requires interpersonal and negotiation skills as well as the new application of employability skills—honesty, ability to work cooperatively, respect for others, pride in one's work, willingness to learn, dependability, responsibility for one's actions, integrity, and loyalty (Lankard, 1987). For years, employers have sought workers with these skills and school curricula have stressed their importance for successful employment. Today, businesses are training their employees in critical thinking and conflict resolution skills required for ethical decision-making. Schools are also focusing on developing students' critical thinking skills, but to date little has been published about the application of those skills in resolving potential ethical dilemmas specific to given jobs/occupations.

Training of Ethics

All levels of workers—management to entry-level—need to recognize the factors that guide ethical behavior and develop strategies for assessing their personal and organizational ethics. Blanchard and Peale (1988) present three "ethics checks" to help individuals decide what is right:

1. Is it legal? Will I be violating either civil law or company policy?
2. Is it balanced? Is it fair to all concerned in the short term as well as the long term? Does it promote win-win relationships?
3. How will it make me feel about myself? Will it make me proud? Would I feel good if my decision was published in the newspaper? Would I feel good if my family knew about it?.

The purpose of training is to make employees aware of the issues they encounter and enable them to deal with those issues in an ethical manner. Training should help employees (1) recognize which decisions involve ethics (not all decisions do); (2) understand values—the organization's, their own, and other people's; and (3) weigh the potential impact of various business options on those values (Kirrane, 1990). Ethics training is beneficial in its focus on ways to apply the organization's credo or code of ethics in a business setting. Ideally, they offer a mechanism for discussion and problem solving to lead workers through the resolution of complex issues. "Actually, ethics training almost invariably pays off in better decisions and in a more committed work force" (Kirrane, 1990).

This view supports the trend noted in recent surveys. "This year's findings of TRAINING's 1990 Industry Report indicate that 36.9 percent of organizations with more than 100 employees provide some type of ethics training compared with 26.6 percent in 1989 and 19.7 percent in 1988. A 1988 survey of 2,000 U.S. corporations...roughly mirrors TRAINING's findings" (Thompson 1990).

Training in ethical decision-making is a critical part of vocational and career development. In *THE MORAL DIMENSION*, Amitai Etzioni recommends integrating ethics training and ethics discussions into the curriculum. He suggests that any decision of consequence has a moral dimension that must be considered in the decision-making process (Thompson, 1990).

Discussions and analyses of case studies are particularly effective in developing ethical decision-making skills. Participating in such learning activities requires active listening, questioning techniques, verbal and nonverbal communication, and reasoning. Talking through a situation to achieve an ethical solution gives students or trainees new insights into the conflicting issues within a situation, the variety of possible options and the consequences of each, and the awareness that they, as workers, will have a personal responsibility in conflict resolution. The selection of case studies should be directed to the day-to-day dilemmas workers in a given occupation will face on the job. The problems and issues must be ones that are relevant to a given job/occupation and ones that are recognized as difficult to resolve.

Another strategy for ethics deliberation—one used frequently by business—is the initiation of organizational ethics committees. Such committees are formed to offer to management and staff objective recommendations on matters that are difficult to resolve. Some organizations have a hotline to which employees can direct their calls for help in resolving an ethical dilemma. As an educational strategy, business leaders could be invited to the classroom to form an "ethics committee" to which students can direct questions they have about ethical dilemmas they expect to encounter.

Although using case studies and resource people to bring workplace situations and experiences into the classroom are good educational strategies, students also need to receive training in critical thinking, conflict resolution, reasoning, communication (speaking and listening), and group process to prepare for the ethical deliberations they will encounter as they progress in their careers. Miller and Coady (1986) point out that today's ethical dilemmas require students to be equipped with higher order decision-making and problem-solving skills necessary to cope with increased individual responsibility for shaping their work environments and managing their career development. Mediation skills promoted by Miller and Coady (1986) include the following:

1. Assertiveness—the ability to stand up for one's rights without infringing on the rights of others.
2. Empathetic listening—the ability to listen to the speaker's complete message and to respond appropriately to the speaker's needs.
3. Principled negotiation—working together to create an agreement fair to all parties, regarding the problem and not the other persons as the enemy.
4. Evaluating risk—recognizing, evaluating, and coping with risk.

Miller and Coady also recommend that in teaching mediation skills the instructor play dual roles of facilitator and participant. As facilitator, the instructor guides the students through the learning process. As a participant, the teacher models the behavior and qualities of an ethical worker (such as showing respect for the ideas of all, a willingness to listen), demonstrating how to learn rather than instructing students in what to learn.

Critical thinking skills required for decision-making and mediation skills required to implement those decisions are important to job progression and success. Most individuals will work for a number of businesses and in a number of jobs. They will be required to participate in decisions affecting both the quality of the work environment and the production process. They will need to interact with a multicultural, diverse group of coworkers to solve job-related problems that have ethical considerations. Courses that offer insight into the unique habits and practices of individuals from various cultures are necessary for the career development of all workers.

Negotiation and Conflict Resolution

Resolving conflict can be mentally exhausting and emotionally draining. But it is important to realize that conflict that requires resolution is neither good nor bad. There can be positive and negative outcomes as seen in the box below. It can be destructive but can also play a productive role for you personally and for your relationships-both personal and professional. The important point is to manage the conflict, not to suppress conflict and not to let conflict escalate out of control. Many of us seek to avoid conflict when it arises but there are many times when we should use conflict as a critical aspect of creativity and motivation (Wertheim: http://iiasa.ac.at/Research/DAS/interneg/training/conflict_overview.html).

Given that organizations are becoming less hierarchical, less based on positional authority, less based on clear boundaries of responsibility and authority, it is likely that conflict will be an even greater component of organizations in the future. Studies have shown that negotiation skills are among the most significant determinants of career success. While negotiation is an art form to some degree, there are specific techniques that anyone can learn. Understanding these techniques and developing your skills will be a critical component of success of any organization.

Potential Positive Outcomes of Conflict	Potential Negative Outcomes of Conflict
• can motivate us to try harder-to "win" • can increase commitment, enhance group loyalty • increased clarity about the problem • can lead to innovative breakthroughs and new approaches • conflict can clarify underlying problems, facilitate change • can focus attention on basic issues and lead to solution • increased energy level; making visible key values • involvement in conflict can sharpen our approaches to bargaining, influencing, competing	• can lead to anger, avoidance, sniping, shouting, frustration, fear of failure, sense of personal inadequacy • withholding of critical information • lower productivity from wasteful conflict • careers can be sidetracked; relationships ruined • disrupted patterns of work • consume huge amount of time-loss of productivity

Major Causes of Conflict

Opposing interests (or what we think are opposing interests) are at the core of most conflicts. In a modern complex society, we confront these situations many times a day, especially in a dynamic society or business environment (Fig 3). The modern organization adds a whole new group of potential causes of conflict that are already present:

- competition over scarce resources, time
- ambiguity over responsibility and authority:
- differences in perceptions, work styles, attitudes, communication problems, individual differences
- increasing interdependence as boundaries between individuals and groups become increasingly blurred
- reward systems: we work in situations with complex and often contradictory incentive systems
- differentiation: division of labor which is the basis for any organization causes people and groups to see situations differently and have different goals
- equity vs. equality: continuous tension exists between equity (the belief that we should be rewarded relative to our relative contributions) and equality (belief that everyone should receive the same or similar outcomes).

The Five Modes of Responding to Conflict

It is useful to categorize the various responses we have to conflict in terms of two dimensions:

1. how important or unimportant it is to satisfy our needs and

Dynamics of Conflict and Culture

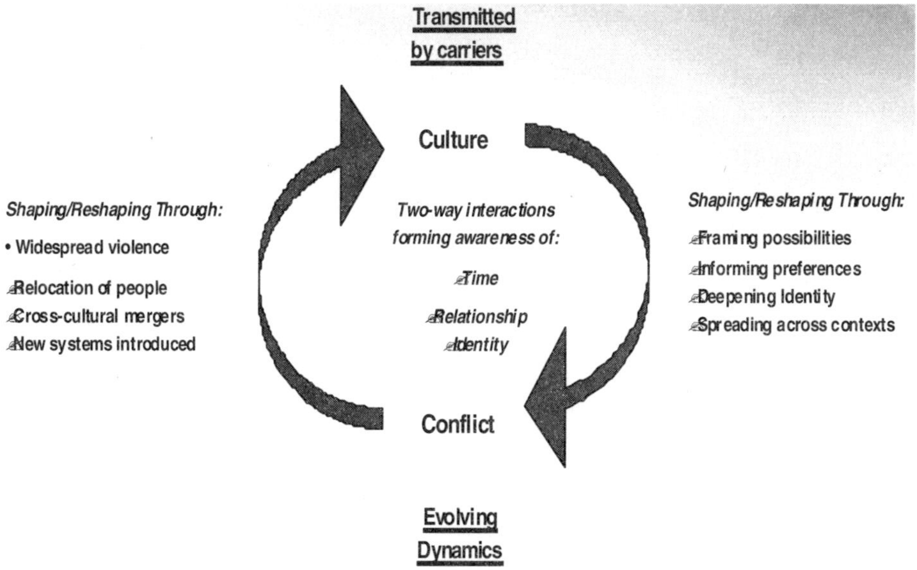

2. how important or unimportant it is to satisfy the other person's needs.

Answering this questions results in the following five modes of conflict resolution. None is these is "right" or "wrong". There are situations where any would be appropriate. For example, if we are cut off driving to work, we may decide "avoidance" is the best option. Other times "avoidance" may be a poor alternative. Similarly, collaboration may be appropriate sometimes but not at other times.

Competition: Distributive (win-lose) bargaining

Satisfying your needs is important; satisfying the other's needs isn't important to you

Collaboration: Integrative (win-win)

Satisfying both your needs and the other's needs is important

Compromising

Satisfying both your needs and the other's are moderately important

Avoiding

You are indifferent about satisfying either your needs or the other's needs: no action is likely

Accommodating

Simply yield (it doesn't matter to you and it matters to the other person)

In general, most successful negotiators start off assuming *collaborative (integrative)* or win-win negotiation. Most good negotiators will try for a win-win or aim at a situation where both sides feel they won. Negotiations tend to go much better if both sides perceive they are in a win-win situation or both sides approach the negotiation wanting to "create value" or satisfy both their own needs and the other's needs.

Now let us focus on the two most problematic types: *Collaborative* (integrative) and *Competitive* (Distributive). Of the two the more important is *Collaborative* since most of your negotiation and conflict resolution in your personal and professional life will (or should) be of this nature. This is because most negotiation involves situations where we want or need an on-going relationship with the other person. While it is important to develop skills in "competitive" bargaining (e.g. when buying a car), or skills that allow us to satisfy our concerns while ignoring the other's goals, this approach has many negative consequences for both our personal lives and for our professional careers especially if we are to have an on-going relationship with the other person.

The key to successful negotiation is to shift the situation to a "win-win" even if it looks like a "win-lose" situation. Almost all negotiation have at least some elements of win-win. Successful negotiations often depend on finding the win-win aspects in any situation. Only shift to a win-lose mode if all else fails.

Reducing Conflict that Already Exists

Organizations also take steps to reduce conflict. The following list suggests some of these ways:

- physical separation
- hierarchy (the boss decides)
- bureaucratic approaches (rules, procedures)
- integrators and third-party intervention
- negotiation
- rotating members
- interdependent tasks and super ordinate goals ("We are all in this together...")
- intergroup and interpersonal training

Rational vs. the Emotional Components of Negotiation

All negotiations involve two levels: *a rational decision-making* (substantive) process and a *psychological* (emotional) process. The outcome of a negotiation is as likely to be a result of the psychological elements as it is the rational element. In most cases, the failure of two people to reach the "optimal" resolution or best alternative stems from intangible factors such as:

Psychological Factors that will affect Negotiations

- how comfortable each feels about conflict

- how each perceives or mis-perceives the other
- the assumptions each makes about the other and the problem
- the attitudes and expectations about the other
- the decisions each makes about trust, about how important "winning" is, how important it is to avoid conflict, how much one likes or dislikes the other; how important it is to "not look foolish."

Understanding the "rational" part of the negotiation is relatively easy. Understanding the "psychological" part is more difficult. We need to understand ourselves and our opponents psychologically. Failure to understand these psychological needs and issues is at the root of most unsuccessful negotiations.

This is made more difficult because norms in most organizations discourage open expression of negative personal feelings. Thus intense emotional conflicts are often expressed and rationalized as substantive issues. People often drum up disagreements on trivial issues to provide justification for an emotional conflict with another individual (Ware and Barnes). The Basic Issues in Conflict Management may be highlighted as follows:

Basic Issues in Conflict Management

- what are the personal and organizational consequences of the conflict
- what are the behavioral patterns that characterize the conflict
- substantive issues vs. emotional issues
- apparent underlying and background conditions leading to the conflict

The Intangibles: Other Elements that affect Negotiation

Intangibles are often the key factors in many negotiations. Some of these intangibles are:

- **Personalities:** be conscious of aspects of your personality such of your own needs and interpersonal style as well as the other person's personality; these factors will play a key role and understanding yourself will be an important factor.
- **Your own personality and style**: how much you trust the person; how free with your emotions; how much you want to conceal or reveal;
- **Physical space:** sometimes where the negotiation takes place can be important; are we negotiating in a space we are uncomfortable and other is comfortable?
- **Past interaction:** if there is a history of conflict resolution with this person, think about how this history might affect the upcoming negotiation?
- **Time pressure:** Think about whether time pressure will affect the negotiation and whether you need to try to change this variable?
- **Subjective utilities**: be aware that people place very different values on elements of a negotiation. For example, in negotiating for a job, you may place a high value on location and relatively lower on salary; it is

important to be aware of your subjective utilities and try to ascertain the other person's subjective utilities; it is difficult to know in advance or even during the negotiation what a particular outcome will mean to the other party. Finding out what is "valued" is one of the key parts of negotiation.

- **Understand the Context for the Conflict**
  - what are the important personal and organizational consequences of the conflict? What are possible future consequences?
  - What behavior patterns characterize the conflict
  - What are the substantive issues? Are the issues biased by each side's perceptions and feelings?
  - What are the underlying or background factors that have lead to the situation and the related feelings, perceptions, and behaviors?

Be an active Listener

Good communication skills are critical although it is easy to forget them in the "heat of battle." Try to separate the problem from the person. Focus on the problem (e.g. "this accounting concept is unclear to me") not the person (e.g. "you did a lousy job explaining this"). When we tie the person to the problem, the other person gets defensive and communication tends to become very difficult

Don't: Talk at the other side, focus on the past, blame the other person.

Do: Be an "active listener.

This involves continuously checking to see if you are understanding the other person. Restate the other's position to make sure you are hearing him or her correctly. Focus on the future; talk about what is to be done; tackle the problem jointly.

How can I change what seems like a "win-lose" situation to a "win-win" (or what if the other person doesn't play by these rules?

There are many advantages to trying to shift a win/lose situation to a win/win. Yet we will be in situations where the other person either doesn't wish to reach a "win-win" or doesn't realize it is in his or her best interest to achieve a collaborative solution. In these situations it is necessary for us to open lines of communication, increasing trust and cooperativeness.

Sometimes conflicts escalate, the atmosphere becomes charged with anger, frustration, resentment, mistrust, hostility, and a sense of futility. Communication channels close down or are used to criticize and blame the other. We focus on our next assault. The original issues become blurred and ill-defined and new issues are added as the conflict becomes personalized. Even if one side is willing to make concessions often hostility prevents agreements. In such a conflict, perceived differences become magnified, each side gets locked into their initial positions and each side resorts to lies, threats, distortions, and other attempts to force the other party to comply with demands.

It is not easy to shift this situation to a win-win but the following lists some techniques that you might use:

- reduce tension through humor, let the other "vent," acknowledge the other's views, listen actively, make a small concession as a signal of good faith
- increase the accuracy of communication; listen hard in the middle of conflict; rephrase the other's comments to make sure you hear them; mirror the other's views
- control issues: search for ways to slice the large issue into smaller pieces; depersonalize the conflict—separate the issues from the people
- establish commonalities: since conflict tends to magnify perceived differences and minimize similarities, look for greater common goals (we are in this together); find a common enemy; focus on what you have in common
- focus less on your position and more on a clear understanding of the other's needs and figure out ways to move toward them
- make a "yes-able" proposal; refine their demand; reformulate; repackage; sweeten the offer; emphasize the positives
- find a legitimate or objective criteria to evaluate the solution (eg. the blue book value of a car)

Is it ethical to "lie or bluff" in negotiations?

The answer to this question depends on one's values, one's culture, and the situation. What might be acceptable in poker would probably not be acceptable in most business situations. What might be acceptable in Cairo might not be acceptable in Boston. Different cultures and different situations contain inherent "rules" about the degree to which bluffing or misrepresentation is deemed acceptable.

In poker and in general negotiations one is not expected to reveal strength or intentions prematurely. But discretion in making claims and statements should not be confused with misrepresentation. In general, in our culture, our "rules" forbid and should penalize outright lying, false claims, bribing an opponent, stealing secrets, or threatening an opponent. While there may be a fine line between legitimate and illegitimate withholding of facts, there is a line and again we are distinguishing between the careful planning of when and how to reveal facts vs. outright lying.

Bluffing, while it may be ethical, does entail risk. The bluffer who is called loses credibility and it can get out of hand. Also remember, that most negotiations are carried out with people with whom you will have a continuing relationship. Again, while our culture supports and encourages those who are careful about how and when to disclose facts, out culture does not condone outright lying.

An old British Diplomat Service manual stated the following and it still might be useful.

Nothing may be said which is not true, but it is as unnecessary as it is sometimes undesirable to say everything relevant which is true; and the facts given may be arrange din any convenient order. The perfect reply to an embarrassing question is one that is brief, appears to answer the question completely (if challenged it can be proved to be accurate in every word), gives no opening for awkward follow-up questions, and discloses really nothing. Skilled negotiators develop techniques to do this. A favorite one is to answer a question with a question to deflect the first question.

Final Advice

Be unconditionally constructive. Approach a negotiation with this— 'I accept you as an equal negotiating partner; I respect your right to differ; I will be receptive.' Some criticize my approach as being too soft. But negotiating by these principles is a sign of strength.

- R. Fisher and R. Ury, "Getting to Yes"

All of us engage in many negotiations during a week but that doesn't mean we become better at it. To become better we need to become aware of the structure and dynamics of negotiation and we need to think systematically, objectively, and critically about our own negotiations. After engaging in a negotiation, reflect on what happened and figure out what you did effectively and what you need to do better.

There is no one "best" style; each of us has to find a style that is comfortable for us. Yet, everyone can negotiate successfully; everyone can reach agreements where all sides feel at least some of their needs have been satisfied. This involves a lot of alertness, active listening, good communication skills, great flexibility, good preparation, and above all it involves a sharing of responsibility for solving the problem, not a view that this is "their" problem.

To summarize the most important keys to successful conflict resolution:

- bargain over interests, not predetermined positions
- de-personalize the problem (separate the person from the problem)
- separate the problem definition from the search for solutions
- try to generate alternative solutions; try to use objective criteria as much as possible
- reflect on your negotiations; learn from your successes and mistakes

Have unlimited patience. Never corner an opponent and always assist the other person to save his face. Put yourself in his shoes-so as to see things through his eyes. Avoid self-righteousness like the devil-nothing is so self-blinding.

CHAPTER 2

Impact of Cross-Culture on Global Business Negotiation

Cross cultural negotiation is one of many specialized areas within the wider field of cross cultural communications. By taking cross cultural negotiation training, negotiators and sales personnel give themselves an advantage over competitors. There is an argument that proposes that culture is inconsequential to cross cultural negotiation. It maintains that as long as a proposal is financially attractive it will succeed. However, this is a naïve way of approaching international business. Let us look at a brief example of how cross cultural negotiation training can benefit the international business person:

> "There are two negotiators dealing with the same potential client in the Middle-East. Both have identical proposals and packages. One ignores the importance of cross cultural negotiation training believing the proposal will speak for itself. The other undertakes some cross cultural training. He/she learns about the culture, values, beliefs, etiquette and approaches to business, meetings and negotiations. Nine times out of ten the latter will succeed over the rival. This is because, (1) it is likely they would have endeared themselves more to the host negotiation team and (2) they would be able to tailor their approach to the negotiations in a way that maximizes the potential of a positive outcome" (http://www.kwintessential.co.uk/cultural-services/articles/cross-cultural-negotiation.html).

The impact of international business in domestic markets compels us to ask a question: "How can we survive in this global playing field, and what can we do to run our businesses more effectively?" Nowadays, businesses of all sizes search for suppliers and customers on a global level. International competition, foreign clients and suppliers may become a danger, but they may also create huge opportunities to develop our business. The increasingly global business environment requires managers to approach the negotiation process from the global business person's point of view. This approach includes aspects which are usually unimportant in domestic negotiations. Some of the components of a cross cultural negotiation process are more complex and difficult, but will increase our success in avoiding barriers and failures in the international business arena.

When doing business internationally, we need to consider (Salacuse, 1991):

1. The negotiating environment
2. Cultural and sub-cultural differences
3. Ideological differences
4. Foreign bureaucracy
5. Foreign laws and governments
6. Financial insecurity due to international monetary factors
7. Political instability and economic changes

If we consider the fact that negotiating with our fellow citizen is not an easy task due to many individual differences, it would be reasonable to suggest that negotiating with foreigners may be even more difficult. The way we perceive and create our own reality may be completely different to our counterpart's way of thinking, behaving and feeling. Unfortunately, knowledge of any foreign language is not enough to face and solve the problem. Language is a cluster of codes used in communication which, if not shared effectively, can act as a barrier to establish credibility and trust. We need more effective tools, and the most important is knowledge of all factors that can influence the proceedings. Nations tend to have a national character that influences the type of goals and process the society pursues in negotiations. This is why specifying and understanding cultural differences is vital in order to perform successfully in inter-cultural communication (Schuster-Copeland 1996, 33). As we better understand that our partners may see things differently, we will be less likely to make negative assumptions and more likely to make progress when negotiating (http://www.calumcoburn.co.uk/articles/cross-cultural-negotiation/).

With the emergence of economic globalization and China's entry into WTO, international business has become increasingly competitive intercultural. As international business relations grow, so does the frequency of business negotiations among people from different countries and cultures creating considerable challenges for business representatives unfamiliar with the cultures of different countries as well as business groups. So the intercultural approach to international business negotiation has attracted increasing attention of the global business community as a whole. Negotiations can easily break down because of a lack of understanding of the cultural component in the negotiation process and appropriate strategic framework to overcome such break-downs. Therefore, to the successful negotiations, the two sides must first understand the cultural differences. Negotiators who take the time to understand the approach that the other parties are likely to use and to adapt their own styles to that one are likely to be more effective negotiators. Thus, in an intercultural negotiation, in addition to the basic negotiation skills, it is important to understand the cultural differences, nuances etc. and to modify the negotiation style accordingly.

The very definition of negotiation, in its modern sense, can vary from culture to culture. What a negotiation is designed to accomplish is seen differently by different groups of people. Before one even comes to the table, such differences in the meaning or purpose of the negotiation affect the negotiation, as how one defines the process of negotiating is culturally determined. Some cultures see it only as an opportunity to bargain, others as the establishment of a lifetime relationship that goes beyond the occasional meeting, still others as an opportunity to demonstrate their capacity for eloquence and debate. Some do not see negotiation as a process at all. For instance, Americans and Europeans tend to see negotiations as a competitive process; the Chinese and the Japanese see it as a collaborative endeavor. So, there are many more challenges in an intercultural environment than in a mono-cultural setting. Intercultural negotiations are negotiation where the negotiating parties belong to different cultures and do not share the same ways of thinking, feeling, and behavior. The negotiation process is generally more complex because cultural norms may undermine effective communication.

This chapter focuses on the different dimensions of culture and different negotiating styles to illustrate the importance of the cultural factors in global business negotiation.

Understanding Culture

Definition of Culture

As early as 1952, Kroeber and Kluckhohn listed 164 definitions of culture that they found in the anthropology literature. Many new definitions have appeared since. Geert Hofstede, an expert on management and cross-cultural differences, defined culture as "the collective programming of the mind which distinguishes the members of one human group from another culture, in this sense, includes systems of values; and values are among the building blocks of culture." Another definition comes from sociologists Zvi Namenwirth and Robert Weber, who considered culture as "a system of ideas" and argued that these ideas constitute "a design for living." Here we follow both Hofstede and Namenwirth and Weber by viewing *culture* as a system of values and norms that are shared among a group of people and that when taken together constitute a design for living and negotiating. By *values* it would mean abstract ideas about what a group believes to be good, right, and desirable. In other words, values are shared assumptions about how things ought to be.

Characteristics of Culture

In order to better understand culture, it is useful to closely examine its characteristics and their ramifications. Regardless of the differences in defining culture, there is a general agreement on its major characteristics. Exploring these characteristics will help us understand why culture differences exert such a huge impact on international business negotiations, and thus help us adjust our mode of communication to the individual culture in which we are negotiating with our counterparts. Cultures around the world share four common characteristics: culture is shared, it is learned, it is based on symbols, and it is integrated. In order for the culture to be transmitted successfully from one person to the next, and from one generation to the next, a system of symbols needs to be created that translates the ideals of the culture to its members.

This is accomplished through language, art, religion, and money. In order to keep the culture functioning all aspects of the culture must be integrated. For example, the language must be able to describe all the functions within the culture in order for ideas and ideals to be transmitted from one person to another. Without the integration of language into the fabric of the culture, confusion and dysfunction would reign and the culture would fail (http://www.associatedcontent.com/article/12134/characteristics_of_culture_and_their.html?cat=) Culture has a number of characteristics. It is: (1) prescriptive, (2) socially shared, (3) learned, (4) subjective, (5) enduring, (6) cumulative, and (7) dynamic. Furthermore, it facilitates communication (http://www.routledge-ny.com/textbooks/0415311330/resources/case/06.pdf).

Culture is Acquired and Transmitted

It can be claimed that learning is the most important of all the characteristics of culture, for without the advantage of learning from those who lived before us, we would not have had culture. Human beings are born with some basic needs—needs that create and shape behavior, but how we go about meeting those needs and developing behaviors to cope with them are learned. From infancy, members of a culture begin to learn consciously or unconsciously from the behavior patterns and thinking patterns of their community until most of these patterns become internalized and habitual, and as a result, all people have far more of their behaviors programmed by cultural learning than by biology.

For a culture to exist and endure, it must be ensured that its crucial message and elements are passed on. It is passed on by other members of a cultural group. It is transmitted by parents, by other adults and institutions such as schools, and by peers. When people find in the process of social evolution certain behaviors and values to be adaptive and helpful, these behaviors and values are often encouraged and preserved. Similarly, non-adaptive and harmful behaviors and values are discouraged and discarded. Over a period of time, useful behaviors, values and artifacts become institutionalized and incorporated as part of cultural traditions. The individual then internalizes these institutionalized practices. Actually, if there are values considered central to a society that have existed for many years, these must be transmitted from one generation to another. Culture is the instrument by which each new generation acquires the capacity to bridge the distance that separates one life from another.

Ethnocentric Character of Culture

People everywhere tend to assume their own culture is right and normal, and to assess all other cultures by how closely they resemble their own. Most people, especially those with little experience of other cultures, believe that their own culture is at the centre of human experience – hence "ethnocentrism". Summer defined ethnocentric as "the technical name for the view of things in which one's own group is the centre of everything, and all others are scaled and rated with reference to it".

Like culture itself, ethnocentrism is usually learned at the unconscious level. For example, schools that teach mainly Chinese history, geography, literature, and government are also, without realizing it, teaching ethnocentrism. When we study only the accomplishment of our Chinese, we are quietly learning ethnocentrism. Exposed to Confucianism as a child, we are learning to judge the world by this standard.

Because we learn ethnocentrism so early in life, and primarily on the unconscious level, it might well be the major barrier to intercultural communication. For example, if males in the dominant culture value women who are thin, young, and dark-haired, then they will perceive women who are stout, older and blonde in a less favourable light. If we perceive privacy as a positive trait while another culture values openness, we again have perceptual differences. If we value vagueness in speech and another culture values directness, we might misinterpret what is being said. These three cases—and there are countless others—are examples of how perception influences communication. With the characteristic of culture in mind, the negotiator at the negotiating table should be conscious of avoiding the negative influence of his ethnocentric culture, which thus facilitates the negotiation process.

The common response in all societies to other cultures is to judge them in terms of the values and customs of their own familiar culture. This is *ethnocentrism*. Being fond of your own way of life and condescending or even hostile toward other cultures is normal for all people. Alien culture traits are often viewed as being not just different but inferior, less sensible, and even "unnatural." For example, European cultures strongly condemn other societies that practice polygamy and the eating of dogs—behavior that Europeans generally consider to be immoral and offensive. Likewise, many people in conservative Muslim societies, such as Afghanistan and Saudi Arabia, consider European women highly immodest and immoral for going out in public without being chaperoned by a male relative and without their bodies covered from head to toe so as to prevent men from looking at them. Ethnocentrism is not characteristic only of complex modern societies. People in small, relatively isolated societies are also ethnocentric in their views about outsiders. Our ethnocentrism can prevent us from understanding and appreciating another culture. When anthropologists study other societies, they need to suspend their own ethnocentric judgments and adopt a *cultural relativity approach*. That is, they try to learn about and interpret the various aspects of the culture they are studying in reference to that culture rather than to the anthropologist's own culture. This provides an understanding of how such practices as polygamy can function and even support other cultural traditions (http://oncampus.malone.edu/documents/Characteristics_of_Culture.pdf).

The emergence of what is essentially a shared global culture is not likely to result in the current major cultures disappearing in the immediate future the same way many of the small indigenous ones have. Language differences and ethnocentrism will very likely prevent that from happening. There are powerful conflicting trends in the world today. At the same time that many people are actively embracing globalism, others are reviving tribalism. The break-up of the former empire of the Soviet Union into largely ethnic based nations is an example of the latter. Likewise, some of the nations in Africa whose boundaries were arbitrarily created by Europeans during the colonial era are now experiencing periodic tribal wars that may result in the creation of more ethnically based countries (http://oncampus.malone.edu/documents/Characteristics_of_Culture.pdf).

Cultural Orientation

Culture is the dominant set of behaviors, values, beliefs, and thinking patterns we learn as we grow and develop in our social groups. Culture determines how we view others and ourselves, how we behave, and how we perceive the world around us. To navigate through an unfamiliar culture, we need to be able to get our bearings by relating ourselves to specific features in the environment the way a sailor uses the sun, the moon, the stars, and the horizon. Cultural orientations are an important aid when we are trying to get our bearings with a new culture. Each culture is built on core value orientations. Value orientations are preferences for certain states of affairs or outcomes over others.

To identify a culture's core values, Walker and Walker (2000) outline eight key cultural dimensions. First of all, each dimension needs to recognize an important aspect of social life. Secondly, each dimension needs to be something to which any socio-cultural environment gives its members a basic orientation as the shared rationale for behavior. Finally, each dimension has practical value to negotiators who need to reconcile, integrate, or transcend cultural difference in order to obtain a desired outcome.

Cultural dimensions of Negotiation may be categorized into following 8 classes:

1. Individualism (individualistic and collectivist): How individuals define their identity.
2. Communication (high-context and low-context; direct and indirect): How individuals express themselves.
3. Time (fluid time and fixed time): How individuals perceive the nature of time and its use.
4. Action (being and doing): How individuals view actions and interactions.
5. Power distance (high power distance and low power distance): How individuals view differential power relationships.

6. Structure (high uncertainty-avoidance and low uncertainty-avoidance): how individuals approach change, risk, ambiguity, and uncertainty.
7. Thinking (linear and systemic): How individuals conceptualize.
8. Environment (harmony and control): How individuals view and relate to the people, objects, and issues in their sphere of influence.

Each of these dimensions contains at least one cultural continuum. Such a continuum is the "field of force" between cultural orientations. Each continuum allows us to identify the directionality of hidden values, expectations, and drives of social phenomena and behavior patterns. These dimensions provide us with a framework for understanding the characteristics of different cultures and for adapting our behaviors. In the next chapter we, by using the eight dimensions, will expound the underlying reasons for the differences between Chinese negotiating styles and American negotiating styles.

Culture is *de facto* Communication

"Culture" has many meanings, but basically it's all about communication. Does it matter to business travelers, who really just want to concentrate on making a deal that will benefit both parties? Well, consider that you can offend a business partner in Japan just by taking off your jacket before getting down to serious negotiation. In France, you'll put them off by making light conversation and asking them if they have kids. In Nepal, they'll be insulted if you hand them papers with your left hand instead of your right. You can't memorize all the "tips and tricks" for all the countries you may ever visit, but you can master the skills of cross-cultural communication that will allow you to observe and analyze small cues that alert you to the possibility of a culture clash and enable you to cross-check with your partners that your communication is coming through clear on their channels.

When we discuss communication and culture, we should be aware of the total spectrum of communication including language, non-verbal communication, customs, perceived values, and concepts of time and space. Do all tourists identify with Canadian traditions and values? Likely not. But the more interesting question is: Why not? The answer lies in the simple fact that most tourists come from different cultures: some vastly different like those from Japan and China, others less different, such as tourists from Eastern Canada or the United States. Even if tourists share the same language, they may have much different customs and values (Gerry & Elizabeth Wilson The University of Calgary-Communication and culture, http://jmm.aaa.net.au/articles/85.htm).What happens when people from different cultures interact face-to-face? One way to appreciate the impact of cultural differences is to look in the mirror. When Americans and Canadians travel to other countries, they look for Cokes, steaks and hamburgers and the same amenities in hotels and other accommodations that they are used to at home. While the host country may offer an authentically different culture, which is one of the reasons people travel, North Americans tourists are notorious for wanting the comforts of home wherever they may be. In many third world countries, North Americans seek out joint venture hotels to enjoy North American food and lodging and to be served by people who speak English. Strangely, what we expect for ourselves in travel is not deemed to be reasonable when we're the hosts dealing with tourists from other countries.

Structural aspect of Culture

Any dictionary of sociology or cultural anthropology would offer us the picture of the "semantic pluralism" of such basic concepts as *social structure, institute, culture* and, more recently, that of *globalisation*. Thus, the term *social structure* is defined in both social anthropology and sociology by the term *institute*, whose semantic field is not clear-cut even within one and the same school. In ethology, the term *social structure* is used to designate the relationships among individuals, animals, or groups using biological (age and sex) criteria (Nadejda Stahovski, http://www.sociology.org/content/vol004.003/romanian.html). *Culture*—a concept of utmost importance in both understanding the motivation of human behaviour and making out how does the social whole function is "too amorphous, hazy and, purely and simply contradictory".

Particularity of the Social Systems

When people of different cultures are engaged in business negotiations, difficulties and misunderstandings all the time occur between the negotiators. For the Americans, the stage of exchanging task-related information in business negotiations is relatively direct, with clear statements of needs and preferences, whereas in Chinese culture, indirect and vague expression is more acceptable than direct and specific references. Ambiguous terminology is preferred. Germans tend to regard time as something that must be planned for the most efficient use whereas in Kuwait, people view time in a more relaxed way, seeing planning as unwise and unnecessary. These and countless other philosophical, ideological, and metaphysical questions need to be answered if we are to navigate through an unfamiliar culture. It is not enough to know that some people bow whereas others shake hands or that some value silence whereas others value talk. Although these behaviors are significant, we also need to know what motivates them. The how and why behind a culture's collective action can be traced to its (1) world view, (2) family structure, (3) history, and (4) education. Working together, these three social forces create, transmit, maintain, and reinforce the basic elements found in all cultures. They are used to tell each member what to expect from life and how to live that life.

World view, according to Hobel and Frost, is defined as "the human being's inside view of the way things are colored, shaped, and arranged according to personal cultural preconceptions."[1[11]] World view thus influences all aspects of our perception and consequently affects our beliefs and value systems as well as how we think. A culture's world view can be thought of as its core. Our world view originates in our culture, is transmitted via a multitude of channels, and can take a variety of forms. But the predominant element of culture that gives us our world view is religion.

Religion, whether or not one is a believer, plays an important part in shaping one's basic value system. A code of conduct – what is right and what is wrong – is set out clearly in every religion. There is, for instance, nothing inherently or naturally wrong in stealing your next neighbor's belongings; all other animals are doing it all the time. But most people do not go about killing, or stealing, or cheating, or whatever. This is because their upbringing and their society's values, which are in turn heavily influenced by the precepts and dictates of their religion, regard these actions as wrong and immortal.

Negotiating Across Cultures

Hendon, Hendon and Herbig (1996) present eight variables in the negotiating process that will lead to a better understanding of negotiating styles: purpose, issues, protocol, communications, arguments, trust, time, and decision-making.

Purpose. Different groups view the purpose and process of negotiation differently. Negotiation may be seen as a conflict in which one side wins and another loses, as a competition to identify who is best, or as a collaborative process to formulate some undertaking. The winner of a negotiation in some countries is the one who gains the most concessions, regardless of the value of the concessions.

Issues. Different groups stress different aspects of the negotiations. Some groups stress the specific substantive issues directly related to the agreement, while others focus on building long-term relationships.

Protocol. Different groups have their own particular etiquette associated with the negotiating process, and their adherence to protocol varies according to its perceived importance. Protocol factors that should be considered are gift giving, entertainment, dress codes, seating arrangements, number of negotiators, and the timing of breaks. The degree of formality or informality is an important component of protocol that should be assessed as well.

Communications. Some cultures rely on verbal communications, others on non-verbal cues such as gestures and silence. The more varied the methods of communication, the more complex the negotiations and the more care must be given to understanding the message. For example, Americans tend to be verbal but the Japanese often use periods of silence and extensive non-verbal gestures in their communications.

Arguments. Various types of arguments are more (or less) effective in different cultures. Some cultures rely on facts and logical arguments, others on tradition and references to the way things were done in the past. Still others focus on intuition or emotion. Some cultures conduct negotiations based on a particular religion or philosophy. *Trust.* All societies seek to establish trust with one another during negotiations. Each group may, however, establish trust on a different basis. Some groups look to experience and records; others rely on intuition and emotion. Still others are most comfortable when sanctions exist to guarantee performance.

Time. In some cultures, time is viewed as limited and precious. Punctuality, agendas, and specified time frames are important to people from those environments. Others view time as plentiful and always available; therefore, they are more likely to expect negotiations to progress slowly and for all parties to be flexible about schedules. For example, Americans view time as a scarce commodity that must not be wasted, while the Japanese view time in the long term.

Decision-making. Decisions are made differently in various groups. They may be made by individuals or by the group as a whole. Within a group, participants may defer to the person of highest status or to the most senior member. Some groups accept the decision of the majority. Other groups seek consensus among members and will not make a decision until all members have agreed.

Ethnocentricity and Cross-cultural Negotiation

Problems in business communication conducted across cultures often arise when participants from one culture are unable to understand culturally determined differences in communication practices, traditions, and thought processing. At the most fundamental level, problems may occur when one or more of the people involved clings to an ethnocentric view of how to conduct business. Ethnocentrism is the belief that one's own cultural group is somehow innately superior to others. It is easy to say that ethnocentrism only affects the bigoted or those ignorant of other cultures, and so is unlikely to be a major factor in one's own business communication. Yet difficulties due to a misunderstanding of elements in cross-cultural communication may affect even enlightened people. Ethnocentrism is deceptive precisely because members of any culture perceive their own behavior as logical, since that behavior works for them. People tend to accept the values of the culture around them as absolute values. Since each culture has its own set of values, often quite divergent from those values held in other cultures, the concept of proper and improper, foolish and wise, and even right and wrong become blurred. In international business, questions arise regarding what is proper by which culture's values, what is wise by which culture's view of the world, and what is right by whose standards. Since no one individual is likely to recognize the subtle forms of ethnocentrism that shape who he or she is, international business practitioners must be especially careful in conducting business communication across cultures. It is necessary to try to rise above culturally imbued ways of viewing the world. To do this, one needs to understand *how* the perception of a given message changes depending on the culturally determined viewpoint of those communicating.

Polycentrism is the principle of organization of a region around several political, social or financial centres. Examples of polycentric cities include the

Ruhr area in Germany and Stoke-on-Trent in the UK. Today, the former is a large city that grew from a dozen smaller cities, the latter a federation of six smaller towns. As a result, these "cities" have no single centre, but several. A county is said to be polycentric if its population is distributed almost evenly among several centres in different parts of the county.

The *theory of polycentrism* was coined by Palmiro Togliatti and was understood as characterization of working conditions of communist parties in comparison between different countries after the de-stalinization in the former Soviet Union 1956 (http://en.wikipedia.org/wiki/Polycentrism). Later the term polycentrism was extended and used for a system with several centres, as *unity in diversity* (politology, architecture, city planning).

In *intercultural competence* the term polycentrism is understood as attitude and openness towards other cultures, opinions and ways of life: when intercultural actions and correlations are interpreted not only with the background of own cultural experiences, but when the independence of other cultures is recognized and appreciated and when cultural values are relativized and seen in the whole context. This in the way of non-ethnocentrism, opposite to ethnocentrism.

Factors affecting Cross-cultural Business Communication

Culture directly affects the communication process in an international business setting through seven variables (http://www.enotes.com/biz-encyclopedia/cross-cultural-international-communication):

1. language
2. environmental and technological considerations
3. social organization
4. contexting and face-saving
5. authority conception
6. nonverbal communication behavior
7. time conception

These seven items form the acronym LESCANT.

Most barriers when communicating across cultures derive from the communicator's misgauge of the LESCANT factors. By assessing in advance the roles these variables play in business communication, one can improve one's ability to convey those messages effectively to an audience from a different culture. The seven LESCANT factors alone do not provide a thorough knowledge of another culture. Moreover, these seven dimensions of culture are not intended to represent the *only* cause of intercultural communication difficulties. Being aware of these factors does, however, provide an underlying foundation on which one can construct a framework for understanding the businesspeople from other cultures. In short, these seven factors represent an approach for asking the right questions needed to see the most significant cultural differences and similarities. The answers to those questions vary according to the individual experiences of those involved.

Language

Among the most often cited barriers to conflict-free cross-cultural business communication is the use of different languages. It is difficult to underestimate the importance that an understanding of linguistic differences plays in international business communication. Difficulties with language fall basically into three categories: gross translation problems, the problems in conveying subtle distinctions from language to language, and culturally-based variations among speakers of the same language.

Gross translation errors, though frequent, may be less likely to cause conflict between parties than other language difficulties for two reasons. First, they are generally the easiest language difficulty to detect. Many gross translation errors are either ludicrous or make no sense at all. Only those errors that continue to be logical in both the original meaning and in the mistranslated version pose a serious concern. Nonetheless, even when easily detected, gross translation errors waste time and wear on the patience of the parties involved. Additionally, for some, such errors imply a form of disrespect for the party into whose language the message is translated.

The subtle shadings that are often crucial to business negotiations are also weakened when the parties do not share a similar control of the same language. In English, for example, the mild distinctions between the words "misinterpret" and "misunderstand" can prove significant in a sensitive situation. To a touchy negotiator, to say that he or she "misunderstands" may imply that he or she is dim-witted. To say that same negotiator "misinterprets" a concept, by contrast, allows the negotiator a way to save face since all interpretations are arguable. He or she has reached an understandable though inaccurate interpretation of the matter. In such a situation, the term applies more objectively to the matter at hand than to the specific negotiator. To a nonnative speaker with inadequate control of the language, however, such subtle distinctions might be lost. When other parties with full control over the language with whom the nonnative speaker communicates assume that knowledge of this distinction exists, conflict deriving from misunderstanding is likely.

Nor do such mistranslations need to actually cross languages in cross-cultural business situations. Dialectical differences within the same language often create gross errors. One frequently cited example of how variations within a single language can affect business occurred when a U.S. deodorant manufacturer sent a Spanish translation of its slogan to their Mexican operations. The slogan read "if you use our deodorant, you won't be embarrassed." The translation, however, which the Mexican-based English-speaking employees saw no reason to avoid, used the term "*embarazada*" to mean "embarrassed." This provided much amusement to the Mexican market, as "*embarazada*" means "pregnant" in Mexican Spanish.

Attitudes toward accents and dialects also create barriers in international business communication. The view that a particular accent suggests loyalty or familiarity to a nation or region is widespread in many languages. The use of Parisian French in Quebec, of Mexican Spanish in Spain, or sub-continental Indian English in the United States are all noticeable and may suggest a lack of familiarity even if the user is fluent. More importantly, regional ties or tensions in such nations as Italy, France, or Germany among others can be suggested by the dialect a native speaker uses.

Finally, national prejudices and class distinctions are often reinforced thorough sociolinguistics—the social patterning of language. For example, due to regional prejudice and racism certain accents in the United States associated with urban areas (e.g., a Bronx accent), with rural regions (e.g., an Appalachian accent), or race (e.g., black English) may reinforce negative stereotypes (usually erroneously) regarding business ability, education level, or acumen among certain U.S. subgroups. Similarly, some cultures use sociolinguistics to differentiate one economic class from another. Thus, in England, distinct accents are associated with the aristocracy and the middle and lower classes. These distinctions are often unknown by foreigners.

Environment and Technology

Technology and pet society or technology and culture refers to the cyclical co-dependence, co-influence, co-production of technology and society upon the other (technology upon culture, and vice-versa). This synergistic relationship occurred from the dawn of humankind, with the invention of the simple tools; and continues into modern technologies such as the printing press and computers. The academic discipline studying the impacts of science, technology, and society and vice versa is called (and can be found at) Science and technology studies (http://en.wikipedia.org/wiki/Technology_and_society). There are an extraordinary number of examples how science and technology has helped us that can be seen in society today. One great example is the mobile phone. Ever since the invention of the telephone society was in need of a more portable device that they could use to talk to people. This high demand for a new product led to the invention of the mobile phone, which did, and still does, greatly influence society and the way people live their lives. Now many people are accessible to talk to whoever they want no matter where any of the two people are. All these little changes in mobile phones, like Internet access, are further examples of the cycle of co-production. Society's need for being able to call on people and be available everywhere resulted in the research and development of mobile phones. They in turn influenced the way we live our lives.

The ways in which people use the technological resources available to them often shifts drastically from culture to culture. Culturally-engrained biases regarding the natural and technological environment can create communication barriers. Most people are accustomed to ways of looking at the environment and the use of technology particular to their own culture. This, in turn, may make it difficult to accept or even to understand those views held by other cultures.

Issues of Environment

Five major areas of attitudes toward a nation's physical characteristics and natural resources are likely to result in cultural environmental presuppositions. These are:

1. climate
2. topography
3. population size
4. population density
5. the relative availability of natural resources

These five sources of environmental differences surface when people communicate on a wide spectrum of business-related subjects. Notions of transportation and logistics, settlement, and territorial organization are affected by topography and climate. For example, transportation and logistics in one culture may seem patently absurd in another. The manager of a Canadian company doing business in South America might never think to ship goods from Chile to neighboring Argentina by the circuitous route of the Panama Canal. Because Canada is relatively flat and has an excellent network of railroads and highways, the Canadian manager might assume that the easiest way to transport goods for any short distance would be overland. This preference would be reinforced by the fact that many Canadian waterways freeze over due to its harsh climate. As a result, the Canadian might well assume or even specify a preference for overland transport in any relevant business communication. What the Canadian might not understand in such a situation is that the rugged physical environment of the Andean terrain and the related absence of cross-Andean railroads and freeways would make such an option unreasonably expensive or even impossible. By contrast, warm water ports and relatively easy access to the Panama Canal or other waterways would reinforce the option of water routes even for such relatively short overland distances.

Population size and the availability of natural resources influence each nation's view toward export or domestic markets. The United States and China, for example, both have gigantic domestic markets and are rich in natural resources. Both nations export out of choice, and have a tendency to internalize their views of foreign markets. Foreign markets in such countries may be culturally reinforced as being secondary markets as a result, with a cultural emphasis on domestic markets. By contrast, Switzerland, with neither a large domestic population nor abundant natural resources, is culturally oriented toward export with foreign markets viewed as their primary markets and the domestic Swiss market as a comparatively negligible secondary market.

Population density and space usage influence the development of different cultural perceptions of how space and materials are used. Thus, how people lay out or use office space, domestic housing, and buildings in general shifts from nation to nation. For example, in many nations the size, layout, and furnishings of a business office communicate a message. The message communicated, however, varies from nation to nation.

Such differences may be subtle or overt. For example, the distinctions between the U.S. and French upper-level executive's office may be quite subtle. In both France and the United States, the size of an office, plushness of its furnishings, and location in the building (corner office or top floor of the building) reflect the status of the office's owner. In France, however, the individual aesthetics of the office decor convey an important statement about the office owner while in the U.S. office the wall decorations and furnishings are often selected by a designer with little input from the office's occupant.

Much more overt is the contrast between the U.S. or French executive office and the "open system" offices of Japan. In the open system office, Japanese department heads have no individual offices at all. Instead, their desks are simply one of numerous other desks placed in a regularly patterned arrangement in a large open area. No partitions are used between the desks at all and no individual offices exist. Yet each person in this office-less open system is strategically placed in a way that communicates his or her rank and status just as surely as the U.S. or French individual office system. Thus, the department heads' desks are normally placed at a point farthest from the door where the department heads can view their whole department easily at a glance. Moreover, further status may be indicated by placement near a window. The messages communicated by such placement in a large open area may be entirely lost on the French or U.S. visitor unfamiliar with it.

Issues of Technology

More seriously, the failure of businesspeople to modify their communication to accommodate environmental differences often derives from ethnocentric inflexibility toward culturally learned views of technology.

Generally, cultures may be divided into three approaches toward technology: (1) control; (2) subjugation, and (3) harmonization.

In control cultures such as those of northern Europe and North America, technology is customarily viewed as an innately positive means for controlling the environment. If a road approaches a mountain in a control culture, a tunnel is blasted through the mountain. If the tunnel collapses, the cultural view is that the technology was inadequate to the task and needs to be improved.

In subjugation cultures such as those of central Africa and southwestern Asia, the existing environment is viewed as innately positive and technology is viewed with some skepticism. If a road approaches a mountain, the road may simply stop at the mountain. If a tunnel is used and does collapse, the cultural view is that the very idea of going through the mountain was misguided, not that the technology was inadequate.

In harmonization cultures such as those common in many Native American cultures and some East Asian nations, a balance is attempted between the use of technology and the existing environment. In these cultures, neither technology nor the environment are innately good and members of such cultures see themselves as part of the environment in which they live being neither subject to it nor master of it.

One major communication stumbling block among those from control cultures is the belief that other cultures wish to be more like them. Control cultures tend to describe themselves as the "industrialized nations." Their members are often acculturated to believe that the way in which people in less industrialized nations use their resources results from inherently inferior technology. Arguably, in some cases this position may be defensible. Often, though, the reason people use the resources available to them in the manner that they do is because it makes good business sense to use them in that fashion within the context of their own cultural views.

Social Organisation

Social organization, as it affects the workplace, is often culturally determined. One must take care not to assume that the view held in one's own culture is universal on such issues reflecting the culture's social organization as nepotism and kinship ties, educational values, class structure and social mobility, job status and economic stratification, religious ties, political affiliation, gender differences, racism and other prejudices, attitudes toward work, and recreational or work institutions.

All of these areas have far-reaching implications for business practice. Choosing employees based on resumes, for example, is considered a primary means of selection in the United States, Canada, and much of northern Europe—all nations with comparatively weak concepts of familial relationships and kinship ties. In these cultures, nepotism is seen as subjective and likely to protect less qualified workers through familial intervention. By contrast, it would seem anywhere from mildly to highly inappropriate to suggest to members of many Arabic, central African, Latin American, or southern European cultures to skip over hiring relatives to hire a stranger. For people in these cultures, nepotism both fulfills personal obligations and ensures a predictable level of trust and accountability. The fact that a stranger appears to be better qualified based on a superior resume and a relatively brief interview would not, as it might for example in the United States or Sweden, affect that belief. Such a suggestion, depending on the situation at hand, could be made. To effectively suggest such a course of action, however, one would need to communicate this in a manner adjusted to the way that employees would likely react to so distressing an order.

Similarly, the nature of praise and employee motivation can be socially determined. For example, a promotion of a single member of a traditional Japanese work group may cause the productivity and morale of both the group and the promoted employee to fall. A similar promotion in the United States, by contrast, might be seen as a reward for the promoted employee and might even be viewed as encouraging the remaining members of the group to work harder for a goal that they too might attain. Thus to communicate such a promotion openly may prove to be a poor policy in Japan but a good policy in the United States.

Finally, it is often difficult to rid business communication of a judgmental bias when social organization varies markedly. For example, those from the United States may find it difficult to remain neutral on class structures prevent upward mobility. For instance, the socially determined inferior role of women in much of the Islamic world, or of lower castes in India—to name just two—may prove particularly disturbing to those from the United States. Nevertheless, if the U.S. businessperson cannot eliminate the attendant condemnation from his or her business communication, then he or she cannot expect to function effectively in that society. An individual may personally believe that a country's social system is inefficient or incorrect. Nevertheless, in the way that individual conducts business on a daily basis, it is necessary to work within the restraints of that culture to succeed. One may choose *not* to do business with people from such a culture but one cannot easily impose one's own values on them and expect to do well.

Factors Influencing Cross-cultural Negotiations

The following factors influence the effectiveness of a cross-cultural negotiation (Michal Zieba-Cross cultural negotiation, http://www.calumcoburn.co.uk/articles/cross-cultural-negotiation/):

Negotiating Goal and Basic Concept: How is the negotiation being seen? Is mutual satisfaction the real purpose of the meeting? Do we have to compete? Do they want to win? Different cultures stress different aspects of negotiation. The goal of business negotiation may be a substantive outcome (Americans) or a long-lasting relationship (Japanese).

Protocol: There are as many kinds of business etiquette as there are nations in the world. Protocol factors that should be considered are dress codes, number of negotiators, entertainment, degree of formality, gift giving, meeting and greeting, etc.

Communications: Verbal and non-verbal communication is a key factor of persuasion. The way we express our needs and feelings using body language and tone of voice can determine the way the other side perceives us, and in fact positively or negatively contributes to our credibility. Another aspect of communication relevant to negotiation is the direct or indirect approach to exchanging information. Is the meaning of what is said exactly in the words themselves? Does "...it's impossible" really mean impossible or just difficult to realize? Always use questions to identify the other side's needs, otherwise assumptions may result in you never finding common interests.

Risk-Taking Propensity—Uncertainty Avoidance: There is always risk involved in negotiations. The final outcome is unknown when the negotiations commence. The most common dilemma is related to personal relations between counterparts: Should we trust them? Will they trust us? Certain cultures are more risk averse than others, e.g. Japan (Hofstede, 1980). It means that less innovative and creative alternatives are available to pursue during the negotiation, unless there is a strong trust-based relationship between the counterparts.

View of Time: In some cultures time is money and something to be used wisely. Punctuality and agenda may be an important aspect of negotiation. In countries such as China or Japan, being late would be taken as an insult. Consider investing more time in the negotiating process in Japan. The main goal when negotiating with an oriental counterpart is to establish a firm relationship, which takes time. Another dimension of time relevant to negotiation is the focus on past, present or future. Sometimes the past or the distant future may be seen as part of the present, especially in Latin American countries.

Decision-Making System: The way members of the other negotiating team reach a decision may give us a hint: who we shall focus on providing our presentation. When negotiating with a team, it's crucial to identify who is the leader and who has the authority to make a decision.

Form of Agreement: In most cultures, only written agreements stamp a deal. It seems to be the best way to secure our interests in case of any unexpected circumstances. The 'deal' may be the contract itself or the relationship between the parties, like in China, where a contract is likely to be in the form of general principles. In this case, if any unexpected circumstances arise, parties prefer to focus on the relationship than the contract to solve the problem.

Power Distance: This refers to the acceptance of authority differences between people. Cultures with low *power distance* postulate equality among people, and focus more on earned status than ascribed status. Negotiators from countries like Britain, Germany and Austria tend to be comfortable with shared authority and democratic structures. When we face a high *power distance* culture, be prepared for hierarchical structures and clear authority figures.

Personal Style: Our individual attitude towards the other side and biases which we sometimes establish all determine our assumptions that may lead the negotiation process towards win-win or win-lose solutions. Do we feel more comfortable using a formal or informal approach to communication? In some cultures, like America, an informal style may help to create friendly relationships and accelerate the problem solving solution. In China, by comparison, an informal approach is proper only when the relationship is firm and sealed with trust.

Non-Verbal Behaviour: Key to Effective Cross-culture Negotiation

Nonverbal behavior may be defined as any behavior, intentional or unintentional, beyond the words themselves which can be interpreted by a receiver as having meaning. Nonverbal behaviors could include facial expressions, eye contract, gestures, body movements, posture, physical appearance, space, touch and time usage are different from culture to culture. Nonverbal behaviors either accompany verbal messages or are used independently of verbal messages. They may affirm and emphasize or negate and even contradict spoken messages. Nonverbal behaviors are more likely to be used unconsciously and spontaneously because they are habitual and routine behaviors (http://www.geocities.com/Athens/Delphi/9158/kwulectureccn8.html).

The wide range of behaviors called non-verbal behavior can be divided into seven categories. Gestures, body movement, facial movement, and eye contact are combined in the kinesic code, commonly called body language. Vocalics refers to call vocal activity other than the verbal context itself. Also called paralanguage, cocalics includes tone, volume, and sounds which are not words. Behaviors which involve touching are placed in the haptics code. The use of space is called proxemics, and the use of time is chronemics. Physical appearance includes body shape and size as well as clothing and jewelry. Finally, artifacts refers to objects which are associated with a person, such as one's desk, car, or books. It should be emphasized that these codes do not usually function independently or sequentially; rather, they work simultaneously. In addition, nonverbal behavior is always sending messages; we cannot not communicate without using them, although, at times, the messages may be ambiguous. This wide range of nonverbal behaviors serves various functions in face-face encounters. Most important emotional messages at the negotiating table are expressed nonverbally by gestures, tone of voice or facial expressions. The other side's interpretation of your statement depends on the non verbal more than what was actually said. Non-verbal communications is significant. What cannot be conveyed through words is sent through gestures and body movements.

Most important emotional messages at the negotiating table are expressed nonverbally by gestures, tone of voice or facial expressions. The other side's interpretation of your statement depends on the non verbal more than what was actually said. Nonverbal messages tend to have more credibility than verbal messages, less likely to be the subject of intentional distortion. When a conflict exists between verbal and nonverbal messages, the latter should be given greater weight (http://www.geocities.com/Athens/Delphi/9158/kwulectureccn8.html).

The meaning of any non-verbal communication act depends upon the individual involved, the context in which the act is performed, and the cultural background of the interacting people. The tremendous impact of the "silent language" on the negotiation process. Everything counts during the negotiation: the time of the negotiation (morning, lunch time, late in the evening) the table (round, square), the lights (white, in the middle of the room), the use of microphones, the breaks, the phone calls, the space between the chairs, the way the negotiators dress, and so on. Everything is important. Effective negotiators are fully aware of the existence of all these factors and that they are able to use them to their advantage. One word of caution: an individual gesture must be approached cautiously. It is clusters of behavior that provide the greatest amount and most accurate nonverbal meanings.

Most of the time we send and receive nonverbal cues without being conscious of them. Between two-thirds and seventy percent of the meaning in social interactions is derived from nonverbal cues. Former United Nations Secretary-General Dag Hammarskjold summarizes the importance of nonverbal behavior in the negotiation process: "The unspoken dialog between two people can never be put right by anything they say." In negotiation, what is not said is in many cases more important than what is openly expressed by the parties involved. Effective negotiators are particularly good at controlling (consciously or unconsciously) their body language and at the same time adjusting to the many non-verbal signals they receive from the opposite negotiators(s). It is important to be aware of nonverbal cues since the negotiator may unintentionally transmit false or confusing messages to the other part, the negotiator may not pick up on or may misinterpret nonverbal cues being transmitted by the other side, or effective communications may require the usage of nonverbal messages. Most important emotional messages at the negotiating table are expressed nonverbally by gestures, tone of voice or facial expressions. The other side's interpretation of your statement depends on the non verbal more than what was actually said. Nonverbal messages tend to have more credibility than verbal messages, less likely to be the subject of intentional distortion. When a conflict exists between verbal and nonverbal messages, the latter should be given greater weight.

Among the most markedly varying dimensions of intercultural communication is nonverbal behavior. Knowledge of a culture conveyed through what a person says represents only a portion of what that person has communicated. Much of nonverbal communication may be broken down into six areas: dress; kinesics, or body language; oculesics, or eye contact; haptics, or touching behavior; proxemics, or the use of body space; and paralanguage. Any one of these areas communicates significant information nonverbally in any given culture.

One of the most apparent differences is the interpretation of dress. The message given by polished shoes, for instance, could easily be lost on a culture in which sandals are the standard footwear. Similarly, a woman's decision to wear her best suit would be lost in a culture in which no women wear business suits. Even when cultures share similar forms of dress, the message inherent in the choice of clothing is not always the same. For instance, the selection of a conservative tie for a formal negotiation might well be shared by several cultures, but exactly what a conservative tie is (even when all parties belong to cultures in which men generally wear ties) remains determined by the standards that prevail in that particular culture. Thus, what is a conservative tie in one culture may seem unconservative or flashy in another, giving a different message altogether.

Just as importantly, people often bring to a cross-cultural meeting ethnocentric prejudices regarding what they believe to be proper dress. Thus, a European or American may condemn as somehow less than civilized a Saudi or Iranian in traditional garb. Conversely, a Saudi or Iranian may well consider as flagrantly immoral the bare face, arms, and legs of a European or American woman in business attire. Nonverbal behavioral differences in kinesics may be less obvious than dress differences. How people walk, gesture, bow, stand, or sit are all, to a large part, culturally determined. In many cases, a kinesic sign well understood in one culture is totally unknown in another culture. In Indonesia and in much of the Arab world, for example, it is offensive to show the soles of one's feet to another. This often clashes with behavior in the United States where foot-crossing is common with no attention to where one's sole points. In Japan, a relatively elaborate system of bowing is common but has no counterpart in the United States. This entire system of nonverbal communication is therefore generally lost on most U.S. businesspeople.

Some kinesic behavior may carry distinctly different meanings in more than one culture. In such cases, all parties recognize the gesture, but interpret it differently. During George Bush's visit to Australia while he was president, he held up two fingers in a V sign. In both countries the symbol is widely understood, but in the United States the "V" emblem is a sign of good will, victory, and solidarity, while in Australia it carries a lewd, sexual meaning.

Haptics or touching behavior also reflects cultural values. In a generally nonhaptic society such as Japan, touching another person in a business setting even with a handshake is traditionally considered foreign. While those Japanese familiar with U.S. handshaking may adapt to its use, one can expect that such cultural compromise would not easily extend to so haptic a response as a pat on the back. The United States itself is a fairly nonhaptic society, particularly between men. In many cultures that behave more haptically, men often walk with arms interlinked or hold hands which to U.S. males might appear effeminate or overly intimate.

Oculesics or the use of eye contact also varies significantly depending on the culture involved. In several cultures, for example, it is considered disrespectful to prolong eye contact with those who are older or of higher status. In many cultures, it is considered improper for women to look men in the eye. By contrast, in the United States, studies have shown that eye contact has less to do with age or rank than with a person's credibility or sense of belonging. While fairly steady eye contact in the United States may indicate the listener's interest and attentiveness, intense eye contact may prove disconcerting.

Finally, proxemics or how far apart people stand when speaking or how far apart they sit in meetings carries significant information to people who share the same culture. Here, too, as with other nonverbal behavior, such information is likely to be garbled across cultures. Personal space is culturally determined. In the United States, for instance, people tend to feel most comfortable in business settings when speaking at approximately arm's length apart from each other.

In many Latin American, southern European, central African and Middle

Eastern cultures, however, a comfortable conversational distance would be much closer. Indeed, in many parts of the world, friendly or serious conversations are conducted close enough to feel the breath of the speaker on one's face. The U.S. or northern European communicator unaware of this may face a very discomforting situation, with the speaker literally backing his or her U.S. or northern European counterpart into a corner as the speaker continues to move closer to the retreating listener. The result in a business situation could be disastrous. The speaker with the closer personal space conception would likely feel distrustful and even spurned by the listener with the larger space conception. Conversely, the person with larger personal space conception might feel the encroaching speaker to be pushy, overly aggressive, or rude.

Examples of Non-verbal Cultural Communications

The Arabs want direct, face-to-face discussions, but do not to bring open disagreements into a formal session. In fact, rather than say that they disagree, many Arabs will say they agree, but then take actions that gently hint they do not agree at all. They hope that the other party will get the message. Arabs will seldom provide a direct 'no,' even if they disagree. Hesitation signals disagreement exists. A person of status is not expected to hesitate over an answer. If you don't know, stall but don't say you don't know. In Algeria, an American consultant said: "My clients never disagree with my recommendations. They just do not try to implement the ones they dislike." Arab men don't hesitate to walk hand in hand, arm in arm in public Saudi Arabians look closely into another's eyes in the belief that they can tell if that person is telling the truth or lying by movements of the pupil. Americans think that keeping direct eye contact is a sign of openness, honesty and assertiveness; other cultures view it as confrontational, aggressive, hostile and rude. Italians, Arabs, and Latin Americans use their hands a great deal to emphasize or support what they are saying. In general, the French shake hands without particular conviction and without even a verbal greeting–which a Germany may misread as indifference.

In Japan and the Arab countries the direct negotiations are combined with social activities. One purpose of these activities is to demonstrate hospitality. Another, more serious purpose is to determine whether you are the sort of person with whom they want to do business. An easy way to create a bad impression is to discuss business at the wrong time. That is, the social process can be as important as the negotiations process. Good manners are so important to the Japanese, and they are so subtle that they have a novel way of punishing boors. The Portuguese prefer that no business be discussed at a meal until the conversation is complete and coffee is served.

The Japanese are willing to meet face-to-face, but they also use third parties much more frequently than we do. They like to have that buffer. They are also so uncomfortable with open conflict that they hardly ever express it directly. They talk around it, or do not react at all, or give indirect hints that they disagree. In fact, they hardly ever say no directly; one must infer it from the way they say yes. When a Japanese says 'yes' he may mean 'no' and often 'maybe' but rarely an unconditional 'yes.' "*Hai*" means 'yes' but it indicates understanding rather than agreement. If he draws breath between his teeth and says something like '*sah*' or 'it is very difficult' he means 'no.' The Japanese claim to have as many as twenty or more ways to say 'no' without having to say it. The Japanese often use little verbal activity, nod frequently, use silence, even close eyes while others are speaking. Silence to a Japanese means one is projecting a favorable impression and is thinking deeply about the problem. When in an impasse in negotiation, the typical Japanese response is silence, withdrawal or change of subject. Japanese more influenced by what is not said. The Japanese interpersonal communication style includes less eye contract, fewer negative facial expressions and more periods of silence.

Flat level tones in English regularly connote boredom or sarcasm. In Russian, on the other hand, the level tone is much more widely used with a natural matter of fact interpretation. A Russian will therefore tend to speak English with many level tone endings. To his own ears the sentence sounds intentionally neutral but to the English listener he sounds uninterested and rude. By the same token the English speaker negotiating in a foreign language has to use the pitch, loudness, speed and rhythm associated with the meaning he intends to convey. The tone of voice interpreted as 'sincere' by Egyptian sounds 'belligerent' to Americans. An Arab speaking English is often thought by Westerners to be shouting, as Arabs tend to speak more loudly than most Westerners. Americans, on the other hand, tend to speak louder than most Europeans and give the impression of assertiveness, even when not intended.

The range and use of emotions drastically differ across the globe. Some cultures, for example Orientals, inhibit emotional expressions while others such as Latin American and Mediterranean cultures, are most more demonstrative. Italians tend to be extremely hospitable but are often volatile in temperament. When they make a point, they do so with considerable gesticulation and emotional expression. Impressed by style, they tend to dress well themselves. Moreover, they enjoy haggling over prices. Indians do not approve of displays of emotion. Chinese negotiators rarely telegraph their next move through a show of emotions. The level of friendliness or impersonality remains the same whether negotiations are approaching agreement or failure. A Thai's laughter in meetings may not indicate amusement. Often it is an embarrassed response when the Thai does not understand the point of the counterpart or simply does not wish to reply.

In Bulgaria, nodding one's head means 'no' while shaking one's head means 'yes.' A 'thumbs up' gesture is considered vulgar in Iran but friendly in Brazil. Folding your arms may be considered disrespectful by a Fijian. Pointing at something with a finger is considered rude in many places in Africa. In Greece, waving may be taken as an insult. The "A-OK" gesture considered perfectly appropriate by an American is likely to be viewed as obscene by a Brazilian.

Stress is the abnormal response by the body to unusual demands placed upon it. Stress can be created in many ways. Stress can be utilized to produce concessions by the other side. For example during the 1972 Nixon-Brezhnex Moscow summit, the Soviet negotiators frequently changed the setting and agenda of the meetings and refused to provide the Americans with access to telecommunications equipment and administrative support. In addition, the U.S. negotiators feared justifiably that the Soviets were electronically monitoring their conversations.

Non-verbal behaviors are often performed too weakly or too strongly for their particular context. The reason for this is that a person's true mood is interfering with the behavior he is trying to project. Gestures and expressions embody subtle complexities. When the performer's mood is inappropriate he fails to convey these complexities to the degree required to convince.

With under- and over-reaction there is a danger when negotiators from different cultures meet that they will misunderstand each other. The man who holds the eye too long as Westerners may believe of Arabs, or is over-familiar or personal as Englishmen may believe of Americans or Indians, may well be looked on as over-reacting. In fact they can be behaving in accordance with the norms of their own cultures where rules in relation to public display have not dampened their actions to the degree they have in the other party's culture. On the other hand the opposer who underplays the intensity of gaze, as a Japanese might do by the standards of American or West European negotiators, may well be regarded as deceitful. As trust is an essential component in effective negotiation, negotiators require to familiarize themselves with the culture with which they are interacting. People often deliberately manipulate clues. The idea which the sender has about himself are converted into body signals which others have to decode. By creating a favorable impression on others, a negotiator can gain material advantages and sustain at the same time a positive and satisfying self-image.

When contradictory signals suggest that the self being presented is not the true one, a negotiator has to refrain from making and emphasizing points which make it clear that he knows this to be so. If a negotiator wishes to be seen to be strong and competent in the eyes of his peers and superiors in his own organization as well as in the eyes of his opposer and follows it with an ease in of demands, this many be looked on as indicating a view of his opposer as a worthy adversary to whom concession must gradually be made. A failure to make any concessions that are perceived as real by the opposer may interpreted as a reflection on the latter's own competence, particularly if he can return to his constituents with some evidence of concessions won. If we destroy his face we have destroyed the relationship.

Negotiating across cultures carries the risk of misperception arising from different in the manipulation of clues. Misinterpretation can introduce antagonisms in the relationship. In many 'Western countries there is something of a taboo on verbal presentation. While Australian have an achievement orientation they also have 'tall poppy syndrome'–one must not take too much credit for one's accomplishment or be seen to stand out above the crowd. Observers have noted a similar attitude in Sweden to setting oneself apart form others in terms of what is said and what is. In counties like India and the Arab counties, on the other hand, this is acceptable social behavior. People are not forced back into non-verbal signals as in these Western and Australian cultures. An understanding and acceptance of these difference direct verbal and non-verbal behavior in a way that can smooth the bargaining process (http://www.geocities.com/Athens/Delphi/9158/kwulectureccn8.html).

Temporal Conception

International business communication is also affected by *cross-cultural differences in temporal conception* or the understanding of time. Most U.S. and northern European businesspeople conceive of time as inflexible, a thing to be divided, used, or wasted. This is not, however, a universal view. How one uses time, consequently, may profoundly affect the way in which business is conducted in various parts of the world.

The various philosophical conceptions of time with which Western culture still operates for the most part (that is, that we use in a day-to-day commonsense way and also within most empirical-seeming schemes for organizing data) were fairly well defined by about the 5th century AD. The exception is the idea of space-time in 20th-century theory of relativity (http://www2.iath.virginia.edu/time/research/cultural.html). Cross-cultural perspectives demonstrate the biases inherent in the concepts of temporality that we take to be intuitive and which serve to organize our social relations into a network of cultural activities in accord with assumptions not universally held within belief systems outside the Euro-centric perception. The relevance of such alternate perceptions to humanistic scholarship requires attention to differences in fundamental concepts of time as well as means of calculating correspondences among distinctly different time-keeping schemes.

While it is dangerous to over-generalize, most cultures fall with varying degrees into two types of temporal conception. The first type adheres to preset schedules in which the schedules take precedence over personal interaction or over the completion of the business at hand. Edward Hall coined the term "monochronic" to describe this system of temporal organization. By contrast, those who follow what Hall termed a "polychronic" temporal organization rank personal involvement and completion of existing transactions above the demands of preset schedules.

Admittedly, not all societies can be easily divided into monochronic and polychronic systems. Often certain subsets within a society will function monochronically, while others within the same culture will function polychronically. For example, most major corporations in the United States follow a strict monochronic system. Many doctors in the United States, however, follow a comparatively polychronic system. Still on the whole, one might generalize that U.S. culture as a whole holds a monochronic conception of time.

Because people generally complete tasks at the expense of scheduling in polychronic societies, people in high authority may become easily overwhelmed with multiple tasks. To prevent overloading people in positions of high authority, those in polychronic societies often use subordinates to screen for them. Once a person can get past those screening, the person in authority will generally see the task through regardless of the relative importance of the task. Because a polychronic system encourages a one-on-one interaction, such cultural organization usually allows for highly personalized relationships to flourish between the person in authority and the task-bringer. The flow of information is open in both directions at all times. Indeed, for the system to work smoothly, it is to the advantage of both superior and subordinate to stay fully aware of all aspects—professional and personal—of each other's lives. This personal involvement makes it even harder for the person in authority to refuse once the task is presented. Thus, in such situations being able to break through those who screen for the person in authority is often the hardest part of having the person in authority assist in a task. No direct barriers exist between the leader and the subordinate; the superior will always welcome the subordinate. This develops a system in which influence and close circles of contacts among those screening for those higher up create an informal and unofficial business hierarchy.

In a monochronic system, personal feelings are rarely allowed to flourish on the job precisely because personal involvement must not be allowed to affect preset schedules if the system is to function smoothly. Personal relationships are determined by the terms of the job. Multiple tasks are handled one at a time in a prescheduled manner. People in authority are, in contrast to those in polychronic societies, available by scheduling appointments. In such a system, time screens tasks for the authority figure rather than the authority figure's subordinates or the personal relationship among the people involved.

The communication strategy for facing a generally polychronic system of time conception differs significantly from the strategy for facing a generally monochronic one. For example, in a polychronic system, one should be aware that people distinguish between insiders and those outside the existing personal relationships. One must therefore try to establish an inside connection to facilitate the effectiveness of a given message. By contrast, in a monochronic society, one needs only to schedule a meeting with the appropriate people. One should not expect people in a monochronic system to give preference to those they know over complete strangers. The outsider is treated in exactly the same fashion as the close associate.

The influence of temporal conception on communication is extensive. This is further complicated by the fact that no culture is exclusively polychronic or monochronic. Members of any culture lean to one direction or the other, although the cultures as a whole may organize their thoughts and conceive of time more one way or the other. The central issue here is to keep alert to communication differences that would indicate that one culture was more monochronic or polychronic in orientation, and to adapt one's communication strategies accordingly.

Interfacing Culture and Negotiation Strategy

A *negotiation strategy* is an integrated set of behaviors chosen because they are thought to be the means of accomplishing the goal of negotiating. All the negotiators have interests, priorities and strategies. These are affected by culture. Culture is the unique character of a social group, including the values and norms shared by members of the group and the group's social, economic, political and other institutions. Cultural values direct the attention of the negotiator to the issues that are more important and influence the negotiators' interests and priorities. Cultural norms define the behaviors that are appropriate and inappropriate in negotiation and influence the negotiators' strategies.

Effects of Culture on Interests and Priorities

- Economic Development
- Preferences for Tradition over Development
- Cultural Blinders

Cultural values may reveal the interests of the negotiators. Negotiators from cultures that value Tradition over change may be less enthusiastic about Economic Development. This was the situation in which Disney found itself after purchasing a large tract of land south of Paris to construct EuroDisney. Although EuroDisney promised jobs and economic development to an area that had high unemployment had few non-farm jobs for youth the local populace valued its traditional agricultural style. EuroDisney management with its American culture had difficulty reconciling the local population's preferences for tradition over development. Negotiators from one Culture expecting preferences to be compatible can not understand the rationality of negotiators from another culture. It is generally unwise in negotiation to label the other party as irrational. Cultural differences in preferences may also act as cultural blinders.

When people negotiate, their behaviors are strategic and their strategies may be culturally based. Not only are there differences in strategic behavior between cultures, but also within cultures and overlap between the cultures. With the result, some members of a culture may negotiate less like their own cultural prototype and more like the prototype of the another culture. Negotiation Strategies are linked with culture because cultures evolve norms to facilitate social interaction. Norms are functional because they reduce the number of choices a person has to make, about how to behave and how others in the culture will behave. Culture may also affect the strategies that the negotiators bring to the table – for example, the way they go about negotiating, whether they confront directly or indirectly, their motivations, and the way they use the information and influence.

- Confrontation
- Motivation
- Influence
- Information

Confrontation is a meeting between negotiators, either directly (face to face or electronically), or indirectly (via third party or non-verbal behavior). People from different cultures vary in their preferences for confrontation in negotiation. Western cultures are characterized by direct confrontation where as the Asian cultures by indirect confrontation.

Motivation is the factor or factors urging a person to act. It is all about negotiators' interests. Negotiators may be concerned about self-interests, about the interests of the other party at the table, or about the collective interests. The relative importance varies by culture. Western cultures prefer self-interests whereas the Asian cultures prefer collective interests.

Influence: Trying to produce a desired effects in another person, usually an attempt to obtain a concession. Power is the ability to influence the other party to accede to your wishes. Negotiators try to influence each other to make concessions by talking about their power. Influence strategies may be direct or indirect. Direct influence strategies include persuasion, argument, substantiation and threats. Indirect influence strategies include appeals to sympathy, references to personal stakes in the negotiation and references to status. A direct influence strategy focuses on the other party's interests, whereas the indirect influence strategy focuses on you.

Information: It is the knowledge or intelligence that is communicated. Information is the currency of negotiation. Negotiated agreements are constructed from information. Negotiators want full information about the other party's interests and priorities and reservation price, but they do not want to reveal the same information about themselves. Sharing information in negotiation makes you vulnerable. When you share information about your interests and priorities, the other party knows what you are willing to give up and what you must have. Negotiators can share information directly or indirectly. Direct information sharing could be a series of questions and answers, comments on mutual interests and differences, or feedback about the correctness of negotiator's influence. Indirect information sharing is a series of proposals and counter proposals, particularly multi-issue proposals.

Culture affecting Negotiation Strategy

The behaviors that negotiators from a culture characteristically use to enact a negotiation strategy are related to other features of that culture including its values and norms. The following features of culture seem to be related to the variability in negotiation strategy across cultures (http://www.indianmba.com/Faculty_Column/FC178/fc178.html):

- Individualism Vs Collectivism

- Egalitarianism Vs Hierarchy
- Low-Context Vs High-Context Communications

Individualism: A cultural value that promotes personal independence and gives self-interest a high priority among important life values.

Collectivism: A cultural value that promotes the interdependence of individuals with the social groups to which they belong and supports collective interests over self-interests as the predominant life value.

Negotiators motivational orientations may also stem from their culture's values for individualism versus collectivism. This cultural value reflects a society's goal orientation. Individualist cultures emphasize self-interests. Collectivist cultures emphasize collective interests.

Egalitarian Culture: A culture that aspires to social equality, especially in political, social and economic affairs.

Hierarchical Culture: A culture that accepts social inequality in political, social and economic affairs. It emphasizes differentiated social status that implies social power.

People in hierarchical cultures may be reluctant to confront directly in negotiation because confrontation implies a lack of respect for social status and may threaten social structures. The norm in such a culture is not to challenge higher-status members.

Low-context communication

- People prefer to communicate directly
- Meaning is on the surface of the message
- Information is explicit, without nuance, and relatively context free.

High-context communication

- People prefer to communicate indirectly
- Meaning is embedded in the context of the message and must be inferred to be understood.

Resolving Disputes

There are three ways to resolve disputes, regardless of whether the confrontation is direct or indirect

- Interests and Culture
- Rights and Culture
- Power and Culture

You can uncover the interests underlying disputants' positions and integrate those interests.

You can determine who is right and who is wrong according to some standard of fairness, contract, and law or precedent. You can determine who is more powerful and therefore who should concede.

Interests: Wants needs or concerns of negotiator, company or the other party.

Rights and Standards: Explicit and implicit rules, procedures and regulations. A trend, traditions, conflicts, asking and telling.

Power Statements: Uncooperative statements to intimidate suggest negative consequences.

Procedures for Resolving Disputes

The following are the main pragmatic approaches that can be used to resolve dispute in the course of negotiation:

- Direct Vs Indirect Confrontation and Culture
- Non-confrontation: Not really an Option
- Direct Confrontation: Negotiating the Resolution of Disputes.
- Indirect Confrontation without Third Parties.
- Indirect Confrontation and Third Party Procedures

Direct Confrontation is a face to face verbal interchange between principals. It is consistent with the action-oriented and solution-minded communication that is characteristic of low context cultures. Characteristics of Western cultures encourage the disputants to confront directly.

Indirect Confrontation is either nonverbal or conducted by agents such as lawyers or intermediaries, or through mediators (mediation skills). Characteristics of Asian cultures encourage disputants to deal with conflict indirectly (Indirect Confrontation).

Characteristics of Western Cultures

- Low-Context Communications
- Self Interests
- Egalitarian Power Distributions

Characteristics of Asian Cultures

- High-Context Communications
- Collective Interests
- Hierarchical Power Distributions

Non Confrontation

Deciding to take a direct or an indirect approach to dispute resolution presumes that unless dealt with somehow, the dispute will have dysfunctional consequences

Direct Confrontation: Negotiating the Resolution of Disputes

To be effective at resolving disputes across cultures, negotiators need to know:

- When to focus on Rights, Power, Facts and Interests.
- How to change the focus from Rights or Power to Interests.
- How to choose among different types of communication

When to focus on Interests, Rights and Power

When you think that you have a rights standard, the other party will recognize the weakness of its own position and come to an agreement.

When you want to make it clear that if the dispute cannot be resolved you will go to the third party.

How to change the focus from Rights or Power to Interests

- Do not reciprocate with an emotional outburst
- Declare the process ineffective
- Combine reciprocity with a change of focus

Choosing how to communicate

- Face to face negotiations
- Electronic negotiations
- Negotiating through agents

Indirect Confrontation without Third Parties

A claimant may use non-verbal behavior to express dismay at a claim's being rejected like slamming doors, pounding fists etc. Another form of indirect confrontation is amassing information that you arrange to have delivered to the other party.

Indirect Confrontation and Third Party Procedures for Dispute Resolution

Procedures with Authority

- Litigation
- Arbitration
- Hierarchy

Procedures without Authority

- Mediation

Government at and around the table

- The Interests of Government in cross-cultural Negotiations may not be cost or profitability but will be social, economic and political.
- Ideology: Private investment, Profits and Individual Rights.
- Advice for dealing with Government Interests, Particularly Human Rights Issues.
- Political and Economic Stability
- Hedging Political Risks
- Hedging Economic Risks
- Power of the Bureaucracy
- Dealing with Corruption
- Advice for making Ethical Decisions in Cross-Cultural Negotiations
- Legal context for Dispute Resolution in Cross-Cultural Negotiations.

Negotiation is about claiming value; how much a set of resources you are going to get and how much the other party gets. Successful Value-Claiming Negotiation leads to a distributive outcome that divides a fixed set of resources such that your interests or the needs underlying your positions are met. But negotiation can also be about creating value; how you and the other party can increase the resources available to divide. Successful Value-Creating Negotiation leads to an agreement that is both integrative and distributive, one that divides an enhanced set of resources.

General Impact of Culture on Business Negotiations

Influences Exerted by Cultural Differences

In international business settings, the progress of the negotiation process and the parties' apprehension of their relationship are under the influence of some factors, among which Cultural differences play a crucial role. Culture is a major determinant of strategies and tactics in international business negotiations, because negotiations involve communication, time and power and these variables differ across cultures. Cultural differences create a challenge to the negotiators involved, and demand understanding as well as flexibility. An ability to assess these differences and properly handle the consequences is essential for achieving success in international business negotiations.

Culture has influences over all the basic elements of negotiation. It can influence the behavioral predispositions of negotiators. For example, some cultures place group over the individual, some to the contrary. This kind of distinction stemming from their respective cultures will inevitably have different influence on people's attitude toward power distance among social members, people's basis for trust, people's goal orientation, people's way of making decisions and people's tendency to take risks.

Culture has impacts on people's perception of negotiation and consequently the strategies they take. Some cultures regard the negotiation as a problem-solving process and are more likely to adopt an integrative strategy while some others tend to see it as a competition and have a strong aversion to the concept of "compromise". People from some cultures are long-term oriented and they can sacrifice short-term profits if they can sense future gains whereas people from some other cultures are short-term oriented and try to get as much as they can in the one-off deal.

Culture also influences the structure of the negotiation. Preference for sites and dates differs across cultures. Composition of the negotiating team also varies greatly. Some cultures regard time as money and would like to set fixed agendas, but some feel that time is abundant and humans should not follow blindly the timetable.

During the negotiation process, culture plays an important role, too. People from different cultures may have different ways of handling issues, some preferring sequential approach while others a holistic one. Some may depend more on verbal communications and some more on non-verbal ones. People also have different outcome orientations. People from some cultures look for a contract while others for a relationship. Some prefer a detailed written agreement, others an agreement with general guidelines.

According to Hendon *et al.* (1996), culture impacts negotiation in four ways: by conditioning one's perception of reality; by blocking out information inconsistent or unfamiliar with culturally grounded assumptions; by projecting meaning onto the other party's words and actions; and by impelling the ethnocentric observer to an incorrect attribution of motive. Negotiators bring to the negotiating table the values, beliefs and background interference of their own culture. These elements influence, without their awareness, their conceptualization of the negotiation process, the objectives they seek in the negotiation, the means they adopt to pursue their goals and the expectations they hold of the behaviors of their partners. Ample evidence exists that negotiation rules and practice differ across cultures.

Consequences Caused by Cultural Differences

Cultural differences have a profound impact on how successfully or unsuccessfully the parties are able to negotiate. They can generate misunderstandings, sow the seeds of distrust, and/or generate negative emotions among the negotiators. When negotiators differ in their basic thought processes, misunderstandings are all but inevitable. For example, Americans are generally not as concerned with building long-term associations as they are with getting their immediate business issues resolved (just as Americans are not as concerned about the long-term business picture as they are about quarterly profits). This means that Americans enter the first meeting expecting an issue-oriented outcome, often through a process of bargaining. For Chinese, however, bargaining too soon can be a sign of untrustworthiness. In Chinese culture it is customary for the negotiators to strive to establish a relationship prior to dealing with task-related issues; resolving a particular issue is simply not the first goal. Their misunderstandings of each other obviously originate from their different thought processes. As a matter of fact, there are a myriad of ways through which conflicting patterns of thinking may impede effective negotiating.

The irony is that negotiators might not even be aware of the fact that they are making biased judgments! The inability to recognize the partiality of the judgments made by negotiators has a number of consequences. First, it can slow down the process of any negotiations, if not disrupt them entirely. Second, misunderstandings prevent negotiators from maximizing joint gains from the business interaction. Moreover, cultural differences can also damage trust between sides in a negotiation, or worse, sow the seeds of distrust. When negotiators do not trust each other they are unlikely to share information for fear of being taken advantage of. They are also likely to be overcritical of the positions advanced by the other negotiator. For example, they may look for flaws or errors where none exist and/or invent reasons as to why the deal may not be possible. Finally, the lack of trust lessens the motivation of the negotiators to bridge the differences that exist between them.

Cultural clashes also have the potential of generating negative emotional reactions between parties in a transaction. The General Motors-Volkswagen conflict and the Enron-India saga are all examples of situations where emotions ran high among the parties. The consequences resulting from cultural differences are a great danger for smooth negotiation in the international setting. Therefore, understanding the different cultural environments that exist among nations and considering cultural differences in all facets of business are of great significance to the operation of international business negotiations. Transcending cultural limits is a formidable but essential task if negotiations with foreign parties are to succeed.

Indian Cultural Values: A Blend of East and West

The Indian culture has been shaped by a wide variety of influences that include Hindu philosophy, British colonialism, Islamic influences and the *real-politik* of the Cold War era. The influences are varied both in terms of the content, their timing and their durability. Clearly, the Hindu philosophy has had a profound impact on the basic belief structure of the Indians, and its importance is self-evident given that more than 80 per cent of the population in India is Hindu. British colonialism or imperialism has sharply coloured the way in which the Indians interact with the West. Islamic influences have no doubt affected the social texture in certain parts of the country, but other than that, and the latent tension between the Hindus and the Muslims, which occasionally erupts, Islam does not play an important role. Finally, with the steady improvement of relations between India and the United States, the tensions of the Cold War era between India and the United States seem to have all but disappeared. Both India and the United States now seem to be showing a new fondness for each other, even though outsourcing concerns, have, of late, highlighted some tensions between the two countries (Rajesh Kumar(2005), Negotiating with the complex, imaginative Indian, Ivey Business Journal March/April 2005: (http://www.iveybusinessjournal.com/view_article.asp?intArticle_ID=544)

(a) Coexistence of Individualism and Collectivism

A unique feature of the Indian mindset is that it combines both individualistic and collectivist tendencies. As individualists, Indians are very goal oriented and aggressive, traits that are not unlike those of the North Americans. At the same time, however, the Indians are a very family-oriented people and confine and ration their loyalties and affections only among those who are close to them.

It is the simultaneous presence of individualism and collectivism that distinguishes the Indian manager not only from his North American counterpart but also from his East Asian peer who is unquestioningly collectivist in his or her orientation. Scholars have long debated whether India is part of the East or the West. They have come to the conclusion that the Indians are, on the whole, more Western than Eastern in their way of thinking. This implies that the Indians can behave either in an individualistic or a collectivist manner, depending on the situation.

The heightened context sensitivity of the Indian manager may make it difficult for the North American manager to fully understand his counterpart's actions. As a Western manager put it, "I feel that the most difficult thing is that the Indians will tell you one thing, think another, and do a third thing, which is not what a Dane would do." A further implication is that the Indian negotiator is not a good team player. Beyond the confines of the familial in-group, the Indian negotiator does not work well as part of a team due to the ingrained belief that he is right and the other person is wrong. I refer to this tendency as "anarchical individualism."

(b) An Idealistic Bent of Mind

To the outside observer, India is a country that has a very well-developed spiritual tradition. Philosophical reflections have loomed large in the Indian cultural context, but it is important to note that these have gone hand in hand with the development of an exceptional ability to analyze. The rapid development of the software industry in India, which has done much to improve the country's image, would not have been possible without such a skill. When transferred to a business-related context, the idealistic mindset means that the Indian manager has high aspirations for what he/she would like to It is the simultaneous presence of individualism and collectivism that distinguishes the Indian manager not only from his North American counterpart but also from his East Asian peer who is unquestioningly collectivist in his or her orientation. It also has the implication that the Indian manager can be very discerning and may easily find flaws in arguments. The idealism that the Indian manager brings to bear is often designed to attain the best possible solution to a problem. This can be both beneficial as well as detrimental to creative problem solving.

(c) Nationalism

A Pew Center study recently found that India was the most nationalistic place on the earth. People are very sensitive to any action by foreigners, and in particular, investment actions that may be viewed as detrimental to the country's welfare. Although such sentiment is not unique to India *per se,* it is probably more easily aroused here than in many other countries. The high degree of nationalistic sentiment is a product both of British imperialism and the strained relations between the United States and India during the Cold War. Nationalistic sentiment has a number of implications. First, foreign investors may be held to a higher standard than the local firms. It also implies that foreign investors' projects, especially highly visible ones, will be evaluated very closely. Third, foreign investors will be constantly under pressure to gain and maintain their legitimacy in the eyes of the stakeholders.

(d) Attitude Towards Time

Unlike North Americans, the Indians have a subjective view of time. A recent study of negotiators from 12 different cultures found that the Indians were the least sensitive to time considerations (Salacuse, 2004). This lack of sensitivity to time stems from the fact that Indians do not feel the same sense of urgency to conquer the world as North Americans. They have more of a "being" than a "doing" orientation, and this difference in the orientation to the world is likely to affect their sensitivity to time.

(e) Hierarchical Culture

The Indian culture is hierarchical. Top-down decision-making is the norm, and more often than not there is only a downward flow of information in an organization. Subordinates will rarely, if ever, disagree with their superiors, even though they may disagree with the nature of the decision or the manner of its implementation. This hierarchical character is accompanied by a parallel tendency for the subordinates to want to be nurtured by their be benevolent towards them, and if this benevolence is reciprocated, the subordinate is also likely to respond by remaining loyal. Cultural values and the Indian negotiating style Negotiation is an important managerial skill. The acceleration of globalization and the opening up of markets in Latin America, Eastern Europe and Asia have underlined the importance of culture in influencing negotiation processes and outcomes.

Much has been written about the role that culture plays in shaping negotiating outcomes, although it would be fair to say that exploration of this matter with respect to India is sparse. A common theme in much of the literature on cross-cultural negotiations is that the negotiating style varies across cultures, and that differences in negotiation styles often lead to a breakdown of negotiations. These differences, if unanticipated and/or not effectively managed, can give rise to negative emotions such as anger and may provoke distrust.

The core Indian cultural values that we have described paint a portrait of the Indian negotiator as a complex, highly imaginative individual. The complexity derives from the fact that his or her behaviour is influenced by cultural values that are associated with inconsistent behavioural patterns. Thus, as an individualist, the Indian negotiator may be highly aggressive; at the same time, as a collectivist, he or she may be passive and reluctant to express his or her views absent consensus. The negotiator's rich imagination may express itself in high aspirations, creative problem solving and/or excessive paranoia in which he or she is able to find problems just about everywhere. This may be further fuelled by a high degree of nationalism.

Factors to be Considered in International Business Environment

The impact of international business in domestic markets compels us to ask a question: "How can we survive in this global playing field, and what can we do to run our businesses more effectively?" Nowadays, businesses of all sizes search for suppliers and customers on a global level. International competition, foreign clients and suppliers may become a danger, but they may also create huge opportunities to develop our business. The increasingly global business environment requires managers to approach the negotiation process from the global business person's point of view. This approach includes aspects which are usually unimportant in domestic negotiations. Some of the components of a cross cultural negotiation process are more complex and difficult, but will increase our success in avoiding barriers and failures in the international business arena. When doing business internationally, we need to consider (Salacuse, 1991):

1. The negotiating environment
2. Cultural and sub-cultural differences
3. Ideological differences
4. Foreign bureaucracy
5. Foreign laws and governments
6. Financial insecurity due to international monetary factors
7. Political instability and economic changes

If we consider the fact that negotiating with our fellow citizen is not an easy task due to many individual differences, it would be reasonable to suggest that negotiating with foreigners may be even more difficult. The way we perceive and create our own reality may be completely different to our counterpart's way of thinking, behaving and feeling. Unfortunately, knowledge of any foreign language is not enough to face and solve the problem. Language is a cluster of codes used in communication which, if not shared effectively, can act as a barrier to establish credibility and trust. We need more effective tools, and the most important is knowledge of all factors that can influence the proceedings. Nations tend to have a national character that influences the type of goals and process the society pursues in negotiations. This is why specifying and understanding cultural differences is vital in order to perform successfully in inter-cultural communication. As we better understand that our partners may see things differently, we will be less likely to make negative assumptions and more likely to make progress when negotiating.

Negotiating Goal and Basic Concept

How is the negotiation being seen? Is mutual satisfaction the real purpose of the meeting? Do we have to compete? Do they want to win? Different cultures stress different aspects of negotiation. The goal of business negotiation may be a substantive outcome (Americans) or a long-lasting relationship (viz.Japanese). These are some of the basic ingredients, linked to the basic concept of negotiation that need to be considered for preparing the negotiation goals:

Protocol: There are as many kinds of business etiquette as there are nations in the world. Protocol factors that should be considered are dress codes, number of negotiators, entertainment, degree of formality, gift giving, meeting and greeting, etc.

Communications: Verbal and non-verbal communication is a key factor of persuasion. The way we express our needs and feelings using body language and tone of voice can determine the way the other side perceives us, and in fact positively or negatively contributes to our credibility. Another aspect of communication relevant to negotiation is the direct or indirect approach to exchanging information. Is the meaning of what is said exactly in the words themselves? Does "...it's impossible" really mean impossible or just difficult to realize? Always use questions to identify the other side's needs, otherwise assumptions may result in you never finding common interests.

Risk-Taking Propensity—Uncertainty Avoidance: There is always risk involved in negotiations. The final outcome is unknown when the negotiations commence. The most common dilemma is related to personal relations between counterparts: Should we trust them? Will they trust us? Certain cultures are more risk averse than others, e.g. Japan (Hofstede, 1980). It means that less innovative and creative alternatives are available to pursue during the negotiation, unless there is a strong trust-based relationship between the counterparts.

View of Time: In some cultures time is money and something to be used wisely. Punctuality and agenda may be an important aspect of negotiation. In countries such as China or Japan, being late would be taken as an insult. Consider investing more time in the negotiating process in Japan. The main goal when negotiating with an oriental counterpart is to establish a firm relationship, which takes time. Another dimension of time relevant to negotiation is the focus on past, present or future. Sometimes the past or the distant future may be seen as part of the present, especially in Latin American countries.

Decision-Making System: The way members of the other negotiating team reach a decision may give us a hint: who we shall focus on providing our presentation. When negotiating with a team, it's crucial to identify who is the leader and who has the authority to make a decision.

Form of Agreement: In most cultures, only written agreements stamp a deal. It seems to be the best way to secure our interests in case of any unexpected circumstances. The 'deal' may be the contract itself or the relationship between the parties, like in China, where a contract is likely to be in the form of general principles. In this case, if any unexpected circumstances arise, parties prefer to focus on the relationship than the contract to solve the problem.

Power Distance: This refers to the acceptance of authority differences between people. Cultures with low *power distance* postulate equality among people, and focus more on earned status than ascribed status. Negotiators from countries like Britain, Germany and Austria tend to be comfortable with shared authority and democratic structures. When we face a high *power distance* culture, be prepared for hierarchical structures and clear authority figures.

Personal Style: Our individual attitude towards the other side and biases which we sometimes establish all determine our assumptions that may lead the negotiation process towards win-win or win-lose solutions. Do we feel more comfortable using a formal or informal approach to communication? In some cultures, like America, an informal style may help to create friendly relationships and accelerate the problem solving solution. In China, by comparison, an informal approach is proper only when the relationship is firm and sealed with trust.

Coping with Culture

Negotiating in the international environment is a huge challenge for any negotiator. How do we cope with the cultural differences? What approach is more efficient and proper when dealing with Japanese, Americans or Germans? There are some very helpful guidelines we can apply (Salacuse, 1991):

1. *Learn the other side's culture*

It is very important to know the commonest basic components of our counterparty's culture. It's a sign of respect and a way to build trust and credibility as well as advantage that can help us to choose the right strategies and tactics during the negotiation. Of course, it's impossible to learn another culture in detail when we learn at short notice that a foreign delegation is visiting in two weeks' time. The best we can do is to try to identify principal influences that the foreign culture may have on making the deal.

2. *Don't be stereotypic*

Making assumptions can create distrust and barriers that expose both your and the other side's needs, positions and goals. The way we view other people tends to be reserved and cautious. We usually expect people to take advantage of a situation, and during the negotiations the other side probably thinks the same way, especially when there is a lack of trust between counterparts. In stead of generalizing, we should make an effort to treat everyone as individuals. Find the other side's values and beliefs independently of values and beliefs characteristic of the culture or group being represented by your counterpart.

3. *Find ways to bridge the cultural gap*

Apart from adopting the other side's culture to adjust to the situation and environment, we can also try to persuade the other side to use elements of our own culture. In some situations it is also possible to use a combination of both cultures, for example, regarding joint venture businesses. Another possible solution is to adopt a third culture, which can be a strong base for personal relationships. When there is a difficulty in finding common ground, focusing on common professional cultures may be the initiation of business relations.

Critical Culture Factors in Business Negotiation

Language goes beyond the spoken word, encompassing nonverbal actions and behaviors that reveal hidden clues to culture. In the negotiation process, interpersonal communication is the key activity that takes place at the verbal, nonverbal, situational contextual level, and a total communication system can assist the negotiator to bridge the gap between utterance and felt meaning. Three key topics such as time, space, body language etc offer a starting point from which negotiators can begin to acquire the understanding necessary to do business in foreign countries.

Time

Two different orientations to time exist across the world: monochromic and polychromic. Monochromic approaches to time are linear, sequential and involve focusing on one thing at a time. These approaches are most common in the European-influenced cultures of the United States, Germany, Switzerland, and the Scandinavia. Japanese people also tend toward this end of the time continuum. Polychromic orientations to time involve working on several activities simultaneously. The time it takes to complete an interaction is elastic, and more important than any schedule. This orientation is most common in Mediterranean and Latin cultures including France, Italy, Greece, and Mexico, as well as some Eastern and African cultures.

Space

Space orientations differ across cultures. They have to do with territory, divisions between private and public, comfortable personal distance, comfort or lack of comfort with physical touch and contact, and expectations about where and how contact will take place. For example, an American etiquette manual advises this about personal space: "When you meet someone, don't stand too close. An uncomfortable closeness is very annoying to the other person, so keep your physical distance, or he will have to keep backing off from you. A minimum of two feet away from the other person will do it." There are large differences in spatial preferences according to gender, age, generation, socioeconomic class, and context. These differences vary by group, but should be considered in any exploration of space as a variable in negotiations.

Body Language

Body Language can be telling as it can help one determine the exact meaning of what the other side is saying and also can help you get your own message across. Likes and dislikes, tensions, and assessing an argument are shown by numerous signs such as blushing, contraction of facial muscles, giggling, strained laughter or simply silence. Wherever a party negotiates, the negotiator must watch and observe the other party. People, when seated, lean forward if they like what you are saying or are interested in listening. They sit back with crossed arms if they do not like the message. Nervousness can manifest itself through nonverbal behavior, and blinking can be related to feeling of guilt or fear.

Hofstede's Five Dimensions of Culture

One well-known way of analyzing human culture is that of Dutch anthropologist, Geert Hofstede, who developed his theories of cross-cultural communication through interviews with international business persons (Hofstede, 2001).

According to Hofstede, each culture must deal with questions that can be resolved according to a series of dimensions, which results in a unique gestalt for each society, depending on the intensity of its tendency towards one or another end of each culture dimension spectrum (http://workabroadtravel.suite101.com/article.cfm/hofstedes_five_dimensions_of_culture).

The Five Dimensions

Individualism/Collectivism: the point here is whether people see themselves at a very deep level as part of a group, or as a single, independent actor. Hofstede emphasizes that the groups are "natural" ones, such as family or clan, not just any group that one happens across. Also, it is important to realize that the dimension does not indicate that some people "like" to be in groups. It is a question of human self-identity.

Uncertainty Avoidance: (Note that the dimensions are not given in any particular order, they work together to describe a culture.) In some cultures, people prefer to have everything spelled out in detail so there will be few, if any surprises. In cultures where Uncertainty Avoidance is low, people have more relaxed expectations and are not anxious when some factors of a situation are unknown.

Power Distance: hierarchy is a feature of most human life, but in some cultures, the relative gap between high and low is wider, making for a society in which people respect the powerful, and there is lower expectation of movement between classes, castes, or levels. In cultures where Power Distance is low, people tend to expect that those in power will have earned it, rather than simply gaining power by virtue of position.

Aggressiveness: within this system, there is a gender gap, and women's values are said to be more similar across cultures. Women are said to value gentleness and consensus seeking, and in cultures with a low Aggressiveness dimension, men also share these values. However, other cultures have more distinctive values for men: competition, assertiveness and "looking out for Number One." In such cultures, the values of women also move somewhat towards the Aggressiveness end of the spectrum, although not as much as men's do.

Long-Term/Short-Term Orientation: long-term planning, thrift, and industriousness are valued in cultures with Long Term orientation, whereas living for the day, celebration, and concerns like "saving face" are more important in those with Short Term orientation. The Long Term end of the continuum is associated with what are sometimes called Confucian values, although cultures not historically connected with this influence can also have a Long Term orientation.

Useful Rules for Crossing Cultures

These five dimensions, taken together, can give important insights for someone wishing to enter a new culture for business, study, or other purposes. It is important to resist the temptation of stereotyping, because these dimensions are *tendencies* not static descriptions of people's behavior. They can be taken to predict actions of groups, societies, or nations, but provide little help in predicting the behavior of individuals.

Hofstede's Five Dimensions theory has been criticized on the grounds of being too static (Holden, Nigel.,2002), or of being based on a weak theoretical foundation (Dahl, Stephan,2004), but it is a well-known framework for cross-cultural dialogue. It will more than repay careful study, and international business persons and others will find it widely used (and misused) all over the world. Any analysis of culture is incomplete without the basic recognition of cultural differences. It has been argued that differences among cultures can be explained according to four dimensions of culture; which in a way characterizes the culture itself (http://workabroadtravel.suite101.com/article.cfm/hofstedes_five_dimensions_of_culture).

Individualism-Collectivism

In individualistic cultures the focus of one's behavior can be unashamedly self-centered. The individual can make objections, state his feelings and be openly judgmental. Success or failure is left to the individual and does not cause the same degree of shame among the group. In individualistic cultures, people tend to put tasks before relationships and to value independence highly. People in these cultures are expected to take care of themselves and to value the needs of the individual over those of the groups, community, or society. Individualistic cultures prefer linear logic and tend to value open conflict.

Members from individualistic societies expect the other side's negotiators to have the ability to make decisions unilaterally. Collectivist negotiators tend to assume that details can be worked out if the negotiators can agree on generalities. Collectivist societies show more concern for the needs of the other party and focus more on group goals than individualistic societies. Members of collectivist societies chafe when members from individualistic societies promote their own positions and ideas during negotiations.

Power Differential

The idea of power differential describes the degree of deference and acceptance of unequal power between people. Cultures where there is a comfort with high power differential are those where some people are considered superior to others because of their social status, gender, race, age, education, birthright, personal achievements, family background or other factors. Cultures with low power differential tend to assume equality among people, and focus more on earned status than ascribed status. Generally speaking, the more unequally wealth is distributed, the bigger will be the power differential in any national setting. National cultures with a high power differential include Arabian countries, Malaysia, the Philippines, Mexico, Indonesia, and India. Negotiators from these countries tend to be comfortable with: hierarchical structures; clear authority figures; the right to use power with discretion. Countries with a low power differential include U.S., Austria, Denmark, Israel, New Zealand, Ireland, Sweden, Norway, Finland, Switzerland, Britain, and Germany. Negotiators from these countries tend to be comfortable with: democratic structures and flat organizational hierarchies; shared authority; the right to use power only in limited circumstances and for legitimate purposes.

Uncertainty Avoidance

The idea of uncertainty avoidance has to do with the way cultures relate to uncertainty and ambiguity, and, how well they may adapt to changes. In general, countries that show the most discomfort with ambiguity and uncertainty include Muslim countries and traditional African countries, where high value is placed on conformity and safety, risk avoidance, and reliance on formal rules and rituals. Trust tends to be vested only in family and close friends. It may be difficult for outside negotiators to establish relationships of confidence and trust with members of these cultures. The United States, Scandinavia, and Singapore are identified as having a higher tolerance for uncertainty. Members of these cultures tend to value risk-taking, problem-solving, flat organizational structures, and tolerance for ambiguity. It may be easier for outsiders to establish trusting relationships with negotiating partners in these cultural contexts.

Masculinity-Femininity

The terms masculinity and femininity are used to refer to the degree to which a culture values assertiveness or nurturing and social support. The terms also refer to the degree to which socially prescribed roles operate for men and women. Countries and regions such as Japan and Latin America are rated as preferring values of assertiveness, task-orientation, and achievement. In these cultures, there tend to be more rigid gender roles and "live to work" orientations. In countries and regions rated feminine, such as Scandinavia, Thailand, and Portugal, values of cooperation, nurturing, relationship and solidarity with those less fortunate prevail, and the moral belief is more one of "work to live". Of course, it is important to remember that associations with gender vary greatly across cultures, so that elements considered masculine in one culture might be considered feminine in another. Negotiators may find it useful to consider the way gender roles play out in the cultural contexts of their negotiating partners.

Negotiating Style

It must be emphasized that there is no one right approach to negotiations. There are only effective and less effective approaches and these vary according to many contextual factors. As negotiators understand that their counterparts may be seeing things very differently, they will be less likely to make negative judgments and more likely to make progress in negotiations. The research and observations by most scholars indicate fairly clearly that negotiation practices differ from culture to culture and that culture can influence "negotiating style"—the way persons from different cultures conduct themselves in negotiating sessions.

For example, U.S. negotiators tend to rely on individualist values, imagining self and other as autonomous, independent, and self-reliant. This does not mean that they don't consult, but the tendency to see self as separate rather than as a member of a web or network means that more independent initiatives may be taken. American negotiators tend to be competitive in their approach to negotiations, including coming to the table with a fallback position but beginning with an unrealistic offer.

Therefore, the American negotiators often act in an impersonal way—"business is business" is their maxim. Besides, American negotiators are always mission-driven—anxious to bring parties concerned into agreement, and they have little interest in building up any relationship. Furthermore, American negotiators like to be openly challenged for the negotiation, and they think it is quite normal if they run into any conflict with any party concerned.

Chinese negotiators also look forward to long-term partnership. Unlike America negotiators, they are not in a hurry to push for an agreement. Generally there is a slow start to "warm up", and then it is followed by some tentative suggestions. Like their Japanese counterparts, Chinese negotiators do not expect any open conflict for whatever reasons, and they are trying to "save face" for both sides.

The Chinese are reserved and known for their hospitality and good manners. The Chinese consider mutual relationships and trust very important. Therefore, time will be spent in the beginning enjoying tea and social talk. However, they are some of the toughest negotiators in the eyes of foreign negotiators. Technical competence of negotiators is necessary, and a non-condescending attitude is important because the Chinese research their opponents thoroughly to gain a competitive advantage during negotiation. Nothing is final until it is signed; and they prefer to use an intermediary. The Chinese delegation will be large. They rarely use lawyers, and interpreters may have inadequate language skills and experience. Although Chinese negotiators imply that there is no compromise or third choice, in reality there is ample room for compromise.

Even as different approaches to negotiation across national cultures are identified, change is constant. International business culture tends to privilege Western approaches to negotiation, centering on problem-solving and linear communication, as do many settings. As Western norms are balanced with Eastern values, and local traditions are balanced with regional and national approaches, negotiation practices continue their global evolution. Culture can influence the way in which persons perceive and approach certain key elements in the negotiating process. Knowledge of these cultural differences may help negotiators to better understand and interpret their counterpart's negotiating behavior and to find ways to bridge gaps created by cultural differences. Equally important, professional and occupational culture may be as important as national culture in shaping a person's negotiating style and attitudes toward the negotiation process. If true, negotiators should at least note two important implications. First, practitioners need to take into account professional culture, as well as national culture, in their studies and analysis of the impact of culture on negotiating table, negotiators from different cultures but with similar occupational or professional backgrounds might seek to the elements of their professional culture in trying to bridge the cultural gap between them.

Culture-Negotiation Nexus

There has been much research in the field of negotiation, and there is fortunately now a good deal of information around that can guide us in our quest to become better negotiators. Most likely, as with many of the other skills mentioned in the paper, we have to learn how to negotiate through trial and error. Most likely, we have developed particular individual styles that we are comfortable with. However, research has shown that there are certain ways of negotiating that are simply more productive than others. Most important to us here, perhaps, is the fact that the research on effective versus less effective international negotiation styles seems to support certain aspects of the way some cultures negotiate, while discouraging other aspects.

Negotiators as members of society are led easily into attitudes of cultural bias. The only way to overcome that bias is to create awareness of one's own cultural system by understanding how other people behave in another system. The negotiator, from his knowledge of his opponent's culture and his sensitivity to it, can adapt his behavior to the situation and serve the interests of the interaction. The more and better the communication, the greater the amount of information shared or extracted, and the greater the build-up of trust, the more likely is the possibility of creating the satisfaction that negotiators are exchanging at the end of the day. In order to be effective the negotiators operate as detectives searching for clues to the values and interests of their counterparts. They avoid assumptions about partner concerns; they look for what does matter to the partner rather than what should matter. In short, they must be careful not to allow cultural stereotypes to determine his or her relations with local businesspersons.

The Impact of Culture on the Negotiation Process

Situations involving negotiation happen more frequently than we imagine in the workplace and in our personal lives. We negotiate with our boss, our co-workers, customers, suppliers, our spouse and our children. The desired outcome of most negotiations is an agreement that both parties find acceptable and can live with (although not always "fair" to both parties). International and cross-cultural negotiations can be particularly problematic because of the complex interaction of business culture, country culture, verbal and non-verbal communication. Like leadership, the process of cross-cultural negotiation brings to bear a complex set of cross-cultural interactions. First, we must understand ourselves and how we are perceived by others in cross-cultural negotiations. The following is a list of positive and negative traits that are displayed by Americans in international negotiations situations (Mark Kenczyk http://www.negotiationtraining.com/images/Cross-Cultural_Negotiations.doc):

Positive American Traits

- Friendliness
- Fairness
- Flexibility
- Innovativeness
- Cooperative
- Good Preparation
- Clear and to the Point
- Pragmatic
- Can See the other Party's Point of View
- Utilize Concessions Effectively
- Decisive

Negative American Traits

- Impatient
- Arrogant
- Quick to Concede
- Underestimate Importance of Relationships
- Overly Focused on Analytics
- Poor Listening Skills (don't perceive the non-verbal cues?)
- Naïveté
- Overly Legalistic
- Short-term perspective
- Too much emphasis on quantitative vs. qualitative issues

Imagine an American businessman negotiating a complex business deal in Southeast Asia. The American is individualistic, decisive, impatient, ego driven, friendly and pragmatic. The Asians may be patient, unassuming, group oriented, decide through consensus, and feel that the relationship and the "person" are more important than the details of the business deal. Without some type of cross-cultural understanding or moderating influence, the negotiations are not going to proceed positively to the benefit of either party. We have a mixture of oil and water.

It is important to remember that cultural differences can influence and change the rules of the game. In some cultures the relationship is far more important than the details of the agreement. In another cultural setting (such as American), the relationship is merely an incidental while the details are critical. When relationships are critical, the negotiator may be the single most important ingredient to a successful negotiation outcome. It is impossible for me or any author to develop a winning list of international negotiation do's and don'ts that would work in most situations. After a lot of study of negotiating techniques and the personal experience of doing business in more than a dozen different countries, I offer the following advice about international business negotiations:

1. Individuals are unique and may differ from cultural generalizations.
2. Increasingly, people involved in international business have developed sophisticated "multi-cultural" styles and are very adaptive to new situations.
3. The cultures in countries, and within individuals, are constantly changing.
4. Every business situation and negotiation is unique and success depends upon an ability to "feel", learn and adapt as the process progresses.
5. Who you are and what you believe in impacts the dynamics of every communication and the outcome of every negotiation.
6. Avoid stereotyping through the rigid application of cultural guidelines and "rules".
7. Rules, guidelines and generalizations will help to minimize cross-cultural pitfalls while you develop your own personal observations and understanding.
8. Try to be free of value judgments.
9. There is no substitute for being polite, patient, flexible, adaptable, and having willingness to change and learn.

Culture-based Negotiation Styles

In an anonymous article, a Japanese writer describes United States negotiators as hard to understand. One of the reasons for this, we are told, is because "unlike Japanese, the Americans are not racially or culturally homogenous." While it is difficult to characterize any national or cultural approach to negotiation, generalizations are frequently drawn. These generalizations are helpful to the extent that the reader remembers that they are only guides. Any generalization holds true or not depending on many contextual factors including time, setting, situation, stakes, history between the parties, nature of the issue, individual preferences, interpersonal dynamics and mood (LeBaron, 2003: http://peacebuilding.caritas.org/index.php/6th_Module_Negotiation,_Conflict_and_Culture)

Any generalization will apply to some members of a group some of the time. This is best seen by considering generalizations about groups to which you belong. If you hear that women or men tend to negotiate in this way, or Americans in another way, what effect does it have on you as a member of these groups? If you want to answer, "Actually, it depends," you are among the majority, for most of us resist easy categorization and broad classifications. At the same time, it can be useful to back up and attempt to see ourselves and others from a distance so that the patterns and habits that define what is "normal" in negotiation can be examined for what they are: culturally bound and culturally defined common sense.

Before outlining these generalizations, a caveat: most of the ways of studying culture, communication, and negotiation are derived largely from Western concepts. When a U.S. or Western European instrument to measure assertiveness in negotiation is translated into Japanese, for example, it retains Western assumptions about the nature of assertiveness. A Japanese idea of assertiveness that included avoidance as an adaptive and appropriate strategy could be easily missed, labeled as unassertive because of cultural assumptions about the natures of assertion and avoidance. Because of the lack of good studies that take an intercultural approach (using a variety of starting points and currencies in developing the research itself and a multicultural team to carry it out), the generalizations that follow are limited. More research is being done on culture-specific approaches by insiders of various non-Western cultures, and some intercultural research is also being conducted—these should be carefully examined as they become available.

Cross-Cultural Negotiations: A Case Study

It is difficult to track the myriad starting points used by negotiators from different national settings, especially as cultures are in constant flux, and context influences behavior in multiple ways. Another complication is that much of the cross-cultural negotiation literature comes from the organizational area. While it cannot be applied wholesale to the realm of intractable conflicts, this literature may provide some hints about approaches to negotiation in various national settings. Dr. Nancy Adler compares key indicators of success as reported by negotiators from four national backgrounds. Her table is reproduced here, ranking characteristics of negotiators in order of importance as reported by Managers in each national setting (see table below)

As Adler points out, Brazilians and Americans were almost identical in the characteristics they identified, except for the final category. The Japanese tended to emphasize an interpersonal negotiating style, stressing verbal expressiveness, and listening ability, while their American and Brazilian counterparts focused more on verbal ability, planning, and judgment. To the Chinese in Taiwan, it was important that the negotiator be an interesting person who shows persistence and determination.

Negotiators also vary in the styles of persuasion they rely upon and their comfort with emotionality. In American settings, appeals tend to be made to logic, relying on "objective" facts. Emotional sensitivity is not highly valued, and dealings may seem straightforward and impersonal. Japanese negotiators value emotional sensitivity highly, and tend to hide emotions behind calm exteriors. Latin American negotiators tend to share the Japanese appreciation of emotional sensitivity, and express themselves passionately about their points of view. Arab negotiators may appeal to emotions and subjective feelings in an effort to persuade others. Russians, in contrast, tend to appeal to ideals, drawing everyone's attention to overarching principles.

Many other cultural differences have been identified by negotiation scholars. Some of these differences are discussed in the other Beyond Intractability essays regarding culture and conflict resolution (Culture and Conflict Resolution, Cultural and Worldview Frames, Cross-Cultural Communication, and/or Communication Tools for Understanding Cultural Differences). This study concludes with negotiating styles associated with national and regional cultures. As with all cultural patterns, these generalizations do not apply to every circumstance or individual. They are general patterns that will shift as cultures and contexts shift.

U.S. Approaches to Negotiation

U.S. negotiators tend to rely on individualist values, imagining self and other as autonomous, independent, and self-reliant. This does not mean that they don't consult, but the tendency to see self as separate rather than as a member of a web or network means that more independent initiative may be

AMERICAN NEGOTIATORS	JAPANESE NEGOTIATORS	CHINESE (TAIWAN) NEGOTIATORS	BRAZILIAN NEGOTIATORS
Preparation and planning skill	Dedication to job	Persistence and determination	Preparation and planning skill
Thinking under pressure	Perceive and exploit power	Win respect and confidence	Thinking under pressure
Judgment and intelligence	Win respect and confidence	Preparation and planning skill	Judgment and intelligence
Verbal expressiveness	Integrity	Product knowledge	Verbal expressiveness
Product knowledge	Demonstrate listening skill	Interesting	Product knowledge
Perceive and exploit power	Broad perspective	Judgment and intelligence	Perceive and exploit power
Integrity	Verbal expressiveness		Competitiveness

taken. Looking through the eyes of the Japanese negotiator who wrote "Negotiating With Americans", American negotiators tend to:

- be competitive in their approach to negotiations, including coming to the table with a fall-back position but beginning with an unrealistic offer;
- be energetic, confident, and persistent; they enjoy arguing their positions, and see things universally, i.e., they like to talk about broad applications of ideas;
- concentrate on one problem at a time;
- focus on areas of disagreement, not areas of commonality or agreement;
- like closure and certainty rather than open-endedness or fuzziness.

Do these generalizations ring true? Clearly, it depends which Americans you are talking about, which sector they represent, and the context surrounding the negotiations. Is this a family matter or a commercial one? Is it about community issues, national policy, or a large public conflict? Strategies change according to context and many other factors.

African Approaches to Negotiation

Many African nations have indigenous systems of conflict resolution that have endured into the present, sometimes quite intact and sometimes fragmented by rapid social change. These systems rely on particular approaches to negotiation that respect kinship ties and elder roles, and the structures of local society generally. In Nigeria, for example, people are organized in extended families (*nnu'*), village (*idu' or obio*), lineage (*'duk*), and lineage groups (*iman*) (Offiong, Daniel, 1997). A belief in the continuing ability of ancestors to affect people's lives maintains social control, and makes the need to have formal laws or regulations minimal. Negotiation happens within social networks, following prescribed roles. Women in conflict with husbands, for example, are to defer and apologize, preparing a ritual meal to symbolize the restoration of harmony.

In the Nigerian Ibibio context, the goal of restoring social networks is paramount, and individual differences are expected to be subsumed in the interest of the group. To ensure that progress or an agreement in a negotiation is preserved, parties must promise not to invoke the power of ancestors to bewitch or curse the other in the future. The aim of any process, formal or informal, is to affect a positive outcome without a "residue of bitterness or resentment." Elders have substantial power, and when they intervene in a conflict or a negotiation, their words are respected. This is partly because certain elders are believed to have access to supernatural powers that can remove protective shields at best and cause personal disaster at worst. In other African contexts, a range of indigenous processes exist in which relationships and hierarchies tend to be emphasized.

Latin American Styles of Negotiation

Role expectations influence negotiation in Latin American contexts. Responsibility to others is generally considered more important than schedules and task accomplishment. Their negotiation approach relates to the polychronic orientation to time and patterns of high-context communication and communitarianism, described earlier. Lederach reports that a common term for conflict in Central America is *enredo,* meaning "entangled" or "caught in a net."(LeBarron Micelle, 2003) He explains that *enredo* signifies the way conflict is part of an intimate net of relations in Guatemala and elsewhere in Central America. Thus, negotiation is done within networks, relationships are emphasized, and open ruptures are avoided. In Central America, people think about and respond to conflict holistically. Lederach contrasts his natural (American) inclination to "make a list, to break [a] story down into parts such as issues and concerns" with his Central American experience, where people tended to respond to requests for naming issues to be negotiated with "yet another story." They preferred a storied, holistic approach to conflict and negotiation, rather than a linear, analytical one. When Central Americans needed help with negotiations, they tended to look to insider partials rather than outsider neutrals, preferring the trust and confidence of established relationships and cultural insight to other credentials or expertise. They referred to the concept of *confianza* to explain this preference. *Confianza* means "trustworthiness," that "they know us" and "we know them" and they will "keep our confidences."

Chinese Approach to International Business Negotiation

While a new, market-driven China has been emerging fast in the global marketplace, Western companies have often reported frustration and confusion when negotiating in China. To identify the roots of the problems, this study investigated what Chinese negotiators are trained to do in the global marketplace by examining China's international business negotiation textbooks used in their training programs. The results indicate the following: (a) The win-win, win-lose, cooperative egoism, and concessive negotiation strategies are taught in China with the win-win recommended and the cooperative egoism controversially recommended, and Chinese negotiators are also trained to probe the counterparts' strategies and then act accordingly; (b) Chinese negotiators are taught a large variety of communication techniques for negotiation arrayed along a continuum from the relationship-based win-win strategy to the pure competition-based win-lose mentality; however, the win-win techniques are taught and used far more frequently; and (c) the Chinese textbooks clearly reflect China's foreign trade and economic cooperation principles: equality, mutual understanding mutual trust, mutual benefit, and long-term cooperation. At the same time, the textbook authors may see a need to emphasize the win-win strategy because in nearly half the cited real-life cases it was not used (The Journal of Business Communication July, 2000).

During the last 22 years, China has made great economic progress and has opened itself to foreign investment. By June 1999, China had approved more than 332,700 foreign-funded enterprises such as automobile, chemical, computer, electronics, food, beverage, retailing, banking, and insurance, with foreign investments of more than $286 billion. According to the International Monetary Fund's (IMF) 1999 World Economic Outlook, China has maintained an average annual GDP growth rate of 9.8% from 1979 to 1998, with a projected growth around 7% for 1999 and 2000, respectively.

While a new, market-driven China has been emerging fast in the global marketplace, numerous U.S. and other Western companies, large and small, have encountered problems when negotiating business ventures with their counterparts in China. U.S. business managers have complained that many times they have been intimidated by U.S. specialists on Chinese culture when attending workshops on how to do business with the Chinese. Many of these specialists were alert only to what might annoy the Chinese and gave little thought to ways of getting ahead of them (Pye, 1982).

Stewart and Keown's (1989) survey of 50 traders with China found the following characteristics: (a) The most important pre-negotiation contacts came from requests from China and from regular sales calls; (b) the Chinese negotiating team typically was twice as large as the Western team; (c) one-third of the negotiation time was spent on talking about technical specifications and another third was spent on price; and (d) although both sides tended to use a cooperative strategy; the Chinese team could make sudden demands, apparently to put the Western team in a disadvantageous position. Stewart and Keown point out that Sun Tzu's (256B.C./1984) Art of War taught the Chinese long ago the value of unsettling the mind and upsetting the plans of one's opponent. Therefore, they conclude that negotiating processes in China are likely to continue to be full of surprises.

Another survey of 163 Hong Kong-based small international companies doing business in China reported that personal relationship is still an important factor for the success of business negotiations with China. Social meetings in restaurants and sending gifts are the two most popular means of building up a relationship (guanxi), followed by sending samples and proposals in the pre-negotiating stage. The major reasons for negotiation failure as reported by the Hong Kong firms are lack of funds on the Chinese side and insincerity. The survey also found that the Chinese negotiators manipulate various strategies such as cooperation, assertiveness, and defensiveness. In addition, they manage to lengthen the negotiation time to put the other side at a disadvantage in order to get concessions.

Adler, Brahm, and Graham (1992) conducted negotiation simulations between American and Chinese business people. Their study found that negotiators in both cultures are more successful when taking a cooperative approach. The Chinese negotiators tend to ask many more questions and to interrupt more frequently than their American counterparts. Such subtle differences point to a potential problem: When the Chinese do not reciprocate with cooperative behavior, their counterparts' economic returns are diminished. Therefore, the researchers suggest further research to identify the signs of Chinese non-reciprocation and to develop proactive measures in Chinese-American negotiations.

These empirical studies have focused on Chinese behaviors during negotiations or on the negotiation outcomes to figure out Chinese negotiating styles and to provide suggestions. No empirical research has been done to investigate (a) how Chinese negotiators are trained for the global marketplace, and (b) what the international business negotiation textbooks that have been used in their training programs say about how negotiations should be conducted. This study attempts to explore the Chinese approach to international business negotiation by examining the negotiation textbooks used in China's training programs. Three research questions guided this study: (a) What key Chinese cultural values are reflected in the Chinese strategies of international business negotiation? (b) What training do the Chinese receive in international business negotiation? And (c) what Chinese government policies about international negotiations are reflected in the textbooks?

The findings of this study can help Western business managers develop appropriate strategies when negotiating in China. Second, the findings enable business educators and trainers to update their curricula and prepare competent business graduates for the global marketplace. Most importantly, the findings provide a database for future comparative studies on national strategies of various countries in training business negotiators for the global marketplace.

Review of Related Literature on Chinese culture

Literature related to the research questions comes from three interrelated areas: cultural dimensions, negotiating strategies, and communication styles.

Cultural Dimensions

China is known as a collectivist culture that values relationships and the harmony, cooperation and facework that nurture them. These cultural dimensions have been shown to be important to successful business interaction with China (Adler & Graham, 1989; Hofstede, 1980, 1983; Hofstede & Bond, 1984, 1988). These findings may help to explain the causes of the frequently reported difficulties of setting up joint ventures in China. Companies, even those from Hong Kong, have cited frustration over the years about the negotiation needed to establish a working relationship. As Tung (1988, 1991) noted, although some of the problems stem from the bureaucracy and the need to get approval from above, much of the delay can be attributed to cultural differences in priorities. Americans like to sign a legally binding agreement and get started with the task, whereas the Chinese wish to have better knowledge of the individuals with whom they are contemplating doing business. Therefore, negotiations do not go forward until the Chinese are satisfied that a harmonious working relationship can be established.

Negotiating Strategies

Culture makes people view and value differently the many social interactions inherent in fashioning any agreement (Hendon, Hendon, & Herbig, 1996). A win-lose strategy does not lead to as productive and satisfactory outcomes as does a win-win strategy (Fisher & Ury, 1981; Neale & Bazerman, 1991). The cultural value of relationship is related to win-win negotiation (Fisher & Brown, 1988; Lewicki, Hiam & Olander, 1996). Other negotiation strategies are also discussed. Bargaining strategies work best when relationships are not important to negotiators. Lebow (1996) suggests that competitive and accommodating strategies in combination are actually what Fisher and Ury (1981) recommend. When negotiators are urged to walk away rather than accept an unattractive compromise, that actually is a competitive strategy. Clearly, while many negotiators practice the win-win strategy, many others resist it and prefer using aggressive strategies guided by the win-lose mindset.

Communication Styles

Poor communication in negotiation can lead to misunderstanding, unhelpful emotions, distrust, sloppy thinking, and poor outcomes (Fisher & Brown, 2998). In cross-cultural business negotiations, communication is even more complicated because of different cultures and languages.

Sino-American Negotiating Styles: A Cross-Cultural Perspective

International Trade Agreement Preamble

In 1991, Crocker and Masten indicated that "the most challenging aspect of developing and maintaining long-term exchange relationships is how to develop efficient contracts to effectively govern exchange". In 1999, Dahlstrom and Nygaard indicated that formal contracts make buyers and sellers in trade harmonize their actions and limit potential opportunistic behaviors, and a formal contract is one in which all duties and rights of all parties are completely prescribed for the duration of period of the contract. In 1993, Crocker and Reynolds indicated that a totally incomplete contract places no prior limitations on the terms under which subsequent trade may occur. International trade is more complicated because it is not easy to understand foreign business partners, evaluate complex product standards, and obtain reliable market information in foreign markets.

Examples of international trade agreements and economic treaties are World Trade Organization (WTO) and North American Free Trade Association (NAFTA). In essence, these agreements replace national law in economy, and it is the highest value to keep free markets in goods and services, and is leading to significant deregulation. Under the WTO agreements, every member has same rights and obligations, and must abide by the agreements because every WTO member is treated equally. WTO Dispute Settlement Mechanism, a key role to provide security and predictability to multi-nations trade, is to resolve trade dispute and has jurisdiction among members. Before Taiwan and Mainland China are one of the members of WTO, they adopt their own laws and policies to govern international trade. After they entered the WTO, they must review and adjust their laws and regulations to meet WTO requirements.

In 1994, the WTO was established to establish multilateral trade agreements, including the GATT. The WTO Agreement made the GATT's substantive provisions more enforceable by requiring WTO members to have their domestic laws conform to the Agreement, and by establishing regulations for resolving trade disputes. WTO agreements include services, procurement, standards, anti-dumping and intellectual property.

In 2001, the WTO formally approved Taiwan and Mainland China for membership into the WTO at the ministerial conference. Between Mainland China and Taiwan, both countries will be forced to adopt WTO rules that all members must treat each other's goods and services equally. The entry of Taiwan and Mainland China into the WTO will speed up market liberalization, lower prices, stimulate their economies and ultimately benefit all consumers who live in Taiwan and Mainland China.

Condon (2003) analyzed the four main contractual segments of international trade transactions: the contract of sale, the contract of carriage, the insurance contract and the payment contract. Tsai (2003) indicated that the contents of contracts/agreements can be divided into two main parts: body of the contract and general terms and conditions. The body of the contract includes quality, quantity, price, package, shipment, insurance, and payment. General terms and conditions include the period of the contract, termination, force of nature, assignment, arbitration clause, jurisdiction, applicable law, entire agreement, amendment clauses, and notice clause.

Japanese Styles of Negotiation

There is a great deal written about Japanese approaches to negotiation, and collisions between American and Japanese approaches are legendary. The following values tend to influence Japanese communication: focus on group goals, interdependence, and a hierarchical orientation. In negotiations, these values manifest themselves in awareness of group needs and goals, and deference to those of higher status. Japanese negotiators are known for their politeness, their emphasis on establishing relationships, and their indirect use of power. Japanese concern with face and face-saving is one reason that politeness is so important and confrontation is avoided. They tend to use power in muted, indirect ways consistent with their preference for harmony and calm. In comparative studies, Japanese negotiators were found to disclose considerably less about themselves and their goals than French or American counterparts. Japanese negotiators tend to put less emphasis on the literal meanings of words used in negotiation and more emphasis on the relationships established before negotiating begins. They are also less likely than their U.S. counterparts to make procedural suggestions.

European Styles of Negotiation

European styles of negotiation vary according to region, nationality, language spoken, and many other contextual factors. One study found the French to be very aggressive negotiators, using threats, warnings, and interruptions to achieve their goals. German and British negotiators were rated as moderately aggressive in the same study.

According to Jordan and Richardson, it seems possible to formulate broad characterizations of the British and European policy processes in terms of the relationship between government and interest groups. There is a preferred type of machinery in Britain, reflecting normative values, which is to avoid electoral politics and public conflict in order to reach consensus or "accommodation" in the labyrinth of consultative machinery. This style is aptly labelled "bureaucratic accommodation" and is a system in which the dominant actors are groups and government departments. Departments readily recognize the "relevant" groups in a given policy area and seek to mobilize the community around agreed policies. The predilection for the avoidance of conflict seems equally apparent in other Western European nations(http://www3.interscience.wiley.com/journal/119547388/abstract?CRETRY=1&SRETRY=0).

Latin American Styles of Negotiation

Role expectations influence negotiation in Latin American contexts. Responsibility to others is generally considered more important than schedules and task accomplishment. Their negotiation approach relates to the polychronic orientation to time and patterns of high-context communication and communitarianism, described earlier. Lederach reports that a common term for conflict in Central America is *enredo*, meaning "entangled" or "caught in a net."He explains that *enredo* signifies the way conflict is part of an intimate net of relations in Guatemala and elsewhere in Central America. Thus, negotiation is done within networks, relationships are emphasized, and open ruptures are avoided.

In Central America, people think about and respond to conflict holistically. Lederach contrasts his natural (American) inclination to "make a list, to break a story down into parts such as issues and concerns" with his Central American experience, where people tended to respond to requests for naming issues to be negotiated with "yet another story." They preferred a storied, holistic approach to conflict and negotiation, rather than a linear, analytical one. When Central Americans needed help with negotiations, they tended to look to insider partials rather than outsider neutrals, preferring the trust and confidence of established relationships and cultural insight to other credentials or expertise. They referred to the concept of *confianza* to explain this preference. *Confianza* means "trustworthiness," that "they know us" and "we know them" and they will "keep our confidences."

Even as different approaches to negotiation across national cultures are identified, change is constant. International business culture tends to privilege

Western approaches to negotiation, centered in problem-solving and linear communication, as do many settings. As Western norms are balanced with Eastern and Southern values, and local traditions are balanced with regional and national approaches, negotiation practices continue their global evolution.

German Style of Communication

Germany is not a melting pot society and Germans are not mobile. Many stay in their geographic region and even the same house for generations. The scale of everything is smaller in Germany than in the Western countries. They love the outdoors, open spaces and treasure forests. Hiking is a popular sport. To the German space is sacred. Homes are protected by a variety of barriers, fences, walls, hedges solid doors, shutters and screening to prevent visual or auditory intrusion. Germans seldom invite anyone who is not a close friend to their home. To be invited is considered an honour. When you arrive bring a small bouquet for the hostess (not red roses which convey romantic attachment). Flowers should be unwrapped before being presented. Positions in things is also important, for example, the right side represents a place of respect. So, in seating arrangements or just walking from one place to another, the senior person or the group leader should be placed on the right (Michalle Le Barron-http://www.beyondintractability.org/essay/culture_negotiation).

The German sense of privacy is very strong. Learn what is considered personal and do not ask questions that may be offensive. Americans feel that Germans do not interact with neighbours and perceive German behaviour as unfriendly. German friends of many years continue to address each other by their last names: "Herr Schmidt" not "Walter". Germans are careful not to touch accidentally or to encourage signs of intimacy. On the other hand, they do maintain direct eye contact in conversations to show they are paying attention. However, the German who speaks most softly and to whom others defer is the one to pay attention to, not the one who makes the most noise.

Order is a dominant theme in German culture. There is order in all things, including space—they are very sensitive to spatial intrusions. One exception to orderliness is behaviour in lines for service, in stores, at ticket counters, or in boarding planes, especially where there is no seat assignment. Germans do not form queues but instead crowd and push and can be very rough. They do not yield when someone says "Excuse me". Their determination to be served overrides their usual need to avoid physical contact. However, these are exceptions. Generally, Germans expect organization and order in all things—everything should be carefully planned, researched thoroughly and carried out in an orderly manner. They have a strong drive for conformity and object strenuously when people fail to obey signs and directions. Westerners feel that things are meant to be used; and if they serve no useful purpose, we dispose of them. The German attitude is that things have great intrinsic value. We feel remiss if we buy books and don't read them. But a German will feel that it is important to own a book even if one can't read it immediately. Sales of hard-cover books exceed sales of paperback books in Germany.

Associated with their demand for high-quality, long-lasting goods is the German abhorrence of waste. Waste is a sin, such as heating, cooling and lighting buildings when it is not necessary. Germans are value-conscious and always insist on getting their money's worth. Don't ever try to sell them goods that are less than high quality. They appreciate, in fact demand, fine workmanship, design and high-quality material.

A television ad that is effective in the U.S. will have to be translated into print media to reach Germans. Germans are print-oriented, which explains in part why there is so little advertising on German TV. Also, Germans are always looking for what is "true" and to them numbers are a way of signaling that a product is exactly as it has been represented. Germans demand facts, facts and more facts.

French Style of Communication and Negotiation

It is not uncommon for Americans to experience difficulty getting the French—even those whom they know and have done business with—to reply to inquiries, even urgent ones. This can be exasperating. The reasons are many, but most have to do with the importance of immediate human contacts to the French. A solution that succeeds when other methods fail is to use a surrogate to relay messages, rather than relying on a letter or a phone call. Why? Because letters and phone calls are not personal enough. If you send a properly placed emissary, one whom the individual you are trying to reach likes and trusts and considers important, you add the necessary personal touch to your message and will thereby release the right response. The French also stress the importance of observing the many rituals of form. If you don't use the right form, the message conveyed is that you are ignorant or ill-mannered or don't care. In any event, the response that is provoked is almost certain to be negative. Remember that the French deplore casualness and informality. Paying attention to the details and being correct in everything you do is the only tactic that releases the right response from the French.

Cultural Intelligence : An Important Factor for Negotiation

Cultural intelligence (CQ) is your capability to grow personally through continuous learning and good understanding of diverse cultural heritage, wisdom and values, and to deal effectively with people from different cultural background and understanding.

Why Cultural Intelligence?

Cultural Intelligence (CQ) – a new domain of intelligence that has immense relevance to the increasingly global and diverse workplace. Some aspects of culture are easy to see, the obvious things like art and music and behavior. However, the significant and most challenging parts of other cultures are hidden. These might include our beliefs, values, expectations, attitudes, and assumptions. "Our cultural programming in these areas shapes everything we do. Most importantly they help us to decide what is 'normal' in our eyes. It is the perceived deviation by other cultures from our version of normality that causes the problems. In short, 'us' and 'them' lives on."

Cultural intelligence will help you manage effectively cross-cultural differences, in particular:

1. lower the cultural barriers caused by 'us' and 'them' and to allow you to predict what 'they' are thinking and how they will react to your behavior patterns
2. harness the power of cultural diversity.

In today's globalizing world, cultural intelligence is a necessary tool for every manager who deals with diverse teams of employees, customers, partners, competitors, government, and other business players.

Manager's Worldly Mindset

People tend to think of the world as an increasingly homogenous place but it is really a collection of worlds within worlds, with definite boundaries and edges. Just because a company sells products globally it may not take into account how those products are perceived and used in different cultures. Managers with a worldly mindset spend time in places where products are made, customers served, and environment threatened.

Attributes of Successful CEOs

The Cultural Fit: A candidate for a top job might look great on paper, but must be culturally compatible in order to build relationships and add true value. Often, hiring managers or boards emphasize the need to challenge old thinking and move in new directions. But if an executive is too far out of step with an organization, the resulting culture clash can overwhelm the benefits.

Signs of a Losing Organization

Discouraging Culture: no shared values; lack of trust; blame culture; focus on problems, not opportunities; diversity is not celebrated; failures are not tolerated; people lose confidence in their leaders and systems.

Corporate Culture

Corporate culture is the collective behavior of people using common corporate vision, goals, shared values, beliefs, habits, working language, systems, and symbols. It is interwoven with processes, technologies, learning and significant events. In addition, different individuals bring to the workplace their own uniqueness, knowledge, and ethnic culture. So corporate culture encompasses moral, social, and behavioral norms of your organization based on the values, beliefs, attitudes, and priorities of its members.

Role of Inspirational Leader

Build teams and promote and teamwork, leverage diversity: Teamwork is essential for competing in today's global arena. Build a star team, not a team of stars. Diversity of thought, perception, background and experience enhance the creativity and innovation. A team should not just be diverse; it has to make the most of it. Involve everyone, facilitate cross-pollination of ideas, build and empower cross-functional teams if you wish to harness the power of diversity. Challenge people from different disciplines and cultures to come up with something better together and achieve creative breakthrough

Cultural Intelligence in International Business Negotiation

Cultural intelligence (CQ), defined as one's capability to adapt to new cultural contexts (Earley, 2002), is a new concept in organizational literature. Earley (2002) identified cultural intelligence as an important individual variable in international business negotiation. He proposed a conceptual model, discussing the impacts of CQ on international negotiation and the potential factors that moderate its impacts. He proposed two methodological issues to give suggestions for future research.

In a global economy, it's a mistake to assume that negotiation strategies are a one-size—fits-all proposition. Understanding the culture of the parties you are negotiating with is vital in order to establish a successful business relationship. With increasing globalization, cultural intelligence becomes only more critical to business success. Livermore points to a study done by The Economist which found that 90% of executives from more than 60 countries said cross-cultural leadership was their top management challenge. The study concluded that "It's important for any business individual from support services all the way up the chain, but especially for a leader who is trying to figure out how do we strategize to remain competitive in a global economy. A leader in particular has to be able to adapt on the fly" (Steve Minter-2009: http://www.industryweek.com/articles/are_you_cued_in_to_cultural_intelligence_20200.aspx).

Livermore offers a four-part plan for developing the cultural intelligence needed to lead abroad:

CQ Drive—The first element involves a self-assessment of your receptivity, confidence and drive for cross-cultural experiences. Are you the person who asks for spicy noodles with hints of squid and fish eyes, Livermore asks, or a traveler who would rather go hungry than take a bite?

CQ Knowledge—Cross-cultural differences influence the way people think and behave. Being ignorant of a culture's impact on people's thoughts, attitudes or behaviors could hamper a person's ability to become culturally intelligent and potentially cost a firm billions of dollars in lost opportunities.

CQ Strategy—CQ Strategy, says Livermore, is the buffer between taking your CQ Knowledge and understanding of a culture and actually applying that knowledge. CQ Strategy helps you determine the best ways to approach a cross-cultural experience and attain the most favorable result.

Cultural Intelligence and Innovation

One advantage of cultural diversity is the potential for innovation arising from the presence of multiple perspectives. Yet, it is clear that not all multicultural teams/organizations are able to harness this benefit. Cultural intelligence (CQ) may enhance the likelihood of innovation success in culturally diverse teams/organizations. CQ facilitates the reconciliation of differences and conflict, and enhances the probability of arriving at culturally synergistic solution that embraces the ideas or interests of various parties.

The Tao of Business Success

The Tao helps you achieve much more with much less effort. This effortless skill comes from being in accord with reality. You can't tell the singer from the song. You can't tell the dancer from the dance. When you are in harmony with the Tao, when you go with its current of energy, your innate intelligence takes over, and the right action happens by itself. The Tao teaches you the art of living and doing business. It gives you advice that imparts perspective and balance. It applies equally well to the managing of a large corporation or the running of a small business, to the governing of a nation or the leading a small team, to your personal development or to the coaching of others

Managing Cross-Cultural Differences

Culture is often at the root of communication challenges. Exploring historical experiences and the ways in which various cultural groups have related to each other is key to opening channels for cross-cultural communication. Becoming more aware of cultural differences, as well as exploring cultural similarities, can help you communicate with others more effectively. Next time you find yourself in a confusing situation, ask yourself how culture may be shaping your own reactions, and try to see the world from the other's point of view

Creating a Culture for Innovation

Virtually all companies recognize intellectually that innovation and culture are both important to success. Yet few have explicitly defined strategies for linking and influencing culture and innovation to achieve specific business goals. Most companies have default innovation cultures in which various values, norms, assumptions and beliefs all compete for influence over employees' actual behavior. The dominant ones that win out ultimately shape the culture. The question for leaders today isn't if culture is important for success but how culture can drive successful innovation – and what, specifically, leaders can do to influence the kind of culture that leads to behavior that's truly innovative

Harnessing the Power of Diversity

Leveraging Opposite Forces

You can inspire innovation and find a strategic competitive advantage in an organizational and cultural context by seeking to leverage, rather than diminish, opposite forces. People with different cultural, educational, scientific, and business backgrounds will bring different frames of reference to a problem and can spark an exciting and dynamic cross-pollination of ideas.

An important but widely overlooked principle of business success is that integrating opposites, as opposed to identifying them as inconsistencies and driving them out, unleashes power," writes Mark Stevens. "This is true on both a personal level (the balanced merger. On an organization level we accept the existence of hard and fast dichotomies because this binary perspective helps to rationalize personal styles, viewpoints, and structures. Polarized thinking is simplistic and misleading. In the business world, ideal approaches are generally painted in gray as opposed to black and white." To be successful in today's complex, rapidly changing and highly competitive world, you must embrace and manage critical opposites.

Characteristics of a Winning Team

Building Synergies

You can inspire innovation and find a strategic competitive advantage in your team by seeking to leverage, rather than diminish, diversity. People with different cultural, educational, scientific, and business backgrounds will bring different frames of reference to a problem and can spark an exciting and dynamic cross-pollination of ideas. A team that builds on core competencies of individual players to develop synergies among them thus makes its members more productive together than independently

Actually, far from it: *Cultural Intelligence—People Skills for Global Business* is full of real life stories depicting what is and is not culturally intelligent behavior in everyday business situations. In addition, the book provides practical guidelines for a variety of international business challenges. As they introduce the concept of cultural intelligence, the authors make a compelling point that success in cross-cultural environments is based on three components: the *Knowledge* to understand cross-cultural phenomena, the *Mindfulness to* observe and interpret particular situations, and the *Behavioral Skills* required to act appropriately and successfully in a range of situations. They argue that mindfulness means switching off one's "cultural cruise control", the tendency of most humans to follow cultural norms that may no longer make sense when working in a different culture. Doing so requires becoming aware of how culture affects perceptions and paying careful attention to the challenges presented by cross-cultural situations.

Thomas and Inkson (2004) investigated the relevance of cultural intelligence in practical business situations, reviewing aspects such as decision-making, communicating, and negotiating across cultures, analyzing cultural concepts of leadership, and discussing what makes multicultural teams effective. Each of these chapters includes practical case studies, a situational analysis that the authors keep refreshingly brief, and a summary of principles that helps readers raise their cultural intelligence. Over time, the book will allow readers to develop a valuable repertoire of behavioral skills for intercultural situations that are common in today's global business environment.

How Cultural Intelligence can Improve Performance

A couple of decades ago, when the world was a simpler place, people who worked internationally simply moved from one culture or country to the next. To-day, all this has changed. Despite working with people from both multiple country and professional cultures, many people who work in the international arena may barely leave home. The ability to do this successfully from any starting point depends on people's level of cultural intelligence.

Culture itself is a shared set of assumptions, values and norms for a group of people that helps them prioritize what they are going to do and how they are going to get things done. It makes it easier to get things done within one's own culture than when working across cultures. Culture also helps to define the group. Cultural intelligence, on the other hand, is key to the success of today's cross culture, cross border, cross organization worker. Cultural intelligence—or the ability to create an impact across different cultures—is much more complex than just working across boundaries. In real terms, it is the ability to understand the relationship between cultural issues, on the one hand, and business issues on the other. The tricky part is understanding both, and putting them back together without losing who you are in the process.

Cultural Intelligence—The Learning Process

Cultural intelligence consists of specific knowledge about different cultures, as well as general knowledge about how cultures work. It is best to create a map of the cultures you are working with – how are they different from and similar to each other? Of course you need to understand your own culture too. You need to have the "I am here" position in order to know how to bridge to others. Cultural intelligence also requires skills—interpersonal, negotiation, listening and cross-cultural. The most important characteristic, however, is cultural mindfulness—or openness to new experiences and ideas and the ability to keep learning.

Mindfulness is really about paying attention. It is what helps a person recognize and understand the differences between cultures. Recent research has shown that if teams or individuals working in cross cultural situations can be persuaded to pay more attention, performance goes up. It really is as simple as it sounds, it's just that we don't usually take the time or effort to pay attention.

The reason that many mergers and acquisitions have a difficult time integrating is usually because they have different norms, values and ways of doing things. This is a classic example of where cultural knowledge, skills, intelligence and mindfulness are very important. Surprisingly, mindfulness in virtual teams tends to be higher than it is in their face-to-face counterparts, although face-to-face contact is an undeniable asset when building a relationship. The virtual context helps people focus and pay attention to the right issues.

When in Rome do as the Romans

Although attempting to adapt in Rome and do as the proverbial Romans did is an automatic response, it is not necessarily the best one. Pretending to be Roman can not only get in the way of one's performance, but may be perceived by other people as insincere or, even worse, manipulative. What is required is enough of a behavior change to show respect, without losing one's sense of self and effectiveness. While nobody expects everyone on a 20-person multicultural team to speak everybody else's languages, the key here is respect in terms of keeping language simple without being offensively overly so.

Cultural and Emotional Intelligence

Cultural intelligence is emotional intelligence across contexts, which makes emotional intelligence a prerequisite for cultural intelligence. And while some people can be very emotionally intelligent in their own culture, a shift across boundaries to some place where the norms and assumptions are different can prove to be a step too far. By the same token, higher emotionally-intelligent people are more likely to pick up cultural differences and develop cultural intelligence too.

It is said that "culture is to people as water is to fish"—and it's all good until the fish is out of water! The best way to get help in understanding a culture is to ask someone from that culture who has been out. "If they haven't been out, they won't know what makes it different for an outsider!"

This is the classic dilemma – how much should I adapt, how much should I expect the others to adapt? The simple answer is this: adapting is the responsibility of anybody who cares about performance. If one person adapts, performance improves a bit. If everybody adapts, performance skyrockets.

Cross-Cultural Training for Global Business

According to Forbes Traveler, 63.7 million Americans traveled internationally in 2006, and a number of other studies show that the weakening economy and fear of terrorism have small to negligible effects on foreign travel numbers. Although *Forbes* did not clarify how many of those overseas travelers went for business and how many for pleasure, it is probable that more than half of them had business as at least part of their reason for traveling. And international business travel requires a new kind of business communication: cultural competence.

Cross-Cultural Negotiations: Constraints Analysis

> All negotiations present problems, but the challenges of international business negotiations are unique. It is critical that you become aware of these challenges before they arise, and take proactive measures to forestall their potentially negative impact.
>
> —*Charles Sheppard, Management Communication Systems, Inc.*

There are several key problems most likely to affect you as an international negotiator. Some of these problems are unique to international business negotiations (such as establishing an international joint venture), while others can occur domestically, but are magnified internationally (such as dealing with a bribe). Let's review the impact of these problems and examine the action steps you must take to overcome them.

Reducing Culture Shock

Culture shock occurs when we are deprived of the familiar "maps" which tell us how to conduct ourselves. These maps encompass both our professional and personal lives, and often guide us during activities that we normally take for granted. In international business negotiations, these might include how to shake hands; what forms of address to use; to whom your comments should be addressed; how direct to be with the other party; determining if the other party means "no" when they say "yes"; and what topics, if any, should be discussed over dinner. Most individuals who work internationally go through unique phases of adjustment to other cultures and negotiating situations. These phases of growth can be very troublesome and perplexing, but they are a normal and expected part of the intercultural journey. Each phase has its own unique characteristics and challenges.

These phases include:

Phase One. The first phase is a time of great excitement and anxiety. Pre-departure anticipation and initial enchantment upon arrival is a powerful combination. There is excitement about the new opportunity to work in a foreign culture, coupled with anxiety about adjusting to the new situation. There is a desire to plunge in and enjoy every aspect of the host culture. You read about the surroundings, history, and architecture, and celebrate the differences between the host culture and the United States. You have a somewhat naive acceptance of the host culture, without much critical analysis of its shortcomings. You feel buoyed by optimism about doing business with the other party. You begin thinking, *"People all over are basically the same."*

Phase Two. This is known as the awakening phase, when you slowly realize that people from different cultures are not, in fact, the same as Americans. Minor annoyances begin to grind one down emotionally. For example, in South America it may seem that your negotiating counterparts are never on time for meetings. They are overly friendly, always grabbing you and hugging you like you were their best friend; they seem more interested in talking about their brandy than about the negotiating issues; they won't give you straight answers to your questions; and four of them talk at once. It takes forever to get a long-distance call through back to the United States, and when you do, the cost seems outrageous. In this phase, you come face-to-face with your own ethnocentrism. This initial culture shock can become permanent and debilitating, unless acknowledged and resolved.

Phase Three. In the next phase you become very specific about what is wrong with the host culture, and with the individuals with whom you must deal. You begin thinking that if only you could extricate yourself gracefully from the negotiation, you would happily board an airplane in the morning and go home. A general feeling of disillusionment is prevalent.

Phase Four. The final phase is characterized by serenity and a realization of what can and cannot be accomplished in the host culture. You realize that the host culture has existed, for centuries in most cases, before your arrival—and will likely survive after your departure. You begin to work creatively and enjoyably among the challenges and opportunities you encounter. The duration and order of these phases differs from person to person. The progression and impact of this series may endure from the first extended trip to the host country through several return visits.

Action Steps for Dealing with Culture-Shock

The following are some of the pragmatic steps that may be followed to deal with impending cultural shock:

- *Find a cultural mentor.* Ask for advice from others who have negotiating experience in the areas of the world where you will be doing business. Talk with people who have had successful negotiating experiences there, and also with those who have had bad experiences there. In this way you can get a balanced view of the host country and its negotiators. The sooner you get this type of information, the better off you will be when it comes to the later phases of adjustment.
- *Be flexible and patient with yourself and with those in the host culture.* Events, services, issues, mechanical devices—in short, practically all aspects of your life—are not going to flow as smoothly and predictably as they do back home.
- *Withhold judgment about the new culture and its people.* Rather than being pre-judicial about your new environment, be post-judicial. Try not to go overboard with either positive or negative reactions.
- *Be aware of the phases of adjustment.* Recognize that the negative feelings you may have at the "awakening" and "disillusionment" stages are normal and appropriate. Annoyances, irritations, and letdowns are to be expected.
- *Keep a sense of humor about yourself and your situation.* This doesn't require joke-telling, but rather, keeping a sense of proportion and a positive attitude about whatever culturally irritating situation you find yourself in.
- *Reduce stress by being as self-sufficient as possible with regard to business services.* "Routine business services" is an oxymoron in some countries. In many emerging economies there are often no secretaries, typewriters, copiers, faxes, or other business fundamentals. There may also be confidentiality issues in many host-country business settings, so don't depend on the other party to type up your bargaining position or other similar material. Take along a portable personal computer (with

appropriate electrical adapters) for your notes, strategies, and other uses Arrange for other services at a large international hotel, or other professional service provider.

The Principles of Value-creating Negotiation

What is meant by "value" in the context of negotiation? We would argue that value is created when two or more parties develop options that allow each to get more of what they care about most, at the expense of things they care about least. A common example: rather than splitting an orange in half, two negotiating parties might ask one another *why* they want it. If one wants the juice and the other the rind to bake a cake, then value has been destroyed by cutting it in half. A more elegant trade would have given each what they needed. Similarly, in the business world, parties often miss opportunities at the negotiating table to do better without risking being any worse off; in many cases, options for joint gain go missing. For example, parties going issue by issue through a contractual agreement, arguing hard and compromising on each issue, may fail to discover that issues are valued differently. Recognizing these differences permits elegant trades:

the buyer agrees a higher price in exchange for speedier delivery, which more than offsets the price increase; or shipping costs shift to the seller, in exchange for a shorter payment cycle granted by the buyer. Over the past 30 years, researchers have shown that negotiators—even experts—fall prey to certain mistakes, including:

- assuming that one's counterpart's needs are diametrically opposite to one's own;
- failing to see the other side's perspective;
- becoming fixated on specific targets or inspirational numbers, even ones generated with little rationale;
- skipping over careful exploration of each side's needs and the kinds of options that might make both better off.

Researchers at the Harvard University-Massachusett's Institute of Technology (MIT), Program on Negotiation (PON), among others, have developed an interest-based theory of negotiation that has been presented in books such as Roger Fisher and William Ury's *Getting To Yes*, Howard Raiffa's *Negotiation Analysis*, and Lawrence Susskind and Jeffrey Cruikshank's *Breaking the Impasse*. These different works all emphasize the importance of (1) distinguishing interests from positions; (2) exploring interests and issues; (3) developing options for mutual gain; (4) using criteria for allocating value that both sides can live with; and (5) rigorous preparation that involves thinking through all sides' alternatives to agreement and all sides' interests. The Consensus Building Institute, working with the PON, has developed a model that incorporates the key findings and prescriptions from several decades of research. The Mutual Gains Approach to Negotiation (MGA) focuses on creating more value for parties, doing so efficiently and in ways that enhance reputations and relationships.

The model has four steps: preparation, value creation, value distribution and follow through. At each step, there are prescribed tasks for increasing the chances that the parties will reach wise, efficient and stable agreements. Central to this model is the notion that parties should clarify their mandate and rank their interests (the kinds of things they care about) prior to negotiations. Moreover, parties should pay equal attention and care to thinking about the other side's interests and alternatives. Even when others show little interest in anything other than a traditional, adversarial approach, using the value-creation process can influence behaviour at the table by, for example, continuing to seek feedback to options as a way of bringing underlying interests and preferences to the surface. The MGA is emphatically *not* about being nice in the hope that others will reciprocate. Rather, it reflects enlightened self-interest and a focus on careful analysis and process management.

The "three deadly sins" of value destruction

The proliferation of strategic sourcing processes in organizations, and their subsequent embedding into procurement best practice, owes much to their proven success in consistently delivering price reduction. We believe there is nothing wrong with strategic sourcing processes *per se*, particularly within relatively straightforward, tactical spend categories. However, the unthinking application of these processes and tactical negotiation, particularly when combined with e-sourcing tools such as e-RFPs and e-auctions, threatens potential for value creation through negotiation. This is especially the case when dealing with suppliers that can genuinely be termed "strategic" – those capable of making a significant contribution to an organization's success, however broadly or narrowly that is defined. E-sourcing delivers well-documented advantages to procurement over a traditional manual approach. However, its widespread adoption has also encouraged practices that, although apparently optimal when viewed through the lens of procurement process, have (largely) unintended consequences that greatly reduce the opportunity for value-creating negotiation.

Sins of Traditional Negotiation

Many CPOs and other procurement managers will already be aware at some level of the idea of creating value through negotiation and using an interest-based approach, but most we've encountered quickly default to a "traditional" mindset.

There are a number of practical problems in most organizations with adopting such an approach:

- The negotiator misses opportunities to create options that could leave all sides better off. He or she spends their entire effort on carving up a value pie that could be made much bigger.

- A typical lack of candour means that each party guesses about what the other really wants, and may hide information that could affect implementation and other commitments down the road, as well as other issues that were not initially contemplated but which could represent enormous new opportunities.
- Agreements become less stable because there are no clear criteria for how or why different options were selected. Each side then seeks to renegotiate terms at the first opportunity because its interests were not well met and compelling criteria for fairness were not identified, so each side could make a strong case for the agreement to its own stakeholders and leadership.
- When key negotiations happen, either ad hoc or through a value-constricting sourcing process, there are limited opportunities for the organization to learn more about what matters to its suppliers, customers, partners and employees.
- Operational and financial relationships are often not enhanced, which means that future negotiations are more difficult and unknown operational risks are potentially incurred because there is no trust built. This often means that problems (actual or potential) in the supply chain are not shared proactively.
- Brand is potentially compromised as counterparts cynically observe that espoused corporate values are apparently irrelevant during negotiation.
- Research has shown that it is extremely stressful for parties to behave in ways that run counter to their own values and standards.

As Jared Curhan at MIT has shown, negotiators have a "subjective utility" for negotiations that is a more powerful predictor of future behaviour towards counterparts that the objective results. Simply put, people who feel uncomfortable with their own actions in a negotiation do not want to negotiate again.

Sins of underestimating the value in relationships

Procurement has traditionally viewed close relationships between internal stakeholders and suppliers with distrust, and there is often a suspicion that side conversations are taking place between insight Procurement's Usual Approach:

- Open with a long list of requirements or demands (typically including an arbitrary price cut figure) without clarifying which are most important.
- Argue why those demands should be met, often using price benchmarking as a weapon.
- Make concessions grudgingly, using each as an opportunity to extract something in return.

- Whenever possible, discredit the other side's data or arguments.
- Use power plays, tricks and tactics to get the other side to give you what you want.
- Adopt a "take it or leave it—we can always find another supplier" stance.

Executives, on the golf course or over lunch, which somehow threatens procurement's attempts to manage suppliers transparently and fairly. These concerns can be particularly acute during a pitch process. However, all business leaders intuitively know and understand that there is enormous value in relationships and open dialogue with key advisers and suppliers. In the world of business and commerce, it's often trusted relationships that enable major deals to get done or significant problems to be resolved. We therefore have an obvious disjunction. On the one hand, business leaders who want to be able to sit down and talk freely with their counterparts, shaping deals and exploring potential options. On the other hand, we have procurement attempting to constrain dialogue within a process that it insists on controlling, seemingly fearful of the very relationships that business leaders want to cultivate. It is therefore not surprising that CPOs often find themselves and their staff excluded from the really key supplier relationships and the vital strategic discussions and decisions. Equally, it's not surprising that procurement's efforts to release value from strategic supplier management activities often fall short, largely as a result of its inability to switch seamlessly from a traditional strategic sourcing approach to a less familiar situation where it has to be able to think and act effectively outside the normal process boundaries.

Imagine a better way Imagine a better (or at least different) way, where CPOs and senior procurement managers view themselves (and are positioned and recognized within the organization) as value-creating commercial specialists first and foremost, and procurement functional specialists second. Where procurement teams are expected to use strategic sourcing processes where it is appropriate to do so, but are also encouraged to experiment with different approaches and to embrace and explore the value of relationships. Where price, while still important, is only one of several metrics of value with which to assess the overall impact of a supplier relationship. Imagine what the potential of procurement might be then. We advocate the following major areas of opportunity for CPOs.

Change the Training Mode

Negotiation training is often viewed as largely generic in terms of content, which is then applied generically to all procurement staff, irrespective of role or seniority. In addition, much existing negotiation training for procurement is more about harnessing and applying power and winning than recognizing that value can be created for both parties. So, careful selection of a negotiation training provider and process of negotiation is key, followed by segmentation of the right kind of training to support a variety of procurement roles. However, training procurement itself is only the beginning of what could be a large untapped opportunity for CPOs to play a different and much broader commercial role. As procurement raises its own negotiation game and is seen to do so through actions as well as results, our experience is that many other functions within a typical organization will start to ask the CPO for help in a variety of ways:

- Requests for procurement to design and deliver negotiation training events to the rest of the organization.
- Requests to deliver negotiation train-the trainer, to enable individual business units to be self-sufficient with their own negotiation training programmes, while delivering a consistent, centrally developed negotiation message and philosophy.
- Requests to coach others as they prepare for, or even during, important negotiations (with the emphasis on negotiation process coaching rather than on content expertise, which is specific to the situation).
- Requests to organize joint training sessions with key suppliers or clients. Each of these has the added benefit of opening up a new constituency of senior business contacts for procurement while clearly positioning the CPO in the role of a valued commercial partner – one who can help facilitate a better outcome for client and supplier organizations alike.

Deal with organizational barriers

Many CPOs will have encouraged and invested in negotiation training for procurement teams in the past, only to be discouraged that months or years later little has changed in the way that negotiations are carried out, with individual behaviours appearing to be struck in a traditional mindset. Organizations that send individuals on training programmes, no matter how entertaining, will not position them to change the way they negotiate. We believe that moving in the direction of a more value-focused process requires a shift in thinking, away from negotiation as an *individual* competence to negotiation as an *organizational* competence. Due attention may be paid to these three areas:

At the Strategic level

There may be scope for the CPO to describe a broader commercial value proposition for procurement, propose a new strategy of alignment with other functions or leaders within the organization, create a new value-based

Spreading the message

WPP and the Consensus Building Institute (CBI) have been working together for three years, exploring how value-creating negotiation can assist in building sustainable client-supplier relationships. During this time, CBI has delivered tailored negotiation training to over 600 senior executives from WPP marketing and communications agencies around the world. In turn, the WPP commercial and procurement services team plays a leading role in internal workshop design and facilitation, and offers "beginner to improver" level negotiation training and train-the-trainer programmes to WPP agencies in all geographic regions. This team has delivered 50 commercial workshops each year for the past three years. Thousands of WPP staff have attended at least one of these workshop programmes. The procurement leadership team in WPP is regularly called upon by agencies within the group as negotiation advisers and process coaches.

Give staff permission to experiment

This is a tough one for CPOs, who for years have been espousing consistency and purity of application of process to drive cost reduction. However, as outlined earlier, the unintended consequences of procurement's process-led approach risk destroying more value than it creates. The recommendations are:

- Give procurement teams permission to step outside the strategic sourcing process where the situation warrants it.
- Encourage pilots of new approaches—for example, instead of issuing an RFP, bring in some valued strategic suppliers and encourage a dialogue about joint aspirations, interests and ideas for the relationship.
- Encourage suppliers to challenge the process—suppliers can only innovate if given the space and opportunity to do so.
- Reward and celebrate procurement teams and suppliers that take a few risks and deliver incremental value as a result.
- For strategic services or products, keep the primary focus on optimization of the output value to the buying organization, as opposed to the primary focus being the input costs. Yes, input costs will always be important to procurement and rightly so, but may be trivial when considered against the broader commercial picture. Getting strategic supplier relationships right can deliver so much more.

Define success differently

While recognizing that traditional savings reporting will always have a role for procurement, we advocate that CPOs take the lead in designing and advocating a different approach to measuring the success of strategic negotiation and supplier relationships. The following observations can be made:

- The debate should start and end with key business stakeholders – this is a business issue, not one solely for procurement.
- Whatever measures of value are chosen, these should be consistent with existing business objectives for client and supplier.
- Measures should reflect a commitment to long-term value, in the form

of innovation, quality improvement, customer satisfaction, revenue growth, cost management, risk management and other key goals.

Procurement processes today tend to be linear and tightly controlled. There is a risk that strategic sourcing has become over-specified and therefore, paradoxically, extremely wasteful. When there is no process for creating value, based on exploiting the differences in the kinds of things each side cares about, then procurement predictably becomes an exercise in making demands, demonstrating marginal short-term savings and ignoring the operational, financial and relational problems that occur downstream when value is compromised.

In this article, we have deliberately tried to be challenging—perhaps even controversial—with the specific intention of challenging CPOs to take themselves and their procurement teams out of a process comfort zone and towards making a more strategic business contribution, both personally and functionally.

The key to making this transition is a willingness to leave behind some of the process baggage that procurement has accumulated over the years and place more trust in the power of relationships and in a set of softer skills and techniques that are more in tune with value creation and less focused on process and price.

Creating a World Class Negotiating Organization

The activities of oil and other energy companies are increasingly being challenged by nongovernmental organizations and media to justify their behavior in ethical terms. Activities that visibly damage the environment have long been challenged by advocacy groups. In recent years public interest has broadened into calls to respect "sustainability," human rights, and other ethical imperatives. This article attempts to set these developments in the context of international promotion of the idea of a global "civil society." Ethical codes reach, by persuasion, beyond coercive legal obligations. They have the character and role of "repeated games." Codes of behavior for business are rooted in national and cultural values, which may conflict at the international level. However, many governments following the lead of the United States are often developing sanctions to promote ethical behavior by businesses, to redress the failure of markets to manage common access to resources and to protect aspects of the natural world for its own sake. Examples are efforts to uphold human rights, fight against corruption, and promote sustainability of resources. Business leaders and the non-government organizations that advocate international values on these subjects have the opportunity to contribute to the development of global civil society by working together to establish persuasive codes that do not require slow and difficult international intervention by government (John V. Mitchell, 2008).

How to avoid pitfalls in Cross-cultural Negotiation: A Case

The work of Arun Kottoli in International sales, marketing, and project coordination has given me rich experience in working with people from other cultures. Cross-cultural communications has always been a tricky subject—particularly when there is business negotiations going on between two parties who are from different cultures (Arun Kottoli: http://arunkottolli.blogspot.com/2007/01/how-to-avoid-pitfalls-in-cross.html).

Business negotiations is always a delicate business—even when the parties are sitting across the table and are from the same culture. The complexity of negotiations increases when the parties are from different cultures. But when both the parties are negotiating via electronic media—the challenges are immense often putting the negotiations at risk.

Cultural Differences are Invisible

Recently Kottoli had written an article on Challenges of Multi-cultural Teams, the problems encountered in managing multi-cultural teams are magnified exponentially when it comes to business negotiations. The problems of parochialism and ethnocentric attitude come into play without people noticing it during negotiations. To illustrate this consider the following example (http://arunkottolli.blogspot.com/2007/01/how-to-avoid-pitfalls-in-cross.html):

Harry in Austin and Harsh in Bangalore—both speak excellent English. Harsh studied in California, watches NBA and listens to rock music. All this makes Harry think that Harsh is just like any other fellow American—and starts the business negotiation right away. After few rounds—the negotiations come to a screeching halt due when Harsh decided to take a break during the negotiations.

The problem? Both parties had different perceptions of the negotiation process itself and misinterpretations of the other's behavior. For Harry, negotiation is about pushing through a quick deal. When Harsh took time—Harry became increasingly impatient and become more forceful in the meetings. Harsh interpreted this with suspicion that Harry was pulling a fast one on him, therefore he needed some more time to study Harry's proposals. Though the negotiations concluded successfully, it took a longer time than Harry initially anticipated. This negotiation example shows how cultural differences are often invisible for both the parties and it affects the negotiations itself—when both the parties ignore the cultural differences.

Negotiating Across Cultures: *Modus operandi*

There is no right way or no perfect way to overcome the cultural differences in negotiations. International negotiations are always a delicate business—requiring skill, tact, and diplomacy. Here are some tips that can help one negotiate with a foreign counterpart. Stepwise negation process across culture can be described as follows:

Tip-1: Take time to setup the negotiation process

This step is very important when you are negotiating with a new partner. People in other cultures have a standardized ritual process for all negotiations—particularly in the initial phase. Indians for example, tend to focus more on confidence building during the initial phase. Chinese on the other had have to establish a relationship before they start the serious negotiations. Americans would go over the main objectives in few minutes and then start off with the main negotiations. This approach is however not appreciated by other cultures. The best way to start negotiations is to start with explaining each one's negotiation process. Take time to explain your process—and ask the other party if they understand it and encourage them to share their process. This helps to build a common ground for all negotiations.

Tip-2: Understand expectations

In any negotiations parties involved will have different expectations—both sides would like to win but they will have different perceptions of victory. In cross-cultural negotiations it is difficult to guess other side's expectations. It may make sense to talk about the expectations of both sides at the beginning of the negotiations—but fall short of disclosing their BATNA. Take time and effort to understand the other side's expectations. Indian, Arab, Chinese and Japanese negotiators do not really like contentious style of negotiations—which is often perceived as "I win—you lose" style negotiations. Instead they prefer a more harmonious "problem solving" approach. It would be therefore useful to frame the negotiations in a problem solving mode when dealing with Asian negotiators and explain that is the approach to them. On the other side, Asian negotiator may assume that the American negotiator will adapt a contentious style and will prepare accordingly. So it will be better to explain the approach in the beginning itself.

Tip-3: Explain the decision-making process

Decision-making is a complex process in most cultures. Unlike in American culture where the decision maker will be at the negotiation table—Asian negotiators may not be the final decision makers. In Indian and most Asian companies, the final decision maker would be different and may not even enter the negotiation process directly but will be watching and monitoring the negotiation process closely. It is important to know who the decision makers are, and how decision will be made—and on what criteria. So take the initiative to explain the decision-making process openly to the other party and encourage them to do the same.

Tip-4: Manage the negotiation process

Multi-country, cross-cultural negotiations often take a long time. In the process the negotiation stalls due to various reasons. When issues are being exchanged or for seeking more information etc., the negotiations may come to a halt because one of the parties may be taking time to verify or find information. And at times negotiations come to a halt when one of the parities get distracted by other business needs. In all such cases, the best solution is to manage the progress of the negotiation in a methodical manner. Ideally it will be best when one person from both sides take up the role of project manager for the negotiation process and manage it like a project. This will prevent the negotiation from getting off course or getting stalled for a prolonged period.

Tip-5: Closing thoughts

Cross-cultural negotiations are always tricky. In most cases parties involved in the negotiation process will not have a good understanding of the other's culture and hence the negotiation process starts off with a set of false set of assumptions and if those assumptions are not tested, the negotiation process will fail. It is therefore a good practice to verify those assumptions and make things transparent and clear at the very onset of the negotiation process and then work towards successful conclusion.

CHAPTER 3

Regulatory Environment in International Trade Negotiation

John S. Odell (1999) of University of California in his paper 'The Negotiation Process and International Economic Organizations' presented in 1999 Annual Meeting of the American Political Science Association, Atlanta underlined the importance of understanding the dynamics of international organizations in conducting research aimed at generalizing about the process of negotiation in those settings. The study of international institutions and the empirical study of negotiation have often been isolated from each other. This has been changing, but many promising opportunities remain unexploited. Research opportunities lie in questions such as what strategies regime negotiators use, what shapes their strategy choices, what effects these strategies have, what coalition-building tactics they use and which work best under what conditions, and how the process is conditioned by its contexts—domestic political institutions, cultures, the security environment, and the international organization context (http://www-rcf.usc.edu/~odell/APSA99.DOC).

The negotiation process may be distinguished from the structures in which it takes place. *Negotiation* (or *bargaining*) is a sequence of actions in which two or more parties address demands and proposals to each other for the ostensible purposes of reaching an agreement and changing the behavior of at least one actor. The process includes which strategies negotiators choose, how markets and negotiators influence each other, whether negotiators add tactics to smoke out joint gains, how much they use tactics to guard against their own biases, and how they go about forming and splitting coalitions. The process includes how the negotiators' moves interact with domestic politics. We have however little standardized evidence showing which strategies and tactics international economic regime negotiators use in general, or with what frequencies, or with what effects.

In this chapter we will try to understand the implications of a regulatory environment which interfaces with International negotiation process in their various manifestations as it extends to International trade practices.

International Trade Negotiation Processes

International trade agreements can be categorized by different rules. For example, the General Agreement on Trade in Services (GATS) focused primarily on trade in services. The General Agreement on Tariffs and Trade (GATT) focused primarily on trade in goods. World Trade Organization (WTO), an institution for administering multilateral trade agreements, focuses primarily on trade in goods including services and intellectual property rights (Ramcharran, 1999). Trade in services is different from trade in goods or merchandise. It is difficult for governments to impose limitations as quotas and tariffs to the types of trade in services, because some services are invisible, intangible, and non-storable (Ramcharran, 1999).

Adam Smith suggested that international trade should be governed by the market (Flory & Kitcher, 2004). Trade theory also indicates that every government or country should adopt liberal trade policies and transact goods and services. Most countries still intervene in international trade because of economics or political reasons to protect their own advantages (Mueller, 2003). According to new trade theory school, the intention of international trade is not to create competitive situations between countries, but is designed to increase mutually beneficial exchange from import and export to obtain goods, services or payment (Jager, 1998).

We will understand the formation and dynamics of international organizations better if we invest in more and better research aimed at generalizing about the process of negotiation in those settings. The study of international institutions and the empirical study of negotiation have often been isolated from each other. This has been changing, over the past decade; and quite dramatically in last one decade as we do have solid empirical knowledge and visible evidences about some regime negotiations, but many promising opportunities remain unexploited and even relatively less understood.

The negotiation process may be distinguished from the structures in which it takes place. *Negotiation* (or *bargaining*) is a sequence of actions in which two or more parties address demands and proposals to each other for the ostensible purposes of reaching an agreement and changing the behavior of at least one actor. Concretely, on international economic issues the process refers to what governments' finance and trade ministers, for example, do with one another. The process includes which strategies negotiators choose, how markets and negotiators influence each other, whether negotiators add tactics to smoke out joint gains, how much they use tactics to guard against their own biases, and how they go about forming and splitting coalitions. The process includes how the negotiators' moves interact with domestic politics.

Many studies of international institutions are dominated by theoretical interests other than the negotiation process. Many revealing negotiation case studies have yet to be integrated under any common analytical framework. An increasing number of studies on institutional bargaining do give us promising foundations to build on. International organizations vary greatly among themselves. Which aspects of organizational structure or behavior make the most difference to the negotiation process? Do some institutional settings make agents willing to be freer with information, more inclined toward value-creating moves?[1] Do some organizations facilitate the formation of coalitions more readily than others, or bias the parties toward certain coalitions and away from others? Do particular international institutions establish specialized negotiation processes such that negotiator behavior differs reliably from one to the other, even when the same governments are involved? For instance, we might compare the process of a typical IMF loan negotiation, the average GATT tariff negotiation, and the typical European Community enlargement negotiation—all as special variations on the general process of economic bargaining. Comparing organizations as to their effectiveness for facilitating gains might suggest fresh innovations to organizations themselves.

Researchers and scholars have made significant strides in this area, mostly with diverse case studies, but methodological problems impede efforts to disentangle such complexities. Also these studies have been designed separately, not under any one theoretical framework, and their findings are not yet commensurable. According to Blair 1993, the OECD's norms and secretariat do not have much discernible effect on governments' negotiation behavior on trade issues or on multiparty outcomes, though more precise rules on one issue enjoy greater compliance than others. Agrawal (1996) reports that the League of Nations did not affect outcomes of debt renegotiations, but the IMF and the Brady Plan did so. Rithstein (1979) and Suskind (1994) were of the view that the U.N. organizational context—UNCTAD for the former and formal universalism in environmental talks for the latter—has impeded valuable settlements that might have been. Winham 1986 sees in the GATT's Tokyo round a transition toward a new system for managing international trade by multilateral negotiation. Martin (1992) reports, from aggregate data as well as contrasting case studies, that when an international organization calls on its members to impose economic sanctions on a country, the level of cooperation among sanctioners increases. Finnmore (1996) reports three historical cases in which an international organization shaped states' very interests and hence their behavior in negotiations and elsewhere. Garrett and Weingast (1993) cite the case of the European Court of Justice and the 1987 EC decision to complete the "internal market" to support an argument that international institutions can help states construct focal points that they might not have found by themselves.

Trade and Investments Agreements and Current Negotiations

This section references example of past, current, and future trade policy topics of general interest, identifies relevant organizations, and links various websites that provide current and more in-depth information (http://www.gov.ns.ca/iga/trade.asp), as are relevant to Trade and Investments, Agreements and Current Negotiations.

World Trade Organization (WTO)—A permanent world trade body was established in 1995 following the conclusion of the Uruguay Round of Negotiations on expanding the General Agreement on Tariffs and Trade (GATT). The objectives of the WTO are to reduce barriers to trade and strengthen international trade rules to ensure that all 142 Members have fair and equal treatment in a global trading system. The Doha Summit (November 2001) launched an ambitious round of new negotiations with the aim of eliminating or reducing trade-distorting subsidies and domestic supports, and to achieve greater market access. A key stated objective of the Doha negotiation round is greater sensitivity to the problems of developing and least developed countries regarding trade obligations and benefits and to provide for capacity-building and technical assistance. Negotiations have been protracted and there is no certainty as to their successful completion. The original 1 January deadline was missed. After that, members unofficially aimed to finish the negotiations by the end of 2006, but the collapse of negotiations in July are not encouraging. The Organization for Economic Co-operation and Development (OECD) carries out parallel research on current and topical trade matters. The WTO site provides extensive background documentation on the global trading system and conducts regular reviews of the trade regimes of member countries through the Trade Policy Review Mechanism.

An important function and role of the WTO is that of providing an effective forum for the resolution of trade disputes, which have witnessed a sharp increase in the last number of years. Canada has been involved in a number of protracted disputes such as the disputes on soft-wood lumber, aircraft subsidies and the application of food safety standards.

North American Free-Trade Agreement (NAFTA)-The Canada—United States Free Trade Agreement of 1989 was the basis for the trilateral North American FTA (NAFTA) in 1993. Given the volume of trade and investment between the United States and Canada the trading relationship is complex and not without problems. In particular, lumber, agri-food, and cultural services have each been topics for continuous consultations and formal dispute settlement. International Trade Canada posts status reports. Equally, the Office of the US Trade Representative (USTR) provides releases, position papers; US trade access interests and status reports, as well as hotlinks to relevant US agencies on its website. www.ustr.gov Information on trade and market access to the United States (and other countries) is available through International Trade Canada and sites such as:

- Export Source: Team Canada
- Canadian Trade Commissioner Service
- Strategies: Industry Canada
- US Customs and Border Protection

Free-Trade Area of the Americas (FTAA) and other FTAs—With the emergence of various trading blocks in Central and South America and the interest in North America in forging closer hemispheric trading and investment links among governments, there was an original undertaking to negotiate a

Free Trade Area of the Americas (FTAA) Agreement by 2005. The scope and timing of any ultimate agreement are unclear following the disagreements and compromises that characterized the Miami ministers meeting in late 2003. Working groups are engaged, however, on various topics and would be expected to draw on generally accepted rules and obligations in the WTO, NAFTA, and other regional agreements. There is now less possibility that some of these negotiations will parallel those under the WTO negotiating track in areas such as services, agriculture, and investment. There is extensive information on the FTAA website.

Asia-Pacific Economic Cooperation (APEC) Forum—Formed in 1989, this 18 country forum has become significant in recent years due to the participation of major trading countries such as the US, Canada, Japan, and China and key new global players that, altogether, represented 50% of world trade by 1995. One of the most important developments in the Asia-Pacific arena was China's accession to the WTO in late 2001. See the APEC website as well as Asia Pacific Foundation of Canada

International Free-Trade Negotiations: Nature of Participation

In international trade, all countries strive to reach a contradictory goal. They would like to foster their exports in order to maximize income and profits for their business and industry and earn foreign exchange to strengthen their economy, while at the same time impose restrictions and tariffs to prevent other countries from exporting to them (http://www.moneyinstructor.com/art/freetrade.asp).

Free trade negotiations try to merge these two interests. Each country's ideal foreign trade policy would be to have unrestricted access to foreign markets for their goods, and impose restrictions on goods from other countries so that they only import what they need and do not import products that will compete in their domestic market. This is, of course, completely impossible as all countries try to achieve this same end. Free trade negotiations are a result of this give and take between nations as they try to maximize exports and minimize imports. Free trade negotiations between nations occur on a global scale around the year, and free trade agreements have been established between trading nations to achieve some compromises in this arena.

The United States is party to the North American Free Trade Association (NAFTA), the Central American Free Trade Association (CAFTA) and the General Agreement on Tariffs and Trade (GATT), the World Trade Organization (WTO) as well as other smaller free trade agreements and organizations. At these organizations, United States trade representatives meet routinely with the representatives of other nations to hammer out the details of how they will trade with one another. Promoters of international trade agreements usually include large corporations who want unrestricted access to as many markets as possible, but have to prove to the domestic public that jobs will not be lost and individuals suffer.

NAFTA, for example, when it was formed in 1994 "promised it would create hundreds of thousands of new high-wage U.S. jobs, raise living standards in the U.S., Mexico and Canada, improve environmental conditions and transform Mexico from a poor developing country into a booming new market for U.S. exports."

Countries use tariffs, quotas, subsidies, import regulations, laws, legislation and regulatory measures as well as restrictions on capital flows and investment in order to control the flow of goods across their borders or protect industries threatened by global trade. Free trade negotiations involve concessions in some of these areas in order to achieve a balance and arrive at fair agreements. Here is an example of free trade negotiations at work. In 2005, the European Union has a maximum ceiling of $19.1billion and the United States a maximum ceiling of $75billion to spend on farm subsidies to protect their agricultural industries. (Subsidies to farmers lead to excess crops, pushing prices down, creating a disadvantage for farmers in other countries. The European Union and Japan, who both subsidize their farmers, have opposed a U.S. plan requiring them to cut that aid.) As part of the Doha trade negotiations in October, 2005, the United States offered to lower their ceiling by 60% if the European Union cut theirs by 80%. (*The Economist* October 15, 2005.) Of course, further rounds of negotiations will take place and a compromise will be agreed upon, as each nation tries to give as little as possible and get as much as possible to protect its interests.

Proliferation of Regional and Bilateral Trade Agreements

Since 1999, the trend of international trade negotiations has changed permanently with the advent of regional and bilateral trade agreements. The failure of the WTO meeting in Seattle in 1999, lack of progress in APEC and ASEAN at the time, and uncertainties in the post Asian crisis environment, all contributed to the phenomenon of economies in Asia which had previously not supported such preferential agreements to begin considering regional and bilateral trade agreements. This included Japan which began considering a Free Trade Area (FTA) with Korea, Singapore and then later followed by Thailand and Malaysia, Australia and New Zealand, signed on to a number of what is now termed as "new age" Comprehensive Economic Partnership Agreements of which a Free Trade Area in goods is a component. China also became ASEAN's first dialogue partner to launch and ASEAN plus one type of agreement, starting with an FTA in goods whereby a subset of goods are subject to immediate tariff reduction (http://www.depdag.go.id/files/publikasi/berita_menteri_perdagangan/data/keynoteaddress-wto_forumfeb2.doc).

The trend of preferential agreements was of course not confined to Asia, but also occurred in other parts of the world and across the Pacific, such as between Singapore and Australia with the US. Other Asian countries are also now entering into negotiations with the US (i.e. Korea, Malaysia and Thailand). Furthermore, other regional agreements that have proliferated in Latin America, including the Free Trade Area of Americas, and in Europe there is the enlargement of the European Union. The trend of regionalism and bilateralism is here to stay, whether we like it or not, and with all the consequences.

The Fate of Multilateral Trade Negotiations: Process and Substance

Meanwhile the failure of Seattle in 1999 unleashed anti globalization sentiment. One of the main reasons for the failure of Seattle was that it was "business as usual" whereby a number of the large developed countries converged to the so called Green Room process to decide on the elements of a new round of trade negotiations. This did not work at all because developing countries, now a large part and active part of WTO membership, were unable to accept this outcome. Seattle saw the last of the Green Room process whereby the fate of so many were decided by major developed countries.

In 2001, in Doha, developing countries were very much included in the dialogue that produced the Doha Development Agenda and they added their long list of demands. Developing countries for the first time negotiation a difficult and tough compromise, and in the aftermath of the September 11, 2001 terrorist attacks, there was a strong sense of not wanting a failure of the WTO Ministerial Meeting. There had to be an outcome for development. At the time 2005 was set at as an end date for negotiations, and even then there was already a sense of this deadline being too optimistic.

In 2003, members attending the WTO ministerial in Cancun tried to describe the end game of negotiations that is the main elements of negotiations. Cancun was yet another failure without any agreement being reached and the talks collapsed. This was a case of little consultation pre Cancun and producing a draft text which included the four controversial so called Singapore issues (i.e. investment, competition policy, government procurement and trade facilitation), which developing countries absolutely did not want to accept. There was a so called Green Room process whereby there were very tough negotiations, conducted in a way which failed to reach compromises and by the time developed countries were ready to make compromises, it was too late and the talks collapsed. During the course of Cancun a number of groups emerged around different issues. The G20 group led by Brazil focused on agriculture trade reform of developed countries; the G33 group led by Indonesia focused on special products and special safeguard mechanism for a subgroup of agriculture products based on food security, rural livelihood and employment; and the G90 group of mainly African and Caribbean developing countries rallied around least developed country issues and other development issues.

Post-Cancun, no agreement could be reached until July 2004 when under the umbrella of the General Council, starting with a draft text, a number of key Ministers met to discuss the way forward and reached several compromises such as dropping all but one of the Singapore issues, that is trade facilitation and accommodating the specific issues raised by different groups such as SP and SSM by G33.

Prior to the Hong Kong meeting, it was decided that a draft Ministerial Text should be prepared. The process in Geneva, especially beginning with the new Director General, Pascal Lamy, was also as much as possible made open and inclusive. The Director General, who was then the EU Trade Commissioner during the failed Cancun talks, had learned about the importance of inclusion of all parties to ensure acceptance of the outcome by all.

What was different about Hong Kong? The main difference is that the groups that formed around issues, many of which comprise of groups of developing countries had done their homework and preparation. G20 had submitted a well-researched proposal of agriculture trade reforms and G33 similarly had come up with proposals justifying the need for SP and SSM. This was a key part of the offensive and defensive strategy. Most importantly the developing country groups supported each other and the coalition lasted throughout the meetings, between G20, G33, G90, the Caribbean countries, and the least developed countries. Furthermore, the process in Hong Kong was deemed as transparent, democratic and inclusive since those in the Green Room or CCG (Chairman Coordinating Group) process comprising of 26 key Ministers, which met intensively during the night, and coordinated with their groups on positions during the day, worked well to ensure that as much as possible all interests were represented.

Whilst Hong Kong did not yield the full negotiating modalities that were targeted, it provided sufficient foundation to build on. The deadlines are now real, negotiating modalities must be completed by April 2006, draft commitments submitted by July 2006 and negotiations completed by end of 2006.

In Davos, at the end of January, 2009 where 20 out of the 26 Ministers met again to discuss ways to ensure that these deadlines can be met. The key factor is of course that there must be movement across a number of fronts, namely that further agriculture trade reform in the developed countries, mainly Europe providing greater market access in their proposal, the US in further reduction in subsidies must also be matched by reduction in industrial tariffs, especially by the large developing countries such as India and Brazil, and improved offer of services by developing countries. That is, there should be agreement to move together, and not wait for one to move before the other moves. Furthermore, there was agreement to come up with clear time schedules in the different areas of negotiations (there are some 48 technical issues to be solved in agriculture and NAMA negotiations alone and only around 60 working days left before the end of April). Other than Agriculture and NAMA, the other areas of negotiations are services, trade facilitation, rules, trade and environment, special and differential treatment.

General Agreement on Tariffs and Trade (GATT)

The *General Agreement on Tariffs and Trade* (GATT) was the outcome of the failure of negotiating governments to create the International Trade Organization (ITO). GATT was formed in 1947 and lasted until 1994, when it was replaced by the World Trade Organization. The Bretton Woods Conference had introduced the idea for an organization to regulate trade as part of a larger plan for economic recovery after World War II. As governments negotiated the ITO, 15 negotiating states began parallel negotiations for the GATT as a way to attain early tariff reductions. Once the ITO failed in 1950, only the GATT agreement was left. The GATT's main objective was the reduction of barriers to international trade. This was achieved through the reduction of tariff barriers, quantitative restrictions and subsidies on trade through a series of agreements. The GATT was a treaty, not an organization. The functions of the GATT were taken over by the World Trade Organization which was established during the final round of negotiations in early 1990s.

The history of the GATT can be divided into three phases: the first, from 1947 until the Torquay Round, largely concerned which commodities would be covered by the agreement and freezing existing tariff levels. A second phase, encompassing three rounds, from 1959 to 1979, focused on reducing tariffs. The third phase, consisting only of the Uruguay Round from 1986 to 1994, extended the agreement fully to new areas such as intellectual property, services, capital, and agriculture. Out of this round the WTO was born.

GATT signatories occasionally negotiated new trade agreements that all countries would enter into. Each set of agreements was called a *round*. In general, each agreement bound members to reduce certain tariffs. Usually this would include many special-case treatments of individual products, with exceptions or modifications for each country.

Inception

The precursor organization to the GATT, called the International Trade Organization (ITO), was first proposed in February 1946 by the United Nations Economic and Social Council. The negotiating countries of the ITO began parallel negotiations for the GATT as a way to introduce early tariff cuts. The plan called for the ITO to take control over GATT, once the ITO was finalized. Owing to the United States failing to implement the ITO, GATT was the only organization left. On 1 January, 1948 the agreement was signed by 23 countries: Australia, Belgium, Brazil, Burma, Canada, Ceylon, Chile, China, Cuba, the Czechoslovak Republic, France, India, Lebanon, Luxembourg, Netherlands, New Zealand, Norway, Pakistan, Southern Rhodesia, Syria, South Africa, the United Kingdom, and the United States. According to GATT's own estimates, the negotiations created 123 agreements that covered 45,000 tariff items that related to approximately one-half of world trade or $10 billion in trade. GATT 1947 in the US.

The GATT, as an international agreement, is a treaty. Under United States law it is classified as a congressional-executive agreement. Based on the Reciprocal Trade Agreements Act it allowed the executive branch negotiating power over trade agreements with temporary authority from Congress. At the time it functioned as a provisional, but promising trade system. The agreement is based on the "*unconditional most favored nation principle*" This means that the conditions applied to the most favored trading nation (i.e. the one with the least restrictions) apply to all trading nations. In the US, there was large opposition against the International Trade Organization (which had been ratified in several countries), and thus President Truman never even submitted it to the Congress (Table 1).

Table 1: GATT & WTO held 8 rounds of Global Negotiations on Strategic Issues

GATT and WTO trade rounds					
Name	**Start**	**Duration**	**Countries**	**Subjects covered**	**Achievements**
Geneva	April 1947	7 months	23	Tariffs	Signing of GATT, 45,000 tariff concessions affecting $10 billion of trade
Annecy	April 1949	5 months	13	Tariffs	Countries exchanged some 5,000 tariff concessions
Torquay	Sept. 1950	8 months	38	Tariffs	Countries exchanged some 8,700 tariff concessions, cutting the 1948 tariff levels by 25%
Geneva II	January 1956	5 months	26	Tariffs, admission of Japan	$2.5 billion in tariff reductions
Dillon	Sept. 1960	11 months	26	Tariffs	Tariff concessions worth $4.9 billion of world trade
Kennedy	May 1964	37 months	62	Tariffs, Anti-dumping	Tariff concessions worth $40 billion of world trade
Tokyo	Sept. 1973	74 months	102	Tariffs, non-tariff measures, "framework" agreements	Tariff reductions worth more than $300 billion dollars achieved
Uruguay	Sept. 1986	87 months	123	Tariffs, non-tariff measures, rules, services, intellectual property, dispute settlement, textiles, agriculture, creation of WTO, etc.	The round led to the creation of WTO, and extended the range of trade negotiations, leading to major reductions in tariffs (about 40%) and agricultural subsidies, an agreement to allow full access for **textiles** and clothing from developing countries, and an extension of intellectual property rights.
Doha	November 2001		141	Tariffs, non-tariff measures, agriculture, labor standards, environment, competition, investment, transparency, patents etc.	The round is not yet concluded.

Annecy Round - 1950

The second round took place in 1949 in Annecy, France. 13 countries took part in the round. The main focus of the talks was more tariff reductions, around 5000 total.

Torquay Round - 1951

The third round occurred in Torquay, England in 1951. 38 countries took part in the round. 8,700 tariff concessions were made totaling the remaining amount of tariffs to three-fourths of the tariffs which were in effect in 1948.

Geneva Round - 1955-56

The fourth round returned to Geneva in 1955 and lasted until May 1956. 26 countries took part in the round. $2.5 billion in tariffs were eliminated or reduced.

Dillon Round - 1960-62

The fifth round occurred once more in Geneva and lasted from 1960 to 1962. The talks were named after U.S. Treasury Secretary and former Under Secretary of State, Douglas Dillon, who first proposed the talks. 26 countries took part in the round. Along with reducing over $4.9 billion in tariffs, it also yielded discussion relating to the creation of the European Economic Community (EEC).

Kennedy Round - 1964-67

The sixth round was the last to take place in Geneva from 1964 until 1967 and was named after the late US President Kennedy in his memory. 66 countries [4] took part in the round. Concessions were made on $40 billion worth of tariffs. Some of the GATT negotiation rules were also more clearly defined.

Tokyo Round - 1973-79

Reduced tariffs and established new regulations aimed at controlling the proliferation of non-tariff barriers and voluntary export restrictions. 102 countries took part in the round. Concessions were made on $190 billion worth.

Uruguay Round - 1986-93

The Uruguay Round began in 1986. It was the most ambitious round to date, hoping to expand the competence of the GATT to important new areas such as services, capital, intellectual property, textiles, and agriculture. 123 countries took part in the round.

Agriculture was essentially exempted from previous agreements as it was given special status in the areas of import quotas and export subsidies, with only mild caveats. However, by the time of the Uruguay round, many countries considered the exception of agriculture to be sufficiently glaring that they refused to sign a new deal without some movement on agricultural products. These fourteen countries came to be known as the "Cairns Group", and included mostly small and medium sized agricultural exporters such as Australia, Brazil, Canada, Indonesia, and New Zealand.

The Agreement on Agriculture of the Uruguay Round continues to be the most substantial trade liberalization agreement in agricultural products in the history of trade negotiations. The goals of the agreement were to improve market access for agricultural products, reduce domestic support of agriculture in the form of price-distorting subsidies and quotas, and eliminate over time export subsidies on agricultural products and to harmonize to the extent possible sanitary and phystosanitary measures between member countries.

GATT and the World Trade Organization (WTO)

Uruguay Round

In 1993 the GATT was updated (GATT, 1994) to include new obligations upon its signatories. One of the most significant changes was the creation of the World Trade Organization (WTO). The 75 existing GATT members and the European Communities became the founding members of the WTO on 1 January 1995. The other 52 GATT members rejoined the WTO in the following two years (the last being Congo in 1997). Since the founding of the WTO, 21 new non-GATT members have joined and 29 are currently negotiating membership. As of October 2007, there were a total of 151 member countries in the WTO.

Of the original GATT members, only the SFR Yugoslavia has not rejoined the WTO. Since FR Yugoslavia, (renamed to Serbia and Montenegro and with membership negotiations later split in two), is not recognized as a direct SFRY successor state; therefore, its application is considered a new (non-GATT) one. The contracting parties who founded the WTO ended official agreement of the "GATT 1947" terms on 31 December, 1995.

Whereas GATT was a set of rules agreed upon by nations, the WTO is an institutional body. The WTO expanded its scope from traded goods to trade within the service sector and intellectual property rights. Although it was designed to serve multilateral agreements, during several rounds of GATT negotiations (particularly the Tokyo Round) plurilateral agreements created selective trading and caused fragmentation among members. WTO arrangements are generally a multilateral agreement settlement mechanism of GATT. The debatable issue is recognition of human rights under GATT. The dimensions of the environmental context include legal and political pluralism, currency fluctuations and foreign exchange, foreign government controls and bureaucracy, instability and change, ideological and cultural differences, and the influence of external stakeholders.

Legal Pluralism

The principle of national sovereignty gives every nation-state the right to make laws that are supposedly in its national interests. An international business transaction must comply with the laws of the countries involved.

Certain laws prohibit certain types of transactions. For example, the United States has legislation that lists the various types of technologies, particularly those with potential military applications that are prohibited from being exported. When Cray Computer Company tried to sell a supercomputer to the Indian government, the U.S. disallowed the sale on the grounds that it was illegal because it hurt American national security interests.

In several countries, certain sectors of the economy, such as telecommunications and automobile manufacturing, are often kept off-limits to wholly owned foreign investments. For instance, a foreign company can enter the Indian and Chinese markets only by forming joint ventures with indigenous companies. General Motors, Ford, Volkswagen, and Mercedes have established manufacturing plants in India in joint ventures with Indian companies; Volkswagen, Citroen, and Peugeot have joint ventures in China. The joint venture requirement undoubtedly affected the negotiations between the two sides over other important aspects, such as managerial and quality control, global marketing rights, valuation of technology transferred, profit sharing, and royalty payments. Negotiators should be forewarned about the legal traps that could transform a supposedly good agreement into a nightmare if the legal implications of the transaction are not carefully examined. It is imperative that negotiators be extremely careful in avoiding the risk of doing something illegal under the laws of either the home country or the host.

Rules of Negotiations under WTO

The WTO and the GATT before it have helped define rules to facilitate international trade and to liberalize markets to expanded trade. The Rules negotiations in the Doha Development Agenda pertain to a subset of internationally agreed rules for international trade and deal with whether modifications to the Antidumping Agreement and the Subsidies and Countervailing Measures (SCM) Agreement should be made, whether additional rules are appropriate for fisheries subsidies, and whether additional clarifications are appropriate for regional trade agreements.

Dumping and subsidies that cause harm have been addressable under international rules since the beginning of the GATT, and under some domestic laws of individual Members before that. Contracting parties to the GATT and Members of the WTO have periodically sought to revisit these areas to clarify rules, improve disciplines or address changing conditions. Since the start of the WTO, many new trade remedy users emerged as they undertook significant trade liberalization in their trade in goods. While trade covered by trade remedies is typically quite small as a percent of total trade (often less than 1%), the use of trade remedies has drawn a lot of attention in the dispute settlement system and remained a topic of interest to many Members before the Doha Ministerial meeting in 2001. A number of countries who viewed their interests as largely exporter-oriented in nature and/or countries who perceived themselves to have defensive interests elsewhere pushed for inclusion of a review of the Antidumping and SCM Agreements as part of the Doha package.

Other countries, particularly the United States, saw limited purpose in reviewing agreements which had just been renegotiated and put into place in 1995.

Because the U.S. Congress has historically viewed a linchpin to public support for expanded trade liberalization being the availability of remedies to address dumping and subsidies that injure U.S. companies and their workers, the United States was willing to have trade remedies included in the negotiations only if the negotiations would both address the underlying causes of dumping and subsidization and if any clarifications and improvements in disciplines preserved "the basic concepts, principles and effectiveness of these Agreements and their instruments and objectives."

Due to concerns regarding the effect of over fishing on sustainable development objectives, it was agreed that participants would "aim to clarify and improve WTO disciplines on fisheries subsidies, taking into account the importance of this sector to developing countries." Doha Ministerial Declaration, para. 28. Free trade agreements (whether bilateral or regional) have exploded in numbers in the last twenty years raising many questions about whether the requirements of GATT Article XXIV are being met (and now the 1979 "Enabling Clause" and GATS Article V). Virtually all WTO Members were partners in at least one RTA, and many were partners in two or more; only Hong Kong, China; Japan; Macau, China; and Mongolia are not currently partners in a RTA."

The number had increased to 215 by December 31, 2006 with many more under active negotiation including by Members not involved just six years earlier. WTO Annual Report 2007 at 50-52. While a mechanism had been developed as part of the outcome of the Uruguay Round to monitor the consistency of RTAs with WTO standards (through the 1994 Understanding on the Interpretation of Article XXIF of GATT, 1994 and the establishment of the a Committee on Regional Trade Agreements, there was continued concern about RTAs at the start of the Doha round. Thus, Members agreed in paragraph 29 of the Doha Ministerial Declaration to clarify and improve "disciplines and procedures under the existing WTO provisions applying to regional trade agreements" while taking "into account the developmental aspects of regional trade agreements."

Despite the importance of regional trade agreements and the interest in trade remedies, the Rules negotiations have typically been viewed as a piece of the overall final agreement but not the primary focus (agriculture, NAMA and services). Thus, for most of the six-year period, Rules, as other areas, tended to follow negotiations in agriculture and NAMA, as can be seen in the draft decision at the Cancun Ministerial in 2003 (draft Ministerial Declaration, para. 7 of Job(03)/150/Rev.2), the decision adopted by the General Council on August 1, 2004, WT/L/579 at 3, para. 1. F, and the Hong Kong Ministerial Declaration (adopted December 18, 2005), WT/MIN (05)/DEC at para 28 and Annex D. The World Trade Organization's Doha Development Agenda.

Some Basic Provisions of Trade Agreements

Trade agreements are separate contracts between the signatories and have their own terms and conditions. Several provisions are common to many agreements. · Trade Rules. Some trade rules, such as those relating to "national treatment" (requiring fair and equal treatment of domestic and foreign companies delivering the same goods) and "least-trade restrictive" solutions (the minimum level of regulation that is possible over a private enterprise) may invalidate local economic and social legislation such as economic preferences granted to local businesses (http://www.nlc.org/assets/3f3c00db0d8c42bcbb28c3dc5794fdd3/ipissuepapertrade041406.pdf).

- *Investment Rules*: These rules are designed to protect both U.S. and foreign companies from arbitrary or discriminatory actions by governments. The agreements allow corporations to bring claims for monetary damages against a national government to the WTO or an arbitration panel if the company believes that the actions of the federal or a state or local government can be considered – directly or indirectly – an expropriation of their investment. In this regard, concerns have been raised that under certain trade agreements foreign companies potentially have stronger claims against the United States than U.S. companies have under U.S. constitutional law when it comes to regulatory takings under the 5th Amendment.
- *Dispute Resolution*: Trade cases outside the jurisdiction of the WTO are decided by tribunals of trade experts selected by the parties under rules governing the resolution of disputes. These experts may or may not be well versed in U.S. constitutional law. Unlike U.S. courts, tribunals are not asked to weigh and balance commercial values with other competing community values. The tribunals may not take U.S. law into consideration and they may conduct their hearings out of public view. State and local governments have no right to represent themselves before international tribunals when a local law or policy is alleged to be in violation of the United States' international obligations. Monetary damages are imposed as penalties against the losing party.

Mandate and Regulatory Provisions of Various Agreements under WTO

The following paragraphs provide a detailed outline as well as account of various Regulatory provisions under some important Acts promulgated under the WTO. Some country-specific examples are also cited to describe as to how these acts are being leveraged to advantage. Alongside, an analysis of implementation modalities, including various constraints faced in implementation are also highlighted.

1. General Agreements of Trade and Services (GATS)

A Note by the UNCTAD Secretariat

The General Agreement on Trade in Services (GATS), negotiated during the Uruguay Round as part of a single undertaking is the first set of multilaterally agreed and legally enforceable rules and disciplines relating to international trade in services. An integral part is the schedules of specific commitments undertaken by individual WTO Members. These commitments, once taken, prevent the Member from introducing more restrictive policies/ regulations that could have an adverse effect on trade. India made initial commitments at the time of entry of GATS into force in 1995 in 33 sub-sectors. While taking commitments, a number of limitations on market access and national treatment were made in the schedules consistent with our national policy objectives. In most cases, these were no more than the autonomously liberalized policies already in force in India.

Negotiations are mandated under Article XIX of the GATS, which states that "in pursuance of the objectives of the Agreement, Members shall enter into successive rounds of negotiations beginning not later than 5 years from the date of entry into force of the WTO Agreements and periodically thereafter, with a view to achieving a progressively higher level of liberalization". Accordingly, a fresh round of negotiation on specific commitment was commenced in the WTO with effect from 1.1.2000. The negotiations are being conducted at the Special Sessions of the Council for Trade in Services (CTS). These negotiations are now part of the Doha Work Programme and were scheduled to be concluded by 1/1/2005 as a single undertaking (http://www.ficci.com/media-room/speeches-presentations/2003/Apr/april17-atbackground.htm).

The main method of negotiations on Trade in Services is the Request and Offer process, under which each country tables its Requests to its trading partners (i.e., their lists of demands, seeking greater market access for their exports from them) and in turn also places its Offers to its trading partners (i.e., the concession that they are willing to offer giving greater market access to imports of services from them) sector-wise. The Doha Ministerial Declaration had mandated that members shall submit initial Requests by June, 2002 and initial Offers by March 2003. Further, it prescribes that the Negotiations shall close by 1 January, 2005. The submission of Requests and Offers is a continuous process which is likely to continue till 2005 or the end of negotiations. The negotiations are being conducted bilaterally, between Groups of Countries and multilaterally. Any commitments agreed to during this process with a particular country or a Group of countries or multilaterally will be made applicable in respect of all other countries at the end of negotiations as part of the MFN obligation.

Under the ongoing negotiations, India has submitted 'requests' to our trading partners in Computer Related services, Architecture services, Health services, Audio-Visual services, Tourism services, Maritime services and Financial services. On the other hand, we have received requests from 23 countries and have to finalize our response to these requests through an "initial offer". The initial offer would point towards the direction in which a Member is willing to liberalize. However, the initial offer has no legal status and can be withdrawn or amended at any time if the Member feels that the trading partners' offers are not satisfactory or adequate. Agreement to liberalize is not reached until all participating Members—including developing countries—are satisfied with the total package being offered. In formulating the offers, Members are not obliged to respond positively to any particular request. Nor is there any requirement for reciprocity. That is, a request made by India in one area/sector/ activity does not impose any obligation to accept a similar request made of it by other countries. Further, the Doha Ministerial Declaration reaffirms the rights of members to regulate and to introduce new regulations on the supply of services. A brief Sector-wise description of the Requests that we have made on our trading partners and the ones that we have received from them can be accessed at the web-site of Department of Commerce (http://commerce.nic.in/wto_counsel_paper.htm).

The mode of supply of particular interest to India and other developing countries is Mode 4, i.e. the Movement of Natural Persons. India, in particular, has a large pool of well-qualified professionals in the services sectors like computer and related services, education services, audiovisual services, accountancy services, architectural services, construction and engineering services, health services and consultancy services. India has fairly large comparative advantage over other Member countries with regard to supply of professional services in these service sectors. Besides, for India modes 1 and 2 are also important as via mode 1 it can deliver professional services electronically and via mode 2 it can provide services such as medical, educational and tourism services to the foreign patients, students and tourists visiting India.

The GATS, in its preamble, explicitly recognizes the right of Members to regulate, and to introduce new regulation, on the supply of services within their territories in order to meet national policy objectives, and given the asymmetries existing with respect to the degree of development of services regulation, the particular need of developing countries to exercise this right. Furthermore, the process of progressive liberalization of trade in services, as provided by Article XIX.2, has to take place with due respect of national policy objectives; and the right of Members to regulate the supply of services in their territories has been further reaffirmed by the Negotiating Guidelines and Procedures adopted for the GATS 2000 negotiations, endorsed by the Doha Ministerial Declaration.1 Nevertheless, the possible impact of the GATS on the regulatory autonomy of the nation state is perhaps one of the issues that have given rise to greater concern among, negotiators, national policy makers, and civil society institutions alike (ICTSD: http://ictsd.net/i/publications/11451).

This is a preliminary checklist of issues prepared by the UNCTAD's Trade

Negotiations and Commercial Diplomacy Branch, on the basis of a first examination of the proposals presented by WTO Members in the context of the GATS negotiations. The purpose of this preliminary checklist is to assist developing countries' delegations in their analysis of numerous proposals submitted to the WTO Council for Trade in Services. It is aimed at providing the first insight into the issues that are detailed in the proposals that may benefit from further attention and consideration by developing countries. The checklist is an overview of "new" issues in the sense that they have not been addressed previously in a particular context. It also aims at identifying those issues that may be commonly found in specific sectoral proposals. Further, an overview of issues contained in the proposals under the specific services sectors is presented. In principle, majority of the proposals have addressed the issues in accordance with the following general themes: (1) General position; (2) Classification and Coverage/Scope; (3) Market Access/National Treatment; and 4) Regulatory Issues.

The work presented is considered as work in progress. The checklist is being regularly updated to account for the forthcoming new proposals. It will be further evolving based on the reactions and feedback received from the delegations, capital based officials and other stakeholders in developing countries. The issues identified in the checklist draw attention to some of them as contained in the proposals, and should not be interpreted as prejudging the issues for the services negotiations, nor as circumscribing the issues for the developing countries in these negotiations. The main purpose of the checklist is to serve as (non-exhaustive) factual tool. In follow up to the points raised in the checklist it is hoped that the position of the developing countries could be more readily elaborated as well as the issues of concern to the developing countries detailed. As it stands now, the checklist is addressing some preliminary views on possible issues of concern for developing countries. They are not intended to give a full picture of the issues contained in the proposals, nor of their implications but only meant to assist in the analysis of proposals and to stimulate their debate, without prejudging the positions of any WTO Member.

I. Overview of the Proposal

Up until the last services week held on 9-18 May 2001, more than 80 sector-specific proposals had been presented. Proposals have been presented under all but health services sector. Such proposals cover the following services sectors: Accountancy; Air transport; Architectural services; Audiovisuals; Business services (other than Professional Services); Computer and related services; Construction and Related Engineering services; Distribution services; Energy services; Engineering services; Environmental services; Financial services; Higher (Tertiary) Education, Adult Education, and Training; Legal services; Logistics and Related Services; Land Transport; Maritime Transport; Postal/Courier services (including Express Delivery); Professional services; Telecommunications; and Tourism.

The WTO Members having submitted individual sectoral proposals are:

Australia, Canada, Chile, the European Communities, Hong-Kong China, Japan, Korea, Norway, Switzerland, the United States and Venezuela. The Dominican Republic, Honduras and El Salvador have tabled two joint submissions, and a third one together with Nicaragua and Panama. The EC, Hong-Kong, China, Japan, Korea, Norway, and Singapore, have also submitted a joint proposal. MERCOSUR countries as a group, have also submitted a proposal on distribution services.

Four more proposals have been tabled on the movement of natural persons/professionals/services suppliers (Mode 4) by Canada, the EC, India, and the United States. Canada has also presented initial negotiating proposals on Regulatory, Transparency and Predictability, and on Small- and Medium-Sized Enterprises. The ANDEAN group has also submitted a proposal on definition and criteria for classification of services.

This draft of a checklist covered at this stage all the sectoral proposals (individual and joint-proposals) submitted by WTO Members up until 14th May 2001. The check-list is divided into two parts: the first one presents possible cross-cutting issues, and the second one provides an identification of possible issues sector by sector.

II. Cross-Cultural Issues

- *Implementation of Article IV*: Most proposals do not address Article IV. Clear exceptions to this are the proposals by Venezuela (Energy), and The Dominican Republic, Honduras and El Salvador (Tourism). It seems that the only differential treatment for developing countries would be accorded in granting periods of transition (Canada) or to support trade liberalization by programs of capacity building (Australia). However, the proposals submitted by developing countries, for example as explicitly indicated by Mercosur, are indicating the sectors of the interest for developing countries in light with the Article IV.
- *Modes of Supply*: Most proposals put emphasis on Modes 3 (commercial presence through establishment) and 1 (cross-border trade). On Mode 4 (movement of natural persons), coverage is generally limited to intra-corporate transferees. However, the EC states in practically all its proposals to be open to hold further discussions on how to improve and facilitate the temporary movement of both intra-corporate transferees and "contractual service suppliers" for the provision of specific services.
- *Standstill*: The US is suggesting that the starting point should be the present situation of liberalization. Both the US and the EC have proposed a commitment on *standstill*. However, most other proposals consider the current schedules (i.e. binding commitments) as the starting point for negotiations.
- *Expanding the GATS Scope*: Some proposals mention goals such as "full privatization", and deregulation (US, on telecommunications). The US proposal is actually more of a proposal on e-commerce than

telecommunications. This was discussed at length during the last services week as most Members felt that it had gone far beyond a proposal on basic telecommunications. Some others address "ownership/acquisition of property or land" as National Treatment limitations (EC, on telecom; Japan on distribution services).

- *E-commerce* is in some cases mentioned as part of these negotiations: either through direct proposals to remove obstacles to the transmission of services across national borders through electronic means (e.g., US proposal on education services and Korea's proposal on distribution services) and to work on extended sectoral coverage to include services that can be delivered electronically (e.g., US proposal on telecommunications); by references to the relevance of the impact/role of e-commerce/Internet on trade in services (e.g. Canadian proposals on financial services and on distribution services; proposal by Hong Kong, China on "Logistics and Related Services"); or indirectly through proposals of certain definitions of services (such as express delivery—US) that include the use of electronic technologies, or proposals that state a need to respect the "principle" of "technological neutrality" (e.g., US on audiovisuals).
- *Linking goods with services*: Some proposals, particularly on energy, environmental and on distribution services, address restrictions for the entry of goods/equipment and tools. Some of them mention the need for the "movement" (entry)/"temporary movement" (entry) of such goods/equipments and tools. Reference to the relevance of GATT disciplines is also made regarding audiovisuals (US proposal).
- *Classification issues*: Notwithstanding ongoing work in the Committee on Specific Commitments, in most sectors there are proposals that suggest sector-specific solutions (exceptions to this are proposals on air and on land transport, and, to a certain extent, on financial services (see below)). Most of these proposals relate to the "improvement" of classifications/broadening of coverage, to include "new" services (e.g., audiovisuals); "additional activities" (e.g., distribution services); "complementary" services (e.g., telecommunications); "related" services (e.g., energy services, environmental services, maritime transport (logistics) services, tourism services).
- *The "Cluster" approach*: Related to the above, many proposals (e.g., on energy services, on environmental services, on tourism services) suggest to consider "related-services" during sectoral negotiations through various options: 1) The "Cluster" approach as a basis for negotiations; or 2) the "Cluster" approach as a check-list to be used only as an *aide memoire*. In any case, a distinction between "core" and "non-core"/"related services" seems to be an issue in many sectors. The guidelines recognize that "The main method for negotiations shall be the request—offer approach."
- *Approaches to the scheduling of commitments*: Different notions/formula

are suggested in different proposals, like the use of models schedules setting up well defined benchmarks for liberalization (maritime transport, energy); the use of pre-determined sets of commitments (Understanding on commitments in financial services).

- *Lack of clarity when addressing barriers*: Many proposals (especially from the US on education, express delivery, distribution, and tourism services) address the question of barriers to trade without differentiating between market access restrictions, and national treatment limitations, and barriers resulting from domestic regulatory provisions.
- *Additional Commitments on Regulatory Issues*: The content of some proposals may raise questions on whether domestic regulatory issues should be solved horizontally (in the Working Party on Domestic Regulation), or through sectoral-specific negotiations. Many of such proposals address issues related to "transparency" of procedures and "fairness of administration" (e.g., distribution services, education services, environmental services, express delivery services). Most US proposals suggest additionally considering other regulatory principles/ disciplines (e.g., the US proposal on financial services considers "prior comment" provisions and other improved/far M reaching "regulatory principles" pertaining to development, adoption and application/ enforcement of regulations).
- *Anti-competitive practices*: Related to the above, the need for Members to establish a pro-competitive regulatory framework in the energy sector is addressed in the form of an invitation (by the EC), as well as in the form of a proposal (by the US and by Norway), for developing a reference paper (RP) in line with the one established for telecommunication services. Regulatory issues, as well as sector-specific "Competitive Safeguards", also similar to the provisions established for telecommunications, are proposed by The Dominican Republic, Honduras and El Salvador to be applied in tourism. A reference paper is also suggested by the EC for the postal/courier sector; this proposal though, does not specify if such an instrument would be meant to prevent anti-competitive practices. No proposal refers to the need to strengthen Article IX on Business Practices.
- *Limited reference to Subsidies*: Except for EC proposal on construction services, no proposal addresses really the issue of distortive effects of trade-related subsidies when referring to barriers to trade. The only clear and specific reference to subsidies appears in the proposal by the US on audiovisuals. Also, in its proposal on environmental services, the EC states its intention to deal with subsidies, among other "horizontal issues", in a possible future proposal. Subsidies are also enumerated as horizontal restrictions in some EC proposals, like for instance on distribution services and on financial services.
- *Technological neutrality*: The US refers in several proposals (e.g., audiovisuals, energy, and telecommunications) to the notion of

"technological neutrality".

- *Absence of proposals on Health services*: There are proposals on practically all services considered in the WTO W/120 classification, except on health services.

Aspect of Transparency under GATS

It is widely recognized that the service industries are among the most heavily regulated areas of most domestic economies. Although some of this regulation is intended to impact on trade, in many cases the regulation takes place strictly for domestic policy purposes. Not only do domestic regulatory authorities generally not intend to make trade policy; often, they are not even aware of the effect that their rules have on international trade. Nevertheless, domestic regulation often does result in serious unintentional trade distortions as well (http://www.wto.org/gatt_docs/English/SULPDF/92020181.pdf).

It is not realistic to expect that services trade can be liberalized through the widespread elimination of domestic regulatory activity. Regulation is and will remain a necessary instrument for achieving each government's social and economic objectives. We should, however, work toward reducing the negative impact of regulation on international service transactions while recognizing each country's need to regulate domestically. One way of accomplishing this is through greater transparency in the regulatory process. Regulatory transparency can be viewed both as an ancillary concept in services trade liberalization and as an important liberalizing principle in its own right. As an ancillary concept, transparency is necessary both for carrying out multilateral trade negotiations and for implementing an agreement. Services trade negotiations can be successful only if the participants have a clear view of the obstacles to trade for which solutions should be sought. Moreover, once an agreement has been reached, the application of the transparency principle is essential in order to assess whether the parties to the agreement are meeting their obligations. If difficulties do arise in implementing the agreement, the consultation procedures which normally accompany transparency provisions are an important means for settling disputes. As a liberalizing principle in its own right, transparency can provide several benefits:

- the publication of regulations gives businesses, (both domestic and international), the information that they need to operate efficiently and to comply with the regulations;
- advance notice of regulatory changes allows businesses to plan effectively and to adjust to a changing regulatory environment;
- consultation provisions allow other governments as well as interested parties in the private sector to make regulators aware of the implications of the regulators' actions for business.

This can assist domestic regulators to assess alternatives for minimizing their negative impact on domestic business and international trade while still achieving their domestic regulatory objectives. They can thus regulate more efficiently. These advantages can significantly outweigh the costs of transparency, which consist mainly of a loss of regulatory flexibility.

2. Trade-Related Intellectual Property Rights (TRIPs)

The World Trade Organization (WTO), which was established in 1995 as a successor to the General Agreement on Tariffs and Trade-1947 (GATT 1947), is the principal international organization governing multilateral trade among Members. The WTO administers the implementation of a set of agreements, which include the General Agreement on Tariffs and Trade, other agreements in the goods sector and in addition, agreements in two other areas, viz., trade in services, and Trade Related Intellectual Property Rights (TRIPs).

The TRIPs agreement is a special agreement which introduced intellectual property law into the international trading system for the first time, and it remains the most comprehensive and all inclusive international agreement on intellectual property to date (Kamath: http://www.indianmba.com/Faculty_Column/FC535/fc535.html).

The WTO administers the implementation of a set of agreements, which include the General Agreement on Tariffs and Trade, other agreements in the goods sector (e.g., agriculture, textiles, sanitary and psycho-sanitary measures, Trade Related Investment Measures-TRIMs, anti-dumping, etc.), and in addition, agreements in two other areas, viz., trade in services, and Trade Related Intellectual Property Rights (TRIPs). Trade Related Intellectual Property Rights (TRIPs) was added to the General Agreement on Tariffs and Trade (GATT) treaty at the end of the Uruguay Round of trade negotiations in 1994. After the Uruguay round, the GATT became the basis for the establishment of the World Trade Organization. Therefore, when GATT was succeeded by WTO in 1995 and all the members of WTO had to sign an agreement related to Intellectual Property Rights if it was interested in multi-lateral trading and also enact mandatorily some regulations related to it in the domestic system. The TRIPs agreement is a special agreement which introduced intellectual property law into the international trading system for the first time, and it remains the most comprehensive and all inclusive international agreement on intellectual property to date.

The TRIPs Agreement tries to bring in uniformity in the standards of intellectual property rights among the WTO irrespective of their development status. While this is expected to result in technology transfer and flow of investment among the Members, the extent of benefits accruing will depend on domestic industries and the status of development of the countries. Intellectual Property Rights (IPRs) refers to the legal ownership of by a person or business of an invention/ discovery attached to a particular product/ process which protects the owner against unauthorized copying or limitation. Intellectual property rights are the rights given to persons over the creations of their minds. They usually give the creator an exclusive right over the use of his/her creation for a certain period of time. The World Trade Organization classifies the IP broadly into two main parts namely copyright and rights related to copyright and industrial property. Let us understand each one of these in greater detail.

TRIPs also specify enforcement procedures, remedies, and dispute resolution procedures.

WTO specifies the three main features of the Agreement as:

- **Standards:** In respect of each of the main areas of intellectual property covered by the TRIPS Agreement, the Agreement sets out the minimum standards of protection to be provided by each Member. Each of the main elements of protection is defined, namely the subject-matter to be protected, the rights to be conferred and permissible exceptions to those rights, and the minimum duration of protection.
- **Enforcement:** The second main set of provisions deals with domestic procedures and remedies for the enforcement of intellectual property rights. The Agreement lays down certain general principles applicable to all IPR enforcement procedures.
- **Dispute settlement:** The Agreement makes disputes between WTO Members about the respect of the TRIPS obligations subject to the WTO's dispute settlement procedures.

Under TRIPs, all countries have to provide for protection of product patents from January 1, 1995. But developing countries like India, which did not have a regime of product patents, had a transition period of ten years-until January 1, 2005, to affect the switch over. During this transition period, it was decided that these economies would accept applications for patents (which would be considered and granted after January 2005) and provide EMR (Exclusive Marketing Rights) for the producers of patented drugs (in the pharmaceutical industry) and agrochemicals.

The transition period for least developed countries was extended to 2016, and could be extended beyond that.

The TRIPs Agreement is a minimum standards agreement, which allows members to provide more extensive protection of intellectual property if they so wish. Members are left free to determine the appropriate method of implementing the provisions of the Agreement within their own legal system and practice.

Why TRIPS?

- Art. 7 defines the main objectives and principles, which mentions that Intellectual Property Rights should contribute to social and economic welfare and to a balance of rights and obligations of the members.
- Art. 8 stipulates prevention of abuse of IPR that will restrain trade or adversely affect international transfer of technology. A liberal and permissible interpretation of these Articles will ensure equity in the application of TRIPS to the benefit of the country's economy and social welfare.

- A weak IPR regime in developing countries leads to losses from "re-engineered products" for the original innovators, namely the Western multinationals and lowers the incentives for local developing country firms to undertake basic R&D themselves. Thus, the countries of the triad, the U.S.A., Europe and Japan, have been working towards the global harmonization of IPR regimes since the last two decades. TRIPs is one of the culminations of their efforts.
- The countries initiating TRIPS based their actions on the presumption that a strong IPR regime is a critical pre-condition for private investment in research and development, and hence economic growth.
- It is contended that an expanded and strengthened protection of IPRs would bring about increased flows of foreign direct investment and technology transfer to developing countries. It would also stimulate local innovation.
- Finally, it would also enable the multinationals of the developed countries to recuperate markets from local imitators. The developing world is, on the other hand, not so confident about reaping benefits from this global IPR regime, since having access to technological knowledge is perceived as being crucial for economic growth.

Property rights are a social institution, not a natural phenomenon. Intellectual property is an invention of the knowledge-based economy. Both free traders and protectionists in the US agree on the need to protect US intellectual property (IP) rights globally in general and in China especially. Of course a protectionist regime has less, if any, leverage at its disposal for combating the violation of intellectual property rights outside its borders. The Uruguay Round in 1986 produced the WTO Trade Related Aspects of Intellectual Property Rights (TRIPS) agreement. It is supposed to be an attempt to narrow the discrepancy in ways these rights are protected in different countries around the world, and to bring them under common international rules. It establishes minimum levels of protection that each government has to give to the intellectual property of fellow WTO members. In doing so, it attempts to strike a balance between the long term benefits and inevitable short term costs to global society at large. Society benefits in the long term when IP protection encourages creation and invention, especially after the limited period of protection expires and the creations and inventions enter the public domain. National governments are allowed to reduce any short term costs through various exceptions, for example to tackle critical time-sensitive public health problems. The WTO dispute settlement system is designed to settle international trade disputes over IP rights before such disputes translate into political tension (http://henryckliu.com/page9.html).

The Agreement on TRIPS, the subject of Annex 1C of the agreement establishing the World Trade Organization, is the latest translation of cultural imperialism into economic imperialism on a global scale. The Schumpeterian "creative destruction" that US Fed Chairman Alan Greenspan tirelessly celebrates, is increasing distorted from the specific idea of a better mouse trap, to the systemic appropriation of the broad notion linking mice to traps. In the US, the self-proclaimed bastion of democracy, the creative destruction of economic democracy through the rule of law is in full force. Not only do the poor economies not have a fighting chance under TRIPS, even the people in the advanced economies are quietly put in technological servitude by the new patent regime. The notion that an individual should be granted permission to stake a personal claim on a nation's natural resource (such as gold, oil and other mineral rights) is undemocratic enough, but now intellectual property rights are defined way beyond any reasonable personal efforts, such as writing a book or a symphony (covered under copyrights), to thoughts while shaving that really amount to wholesale robbery from the public domain. On a corporate level, intellectual property rights has become an economic weapon of mass destruction, preventing creativity from ever seeing sunlight. US annual revenue from patent licenses now exceeds $100 billion, which is larger than the foreign exchange reserves of most countries. Through TRIPS, US patents gain global status without the burden of sharing patent fees with other governments.

General Provisions and Basic Principles under TRIPS

Article 1: Nature and Scope of Obligations

1. Members shall give effect to the provisions of this Agreement. Members may, but shall not be obliged to, implement in their law more extensive protection than is required by this Agreement, provided that such protection does not contravene the provisions of this Agreement. Members shall be free to determine the appropriate method of implementing the provisions of this Agreement within their own legal system and practice (http://www.wto.org/english/tratop_e/trips_e/t_agm3_e.htm).
2. For the purposes of this Agreement, the term "intellectual property" refers to all categories of intellectual property that are the subject of Sections 1 through 7 of Part II.
3. Members shall accord the treatment provided for in this Agreement to the nationals of other Members. (1) In respect of the relevant intellectual property right, the nationals of other Members shall be understood as those natural or legal persons that would meet the criteria for eligibility for protection provided for in the Paris Convention (1967), the Berne Convention (1971), the Rome Convention and the Treaty on Intellectual Property in Respect of Integrated Circuits, were all Members of the WTO members of those conventions. (2) Any Member availing itself of the possibilities provided in paragraph 3 of Article 5 or paragraph 2 of Article 6 of the Rome Convention shall make a notification as foreseen in those provisions to the Council for Trade-Related Aspects of Intellectual Property Rights (the "Council for TRIPS").

Article 2: Intellectual Property Conventions

1. In respect of Parts II, III and IV of this Agreement, Members shall comply with Articles 1 through 12, and Article 19, of the Paris Convention (1967).
2. Nothing in Parts I to IV of this Agreement shall derogate from existing obligations that Members may have to each other under the Paris Convention, the Berne Convention, the Rome Convention and the Treaty on Intellectual Property in Respect of Integrated Circuits.

Article 3: National Treatment

1. Each Member shall accord to the nationals of other Members treatment no less favourable than that it accords to its own nationals with regard to the protection (3) of intellectual property, subject to the exceptions already provided in, respectively, the Paris Convention (1967), the Berne Convention (1971), the Rome Convention or the Treaty on Intellectual Property in Respect of Integrated Circuits. In respect of performers, producers of phonograms and broadcasting organizations, this obligation only applies in respect of the rights provided under this Agreement. Any Member availing itself of the possibilities provided in Article 6 of the Berne Convention (1971) or paragraph 1(b) of Article 16 of the Rome Convention shall make a notification as foreseen in those provisions to the Council for TRIPS.
2. Members may avail themselves of the exceptions permitted under paragraph 1 in relation to judicial and administrative procedures, including the designation of an address for service or the appointment of an agent within the jurisdiction of a Member, only where such exceptions are necessary to secure compliance with laws and regulations which are not inconsistent with the provisions of this Agreement and where such practices are not applied in a manner which would constitute a disguised restriction on trade.

Article 4: Most-Favoured-Nation Treatment

With regard to the protection of intellectual property, any advantage, favour, privilege or immunity granted by a Member to the nationals of any other country shall be accorded immediately and unconditionally to the nationals of all other Members. Exempted from this obligation is any advantage, favour, privilege or immunity accorded by a Member:

(a) deriving from international agreements on judicial assistance or law enforcement of a general nature and not particularly confined to the protection of intellectual property;
(b) granted in accordance with the provisions of the Berne Convention (1971) or the Rome Convention authorizing that the treatment accorded be a function not of national treatment but of the treatment accorded in another country;

(c) in respect of the rights of performers, producers of phonograms and broadcasting organizations not provided under this Agreement;
(d) deriving from international agreements related to the protection of intellectual property which entered into force prior to the entry into force of the WTO Agreement, provided that such agreements are notified to the Council for TRIPS and do not constitute an arbitrary or unjustifiable discrimination against nationals of other Members.

Article 5: Multilateral Agreements on Acquisition or Maintenance of Protection

The obligations under Articles 3 and 4 do not apply to procedures provided in multilateral agreements concluded under the auspices of WIPO relating to the acquisition or maintenance of intellectual property rights.

Article 6: Exhaustion

For the purposes of dispute settlement under this Agreement, subject to the provisions of Articles 3 and 4 nothing in this Agreement shall be used to address the issue of the exhaustion of intellectual property rights.

Article 7: Objectives

The protection and enforcement of intellectual property rights should contribute to the promotion of technological innovation and to the transfer and dissemination of technology, to the mutual advantage of producers and users of technological knowledge and in a manner conducive to social and economic welfare, and to a balance of rights and obligations.

Article 8: Principles

1. Members may, in formulating or amending their laws and regulations, adopt measures necessary to protect public health and nutrition, and to promote the public interest in sectors of vital importance to their socio-economic and technological development, provided that such measures are consistent with the provisions of this Agreement.
2. Appropriate measures, provided that they are consistent with the provisions of this Agreement, may be needed to prevent the abuse of intellectual property rights by right holders or the resort to practices which unreasonably restrain trade or adversely affect the international transfer of technology.

Section 1: Copy Rights and Related Rights

Article 9: Relation to the Berne Convention

1. Members shall comply with Articles 1 through 21 of the Berne Convention (1971) and the Appendix thereto. However, Members shall not have rights or obligations under this Agreement in respect of the rights conferred under Article 6*bis* of that Convention or of the rights derived therefrom.

2. Copyright protection shall extend to expressions and not to ideas, procedures, and methods of operation or mathematical concepts as such.

Article 10: Computer Programs and Compilations of Data

1. Computer programs, whether in source or objects code, shall be protected as literary works under the Berne Convention (1971).
2. Compilations of data or other material, whether in machine readable or other form, which by reason of the selection or arrangement of their contents constitute intellectual creations shall be protected as such. Such protection, which shall not extend to the data or material itself, shall be without prejudice to any copyright subsisting in the data or material itself.

Article 11: Rental Rights

In respect of at least computer programs and cinematographic works, a Member shall provide authors and their successors in title the right to authorize or to prohibit the commercial rental to the public of originals or copies of their copyright works. A Member shall be exempted from this obligation in respect of cinematographic works unless such rental has led to widespread copying of such works which is materially impairing the exclusive right of reproduction conferred in that Member on authors and their successors in title. In respect of computer programs, this obligation does not apply to rentals where the program itself is not the essential object of the rental.

Article 12: Term of Protection

Whenever the term of protection of a work, other than a photographic work or a work of applied art, is calculated on a basis other than the life of a natural person, such term shall be no less than 50 years from the end of the calendar year of authorized publication, or, failing such authorized publication within 50 years from the making of the work, 50 years from the end of the calendar year of making.

Article 13: Limitations and Exceptions

Members shall confine limitations or exceptions to exclusive rights to certain special cases which do not conflict with a normal exploitation of the work and do not unreasonably prejudice the legitimate interests of the right holder.

Article 14: Protection of Performers, Producers of Phonograms (Sound Recordings) and Broadcasting Organizations

1. In respect of a fixation of their performance on a phonogram, performers shall have the possibility of preventing the following acts when undertaken without their authorization: the fixation of their unfixed performance and the reproduction of such fixation. Performers shall also

have the possibility of preventing the following acts when undertaken without their authorization: the broadcasting by wireless means and the communication to the public of their live performance.

2. Producers of phonograms shall enjoy the right to authorize or prohibit the direct or indirect reproduction of their phonograms.
3. Broadcasting organizations shall have the right to prohibit the following acts when undertaken without their authorization: the fixation, the reproduction of fixations, and the rebroadcast by wireless means of broadcasts, as well as the communication to the public of television broadcasts of the same. Where Members do not grant such rights to broadcasting organizations, they shall provide owners of copyright in the subject matter of broadcasts with the possibility of preventing the above acts, subject to the provisions of the Berne Convention (1971).
4. The provisions of Article 11 in respect of computer programs shall apply *mutatis mutandis* to producers of phonograms and any other right holders in phonograms as determined in a Member's law. If on 15 April 1994 a Member has in force a system of equitable remuneration of right holders in respect of the rental of phonograms, it may maintain such system provided that the commercial rental of phonograms is not giving rise to the material impairment of the exclusive rights of reproduction of right holders.
5. The term of the protection available under this Agreement to performers and producers of phonograms shall last at least until the end of a period of 50 years computed from the end of the calendar year in which the fixation was made or the performance took place. The term of protection granted pursuant to paragraph 3 shall last for at least 20 years from the end of the calendar year in which the broadcast took place.
6. Any Member may, in relation to the rights conferred under paragraphs 1, 2 and 3, provide for conditions, limitations, exceptions and reservations to the extent permitted by the Rome Convention. However, the provisions of Article 18 of the Berne Convention (1971) shall also apply, *mutatis mutandis*, to the rights of performers and producers of phonograms in phonograms.

Section 2: Trade Marks

Article 15: Protectable Subject Matter

1. Any sign, or any combination of signs, capable of distinguishing the goods or services of one undertaking from those of other undertakings, shall be capable of constituting a trademark. Such signs, in particular words including personal names, letters, numerals, figurative elements and combinations of colours as well as any combination of such signs, shall be eligible for registration as trademarks. Where signs are not inherently capable of distinguishing the relevant goods or services, Members may make registrability depend on distinctiveness acquired

through use. Members may require, as a condition of registration, that signs be visually perceptible.

2. Paragraph 1 shall not be understood to prevent a Member from denying registration of a trademark on other grounds, provided that they do not derogate from the provisions of the Paris Convention (1967).
3. Members may make registrability depend on use. However, actual use of a trademark shall not be a condition for filing an application for registration. An application shall not be refused solely on the ground that intended use has not taken place before the expiry of a period of three years from the date of application.
4. The nature of the goods or services to which a trademark is to be applied shall in no case form an obstacle to registration of the trademark.
5. Members shall publish each trademark either before it is registered or promptly after it is registered and shall afford a reasonable opportunity for petitions to cancel the registration. In addition, Members may afford an opportunity for the registration of a trademark to be opposed.

Article 16: Rights Conferred

1. The owner of a registered trademark shall have the exclusive right to prevent all third parties not having the owner's consent from using in the course of trade identical or similar signs for goods or services which are identical or similar to those in respect of which the trademark is registered where such use would result in a likelihood of confusion. In case of the use of an identical sign for identical goods or services, a likelihood of confusion shall be presumed. The rights described above shall not prejudice any existing prior rights, nor shall they affect the possibility of Members making rights available on the basis of use.
2. Article 6*bis* of the Paris Convention (1967) shall apply, *mutatis mutandis,* to services. In determining whether a trademark is well-known, Members shall take account of the knowledge of the trademark in the relevant sector of the public, including knowledge in the Member concerned which has been obtained as a result of the promotion of the trademark.
3. Article 6*bis* of the Paris Convention (1967) shall apply, *mutatis mutandis,* to goods or services which are not similar to those in respect of which a trademark is registered, provided that use of that trademark in relation to those goods or services would indicate a connection between those goods or services and the owner of the registered trademark and provided that the interests of the owner of the registered trademark are likely to be damaged by such use.

Article 17: Exceptions

Members may provide limited exceptions to the rights conferred by a trademark, such as fair use of descriptive terms, provided that such exceptions take account of the legitimate interests of the owner of the trademark and of third parties.

Article 18: Term of Protection

Initial registration and each renewal of registration, of a trademark shall be for a term of no less than seven years. The registration of a trademark shall be renewable indefinitely.

Article 19: Requirement of Use

1. If use is required to maintain a registration, the registration may be cancelled only after an uninterrupted period of at least three years of non-use, unless valid reasons based on the existence of obstacles to such use are shown by the trademark owner. Circumstances arising independently of the will of the owner of the trademark which constitute an obstacle to the use of the trademark, such as import restrictions on or other government requirements for goods or services protected by the trademark, shall be recognized as valid reasons for non-use.
2. When subject to the control of its owner, use of a trademark by another person shall be recognized as use of the trademark for the purpose of maintaining the registration.

Article 20: Other Requirements

The use of a trademark in the course of trade shall not be unjustifiably encumbered by special requirements, such as use with another trademark, use in a special form or use in a manner detrimental to its capability to distinguish the goods or services of one undertaking from those of other undertakings. This will not preclude a requirement prescribing the use of the trademark identifying the undertaking producing the goods or services along with, but without linking it to, the trademark distinguishing the specific goods or services in question of that undertaking.

Article 21: Licensing and Assignment

Members may determine conditions on the licensing and assignment of trademarks, it being understood that the compulsory licensing of trademarks shall not be permitted and that the owner of a registered trademark shall have the right to assign the trademark with or without the transfer of the business to which the trademark belongs.

Section 3: Geographical Indications

Article 22: Protection of Geographical Indications

1. Geographical indications are, for the purposes of this Agreement, indications which identify a good as originating in the territory of a Member, or a region or locality in that territory, where a given quality,

reputation or other characteristic of the good is essentially attributable to its geographical origin.

2. In respect of geographical indications, Members shall provide the legal means for interested parties to prevent:
   (a) the use of any means in the designation or presentation of a good that indicates or suggests that the good in question originates in a geographical area other than the true place of origin in a manner which misleads the public as to the geographical origin of the good;
   (b) any use which constitutes an act of unfair competition within the meaning of Article 10*bis* of the Paris Convention (1967).
3. A Member shall, *ex officio* if its legislation so permits or at the request of an interested party, refuse or invalidate the registration of a trademark which contains or consists of a geographical indication with respect to goods not originating in the territory indicated, if use of the indication in the trademark for such goods in that Member is of such a nature as to mislead the public as to the true place of origin.
4. The protection under paragraphs 1, 2 and 3 shall be applicable against a geographical indication which, although literally true as to the territory, region or locality in which the goods originate falsely represents to the public that the goods originate in another territory.

Article 23: Additional Protection for Geographical Indications for Wines and Spirits

1. Each Member shall provide the legal means for interested parties to prevent use of a geographical indication identifying wines for wines not originating in the place indicated by the geographical indication in question or identifying spirits for spirits not originating in the place indicated by the geographical indication in question, even where the true origin of the goods is indicated or the geographical indication is used in translation or accompanied by expressions such as "kind", "type", "style", "imitation" or the like.
2. The registration of a trademark for wines which contains or consists of a geographical indication identifying wines or for spirits which contains or consists of a geographical indication identifying spirits shall be refused or invalidated, *ex officio* if a Member's legislation so permits or at the request of an interested party, with respect to such wines or spirits not having this origin.
3. In the case of homonymous geographical indications for wines, protection shall be accorded to each indication, subject to the provisions of paragraph 4 of Article 22. Each Member shall determine the practical conditions under which the homonymous indications in question will be differentiated from each other, taking into account the need to ensure equitable treatment of the producers concerned and that consumers are not misled.

4. In order to facilitate the protection of geographical indications for wines, negotiations shall be undertaken in the Council for TRIPS concerning the establishment of a multilateral system of notification and registration of geographical indications for wines eligible for protection in those Members participating in the system.

Article 24: International Negotiations; Exceptions

1. Members agree to enter into negotiations aimed at increasing the protection of individual geographical indications under Article 23. The provisions of paragraphs 4 through 8 below shall not be used by a Member to refuse to conduct negotiations or to conclude bilateral or multilateral agreements. In the context of such negotiations, Members shall be willing to consider the continued applicability of these provisions to individual geographical indications whose use was the subject of such negotiations.
2. The Council for TRIPS shall keep under review the application of the provisions of this Section; the first such review shall take place within two years of the entry into force of the WTO Agreement. Any matter affecting the compliance with the obligations under these provisions may be drawn to the attention of the Council, which, at the request of a Member, shall consult with any Member or Members in respect of such matter in respect of which it has not been possible to find a satisfactory solution through bilateral or plurilateral consultations between the Members concerned. The Council shall take such action as may be agreed to facilitate the operation and further the objectives of this Section.
3. In implementing this Section, a Member shall not diminish the protection of geographical indications that existed in that Member immediately prior to the date of entry into force of the WTO Agreement.
4. Nothing in this Section shall require a Member to prevent continued and similar use of a particular geographical indication of another Member identifying wines or spirits in connection with goods or services by any of its nationals or domiciliary who have used that geographical indication in a continuous manner with regard to the same or related goods or services in the territory of that Member either (*a*) for at least 10 years preceding 15 April 1994 or (*b*) in good faith preceding that date.
5. Where a trademark has been applied for or registered in good faith, or where rights to a trademark have been acquired through use in good faith either:

   (a) before the date of application of these provisions in that Member as defined in Part VI; or

   (b) before the geographical indication is protected in its country of origin;

Measures adopted to implement this Section shall not prejudice eligibility for or the validity of the registration of a trademark, or the right to use a trademark, on the basis that such a trademark is identical with, or similar to, a geographical indication.

6. Nothing in this Section shall require a Member to apply its provisions in respect of a geographical indication of any other Member with respect to goods or services for which the relevant indication is identical with the term customary in common language as the common name for such goods or services in the territory of that Member. Nothing in this Section shall require a Member to apply its provisions in respect of a geographical indication of any other Member with respect to products of the vine for which the relevant indication is identical with the customary name of a grape variety existing in the territory of that Member as of the date of entry into force of the WTO Agreement.
7. A Member may provide that any request made under this Section in connection with the use or registration of a trademark must be presented within five years after the adverse use of the protected indication has become generally known in that Member or after the date of registration of the trademark in that Member provided that the trademark has been published by that date, if such date is earlier than the date on which the adverse use became generally known in that Member, provided that the geographical indication is not used or registered in bad faith.
8. The provisions of this Section shall in no way prejudice the right of any person to use, in the course of trade, that person's name or the name of that person's predecessor in business, except where such name is used in such a manner as to mislead the public.
9. There shall be no obligation under this Agreement to protect geographical indications which are not or cease to be protected in their country of origin, or which have fallen into disuse in that country.

Section 4: Industrial Designs

Article 25: Requirements for Protection

1. Members shall provide for the protection of independently created industrial designs that are new or original. Members may provide that designs are not new or original if they do not significantly differ from known designs or combinations of known design features. Members may provide that such protection shall not extend to designs dictated essentially by technical or functional considerations.
2. Each Member shall ensure that requirements for securing protection for textile designs, in particular in regard to any cost, examination or publication, do not unreasonably impair the opportunity to seek and obtain such protection. Members shall be free to meet this obligation through industrial design law or through copyright law.

Article 26: Protection

1. The owner of a protected industrial design shall have the right to prevent third parties not having the owner's consent from making, selling or importing articles bearing or embodying a design which is a copy, or substantially a copy, of the protected design, when such acts are undertaken for commercial purposes.
2. Members may provide limited exceptions to the protection of industrial designs, provided that such exceptions do not unreasonably conflict with the normal exploitation of protected industrial designs and do not unreasonably prejudice the legitimate interests of the owner of the protected design, taking account of the legitimate interests of third parties.
3. The duration of protection available shall amount to at least 10 years.

Section 5: Patents

Article 27: Patentable Subject Matter

1. Subject to the provisions of paragraphs 2 and 3, patents shall be available for any inventions, whether products or processes, in all fields of technology, provided that they are new, involve an inventive step and are capable of industrial application. Subject to paragraph 4 of Article 65, paragraph 8 of Article 70 and paragraph 3 of this Article, patents shall be available and patent rights enjoyable without discrimination as to the place of invention, the field of technology and whether products are imported or locally produced.
2. Members may exclude from patentability inventions, the prevention within their territory of the commercial exploitation of which is necessary to protect *ordure public* or morality, including to protect human, animal or plant life or health or to avoid serious prejudice to the environment, provided that such exclusion is not made merely because the exploitation is prohibited by their law.
3. Members may also exclude from patentability:
   (a) Diagnostic, therapeutic and surgical methods for the treatment of humans or animals;
   (b) Plants and animals other than micro-organisms, and essentially biological processes for the production of plants or animals other than non-biological and microbiological processes. However, Members shall provide for the protection of plant varieties either by patents or by an effective *sui generis* system or by any combination thereof. The provisions of this subparagraph shall be reviewed four years after the date of entry into force of the WTO Agreement.

Article 28: Rights Conferred

1. A patent shall confer on its owner the following exclusive rights:
   (a) Where the subject-matter of a patent is a product, to prevent third parties not having the owner's consent from the acts of: making, using, offering for sale, selling, or importing for these purposes that product;
   (b) Where the subject matter of a patent is a process, to prevent third parties not having the owner's consent from the act of using the process, and from the acts of: using, offering for sale, selling, or importing for these purposes at least the product obtained directly by that process.
2. Patent owners shall also have the right to assign, or transfer by succession, the patent and to conclude licensing contracts.

Article 29: Conditions on Patent Applicants

1. Members shall require that an applicant for a patent shall disclose the invention in a manner sufficiently clear and complete for the invention to be carried out by a person skilled in the art and may require the applicant to indicate the best mode for carrying out the invention known to the inventor at the filing date or, where priority is claimed, at the priority date of the application.
2. Members may require an applicant for a patent to provide information concerning the applicant's corresponding foreign applications and grants.

Article 30: Exceptions to Rights Conferred

Members may provide limited exceptions to the exclusive rights conferred by a patent, provided that such exceptions do not unreasonably conflict with a normal exploitation of the patent and do not unreasonably prejudice the legitimate interests of the patent owner, taking account of the legitimate interests of third parties.

Article 31: Other Use without Authorization of the Right Holder

Where the law of a Member allows for other use of the subject matter of a patent without the authorization of the right holder, including use by the government or third parties authorized by the government, the following provisions shall be respected:

(a) Authorization of such use shall be considered on its individual merits;
(b) such use may only be permitted if, prior to such use, the proposed user has made efforts to obtain authorization from the right holder on reasonable commercial terms and conditions and that such efforts have not been successful within a reasonable period of time. This requirement may be waived by a Member in the case of national emergency or other circumstances of extreme urgency or in cases of public non-commercial use. In situations of national emergency or other circumstances of

extreme urgency, the right holder shall, nevertheless, be notified as soon as reasonably practicable. In the case of public non-commercial use, where the government or contractor, without making a patent search, knows or has demonstrable grounds to know that a valid patent is or will be used by or for the government, the right holder shall be informed promptly;

(c) the scope and duration of such use shall be limited to the purpose for which it was authorized, and in the case of semi-conductor technology shall only be for public non-commercial use or to remedy a practice determined after judicial or administrative process to be anti-competitive;

(d) Such use shall be non-exclusive;

(e) Such use shall be non-assignable, except with that part of the enterprise or goodwill which enjoys such use;

(f) Any such use shall be authorized predominantly for the supply of the domestic market of the Member authorizing such use;

(g) Authorization for such use shall be liable, subject to adequate protection of the legitimate interests of the persons so authorized, to be terminated if and when the circumstances which led to it cease to exist and are unlikely to recur. The competent authority shall have the authority to review, upon motivated request, the continued existence of these circumstances;

(h) The right holder shall be paid adequate remuneration in the circumstances of each case, taking into account the economic value of the authorization;

(i) The legal validity of any decision relating to the authorization of such use shall be subject to judicial review or other independent review by a distinct higher authority in that Member;

(j) Any decision relating to the remuneration provided in respect of such use shall be subject to judicial review or other independent review by a distinct higher authority in that Member;

(k) Members are not obliged to apply the conditions set forth in subparagraphs (b) and (f) where such use is permitted to remedy a practice determined after judicial or administrative process to be anti-competitive. The need to correct anti-competitive practices may be taken into account in determining the amount of remuneration in such cases. Competent authorities shall have the authority to refuse termination of authorization if and when the conditions which led to such authorization are likely to recur;

(l) where such use is authorized to permit the exploitation of a patent ("the second patent") which cannot be exploited without infringing another patent ("the first patent"), the following additional conditions shall apply:

   (i) The invention claimed in the second patent shall involve an important technical advance of considerable economic significance in relation to the invention claimed in the first patent;

(ii) The owner of the first patent shall be entitled to a cross-licence on reasonable terms to use the invention claimed in the second patent; and

(iii) The use authorized in respect of the first patent shall be non-assignable except with the assignment of the second patent.

Article 32: Revocation/Forfeiture

An opportunity for judicial review of any decision to revoke or forfeit a patent shall be available.

Article 33: Term of Protection

The term of protection available shall not end before the expiration of a period of twenty years counted from the filing date

Article 34: Process Patents: Burden of Proof

1. For the purposes of civil proceedings in respect of the infringement of the rights of the owner referred to in paragraph 1(b) of Article 28, if the subject matter of a patent is a process for obtaining a product, the judicial authorities shall have the authority to order the defendant to prove that the process to obtain an identical product is different from the patented process. Therefore, Members shall provide, in at least one of the following circumstances, that any identical product when produced without the consent of the patent owner shall, in the absence of proof to the contrary, be deemed to have been obtained by the patented process:

   (a) if the product obtained by the patented process is new;

   (b) if there is a substantial likelihood that the identical product was made by the process and the owner of the patent has been unable through reasonable efforts to determine the process actually used.

2. Any Member shall be free to provide that the burden of proof indicated in paragraph 1 shall be on the alleged infringer only if the condition referred to in subparagraph (a) is fulfilled or only if the condition referred to in subparagraph (b) is fulfilled.
3. In the adduction of proof to the contrary, the legitimate interests of defendants in protecting their manufacturing and business secrets shall be taken into account.

Section 6: Lay-out Designs of Integrated Circuits

Article 35: Relation to the IPIC Treaty

Members agree to provide protection to the layout-designs (topographies) of integrated circuits (referred to in this Agreement as "layout-designs") in accordance with Articles 2 through 7 (other than paragraph 3 of Article 6),

Article 12 and paragraph 3 of Article 16 of the Treaty on Intellectual Property in Respect of Integrated Circuits and, in addition, to comply with the following provisions.

Article 36: Scope of the Protection

Subject to the provisions of paragraph 1 of Article 37, Members shall consider unlawful the following acts if performed without the authorization of the right holder: importing, selling, or otherwise distributing for commercial purposes a protected layout-design, an integrated circuit in which a protected layout-design is incorporated, or an article incorporating such an integrated circuit only in so far as it continues to contain an unlawfully reproduced layout-design.

Article 37: Acts Not Requiring the Authorization of the Right Holder

1. Notwithstanding Article 36, no Member shall consider unlawful the performance of any of the acts referred to in that Article in respect of an integrated circuit incorporating an unlawfully reproduced layout-design or any article incorporating such an integrated circuit where the person performing or ordering such acts did not know and had no reasonable ground to know, when acquiring the integrated circuit or article incorporating such an integrated circuit, that it incorporated an unlawfully reproduced layout-design. Members shall provide that, after the time that such person has received sufficient notice that the layout-design was unlawfully reproduced, that person may perform any of the acts with respect to the stock on hand or ordered before such time, but shall be liable to pay to the right holder a sum equivalent to a reasonable royalty such as would be payable under a freely negotiated licence in respect of such a layout-design.
2. The conditions set out in subparagraphs (a) through (k) of Article 31 shall apply *mutatis mutandis* in the event of any non-voluntary licensing of a layout-design or of its use by or for the government without the authorization of the right holder.

Article 38: Term of Protection

1. In Members requiring registration as a condition of protection, the term of protection of layout-designs shall not end before the expiration of a period of 10 years counted from the date of filing an application for registration or from the first commercial exploitation wherever in the world it occurs.
2. In Members not requiring registration as a condition for protection, layout-designs shall be protected for a term of no less than 10 years from the date of the first commercial exploitation wherever in the world it occurs.
3. Notwithstanding paragraphs 1 and 2, a Member may provide that protection shall lapse 15 years after the creation of the layout-design.

Section 7: Protection of Undisclosed Information

Article 39

1. In the course of ensuring effective protection against unfair competition as provided in Article 10*bis* of the Paris Convention (1967), Members shall protect undisclosed information in accordance with paragraph 2 and data submitted to governments or governmental agencies in accordance with paragraph 3.
2. Natural and legal persons shall have the possibility of preventing information lawfully within their control from being disclosed to, acquired by, or used by others without their consent in a manner contrary to honest commercial practices so long as such information:
   (a) is secret in the sense that it is not, as a body or in the precise configuration and assembly of its components, generally known among or readily accessible to persons within the circles that normally deal with the kind of information in question;
   (b) Has commercial value because it is secret; and
   (c) Has been subject to reasonable steps under the circumstances, by the person lawfully in control of the information, to keep it secret.
3. Members, when requiring, as a condition of approving the marketing of pharmaceutical or of agricultural chemical products which utilize new chemical entities, the submission of undisclosed test or other data, the origination of which involves a considerable effort, shall protect such data against unfair commercial use. In addition, Members shall protect such data against disclosure, except where necessary to protect the public or unless steps are taken to ensure that the data are protected against unfair commercial use.

3. Trade Related Investment Measures (TRIMs)

The Agreement on Trade Related Investment Measures (TRIMs) is one of Agreements covered under Annex IA to the Marrakech Agreement, signed at the end of the Uruguay Round (UR) negotiations. The Agreement addresses investment measures that are trade related and that also violate Article III (National treatment) or Article XI (general elimination of quantitative restrictions) of the General Agreement on Tariffs and Trade. An illustrative list of the measures that are violative of the provisions of the Agreement is annexed to the text of the Agreement. These pertain broadly to local content requirements, trade balancing requirements and export restrictions, attached to investment decision-making (http://commerce.nic.in/wtotrims.htm).

The *Agreement on Trade Related Investment Measures* (TRIMs) are rules that apply to the domestic regulations a country applies to foreign investors, often as part of an industrial policy. The agreement was agreed upon by all members of the World Trade Organization (http://en.wikipedia.org/wiki/Agreement_on_Trade_Related_Investment_Measures).

Policies such as local content requirements and trade balancing rules that have traditionally been used to both promote the interests of domestic industries and combat restrictive business practices are now banned.

Trade Related Investment Measures is the name of one of the four principal legal agreements of the WTO trade treaty.

TRIMs are rules, which restrict preference of domestic firms and thereby enable international firms to operate more easily within foreign markets.

In the late 1980s, there was a significant increase in foreign direct investment throughout the world. However, some of the countries receiving foreign investment imposed numerous restrictions on that investment designed to protect and foster domestic industries, and to prevent the outflow of foreign exchange reserves. Examples of these restrictions include local content requirements (which require that locally-produced goods be purchased or used), manufacturing requirements (which require the domestic manufacturing of certain components), trade balancing requirements, domestic sales requirements, technology transfer requirements, export performance requirements (which require the export of a specified percentage of production volume), local equity restrictions, foreign exchange restrictions, remittance restrictions, licensing requirements, and employment restrictions.

These measures can also be used in connection with fiscal incentives as opposed to requirement. Some of these investment measures distort trade in violation of GATT Article III and XI, and are therefore prohibited. Until the completion of the Uruguay Round negotiations, which produced a well-rounded Agreement on Trade-Related Investment Measures (hereinafter the "TRIMs Agreement"), the few international agreements providing disciplines for measures restricting foreign investment provided only limited guidance in terms of content and country coverage. The OECD Code on Liberalization of Capital Movements, for example, requires members to liberalize restrictions on direct investment in a broad range of areas. The OECD Code's efficacy, however, is limited by the numerous reservations made by each of the members. In addition, there are other international treaties, bilateral and multilateral, under which signatories extend most-favoured-nation treatment to direct investment. Only a few such treaties, however, provide national treatment for direct investment. Moreover, although the APEC Investment Principles adopted in November 1994 provide rules for investment as a whole, including non-discrimination and national treatment, they have no binding force.

Legal Framework

GATT 1947 prohibited investment measures that violated the principles of national treatment and the general elimination of quantitative restrictions, but the extent of the prohibitions was never clear. The TRIMs Agreement, however, contains statements prohibiting any TRIMs that are inconsistent with the provisions of Articles III or XI of GATT 1994. In addition, it provides an illustrative list that explicitly prohibits local content requirements, trade balancing requirements, foreign exchange restrictions and export restrictions (domestic sales requirements) that would violate Article III:4 or XI:1 of GATT 1994. TRIMs prohibited by the Agreement include those which are mandatory or enforceable under domestic law or administrative rulings, or those with which compliance is necessary to obtain an advantage (such as subsidies or tax breaks). Figure 8-1 contains a list of measures specifically prohibited by the TRIMs Agreement. Note that this figure is not exhaustive, but simply illustrates TRIMs that are prohibited by the TRIMs Agreement. The figure, therefore, calls particular attention to several common types of TRIMs. We would add that this figure identifies measures that were also inconsistent with Article III:4 and XI:1 of GATT 1947. Indeed, the TRIMs Agreement is not intended to impose new obligations, but to clarify the pre-existing GATT 1947 obligations. Under the WTO TRIMs Agreement, countries are required to rectify any measures inconsistent with the Agreement, within a set period of time, with a few exceptions.

Provisions on elimination of notified TRIMs by WTO Members

The Agreement requires all WTO Members to notify the TRIMs that are inconsistent with the provisions of the Agreement, and to eliminate them after the expiry of the transition period provided in the Agreement. Transition periods of two years in the case of developed countries, five years in the case of developing countries and seven years in the case of LDCs, from the date of entry into force of the Agreement (i.e. 1st January 1995) are provided in the Agreement.

Temporary deviation on BOP grounds

The Agreement allows developing countries to deviate temporarily from its provisions on balance of payments (BOP) grounds (as per the provisions of Article XVIII.B of GATT, 1994).

India's notified TRIMs

As per the provisions contained in Art. 5.1 of the TRIMs Agreement, India had notified three trade related investment measures as inconsistent with the provisions of the Agreement:

Local content (mixing) requirements in the production of News Print,

Local content requirement in the production of Rifampicin and Penicillin – G, and Dividend balancing requirement in the case of investment in 22 categories consumer goods.

Such notified TRIMs were due to be eliminated by 31st December, 1999. None of these measures is in force at present. Therefore, India does not have any outstanding obligations under the TRIMs agreement as far as notified TRIMs are concerned.

Present Status

The transition period allowed to developing countries ended on 31st December, 1999. However, Art. 5.3 provides for extension of such transition periods in the case of individual members, based on specific requests. In such cases individual Members have to approach the Council for Trade in Goods with justification based on their specific trade, financial and development needs. Accordingly 9 developing countries (Malaysia, Pakistan, Philippines, Mexico, Chile, Colombia, Argentina, Romania and Thailand) have applied for extension of transition period in respect of certain TRIMs which had been notified by them. Examination of their requests is underway in the Council for Trade in Goods of WTO.

India had proposed during the Seattle Ministerial Conference that:

- Extension of transition period for developing countries should be on a multilateral basis and not on an individual basis;
- Another opportunity should be provided to developing countries to notify un-notified TRIMs and maintain them for an extended transition period;

The Seattle Ministerial Conference was inconclusive and no decision could be taken on the proposals.

However, during the General Council meeting of 8th May, 2000, the following decisions, *inter-alia*, were taken:

> Members agree to direct the Council for Trade in Goods to give positive consideration to individual requests presented in accordance with Article 5.3 by developing countries for extension of transition periods for implementation of the TRIMs Agreement".
>
> "Members have noted the concerns of those Members who have not notified TRIMs or have not yet requested an extension. Consultations on the means to address these cases should also be pursued as a matter of priority, under the aegis of the General Council, by the Chairman of the Council for Trade in Goods".

Mandated Review of the Agreement

Art. 9 of the Agreement envisage its review within five years of its coming into operation, i.e. by 1-1-2000.

The Council for Trade in Goods is to review the operation of the Agreement and, as appropriate, propose to the Ministerial Conference amendments to its text. The process of review has started but no specific proposals have been made by any Member as yet.

Investment Policy and Competition Policy

In the course of this review, the Council for Trade in Goods shall consider whether the Agreement should be complemented with the provisions on investment policy and competition policy. The Singapore Ministerial Conference which established the two parallel Working Groups to study the relationship between Trade and Investment on the one hand and Trade and Competition Policy on the other had stipulated that future negotiations, if any, regarding multilateral disciplines in these areas will take place only after explicit consensus decision by the Members. The Working Group process is still on.

Likely issues during the review

The review of the Agreement is likely to address the following issues:

A. Issues related to the operation of the Agreement during the last five years, and
B. Issues related to the coverage of the Agreement

A. Issues related to the operation of the Agreement

Art. 4 provide that a developing country Member shall be free to deviate temporarily from the obligations arising out of this agreement to the extent and in such a manner as Art. XVIII of GATT 1994, the Understanding on the Balance of Payments Provisions of GATT 1994, and the Declaration on Trade Measures Taken for Balance of Payments Purpose adopted on 28th November, 1979. Issues related to operationalization of this provision would be raised by developing countries;

The question of transition period of five years for developing countries has ended before the review of the operation of the Agreement. The issue of transition periods and the need for general exemption, rather than based on individual request, is a matter of concern for developing countries;

Art. 5.3 which provides for request for extension of transition period on individual basis, stipulates that such Members should demonstrate particular difficulties in implementing the provisions of the Agreement. This leaves the decision to the discretion of WTO Members. There is likely to be demand for objective criteria;

The role of the Committee on Trade–Related Investment Measures has so far been confined to monitoring the notification requirements. A changed role could be considered.

B. Issues related to the coverage of the Agreement

The present agreement prohibits trade related investment measures that are violative of the Art. III nd of the Article XI of the General Agreement on Tariffs and Trade (GATT). Local content requirements, trade balancing requirements, and export restrictions are prohibited. The efforts of developing countries would be to reduce the prohibitions in view of the experience of these countries based on the operation of the agreement. Developing countries (the Like Minded Group) have submitted certain proposals in this regard in the context of review of implementation of the Uruguay Round Agreements.

The TRIMs Agreement has been found by the developing countries to be standing in the way of sustained industrialization of developing countries, without exposing them to balance of payment shocks, by reducing substantially the policy space available to these countries. Developed countries, on the other hand, have been arguing for a further expansion in the list of prohibited TRIMs.

4. Non-Tariff Barriers (NTBs) to International Trade in Agriculture Commodities

The *Agreement on Agriculture* resulting from the Uruguay Round of negotiations significantly affected international trade policies on agricultural commodities. For example, the new tariff system made trade more transparent by changing import-restricting measures such as quotas into customs tariffs subject to minimum market access. However, some international organizations, such as the Organization for Economic Co-operation and Development (OECD), have noted that, as a result of these scheduled reductions in customs tariffs, NTBs could become the main hindrances to international trade in agricultural commodities. Domestic food safety regulations have been identified as a particular source of protectionism. In Europe, for example, the moratorium on certain Genetically Modified Organisms (GMOs) and the ban on cattle that have been given growth hormones are NTBs that affect agriculture in Canada.

International Agreement

Two main international agreements resulting from, or reinforced by, the *Agreement on Agriculture* affect the technical and sanitary aspects of international trade in agricultural commodities:

- the Sanitary and Phytosanitary Agreement (SPA); and
- the Technical Barriers to Trade Agreement (TBTA).

The *SPA*, signed as part of the Uruguay Round, came into force in January 1995 when the World Trade Organization (WTO) was created. It covers food safety, animal health protection, and plant preservation. It defines the basic rules for ensuring a healthy food supply while preventing domestic safety and security regulations from being used as a pretext for protecting domestic production. It also authorizes countries to set their own standards, which must have a scientific basis. Countries are encouraged to use existing international standards, particularly those developed by the *Codex Alimentarius* Commission with respect to human health, the *International Plant Protection Convention (IPPC)* with respect to plant health, and the International Office of Epizootics (IOE) with respect to animal health. (These organizations are described in the Appendix.) However, countries may set stricter standards if these are justified on the basis of science or risk assessment, provided the approach is consistent and not arbitrary.

The *TBTA*, resulting from the Tokyo Round, has existed since 1979; its present version was established during the Uruguay Round. Like the *PSA*, it aims to ensure that domestic regulations do not create undue trade barriers. It covers all technical regulations, standards, and compliance assessment procedures, except for safety measures defined in the *SPA*; thus the *SPA* is an exception to the more general *TBTA*.

Since the scope of the *SPA* is quite specific, some measures related to human health, such as the allergenic properties of foods, may be covered by the *TBTA*. Where agriculture and agri-food are concerned, the *TBTA* covers regulations on labelling, packaging, and claims with respect to the nutritional and allergenic properties of foods, for example. Although the *TBTA* also encourages countries to adopt international standards, unlike the *SPA* it also allows stricter standards to be justified on non-scientific grounds, including major technical problems and geographic location.

Other WTO agreements cover more specific technical problems that could constitute barriers to trade in agricultural commodities. Examples include the *Rules of Origin Agreement*, which requires member countries to adopt transparent rules of origin, and the *Agreement on Trade-Related Aspects of Intellectual Property Rights* (*TRIPS Agreement*), which governs the use of geographic terms such as "champagne," "scotch" and "Roquefort" on food products. Other non-WTO agreements may affect technical and sanitary aspects of international trade in agricultural commodities; for example, the bio-security protocol would govern trans-border movements of living modified organisms such as genetically improved seed.

Dispute Settlement

Since the Uruguay Round, the WTO has had a dispute settlement procedure. If consultations between the countries concerned fail, the WTO Dispute Settlement Body (DSB) may set up a panel to investigate the complaint. The panel submits a report to the DSB, which makes a decision that is binding on the offending country. Although an appeal may be brought, at the conclusion of the process the losing country is required to take appropriate measures. This procedure applies to all trade disputes between two or more WTO member countries, not only to disputes about trade in agricultural commodities or the technical and sanitary aspects of such trade. The DSB, created in 1995, must promote the establishment of jurisprudence and the clarification of the terms of the *SPA* and the *TBTA*.

The *SPA* recommends that the *Codex Alimentarius* Commission, *IPPC*, and IOE standards be consulted during the settlement of international disputes involving scientific issues. Panels have used the standards of the *Codex Alimentarius* Commission to settle certain disputes, thus potentially making these standards authoritative. The best-known *SPA* and *TBTA* dispute settlement dealt with the European Union (EU) ban on the import of live animals that had been given growth hormones and the meat of such animals.

Furthermore, a March 1999 report published by the *SPA* Committee points out that many disputes have been avoided by means of discussions held in accordance with the *SPA*, in particular the section on transparent implementation of sanitary and phyto-sanitary measures. The report refers to measures taken by various countries following the spongiform bovine encephalitis ("mad cow disease") crisis, and a United States import ban placed on certain packaging materials in order to combat an Asian beetle infestation; in some cases, measures were amended after discussions at the *SPA* Committee or another forum provided for under the *SPA*.

Current Issues

A. Interpretation of International Agreements

There is considerable debate over the accurate interpretation of the agreements resulting from the Uruguay Round. Emerging jurisprudence on the *SPA* and the *TBTA* may clarify the limits these set and influence negotiations for their revision. In its 1997 decision on the EU ban on the meat of animals that had been given growth hormones, the DSB relied heavily on the standards of the *Codex Alimentarius* Commission, stating that existing international standards must be accepted. In practical terms, the result has been the free circulation of any product that meets the standards of the *Codex Alimentarius*, which are now seen as authoritative and as having precedence over domestic rules. The DSB decision on appeal seems to alter the interpretation of the *SPA* and the potential role of the *Codex Alimentarius* Commission standards, although it maintains that the import ban is incompatible with certain sections of the *SPA*. The DSB decision does point out that a country may set stricter standards, provided these have a scientific basis, and suggests that a balanced scientific opinion, even a minority one, may be taken into consideration. There also seems to be a trend toward requiring countries that consider measures illegal to provide conclusive evidence of this. Although these decisions do not necessarily establish jurisprudence, they do clearly illustrate that there are various interpretations of the *SPA*.

There is also debate over the *SPA* section on risk assessment, which is required when a country adopts standards stricter than those of the *Codex Alimentarius* Commission or IOE. Although the *Codex Alimentarius* Commission has set stages for risk assessment, there is not one methodology, or any one agreement on acceptable risk levels or what constitutes acceptable risk. There is a full range of opinions, from the desire to eliminate risk (by, for example, sterilizing mineral water, or banning raw-milk cheese) to the possibility of properly managing risk (by, say, bottling mineral water at source, or applying the World Health Organization (WHO) Hazard Analysis Critical Control Point (HACCP) system).

The *SPA* clearly provides that measures taken under it must have a scientific basis: only human, animal or plant health factors—not those that are ethical, cultural or moral—may justify domestic regulations limiting imports of agricultural commodities. However, in 1997, during the *Codex Alimentarius* Commission debate on setting a Maximum Residue Limit (MRL) for recombinant bovine Somatotropin (rbST), the Netherlands moved a motion requesting a review of the consideration of legitimate non-scientific factors in setting *Codex Alimentarius* Commission standards. In fact, non-scientific factors are often seen as the means of determining whether risk is acceptable and scientific factors only as the means of quantifying risk. In response to this motion, the *Codex Alimentarius* Commission's General Principles Committee is considering the role of scientific factors and the extent to which other factors are taken into consideration, particularly in assessing risk. Thus it is possible that, when the *SPA* is renegotiated, some countries will want to have non-scientific factors taken into consideration in justifying domestic regulations.

It is often claimed that the *SPA*, by providing that domestic regulations must be justified on available scientific bases, does not respect the precautionary principle. There are a number of definitions of this principle, which essentially states that, in the absence of scientific certainty, precautionary measures must be taken. The precautionary principle is recognized in a number of international legal instruments, including the *Rio Declaration* and the *UN Framework Agreement on Climate Change*, and is often invoked by consumer and environmental groups. Thus some public expectations that rely on these international agreements may clash with the development of domestic regulations provided for in the agreements that govern the technical and sanitary aspects of international trade.

B. Codex Alimentarius Commission and Other Standard-Setting Organizations

The main fear of consumer and producer groups is that Canadian food safety standards will be lowered to correspond to international standards for facilitating trade. Thus public and national confidence in standard-setting organizations such as the *Codex Alimentarius* Commission, the *IPPC*, and the IOE is of the utmost importance if international standards are to be accepted.

Sometimes criticized are the operations of the *Codex Alimentarius* Commission and some of its advisory committees, including two of the joint expert committees of the WHO-UN Food and Agriculture Organization (FAO) —the Joint Expert Committee on Food Additives (JECFA) and the Joint Meeting on Pesticide Residues (JMPR). In a March 1999 report, Canada's Standing Senate Committee on Agriculture and Forestry, noting that officials from some countries on these committees are representatives of industry, expressed concern about potential conflict of interest. As well, since experts are selected on the basis of their scientific competence, some countries are very well represented on expert committees such as the JECFA and the JMPR, and there is said to be lack of transparency in the selection of these experts. As WTO panels gradually determine the authority of the *Codex Alimentarius* Commission, controversy may arise about the representation of countries and the role accorded to industry at future trade negotiations.

The 1991 conference on food standards among the FAO, the WHO, and the General Agreement on Tariffs and Trade (GATT) noted that recognition in the proposed *SPA* of the special value of the *Codex Alimentarius* Commission's conclusions would change the status of those conclusions. The 1997 decision by the WTO panel on beef led the European Commission to criticize both the procedure used, which it claimed gave the *Codex Alimentarius* Commission's conclusions the value of standards, and the pressure exerted by economic considerations on *Codex Alimentarius* Commission and IOE experts, who ought to be neutral, since different countries do have different regulations for similar products. Debate on the scientific objectivity of the international standard-setting organizations could result, particularly since science has limitations and standards are sometimes set on the basis of technical and economic feasibility; for example, standards on radioactivity levels were set only after their effects on human health had been observed. Moreover, it has been noted that *Codex Alimentarius* Commission votes reflect political, economic, and former colonial considerations as well as those that are objective and scientific.

SPS and TBT issues

The rising incidence of non-tariff barriers, in the form of Sanitary & Phyto-sanitary (SPS) Measures and Technical Barriers to Trade (TBT), has emerged as a major trade concern. New SPS and TBT-related measures are being formulated with the implicit objective of protecting the domestic industries. This has market access implications for us and hence, needs to be addressed adequately.

The SPS and the TBT Agreements provide that while WTO Members have the right to adopt measures to ensure appropriate level of protection for animal, plant and human lives and health (SPS Agreement) and also to achieve national objectives like protection of environment, consumer protection (TBT Agreement), the member countries do not use such measures to create unnecessary restrictions on international trade. In order to ensure this, adequate transparency provisions have been built in. To ensure compatibility with the transparency provisions, three SPS-related Enquiry Points were established to handle all reasonable queries/comments on the SPS notifications/regulations viz. the Department of Agriculture & Cooperation (DoAC), Ministry of Agriculture for plant health and life, the Ministry of Health & Family Welfare for human health and life, and the Department of Animal Husbandry, Dairying & Fisheries, Ministry of Agriculture for animal health and life. For the TBT related issues, the Bureau of Indian Standards (BIS) has been designated as the National Enquiry Point. The Department of Commerce continues to be the National Notifying Authority to the WTO for both the SPS measures and the TBT regulations (http://commerce.nic.in/annual2006-07/html/chapter10.html).

During the year 2006-07 (April 2006-January 2007), India notified 14 SPS related measures to the WTO. Out of this, nine related to food safety, issued by the Ministry of Health & Family Welfare under the PFA Act; four from Ministry of Agriculture on plant health and life; and one from the Department of Animal Husbandry, Dairying & Fisheries under the Ministry of Agriculture.

During the same period, India notified 20 TBT related regulations. These were on various aspects, and were issued by the Ministry of Health & Family Welfare, Ministry of Environment and Forests, BIS, Ministry of Consumer Affairs and Public Distribution.

An analysis of the TBT notifications by various countries shows that the consumer protection and safety is an important aspect of the TBT notifications. The distribution (in per cent age terms) of the objectives of TBT notifications is given below:

Consumer Protection	23%
Environment protection	22%
Health Requirement	18%
Avoiding Deceptive consumer practices	16%
Consumer Information	10%
Safety	11%

To address such challenges and prepare for appropriate response with the objective of trade enhancement and fulfilling socio-economic objectives, the Department of Commerce has identified the following strategy:

- identifying sectors or commodities which are of existing and potential export interest to us and take appropriate steps for preparing the firms to modify their production, post-harvest, processing and treatment technologies in these sectors or commodities;
- strengthening information system and preparing database of standards in these sectors and commodities and also developing a system for information dissemination to exporters and other stakeholders;
- ensuring effective participation in International Standards Setting bodies, evolving National Standards and strengthening accreditation & certification systems; resourcing universities to build databases for standards developments.
- improving coordination between industry and standards institute so as to encourage industry to carry out research and analysis to support standardization activities.
- building capacity for compliance, including testing activities, risk analysis and assessments; improving consumer awareness so that consumer associations start reacting to standards' development.

The Department of Commerce has also taken a number of steps to deal with such barriers to trade. For increasing the awareness among the various stake-holders, a number of seminars and workshops were organized during the year in collaboration with BIS, various industry bodies, etc. A workshop was also organized for the officials from the Central and the State Government Departments, scientists, and other technical persons on risk analysis and assessment on the issues related to human health and life, and animal and plant health and life. The workshop was organized under the Standards and Trade Development Facility (STDF) of the WTO.

During the various rounds of the multilateral trade negotiations, efforts have been made to clarify the technical and sanitary aspects of trade in agricultural commodities. The various agreements signed provide a framework for addressing the ensuing debates and settling disputes. Although the DSB has been fairly effective, it has also shown that various interpretations of the agreements could affect how these are renegotiated. NTBs represent only one factor in integrating agriculture into the world economy; others are customs tariffs, domestic production support policies, and export subsidies.

5. Agreement on Trade Barrier to Trade (TBT)

The Key Features of TBT

- The Trade Barrier to Trade (TBT) Agreement sets out the new disciplines that will govern trading practices at the international level for all consumer type products. It sets out the rights and obligations of WTO Members when applying technical regulations and standards and conformity assessment procedures to traded goods.
- The Agreement tries to prevent standards becoming obstacles to trade by insisting on products imported from any WTO Member receiving no less favourable treatment than that given to similar products of national origin or originating in any other country. Standards should be based on legitimate objectives, be drafted in terms of performance rather than design, and not create an unnecessary obstacle to trade.
- Governments must notify each other of standards in the course of preparation.
- Members are encouraged to adhere to international standards where possible.
- Members should seek to accept the standards of other countries as equivalent even if different where they meet the objectives of their own regulations.
- Foreign suppliers should have access to conformity assessment procedures on terms no less favourable than domestic producers.

The Agreement on Technical Barriers to Trade (TBT) resulting from the Uruguay Round of Multilateral Negotiations is a revision of the Agreement of the same name that emerged from negotiations during the Tokyo Round of GATT negotiations held in the 1970s. The objective of the Agreement is to prevent the use of national or regional technical requirements as unjustified technical barriers to trade. The Agreement covers all types of consumer products and any existing standards including quality requirements for foods. It does not apply to *requirements that are related to sanitary and phytosanitary measures covered by the SPS Agreement*. The TBT Agreement covers measures designed to protect the consumer against deception and economic fraud. It states that all technical standards and regulations must have a legitimate purpose and that the impact or cost of implementing the standard must be proportional to the purpose of the standard. It also says that if there are two or more ways of achieving the same objective, the least trade-restrictive alternative should be followed.

The TBT Agreement emphasizes the use of international standards. WTO Members are obliged to use international standards or parts of them where they exist, except where the international standards would be ineffective or inappropriate in the national situation. Like the SPS Agreement, the TBT Agreement also calls for harmonization of standards and obliges Members to fully participate, within the limitations of available resources, in developing and adopting standards at the international and regional levels.

Article 1: General Provisions

This article states that the definitions for terms listed in Annex 1 apply when used in this Agreement and that other terms have the meaning as defined by the United Nations system and international standardizing bodies. Further, the Agreement:

- covers all products, including industrial and agricultural products;
- covers standards drafted as process or production methods if product related (in contrast to the Standards Code agreed in the Tokyo Round which only covered standards drafted as product characteristics);
- excludes purchasing specifications prepared by government bodies for use by government bodies;
- does not apply to sanitary and phytosanitary measures; and
- technical regulations, standards, and conformity assessment procedures include all amendments, additions and changes.

Article 2: Preparation, Adoption and Application of Technical Regulations by Central Government Bodies

Article 2 contains important provisions that establish the basic requirements of the Agreement. The text and requirements in this Article also serve as a pattern for the requirements for local government bodies and non-government bodies in matters related to establishing product standards and in establishing conformity assessment procedures discussed further on in the Agreement.

First, Members are to treat foreign goods as they would their own goods. Second, Members are to ensure that technical regulations are not prepared, adopted or applied in a manner which would create unnecessary barriers to international trade and that they are not any more trade restrictive than necessary to fulfil a legitimate purpose. Some examples of legitimate purposes for technical regulations are given in the text of this Article. These include national security requirements, prevention of deceptive trade practices, protection of human health or safety and animal or plant life or health, or the environment. Scientific and technical information is to be used in the assessment of the risks associated with the intended purpose of the technical regulation, along with processing technology and intended end-uses of the product.

Technical regulations are to be removed when no longer needed or are no longer appropriate. International standards are to be used if they exist, unless they are ineffective or inappropriate for the objective of the regulation. Justification for the regulation shall be provided upon request from other Members whose trade may be significantly effected by the regulation. Members are to play a full part, within the limits of their resources, in the preparation by appropriate international standardizing bodies of product standards they have adopted or expect to adopt.

Members are also to give consideration to accepting other Members' technical regulations as equivalent and technical regulations are required to be based on performance rather than design or descriptive characteristics.

Paragraph 2.9 states that if international standards do not exist, or the technical regulation is not in compliance with an international standard that does exist, and the technical regulation has a significant effect on trade of other Members, then the Member shall:

- Publish a notice in a publication to allow interested parties to become acquainted with the requirements;
- Notify other Members through the TBT Committee Secretariat, indicating the objective and rationale for the technical regulations;
- Provide other Members, upon request, with copies and particulars, including describing those parts of the technical regulation which differ from the international standard; and,
- Allow reasonable time for other Members to provide written comment, hold discussions and then to take these views into account.

In all of the above circumstances, the notifications must be done promptly.

Paragraph 2.10 provides special provisions that apply in urgent or emergency situations related to safety, health, environmental protection or national security. In these situations, some steps listed above in paragraph 2.9 may be omitted, particularly the first step of publishing a notice in a publication for interested parties.

Article 3: PreparAtion, Adoption and Application of Technical regulations by Local Government Bodies and Non-Government Bodies and Non-Government Bodies

This article confirms the responsibility of the Members to take all reasonable measures necessary to ensure that local government and non-government bodies comply with the provisions of Article 2. Central government of the Member is responsible for notification of the technical regulations of local government under 2.9 and 2.10. Contact between Members on matters related to 2.9 and 2.10 should be made at the central government level.

Article 4: Preparation, Adoption and Application of Standards

Standardizing bodies must accept and comply with the Code of Good Practice for the Preparation, Adoption and Application of Standards, as written in Annex 3 of the Agreement. It is the responsibility of the Member to ensure that the central and local governments and non-government standardizing bodies within their territories are "members, accept and comply" with this Code. If they are not a Member of the Code, or do not accept the Code, then the Member must still ensure that they will comply with the Code irrespective of their willingness to accept the Code.

Article 5: Procedures for Assessment of Conformity (CAPs) by Central Government

This article concerns the provisions to be applied to foreign goods by central governments when conformity with technical regulations and standards are required. First, the procedures to be followed are prepared, adopted and applied to grant foreign suppliers no less favourable conditions than domestic suppliers, and Conformity Assessment Procedures (CAPs) are not of themselves to be unnecessary obstacles to international trade. The assessments are to be undertaken and completed as expeditiously as possible. The standard time anticipated for the assessments is to be published so that the supplier knows what to expect in advance in terms of the assessment time and other administrative procedures, such as application review etc. These procedures are not to cause any undue delay in processing.

Only information that is considered necessary to have is to be requested and confidentiality of the information is to be respected. Any fees imposed are to be equitable when compared to the fees charged for identical or similar services for domestic procedures. The location of the facilities where assessments are to be made should not be unnecessarily inconvenient to the supplier. For those products where changes have been made, only the changes will be assessed during subsequent conformance assessments, unless the changes do not permit the complete evaluation of the product's compliance with the technical regulation or standard. Finally, the CAPs should have a procedure to investigate complaints related to the operation of a conformity assessment procedure and to take corrective action when justified.

In all cases where products are to comply with technical regulations or standards, Members are to ensure that central governments use international standards, recommendations or guidelines where they exist or where their completion is imminent, or any applicable parts of the international standards, as a basis for the conformity standards, if appropriate. Harmonization is to take place by the Member's full participation, within the limits of available resources, in the international standardizing body's preparation of recommendations and guidelines for conformity assessment procedures.

As with the issuance of technical regulations discussed in Article 2, the Agreement also provides, under paragraph 5.6, the procedures to apply the implementation of CAPs under specific circumstances. If international guidelines and recommendations do not exist, or if the technical content of a CAP is not in accordance with an international guideline or recommendations, and if the CAP may have a significant effect on trade of other Members, then the Member SHALL, as for technical regulations (Article 2), publish a notice, notify other Members, provide Members with copies of the CAP and allow time for the Members to make comments.

In all of the above circumstances, the notifications must be done promptly.

Again, as in Article 2, paragraph 5.7 of this Article provides special considerations that apply in urgent or emergency situations related to safety, health, environmental protection, or national security. In these situations, some of the steps listed in paragraph 5.6 may be omitted, particularly the first step regarding publishing a notice in a publication for interested parties.

Article 6: Recognition of Conformity Assessment by Central Government Bodies

Under this Article Members are to recognize the results of conformity assessments of other Members where there is confidence that the procedures are equivalent, even if different. This may be established through prior consultations taking into account the technical competence of the assessment bodies, verification procedures, accreditation and other relevant information. Mutual Recognition Agreements related to recognition of CAPs and the results of assessments are encouraged between Members.

Article 7: Procedures of Assessment of Conformity by Local Government Bodies

Members are responsible for ensuring the local government bodies comply with Articles 5 and 6 of the Agreement. They must provide the required notifications as indicated under paragraphs 5.6.2 and 5.7.1 of the Agreement. This and all other communications and contacts made related to conformity assessment should to be made at the central government level.

Article 8: Procedures for Assessment of Conformity by Non-Government Bodies

Members are also responsible for ensuring that non-government bodies, which also operate conformity assessment procedures, comply with Articles 5 and 6 of the Agreement. Also, central governments shall ensure that they only rely on the results of assessments carried out by those non-government bodies that are in compliance with Articles 5 and 6 of the Agreement.

Article 9: International and Regional Systems

Members are required to, wherever practicable, formulate and adopt international systems for conformity assessment and become members or participate in them. They are also to ensure that international and regional systems of conformity assessments for which they participate, or for which conformity assessment bodies within the country participate, comply with the provisions of Articles 5 and 6, and central governments rely on these assessment systems only if they comply with these same articles.

Article 10: Information about Technical regulations, Standards, and Conformity Assessment procedures

The provisions in this Article pertain to the establishment of an Enquiry Point. Each Member is to establish an enquiry point for the purpose of providing other Members with requested information. Such information includes:

- technical regulations;
- standards, conformity assessment procedures;
- location of published notices; and
- answers to other type questions

The Enquiry Point would also be the source of information related to the international standards setting bodies for which the Member is a member or participant, including those bodies for which the central and local governments and non government organizations are members or participants.

Article 11: Technical assistance to Other Members

Members are to provide advice to other Members, especially developing country Members. Technical advice and assistance can be provided on the preparation of technical regulations and establishing standardizing bodies. Additional assistance can be provided to enable developing country Members to participate in the activities of international standardizing bodies in the development of CAPs and the operation of conformity assessments. Finally, assistance can be provided in establishing institutions and legal frameworks to enable them to fulfil their obligations under the Agreement.

Article 12: Special and Differential Treatment of developing Country Members

Members are to provide differential and more favourable treatment to developing country Members by recognizing that these countries have special development, financial and trade needs and these needs should be taken into account in the operation of the Agreement. For instance, the Agreement states that Members shall take into account these needs in the preparation and implementation of technical regulations, standards, and conformity assessment procedures. There should be recognition that developing countries have an interest in the protection of their indigenous technology and production methods and through their technical regulations, standards and CAPs aim at preserving these indigenous technologies and production methods and processes compatible with their development needs. Therefore, developing countries should not be expected to use international standards as a basis for their technical regulations or standards which are not appropriate to their development, financial or trade needs. International standardizing bodies are encouraged also to take into account the needs of developing countries in developing standards which are within the interest of developing country Members. Developing countries, with infrastructure and institutional problems, are to be given consideration by the TBT Committee, upon their request, for specified and time limited exceptions in whole or in part from obligations under this Agreement.

Article 13: The Committee of technical Barriers to Trade

The provisions of this Article establish the operating committee for the Agreement, the Committee on Technical Barriers to Trade, and list the authorities and procedures.

Article 14: Consultation and Disputer Settlement

The provisions of this Article establish the Consultation and Dispute Settlement procedures under this Agreement as those established in Article XXII and XXIII of GATT, 1994. The dispute panel may establish technical expert groups to assist in issues in a technical nature. The procedures that govern such groups are provided in Annex 2 to the Agreement.

Article 15: Final Provision

This is the final provision and indicates that reservation to any provision of the Agreement is allowed only with the consent of the other Members. In addition, Members were to notify the TBT Committee of existing measures in order to ensure prompt implementation of the Agreement following the date of entry into force. This Article also calls for a review of the operation and implementation of the agreement in three years. The TBT Agreement came into force on 1 January 1995.

ANNEXES 1-3

Annex 1—Terms and their Definitions for the Purpose of this Agreement

This annex provides definitions for the terms Technical Regulation, Standard, Conformity Assessment Procedures, International body or system, Regional body or system, Central Government body, Local Government body, and Non-governmental body.

Annex 2—Technical Expert Group

This Annex describes the procedures which shall apply to technical expert groups established in accordance with the provisions of Article 14, related to Consultations and Dispute Settlement Procedures. The annex explains the role of the technical expert group and the rights of those parties to the dispute in relation to the activities of the technical expert group.

Annex 3—Code of Good Practice for the Preparation, Adoption and Application of Standards

The Code is open to acceptance by any standardization body within the territory of any Member of the WTO and acceptance (or withdrawal) requires notification to the International Standards Organization/International Electrotechnical Commission (ISO/IEC). The procedures are a summary of those requirements which express the intent and spirit of the Agreement to prevent and ensure that technical regulations, standards and conformity assessment procedures do not create unnecessary obstacles to international trade, do not discriminate, and, are harmonized, transparent, and based on performance rather than design or descriptive characteristics.

Structural Barriers to Agreement on Trade Transaction

It is common, in discussing intractable conflicts, to frame the conflict in terms of the actors involved and their preferences. But there are many situations in which, even given matching preferences, there is no way to reach an agreement. This is often because of *structural impediments.*

Structural impediments or barriers can be understood as aspects of the external environment that limit negotiating options, to the extent that there are no possible points of agreement. Even agreements-in-principle can be disrupted by structural impediments, as the nature of the system in which the actors operate confounds their efforts to follow through with the provisions of the agreement. This essay will discuss some major structural barriers to reaching agreements. Before doing so, it is necessary to define structure, in this context.

Defining Structure

Kenneth Waltz, a political scientist, (*Theory of International Politics* by Kenneth N Waltz) presented one of the first structural theories of international relations. Waltz argued that a structural theory of politics eschews actor preferences and institutional organization, in favor of explanations that focus solely on the rules of the game. Any discussion of the structural barriers to agreement must be seen in a similar light.

One way of defining structural impediments is by defining what not structural impediments are. Structural impediments are not:

- Individual beliefs, preferences, or identities;
- Differences between one group or institution and another.

Instead, structural impediments are:

- Formal and informal rules that regulate an entire system of interaction;
- The physical limitations of an environment.

Any interaction between two actors is thus defined, if not limited, by the social and physical constraints of the environment. Social structures or systems, as Bounding calls them, create patterns of interaction. Social systems encourage certain choices while discouraging others. Although this may be accomplished by a formal set of rules or a rule of law, there may also be informal rules, customs that regulate behavior. For example, in situations structured by fear and hate of an ethnic group, even if an individual wants to operate differently, he or she is discouraged from doing so. As another example, there are no laws in the United States that require a university education, but the pattern of incentives and disincentives in the workplace strongly encourages one. In this way, the combination of formal and informal rules defines not only what is acceptable, but also what is conceivable. In intractable conflicts, it is often the case that structural limitations are hardened to the point that abstract agreements-in-principle are unimaginable, given the general pattern of incentives and disincentives.

Some examples of structural impediments might be group identities, political and legal institutions, mountains and oceans, or production and trade patterns in a region. Structural impediments are domain-specific. Some structural limits may exist for one person in one conflict, but not for the same person in a different conflict. For example, a legal institution can be a structural barrier in a local environmental dispute because it limits the possible outcomes. The same corporation that may be involved in this local dispute will not be constrained by that legal system in the international realm. There is no overarching enforcement mechanism at the international level to constrain the corporation. Similarly, states, it is argued, exist in an environment of anarchy.

This section will focus on a handful of examples in order to show how these barriers limit conflict resolution, and to discuss possibilities for overcoming the limits imposed by structural limitations. The number of parties involved can be important determinants of possible agreements; institutions, beliefs and information, and physical limitations are also important constraints on possible agreements and their implementation.

Types of Structural Barriers

Number of Parties

The number of parties can be understood in a couple of different contexts. The first structural barrier involving parties is the complexity of negotiations. Game theory and rational-choice theory assume that actors choose actions for a reason, actions are purposeful and that the reason for any given action is to maximize utility. In game theory, scholars use this assumption to model how two actors in competition will choose to maximize a given set of preferences. As the number of actors increases beyond two, the models become increasingly complex. This is because the range of possible solutions decreases dramatically. As Kahler points out, negotiations involving large numbers of groups are not impossible, but they are difficult. In the case of intractable conflict, it is often important to include as many parties as possible lest some parties withdraw entirely from the negotiations and actively attempt to sabotage any possible resolution. The second problem with parties is this "spoiler" problem. Outside parties that have an interest in the outcome of a negotiation can upset the implementation of an agreement. Even in cases where parties involved in the negotiations agree to a settlement, outside parties can disrupt the implementation of the agreement. As the number of spoilers increases, the difficulty of implementation increases dramatically.

It is a double-edged sword. On one hand, as the number of parties involved in negotiations increases, there is less possible room for agreement. On the other hand, as the number of spoilers left out of the negotiations increases, it becomes more difficult to implement the agreement. Thus, there is no attractive trade-off in terms of the number of parties. However, including all important parties in the negotiations, but dividing the negotiations among committee groups, might be a more attractive alternative. The benefit of a committee system is the ability to disentangle one issue from another. Intractable conflicts tend not to revolve around a single easily identifiable issue, but instead around many issues those are murky and linked in surprising ways. When the number of parties involved increases the complexity of negotiations, it is useful to decrease complexity and pressure in other ways. In particular, the use of committees allows each issue to be discussed on its own merits.

Beliefs and Information Flow Scene

In order to make similar decisions, opponents need similar sets of information, but in intractable conflicts there is an incentive to withhold information. One way of analyzing an intractable conflict is to use the strategic setting framework developed by Lake and Powell. Lake and Powell distinguish four key features of a strategic setting: information, institutions, beliefs, and preferences. *Information* and *institutions* are part of the external environment that dictates what an actor can know and do in any given situation. *Beliefs* and *preferences* define the cognitive framework of the actor. By considering all these factors, an outside observer can analyze what is desired, what is possible, and specify the parts of the environment that limit any choice.

In this context, beliefs and information represent two key constraints on possible agreements. Fearon notes that in most situations there is a possible agreement that is mutually beneficial to the parties involved, but that withheld information can sabotage the possible agreement. Information, in the form of capacities, objectives, and constraints, lets the parties involved know the possible agreement points of which any individual actor is capable. If information is concealed, proposed solutions must be made and rejected while only knowing one side of the equation. *The Prisoner's Dilemma* is an example of imperfect decision-making because of a dearth of information. In the Prisoner's Dilemma, individuals will tend to minimize losses instead of maximizing gains. As more information is communicated between the two parties, it becomes possible to maximize benefits instead of minimizing losses.

Returning to the definition of structure as a pattern of incentives and disincentives, it becomes understandable why information could be a structural barrier. An individual coming to a fork in the road, without a map, would have no way of knowing which path to take to get to his or her destination. However, as information is provided, the choice becomes easier. A rudimentary map may provide some information, a topographical map yet more, a topographical map with marked roads still more. As information increases, better agreements are possible and are easier to arrive at.

In intractable conflicts, there is often an implicit or explicit prohibition against the involved parties sharing information. Milner suggests that the best way to overcome information limitations is the use of interest groups. Any number of groups, from NGOs to intervening international organizations and states, can create communication channels between parties that would not communicate directly. These communication channels will increase the amount of shared information in any conflict. By creating a common informational environment, choices based on self-interest can lead to agreements. Rational actors seeking to improve their own situation find themselves in a better situation to cooperate, as more information is provided. As information increases, and with it the number of people who share the same information, the possibility for agreement increases substantially. This does not guarantee agreement, but instead helps to manage one structural barrier.

Beliefs, at a very basic level, provide a pattern of incentives and disincentives by ordering self-perception vis-à-vis the outside world and the outside world vis-à-vis the self. Beliefs about likely outcomes and about what is possible represent one sort of belief system. Group identities represent another sort of belief system. Group identities, for example, determine which actions are acceptable to many members of the group. Group identities encourage group censorship and self-censorship of individual actions, according to what is deemed acceptable. One can think of Catholicism in this regard. The Catholic religion prohibits certain actions, such as adultery, murder, and abortion, and strictly observant Catholics find such actions by other Catholics to be unacceptable. In addition, Catholic individuals may censor themselves according the same rules, though others, who are less strict, may not.

People outside the group will tend to stereotype the people of a group, which may affect interactions between people in different groups. In civil wars, group identities are often difficult to overcome. Elites must balance attempts at conciliation with rival groups with maintaining authenticity within their own group. Group identities thus create a two-level game that elites must play in order to reach an agreement. Group identities represent just one form of a belief system, but an important one that can provide a sometimes insurmountable barrier to agreements. Belief systems are very difficult to change. In fact it is probably counterproductive to try to change a party's belief systems early in an intractable conflict, when they may be very resistant to change. It is not impossible, but in the context of intractable conflicts, belief systems will change only very slowly, through repeated positive interactions in an environment of trust.

Political and Legal Institutions

Intractable conflicts at all levels are constrained by the rules, regulations, and political coalitions that define the institutional environment. This environment varies widely as one moves from conflicts within states, to conflicts between states, to conflicts in failed states. In conflicts between states and in failed states, the institutional environment is structured by power and anarchy. That is, agreements are limited by the lack of an overarching government that can provide effective sanctions against illegal actions. Thus, some argue, power rules and Might Makes Right. One challenge in this sort of anarchy is to overcome prevailing conceptions of Might Makes Right, in order to create reasonable solutions that foster agreement. Reasonable solutions are not necessarily fair agreements unstructured by power differentials, but are instead pragmatic agreements that recognize issues other than power. In failed states torn apart by civil war, the structure of the state is often at the core of the conflict. The structure of society is the most important determinant of the justice of the society. In states weakened by war, poverty, and resource scarcity, the justice of the institutions is a strong determinant of the stability of any peace agreement.

Conflicts that occur within states must be resolved according to law, and possible agreements must fall within the range of legally and politically acceptable options. On occasion, the laws themselves create a problem and must be changed. Campaign-finance reform is a good example of an intractable conflict in the United States. Incumbents and challengers alike would probably like to forego fund-raising in favor of focusing on and debating the issues, but the laws that determine elections encourage putting maximum effort towards fund-raising. Changing the rules, however, would tend to even the playing ground putting incumbents at a disadvantage. Because incumbents are the very same people who will vote on a law, they are unlikely to pass a law that will put them at a disadvantage relative to the status quo. In similar ways, the political and legal status quo is often a strong structural barrier to possible agreements within states. Individuals and groups that are in conflict with each other must mobilize not only like-minded individuals, but people who may not care about the conflict at all. Mobilizing the apathetic is the biggest barrier to changing institutions within stable states.

Institutional barriers to agreement are not as intransigent as belief systems, but they can be quite difficult to overcome. In relatively peaceful social settings, the institutional structure and its consequences for distribution of resources are likely to be relatively fixed, whereas in failed states the institutional structure is likely to be in a rather severe state and in flux. These two extremes and the wide range of intermediate possibilities present different challenges to reaching an agreement. In relatively stable situations, the debate is likely to revolve around particular rules or the distributional consequences of particular legal frameworks. Women's ownership of property and ability to divorce, for example, were key issues to the first generation of feminists in the United States. Changing these rules was important to reaching an agreement over women's moral, legal, and intellectual equality.

Physical Limitations

The oldest and some of the most difficult structural barriers are simple physical limitations to an agreement. These are literal barriers to communication, such as mountains, rivers, jungles, deserts, oceans, and scarce resources, and they can limit the ability to communicate or to provide the material underpinnings of an effective agreement. Some scholars cite resource scarcity as both a cause of intractable conflicts and an impediment to possible solutions. Scarcity problems tend to intensify group identities, as competition over resources creates incentives for belonging to one group or another. Kaplan has cited increasing competition over resources such as water as one of the key conflicts in developing countries. In civil wars, the presence of exportable primary goods, such as timber and diamonds in Ivory Coast and cocaine in Colombia, can exacerbate conflicts because the resources fund the conflict and become spoils to the victor.

Physical barriers such as deserts and oceans limit possible agreements as well. In intractable conflicts, it is unlikely that two groups are separated by significant physical barriers; it is their very proximity that usually causes the conflict. But physical barriers place important constraints on third-party involvement. Even in situations where two parties to a conflict may desire intervention, they are not likely to be able to cover the cost. As the cost of overcoming barriers mounts, it is less likely that third parties will be available to provide the vital input necessary to resolve a conflict. In an environment where high levels of scarcity and low levels of development are pervasive, relations are likely to remain strained. One of the best and easiest ways to begin to resolve intractable conflicts is to attack the underlying material conditions that create the problem. Problems of scarcity in ecologically stressed environments can rarely be solved in the environment itself.

Activities Relating to other International Trade Organizations

Economic and Social Commission for Asia and Pacific (ESCAP)

India is one of the founding members of ESCAP, the regional development arm of the United Nations, which serves as the main economic and social development centre for the United Nations in Asia and the Pacific. Its mandate is to foster cooperation between its 53 members and 9 associate members. The ESCAP provides the strategic link between global and country-level programmes and issues. It supports Governments of the region in consolidating regional positions and advocates regional approaches to meet the region's unique socio-economic challenges in a globalizing world. The major works of the Organization are (http://commerce.nic.in/annual2006-07/html/chapter10.html):

- Regional Economic Cooperation;
- Poverty Alleviation through Growth and Social Development;
- Environment and Sustainable Development;
- Development of Transport Communications, Tourism and Infrastructure Development in the region; and
- Enhancing capabilities of National Statistical Organizations.

The 62nd Annual Session of ESCAP was held in Jakarta between 6th and 12th April, 2006 with a theme "Enhancing Regional Cooperation in Infrastructure Development, including that related to Disaster Management". The Session was attended by delegates from 50 member countries and associate member countries. Various issues relating to poverty reduction, emerging economic and social issues, institutional reform managing migration, development of health systems etc. were also deliberated upon in the senior officials meetings of the Annual Session. India has worked in close cooperation with ESCAP during the year and has committed financial support to the following four regional institutions of ESCAP:

- Asian and Pacific Centre for Transfer of Technology (APCTT), New Delhi, India;
- Centre for Alleviation of Poverty through Secondary Crops Development in Asia and Pacific (CAPSA);
- Statistical Institute for Asia and Pacific (SIAP); and
- Asia and Pacific Centre for Agriculture and Engineering Machinery (APCAEM).

The 63rd Annual Session of ESCAP is scheduled to be held at Kazakhstan from 17 to 23 May, 2007 with a theme: "Health Systems Development in Asia and the Pacific".

1. United Nations Conference on Trade and Development (UNCTAD)

The United Nations Conference on Trade and Development (UNCTAD) aims at development-friendly integration of developing countries into the world economy. The UNCTAD serves as the focal point within the United Nations for the integrated treatment of trade and development and the interrelated issues in the areas of finance, technology, investment and sustainable development. The Ministerial Conference, which meets in every four years, is the UNCTAD's highest decision-making body. It sets priorities and guidelines for the organization and provides an opportunity to debate and evolve policy consensus on key economic and development issues.

The three pillars of UNCTAD's existing mandate are: (a) independent policy analysis; (b) consensus building; and (c) technical assistance. The main goals of UNCTAD are to maximize the trade, investment and development opportunities of developing countries and assist them in their efforts to integrate into the world economy on an equitable basis. It serves as a forum for intergovernmental consensus building in the areas of international trade, investment, enterprise development and technology, globalization and development, services infrastructure, transport and trade efficiency, human resource development and least developed, landlocked & island developing countries. It also undertakes research, policy analysis and data collection in order to provide substantive inputs for the discussion of experts and government representatives. In co-operation with other organizations and donor countries, it provides technical assistance tailored to the needs of the developing countries, with special attention being paid to the needs of the least developed countries and countries with economy in transition.

Eleven Conferences of UNCTAD have taken place so far. The UNCTAD XI was held in Sao Paulo, Brazil on 13-18 June, 2004 with a Theme: "Enhancing coherence between national strategies and the global economic processes towards economic growth and development, particularly of developing countries". The Conference mainstreamed three related issues-trade and poverty, trade and gender and trade and creative industries which were discussed both in the inter-governmental meetings and in a series of seminars and workshops designed to enrich the Conference dialogue and debate. India, as a member of UNCTAD, participated in the Conference. The Conference provided India a unique opportunity to participate in the international policy dialogue and analysis of the current process of globalization, how this will impact on developing countries and the policy responses required both at the national and international level, to ensure that globalization is responsive to and serves the development needs of developing countries. The discussions and the outcome of the Conference reflected our concerns on trade and development, including on specific issues relating to the international trading system and trade negotiations. A major achievement of the Conference was the launching of the Third Round of Negotiations under the Global System of Trade Preferences among Developing Countries (GSTP). The new round of negotiations through broader and deeper exchange of tariff preferences amongst developing countries has commenced in November 2004 and is expected to revitalize the GSTP Agreement.

2. Global System of Trade Preferences (GSTP)

The Agreement establishing the Global System of Trade Preferences (GSTP) among developing countries was signed on 13th April, 1988. The GSTP establishes a framework for the exchange of trade concessions among the members of the Group of 77. It lays down rules, principles and procedures for conduct of negotiations and for implementation of the results of the negotiations. So far, only two Rounds of negotiations have been held under GSTP. The third round of negotiations is underway. A meeting of the senior officers of the Negotiating Committee on GSTP was held on 11-12 December 2006 in Geneva. Several countries including India have indicated their preference to conclude the Third Round by end of 2007.

3. Asia Pacific Trade Agreement (APTA)

The Asia Pacific Trade Agreement (APTA) was signed on 2nd November, 2005 in Beijing, China. The Agreement is operational among five countries namely, Bangladesh, China PR, India, Republic of Korea and Sri Lanka. Three Rounds of Trade Negotiations have taken place so far. The third round of tariff concessions were implemented from 1st September 2006 which has consolidated the concessions granted in all the three rounds of negotiations. The revised Rules of Origin under APTA have been notified on 31st August, 2006.

4. *Bay of Bengal Initiative for Multi-Sectoral Technical and Economic Cooperation (BIMSTEC)*

The Frame work Agreement on the BIMST-EC Trade Area was signed in 2004 with a view to establish economic cooperation among Bangladesh, India, Sri Lanka, Thailand, Myanmar, Bhutan and Nepal. With the admission of Bhutan and Nepal as its member in 2004, the initiative was named as Bay of Bengal Initiative of Multi-Sectoral Technical and Economic Cooperation (BIMSTEC). The Cooperation involves 5 members of SAARC (India, Bangladesh, Bhutan, Nepal & Sri Lanka) and 2 members of ASEAN (Thailand, Myanmar). BIMSTEC is visualized as a 'bridging link' between two major regional groupings i.e. ASEAN and SAARC. BIMSTEC is an important element in India's "Look East" strategy and adds a new dimension to our economic cooperation with South East Asian countries. It was agreed that the Cooperation should aim and strive to develop into a Free Trade Area, and should focus on activities that facilitate trade, increase investment & promote technical cooperation among member countries. The Framework Agreement signed includes provisions for negotiations on FTA in goods, services and investment. The negotiations on FTA in goods are at an advanced stage. The negotiations on the agreement on services & investment have also commenced.

Prospects for New WTO Trade Negotiations

Trade ministers from the 135 member countries of the World Trade Organization met in Seattle in early December 1999 but failed in their efforts to launch a new round of multilateral trade negotiations. To be sure, the violent protests complicated their task. More important, however, the ministers were unable to bridge major differences both among developed countries and between developed and developing countries regarding what should be on the agenda of the new WTO Round. In large measure, the developed countries were reluctant to address their own barriers to trade in goods and services but demanded that the new talks target protectionism in developing countries. For their part, developing countries argued that new concessions should await the fulfillment of the Uruguay Round reforms by developed countries (especially regarding textiles, compliance with dispute rulings, and "best efforts" commitments to encourage technology transfer). Everyone seemed to want the Uruguay Round accords to be faithfully implemented, but developed countries talked about adhering to the new trade rules, for example, deadlines for Trade-Related Aspects of Intellectual Property and Trade-Related Investment Measures, while developing countries focused on commitments to liberalize trade barriers. In particular, U.S. and European Union commitments to eliminate textile quotas and their "alleged" efforts to undercut market access commitments with anti-dumping measures (Jeffrey J. Schott, 2004: http://www.cato.org/pubs/journal/cj19n3/cj19n3-5.pdf).

Everyone wanted to expand the WTO agenda beyond the issues mandated by the Uruguay Round accords (the so-called "built-in" agenda), but countries differed markedly on which new subjects deserved priority. The United States, for example, pushed for new WTO initiatives on electronic commerce and on trade-related labor issues; the European Union wanted more attention given to investment and competition policy issues. By contrast, developing countries wanted to focus efforts on more traditional issues such as tariffs and agricultural restrictions. In services, developing countries placed priority on removing barriers in sectors in which they are competitive such as labor, maritime, and entertainment services; developed countries favored their own "winners" such as financial, air transport, information, and professional services. "Priorities" of some countries were "nonstarters" for others.

The chief example of these conflicting interests involved U.S. efforts to establish a new WTO Working Group on Trade and Labor. In the aftermath of the China WTO deal, U.S. negotiators were under great pressure to secure agreement on their proposal to open a WTO forum on these issues. The U.S. proposal was much more modest in this area than earlier U.S. initiatives that were soundly rebuffed by most other WTO members. But opposition from developing countries remained intractable. It is hard to conceive of their changing course unless the United States responds more favorably to issues of priority concern to developing countries in the negotiations. Lest one think that all of the problems fell along a North-South divide, it is important to emphasize that one of the biggest hurdles to a successful meeting in Seattle involved substantive differences on numerous issues among the Quad countries (United States, European Union, Japan, and Canada). The United States wanted deeper cuts than Europe or Japan in farm subsidies and tariffs, but opposed those countries' demands for new talks on investment and competition policy. Japan wanted to reexamine anti-dumping provisions, and Europe and Canada wanted to explore cultural exemptions, both of which conflicted with U.S. proposals. The end result: a leadership vacuum at the heart of the trading system.

Crafting a Workable Agenda

Given the failure in Seattle, WTO members have the following options in crafting a workable agenda for new trade negotiations:

First, they could rely primarily on existing mandates and possibly supplement them with new initiatives during the course of the negotiations (as was done in both the Tokyo and Uruguay Rounds). Under the WTO's built-in agenda, negotiations on agriculture and services were launched in early 2000. Unfortunately, the experience under the General Agreement on Tariffs and Trade (GATT) demonstrates that self-standing negotiations on agriculture never succeed; recent services accords have fared somewhat better (but only when developing countries accepted deals that did not require significant changes in U.S. and European practices). A broader bargain will be needed to enable countries to trade off concessions across sectors and issues and undertake obligations to liberalize long-standing and politically sensitive trade barriers.

Second, they could follow the current U.S. approach— which seeks to limit the negotiating agenda by focusing primarily on sector and product-specific reforms, and not on revising the terms of the Uruguay Round accords to avoid protracted negotiations. Here again, the proposed U.S. agenda does not encompass a "critical mass" of issues to ensure that agreements can be reached that accommodate the diverse interests of the developed and developing countries. To take into account the diverse perspectives of WTO member countries, new talks will have to encompass a broad range of issues. New WTO negotiations thus will have to pursue several initiatives simultaneously:

- Trade liberalization in industry and agriculture and in developed and developing country markets
- New rule-making that establishes rights and obligations in areas not yet subject to, or inadequately covered by, WTO provisions
- Institutional reforms that remedy flaws in the WTO's dispute settlement procedures, that make WTO operations more transparent, and that help promote economic development for the betterment of all citizens of WTO member countries

In uncertain terms, some trade officials tend to worry that WTO talks will bog down if negotiators cover too many issues, including subjects that do not seem "ripe" for resolution in the near future. They fear that the requirement that the new round be a "single undertaking"— in which nothing is agreed on until all aspects of the package of accords are agreed on— would make concluding new trade pacts promptly quite difficult because negotiations in some areas will require many years to be fully resolved.

A Round-up of Agreements

Unfortunately, many trade officials still think of new WTO talks as a fixed-length, one-shot GATT round, even though they admit that the old GATT approach no longer fits the fast-paced world of global commerce. Instead, they should adopt a broader, yet more pragmatic, strategy for trade negotiations. Fortunately, the WTO has already upgraded the GATT model; its new institutional framework accommodates continuous negotiations. WTO ministers can start and finish talks on some issues while other subjects remain under debate and new issues are added to the agenda. Trade ministers could use their regularly scheduled meetings as action forcing events to put together a package of trade agreements in what I have called a "round-up" (Schott, 1998). In this way, countries can conduct a series of seamless trade negotiations; with new talks starting immediately after a package of trade agreements is concluded. Each round-up would build on the results of the previous accord.

Over a decade, the WTO could produce three or four round-ups, which cumulatively liberalize significant trade barriers and strengthen a member country's rights and obligations. Each round-up or set of agreements would be a single undertaking but would not require that all aspects of all issues under negotiation be completed before a deal could be concluded. Because the WTO is a forum for continuing negotiations, not all of the problems in a given sector need to be resolved in the first phase of talks or the initial round-up, nor would each round-up have to include all issues. Each package, however, would have to include reforms of interest to both developed and developing countries, so that each member could "bring home" concessions that reinforce domestic political support for the trade pacts and for implementing reforms of their own trade barriers.

Such an approach still requires complicated horse trading among a large number of countries on a large number of issues. But crafting such packages of agreements, I believe, is essential to accommodate trade-offs across sectors and issues, involving both product-or sector-specific liberalization and acceptance of new trade obligations. Without such grand bargains (even on the more limited scale envisaged by my round-ups), WTO members will likely fail to dent the strongest trade barriers protecting domestic industries in their key export markets. In that regard, the three-year timetable for the WTO talks, as proposed by the United States and others, will clearly be ambitious, especially if the lack of fast track and electoral politics in 2000 limit the flexibility of U.S. negotiators to address politically sensitive U.S. trade barriers until well into 2001. Under such a scenario, WTO talks probably can't be launched until late 2001 and surely can't be concluded three years hence during the 2004 election campaign.

A Need for U.S. Leadership

Under the given scenario, the United States has to exert a more positive leadership role in the negotiations. The United States has broad-based economic and political interests in a successful WTO Round. Most of its objectives involve liberalizing foreign trade barriers down to U.S. levels and strengthening WTO rules so that foreign trade laws and regulations move up toward U.S. norms. But the United States will also have to contribute to the party. Although the U.S. market is arguably the most open in the world, there are a few notable barriers whose partial liberalization could yield large dividends in both foreign trade concessions and U.S. economic welfare, such as reductions in peak tariffs (including textiles and clothing), perhaps capped at a level of 15 percent or below; reductions in agricultural protection, including cuts in domestic subsidies and enlargement of tariff-rate quotas on sugar, citrus, and dairy products; increased *de minimis* thresholds for the application of anti-dumping duties; and new guidelines on the provision of temporary labor services by professional and other workers. The United States is the leader of the world trading system, and it must lead by example.

Inter-Business Collaboration via Contract Negotiation and Enactment

The increasing complexity of products and services encourages more and more companies to form collaborative networks. As these companies are independent organizations there is often an issue of governance. In the given circumstances it would be apt to suggest a possible architecture for such a business network that proposes a contract as the principal means of coordination and describes how such a contract can be designed and enacted (http://jobfunctions.bnet.com/abstract.aspx?docid=321594).

Today one can witness two seemingly opposed trends in the cooperation between businesses: On the one hand companies are forced to concentrate on their core competencies and to outsource all activities that lie outside the core. On the other hand customers demand that a supplier covers an increasing range of products and services. They want to buy a complete solution from only one supplier instead of buying bits and pieces from many. This latter point seems to suggest an increased amount of "in-sourcing". The solution to both is that companies have to engage in closer cooperation, each concentrating on its area of expertise, but jointly offering a complete suite of related products and services that are well matched (one face to the customer). But this scenario represents an enormous challenge both in terms of organization and regarding the information system support (Peter Rittgen: Supporting Inter-Business Collaboration via Contract negotiation and enactment (http://www.aifb.uni-karlsruhe.de/Forschungsgruppen/BIK/wi2007/papers/wi-2007-1-041.pdf).

In an e-commerce environment, contracts are important for attaining business process interoperability and enforcing their proper enactment. An e-contract is the computerized facilitation or automation of a contract in a cross-organizational business process (http://www.springerlink.com/content/2bed0u8tt8a89pg5/).

Companies that want to engage in a closer cooperation, e.g. a value network, a virtual enterprise or the like, bring into this cooperation not only their different organizational cultures but also different, often incompatible, information systems. A successful cooperation therefore requires the alignment or integration of both the business processes and the information systems to a certain degree. In some industries, such as the automotive industry, this can go as far as the customer forcing the suppliers to introduce the ERP system of the customer's choice (e.g. SAP). But on the whole it is more common that the organizations involved will strive for some kind of mutual adaptation of their business processes and information systems. In a very simple case this could be the introduction of a file transfer accompanied by suitable import and export functionalities and some organizational measures for providing and handling the new data. In more advanced cases it will imply substantial reorganization of business processes and changes to existing information systems and/or introduction of new ones.

In this regard, the goal should be to support the set-up and operation of a business network. The first phase consists mainly of the design of a contract that can be used to coordinate the behavior of network actors. The design process is cooperative, i.e. the actors negotiate this contract among themselves. Such negotiations can be either bilateral or multilateral but both types will contribute to creating one common contract that is binding for all parties involved. We also call this negotiation process a co-design process. Negotiation is a social process that can be supported by a negotiation support system. This eliminates the need for partners to meet face to face and contributes to a flexible set-up of the business network. It implies that the lead-times for setting up the network are relatively short and replacing members that have left and adding new ones can be done with a minimum of effort. These are crucial issues for a business network.

The second phase, operation, consists of enacting the behavior specified in the contract. Here the business logic concerning the coordination of actors is incorporated into the communication network. In this we phase "translates" from the business network to the communication network by managing the respective message exchange via the technical network and a coordination server. We have used this approach to improve the governance of an existent network that consisted of three partners: the headquarters of a retail chain in the home textile and home decoration industry, the shops of this chain and a third-party logistics provider. Although this is a minimal case of a business network it nevertheless provides fundamental insights into the workings of such networks. The contribution of work would ideally consist in outlining a method for governing business networks by negotiating and enacting contracts that take the form of business process models. It is based on existing methods for contract negotiation, business process modeling and workflow management. Apart from combining these methods one can also enrich them, e.g. by extending the concept of a trade contract to cover process aspects.

Negotiating International Environmental Agreements

Addressing international environmental problems requires the cooperation of all nations. In 1972, a growing awareness of global and transnational environmental issues led to the United Nations Conference on the Human Environment in Stockholm, Sweden, and the formation there of the United Nations Environmental Programme. Over the next few years, nations signed on to international treaties to preserve natural and cultural heritage, control the trade in endangered species and reduce air and ocean pollution. These agreements led to others to protect the ozone layer, to regulate the use of ocean resources and to control trans-boundary movements of hazardous waste.

By the late 1980s, dozens of international treaties and agencies existed, yet new challenges had come up. Developing countries around the world were finding it impossible to meet their obligations to protect globally important resources, and it became apparent that global environmental problems could not be solved in isolation from the social and economic challenges facing individual nations. The leaders of the 1992 United Nations Conference on Environment and Development in Rio de Janeiro, Brazil—known as the Earth Summit—embraced the concept of sustainable development and of common, but differentiated, responsibilities among rich and poor nations concerning the protection of global resources. The summit included the adoption of treaties on global warming and biodiversity that incorporated these principles. The summit also raised recognition of the important role that citizen organizations play in holding global financial and trade institutions accountable for their lending practices and decisions.

Since the 1970s, the world community has developed a large body of international environmental laws, including more than 1000 treaties. Yet this process has not included sufficient attention to the implementation and enforcement of these commitments. The 2002 World Summit on Sustainable Development in Johannesburg, South Africa, encouraged the creation of more informal partnerships among governments, agencies, businesses and citizen groups to take action on existing promises related to sustainable development. Some nations have called for the creation of a global environmental organization with real international regulatory powers. We can expect the debate over how best to protect the planet to continue and grow in the coming years.

Landmarks in international environmental cooperation (NRDC—The Evolution of International Environmental Governance: http://www.nrdc.org/international/fgovernance.asp)

- The United Nations Conference on the Human Environment, held in Stockholm, Sweden, in June 1972, marked the emergence of international environmental law. There, countries adopted the Declaration on the Human Environment or Stockholm Declaration which set out the principles for many international environmental issues, including human rights, natural resource management, pollution prevention and the relationship between the environment and development. The conference led to the creation of the United Nations Environment Programme.
- The United Nations Conference on Environment and Development, held in Rio de Janeiro, Brazil, in June 1992, marked a turning point in the history of international environmental cooperation. The Earth Summit attracted more than 110 presidents and prime ministers and thousands of nongovernmental organizations. The Earth Summit developed the Rio Declaration on Environment and Development and Agenda 21. It also led to the establishment of the United Nations Commission on Sustainable Development and the Global Environment Facility..
- The World Summit on Sustainable Development held in Johannesburg, South Africa, in August 2002 helped heighten attention to the critical role of civil society in a globalized world. The summit stimulated the announcement of more than 200 partnerships and initiatives involving not only governments, but also citizen groups and businesses for implementing commitments at the domestic level.

The development of international environmental law has been one of the most rapidly evolving fields in international relations over the last decade. Under the auspices of the United Nations (UN), the progressive development of such legal arrangements has burgeoned. Through the development of this expanding body of environmental law, the international community has been able to craft innovative responses, building and enhancing processes to address the most pressing environmental challenges. The negotiation of multilateral environmental agreements (MEAs) is thereby playing an increasingly important role in promoting the integration of environment and development, and in providing an effective legal and regulatory framework to underpin the efforts of the international community in the field of the environment (http://books.google.co.in/books?id=YzcxrYZqJbcC&pg=PA136&lpg=PA136&dq=Negotiating+ International+ Environmental+ Agreements &source=bl&ots=tWc Ojs3yi_&sig=4zyfwRDjm7M1YJuRYRggex GUlPM&hl =en&ei= vdvmSu7OHZPo6gPntK jlBQ&sa=X&oi=book_result&ct =result &resnum=1&ved=0CA8Q6AEwADgK#v=onepage&q=Negotiating %20International%20Environmental%20Agreements&f=false).

Clearly, the definition, negotiation and creation of the various legally binding conventions and protocols in the field of the environment, represents an outstanding achievement of the international community. Conventions represent the collective will of the international community to legally commit to protecting the environment. Binding international conventions now exist in areas as diverse as climate change, biological diversity, desertification and, more recently, prior informed consent of trade in hazardous chemicals and pesticides. The total number of such MEAs is steadily rising, while the average time taken to negotiate each treaty is decreasing. Within this same timeframe, the scale of problems to be addressed has widened – from the regional through the hemispheric to the global – while the total number of sovereign States that participate in the negotiation of such legal arrangements has grown. Moreover, new concerns and principles – precaution, inter- and intra-generational equity, scientific uncertainty, and sustainable development – have also arisen in recent years and now need to be factored into negotiation processes.

A milestone in the evolution of environmental agreements and legislation was the United Nations Conference on Environment and Development (UNCED), the Earth Summit, held in Rio de Janeiro in 1992. With all but six member states of the UN represented, the conference was a landmark in the history of environmental law, confirming the global character of environmental protection and its integration with development. Two new conventions were opened for signature: the UN Convention on Climate Change (UNFCCC), which is sectoral in that it deals with climate and the atmosphere, but holistic in addressing their effects, and the Convention on Biological Diversity (CBD) which brings together agriculture, forestry, fishery, land use and nature conservation in new ways. The negotiation of the UNFCCC and CBD demonstrated the difficulty of pursuing agreements that affect multiple sectors. Both agreements were highly politicized with major diplomatic battles taking place during negotiations. This illustrates the fact that as more holistic, multi-sector agreements involve so many different and crosscutting areas of law, policy and politics, they can engender more conflict and problems than the earlier generation of sectoral MEAs.

The Rio Conference also encouraged the development of other MEAs, including the Convention to Combat Desertification (CCD, 1994), and the Rotterdam Convention on Prior Informed Consent (PIC) on Hazardous Chemicals (1998), as well as new regional MEAs including, the Regional Agreement on the Transboundary Movement of Hazardous Wastes in Central America (1992), the Convention on Cooperation for the Protection and Sustainable Use of the Danube River (1994) and the Agreement on Cooperation for the Sustainable Development of the Mekong River Basin (1995). In this regard, it is significant to note in the past quarter of a century, thirteen regional Action Plans and nine Regional Seas Conventions and their protocols have been formulated, making up a web of detailed obligations for the majority of coastal states.

Since its inception in 1972, UNEP has played a pivotal role in supporting the development and implementation of environmental law. In Agenda 21, UNEP was specifically called upon to give priority to the further development of international environmental law. Five years later, the General Assembly, in the Programme for the Further Implementation of Agenda 21, stated that, consistent with the Nairobi Declaration on the Role and Mandate of UNEP (adopted earlier in 1997), the role of UNEP in the further development of international environmental law should be strengthened, including through the development of coherent inter-linkages among relevant conventions, in cooperation with their respective COPs or governing bodies. It further stated that, in performing its functions related to the conventions signed at UNCED or as a result of it, and other relevant conventions, UNEP should strive to promote the effective implementation of those conventions in a manner consistent with the provisions of the conventions and the decisions of the COPs.

As such, UNEP has undertaken a series of initiatives, in cooperation with the respective governing bodies of the environmental conventions, to develop coherent inter-linkages among the conventions with a view to achieving synergies and multiple benefits and promoting coherence of policies and actions. UNEP is putting an increased emphasis on facilitating collaboration and identifying synergies amongst conventions, utilizing the capabilities of the entire Programme to contribute to the objectives agreed to under the various global and regional conventions and action plans. UNEP's effort to promote collaboration and synergies amongst conventions has been launched on the basis of the following priorities; promoting information exchange amongst convention secretariats; strengthening collaboration amongst the conventions' scientific and technical bodies; revitalizing UNEP's support to the regional seas conventions and actions plans; making international trade and environmental regimes more compatible; and streamlining national reporting for the environmental conventions. One important initiative that UNEP collaborated on in this area was the UNU international conference on 'Synergies and Coordination between Multilateral Environmental Agreements' held in Tokyo, Japan, in July 1999.

Critical to any MEA is credible scientific information to underpin the negotiation process, for example the authoritative assessments undertaken by the Intergovernmental Panel on Climate Change (IPCC) and the various assessments in the area of Ozone. Forging international consensus around such information has been another key objective of the UN Environment Programme in the field of international environmental law, UNEP is working to build its capacity and networks to ensure the scientific underpinning of conventions, and facilitate their implementation. Recently, UNEP developed a central strategy to strengthen its capacity in the area of information, monitoring and assessment of environmental trends and threats, building on the capacity of a network of centres of excellence in developed and developing countries.

The global conventions developed since Stockholm is supported by a COP. The COP exists to: review implementation based on reports submitted by governments; consider new information from governments, NGOs and individuals to make recommendations to the Parties on implementation; make decisions necessary to promote effective implementation; revise the treaty if necessary (adopting amendments and additional protocols to help them adapt to new circumstances, i.e. the Montreal Protocol of the Vienna Ozone Convention and the Kyoto Protocol of the UNFCCC); and act as a forum for discussion on matters of importance. The meetings of COPs are open to representatives of the Parties and others. This helps ensure transparency of operation and cooperation with other intergovernmental bodies and non-state actors. For example, more than 200 intergovernmental and NGOs were represented at the meetings of the COP of the UNFCCC in Bonn in 1995 and in Kyoto in 1997.

It is also significant to note that non-binding instruments are often forerunners of binding policy instruments and have at times had a more profound effect on environmental policy than binding ones. Non-binding instruments have also helped to bring about changes in attitudes and perceptions at all levels of society. While binding instruments receive the bulk of attention from policy makers and the public alike, non-binding instruments have played and are likely to continue to play a major role in the management of global and regional environmental problems.

Non-binding instruments, rather than creating commitments for action in the form of legally binding targets and timetables, provide a looser framework. In some cases, the main aim is to set out important issues and priorities, foster discussion and attention, and stimulate new thinking and understanding about the relation of humans to the natural world. In other cases, such as the non-binding Prior Informed Consent (PIC) system for chemicals and pesticides, jointly administered by UNEP and FAO, non-binding instruments provide international procedures and arrangements that contributed to the development of a legally binding regime, the 1998 Rotterdam Convention.

Examples of important non-binding instruments include the Rio Declaration, Agenda 21, and the Global Programme of Action for the Protection of the Marine Environment from Land-Based Activities (GPA). Agenda 21 is probably the most prominent, significant and influential non-binding instrument in the environmental field and has become the guiding document for environmental management in most regions of the world. Its most important impact, through its core concept of sustainable development, has been to extend the environmental debate beyond environmental departments and NGOs. It provides policy makers with a starting point for linking environmental and socio-economic issues.

The Rio Declaration is also a very significant non-binding instrument, in that it includes several established and emerging principles, including common but differentiated responsibilities of states, the precautionary principle and the polluter pays principle. Many of the environmental agreements drawn up since UNCED include principles contained in the Rio Declaration that are now becoming part of international law. These include the right of people to an appropriate environment, the right to information, the right to participate in environmental management, and the precautionary principle.

The recently adopted Cartagena Protocol to the CBD on Biosafety is the first global treaty that reaffirms, incorporates and operationalizes the precautionary principle enunciated in the Rio Declaration. The protocol outlines procedures to deal with issues arising from the trans-boundary movement, transit, handling and use of genetically modified organisms (GMOs) – and commodities containing them – that may adversely affect the conservation and sustainable use of biological diversity or pose risks to human health and the environment. The precautionary principle is reflected in a key provision of the protocol which states that countries do have not to have complete "scientific certainty" to block imports of a GMO they fear could be harmful to biological diversity and, by extension, human health.

After five years of often difficult and tense negotiations, Governments meeting in Montreal in January 2000 finalized the Cartagena Protocol on Biosafety. The Montreal session followed the suspension of the First Session of the Extraordinary COP in February 1999 in Cartagena, Colombia, when officials were unable to finalize the text of a Biosafety Protocol in the time available due to a number of outstanding differences. In the interim period, the President of the Extraordinary Session, the Environment Minister of Colombia, held two rounds of open-ended informal consultations. At these meetings, representatives of all the negotiating groups that emerged from the Cartagena meeting expressed their commitment to concluding a Biosafety Protocol and confirmed that the political will did exist to achieve this. The negotiating groups were the Miami Group (Argentina, Australia, Canada, Chile, Uruguay, and the US), the European Union, the Central and Eastern European Countries, the Compromise Group, and the Like-Minded Group of Countries (which includes most of the developing countries).

The bio-safety talks reflected growing public concerns about the potential risks of biotechnology. While many of the countries with modern biotechnology industries have domestic legislation, there existed no binding international agreements covering LMOs. Another concern was that many developing countries lack the technical, financial, institutional, and human resources to address bio-safety. They need greater capacity for assessing and managing risks, establishing adequate information systems, and developing expert human resources in biotechnology.

The talks stalled over a number of issues. In particular, governments disagreed over the proposed scope of the treaty's regulatory powers. Some wanted to restrict the scope of the Protocol to Living Modified Organisms (LMOs) intended for introduction into the environment, such as seeds. Others argued for a broader scope that would include LMOs that are agricultural commodities or that are used for food, feed, or processing. Another contentious issue was liability: if LMOs enter the environment and cause damage, which pays? Also unresolved was how to minimize the potential socio-economic impacts, such as the competitive decline of traditional crops faced with LMO imports.

One of the most contentious issues related to the Protocol's relationship to other international agreements, particularly those under the World Trade Organization (WTO). So why is biotechnology also a trade issue? And why did the relationship with the WTO cause such obstacles in the negotiation of the Cartagena Protocol? The commercialization of biotechnology has spawned multi-billion-dollar industries for foodstuffs and pharmaceuticals that continue to grow at a dramatic pace. Under WTO regulations, the regulation of trade must be based on "sound scientific knowledge". Yet under environmental regimes, the standard of proof is the "precautionary principle". The WTO also does not accept socio-economic concerns, such as the risk that exports of genetically engineered crops may replace traditional ones and undermine local cultures and traditions in importing countries. The subsidiary agreements of the WTO, including the Sanitary and Phytosanitary Agreement (SPS), Technical Barriers to Trade Agreement (TBT), and the Agreement on Trade-Related Intellectual Property (TRIPs), also contain specific provisions that apply to the bio-safety issue. In the end, the compromise reached, and approved by representatives of more than 130 countries, was that in the preamble, it is emphasized that the protocol "shall not be interpreted" as changing the rights and obligations of countries under other international pacts, such as the WTO. The preamble also recognizes that trade and environmental agreements should be mutually supportive and the protocol is not subordinate to other international pacts.

Under the Cartagena Protocol, signatories will signal whether or not they are willing to accept imports of agricultural commodities that include (LMOs) by communicating their decision to the world community via an Internet-based Biosafety Clearing House. In addition, shipments of these commodities that may contain LMOs are to be clearly labelled. Stricter Advanced Informed Agreement procedures will apply to seeds, live fish, and other LMOs that are to be intentionally introduced into the environment. The aim is to ensure that recipient countries have both the opportunity and the capacity to assess risks involving the products of modern biotechnology. The agreed text of the Biosafety Protocol will be opened for signature at UNEP headquarters in Nairobi from 15 to 26 May, on the occasion of the Fifth Session of the COP to the CBD. The Protocol will then enter into force for its members after 50 countries have ratified it.

Another interesting example of an intergovernmental negotiation process is the major new MEA on Persistent Organic Pollutants (POPs), currently being developed under the auspices of UNEP. The treaty, which aims to ban the "dirty dozen" list of POPs, such as DDT, dioxins and PCBs, which have been linked to cancer, birth defects and other health problems, is expected to be opened for signature early in 2001. The fourth round of inter-governmental negotiations held last month made important progress on a number of key issues, and reaffirmed the eventual elimination of those POPs as the goal of the Convention and stressed the need to include exemptions, inter alia, for use of DDT in controlling malaria mosquitoes, subject to periodic review. Intensive discussions also laid the basis for deciding on technical and financial assistance at the last round of negotiations, to be held in December 2000 in Johannesburg, South Africa.

While it is considered that negotiators are now in a good position to reach agreement on the treaty by the end of 2000, the deadline in the mandate from the Governing Council of UNEP, a number of contentious issues are outstanding. For example, negotiators recognized that technology and funding are critical to successful implementation of the convention, and that developing countries and countries with economies in transition would need funds and environmentally sound technology to allow them to meet their obligations, however the modalities for achieving this are under discussion. As such, proposals for ensuring access to funding were considered, including several which, if adopted, would build on the Global Environment Facility (GEF), in recognition of its potential for addressing global environmental issues. The Group of 77 (G77) developing countries and China take the position that the nature of the POPs issue, and experience with existing mechanisms, reflect the need for a dedicated financial mechanism, which should include an independent multilateral fund (such as the one that exists for Ozone, under the Montreal Protocol). This will be one of the issues that will be discussed during a planned intercessional meeting, which will seek to establish common ground and help bring about resolution in December.

Another interesting example of the issues that are impacting the negotiation and implementation of MEAs can be seen in discussions currently being held to adapt certain provisions under a well-established treaty, namely, CITES. The 11th COP of the Convention on International Trade in Endangered Species is being held at UNEP's headquarters in Nairobi. The discussions reflect the increasing appreciation of the need to complement conservation efforts and trade controls with stronger support for the sustainable use of wildlife. Sustainable use is key to building support for conservation among local communities while directly raising funds for protecting endangered species.

There is also an increasing recognition that developing countries need more capacity building in order to monitor and control both wildlife trade and wildlife populations.

This CITES meeting will establish a five-year "strategic vision" to guide the work of the CITES through the year 2005. It is also considering proposals to amend the lists of species subject to trade controls or bans. The proposals cover over 60 species, ranging from the African elephant and the mink whale to Malagasy poison frogs and the monkey puzzle tree. Perhaps the most high profile proposals involve whether or not to authorize annual sales of ivory from southern African elephants. Passions are running high over proposals to relax global bans on the trade in elephants. At the last CITES conference, in Harare in 1997, governments agreed that Botswana, Namibia, and Zimbabwe could make a one-time and highly controlled experimental sale of existing ivory stocks to Japan. Together with South Africa, these countries now propose a further authorization for trade in elephant products under strict conditions. The proceeds would be devoted to elephant monitoring and conservation. Kenya and India, among others, are opposed and propose a total ban on such trades, contending that CITES-approved, one-time sales last year sparked an increase in elephant poaching. Kenya says that it opposes lifting the ivory ban until such time as an effective monitoring capacity is established and is operational. The debate over the ivory trade embodies the emerging tensions between saving endangered animals and raising the resources to sustain them. For example, Zimbabwe wants to sell ivory, as otherwise they contend that there will not be sufficient funds toward conservation for the elephants, while Kenya's economic reliance on elephant-related tourism puts it at the forefront of those who want a stricter ban. Africa's elephant population was halved in the 1970s and 80s, with some 650,000 killed, but the numbers recovered somewhat after CITES imposed a total ban on ivory trade in 1989.

In another emotional-charged debate, the issue of whales is also being revisited. Japan and Norway believe that certain stocks of gray and minke whales are healthy enough to be transferred from CITES Appendix I (which bans all trade) to Appendix II (which regulates trade through a system of permits) on the basis of their good conservation status. Similar proposals were rejected by CITES in 1997, but fell only nine votes short of victory. In 1986, the International Whaling Commission banned all commercial whaling. Japan argues that with 1 million minkes worldwide and 760,000 around Antarctica alone, the creatures do not deserve the level of protection reserved for endangered species. Japan also says the plentiful minkes have depleted food supplies for the rarer blue whales. Environmentalists contend that renewed whaling for minkes could threaten other species as well, and that it is nearly impossible to tell one species of minke from another, with not all of the species falling under CITES' protection. Environmentalists have also warned that Russia is looking for the hard currency that whaling could produce.

Among the other issues on the CITES agenda, Cuba wants the right to sell stockpiles of shells from the endangered hawksbill turtle, and Australia, the

United States and the United Kingdom will propose measures to protect sharks. Tigers, dolphins, snake and spiders are among the other species under consideration.

The Vienna Convention and its Montreal Protocol on Substances that Deplete the Ozone Layer are now acknowledged as outstanding successes and as examples to be followed for the solution of global environmental problems through global cooperation and partnership. The Vienna Convention committed parties to protecting human health and the environment against the adverse effects of depletion of the ozone layer due to human activities. It set out broad principles of ozone layer protection, rather than establishing the detailed phase-out schedule of ozone-depleting substances, which were later, included in the Montreal Protocol in 1987. The Convention committed States to cooperate in researching the causes and effects of ozone depletion as well as alternative technologies; to cooperate on adopting legal and policy measures to counteract activities that are harmful to the atmosphere and to facilitate the transfer of technology and transmission of information, especially to developing countries.

Both the Convention and the Protocol allowed the Parties thereto to progress step-by-step in building ownership of the process by all Governments, industry, NGOs and academia, among others. At its adoption on 22 March 1985, 28 countries signed the Convention. There are now 173 Parties to the Vienna Convention. These Parties have phased out 84 per cent of consumption of the chemicals that destroy the ozone layer. This path must continue to ensure recovery of the ozone layer by the year 2050.

A key to the Vienna Convention's success has been its flexibility and ability to adapt to new scientific evidence and make amendments accordingly, coupled with strong political will and the engagement of the private sector. It serves as a laudable example of how to negotiate an effective multilateral environmental agreement, and it can even serve as a model for forging international treaties in other fields.

United Nations Climate Change Conference

An emission trading is an economic system by which regulated entities can buy or sell allowances or permits for emissions, or credits for reductions in emissions of specified pollutants. Once created, emission allowances are fully fungible commodities, meaning they can be bought, sold, traded or banked for future use. They may even be retired by the regulating entity to create an environmental benefit. Companies are attracted to the prospect of gaining experience and acquiring credits at lower prices prior to formal trading under national schemes or the Kyoto Protocol. A number of companies have begun preparing for emissions trading by participating in voluntary emissions trading schemes or implementing internal trading systems (http://www.blakes.com/english/view_disc.asp?ID=115).

At the international level, emissions trading under the Kyoto Protocol represent a basic buyer-seller transaction between two countries. This activity is expected to be delegated by governments to corporations directly or indirectly through the coordination of national implementation schemes. It is anticipated that a global emissions trading market will begin in 2008. However, domestic emissions trading systems are being put in place prior to the start of global trading. Emission rights will be able to be transferred between multiple entities in national "pools" of Assigned Amount Units (AAUs). The AAUs are tradable divisions of each country's respective Kyoto Protocol caps, which correspondingly rise and fall with each transaction. If it is relatively unfettered by rules and restrictions, many experts believe that this mechanism holds the greatest potential for reducing the cost of achieving the Kyoto Protocol's commitments. Negotiations on a successor to the Kyoto Protocol dominated the 2007 United Nations Climate Change Conference. A meeting of environment ministers and experts held in June called on the conference to agree a road-map, timetable and 'concrete steps for the negotiations' with a view to reaching an agreement by 2009.

Regulatory Aspects of Emissions Trading

The Kyoto Protocol introduces a fairly new approach for reducing CO_2 emissions. Traditionally, the United States has applied a "command and control" method to deal with pollution. For ex ample, with air pollution, the Clean Air Act (CAA) authorizes the Environmental Protection Agency (EPA) to set national ambient air quality standards (NAAQS). The EPA and states then establish a source specific technology-based emissions limit to assist individual polluters in meeting the NAAQS. Many economists and scholars argue that the command and control method unnecessarily increases cleanup costs. For example, the 1977 Amendments to the CAA required all utilities to install expensive scrubbers to remove sulfur dioxide (SO_2) from emissions even though many utilities could have reduced SO_2 emissions by switching to low sulfur coal. Many also believe that command and control discourages innovative pollution control technology. Since the EPA sets cleanup goals based on currently available technology, little incentive exists for firms to spend money on research and development of new pollution control methods.

An alternative to the command and control system is taxing producers for each unit of pollution they emit. The tax would force producers to take into account the cost of pollution. Without the tax and without command and control, the emitted pollution and its effects on the environment are only externalities that are not included when producers analyze costs. In theory, the efficient firm would try to reduce pollution until the incremental cost of reducing pollution equals the incremental benefits of further pollution reduction. This would result in a socially optimal level of pollution at the lowest cost. However, there are extreme difficulties with implementing an emissions tax. It is often difficult to assess the social costs of pollution. Many costs are measured in terms of aesthetic damage or damage to a person's health. In many cases, it is not possible to foresee all the damages polluting can cause. Even if costs could be estimated, regulators would have to constantly update the taxes to include changes in economic activity, inflation, or other changes in the level or impact of that particular source's pollution. Finally, it will be politically difficult to implement a tax-based pollution control since the tax would mean higher costs to producers which would probably be passed on to the consumers.

A transferable pollution permitting system, or emissions trading system, is an alternative to the emissions tax. Under an emission trading system, regulators establish the allowable pollution level for a given area and grant permits to existing producers so that emissions do not exceed prescribed pollution levels. Each producer is allocated permits based on the "producer's past pollution levels or through a competitive bidding auction." Firms that reduce their pollution emissions below their allocated level can sell their surplus permits to other firms or individuals. Firms that cannot reduce their pollution emissions to meet their allocated level can purchase more permits. Under this system, firms can choose the most cost-effective way to stay within their allocated emissions level. The ability to profit from the selling of emission credits encourages firms to develop innovative pollution control devices.

The emissions trading system has several advantages over the emissions tax system. First, an emission trading system fits well with current regulatory schemes such as the CAA, which establishes allowable pollution levels. Regulators set allowable pollution levels while the market decides the price of the tradable permits. Under the emissions tax system, regulators must somehow calculate the price of the emissions tax and make the tax high enough so that the desired level of pollution reduction can be achieved. Second, under the emissions trading system, regulators will not have to worry about adjusting prices for inflation or changes in economic activity because the market would make these adjustments automatically. Third, while both programs would reduce emissions, a tax imposes additional financial burdens on industry. Not only would firms have to pay for the cost of reducing emissions, firms would also have to pay for the tax liability of remaining emissions.

Proponents for emissions trading markets have determined four requirements for a successful program. First, there must be enough participants in the market; both to sell and to buy emissions credits. Without enough participants, price information would be difficult to establish and prices for credit might not accurately reflect actual supply and demand. Second, transaction costs must be kept low Otherwise, buyers and sellers will be discouraged from trading in a market that could have been beneficial to both. Robert Hahn and Gordon Hester identified high transaction costs as the single most important obstacle to the success of pollution markets. Third, in order for a market-based program to work, there must be effective enforcement. Both monitoring and sanctions are needed for effective enforcement to exist. Without effective enforcement, the market will become distorted and inefficient. Finally, the regulatory system must engender confidence in market participants of its stability. In a market system, there will be tension between the participants' need for stability and the regulators' need to change the rules as new information becomes available. Though this problem exists for most markets, it is particularly important in the area of pollution control because the commodity, pollution credits, only retain their value if the government maintains the market.

2009 United Nations Climate Change Conference at Copenhagen

2009 United Nations Climate Change Conference at Copenhagen

Copenhagen will be the center of climate change negotiations in 2009. The 2009 conference is scheduled to be held in December 2009 in Copenhagen, Denmark, and the treaty succeeding the Kyoto Protocol is expected to be adopted there. Potential topics to be discussed in the UNFCC Summit include carbon capture and storage, biofuels, adaptation financing, technology transfer, sustainable agriculture, emissions targets, tropical forests and rural and transport electrification (plug-in hybrids). Development of technologies will be important to reduce carbon emissions. Even if all carbon emissions stopped tomorrow, global warming would continue for the next 30 years. James E. Rogers, CEO of Duke Energy and member of Copenhagen Climate Council said "It is a myth that we have the technologies to do the job. We don't. New technologies are crucial as is further development of existing technology."

The Kyoto Protocol: Implications for Emissions Trading

The Issue

In historic negotiations in 2001, nearly every nation in the world agreed to the terms of the Kyoto Protocol with the goal of reducing the emission of greenhouse gases (GHG). The form of the agreement finally agreed upon by signatory nations included provisions for the creation of an emissions trading system. This idea attempts to assist countries in complying with the protocol by allowing them to "trade" excess pollution for emissions credits earned by nations that remain under their pollution caps. The complex nature of such a trading system, as well as its potentially effect on most of the nations of the world, points to several international legal and trade issues. The resolution of those issues as embodied in some future emissions trading system will determine—in all likelihood—whether or not the Kyoto Protocol successfully reduces GHG emissions (http://www1.american.edu/TED/kyoto-emissions.htm).

Description

The perceived need to reduce the world's output of greenhouse gases (GHGs) motivated most of the world to create and sign the Kyoto Protocol. The agreement was designed to combat the problems of global warming, which, according to many scientists, threatened the world's environment over the course of the next few hundred years. Even as they signed this accord, however, many nations held reservations. The Kyoto Protocol required industrialized nations to make emissions reductions—steps that have economic consequences for people in each country involved. The goal of improving the world's environment was thus weighed against the economic well-being of individuals, corporations and national economies. The United States refused to sign the treaty because of these concerns. Japan reluctantly joined the accord after it received some concessions that facilitate its ability to comply with treaty mandates.

Such assistance came as a way to balance competing environmental and economic interests. The Kyoto agreement contained a system of emissions trading. Some countries who signed the agreement were clearly more prepared to make emissions reductions than others. In theory, this creates the possibility for countries with painful economic adjustments to take advantage of favorable environmental movement in other parts of the world. If Japan perceived dangerous economic consequences of reducing its emissions too quickly, it could buy credits from those countries that easily remained underneath mandated emissions caps. Though the principle is simple, the issue is complex. No international system can function without a basis in international law. The rules of any emissions trading system must be both clearly established and universally recognized. Additionally, a new system will have to be reconciled with existing international agreements regarding international trade. The legal and economic ramifications of Kyoto-inspired emissions trading will be both far reaching and significant. With so much of the world ready to establish an emissions market and with such perceived environmental problems at stake, it is clear that the way seemingly trivial points of international law and trade are interpreted will have a broad influence over the global environment. Some (but by no means all) of the major issues involved in the establishment of an international emissions trading system are discussed in the clusters below.

Agreement in Progress

Signatory nations brought the Kyoto Protocol into force in 2001. The agreement included three sections concerning an emissions trading regime. Article 17 provides for trading of assigned amounts of emissions between industrialized countries (referred to as Annex B countries in the Kyoto text). Article 12 empowers industrialized countries to engage in emissions-reducing activities in developing countries, facilitating sustainable development in the process. Finally, Article 6, joint implementation, deals with the transfer of emission reduction units between nations ("Kyoto Protocol").

Though these three articles were included in the original agreement, they do not establish the formal guidelines for an emissions trading system. The Kyoto agreement foresees the development of such a system and has ensured that a future trading regime will be compatible with the original protocol, but it did not create a system on its own. There are two types of disputes that could emerge under a global emissions trading system: verification and compliance.

Verification, both of the amounts of emissions credits a country is entitled to, and of the amount of reduction a nation achieves, is a crucial part of any system. Only if all nations are confident that emissions are fairly and uniformly measured can there be a fair market in which emissions can be traded. UNCTAD has speculated about a two-level process: "Certification would be the first step towards creating a tradable credit. The certification process would occur whenever a Party not subject to an assigned amount wished to create a tradable credit. Its purpose would be to assure that a specific quantified reduction from a baseline could be expected from the credit-creating action. Verification, the second step, would provide assurance that the reductions actually occurred." In other words, before selling an emissions credit, a country would have to gain certification that it was capable of making enough of an emissions reduction to believe that the credit would actually be available and then allow its reductions to be verified after emissions reductions were completed (Tietenberg, *et. al.*, 2000).

The treaty must also guarantee compliance by all member nations. There is little reason to have a treaty if nations have no incentive to follow its mandates. In other words, to preclude cheating, the treaty must be enforceable. One of the most obvious examples of emissions trade cheating is referred to as "overselling"—when a country sells allowances (emissions credits) that it does not have or that it needs to meet its own treaty obligations. There are two ways to combat this problem. "On the one side of the spectrum is an approach that would rely on an already contemplated compliance framework that would not impose up-front restrictions on emissions trading but would punish noncompliance with sanctions. On the other side of the spectrum is an approach that would not allow trading until after the deadline for meeting the emission limitation and reduction commitments and then would limit trades to allowances not needed to meet those commitments" (Nordhaus, *et. al.*, 2000).

Unfortunately, both options have problems. There are two reasons why nations might end up overselling emissions credits. First, even though a country might wish to reduce emissions and expect to have credits to sell, it may be unable to administer those desired and anticipated reductions. Consequently, administrative inadequacies could result in a larger number of credits being sold than are actually available. Second, nations might willfully oversell, hoping to make money off of the emissions trading system while betting that the Kyoto-inspired trading regime will not be able to penalize such behavior (Nordhaus, *et. al.*, 2000).

Enforcing Kyoto's mandates, particularly if there is any level of cheating involved, will probably end up causing international trade disputes at one time or another. Such trade disputes might be within the jurisdiction of the WTO, of which many treaty signatories are members. An UNCTAD newsletter monitoring issues related to emissions trading succinctly summarized the problems international negotiators face when attempting to reconcile Kyoto Protocol provisions with existing WTO structures. For example, the principle of Most Favored Nation (MFN), a key part of the WTO, might be undermined under Kyoto if industrialized countries (appearing on the Annex B) list are not allowed to trade credits in the same ways as Annex I countries. The newsletter also cited potential problems for energy exporters whose products (like petroleum) might be denied into a country that lacked enough allowances to use the energy ("Global Greenhouse"). Thus, the Kyoto Protocol envisions an emissions-trading system but the lack of formal rules points to several potential legal problems. Actual emissions levels of each nation involved must be verified by the international community to determine the number of emissions credits available for trade. Each nation must then be willing to abide by the results of those verifications and not engage in "overselling." Otherwise, disputes will probably have to be dealt with by other international organizations, like the WTO, which may not resolve disputes with the same goals of global emissions reductions that the Kyoto Protocol possesses.

Legal Standing: Treaty

Relevant International Organizations/Regimes

- The Kyoto Protocol—agreed upon in 1997, international ratification pending.
- The World Trade Organization—established in 1995.

Any global emissions trading regime is still in its initial stages of development. UNCTAD research suggests that there might be several evolutionary phases. The first stage involves the development of domestic emissions markets in many nations (where emissions credits are traded between companies). This would be followed by a second stage where nations would mutually recognize the emissions credits and allowances of the other markets. A third and final stage would involve the establishment of a multilateral trading system, consistent with the mandates of the Kyoto Protocol (Aslam *et. al*, 2001).

Type of Measure: Import Standard

There are currently several proposals for carbon emissions trading that might ultimately be adopted by Kyoto signatories; two broad conceptions of emissions credit generation have emerged.

First, nations could earn emissions credits by remaining underneath the pollution ceiling established by the Kyoto agreement. Kyoto requires signatory nations to make percentage reductions in their 1990 emissions levels. Since it is usually assumed that one metric ton of carbon dioxide emission (CO_2) is equal to one tradable emissions allowance, a country observed to be underneath its predetermined emissions cap would receive one emissions credit for each metric ton saved. A hypothetical example is in order. Assume that Country A emitted 100 million metric tons of (CO_2) in 1990 and was expected to make a 10 percent reduction by year X. If Country A was able to reduce its emissions by 20 percent to 80 million metric tons—it would be recognized for having met its emissions target and rewarded with 10 million emissions credits for its extra reductions. Those credits could then be sold on the international marketplace to nations that exceeded their pollution limits. The resulting carbon commodity market would be responsible for establishing the monetary value of the credits. If several countries polluted excessively, emissions credits would be scarce, raising their value. In theory, then, nations that exceed their pollution limits would have a financial incentive to make emissions reductions, lest they be forced to buy expensive emissions credits (Nordhaus *et.al*, 2000.).

Second, many nations have argued that they should be able to earn credits for environmentally friendly initiatives. If a country were to take positive steps to manage national forests or provide assistance to other nations to reduce their emissions, it seems logical that such a nation should be rewarded with emissions credits it could sell in the international marketplace. This system, of course, has its problems. One, the Kyoto Protocol's reliance on 1990 emissions levels for its "measuring stick" may create a dubious distribution of emissions credits. Countries like Russia experienced large reductions in industrial production that coincided with the downfall of the communist system. This reduction in production has brought Russia underneath its 1990 pollution level, not because Russia has become more environmentally conscious, but because its industries have become dormant. The system as currently envisioned would give Russia a large number of emissions credits without any Russian environmental progress. Too many environmentalists are concerned that nations with pollution problems will continue to pollute and offset their carbon emissions by planting trees or adopting other eco-friendly policies that do not interfere with their pollution rates. Scientists and bureaucrats alike are still debating the value of forests relative to a nation's emission levels. How their conclusions are embodied in any emissions trading regime will have a great effect on the overall success of the system (Hertsgaard, 2001).

Trans-boundary Asymmetric Issues

International relations are increasingly marked by agreements that govern multilateral issues like trade and the environment. One of the most important international environmental issues concerns global warming and the perceived need for international action. This is because environmentally destructive behaviors in one country are almost certain to eventually effect the environment of other countries. Nations that are relatively environmentally responsible do not wish to experience the negative impacts of lax environmental standards elsewhere. Some international relations scholars have even suggested that the failure to recognize the trans-national nature of environmental problems like global warming may impede nations (such as the United States) from achieving its national interests (Mathews).

WTO Negotiations for Liberalizing Trade in Services

The Importance of Service Industries

Service industries are growing in importance as the basic infrastructure for the economic activities of corporations and consumers, not only in developed countries but also in the developing world. These efficient and highly productive service industries help to strengthen the competitiveness of the mining, manufacturing, and agricultural industries, and contribute to improvements in the quality of life.

Trade in services has played an important role in the development of efficient and highly productive service industries in every country. In particular, the General Agreement on Trade in Services (GATS), which entered into force in 1995, laid the groundwork for the promotion of trade in services. However, the history of GATS is very brief, and in many countries, there unfortunately remain various barriers to service-related business activities. Based on this situation, we strongly support negotiations for the liberalization of trade in services within the WTO. It is fervently hoped that through such negotiations, trade in services amongst member countries will be further liberalized, and efforts will be made towards strengthening WTO rules (November 2000, Japan Services Network, Mission to Geneva: http://www.keidanren.or.jp/english/policy/2000/066.html).

However, as an increasing number of countries would not benefit sufficiently from services negotiations alone, there are concerns that such negotiations will not gain strong enough momentum. Consequently, the early launch of a new round of WTO negotiations, which encompasses a comprehensive agenda and incorporates services negotiations, has become an urgent issue. In particular, within the new round of negotiations, it is important that developed countries make efforts to improve market access for products from developing countries, and that discipline is strengthened in order to prevent the arbitrary imposition of restrictive trade policies such as anti-dumping measures.

Towards the Promotion of Negotiations

The importance of practical guidelines for negotiations

In order to facilitate services negotiations, it is expected that every country by the end of the year will actively make proposals to promote the further liberalization of trade in services, based on the Roadmap for the Negotiations adopted in May 2000.

Also, in conjunction with these activities, it will be important to draft the Negotiations Guidelines. In order to serve as a foundation for future negotiations, the Guidelines must be practical and take into consideration the viewpoints of and benefits to all WTO member countries. In particular, at the outset of negotiations, the current schedule of commitments should serve as a basis, and sufficient credit should be given to previously independent liberalization efforts should they be bound in the schedule.

Furthermore, references in the Guidelines to final deadlines for services negotiations are thought to be premature in consideration of continuing efforts towards launching a new round of negotiations.

Consideration towards Developing Countries

The proactive participation of developing countries in services negotiations is an essential factor in their success. Consequently, it is important that the negotiations accurately reflect the needs of developing countries and make the utmost cooperative efforts to meet these demands. In conjunction, it is necessary for developed countries to strengthen technical assistance towards capacity-building in developing countries.

Handling of the Most-Favored Nation (MFN) Exception

MFN status is a basic principle of the WTO, but unfortunately, many countries, including the U.S. and European nations, register MFN exemptions. The MFN Review Meetings held recently are appreciated as the first step towards abolishing the exemptions. In the future, it is imperative that all countries continue to make efforts towards the early abolition of MFN exemptions, which run contrary to the fundamental spirit of the WTO.

Greater Transparency of Domestic Regulations

Basic Concept

Domestic regulations exercise great influence over services negotiations. We welcome the fact that the transparency and necessity of regulations is being discussed in the Working Party on Domestic Regulation. Furthermore, it is expected that this Working Party will review not only "measures relating to qualification requirements and procedures, technical standards and licensing requirements" stipulated in Article 6.4 of the General Agreement on Trade in Services (GATS), but will investigate all service-related regulations. In particular, it is considered important to create rules regarding the transparency of cross-sectional domestic regulations. Furthermore, it will be necessary to exchange views with the regulating authorities in creating these rules.

Greater Transparency of Regulations

Companies face various hurdles to conducting services-related business in foreign countries, such as incomplete and opaque legal systems, sudden changes, arbitrary operation, and opaque and unreasonable licensing requirements and procedures (licensing criteria and fees, for example). Fundamentally, it is preferable to ensure transparency in all aspects of domestic regulations, including (1) the process of establishing the regulations, (2) the regulations themselves, and (3) actual application of the regulations.

However, considering the administrative burden on each country, the realization of greater transparency of the legal system (including the availability of all laws and ministerial ordinances; establishment and announcement of investigation criteria for permits; and documentation of oral guidance) will be a necessary first step. Furthermore, as there have been cases of developing countries with no established legal system governing businesses, such as bankruptcy laws, it is desirable that developed countries provide technical assistance for the establishment of such a legal system.

The second step is to create rules to correct the excessive discretion of regulatory authorities regarding permission and approval. Specifically, it is important to establish legal systems and regulations for administrative procedures (such as the obligation to initiate investigations; the establishment and announcement of standard process timeframe; and the disclosure of reasons in cases where permission or approval is denied).

Furthermore, if possible, the introduction of so-called "public comment system" related to the establishment, revision, and abolition of regulations through national laws and ministerial ordinances should be considered.

The Necessity of Regulations

The concept of "not more burdensome than necessary" and "unnecessary barriers to trade in services" should be clarified in the discussions on the "necessity" of domestic regulations held by the Working Party on Domestic Regulation, thereby being reflected in the improvement of systems in of each country.

Negotiations in the WTO: Focus on Market Access Strategy

1. Improvement of market access

For the improvement of market access related to electronic commerce, it is necessary to liberalize both the infrastructure fields relevant to electronic commerce and the content of trade.

Clusters Approach

Concerning the method of progressing with negotiations on liberalization of the infrastructure field of electronic commerce, there is one train of argument that calls for the adoption of a cluster approach, with which a number of industry sectors are gathered together to be negotiated. For example, telecommunications and finance have been cited as one industrial field in which a cluster could be created, and of these, each one comprises one main service industry, which is in actual fact the target sector of the current services negotiations.

When and whether to adopt the so-called clusters approach of package negotiations should be based on considerations of the ease of proceeding with negotiations, and the creation of an environment in which many countries can proactively participate. From this perspective it is therefore thought to be effective to adopt the cluster approach as something of a negotiation checklist from the aspect of a cross-sectoral viewpoint.

Modes of supply

With regard to contents, due to the rapid progress of electronic commerce, while there are currently many services which can be supplied only through mode 3 (foreign commercial presence) and mode 4 (movement of natural persons), electronic means are now making possible the supply of services. There are still many cases for these services, where it is written in schedules of commitment that "unbound due to technical feasibility." However, it if necessary for all countries in the future to press forward with active commitments to liberalization aiming to further promote electronic commerce. In this connection, it is therefore of importance to sufficiently coordinate modes with electronic commerce (especially mode 1 and mode 2).

Classification

In cases where digital contents, such as music software, originally traded in a format such as CD are now being traded by electronic means, it is necessary to apply the existing GATT disciplines. In addition, in cases where services are provided by electronic means that already come under provisions of the rules of the General Agreement on Trade in Services (GATS), then these rules should be applied regardless of the means of provision.

Further, for example, with regard to new services such as Application Services Providers, in order not to create needless new classifications, further review should be made as to whether the classification meets the needs of reality, including application of the existing GATS classifications.

(ii) Domestic regulations

Domestic regulations have a significant effect on electronic commerce and as such it is necessary to secure the transparency of related domestic regulations through WTO review, in order that domestic regulations are not in actual fact camouflaged trade restriction measures.

(iii) Continuation of the moratorium on customs duties

It is important that member countries come to a decision on the continuation of the moratorium on customs duties for digital transmissions. Until then, the status quo should be maintained.

Support for Developing Countries

When considering the international expansion of electronic commerce and the development of IT and the Internet, it is of urgency to bring WTO negotiations to a prompt and successful conclusion and to promote the development of systems and cultivation of an environment in developing countries whereby utilization of electronic commerce could be promoted. In addition, it is also important to review the modalities of support for developing countries in this area by developed countries

Ensuring the Free Movement of Personnel

When enterprise perform trade in services (particularly mode 3), it is important that the dispatch of company personnel (managers and persons with expertise and technical skills) abroad be conducted smoothly. However, in many countries companies are facing problems such as: (1) acquiring visas and labor permits; (2) residency requirements for company executives and employees; and (3) obligations to employ local personnel.

Each country should, through improvement of its schedule of commitments aim to realize the securing of the free movement of business-related personnel. In addition, it is also hoped that discussions can be made on achieving clarification and simplification of visa and labor permit procedures, and of requirements, while at the same time shortening the process of issuance of visas and permits.

Safeguards

The Basic Concept

Japanese industry does not feel any particular need for the imposition of safeguard measures. On the other hand, as developing countries move forward with liberalization, cases could be anticipated where safeguards need to be imposed in order to alleviate the sudden impact of such liberalization on domestic society. However, since trade in services is an area in which statistics have not been sufficiently developed, clear and objective rules therefore need to be formulated in GATS in order that they are not arbitrarily imposed, if regulations are to be organized for safeguard measures.

Necessity for Objective Rules

To this end, firstly, it is therefore necessary that detailed discussions be undertaken on what these clear objective rules or standards should be. In addition, since safeguard measures are primarily aimed at the protection of domestic industries, the stopping or limiting of activities in enterprises which have already established a presence in the supply of services (mode 3), or limitations on the establishment of new branch offices and increase in capital, should, in principle, not be permitted. If it were the case that such limitations were to be placed, then they should only be place under non-discriminatory conditions with other domestic enterprises. In the same way as Article XIX of the GATT, it is necessary to incorporate conditions for the imposition of safeguard measures where domestic industry has been damaged or could be damaged" as a result of unforeseen developments".

Prompt Withdrawal of Measures

Safeguards are emergency measures and as such should only be permitted over a given duration that is necessary in order to stop or prevent serious damage. In order to avoid extensive application of the measures, the duration and review of safeguard measures such as Article 7.4 of the Agreement on Safeguards should be included. Room must also be left for such restrictive measures to be withdrawn or relaxed, reflecting economic/social changes in the country.

Position on Sector-Specific Liberalization-based Negotiations

Negotiation Approach

In liberalization negotiations, Japanese industry expects that, through improvement of national schedules, among others the following will be realized: (i) limitations on foreign ownership restrictions; (ii) abolition of nationality and residency requirements for directors and employees; and (iii) the abolition of domestic and industry practices that discriminate between domestic and foreign industries. Currently, various negotiation approaches are being discussed, and each approach has its merits and demerits. In the future, while discussions will be based on a request-offer approach, it is still necessary to cast light on the characteristics of each sector, and conduct individual specific review into whether model schedules or the cluster approach can be complimentarily applied.

Financial Services

Basic concept

The WTO Financial Services Agreement of 1997, made a large contribution to the stable development of the financial markets by heightening the stability of the financial measures of each country and investor predictability. The progress of liberalization has brought about merits for both foreign enterprises investing inwards and domestic enterprises, and it is therefore important that all countries proceed with the steady implementation of their national schedules in accordance with the WTO Financial Services Agreement of 1997.

Domestic regulations

Objectivity and transparency in regulations should be ensured. For example, it is important to address oral explanations of new regulations and the lack of legal precedents, and have regulations announced in written form, so as to control sudden regulatory changes. In addition, it is vital to secure the objectivity and transparency of issuance requirements and procedures for business licenses, and the abolition of a number of restrictions on the issuances of business licenses. Systemic obstructions should be abolished such as foreign ownership restrictions; restrictions on the establishment of branches and subsidiaries; nationality and residence requirements for executives and employees; obligation of reinsurance to state reinsurance agencies; foreign remittance regulations, etc.; the monopoly of domestic or government-affiliated companies over certain areas of insurance; and discriminatory tax treatment of foreign companies, etc.

MFN exemptions

Regarding the case of the individual exemption of most favored nation status, it is expected that appropriate negotiations will be taken on reduction and abolition, in accordance with the provisions of the Annex on Article II exemptions.

Grandfathering

With regard to the grandfathering clause, from the perspective of ensuring fair and competitive conditions, cases need to be carefully and individually judged. It is to be hoped that rights acknowledged in the grandfathering clause can be enjoyed by all member nations on an MFN basis.

Measures for Prudential Reasons

With regard to measures for prudential reasons based on Paragraph 2 of the GATS Annex on Financial Services, member countries should seek to harmonize the necessary measures they take under the scheme of international institutions, which have more expertise and technical skills rather than in WTO negotiations.

Maritime Transport Services

Basic concept

Despite the importance of maritime transport services, the Uruguay Round Negotiations on maritime transport did not reach an agreement, leaving this area outside GATS coverage. With the start of the services negotiations, the Extended Negotiations should be resumed.

Areas for Negotiation

Under the recognition that competitive marine transport services contribute to the development of international trade, it is necessary that in addition to abolishing restrictions on the establishment of local entities and the scope of their work, and the abolition of policies for the protection of national maritime transport industries, debate must be advanced aimed at the liberalization of international maritime transportation services (international shipping). In conjunction with this, liberalization should be actively progressed with regard to auxiliary services (maritime agency services, freight-forwarding services, etc.), and port services (pilotage, towing and tug, water supplies, fuel supplies).

Air Transport Services

The three "Soft rights" areas

There are many countries which have only yet committed themselves to partial liberalization under the following three areas in framework of the GATS rules, the so-called "soft rights" areas: the selling and marketing of air transport services with the exception of price setting; computer reservation system (CRS) services; and aircraft repair and maintenance. Based on the review of the Annex on Air Transport Services that is currently underway, liberalization should be promoted in the area of the three "soft rights" in each country.

Expansion of the scope of GATS

There would be significance in reviewing on a case-by-case basis the liberalization of those services which currently do not fall under the scope of GATS, such as ground handling and airport management.

Problems associated with "Hard rights"

Concerning the liberalization of services directly related to transportation rights (hard rights), bilateral agreements should be advanced, bearing in mind the various situations in each country.

Energy Services

Basic concept

Liberalization negotiations in the energy sector must be advanced on the basis of a balance between public interest (ensuring security, harmony with the environment, the provision of universal services, high supply credibility) and greater efficiency.

Problems of classification

In energy service negotiations it is necessary to review classifications, having first clarified the items targeted for negotiation. Target items: Production of energy is considered to be the production of goods as applicable under the scope of the GATT, but not to be included in energy services. In addition, with regard to items which are additional services in the energy sector and are covered under other classifications in the national schedule of commitments, should be placed outside the scope of energy services.

Method of classification: Classification should reflect the situation in the energy industry of each country. In particular, from the point of view of increasing efficiency, many countries have a vertically integrated system run by domestic operators and this might make detailed classification inappropriate.

Other Important Sectors

Telecommunications

In order to ensure the smooth entry into the market of new companies, it is necessary to review the implementation status of national schedules of commitments on basic telecommunications, in addition to achieving an actual expansion of the number of countries that submit national schedules and a qualitative improvement in the content of the commitment. It is of particular importance to abolish or alleviate restrictions on foreign ownership, and improve transparency and clarification of the conditions and procedures for the granting of business licenses.

Construction

Construction services are provided primarily through establishment of a local base, and the following improvements, among others, are called for: (i) Improvement in restrictions on foreign ownership; (ii) improvement in restrictions on business modes; (iii) improvements in domestic and business regulations which discriminate against foreign business; and (iv) favoring local companies and qualification restrictions in regard to public works.

Distribution: A relaxation is called for in such areas as restrictions on foreign ownership of import, retail sales and after-sales service industries, and restrictions on the establishment of business premises and the use of these in some developed countries.

CHAPTER 4

Negotiations under International and Regional Trade Agreements with Country-Specific Implications

Negotiations that takes place across companies within country will be vastly different form such negotiations that take place across countries within a region, inter-regionally and internationally. And this scenario gets fairly complicated and broad-based when cross-country negotiations suffer for instance from cross-cultural barriers, entry barriers (viz. in the forms of tariff and regulatory aspects) etc. This would by implication need country-specific scenario analysis to know exactly about the type of *modus operandi* towards the preparatory requirements and transaction requirements etc. to be able to make a break-through in the conduct of negotiations successfully. In the following paragraphs we will describe the different contexts of negotiations that actually take place under various International as well as Regional Trade Agreements with Country-specific Implications.

Principles and Evolution of International Trade Agreements

Trade Agreements: Definition

Trade Agreement is any contractual arrangement between states concerning their trade relations. Trade agreements may be bilateral or multilateral, that is, between two states or more than two. Trade agreement is, usually between or among governments that encourages, regulates, and/or restricts elements of trade among the respective countries. For most countries international trade is regulated by unilateral barriers, including tariffs, non-tariff barriers, and government prohibitions. Trade agreements aim to reduce such barriers and thus provide all parties with the benefits of increased trade. Reciprocity is a necessary feature of trade agreements, since neither state will be willing to sign the agreement unless it expects to gain as much as it loses. Another common feature is a most-favoured nation (MFN) clause, which provides against the possibility that one of the parties to the current agreement will later offer lower tariffs to another country. Agreements often include clauses providing for "national treatment of non-tariff restrictions," meaning that both states promise not to duplicate the properties of tariffs with non-tariff restrictions such as discriminatory regulations, selective excise taxes, quotas, and special licensing requirements. Unilateral trade agreement would be any agreement that is imposed on one national by another, and benefits one nation only. Many smaller, developing nations are afraid of trade agreements involving developed nations because the imbalance of power could result in a unilateral benefit to the developed nation. No country would willingly enter a unilateral trade agreement, but fear of such an agreement has stymied many negotiations (http://useconomy.about.com/od/glossary/g/Unilateral.htm).

General multilateral agreements are sometimes easier to reach than separate bilateral agreements, since the gains to efficient producers from worldwide tariff reductions are large enough to warrant substantial concessions. The most important modern multilateral trade agreement was the General Agreement on Tariffs and Trade (GATT), which reduced world tariff levels and greatly expanded world trade. Such agreements continue under the aegis of the World Trade Organization (WTO), which replaced GATT in 1995.

Treaty (such as FTAA or NAFTA) is between two or more countries to establish a free trade area where commerce in goods and services can be conducted across their common borders, without tariffs or hindrances but (in contrast to a common market) capital or labor may not move freely. Member countries usually impose a uniform tariff (called common external tariff) on trade with non-member countries (http://www.businessdictionary.com/definition/free-trade-agreement.html).

History of Trade Agreements

Ever since Adam Smith published *The Wealth of Nations* in 1776, the vast majority of economists have accepted the proposition that Free trade among nations improves overall economic welfare. Free trade, usually defined as the absence of tariffs, quotas, or other governmental impediments International Trade, allows each country to specialize in the goods it can produce cheaply and efficiently relative to other countries. Such specialization enables all countries to achieve higher real incomes.

Although free trade provides overall benefits, removing a trade barrier on a particular good hurts the shareholders and employees of the domestic industry that produces that good. Some of the groups that are hurt by foreign competition wield enough political power to obtain protection against imports. Consequently, barriers to trade continue to exist despite their sizable economic costs. According to the U.S. International Trade Commission, for example, the U.S. gain from removing trade restrictions on textiles and apparel would have been almost twelve billion dollars in 2002 alone. This is a net economic gain after deducting the losses to firms and workers in the domestic industry. Yet, domestic textile producers have been able to persuade Congress to maintain tight restrictions on imports.

While virtually all economists think free trade is desirable, they differ on how best to make the transition from tariffs and quotas to free trade. The three basic approaches to trade reform are unilateral, multilateral, and bilateral. Some countries, such as Britain in the nineteenth century and Chile and China in recent decades, have undertaken unilateral tariff reductions—reductions made independently and without reciprocal action by other countries. The advantage of unilateral free trade is that a country can reap the benefits of free trade immediately. Countries that lower trade barriers by themselves do not have to postpone reform while they try to persuade other nations to follow suit. The gains from such trade liberalization are substantial: several studies have shown that income grows more rapidly in countries open to international trade than in those more closed to trade. Dramatic illustrations of this phenomenon include China's rapid growth after 1978 and India's after 1991, those dates indicating when major trade reforms took place.

For many countries, unilateral reforms are the only effective way to reduce domestic trade barriers. However, multilateral and bilateral approaches—dismantling trade barriers in concert with other countries—have two advantages over unilateral approaches. First, the economic gains from international trade are reinforced and enhanced when many countries or regions agree to a mutual reduction in trade barriers. By broadening markets, concerted liberalization of trade increases competition and specialization among countries, thus giving a bigger boost to efficiency and consumer incomes.

Second, multilateral reductions in trade barriers may reduce political opposition to free trade in each of the countries involved. That is because groups that otherwise would oppose or be indifferent to trade reform might join the campaign for free trade if they see opportunities for exporting to the other countries in the trade agreement. Consequently, free trade agreements between countries or regions are a useful strategy for liberalizing world trade.

The best possible outcome of trade negotiations is a multilateral agreement that includes all major trading countries. Then, free trade is widened to allow many participants to achieve the greatest possible gains from trade. After World War II, the United States helped found the General Agreement on Tariffs and Trade (GATT), which quickly became the world's most important multilateral trade arrangement.

The major countries of the world set up the GATT in reaction to the waves of protectionism that crippled world trade during—and helped extend—the *Great Depression* of the 1930s. In successive negotiating "rounds," the GATT substantially reduced the tariff barriers on manufactured goods in the industrial countries. Since the GATT began in 1947, average tariffs set by industrial countries have fallen from about 40 percent to about 5 percent today. These tariff reductions helped promote the tremendous expansion of world trade after World War II and the concomitant rise in real per capita incomes among developed and developing nations alike. The annual gain from removal of tariff and non-tariff barriers to trade as a result of the Uruguay Round

Agreement (negotiated under the auspices of the GATT between 1986 and 1993) has been put at about $96 billion, or 0.4 percent of world GDP.

In 1995, the GATT became the World Trade Organization (WTO), which now has more than 140 member countries. The WTO oversees four international trade agreements: the GATT, the General Agreement on Trade in Services (GATS), and agreements on trade-related *Intellectual Property rights* and trade-related Investment (TRIPS and TRIMS, respectively). The WTO is now the forum for members to negotiate reductions in trade barriers; the most recent forum is the Doha Development Round, launched in 2001.

The WTO also mediates disputes between member countries over trade matters. If one country's government accuses another country's government of violating world trade rules, a WTO panel rules on the dispute. If the WTO finds that a member country's government has not complied with the agreements it signed, the member is obligated to change its policy and bring it into conformity with the rules. If the member finds it politically impossible to change its policy, it can offer compensation to other countries in the form of lower trade barriers on other goods. If it chooses not to do this, then other countries can receive authorization from the WTO to impose higher duties (i.e., to "retaliate") on goods coming from the offending member country for its failure to comply.

As a multilateral trade agreement, the GATT requires its signatories to extend most-favored-nation (MFN) status to other trading partners participating in the WTO. MFN status means that each WTO member receives the same tariff treatment for its goods in foreign markets as that extended to the "most-favored" country competing in the same market, thereby ruling out preferences for, or discrimination against, any member country.

Although the WTO embodies the principle of nondiscrimination in international trade, article 24 of the GATT permits the formation of free-trade areas and "customs unions" among WTO members. A free-trade area is a group of countries that eliminate all tariffs on trade with each other but retain autonomy in determining their tariffs with nonmembers. A customs union is a group of countries that eliminate all tariffs on trade among themselves but maintain a common external tariff on trade with countries outside the union (thus technically violating MFN).

The customs union exception was designed, in part, to accommodate the formation of the European Economic Community (EC) in 1958. The EC, originally formed by six European countries, is now known as the European Union (EU) and includes twenty-seven European countries. The EU has gone beyond simply reducing barriers to trade among member states and forming a customs union. It has moved toward even greater economic integration by becoming a common market—an arrangement that eliminates impediments to the mobility of factors of production, such as capital and labor, between participating countries. As a common market, the EU also coordinates and harmonizes each country's tax, industrial, and agricultural policies. In addition, many members of the EU have formed a single currency area by replacing their domestic currencies with the *euro*. The GATT also permits free-trade areas (FTAs), such as the European Free Trade Area, which is composed primarily of Scandinavian countries. Members of FTAs eliminate tariffs on trade with each other but retain autonomy in determining their tariffs with nonmembers.

One difficulty with the WTO system has been the problem of maintaining and extending the liberal world trading system in recent years. Multilateral negotiations over trade liberalization move very slowly, and the requirement for consensus among the WTO's many members limits how far agreements on trade reform can go. As a result, many countries have turned away from the multilateral process toward bilateral or regional trade agreements. One such agreement is the North American Free Trade Agreement (NAFTA), which went into effect in January 1994. Under the terms of NAFTA, the United States, Canada, and Mexico agreed to phase out all tariffs on merchandise trade and to reduce restrictions on trade in services and foreign investment over a decade. The United States also has bilateral agreements with Israel, Jordan, Singapore, and Australia and is negotiating bilateral or regional trade agreements with countries in Latin America, Asia, and the Pacific. The European Union also has free-trade agreements with other countries around the world.

The advantage of such bilateral or regional arrangements is that they promote greater trade among the parties to the agreement. They may also hasten global trade liberalization if multilateral negotiations run into difficulties. Recalcitrant countries excluded from bilateral agreements, and hence not sharing in the increased trade these bring, may then be induced to join and reduce their own barriers to trade. Proponents of these agreements have called this process "competitive liberalization," wherein countries are challenged to reduce trade barriers to keep up with other countries. For example, shortly after NAFTA was implemented, the EU sought and eventually signed a free-trade agreement with Mexico to ensure that European goods would not be at a competitive disadvantage in the Mexican market as a result of NAFTA. But these advantages must be offset against a disadvantage: by excluding certain countries, these agreements may shift the composition of trade from low-cost countries that are not party to the agreement to high-cost countries that are.

Critics of bilateral and regional approaches to trade liberalization have many additional arguments. They suggest that these approaches may undermine and supplant, instead of support and complement, the multilateral WTO approach, which is to be preferred for operating globally on a nondiscriminatory basis. Hence, the long-term result of bilateralism could be a deterioration of the world trading system into competing, discriminatory regional trading blocs, resulting in added complexity that complicates the smooth flow of goods between countries. Furthermore, the reform of such issues as agricultural export subsidies cannot be dealt with effectively at the bilateral or regional level.

Despite possible tensions between the two approaches, it appears that both multilateral and bilateral/regional trade agreements will remain features of the world economy. Both the WTO and agreements such as NAFTA, however, have become controversial among groups such as anti-globalization protesters, who argue that such agreements serve the interests of multinational Corporations and not workers, even though freer trade has been a time-proven method of improving economic performance and raising overall incomes. To accommodate this opposition, there has been pressure to include labor and environmental standards in these trade agreements. Labor standards include provisions for *Minimum Wages* and working conditions, while environmental standards would prevent trade if environmental damage was feared.

One motivation for such standards is the fear that unrestricted trade will lead to a "race to the bottom" in labor and environmental standards as multinationals search the globe for low wages and lax environmental regulations in order to cut costs. Yet there is no empirical evidence of any such race. Indeed, trade usually involves the transfer of technology to developing countries, which allows wage rates to rise, as Korea's economy—among many others—has demonstrated since the 1960s. In addition, rising incomes allow cleaner production technologies to become affordable. The replacement of pollution-belching domestically produced scooters in India with imported scooters from Japan, for example, would improve air quality in India.

Labour Unions and environmentalists in rich countries have most actively sought labor and environmental standards. The danger is that enforcing such standards may simply become an excuse for rich-country protectionism, which would harm workers in poor countries. Indeed, people in poor countries, whether capitalists or laborers, have been extremely hostile to the imposition of such standards. For example, the 1999 WTO meeting in Seattle collapsed in part because developing countries objected to the Clinton administration's attempt to include labor standards in multilateral agreements.

General Agreement on Tariffs and Trade (GATT) in the Context of Negotiations

The most important general trade agreement is called, simply enough, the General Agreement on Tariffs and Trade (GATT). GATT was signed in October 1947 to liberalize trade, to create an organization to administer more liberal trade agreements, and to establish a mechanism for resolving trade disputes. The GATT organization is small and located in Geneva. More than 110 nations have signed the general agreement, which originally was signed by 24 nations, including the United States. To a large degree, the role of GATT as an organization has been superceded by the World Trade Organization. Since GATT was signed, several "rounds" of talks to liberalize trade have occurred. The most significant of these were the Kennedy rounds, which eventually led to a one-third reduction in tariffs and, more recently, the Uruguay rounds. The Uruguay rounds dealt with general barriers to trade and the relatively new issues of intellectual property rights, fishing practices, and environmental concerns. A major trend of the past 25 years has been the creation and growth of free trade zones among nations agreeing to form regional trade blocs. The agreements that create free trade zones all share the same aims: to liberalize trade, promote economic growth, and provide equal access to markets among the member nations. The most significant free trade zones are the European Union (EU), the North American Free Trade Agreement (NAFTA), and the Association of Southeast Asian Nations (ASEAN).

In the mid 1800's, a number of regional agreements that provided preferential treatment for specific countries were made among European countries to reduced trade barriers. These agreements began the movement towards freer trade. Meanwhile, the U.S. had an inconsistent stance on free trade as a number of trade barriers were reduced and then reinstated. By the 1920's, the U.S. had a tariff rate as low as 20 percent, but in 1930, the U.S. had a radical shift in policy by instituting the Smoot Hawley tariff that significantly increased U.S. tariffs. Within a few short years, the U.S. recognized the harmful effects of this tariff and started to make international regional agreements (referred to as Reciprocal Trade Agreements) that provided preferential treatment to selected countries. In the course of the next 60 years, the U.S. entered a number of agreements that provided both preferential and equal treatment to world trading partners. Each of these trade agreements has made a significant contribution towards free trade through the reduction of trade barriers including tariff rates.

GATT is an agreement that exemplifies equal treatment and the MFN principle is the General Agreement on Tariffs and Trade (GATT). A country that gains membership into GATT automatically gains access to the rest of the members of the world trading system on a MFN principle. The agreement creates an incentive for member countries to specialize in industries for which they have a competitive advantage, rather than specializing in industries they already have. In the end, and although not perfect, GATT has led to greater competition and reduced cost of production for industries across countries.

The World Trade Organization is a global international organization dealing with the rules of trade between nations. The Trade Negotiations Committee was set up by the Doha Declaration, which in turn assigned it to create subsidiary negotiating bodies to handle individual negotiating subjects, and other work including issues concerning the implementation of the present agreements. The website of the negotiations committee features a searchable database for negation documents that include the following subjects: agriculture; cotton; development; dispute settlement; environment; intellectual property rights; market access; regional trade agreements; services; and trade facilitation.

The General Agreement on Trade in Services (GATS) a trade agreement that establishes a multilateral framework of principles and rules for trade in services. It is the companion piece within the World Trade Organization (WTO) of the goods-specific Multilateral Agreements on Trade in Goods. It covers all services except those provided in the exercise of governmental authority, is a framework for multilateral obligations as well as commitments to continuous liberalization in the trade in services. Its objectives are:

- To expand services trade under conditions of transparency and progressive liberalization
- To promote the economic growth of its trading partners. In addition to a general framework of principles

The GATS requires its Members to set out a specific schedule of commitments defining how much market access service providers are allowed for specific service sectors, and under what national treatment conditions. The obligations and commitments that Members of the GATS make are subject to enforcement through the WTO. Once commitments on specific services have been undertaken, they cannot be withdrawn without compensating the other members. However, the fact that a country is a signatory to the GATS does not guarantee that it has made far-reaching commitments to open its markets in all sectors and/or for all measures affecting the supply of services. The level of commitments varies significantly among WTO Members.

WTO: Mandated to Trade Facilitation through Negotiations

Over the past few years, a wealth of empirical evidence has been gathered on the transaction costs that are imposed on international trade by poor-quality border management and logistics. Moving goods from the farm or factory gate to markets overseas often involves a long and complicated supply chain, with the risk that a single bottleneck along the way can seriously affect the entire process. Connecting efficiently to markets is particularly critical for developing countries, whose firms and farmers typically do not enjoy a high enough margin of competitiveness internationally to be able to absorb high Global transaction costs. Their ability to move their produce across borders quickly, reliably, and cheaply can mean the difference between their success or failure in integrating into the global economy. The WTO Trade Facilitation negotiations do not pretend to target the entire logistical supply chain. A significant share of the costs of getting goods to markets arises in areas such as ocean and inland transport, port management, and warehousing. For the most part, these areas lie well outside the purview of the WTO, although the Doha Round negotiations on Trade in Services can play an important role in helping to increase competitiveness, productivity, and efficiency in these activities. The Trade Facilitation negotiations cover a relatively narrow, but still significant, link in the chain—the actions that governments take to control and administer the way in which goods move across their national borders, through the various documentary and physical inspection stages to clearing customs and receiving approval from border agencies such as the health and safety or revenue authorities.

There are no precise figures of the costs that poor trade facilitation, narrowly defined, imposes on business and consumers, but data collected by the World Bank for its excellent annual report on the costs of "Doing Business" in its member countries come close. These data cover all of the official procedural requirements involved in exporting and importing a standardized container of goods, and measure them in terms of the number of documents required, the time taken from start to finish, and the overall cost of meeting the requirements. The Organization for Economic Co-operation and Development (OECD) countries set the benchmark for best practice as a regional group, requiring on average about 5 separate documents and clearing the goods in an average of 10 days at an average cost of about US$950 per container. In contrast, in sub-Saharan Africa almost double the number of documents are required: goods take from 35 days (for exports) to 44 days (for imports) to clear at an average cost per container of between US$1,660 (for exports) and US$1,986 (for imports).

The overall world champion at trade facilitation is Singapore, where 4 documents are required and goods are cleared in, at most, 5 days at an average cost of around US$400 per container. At the other end of the scale are many of the low-income developing countries, in particular the landlocked developing countries whose trade facilitation costs can mushroom as a result of the effort required to move goods in transit by road or rail through their neighbors to their nearest international port. Handicapping the world's least competitive producers and poorest consumers with additional transaction costs of US$1,000 or more for each container of goods that they manage to export or import is clearly absurd. The trade barriers they face in their main export markets are, in most cases, far less significant than these transaction costs, and for many of them the costs of poor trade facilitation have a bigger impact than their tariffs on the domestic price of imported goods. In short, the stakes involved in completing the Trade Facilitation negotiations and implementing the results successfully are high for many WTO Members, particularly the majority of developing countries.

Negotiating Objectives

Mandates for formal WTO negotiations are often fought over bitterly by governments, since they set the parameters for the final results. These mandates can end up laced with compromise language that conceals unresolved differences at the time a Round is launched, and when these surface further down the road, as inevitably they do, they risk bringing the negotiations to a halt while they are sorted out. The mandate for the Trade Facilitation negotiations is refreshingly clear and straightforward. It sets out three objectives:

- to clarify and improve GATT rules on the movement, release, and clearance of goods, including goods in transit, with the aim of reducing the transaction costs of trade;
- to develop special provisions for developing countries and least-developed countries (LDCs) and provide them with technical assistance and capacity building support that will help them to implement better

trade facilitation policies and practices; and
- to improve communication and cooperation between the customs authorities of WTO Members.

The most important target of these negotiations is to assist developing countries and LDCs to implement trade facilitation reforms and to adopt better practices that will enable them to move goods across their borders more efficiently than they do today. The negotiations are not inconsequential for the industrial countries such as the United States or those in the European Union. They too have scope to make reforms and improve their practices, and better GATT rules will bring outside pressure on them to move in that direction as well as helping to avoid unnecessary trade disputes between them from flaring up, as they have done at times in the past. Overall, however, it is the developing countries and LDCs that have the most to gain. They have the biggest deficit to make up in reaching standards of international best practice and the accent has been placed firmly on assisting them do that in practical terms by providing them with technical and, where necessary, financial support, not on litigating against them through the WTO's legal system.

Clarifying and improving GATT rules Three GATT Articles are at the center of the Trade Facilitation negotiations: Article V, on facilitating transit trade, Article VIII on limiting border fees and formalities, and Article X on making trade regulations transparent so that foreign traders can understand them and work with them more easily in their day-to-day business activities. These Articles all date back to the original GATT agreement of 1948, and although they have stood the test of time remarkably well they are undoubtedly in need of modernization to reflect the ways in which commercial and business practices have changed. A good example is the use of the Internet to publish trade regulations, to allow documentation requirements to be completed online, and to help border agencies use modern information technology to improve the efficiency and cost-effectiveness of their own operations. Other proposals that have been tabled under the rubric of clarifying and improving GATT Article X to create better and easier access to information for traders include the establishment of national enquiry points that serve as a one-stop shop for information about trade related legislation and procedures; procedures to notify traders of upcoming changes in laws and regulations so that they can adjust their business practices ahead of time and avoid running into problems after the goods have already arrived at the docks; the provision of advance rulings about how goods will be treated when they arrive at customs, in terms of tariff classification or customs valuation, for example; and the creation of appeal procedures for traders to allow them, where necessary, to challenge decisions of customs or other border agencies in an objective and transparent manner.

The task of updating GATT Article VIII on border fees and formalities has attracted the largest number of proposals. These cover a lot of ground. One proposal aims to reduce border fees and charges by requiring that they be set in line with the actual costs of border administration. Another is to agree on common standards that can be used to simplify documentation requirements and harmonize them internationally as far as possible. A particularly valuable proposal for many traders is the establishment of a "single window" that allows all documentation and data requirements for importation, exportation, and transit to be submitted at the same time and once only, cutting out the duplication of effort that is involved in dealing with many different border authorities and agencies separately.

Other proposals are that WTO Member governments should eliminate requirements for pre-shipment inspection, stop charging consular fees, and open up any system they have of mandatory customs brokers to much wider participation by foreign traders than is the case at present. There are proposals, too, to recognize and adopt modern customs practices, such as allowing the expedited release and clearance of goods, using risk assessment techniques and authorized trader schemes, and carrying out post-clearance audits. Steps to facilitate transit traffic are the major objective of these negotiations for many landlocked countries that, as noted in the figures cited from *Doing Business,* are paying a very expensive price to get their exports and imports to and from their nearest ports. Proposals have been made to strengthen the nondiscrimination provisions (most-favored nation, or MFN, and national treatment) of GATT Article V, to reduce transit fees and charges and simplify transit formalities and documentation, to limit inspections and controls by using bonded transport, and to promote regional transit arrangements. In one respect at least, these proposals may be tricky to deal with since for transit countries, many of whom are themselves low-income developing countries, the prospect of dealing with substantially increased transit traffic from their neighbors can threaten to overload their road and rail infrastructure, which is already weak.

This is an area, therefore, in which the logistical supply chain needs attention—not only through the WTO negotiations but also by development agencies and bilateral donors to help invest in upgrading transport facilities and creating new transit corridors. Trying to restrict or regulate transit traffic through excessive border controls is, in every respect, a second-best alternative. In total, proposals for new or improved GATT disciplines have been tabled on about 50 issues. Part of the success of the Trade Facilitation negotiations is the fact that these proposals have originated from across the whole spectrum of WTO Member governments, reflecting a high level of engagement by developing countries and LDCs. In several cases, they have joined forces with the major industrialized countries to help get their point across.

The original negotiating proposal to eliminate consular fees, for example, was jointly sponsored by Uganda and the United States, and Switzerland has cosponsored proposals on improving transit rules with a number of low-income, landlocked, developing countries as well as landlocked countries in Eastern Europe. While alliances of this sort are not unheard of in other areas of the Doha Round, they have been particularly evident in the Trade

Facilitation negotiations and they have created the sense of common purpose that is so important for crafting a multilateral consensus around an agreement that aims to serve the collective welfare of the whole membership. All WTO Members are both importers and exporters of merchandise trade, and all of them have a vested commercial interest in seeing the transaction costs of their trade reduced, in their own countries as well as in their trading partners. The prospect is for a win-win outcome for all concerned. Support for developing countries.

One reason that the start of negotiations on Trade Facilitation was delayed until 2004 was opposition from developing countries to including the package of "Singapore Issues" in the Doha Round. These issues—Foreign Investment, Competition Policy, Government Procurement, and Trade Facilitation—were promoted heavily, by the European Union in particular, at the WTO's Ministerial Conference in Singapore in 1996. Trade Facilitation was always the least contentious of the four issues, but even so it did raise concerns, especially among low-income developing countries, that it would overload the capacity of these countries to upgrade their trade infrastructure by requiring them to take on additional, expensive but unfunded WTO obligations. When proposals to launch negotiations on the other three Singapore Issues were finally dropped at the WTO's Cancun Ministerial Conference in 2003, attention turned to crafting a negotiating mandate for Trade Facilitation that would allay these concerns. The result provided *ex ante* assurance to developing countries and LDCs on three points: they would receive help to participate fully in the negotiations so that the substantive issues of most commercial interest to them would be taken fully on board; they would receive generous technical assistance and capacity-building support to implement the results of the negotiations; and, on a somewhat more defensive note, they would not be required to undertake new WTO obligations until that assistance and support has been provided. Once the negotiations got going and it became clear that developing countries and LDCs were enthusiastic about sharing fully in the potential benefits of a final agreement, attention turned to designing an effective delivery mechanism to ensure that the technical assistance and capacity building support is provided and that it does produce real trade facilitation results on the ground, where it counts.

Enhancing the ability of low-income developing countries to participate effectively in the negotiating process may sound like a mere detail, but it matters a great deal for those that can afford to maintain only a very limited staff at their permanent missions in Geneva and that require the presence of customs and other experts from capitals at the negotiating table to make sure that their own commercial interests are well represented. A facility has therefore been set up to cover the costs of periodically bringing experts from low-income countries to Geneva for the negotiating sessions, thanks to funding that, to date, comes from Norway and the United Kingdom.

As for the second and third points of assurance provided in the negotiating mandate, negotiations to create an effective delivery mechanism for technical assistance and capacity-building support are still underway, but the broad lines that will be involved are already fairly clear. The first step, which is already being organized by the WTO Secretariat, involves expert support to individual developing countries to help them review their current trade facilitation practices and to assess what more they would need to do to implement in full the package of draft proposals that is on the table today. About 70 WTO Member governments have requested assistance under this needs-assessment program, and the secretariat is organizing missions at the rate of five or six countries per month to respond to these requests, with the help of customs experts from other intergovernmental agencies such as the World Bank and the World Customs Organization as well as from the national administrations of other WTO Members. Over the course of a one-week workshop held in each country's national capital, representatives from all relevant border agencies meet together to study the proposals, learn from the experts how other countries manage their customs and border procedures, and assess what steps they would need to take to raise their own trade facilitation practices up to international norms.

Experience has shown that, beyond the preparation of a detailed needs assessment, one of the most valuable and rewarding results of the exercise is to generate better understanding and closer cooperation among the different national agencies involved in the border management process. That alone can begin yielding practical results on the ground and lower the transaction costs of the country's trade, even before official negotiations have been completed. The finished needs assessment for each WTO Member government is an important input to the completion of the negotiating process back in the WTO headquarters in Geneva. Negotiators are currently working on a framework to implement the eventual Trade Facilitation agreement that would see developing countries and LDCs scheduling their trade facilitation reforms in three categories:

- those reforms that they have already undertaken or that they consider can be undertaken relatively easily and that they can therefore agree to implement straight away, as soon as the agreement is finalized;
- a second category that the national needs-assessment exercise has shown they would require time to carry out; and
- a third category for which they require not only time but also technical assistance and capacity building support in order to complete satisfactorily.

Since the trade facilitation situation on the ground differs from country to country, each Member government's schedule is likely to differ too, but that is not a real concern. The aim is not to line up all WTO Members at the start, but to help them all to reach the finish successfully, especially those that need the help most. Following up on the third category of commitments in a Member government's schedule—those that require not only time but also technical assistance and capacity building support to implement fully—will clearly be an essential part of the process. It will require close cooperation between the WTO and other intergovernmental agencies with expertise and experience in the area of trade facilitation as well as direct cooperation among individual WTO Members—those that require assistance on the one hand and those that are in a position to supply it on the other. The WTO is not a development agency, much less a development bank, and it has no intention of moving into that area of activity. Under its Aid-for-Trade program, the WTO aims to help its low income Member governments to advocate their case for increased development financing from development banks and bilateral donors to allow them to build trade related capacity. It will use that program to make the case for providing capacity-building support for trade facilitation projects, among others. Completing the implementation of this third category of commitments will take time, but—given the size of the returns that can confidently be expected from each dollar invested in facilitating trade—there should be no doubt about its eventual success.

Trade Facilitation Process and Prospects for success

Although the Trade Facilitation negotiations began only three years after the rest of the Round had been launched, they have more than made up for their late start. At the time of writing, all of the main elements of an eventual Trade Facilitation agreement have been tabled in proposals by WTO Member governments, the process of reviewing and refining those elements and turning them into draft legal provisions has begun, and an extensive program of technical assistance for developing countries LDCs is well underway in their capitals to help each of them assess what reforms they will need to carry out in order to implement the agreement when it finally comes into force.

Trade Facilitation is being treated as part of what is termed the "Single Undertaking" of the Doha Round. This means that it cannot be split off or completed separately from other subjects under negotiation, such as Agriculture and Services. Accepting the Single Undertaking formulation was a necessary condition for some Member governments to agree to start negotiations on Trade Facilitation. It is a formulation that is credited with having made the Uruguay Round negotiations a comprehensive success in the 1990s. Tying all of the negotiating subjects together prevents any attempt at cherry-picking when it comes to agreeing on the overall results, and results that are broadly popular for all WTO Members (such as Trade Facilitation) can help leverage through others for which finding consensus is an altogether more difficult affair. Equally, of course, the Single Undertaking may cause delays to Trade Facilitation if problems develop elsewhere on other negotiating issues, but at the moment there is no sign of that having happened to any significant extent.

One hallmark of these negotiations has been the engagement of developing countries, including many of the LDCs. This reflects their belief that the eventual Trade Facilitation agreement will yield significant benefits for their trade expansion and economic development. Great care is being taken to craft meaningful development provisions—in WTO jargon," Special and Differential Treatment" provisions—into the agreement that will ensure it produces genuine change and makes a real difference to the ease with which developing countries can expand their trade. In sum, the prospects for a successful conclusion to the Trade Facilitation negotiations are good, and the benefits for business and consumers from a new agreement will be significant. These negotiations do not have the high political profile of some other parts of the Doha Round, but that is no bad thing when it comes to making steady progress at the technical expert level in Geneva. Once completed, the new agreement will add another page to the WTO rulebook that underwrites the openness and stability of the international trading system, and it will signal real changes on the ground in Member governments' trade facilitation policies and practices that will allow traders to get goods across borders more quickly, reliably, and cheaply than they can today.

Need for a "Crisis Round" of Trade Negotiations

Protectionism is steadily mounting. The wide spectrum of new protectionist measures shares two features: They are WTO-legal and largely unaddressed by the ongoing Doha Round. The current solution adopted by the world's leading countries in the G-20 is a restatement of good intentions: not to erect new barriers and to try, yet again, to complete the Doha Round. The former has clearly not worked because seventeen of the G-20 countries have imposed restrictions. And focusing on Doha alone could delay action to head off the protectionist pressures that are emerging. It is time to find an urgent solution to this problem (http://www.petersoninstitute.org/publications/papers/paper.cfm?ResearchID=1173).

The following Para brings about the rationality of the need for a Crisis Round of Negotiation to break away from the syndrome of Protectionisms (Mattoo & Subramanium, 2009, http://www.voxeu.org/index.php?q=node/3367).

The Pre-Doha Equilibrium

Since the conclusion of the Uruguay Round in the mid-1990s, the multilateral trading system has been in a kind of equilibrium, in which few demands have been made of the World Trade Organization (WTO) to deliver more opening of markets. Emerging-market countries steadily lowered their barriers to flows of goods, services, and capital, either on their own or in the context of regional agreements. Many developing countries also drastically reduced barriers to foreign investment and international trade in most of their service sectors, including finance, telecommunications, transport, and retail.

Industrial countries, apart from pockets of protection in agriculture, clothing, and labor services, maintained open markets. This state of affairs was a reasonably stable equilibrium; private-sector interests in the industrial world, the usual demandeurs of multilateral trade liberalization, did not seriously push their governments for multilateral market opening. This explains why repeated efforts at reviving WTO trade negotiations (such as Seattle in 1999) failed. This also explains why, when the Doha Round was launched in a burst of post-9/11 international solidarity, its ambitions were relatively moderate, yet even these ambitions have proved difficult to realize.

Global Financial Crisis

The global financial crisis has disturbed this equilibrium. The economic downturn and the resulting underemployment of resources have created new macroeconomic sources of protectionist pressure. In terms of the constituents of aggregate demand, consumption and investment are in wholesale retreat, creating a temptation to reduce imports and increase exports through protectionist actions. Furthermore, as countries inject demand into the economy via fiscal reflation, they are anxious to not let this demand "leak" abroad. The Buy America provisions in the US fiscal stimulus package and the French attempt to condition auto subsidies on locating investment in France illustrate this anxiety.

The Nature of New Protectionism

We have witnessed protection imposed through traditional instruments, such as tariff increases, restrictive import licensing, state aid (especially in the automobile and financial sectors), antidumping actions, and discriminatory government procurement, which has assumed greater importance in industrial countries because of the increased role of the state and higher government expenditures. There have also been newer forms of protection, including undervalued exchange rates, environmentally motivated trade restrictions, resource nationalism (such as when countries restricted the export of food during last year's commodity crisis), and now financial nationalism, whereby financial resources are directed to national firms. These differing forms of protection share two common features: They are consistent with current WTO rules and, for the most part, are not being addressed in the Doha Round.

International Policy Responses

Two possible scenarios loom ahead. In the first, low-grade protectionism, limited in scope and intensity and pursued by a narrower range of actors, would prevail. This is a world that would reflect the expediency of Prime Minister Vladimir Putin's words at Davos: "Although additional protectionism will prove inevitable during the crisis, all of us must display a sense of proportion."But low-grade protectionism is not the only possible outcome. There is a gloomier scenario in which protectionist actions become more serious. The probability of this outcome is currently low, but its likelihood will increase with the depth and length of the global recession. In this scenario, an exclusive focus on completing Doha could delay action to head off the protectionist pressures that are emerging. Even the signaling value of completing Doha would be doubtful. Imagine that Doha were completed while antidumping actions rose, dollops of subsidies were doled out, procurement became discriminatory, environmentally motivated protectionism were unleashed, and mercantilism took hold. How would it help the credibility of the WTO system to have spent time negotiating some tariffs reductions and limits on agricultural subsidies while trade was rapidly declining due to a range of new protectionist actions?

Historically, once protection is in place, it is painfully difficult to negotiate away; the high depression-era tariffs were only eliminated decades later. If this scenario is at all likely, the world must act now to head off the new protectionist pressures. We need a crisis round.

The Crisis Round

We suggest that the Crisis Round be immediately launched at the G-20 London Summit. Its key aim would be to preserve something close to the current level of global openness. The crisis nature of the round would have implications for its agenda, ambitions, and actors.

Agenda

First, the agenda would be confined to the key protectionist measures. These include trade restrictions and subsidies in agriculture, manufacturing, and services; antidumping actions; preferential government procurement; and environmentally motivated trade interventions. While exchange rate mercantilism could merit inclusion, it is a much harder issue to address and would in any case require a high degree of institutional coordination. Similarly, financial protectionism needs to be tackled but this is best done through coordination between national financial regulators rather than through WTO legal mechanisms.

Table 1 spells out the broad aims of the Crisis Round, but specific elements would have to be negotiated by countries of course.

Future Outlook

A crisis round would moderate the level of ambition in some policy areas and temporarily raise it in others. It would not seek new liberalization but aim to bind, for a fixed period of time, say three years, the current level of openness across the board in the WTO. For the Crisis Round to have timely effect, it would have to be concluded within 12 months.

For developing countries, the aim would be to bind all tariffs in industry and agriculture as well as restrictions in services at currently applied levels. For industrial countries, the aim would be to bind current levels of subsidization in agriculture, current levels of aid to industry (including that handed out in the current crisis), and current levels of access in cross-border trade in services (the latter would head off the temptation to reduce outsourcing). For both sets of countries, to reduce the threat of antidumping actions, there would be an effort to raise the threshold for such actions (by amounts to be negotiated).

On government procurement, the crisis may offer an opportunity to strike

Table 1: Commitments under the Doha Round and the Proposed Crisis Round

Sector / Area	Doha agenda's likely outcome	Crisis round agenda
Agricultural tariffs (developing)	Some liberalization, but bound tariff rates above current applied levels	No liberalization, but bound tariff rates at current applied levels
Manufacturing tariffs (developing)	Some liberalization, but bound tariff rates above current applied levels	No liberalization, but bound tariff rates at current applied levels
Agricultural tariffs (industrial)	Some liberalization, but bound tariff rates above current applied levels	No liberalization, but bound tariff rates at current applied levels
Manufacturing tariffs (industrial)	Some liberalization	No liberalization
Services	Limited increase in scope of bound tariff rates	All countries bound at current access
Antidumping	Limited changes to rules; may even lead to permissiveness	Raise *de minimis* dumping margin and *de minimis* volume of dumped imports
Government procurement	No change	All countries to bind existing procurement regime on MFN basis
State aid in manufacturing	No change	Bind at current levels
Environment-related trade measures	No change	No trade-related actions pending conclusions of global climate change negotiations

a bargain that has hitherto proved elusive. Existing signatories to the WTO's Government Procurement Agreement would extend the benefits of this agreement to the larger developing countries. In return, the latter would assume the agreement's transparency obligations and transparently bind their current practice. Given that environmentally motivated trade restrictions are becoming a major concern, there would be a commitment by all countries to desist from such actions until an international agreement on climate change is negotiated. In effect, this would be like a peace clause, pending political agreement on the key issues of burden-sharing on climate change.

Another innovation that might need to be considered is an accelerated dispute settlement procedure to deal expeditiously with complaints. The object of preserving the status quo would be defeated if prolonged violations were tolerated simply because of the tardiness of the dispute settlement process. A possible model could be the provision for expeditious arbitration in current WTO dispute settlement procedures.

Actors

A crisis round would allow for another innovation, namely variable geometry. Since the major threats to the global economy come from actions by the large trading partners, it is these countries that must make commitments to desist from protectionism. The G-20 would be a natural forum for initiating these commitments, but other important trading countries may also have to be brought in to constitute a critical mass. Insofar as the benefits of these bindings would be extended on a most-favored nation (MFN) basis to all WTO members, the interests of the small and poor countries would be naturally protected.

Survival Prospect of Crisis Round

One advantage of initiating a crisis round along these lines would be that it would specifically address the current forms of protection. Trade history tells us that countries are more likely to resist protectionist pressures if there is a serious ongoing process aimed at addressing those pressures. In the Uruguay Round, for example, there was a standstill and rollback commitment that was broadly respected because all countries were engaged in serious negotiations to bring down barriers. Thus, even the initiation of a crisis round with the aim of legally binding specific instruments of protection would lend greater force to the current political (and somewhat nebulous) standstill commitment.

In the current political climate, Doha seems to be doing both too much and too little. Too much because it is aiming for new liberalization in agriculture and industry when the climate for holding the line on openness, let alone achieving market opening, is proving politically difficult. At the same time, the Doha agenda is also doing too little because it is not addressing the protectionist pressures emerging in new areas in new forms.

The Crisis Round would address both these problems. Because its major thrust would be to lock in the current state of openness, it would not require any incremental liberalization. And by extending this lock-in more widely than the Doha agenda, it would be more effective. Its feasibility would be facilitated by the fact that the envisaged commitments are time-bound. Ultimately, though, the success of the Crisis Round would depend on whether major trading players see it as providing a mutually acceptable balance of gains and losses. Table 2 suggests that such a broad balance is achievable.

In some ways, the crisis is an opportunity for the WTO to respond nimbly and effectively in pre-empting protectionism. In a crisis, there can be experimentation that would be difficult in normal times (for example, variable geometry). In the long run, the WTO should take on a wider liberalization agenda. But first, the trading system must survive these potentially perilous times. That survival requires calibrating the agenda and ambition to stem the protectionist tide. Ambition can return when this tide recedes. And it is even possible that an innovative response to the crisis would enhance the WTO's credibility and provide experience and ideas that would facilitate the successful conclusion of Doha or even a more ambitious effort.

Table 2: Gains and Concessions for major Trading Countries in the Proposed Crisis Round

	Gains	Concessions
US	Government procurement in developing countries (DCs) Manufacturing in DCs Agriculture and services globally	Agricultural protection Preferential procurement Environment
EU	Government procurement in DCs Manufacturing in DCs Agriculture and services globally	Agricultural protection Preferential procurement Environment
Brazil	Agriculture globally Environmental measures	Manufacturing and services Preferential procurement
India	Services globally Environmental measures Government procurement	Manufacturing and agriculture Preferential procurement
China	Manufacturing in DCs Environmental measures Government procurement	Services Preferential procurement

As Mattoo and Subramanian noted in a 2008 article in *Foreign Affairs*, the Doha agenda has focused on further limited liberalization of bound border barriers on trade in goods. These barriers are no longer the strategic constraints to international economic integration. The time has come to move on to limiting uncertainty about the way existing rules and disciplines will be applied as well as to address new issues such as food, energy, and economic security. If work on these issues is held hostage progress on old issues, more and more action will shift to the negotiation of discriminatory preferential trading arrangements (Andrew Elek-Crisis & Reinventing WTO Negotiation, http://www.eastasiaforum.org/2009/04/15/the-crisis-and-reinventing-wto-negotiations/)

International Trade Barriers

When we talk about international trade we mean the exchange of goods and/or services. This exchange usually takes place between two parties from different countries or between two countries located anywhere on the globe. If the international trade takes place between two parties, it is known as bilateral trade and if the trade takes place between more than two parties, it is known as multi-lateral trade.

There are basically three barriers to international trade that are used by countries, and they are as follows:

1. *Non-tariff Barrier*

Usually this type of barrier is imposed by a country on imports so that the quantity of imported items is restricted. Due to this, the availability of the imported item or items is restricted in the domestic market and the price too is very high.

2. *Tariff Barrier*

This is barrier is in the form of duties, taxes, quotas etc. Because of this barrier, imports decrease and price of imported products increase which results in the fall in the demand giving boost to domestic products.

3. *Voluntary Constraint*

This is a type of international trade barrier wherein a country voluntarily restricts or stops imports from coming in. This is usually used to limit the competition that domestic industries will face with the coming in of imported goods. Whenever a country starts international trade with another country, these three barriers to international trade are always taken into account. It has been seen that lower developed countries and developing countries tend to favor these three barriers to international trade as the countries can earn foreign exchange by introducing tariff and non-tariff barrier, the local industries are protected from competition by foreign companies and industries and as less imported goods are available in the country, consumers tend to buy local products giving the local industries a boost (http://www.bangkoklogistics.com/international-business/Three-Barriers-To-International-Trade.html).

A number of trade barriers have been employed in order to protect industries, to raise revenue, and to counter the barriers erected by other foreign countries. These barriers create a distortion of relative prices across countries and, consequently, distort individual consumption patterns and lower individual welfare. A general discussion of these barriers and their consequences is provided below.

Tariffs

Tariffs have been a means of protecting domestic industries and creating revenue for centuries. A tariff is really nothing more than a tax placed on goods imported into a country. In the early years of the U.S., tariffs were the main source of revenue for the Federal government and continued to be an important source of revenue up until the 1930's. Today, the average tariff rates across goods and across countries are between 10 and 15 percent and are not a significant source of revenue for most countries.

However, tariffs still present a significant barrier to trade among nations. By placing a tax on imported goods, a tariff raises the price of goods and allows certain domestic producers to produce at higher levels. In doing so, resources may be diverted away from industries for which a country has a competitive advantage to industries for which the country does not have a competitive advantage. Diversion of resources creates higher prices and lower quality for goods that are produced domestically. Therefore, a tradeoff exists between saving jobs in specific industries versus the welfare of consumers.

Quotas

A quota, also referred to as a quantitative restriction, is a policy tool to restrict trade by placing a ceiling on the amount of a product that can be imported during a given period. As a result, the restriction will create artificially high prices on goods and reduce the amount of competition within that industry. A variation of the quota system is a voluntary export restriction (VER). Under VER, an exporting country is asked to restrict their exports under the threat of explicit restrictions and trade barriers. In general, the goods that have quotas placed against them are goods that the country does not have a competitive advantage in and yet they produce them. Because the country does not have a competitive advantage in the goods, the cost of producing the goods will be higher than the cost of other countries, and therefore, the selling price will be higher than the world price of the goods. In the end, consumers are the ones who suffer the consequences by paying higher prices for the goods that have restrictions placed on it.

Duties

A duty is a tax imposed on imported goods by the customs authority. It is often applied as an ad valorem tax and is either based upon the value of the good or the weight or quantity of the good. A duty has a similar effect as a tariff in that it raises the price of imports and distorts the relative price of goods and consumption patterns. Therefore, duties create a consumer welfare loss.

Exchange Rate Controls

Many third world countries try to be protective of their unstable and struggling economies. Therefore, they want to be self-reliant as much as possible to encourage their domestic industries. In an attempt to protect their domestic industries, third world countries will often create exchange rate barriers to reduce the influx of foreign currency, which reduces the ability of a country to purchase imports. Consequently, residents will be forced to purchase goods from domestic producers which create an artificially diversified domestic economy that produces a number of goods for which the country does not have a competitive advantage. As a result, consumers will have to pay a higher price on goods and services and resources will be diverted away from industries for which they have a competitive advantage.

Dumping Policy

Dumping occurs when a producer sells a product in a foreign market at prices below that of their own domestic market. Dumping could be just a strategy of a producer (predatory dumping practices), or it could be the result of foreign government subsidies. This will not only enable a domestic producer to crack the foreign market, it may, eventually, drive out competition in that foreign market.

Subsidies

Subsidies come in the form of grants, concessionary loans, loan guarantees, and tax credits that are provided by a government to provide financial benefits on the production, manufacturing, and distribution of goods or services to foreign markets. Once again, these subsidies distort the relative price of goods and distort individual consumption patterns. Furthermore, it is an anticompetitive practice that restricts the ability of foreign producers to compete in a worldwide market. Subsidies have been widely used in the agriculture industry.

Fair Trade Practices

Policies that are recognized as countervailing polices of trade can become protectionary policies as well. Trade policies such as anti-dumping, safeguards, and countervailing duties can be used to restrict trade and actually hurt free trade when these techniques are abused. When one country tries to retaliate against another country by using these policies, they can also create an escalating trading war that hurts consumers and producers of each country.

Price Bands

Many countries use what is referred to as "price bands" to restrict the importation of agriculture products. Price band is a policy instituted by the government that calculates the price range of a product from a time series analysis of international prices for that product. For example, a government may examine the prices of a product for a 60 month time period. Out of these prices, a portion of the highest and lowest prices will be eliminated. The remaining highs and lows establish the price band. Imports entering within the price rage are assessed a standard tariff rate. Imports entering above that price range are assessed a lower tariff rate, while imports entering below that market rate are assessed a very high tariff rate. Therefore, if a particular country has low prices for a good because of excessive supply, their goods will have a higher tariff rate assessed to the product.

Other Barriers

While there has been a decline in tariff rates across countries, a number of other barriers have often taken the place of the tariff. These barriers include licensing requirements, government procurement practices, technical standards, and domestic-content rules. Often, a country can require a license, which is a property right to export to a country. The country will only issue so many licenses and they are then bought and sold among producers who want to export to the country.

Trade agreements have created an ever-shrinking world that has progressively been moving towards a global market. On a daily basis, U.S.

consumers buy goods that are produced in places like China, Germany, and Brazil, while U.S. companies produce goods that are consumed by people in places like Australia, Mexico, and Russia. This increase in trade can be attributed to a number of factors including the reduction in the cost of communication and transportation, as well as other socioeconomic factors which have lead to higher worldwide disposable income. Another key factor is an almost century long series of continuously evolving international negotiations that have led to numerous agreements to reduce barriers to trade.

These trade agreements include both global and regional agreements. Examples of global agreements include the General Agreement on Tariffs and Trade (GATT) and the World Trade Organization (WTO). Examples of regional agreements include the Latin American Free Trade Agreement (LAFTA), the Andean Pact, the Central American Common Market (CACM), the European Economic Community (EC), the Association of South East Asia (ASEAN), and the North American Free Trade Agreement (NAFTA). Ultimately, the global economy is progressing towards conditions involving free movement of goods across borders with fewer restrictions to what people can buy.

REDUCING INTERNATIONAL TRADE BARRIERS

A number of organizations work to ease barriers to trade, and more countries are joining together to promote trade and mutual economic benefits. Let's look at some of these important initiatives.

Trade Agreements and Organizations

Free trade is encouraged by a number of agreements and organizations set up to monitor trade policies. The two most important are the General Agreement on Tariffs and Trade, and the World Trade Organization.

General Agreement on Tariffs and Trade

After the Great Depression and World War-II, most countries focused on protecting home industries. As a result, international trade was hindered by rigid trade restrictions. To rectify this situation, twenty-three nations joined together in 1947 and signed the General Agreement on Tariffs and Trade (GATT), which encouraged free trade by regulating and reducing tariffs and by providing a forum for resolving trade disputes. The highly successful initiative achieved substantial reductions in tariffs and quotas, and in 1995 its members founded the World Trade Organization to continue the work of GATT in overseeing global trade.

World Trade Organization

Based in Geneva, Switzerland, with nearly 150 members, the World Trade Organization (WTO) encourages global commerce and lower trade barriers, enforces international rules of trade, and provides a forum for resolving disputes. It is empowered, for instance, to determine whether a member nation's trade policies have violated the organization's rules, and it can direct "guilty" countries to remove disputed barriers (though it has no legal power to force any country to do anything it doesn't want to do). If the guilty party refuses to comply, the WTO may authorize the plaintiff nation to erect trade barriers of its own, generally in the form of tariffs. Affected members aren't always happy with WTO actions. In 2002, for example, the Bush administration imposed a three-year tariff on imported steel. In ruling against this tariff, the WTO allowed the aggrieved nations to impose counter-tariffs on some politically sensitive American products, such as Florida oranges, Texas grapefruits and computers, and Wisconsin cheese. Reluctantly, the administration lifted its tariff on steel.

Financial Support for Troubled Economies

The key to helping developing countries become active participants in the global marketplace is providing financial assistance. Offering monetary assistance to some of the poorest nations in the world is the shared goal of two organizations: the International Monetary Fund and the World Bank. These organizations, to which most countries belong, were established in 1944 to accomplish different but complementary purposes (http://www.flatworldknowledge.com/pub/1.0/exploring-business/28031):

The International Monetary Fund

The International Monetary Fund (IMF) loans money to countries with troubled economies, such as Mexico in the 1980s and mid-1990s and Russia and Argentina in the late 1990s. There are, however, strings attached to IMF loans: in exchange for relief in times of financial crisis, borrower countries must institute sometimes painful financial and economic reforms. In the 1980s, for example, Mexico received financial relief from the IMF on the condition that it privatize and deregulate certain industries and liberalize trade policies. The government was also required to cut back expenditures for such services as education, health care, and workers' benefits.

Criticism of the IMF and the World Bank

In recent years, the IMF and the World Bank have faced mounting criticism, though both have their supporters. Some analysts, for example, think that the IMF is often too harsh in its demands for economic reform; others argue that troubled economies can be turned around only with harsh economic measures. Some observers assert that too many World Bank loans go to environmentally harmful projects, such as the construction of roads through fragile rain forests. Others point to the World Bank's efforts to direct funding away from big construction projects and toward initiatives designed to better the lot of the world's poor—educating children, fighting AIDS, and improving nutrition and health standards.

Trading Blocs

So far, our discussion has suggested that global trade would be strengthened if there were no restrictions on it—if countries didn't put up barriers to trade or perform special favors for domestic industries. The complete absence of barriers is an ideal state of affairs that we haven't yet attained. In the meantime, economists and policy makers tend to focus on a more practical question: Can we achieve the goal of free trade on the *regional* level? To an extent, the answer is yes. In certain parts of the world, groups of countries have joined together to allow goods and services to flow without restrictions across their mutual borders. Such groups are called trading blocs. Let's examine two of the most powerful trading blocks—NAFTA and the European Union. Other countries have also opted for economic integration. Four historical rivals in South America—Argentina, Brazil, Paraguay, and Uruguay—have established MERCOSUR (for *Mercado Commun del Sur*) to eliminate trade barriers. A number of Asian countries, including Indonesia, Malaysia, the Philippines, Singapore, and Thailand, are cooperating to reduce mutual barriers through ASEAN (http://www.flatworldknowledge.com/pub/1.0/exploring-business/28031).

North American Free Trade Association

The North American Free Trade Association (NAFTA) is an agreement among the governments of the United States, Canada, and Mexico to open their borders to unrestricted trade. The effect of this agreement is that three very different economies are combined into one economic zone with almost no trade barriers. From the northern tip of Canada to the southern tip of Mexico, each country benefits from the comparative advantages of its partners: each nation is free to produce what it does best and to trade its goods and services without restrictions. When the agreement was ratified in 1994, it had no shortage of skeptics. Many people feared, for example, that without tariffs on Mexican goods, more U.S. manufacturing jobs would be lost to Mexico, where labor is cheaper. A decade later, most such fears have not been realized, and, by and large, NAFTA has been an enormous success. Since it went into effect, the value of trade between the United States and Mexico has grown substantially, and Canada and Mexico are now the United States' top trading partners.

The European Union

The forty-plus countries of Europe have long shown an interest in integrating their economies. The first organized effort to integrate a segment of Europe's economic entities began in the late 1950s, when six countries joined together to form the *European Economic Community* (EEC). Over the next four decades, membership grew, and in the late 1990s, the EEC became the European Union. Today, the European Union (EU) is a group of twenty-seven countries that have eliminated trade barriers among themselves.

At first glance, the EU looks similar to NAFTA. Both, for instance, allow unrestricted trade among member nations. But the provisions of the EU go beyond those of NAFTA in several important ways. Most importantly, the EU is more than a trading organization: it also enhances political and social cooperation and binds its members into a single entity with authority to require them to follow common rules and regulations. It is much like a federation of states with a weak central government, with the effect not only of eliminating internal barriers but also of enforcing common tariffs on trade from outside the EU. In addition, while NAFTA allows goods and services as well as capital to pass between borders, the EU also allows *people* to come and go freely: if you possess an EU passport, you can work in any EU nation.

Many EU initiatives have been less successful than those of NAFTA, yet it can claim at least one very important exception: the introduction of a common currency. A key step toward unification occurred in 1999, when most (but not all) EU members agreed to abandon their own currencies and adopt a joint currency. The actual conversion occurred in 2002, when a common currency called the *euro* replaced the separate currencies of participating EU countries. The common currency facilitates trade and finance because exchange-rate differences no longer complicate transactions. Its proponents argue that the EU will not only unite economically and politically distinct countries, but further will create an economic power that can compete against the dominant players in the global marketplace. Individually, each European country has limited economic power, but as a group, they could be an economic superpower.

Challenges before International Trade Regime

The opportunities and challenges of international trade have been an issue of major concern for the economists and policy makers of the contemporary world. As far as the challenges facing the international trade are concerned, they vary with the economic and social scenarios of the countries involved in cross border trade. Be it a developed or developing economy, the primary challenge of global trade is to maximize the gains from trade. The countries involved in international trade always try to focus on the efficient utilization of the opportunities derived from exchange of goods and services with their trading partners. To utilize the benefits of the open market economy is another major challenge before world trade.

In this era of globalization, international trade has a crucial role to play so as to bring about economic and social harmony among the developed and developing nations of the world. With openness to trade becoming more popular, the issues of trade solidarity both at the domestic and multilateral level have gained huge importance across the world. Globalization and the resulting economic liberalization have opened up an array of challenges before the developed and less developed economies that are involved in international trade. One of the major challenges that are crucial in the context of relatively backward economies is that the macroeconomic policies of these countries are not always proportionate to utilize the gains from world trade. International trade can be beneficial if the gains derived from it can be distributed evenly across the different layers of the society. Here lies the importance of "trickle-down" effect.

Domestic trade involves exchange of factors of production at the regional level; whereas international trade ensures greater mobility of latest technology and goods and services across the nations. World trade helps the developing countries to have ready access to the modern techniques of production. However, the challenge here is to use these techniques in an efficient manner. The industrial setup and social infrastructure need to be developed as per the global standard to optimize the benefits from international trade.

There are instances of African nations, which have failed to utilize the gains from trade due to inappropriate macroeconomic setups. Before opening up the economy, the backward nations need to safeguard the interests of the domestic entrepreneurs. The liberalization policies need to be taken up gradually so as to help the infant industries face the challenges of the changing economic scenario. So the challenges before international trade may arise from different fronts. The countries involved in world trade need to adopt proportionate policy measures to make use of the gains from trade for the overall development of their economies.

A number of other multilateral tools have been developed over the years. The expert group of the United Nations Conference on Trade and Development (UNCTAD) has developed a set of principles and rules to govern the conduct of governments and businesses in regard to the international control of restrictive trade practices, consultation and cooperation. For its part, the OECD has developed the *Revised Recommendation Concerning Co-operation between Member Countries on Anticompetitive Practices Affecting International Trade* and the *Council Recommendation Concerning Effective Action against Hard Core Cartels.* These instruments are useful references for encouraging cooperative efforts between competition authorities. However, their scope is largely restricted to the members of these organizations, and compliance remains essentially voluntary and often uneven. Nonetheless, efforts are still being made to develop greater convergence and cooperation among the various competition agencies around the world. Special attention is being given to integrating the developing economies and to increasing the operational capabilities of the new agencies.

Some initiatives deserve mention here (Dominique Burlone: http://www.apeccp.org.tw/doc/Canada/Policy/1b.htm)

- A considerable amount of work being done within such regional and international organizations as the OECD, UNCTAD, the WTO and Asia-Pacific Economic Cooperation (APEC) is making it possible to more clearly identify, explain and disseminate best practices associated with the enforcement of competition laws, and to have a better understanding of the issues arising at the interface between competition policy and trade.
- A chapter on competition within the FTAA, which is presently being

negotiated, might eventually lead to a hemisphere-wide competition framework for the Americas.
- The creation of a worldwide discussion forum has recently been proposed, which would bring together competition authorities from the industrialized world and from the world of developing countries, and also representatives of various stakeholder groups.

The discussions on competition policy within the OECD have allowed, and continue to foster, greater convergence among the leading developed countries that have well-established systems and institutions.

The Rationale for a Multilateral Approach

The multilateral path is a complex and lengthy process. The Kennedy Round took five years, the Tokyo Round went for seven and the Uruguay Round ran for almost eight—double the original target. Negotiations of this duration are a heavy commitment, but testify to the fact that the parties see the rewards as justifying the effort. This is not surprising when one looks at the history. The eight multilateral trade negotiating rounds over the past fifty years have transformed a protectionist post-war environment to a much freer trading world, with tariffs on manufactures alone cut by an average of 90 per cent (http://www.dfat.gov.au/media/speeches/department/990428_mtn_challenge.html). Through the development of contractual rules, the trading system is much less vulnerable to economic shocks. Global trade has expanded dramatically, increasing fifteen-fold since 1960. This helped quadruple world economic production and more than double world per capita income over that period. The GATT, now WTO, system has been a fundamental underpinning of post-war economic growth.

The following Para explains the nature and extent of negative influences of Trade barriers in maintaining regulated Food safety Standards in the International market and trading systems.

Trade Barriers and Food-Safety Standards

International trade in agricultural and food products remains one of the most sensitive issues in the commercial relations of nations. For agricultural products, the principal traditional issues are: the lack of market access caused by tariffs and tariff rate quotas; the levels and nature of domestic support, much of which is still provided through trade-distorting instruments; and assistance to exports in the form of subsidies. There remains a considerable gulf between governments on each of these topics in the current trade negotiations taking place in the World Trade Organization (WTO). Trade in agricultural products is also curtailed by sanitary and phyto-sanitary (SPS) barriers but, since the introduction of the WTO Agreement on the Application of Sanitary and Phyto-sanitary Measures in 1995, with a few exceptions (e.g., the Canada-Australia salmon case), there does not appear to have been too much disharmony in the context of reducing tensions in the areas of plant health and animal health. Indeed, in the current negotiations, there have been no proposals to re-open the Agreement on those grounds (IATRC, 2001). For International trade in food products, food safety (and quality) is perhaps the major issue, although disquiet in developing countries about the continued use by developed countries of escalating tariffs, remains important. In the context of food safety, the SPS Agreement has been less successful in resolving disagreements (e.g., the EU-U.S. beef hormones case) because of the fundamental tension that exists between consumers' preferences and consumer protection on the one hand and consumers' gains from trade on the other (IATRC, 2001). Moreover, the Agreement was motivated originally by the need to constrain the protection afforded to producers from import barriers and not by protection for consumers from imports (Perdikis *et al.*, 2001).

It is clear from the various negotiating proposals which have been put forward to the WTO Committee on Agriculture as part of the agricultural negotiations, that food safety, as well as other aspects of food (e.g., geographic indications, shelf-life labelling and GM foods), is regarded as an important "non-trade' concern by a number of countries. With the rapid pace of technological change in the food processing industry, with improved transportation and with increasingly international supply chains, the perception is growing that imported food may be a source of increased health risks for food consumers. The erection of import barriers by governments to regulate that risk and to secure the health of their human populations is also governed by the SPS Agreement. It is important to make a distinction between the objectives of trade negotiations in the traditional areas and those on SPS matters. In the former, the aim is to secure a movement towards freer international markets by reducing trade barriers in order to increase national incomes everywhere: in the latter, the aim is to define a set of standards or regulations which will be minimally trade distorting but which will yet achieve different countries' social objectives about the extent to which their citizens are exposed to unsafe or low-quality foods. In the context of the traditional areas, the welfare gains from trade liberalization are assumed to apply generally, as a principle, across all products and all countries; in the second, because of market failure, the welfare gains need to be evaluated on a case-by-case basis without there being any presumption of general application (MacLaren,D: (http://rspas.anu.edu.au/economics/publish/papers/aciar/aciar_2002_mclaren.pdf).

In matters to do with sanitary and phyto-sanitary measures, the issue is the extent to which individual governments should be constrained in defining their domestic regulations; regulations which may reduce the benefits from trade for other countries should such regulations prove to be unnecessarily strict. The onus appears to be on the importing countries to define their barriers to imports in a way which is consistent with the Agreement; there does not appear to be any requirement, other than commercial self-interest, on exporting countries to ensure that the food which they export is safe (Charnovitz, 2002). The SPS Agreement curtails not only what a government may do 'at the border', the traditional view of trade policy, but also what a government may do.

The *Codex Alimentarius* Commission has produced a Code of Ethics for International Trade in Food, one of the principles in which is that no food should be in international trade which contains anything injurious to health (Charnovitz, 2002). Hence, the SPS Agreement is a substantial departure from the original activities of the GATT which stopped at national borders. In the traditional areas of trade negotiations for agricultural products it is assumed that there are no market failures. In the area of food safety, there is a potentially serious market failure in the form of imperfect information amongst consumers in importing countries. The implications of imperfect and asymmetric information are outlined. The SPS Agreement is underpinned by standards which are defined by one of three international organizations or through a risk assessment undertaken by a national government. For internationally recognized standards dealing food safety and human health, the relevant organization is the *Codex Alimentarius* Commission (CODEX). The key elements of the Agreement are explained (Section 3).One element of the risk assessment undertaken by the *Codex Alimentarius* Commission or by national governments is estimation of the probabilities of certain risks. However, the way in which these probabilities are used in assessing the risks involved in consuming a particular food product and in defining the risk management strategy, may not be appropriate. An elaboration of this observation is provided.

To sum up it can be stated that barriers to international trade in agricultural and food products exist for several reasons, one of which is to ensure food safety. Food safety is credence characteristic and this attribute causes market failure through imperfect and asymmetric information. One way in which government intervention in importing countries can improve upon the market outcome is to impose trade regulations as a way of providing the missing information. Any such regulations need to be consistent with the SPS Agreement. It is also in the interests of governments in exporting countries to overcome the market failure by putting in place regulations to ensure that their exports of food meet minimum levels of food safety. The issue for them is whether their regulations should be enforced through public or private agencies. Because of the credence characteristic of food safety, it is not possible for private firms credibly to commit to the provision of high-quality food exports in the absence of regulation.

In the application of the SPS Agreement to the area of consumer health and food safety, there is no scope for consumers' preferences to be taken into account. The consistency of import regulations is based on risk assessment involving only estimates of probabilities. There is no place for consumers' preferences about risk or for economic considerations. This omission is perhaps the outcome of the original negotiations based upon pragmatism and the need to get agreement but it is an inherently unsatisfactory aspect of the Agreement. A better approach would be to incorporate consumers' preferences and nonadditive probabilities into a more comprehensive decision-making framework. The link between food-safety standards, trade barriers and the gains from trade would then be better defined.

Trade Integration and Food-Security

According to FAO (FAO—Regionalism & Food Security, http://www.fao.org/docrep/004/y4793e/y4793e09.htm) Food security will be affected by international trade in general and agricultural trade in particular. To the extent (a) that increased intra-regional trade fosters economic growth and increases employment prospects and the income-earning capacities of the poor, it will enhance access to food. The lesson from Chapter 2 is that whether regional integration promotes overall economic growth will depend on the design of the agreement, and whether it succeeds in promoting more trade creation rather than trade diversion. Increased intra-regional agricultural trade could also promote food security in two further ways: (b) by augmenting domestic food supplies to meet consumption needs and (c) by reducing overall food supply variability.

To evaluate the food security effects of RTAs, however, a more nuanced analysis is required. Lower trade barriers generate the potential for trade creation. However, potential beneficiaries of regional integration among low-income farm households may be unable to take advantage of increased market access opportunities in the presence of supply-side constraints. Accompanying measures may be needed to assist them to increase both the volume and quality of their output to take advantage of the market opportunities created. This implies the need for targeted interventions focused on training of and investment by low-income farm households in the context of regional integration strategies. This will be particularly important in Africa where increasing numbers of small-scale farmers have withdrawn from market production in the wake of domestic liberalization.

There will also be those who either fall behind or lose out in the regional integration process. Thus, while trade integration may contribute positively to higher production and output growth, if those who lose out are concentrated disproportionately among food-insecure households, then the overall impact on food insecurity in the short run may be negative. In countries with dualistic agricultural structures, it may be the larger commercial farms already well-integrated into food markets which benefit, while semi-subsistence smallholders are simply too constrained to take advantage of the new market opportunities and may even lose out from greater import competition on the domestic market.

In the context of developed countries, that analysis of the distributional effects of regional integration for farm households is a new research topic with, at present, few definitive answers. He argues that how a farm household will fare following integration depends on both its commodity exposure and its asset exposure (its tenure situation and the sector specificity and diversification of its assets). The risks of trade integration point to the need for country-specific and region-specific evaluations of market integration on the overall status of food insecure households. Where supply constraints are identified, regional integration strategies should include investment and training interventions to address these constraints, including technology transfer and rural extension; new production alternatives, labor training on new farming practices and for off-farm activities; and possible ways to integrate smallholders with more commercial farm enterprises. Where negative impacts are identified, then a regional integration strategy which is food-security aware should be accompanied by flanking measures to address these negative impacts.

Regional Cooperation and Food-Security

Because regionalism, especially among developing countries, was seen as an instrument of industrialization in the past, there is relatively little literature on its potential to contribute to food security. Thus recent thinking in both FAO and the EU Commission on how regional initiatives can promote food security is of particular interest.

Regional Strategies

FAO has developed its ideas in the context of the Regional Strategies for Agricultural Development and Food Security and the follow-up Regional Programs for Food Security (RPFS) which twelve regional economic groups have prepared with FAO assistance. The Regional Strategies were based on the key policy recommendations emerging from the World Food Summit follow-up Strategy Papers on National Agricultural Development prepared by the individual members of each grouping. They identify areas requiring investment and technical support for agricultural development and food security, including the national Special Program for Food Security in those countries where it is operative. The Regional Programs (RPFS) are designed to implement the key elements in the Regional Strategies and usually consist of three components:

- trade facilitation
- harmonization of national agricultural policies
- support to the national Special Programs for Food Security

The trade facilitation component generally includes proposals to support modernizing food safety control systems and standards, standardizing phyto-sanitary and zoo-sanitary standards, promotion of intra-regional trade through identification of trade barriers, preparation of development programs for major export commodities, review of the impact of implementing the relevant WTO Marrakech Agreements and assistance in participating in the current WTO negotiations. Under the other two headings, support is envisaged to identify investment programs and to prepare feasibility studies of bankable investment proposals. In addition, agricultural policy assistance is envisaged both to strengthen each regional grouping (and especially its capacity to formulate a common agricultural policy for the region and to monitor and contribute to the investment strategy envisaged under the RPFS) as well as to support individual ministries, public institutions and those responsible in civil society for agricultural development.

Effect of Negotiations on International Trade Agreements

Globalization and Legal Harmonization

(A) Economic and Legal Integration

The globalization phenomenon that is currently reshaping our world and way of life is a multifaceted concept. While it encompasses a wide range of human activities such as employment, technology, finance, business, politics, environment, culture and entertainment, it primarily refers to an economic process related to a world-wide integration of markets. Economic integration is basically the process of eliminating discrimination, through the mechanism of free trade, among the economies of a group a countries.

The effort was first initiated after World War II with the creation of the Bretton Woods institutions and the General Agreement on Tariffs and Trade (GATT), which has fostered unprecedented trade liberalization at the global scale through eight rounds of multilateral trade negotiations. The end of the Cold War and the collapse of the communist system then contributed to the consolidation of the global economic regime. Indeed, the conclusion of the Uruguay Round represented an enormous step along in the path of worldwide trade liberalization and a consecration of multilateralism that materialized in the creation of the World Trade Organization (WTO) in 1995, the first post-Cold War global institution. Liberal economic policies, international trade and new technologies of communication have progressively converged towards the establishment of a multi-level integrated world system.

Multilateral economic integration is regulated through the GATT-WTO framework that constitutes the basic set of rules regulating the global trading order, its core principles being non-discrimination, reciprocity and transparency. However, numerous states are also members of regional trading agreements, i.e. geographically discriminatory arrangements among a subset of countries, which in fact discriminate trade of non-members. A special provision was made with GATT Article XXIV to allow for the existence of these agreements inconsistent with the non-discrimination principle. Those regional trading agreements are varied in structure, level of integration and significance, as are the motives for creating such groupings. However, they have been multiplying and nearly all of the WTO's members have now concluded such arrangements with other countries. Most notably, the countries of the Americas have been particularly active in establishing a multitude of bilateral and regional trade agreements amongst them.

A form of macro-level regulatory convergence among a subset of countries will happen through the implementation of commitments undertaken through negotiations aiming at the closure of a multilateral trade round or at the establishment of a regional free trade or other preferential agreements. But as processes of economic integration go deeper among a subset of countries, a certain degree of concrete "bottom-level" legal harmonization also becomes highly desirable or even necessary in order to benefit from the commercial advantages spurred by such integration. Any integrated system requires a certain co-ordination and legal uniformity at the domestic level in order to function effectively, and this facilitates exchanges between private parties located in different jurisdictions and other transnational business activities. In other words, a certain level of legal integration should follow economic integration.

B. Harmonization

Harmonization processes are varied and can take many forms, at the domestic, international, or multilateral level. For instance, such a process can be embodied in (a) the revision of a national code (e.g. Mexico modernizing and harmonizing the *Código Comercial* and related statutes, or the National Commissioners on Uniform State Laws and the American Law Institute working on revisions of the *Uniform Commercial Code* (UCC)), (b) the creation of an international code such as the *Convention on the International Sales of Goods* (CISG by UNICTRAL), (c) an international restatement such as the UNIDROIT *Principles of International Commercial Contracts*, (d) the adoption of regional choice of law conventions such as the Rome Convention (1980 *European Convention on the Law Applicable to Contractual Obligations*) or the Mexico City Convention (1994 *Inter-American Convention on the Law Applicable to International Contracts*), (e) the adoption of uniform private rules such as the *Uniform Customs and Practices on Documentary Credits* (UCP), and (f) the universal adoption of arbitral regimes in commercial disputes.

The more radical form of legal integration is uniformization, which the legal technique is seeking to erase the differences between the national provisions by replacing them with a unique and identical text for all the states involved in the legal integration process. Two possibilities then follow: the text is submitted to national parliaments who may adopt it as is, modify it or even reject it, or the adopted text contains the principle of supra-nationality, by which the uniform norm is directly integrated into the domestic legal order.

Harmonization is a less radical technique than pure uniformization. It basically consists of modifying domestic provisions from various countries that are not similar in order to make them all coherent, or update them with a reform. Therefore, while respecting the particularities of various national legal regimes, harmonization permits to reduce their differences in specific areas, or to promote increased legal cooperation between the countries[1] . Generally, such a result is obtained through the directives or recommendations adopted by an international organization who then directs them to its member states for implementation. Member states remain free to choose the form of adoption of the new instruments, as long as the result is the incorporation of the new harmonized norm (of course, provided that there is sufficient incentive to do so), thus leaving much more flexibility.

Since the advent of modern international trade, efforts towards the international unification of law have essentially taken the form of binding instruments, such as supranational legislation or binding international conventions. However, despite some successes, the majority of bilateral or multilateral treaties of unification or harmonization have generally not been very effective, as demonstrated by their subsequent limited use. It seems that the development of a truly successful harmonized solution does not fit with the rigidity of the traditional treaty-making process, where unification cannot go beyond the terms of the treaty and amendments are difficult to adopt. But calls have been increasingly made for recourse to non-legislative or non-binding means of unification or harmonization of law, for example, through model laws or model clauses and contracts formulated on the basis of current trade practices, or even through international restatement of general principles of some particular legal domain, such as the *UNIDROIT Principles of International Commercial Contracts* for contract law, which have been very successful. As levels of integration deepen, increased legal convergence would become useful for the Americas, specifically through processes of informal harmonization. Informal harmonization may consists merely in a new awareness among the participants to a new initiative, but generally refers to the development of new soft law, i.e. non-binding instruments such as model laws, codes of conduct, guiding principles, etc., which presents the advantage of flexibility.

Standardization in International Business Law

In a strict definition, business law generally refers to commercial law. However, if taken in a broader context, business law includes many other areas relating to the regulations applicable to all economic activities (production, distribution, consumption), such as its legal framework (antitrust and competition, credit), its actors (businessman, companies, agents) and the corresponding goods and services. Therefore, under the general term business law could be included legal areas such as commercial law, law of sales, company laws, labor law, competition law, securities, bankruptcy law, debt collection, enforcement law, accounting, arbitration, etc., in short, all the legislation relating to the economic environment.

International business transactions are complex operations that involve identifying and coordinating many issues such as the corporate, antitrust/ competition, tax, and regulatory requirements in different countries and multinational jurisdictions. A broad range of legal sub-topics can arise in the course of closing such a transaction. For instance, the determination of the structure of the proposed investment (asset vs. share investment, setting up branches or foreign subsidiary, franchising or joint venturing, mergers and acquisitions, international project financing and cross-border lending), the selection of international representation (international agency and distributorship law), taking into account foreign domestic considerations such as securities regulations, protection of intellectual property rights, regulations applicable to consumer contracts, international technology transfers, etc. Other concerns relate to choosing the applicable law and jurisdiction, and international commercial arbitration.

Basically, issues arising can be grouped into three different sections: transactional issues, litigation issues, and regulatory issues. Transactional issues to take into account will include, for instance, those related to agency and distributorship law, sale of goods and services and letters of credit, international contract problems, regulation of international trade including customs law, cross-border mergers and acquisitions, project financing and structure of the foreign investment. Litigation matters will arise in connection to choice of law and forum issues, force majeure events or ex-propriatory conduct, foreign domestic rules of procedure and evidence, enforcement of judgements, sovereign immunity and international commercial arbitration. Regulatory issues facing international business are also very important since they relate to the wide scope of regulations in connection with trade transactions and financing (bank, securities, etc.), tax regimes, bankruptcy and competition or antitrust law in an international economy. International instruments seeking to harmonize some of the aspects of cross-border transaction issues may then cover a wide range of topics, establishing new substantive and/or procedural norms for international transactional, litigation or regulatory issues.

Business-to-Business (B2B) Negotiation

Conservative advances to business-to-business negotiations for import and export make use of primary terms like order quantity or price analysis without paying due attention to deeper negotiation terms including resource management and corporate culture. Furthermore, B2B negotiation asks for a practical framework whereby past negotiation databank is reused to carry out critical analysis. A historical case study of B2B negotiations facilitates their implementation to current import/export problems with B2B ahead of decision-making to simulate various instances of negotiation. A structured approach must be used for evaluating the validity of any purported possibility established on B2B negotiation experts' opinions. Going by statistical tests, the planned framework could be applied to significantly improve the performance of decision in B2B negotiations. Global sourcing customers react to hard B2B negotiations circumstances when confronted by "take-it or leave-it" B2B offers from solitary source providers. So, an automated business to business (B2B) negotiation solution is the pressing need of the hour to overcome B2B monopoly.

Flexibility in B2B for Channelized Global Sourcing

Conservative advances to business-to-business negotiations for import and export make use of primary terms like order quantity or price analysis without paying due attention to deeper negotiation terms including resource management and corporate culture. Furthermore, B2B negotiation asks for a practical framework whereby past negotiation databank is reused to carry out critical analysis. A historical case study of B2B negotiations facilitates their implementation to current import/export problems with B2B ahead of decision-making to simulate various instances of negotiation. A structured approach must be used for evaluating the validity of any purported possibility established on B2B negotiation experts' opinions. Going by statistical tests, the planned framework could be applied to significantly improve the performance of decision in B2B negotiations. Global sourcing customers react to hard B2B negotiations circumstances when confronted by "take-it or leave-it" B2B offers from solitary source providers. So, an automated business-to-business (B2B) negotiation solution is the pressing need of the hour to overcome B2B monopoly.

International and Regional Agencies for Trade Negotiations

There are various established International as well as Regional Agencies that are actively involved as mediators to effect and facilitate Trade and allied negotiations. The following section highlights the core activities of some such Agencies.

Agency for International Trade Information and Cooperation (AITIC)

http://www.acici.org/aitic/index.html

The Agency for International Trade Information and Cooperation is an intergovernmental organization that aims to help less-advantaged countries (LACs) by assisting them in taking a more active part in the work of the World Trade Organization (WTO) and other trade-related organizations in Geneva, as well as the negotiations under the auspices of the former. The website features the Trade Portal which provides info on WTO trade topics and legal texts; preferential and regional trade agreements; international conventions, rules and model laws; trade and development-related sites; development agencies and regional development banks; training and technical assistance; statistics and data; news sources; reference tools and more. Furthermore, AITIC offers Background Notes; Information Briefs and Reports on Meetings.

Bilaterals

http://www.bilaterals.org/

Bilaterals is a web site critical to bilateral trade and investment agreements and offers a wide range of background information on ongoing negotiations, recently finalized agreements, as well as agreements already in work. The Negotiations webpage of Bilaterals offers news and analyses about major bilateral and regional agreements currently under negotiation; including implications and impact, who is pursuing what, etc. Once signed, the texts of the agreements can be found under "Treaties and Agreements."

Centre for Socio-Economic Development (CSEND)

http://www.csend.org

The Centre for Socio-Economic Development works to strengthen public administrations and public-sector enterprises by designing and implementing comprehensive institution development and capacity-building projects. Diplomacy Dialogue is a branch of CSEND that aims at to open channels for dialogue and participation amongst stakeholders involved in public concerns with the aim to resolve conflicts, may they be commercial, economic, communal or political, through dialogue, diplomacy and negotiations; and to promote equitable, sustainable and integrated development.

DilploFoundation

http://www.diplomacy.edu/

The DilploFoundation offers courses, tools, web sites, and publications and references on several aspects of diplomacy. It features the *DiploPortals*, a series of web portals with the objective of furnishing the diplomatic community with a stream of up-to-date knowledge on various facets of diplomacy and international relations. Selected portals are DiploKnowledge which offers definitions and useful references on the use of knowledge management in diplomacy and DiploTools which offers a set of software applications custom designed for diplomats and others who work in international relations. The applications are intended to assist with the preservation, management and sharing of information and knowledge.

Economic Diplomacy

http://textus.diplomacy.edu/textusBin/BViewers/oview/Economic Diplomacy/oview.asp

This portal explores the multiple dimensions of modern economic diplomacy as a component of international relations. The portal's principal content is derived from a book on the economic aspects of diplomatic activity, Last updated April 2006 published by the DiploFoundation. Chapters 4 'Economics and Diplomacy' and 5 'Trade, Investment, Aid and Technology' are available. The web page offers a wide array of references and resources topics such as trade and export promotion; aid diplomacy; multilateral economic diplomacy; as well as practitioner's accounts and country's experiences.

Economic Negotiation Network

http://www-rcf.usc.edu/~enn/

The Economic Negotiation Network is an informal network of scholars, officials and others who share an interest in explaining, generalizing about, and improving negotiations concerning international trade, finance, investment, migration, or the environment. Its focus is on the process of international negotiation on economic or environmental issues. The website offers links to other sources, a selected bibliography and contact details of members.

Global Trade Negotiations Homepage
http://www.cid.harvard.edu/cidtrade/

The Global Trade Negotiations Homepage of the Centre for International Development at Harvard University provides a centralized information resource on global trade negotiations. It gathers and disseminates information and research on the multilateral trade system.

Institute for Trade and Commercial Diplomacy (ITCD)
http://www.commercialdiplomacy.org/index.html

The Institute for Trade and Commercial Diplomacy promotes training in commercial diplomacy by developing and disseminating training materials and by assisting the establishment of a global network of training programmes in the field. The website offers commercial diplomacy dictionaries; trade policy articles; instructional modules; case studies; simulated cases; news and relevant links. Access is free, but registration is required.

International Centre for Trade and Sustainable Development (ICTSD)
http://www.ictsd.org/issarea/dsu/index.htm

The International Centre for Trade and Sustainable Development contributes to a better understanding of development and environment concerns in the context of international trade. The Dispute Settlement website presents news and analysis on WTO disputes between the crux of trade and sustainable development, resources and events, regional dispute settlement news and updates.

Processes of International Negotiation Network (PIN)
http://www.iiasa.ac.at/Research/PIN/index.html?sb=1

The Processes of International Negotiation Network is a group of international scholars whose secretariat is based at the International Institute for Applied Systems Analysis (IIASA), a non-governmental research organization. The network organizes and conducts research on a broad spectrum of topics related to the theory and application of negotiation in various fields. The network seeks to broaden dissemination of new knowledge about negotiation; develop networks of interested scholars and practitioners; and further the improved study and practice of negotiation.

UNCTAD, Trade Negotiations and Commercial Diplomacy Branch (TNCDB)
http://www.unctad.org/Templates/StartPage.asp?intItemID=1917&lang=1

The Trade Negotiations and Commercial Diplomacy Branch contributes to maximizing the trade and development prospects of developing countries and economies in transition, assisting them in integration into the globalizing and liberalizing world economy and the international trading system, and effectively implementing the Millennium Declaration commitment "to an open, equitable, rule-based, predictable, and non-discriminatory multilateral trading and financial system". TNCDB offers technical assistance and capacity building, access to training modules and publications, as well as various reports.

World Trade Law net's Dispute Settlement Commentary (DSC)
http://www.worldtradelaw.net/

The Dispute Settlement Commentary service is a comprehensive legal research tool for WTO dispute settlement. Features include summary/analysis of all reports/arbitrations; up-to-date keyword index; and a database of dispute settlement tables/statistics. Parts of the website are accessible for paying subscribers only, however, there are a number of free resources on trade law cases and agreements, including GATT/WTO dispute settlement reports; Last updated April 2006. GATT/WTO legal texts; frequently used Uruguay Round agreements and other legal texts; WTO negotiating history; bilateral and regional trade agreements; and a discussion forum.

Regional Trade Agreements (RTAs)

The Rationale for a Multilateral Approach

The multilateral path is a complex and lengthy process. The Kennedy Round took five years, the Tokyo Round went for seven and the Uruguay Round ran for almost eight—double the original target. Negotiations of this duration are a heavy commitment, but testify to the fact that the parties see the rewards as justifying the effort. This is not surprising when one looks at the history. The eight multilateral trade negotiating rounds over the past fifty years have transformed a protectionist post-war environment to a much freer trading world, with tariffs on manufactures alone cut by an average of 90 per cent. Through the development of contractual rules, the trading system is much less vulnerable to economic shocks. Global trade has expanded dramatically, increasing fifteen-fold since 1960. This helped quadruple world economic production and more than double world per capita income over that period. The GATT, now WTO, system has been a fundamental underpinning of post-war economic growth (http://www.dfat.gov.au/media/speeches/department/990428_mtn_challenge.html).

Total number of notified regional trade agreement (RTAs) increased to 177 in December 2002 Most WTO members are now party to at least one RTA, and many to several. Almost half of the world trade in now conducted under RTAs (Das, 2004). In February 1996, the WTO General Council set up a single committee to oversee all RTAs, replacing separate "working parties", each dealing with a separate agreement. It was called the Regional Trade Agreement Committee (RTAC). Issues in the on-going regional debate are complex. Some are primarily legal, while others are institutional. More importantly, several issues have an economic dimension. The RTA debates is concerned with the question of the impact of regional agreements on the future shape of the world trade, given the large and increasing number of RTAs and their overlapping membership. In the foreseeable future, RTAs will be one of the biggest challenges facing the policy-making community in all continents. The relationship between regionalism and multilateralism has continued to be a critical systemic issue. The Doha mandate on RTAs is to clarify and improve disciplines and procedures under the existing WTO provisions applying to RTAs. The Negotiating Group on Rules set up in February 2002, noted in the preceding paragraph, and organized a seminar on regionalism in April 2002 in Geneva. It helped raise awareness of the significance of regional agreements in world trade. A listing of all the RTA related issues raised in various WTO councils and committees was prepared in August 2002. The RTAC would aid the work of Negotiating Group on Rules on RTAs. The Negotiating Group on Rules decided to address the procedural issues (like transparency) first and the systemic issues later. It has identified four systemic issues for early consideration (http://www.cid.harvard.edu/cidtrade/Papers/das2003.pdf).

A good deal of work was to be done on trade and environment related issues. The WTO members agreed to start negotiations on trade and environment linkage at Doha. It was decided that the future focus of these negotiations would be specific and cover the following four areas: (1) clarification of the relationship between WTO rules and specific trade obligations set out in the multilateral environment agreements (MEAs), (2) exchange of information between the WTO and MEA secretariats, (3) the norms and criteria for granting observer status to other international organizations, and (4) liberalization of trade in environmental goods and services. These negotiations have been in progress in the special sessions of the Trade and Environment Committee (TEC).

Regional trade agreements (RTAs) have emerged as an alternative to achieve trade liberalization as multilateral efforts have faced political and economic obstacles. The difficulties of reaching agreements on sensitive issues like agriculture and services have been evident in the Doha Round. The previous rounds were also marked by complex and slow negotiation processes. For one, as the number of participants' increases, it has been more difficult to address each country's demands for special considerations.

RTAs convey advantages as well as limitations. By reducing the numbers of participants in the negotiation they can help expand the discussion to include more dimensions of economic integration. Compared with unilateral liberalization, political support for RTAs also seems to be greater given the perception of reciprocity from other member countries. However, since the early work of Viner (1950), these benefits have been weighted against distortions that RTAs can create. By *de facto* discriminating against nonmembers, RTAs distort resource allocation, favoring regional producers to the potential detriment of local consumers. Recent research also emphasizes the global consequences of multiple and overlapping RTAs in terms of the transaction costs they impose (Feridhanusetyawan, 2005).

Although RTAs have varied components, these agreements include some or all of the following eight elements. Bhagwati and Panagariya (1996) provide an overview of RTA 's functional modalities: (i) a tariff liberalization program—TLP (transformation of nontariff barriers, e.g. quotas, to their tariff equivalent and the sequential reduction of tariffs; special considerations to least developed countries4 are not uncommon); (ii) sensitive lists (goods or services to be exempt from the tariff reduction program); (iii) rules of origin—ROO (prevention of the application of the preferential tariffs to non regional goods or services as defined by the agreement); (iv) Institutional arrangements (establishment of a council or administrative committee responsible for the administration and implementation of the agreement); (v) trade facilitation policies (collection of instruments to reduce transaction costs of importing and their degree of trade barrier reductions. RTAs refer to agreements involving regional partners. Free Trade Agreements (FTAs) refers to agreements that includes the full elimination of tariffs (and trade barriers) while Preferential Trade Agreements (PTAs) refer to agreements involving partial tariff elimination. For example, SAPTA is South Asia's PTA and SAFTA is South Asia's FTA exporting, including homogenization of customs practices and technical assistance specially to the least-developed members); (vi) dispute settlement mechanism (procedures to report and deal with violations to the agreement); (vii) safeguards measures (suspension of preferential treatment on grounds that imports are causing or threatening to cause serious injury to the domestic industrial base); and (viii) parallel reduction in foreign investment barriers and/or trade in services.

South Asia (Bangladesh, Bhutan, India, Maldives, Nepal, Pakistan and Sri Lanka) has been involved in setting up its own RTA. The South Asian Association for Regional Cooperation (SAARC) was formed in 1985 with the objective of exploiting "accelerated economic growth, social progress and cultural development in the region" for the welfare of the peoples of South Asia (SAARC Secretariat, 2006). In 1995, its corresponding RTA (SAPTA) came into force. South Asian Free Trade Agreement (SAFTA) has been ratified and entered into force in mid-2006.

Extending SAFTA toward other Blocs

Two features of South Asian countries' trade pattern generate the result that looking outside the region to form RTAs would be beneficial. First, except for Bhutan and Nepal, South Asian countries rely more heavily on non regional partners for their trade relations. Second, on average, South Asian countries have a more restrictive trade policy toward non-regional partners. In fact, three out of the seven countries apply lower tariffs to SAFTA members than to any other bloc. The results of the simulation are provided for three indicators (trade flows, trade balance and customs revenue) for South Asia as an aggregate and for individual countries in South Asia. The relative attractiveness of each hypothetical RTA varies across individual countries.

Trade agreements with NAFTA, EU or ASEAN would generate higher trade flows than candidate for SA further liberalization efforts (Baysan *et al*, 2006)—would likely generate smaller trade flows than NAFTA or EU. Once again an important determinant is the fact that current trade relations with the European Union and NAFTA are of greater importance than bilateral flows with ASEAN members; however, an additional factor worth further exploration is the similarity between the main exports and imports of South Asia and ASEAN's members that would make their offerings of goods and services substitutes rather than complements.

Negotiating RTAs usually involve the conciliation of differing interests of member countries and the simulations show that deciding on new trading partners is no exception. For some of these countries (especially Bhutan and Nepal) regional trade is their main commercial channel, and SAFTA represents the highest increase in trade flows they could expect to obtain from a menu of RTAs. Maldives is an interesting case due to the unusual importance of ASEAN countries in its trade flows, and would experience the highest increase in trade flows from an expansion to this bloc. If the objective of a country was to minimize trade imbalances, SA + NAFTA would receive support from Bangladesh, Sri Lanka, and the Maldives; SAFTA would be favored by India and Pakistan.

Regional trade agreements have been, and will likely remain, an important tool for trade liberalization. While theory is skeptic about RTAs, most empirical studies find that trade creation dominates trade diversion. In practice several factors increase the benefits of RTAs, including large and diverse membership, low external most-favored-nation tariffs, comprehensiveness, liberal rules of origin, and trade facilitation measures. On these grounds, SAFTA offers room for improvement. Restrictive rules of origin, extensive sensitive lists and uncoordinated efforts currently threaten to limit the trade potential of the region. SAPTA was a clear example of the limitations of imposing restrictive rules of origin as well as of the negative role played by exclusion lists that in some cases covered the vast majority of the existing trade (Baysan *et al*, 2006). The India-Sri Lanka FTA suffered similar restrictions and yet has significantly increased trade between India and Sri Lanka, showing the vast potential of unexplored commercial linkages.

Not all RTAs are created equal. They vary in terms of their capacity to generate additional trade, overall economic integration, and distribution of benefits among members. Focusing on the tariff reduction component of RTAs, South Asian benefits would be distributed toward the smallest countries. There is also evidence that extending SAFTA to other RTAs including NAFTA, EU, Plus 3 or ASEAN confers benefits. There are important additional gains from pursuing a coordinated approach to deeper economic integration. Some of South Asian's members are currently pursuing individual trade agreements with NAFTA and with other Asian countries, however the added complexity of cascading trade barriers could turn this approach into a losing proposition for not only the region as a whole but also for, ironically, the very negotiating countries (World Bank, 2004).

Multilateral Agreements under RTA

The influence of special interest groups is, however, more dominant in RTAs versus multilateral negotiations, resulting in sensitive trade areas being left out of RTAs completely. The major driver for the use of RTAs as a trade policy tool is the relative speed and flexibility possible in their negotiation. The appeal of RTAs is evident in their proliferation over the last 13 years. The WTO (established 1995) has been notified of close to 300 RTAs, as compared to the GATT's 47-year existence when notifications only numbered 124. Currently, there have been over 400 regional trade agreement notifications sent to the WTO and 230 in force. The United States has 14 trade agreements (TAs) in place, with four additional agreements under negotiation. In order to maintain of multilateral trade talks at the WTO, the Doha Round, has stalled. Disagreements over domestic agricultural subsidies blocked an agreement in July, 2006.

In 2007, no agreement was reached due to conflicts regarding opening agricultural and industrial markets and farm subsidies of developed nations. A disagreement over a Special Safeguard Mechanism requested by certain developing countries blocked an agreement in July 2008. While multilateral trade agreements may be considered a better tool for reducing discriminatory trade practices and encouraging governance reform among member countries, current talks remain stalled.

However, in the interest of producers, it is important to continue talks. Of particular importance to the globally significant agricultural sector, is that such negotiations are critical to open and expanded trade relations. While multilateral negotiations are currently stalled, the opportunity exists for continued trade development at the bilateral and regional level. While not a substitute for multilateral negotiations, development can continue through regional trade agreements (RTAs) with fewer complications in the negotiations. Virtually all members of the WTO use regional trade agreements as a trade policy tool. Such Agreements allow countries to open their markets to one another through the granting of preferential access. These regional agreements are used as a policy tool in addition to multilateral trade liberalization is usually the first casualty of a recession. There has been a proliferation of Regional/Bilateral Trade Agreements (RTA's) in recent years. Are these a substitute for multilateral liberalization?

Regional Trade Agreements (RTAs) have become an integral feature of today's international trading system. Their proliferation in the past decade has led to the prominence of such agreements in recent trade discussions, thereby making the topic a very pertinent one to discuss. However, in order to deepen the debate, one should first explore the degrees of integration of RTAs. The main types include Free Trade Areas (FTAs), Customs Unions, Common Markets, and Economic Unions. While exploring these trade tools, an interesting question emerges: which method is best suited to achieving the generally agreed upon maxim of Free Trade? The most recent trend is the movement to ever greater economic integration, as in the EU. Nevertheless, the United States, the world's largest economy, seems to prefer a network of FTAs. The resulting conflict of views has spurred a worldwide debate on the matter, one likely not to be settled without difficulty.

Proliferation of Regional Trade Agreements

As previously stated, vast numbers of RTAs have been emerging in the last ten years. This trend is still accelerating even today. "Between January 2004 and February 2005 alone, 43 RTAs have been notified to the WTO, making this the most prolific RTA Maxey/Macor period in recorded history." Indeed the overall tendency in the world is to favor one kind of RTA or another. The number of these agreements in force is 170, while many more are under negotiation. It must be mentioned, though, that the intensification of the agreements has occurred particularly strongly in the West and the Asia-Pacific region.

At first glance, these types of agreements appear counter productive to the WTO's principle of Most Favored Nation (MFN), as applied to lowering trade barriers evenly and indiscriminately. The idea was to spread out this principle and presumably build a world of free trade based off of it. RTAs on the other hand, represent a clear kind of Trade Bloc, with the inherent notion of discrimination. "RTAs are being embraced by many WTO members as trade policy instruments and, in the best of cases, as complementary to MFN." However, this sentiment is not universal, and while there may be benefits to RTAs there are also plenty of challenges involved.

The promotion of free trade at a preferential level may help developing economies to implement domestic reforms and open up to competitive market pressures at a sustainable pace, thus facilitating their integration in the world economy. This may also benefit the multilateral process by exerting leverage for openness and competitive liberalization in international trade relations. Yet, the development of complex networks of non-MFN trade relations and of regulatory regimes which increasingly touch upon policy areas uncharted by multilateral trade agreements may place developing countries, in particular, in a weaker position than under the multilateral framework. As for the multilateral trading system, such RTA proliferation is already undermining transparency and predictability in international trade relations, which are pillars of the WTO system. This may ultimately alter global trade patterns with severe implications for WTO Members through, among others, trade and investment diversion and diminished attention to the multilateral system. As is evident, the future implications of the movement towards RTAs are as of yet unknown; they may be ultimately a very destructive element against the push for free trade or they may be the key to resolving the matter.

In regards to the types of RTAs that we observe in the real world, the most proliferated is by far the FTA, occupying 84 percent of the RTAs in force today. An FTA itself is agreement under which the member nations remove all trade barriers between themselves, while maintaining individual national barriers in respect to the rest of the world (for example, NAFTA). The next type of RTA is the Customs Union, coming in at 8 percent of the current agreements. This arrangement follows the same principles as an FTA, but indeed eliminated differences in national barriers. There is only one common set of trade barriers applied to non-members of the Customs Union (i.e., MERCOSUR).

The next two important classifications of RTAs are common market and economic union. A common market is essentially a Customs Union, with the added stipulation of freedom of factor flows. An Economic Union entails full economic integration (the closest example of which is the EU, although it is not yet entirely integrated). Obviously, the percentage of active agreements falling under either of these categories is negligible, but their percentage of trade flows is quite significant. "The predominance of FTAs over Customs Unions (Common Markets and Economic Unions included) is probably due to the fact that they are faster to conclude and require a lower degree of policy coordination among the parties since in an FTA each party maintains its own trade policy vis-à-vis third parties." The easiness of an FTA is inherent in its makeup, and the benefits seem to clearly outweigh the hassles of negotiating such an agreement. "Customs Unions, on the other hand, require the establishment of a common external tariff and harmonization of external trade policies, implying a greater loss of autonomy over the parties' commercial policies and longer and more complex negotiations and implementation periods." This has serious repercussions in regards to a nation's sovereignty. The inevitable question is what policies are under the jurisdiction of the Customs Union, and which policies are in the realm of the national government? Obviously, ground rules are determined on a case by case basis, nonetheless, this is an insight into the complicated nature of Custom Union agreements. "Furthermore, the majority of FTAs are concerned with strategic market access, often unbound by geographical considerations; in Customs Unions, on the other hand, geographical considerations play a pivotal role in defining the objective of economic (and often political) integration among the parties concerned."

Nevertheless, deeper integration beyond FTAs has garnered extensive media coverage in recent years, especially where concerning the European Union. While originally established as a Customs Union by the Treaty of Rome in 1957 (stemming from the trade of the prime materials coal and steel), it has since become a much more deeply integrated Union. All monetary and trade policy of the members is determined by a representative governing council (involving multiple organs, including the Council of the European Union, the European Commission, the European Parliament and the European Court of Justice). This leaves the fiscal policy up to the individual nation, however it is easy to imagine a situation involving fiscal policy counter acting monetary policy, especially where the two do not coincide in final aims. Regardless, beyond these policies, the EU shares also a common currency and common borders. An even more obvious, but often overlooked fully integrated Economic Union is the case of the United Kingdom. The independent nations of England, Scotland, Wales, and Northern Ireland operate under the economic policies dictated by the supranational organizational structure of the UK. In other words, it is not fair to fully disregard the possibility of a completely integrated European Union; however, the completion of the integration would appear to be fairly far into the future.

As a final example, one can cite the example of an African Customs Union, namely The Southern African Customs Union. The five members of the Union are Botswana, Lesotho, Namibia, South Africa, and Swaziland. The dominant member, South Africa, collects levies from customs, sales, and excise duties for all five members, sharing out proceeds based on each country's portion of imports. The future of RTAs seems to be an interesting combination of the ideas of a bilateral agreement based upon plurilateral agreements. "A noteworthy development expected in the next five years, which reflects the growing consolidation of established trading relationships, is the emergence of a new category of agreement, namely RTAs where each party is a distinct RTA itself." This may in fact be evidence towards the assertion of some WTO Members that RTAs do indeed enhance the progression towards international free trade. We must keep in mind however, that "the fact that several such RTAs have been under negotiation for some time, but that none, thus far, has been concluded suggests that such RTAs are complex to negotiate." Again, the suggestion is that such high hopes as free trade are not reasonably expected for a long time to come. Nevertheless, the possibility does not seem negated.

Limitations of Regional Trade Blocs

Trade blocs, free trade areas, and bilateral agreements are emerging far and wide in international trade. In 2001, regional trade agreements (RTAs) accounted for 43% of world trade, and the rate was expected to reach 55% by the year 2005. The emergence of RTAs has added diversity and complexity thereby creating a web in international trade relations. Growth in trade is observed as a result of these negotiations, but are they really the best method of liberalizing trade on a global level? The rapid surfacing of RTAs evokes concerns for the future of free trade, and in general the welfare of the world economy in the long run. There are six dominant concerns involving the efficiency and limitations of RTAs.

Trade Diversion

Efficiency is a great concern surrounding the creation of trade blocs. Trade diversions can be the unfortunate effect of these preferential trade agreements. Trade diversions are created when trade barriers are lowered in a bloc or region, thus making prices on imports from outsiders comparatively higher, even if they are the low-cost supplier. Trade is then diverted away from the low-cost supplier, to the less efficient incumbent. These breaches in efficiency have welfare effects.

"Competitive Regionalism," Costly Negotiation Process and Overlapping Agreements Establishment of regional trade agreements has gained momentum. Small countries in particular are vulnerable to pressures to join trade blocs in order not to be left out of benefits from increased trade volume. This tendency is referred to as "competitive regionalism." The pressure to quickly regionalize may also distract efforts from the greater goal of multilateral liberalization of trade. Since the pace of multilateral talks is generally slow (the Uruguay

Round took seven years) requiring extensive negotiations; countries that would prefer liberalization of trade on a multilateral level are, in the mean time, scrambling to regionalize. Furthermore, the negotiation process is costly, particularly to smaller countries, and given the "cost of non-participation" in RTAs, efforts are concentrated on quick regional agreements. Given the pressures to regionalize, and limited negotiation resources, countries may hastily create trade blocs. This "competitive regionalism" can ultimately divert efforts away from greater free trade, and rather create complex barriers among blocs.

The rapid creation of regional agreements may also hinder the greater goal of free trade by creating a complex web of agreements, thus posing a challenge to and complicating multilateral solutions through the WTO. Agreements with too much red tape can initially look attractive, but if not in harmony with greater global negotiations; the participants can find themselves at a disadvantage in the future. In this light, it is warned that the benefits given by the preferential treatment through regionalization, may be short lived, and unable to exceed the costs of continuous administration of the bloc. *Preferential Liberalization Can Potentially Increase Vulnerability* Entering into a trade bloc makes all parties vulnerable to the decisions and practices of all countries involved. For political or other reasons an incumbent of the region may revoke or modify the preferential treatment granted by the agreement. This situation is particularly dangerous when there is a dominant trade partner in the bloc that may shift its weight around for political gains. Furthermore, the preferential agreement may shelter industries and hamper inefficiencies within the bloc. In the case that the bloc should expand, or the terms of the agreement change, the margins of preference are eroded, and the countries are worse off. A more stable system would be multilateral reduction of barriers within a common set of rules (Hilaire, Alvin and Yongzheng Yang, 2003).

Inclusion of Additional Elements in RTAs

It is common for RTAs to include elements unrelated to trade, that may in fact serve to restrict trade rather than promote trade in the long run. RTAs, especially many involving the US, oftentimes contain parameters on labor standards, environmental issues, intellectual property rights, and capital movements. In some cases noncompliance with the agreed parameters results in trade sanctions or other forms of punishment. These types of standards could be detrimental to trade growth especially for countries in which institutions are weak.

Regional Trade Agreements under World Trade Organisation (WTO) Rules

Within the WTO, regionalism is viewed as 'actions by governments to liberalise or facilitate trade on a regional basis, sometimes through free-trade areas or customs unions'. A trading arrangement among a subset of countries in which members trade on preferential terms with discriminatory removal of trade barriers among themselves broadly describes an Regional Trade Agreement (RTA). RTAs usually begin with tariff preferences but often extend into services, intellectual property rights, government procurement and other areas. These may take the forms of (http://www.berr.gov.uk/whatwedo/europeandtrade/regional-trade/tradeagreements-wto-rules/page27097.html):

Free trade areas—where reciprocal preferences for goods or services are exchanged but members retain their own tariff rates.

Customs unions—where a common external tariff is implemented in addition to the exchange of reciprocal preferences.

Asymmetrical agreements—where preferences are not strictly reciprocal, for example one party may be allowed longer than another to implement certain goods or services preferences.

The **North American Free Trade Area (NAFTA)** is an example of a free trade area, the European Communities (EC) is an example of a customs union and many EC Association Agreements (such as those with North African countries) are examples of asymmetrical agreements.

Regional Trade Agreements play an ever-increasing role in world trade, accounting for an estimated 60 percent of global transactions today. Regional Trade Agreements are expanding in both number and scope. Currently, 197 RTAs notified with the WTO are in force; the number exceeds 300 if those being negotiated, those in the proposal stage, and ones that are signed but not yet in force are counted.

The Most Favoured Nation (MFN) clause under Article I of the GATT enshrines the fundamental principle of non-discrimination. This implies that in the trade of goods and services (under the GATS), all imported products should receive the same tariff or non-tariff treatment irrespective of their country of origin. Under WTO rules, WTO Members are allowed to enter into RTAs provided those Agreements meet certain criteria about their coverage of trade, implementation periods and so on. Article XXIV of GATT permits signatories to set up regional FTAs and Customs Unions (CUs) for trade in goods, Article V of the GATS for services, and the Enabling Clause provides legal cover for preferential trade agreements among developing countries.

The WTO has a clear brief to monitor the spread of RTAs and review their consistency with prescribed regulations. At the WTO Ministerial Conference held in Doha in 2000, it was agreed that there should be negotiations to clarify and improve disciplines and procedures under the existing WTO provision applying to regional trade agreements. The Committee on RTAs (CRTA) has the primary responsibility to conduct the review of RTAs, aided by other WTO bodies, and examines members' agreements to ensure they comply with WTO rules.

The review process is to examine whether a given agreement is in harmony with the criteria prescribed. Effectively, trade barriers must not be raised against non-members; they must be eliminated on "substantially all trade" among members; and formalities leading to RTAs must be completed within

10 years. In this context, a new WTO transparency mechanism has been developed, aimed at facilitating the process of notification of RTAs, and also to expedite reviews of RTAs and examine their consistency with WTO prescriptions.

Current Status of Services Negotiations under GATS

The creation of the GATS was one of the landmark achievements of the Uruguay Round, whose results entered into force in January 1995. The GATS for the first time extended internationally agreed rules and commitments into the rapidly growing area of international trade viz., service, which was never done before. The GATS was based on the same objectives as that of GATT of creating a credible and reliable system of international trade rules; ensuring fair and equitable treatment of all participants (principle of non-discrimination); stimulating economic activity through guaranteed policy bindings; and promoting trade and development through progressive liberalization.

Further negotiations for progressive liberalization commenced by 1.1.2000, as mandated under GATS. The Doha Ministerial Conference has given a further direction to these negotiations by mandating that members should submit initial requests for specific commitments by 30 June 2002 and initial offers by 31 March 2003. According to the paragraph 15 of the Ministerial Declaration, there is an agreement on. "Negotiations on trade in services shall be conducted with a view to promoting the economic growth of all trading partners and the development of developing and least-developed countries. We recognize the work already undertaken in the negotiations, initiated in January 2000 under Article XIX of the General agreement on Trade in Services, and the large number of proposals submitted by Members on a wide range of sectors and several horizontal issues, as well as on movement of natural persons. With a view to achieving the objectives of the General Agreement on Trade in Services, as stipulated in the Preamble, Article IV and Article XIX of that Agreement. Participants submitted initial requests for specific commitments by 30 June 2002 and initial offers by 31 March 2003. To take stock of the progress of the Doha Round of trade talks, a Ministerial meeting was held in Hong Kong from 13th-18th December, 2005, in which the following timelines were agreed to:

(a) 28th February, 2006, for submitting plurilateral requests;
(b) 31st July, 2006, for submitting the second round of Revised Offers; and
(c) 31st October, 2006, for submitting the draft final schedule of commitments.

The Hong Kong Ministerial declaration provided guidance to WTO Members to take forward the Services negotiations as per the provisions included in Annex C of the declaration. In a sense, Hong Kong was a watershed in the Services negotiations in a number of aspects, some of which are:

- Guidance on the various Modal targets aimed at making services trade less restrictive and more transparent.
- Agreement to begin plurilateral negotiations, which would be complementary to the bilateral Request-Offer process.
- Agreement on developing disciplines in domestic regulations before the end of the current Round.

In pursuance of the Hong Kong Ministerial Declaration, the plurilateral process has begun in Geneva. 21 plurilateral groups have been formed in various service sectors and two plurilateral group meetings have been held so far.

Presently the negotiations are suspended. The Revised Offers by the Member countries will be submitted once the negotiations are resumed.

The first and second rounds of meetings of all plurilateral groups were held from 28th March to 6th April 2006 and 15th-24th May 2006 respectively. India is the coordinator of Mode-1 (Cross Border Supply) and Mode-4 (Temporary Movement of Natural Persons) plurilateral groups. India has also participated as a requesting member in the Computer and Related Services (CRS) group and Architecture, Engineering and Integrated Engineering Services (AEI) group. As a part of the plurilateral process, India has also received a number of plurilateral requests in all the sectors/areas listed in Para 4.2 above except for the Horizontal Request in Mode 3 (Commercial presence), MFN Exemptions (General) and MFN Exemptions (Financial Services).

The *World Information Technology and Services Alliance* (WITSA) recognizes the World Trade Organization (WTO) as the international body dealing with the rules of trade between nations. WTO agreements provide the legal ground-rules for international commerce and for trade policy. These multilateral agreements have three main objectives: to help trade flow as freely as possible, to achieve further liberalization gradually through negotiation, and to set up an impartial means of settling disputes. A number of simple, fundamental principles run throughout all the WTO agreements: non-discrimination ("most-favored-nation" treatment and "national" treatment), freer trade, predictable policies, and encouraging fair competition. With stability and predictability, the multilateral trading system should encourage trade and investment flows, create jobs, and provide consumers the benefits of competition—expanded choice and lower prices. WITSA strongly supports the WTO and its objectives in creating an open trading system free of barriers. WITSA is committed to maintaining open markets, reducing protectionism and sustaining the momentum of liberalization achieved by the General Agreement on Tariffs and Trade (GATT)/WTO over the last forty years and, more recently, the General Agreement on Trade in Services (GATS).

WITSA supports the new round of multilateral trade negotiations, which provides an opportunity to embark on further liberalization of barriers to international trade, including trade in information technology goods and services (http://www.witsa.org/papers/WTOCancun03.pdf). WITSA also recognizes and supports the WTO work program on electronic commerce, which since its inception in 1998 has included a thorough examination of issues related to electronic by the Goods, Services and TRIPS (intellectual property) Councils, and the Trade and Development Committee.

The November 2001 decision by WTO Trade Ministers to launch a comprehensive trade round adds greater urgency to the negotiations on services, which have been underway since 2000. The Doha Declaration launching the trade round called for countries to make "requests" of trading partners in the services sectors by June 30, 2002 with offers by March of 2003. Early results from these processes are promising with country offers generally extending earlier commitments to Internet and web-based services. The current schedule calls for conclusions of the negotiations on January 1, 2005. Information and communication technology (ICT) industries must work with their governments to determine how to negotiate trade commitments affecting these critical sectors over the next few months. This collaborative effort should establish the ICT industry's goals for the Doha negotiations and the negotiating methodology best suited to achieve those goals.

Agreements under Free Trade Area (FTAs)

Free trade area is a type of trade bloc, a designated group of countries that have agreed to eliminate tariffs, quotas and preferences on most (if not all) goods and services traded between them. It can be considered the second stage of economic integration. Countries choose this kind of economic integration form if their economical structures are complementary. If they are competitive, they will choose customs union.

Unlike a customs union, members of a free trade area do not have a common external tariff (same policies with respect to non-members), meaning different quotas and customs. To avoid evasion (through re-exportation) the countries use the system of certification of origin most commonly called rules of origin, where there is a requirement for the minimum extent of local material inputs and local transformations adding value to the goods. Goods that don't cover these minimum requirements are not entitled for the special treatment envisioned in the free trade area provisions.

Cumulation is the relationship between different FTAs regarding the rules of origin—sometimes different FTAs supplement each other, in other cases there is no cross-cumulation between the FTAs. A free trade area is a result of a free trade agreement (a form of trade pact) between two or more countries. Free trade areas and agreements (FTAs) are cascadable to some degree—if some countries sign agreement to form free trade area and choose to negotiate together (either as a trade bloc or as a forum of individual members of their FTA) another free trade agreement with some external country (or countries)—then the new FTA will consist of the old FTA plus the new country (or countries).

Within an industrialized country there are usually few if any significant barriers to the easy exchange of goods and services between parts of that country. For example, there are usually no trade tariffs or import quotas; there are usually no delays as goods pass from one part of the country to another (other than those that distance imposes); there are usually no differences of taxation and regulation. Between countries, on the other hand, many of these barriers to the easy exchange of goods often do occur. It is commonplace for there to be import duties of one kind or another (as goods enter a country) and the levels of sales tax and regulation often vary by country.

The aim of a free trade area is to so reduce barriers to easy exchange that trade can grow as a result of specialization, division of labour, and most importantly via (the theory and practice of) comparative advantage. The theory of comparative advantage argues that in an unrestricted marketplace (in equilibrium) each source of production will tend to specialize in that activity where it has comparative (rather than absolute) advantage. The theory argues that the net result will be an increase in income and ultimately wealth and well-being for everyone in the free trade area. However the theory refers only to aggregate wealth and says nothing about the distribution of wealth. In fact there may be significant losers, in particular among the recently protected industries with a comparative disadvantage. The proponent of free trade can, however, retort that the gains of the gainers exceed the losses of the losers.

Free trade agreements (FTAs) have proved to be one of the best ways to open up foreign markets to U.S. exporters. Today, the United States has FTAs with 14 countries. In 2006, six new FTAs were implemented: with Bahrain, El Salvador, Guatemala, Honduras, Morocco, and Nicaragua. Last year, trade with countries that the United States has FTAs was significantly greater than their relative share of the global economy. Although comprising 7.5 percent of global GDP (not including the United States), those FTA countries accounted for over 42 percent of U.S. exports (http://www.trade.gov/fta/index.asp).

Free Trade Agreement Partners in the Global Economy

Percent of World GDP, 2006 **Percent of U.S. Exports, 2006**

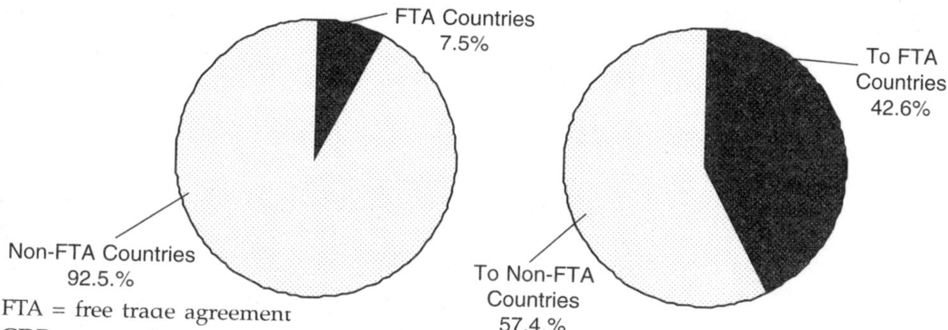

FTA = free trade agreement

GDP = gross domestic product

Note: World GDP excludes the United States. GDP percentage shares are based on GDP figures on a purchasing power parity basis. Export figures are for total U.S. Exports. Free trade agreement countries include all countries with free trade agreements with the United States (Australia, Bahrain, Canada, Chile, Dominican Republic, El Salvador, Guatemala, Honduras, Israel, Jordan, Mexico, Morocco, Nicaragua, and Singapore).

Sources: International Monetary Fund, World Economic Outlook Database, April 2007); U.S. Department of Commerce, International Trade Administrations, and Bureau of the Census.

Free Trade Agreement Partners and the U.S. Trade Balance, 2006

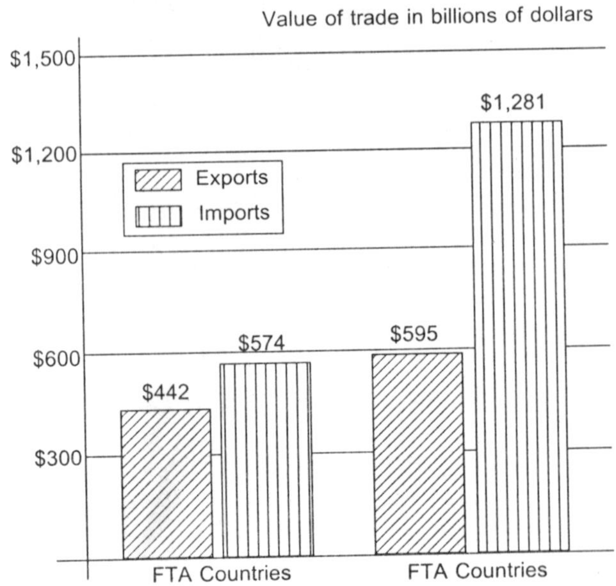

Source: U.S. Department of Commerce.

U.S. Free Trade Agreements

Trade agreements help open markets and expand opportunities for American workers and businesses and can help your company enter and compete more easily in the global marketplace. Trade agreements are also a tool for promoting fair competition and encouraging foreign governments to adopt open and transparent rulemaking procedures as well as non-discriminatory laws and regulations. Trade agreements can strengthen the business climate by including commitments on issues of concern along with the reduction and elimination of tariffs. Trade agreements may include commitments on topics such as (http://www.export.gov/fta/):

- Improving intellectual property right protection
- Enhancing labor rights
- Government procurement
- Opening service sectors to competition
- Enhancing rules on foreign investment
- Environmental standards
- Improving customs facilitation

The United States is party to many bi-lateral and multi-lateral trade agreements. Countries with which the U.S. has active bi-lateral trade agreements include: Australia, Bahrain, Chile, Israel, Jordan, Morocco, Peru, Oman, and Singapore. The active multi-lateral trade agreements that the U.S. has signed include the North American Free-Trade Agreement and the Central America-Dominican Republic Free Trade Agreement (CAFTA-DR). The U.S. is also party to the General Agreement on Tariffs and Trade (GATT, overseen by the WTO) along with 152 other countries. U.S. trade agreements with Panama, Korea, and Columbia are pending congressional approval. The U.S. is also in negotiations on trade agreements with Malaysia, Thailand, the United Arab Emirates, and the Southern African Customs Union (SACU) which includes Botswana, Lesotho, Namibia, South Africa, and Swaziland.

Country-specific trade agreement information is available by clicking on an area of interest on the right in the "Main Topics" box or in the table below. The table 1 below shows the growth in U.S. exports to its trade agreement partners from 2007 to 2008.

Country	2007 MMUSD	2008 MMUSD	Percent Change
NAFTA	332,499	353,931	6.45%
Canada	213,118	222,424	4.40%
Mexico	119,381	131,507	10.20%
CAFTA-DR	21,274	23,922	12.45%
Costa Rica	4,224	5,047	19.50%
Dominican Rep	5,793	6,293	8.60%
Guatemala	3,872	4,493	16.00%
Honduras	4,327	4,699	8.60%
Nicaragua	846	1,030	21.70%
El Salvador	2,209	2,357	6.70%
Australia	17,916	20,948	16.90%
Bahrain	565	779	37.80%
Chile	7,610	11,366	49.40%
Israel	9,940	10,238	3.00%
Jordan	831	904	8.70%
Morocco	1,333	1,506	12.90%
Oman	1,034	1,380	33.40%
Peru	3,764	5,686	51.10%
Singapore	23,576	25,655	8.80%
Total	**420,348**	**456,319**	**8.60%**

Table 1: Growth in Total U.S. Exports to Free Trade Agreement Countries.

Source: www.usitc.gov, data compiled from tariff and trade data from the U.S. Department of commerce and the U.S. International Trade Commission.

Different International Models of FTA's are described below:

I. FTA's in Asia-Europe Relations

The European Commission decided to propose launching FTA negotiations with ASEAN in October 2006 only after its strategies within ASEM and in the ASEAN-EU context failed to achieve their goals, and individual ASEAN members had already concluded FTAs with Japan and/or the US. The process leading up to the decision to negotiate an FTA deserves closer scrutiny, as do the ideas of the ASEAN-EU Vision Group Report and the European Commission regarding the rationale of an FTA.ASEM—Market Access through Trade Facilitation and Investment Promotion.

2. The ASEM process was initiated in 1996, following a Singaporean proposal. Six summits have been held (Bangkok, 1996; London, 1998; Seoul, 2000; Copenhagen, 2002; Hanoi, 2004; and Helsinki, 2006), in addition to seven meetings of Foreign Ministers, six of Economic Ministers, seven of Finance Ministers, two of Culture Ministers, and one of Labor and Employment Ministers, and ten (the ASEM record) of the Senior Officials on Trade and Investment. The Asia-Europe People's Forum meets at the same time as the summit, but is not part of the official process.

3. The original participants on the Asian side were the seven ASEAN members (Brunei, Indonesia, Malaysia, the Philippines, Singapore, Thailand and Vietnam), together with China, South Korea and Japan; and on the European side, the fifteen EU members (Austria, Belgium, Denmark, Finland, France, Germany, Greece, Ireland, Italy, Luxembourg, Netherlands, Portugal, Spain, Sweden and the UK), together with the European Commission. In 2004, after considerable controversy, the three new ASEAN members (Burma/ Myanmar, Cambodia, and Laos) and the 10 new EU members (Cyprus, the Czech Republic, Estonia, Hungary, Latvia, Lithuania, Malta, Poland, Slovakia, and Slovenia) were admitted. In 2006, it was decided that India, Mongolia, Pakistan and the ASEAN Secretariat on the Asian side, and Bulgaria and Rumania on the European side, would be allowed to participate in the next summit, scheduled to take place in Beijing in 2008.

4. The EU's main concern in East Asia, as in other regions of the developing world, has been market access, as the Commission very frankly announced in its Market Access Strategy, published one month before ASEM(European Commission, 1996).

5. Market access could be achieved by convincing the Asians to modify their laws and regulations, as announced in the EU's New Asia Strategy, (European Commission 1994) and by using ASEM as a forum to facilitate negotiations in other international fora (mainly the WTO), (ASEM, 1998) without ASEM itself becoming a negotiating forum.

6. The EU has sought to achieve its aims by urging the Asians to follow EU Models and approaches used therein. (http://ipdprojects.org/aepf/index.php?option=com_content&view=article&id=54:ftas-in-asia-europe-relations&catid=37:articles&Itemid=61):

- to implement their Uruguay Round commitments;
- to support the launching of a new WTO round, which would cover the four Singapore issues (trade facilitation, investment, competition, and government procurement);
- to implement the allegedly non-binding plans that cover two of the four Singapore issues: The Trade Facilitation Action Plan (TFAP) and the Investment Promotion Action Plan (IPAP).

7. A free trade area was proposed in 1999 by the Asia-Europe Vision Group, which advocated a step-wise approach and a 2025 deadline. Differences in levels of development (between the EU and the Asian states? among the Asian states?) were supposed to be taken into account, but how this was to be done was not explained (Asia-Europe Vision Group Report, 1999: http://www.mofa.go.jp/POLICY/economy/asem/asem2/vision.html). However, the recommendation was purely and simply ignored by ASEM participants. This rejection has never been officially explained, but it is likely that the EU feared that a free trade area would cause its trade deficit with several Asian countries to balloon.

8. Instead, ASEM adopted plans for trade facilitation and investment promotion. The two terms should not mislead the observer. Neither of them implies the funding by the EU of projects, such as transfers of technology, trade missions, participation in trade fairs, feasibility studies, the establishment of joint ventures or the lending of money to governments and/or firms for marketing campaigns or product development. In ASEM jargon, these two terms refer to amendments of domestic regulations of Asian countries that the EU and European firms find objectionable.

9. Within the ASEM framework, two lists were prepared: "Consolidated and Prioritized List of the Major Generic Barriers to Trade" under the TFAP and "Most Effective Measures for Attracting Foreign Direct Investment" under TFAP. The two lists give us an idea of the demands of the EU and European firms. For example, the EU objects in the area of government procurement to requirements that companies must have a minimum level of domestically-held shares and domestic content in products. In distribution, European firms do not wish to see any requirements of domestic partnership and joint ventures, obligations on foreign retailers to buy local products for their supermarkets, or the promotion of local products. European companies complain about limits on duration of visas. In the area of investment, Europeans argue that removal of performance requirements (e.g., local content, export and transfer of technology) would attract foreign direct investment. They find unacceptable the obligation to form joint ventures, the prohibition to invest in some sectors, and limits on the number of intra-corporate transferees and on the employment of foreigners in management (Robles, 2005).

10. After a first round of reporting on the allegedly "voluntary" TFAP and IPAP in 2002, the working groups' activities slowed down. In response, calls were heard for "immediate action for the reduction of trade barriers." The sixth ASEM summit also noted the need to consider further action within TFAP and IPAP.

11. The slowing down of ASEM activities demonstrates the growing lack of interest of the Asian countries in the ASEM process. This disinterest is confirmed by the strategy of individual ASEAN members since 2001, consisting in the negotiation of FTAs with the US and/or Japan.

Aware of the intensifying competition with the latter two countries, the EU attempted to ward off the threat by proposing substitutes for FTAs – the Partnership and Cooperation Agreements.

II. EU-ASEAN Partnership and Cooperation Agreements (PCAs): Regulatory Convergence

12. In 2003, the EU Commission proposed a new partnership with Southeast Asia (European Commission (2003)). The partnership's economic component was to be embodied in an action plan called "Trans-Regional EU-ASEAN Trade Initiative (TREATI), which would establish a framework for dialogue and regulatory cooperation on trade facilitation, market access and investment. The aim was supposedly to inform each side of the other's regulatory systems (one wonders if the Internet was not sufficient for this purpose). The dialogue might eventually "develop into an exercise of approximation and harmonization".

13. We may get an idea of the nature of the regulatory dialogue that the EU had in mind by turning to the Japan-EU Regulatory Reform Dialogue, which has been held for over a decade now. Analysis of the dialogue reveals that in its efforts to convince Japan to change Japanese regulations, the EU uses three arguments. First, the EU proposed action conforms to WTO rulings. Second, the EU proposal follows EU regulations, which offer models that the EU urges Japan to adopt. If the two arguments fail, the EU simply states that the Japanese regulations are disadvantageous for EU interests and for this reason should be changed. Based on the experience of this dialogue, the EU's aims in proposing TREATI were not very different from those it pursued through ASEM—the modification of Asian laws and regulations in order to ensure market access for European firms. The expression "regulatory convergence" in reality refers to the adoption by the EU's partner of EU-style regulations. In the Japan-EU Regulatory Dialogue, it has practically never happened that the EU has adopted a Japanese regulation as a model, even if the EU sometimes agrees to Japanese requests.

14. Realizing the sensitive nature of such a dialogue, the EU proposed to start meetings on TREATI as soon as at least two ASEAN member states indicated that they were ready for it. From the ASEAN perspective, this strategy could have had the effect of a divide-and-rule strategy. The EU probably hoped that if two ASEAN states engaged in a dialogue with the EU, the others, fearing that they might not benefit from any resulting EU concessions, would be convinced to jump on the bandwagon.

15. The EU noted that even at this stage, ASEAN had already expressed a desire for an FTA with it, but the European Commission was reluctant to consider the proposal. According to the Commission, an FTA could only come after several conditions had been fulfilled: successful conclusion of the WTO negotiations; sufficient progress on regulatory governance; and preparation with the TREATI framework. In other words, the EU first wanted ASEAN members to adopt EU-style economic regulations before the EU might even consider the possibility of an FTA. There was no guarantee that an FTA might

indeed be negotiated. Once more, it is probable that the EU's caution was attributable to its fears for its trade deficit with individual ASEAN members.

16. At ASEM, held in Hanoi in October 2004, the EU, Singapore and Thailand announced that they were initiating negotiations for PCAs. It has been reported that such negotiations are also underway with Brunei, Indonesia, Malaysia and the Philippines. However, the absence of reports of progress being made in the negotiations is remarkable. Perhaps, this is simply the reflection of the extraordinary lack of transparency of the process. Alternatively, it may be an indication that the negotiations have not been making much headway. If so, it could explain the EU's change of heart and its agreement to launch FTA negotiations with ASEAN.

III. Towards an ASEAN-EU FTA

The Association of South East Asian Nations (ASEAN) encompasses 10 South East Asian countries: Brunei Darussalam, Cambodia, Indonesia, Laos, Malaysia, Burma/Myanmar, Philippines, Singapore, Thailand and Vietnam). The ASEAN region is the fifth largest export market of the EU and the fifth largest trading partner of the EU. The EU is the second largest trading partner for most countries in ASEAN after the US. ASEAN exports to the EU are account for about 13% of its total exports. EU exports to ASEAN account for around 4% of its total exports.

Building Region-to-Region ties

The EU and ASEAN have focused on promoting region-to-region economic relations. Last year ASEAN celebrated the 40th anniversary of the founding of its regional cooperation process. In October 2003, ASEAN leaders at their 9th Summit Meeting signed the Bali Concord II, a landmark treaty for the future integration of ASEAN, calling for the creation of an ASEAN Community by the year 2020. At their 13th Summit Meeting in Singapore last November, ASEAN Leaders approved the Blueprint of the ASEAN Economic Community, which sets the roadmap for economic integration by 2015 (http://trade.ec.europa.eu/doclib/docs/2008/may/tradoc_138792.pdf).

The Trans-Regional EU-ASEAN Trade Initiative (TREATI)

In 2003 the EU and ASEAN launched the Trans-Regional EUASEAN Trade Initiative (TREATI) as a framework for dialogue and regulatory co-operation between the two regions. The priority areas for co-operation under TREATI are closely linked to ASEAN's own moves towards closer economic integration: sanitary standards agriculture and fisheries, industrial product standards and technical barriers to trade. It also covers closer cooperation in investment. The positive experience with the TREATI encouraged both sides to consider deeper economic integration through an FTA. In April 2007 the European Commission was given a mandate by European Member States to negotiate an FTA with countries of ASEAN, as part of the Commission's Global Europe strategy. These negotiations were launched in May 2007.

The Benefits of an FTA

Independent research commissioned by the European Commission suggested that the likely economic benefits for both ASEAN and the EU from an EU-ASEAN FTA were considerable. ASEAN could see its exports to the EU rise by 18.5%—and expect economic gains equivalent to 2% of its GDP by 2020. The EU could see its exports to ASEAN increase significantly—also increasing total EU global exports by almost 2%. One of the biggest areas of gains for both sides would be in the area of businesses services—one of the key reasons why the EU-ASEAN FTA needs to tackle services trade.

17. As mentioned above, it was the ASEAN that first expressed interest in an FTA with the EU. The proposal was reportedly made at the September 2004 meeting of ASEAN Economic Ministers in Jakarta. Philippine Trade Secretary Cesar Purisima told the Press that then EU Trade Commissioner Pascal Lamy made it clear that the EU preferred multilateral arrangements under the WTO and that the EU was only pursuing FTA negotiations that had been started before 1999 (Lawrence Agcaoili). Strictly speaking, this second statement was not accurate, since the EU negotiations for Economic Partnership Agreements (EPAs), which included FTAs, with African, Caribbean and Pacific (ACP) countries had started several years after the failed WTO meeting in Seattle.

18. According to press reports, the ASEAN members were led by Singapore in the effort to convince the EU to negotiate a trade agreement with the organization (John Burton, 2006). This leadership role would be consistent with the policy that Singapore has pursued since the late 1990s, which is driven by impatience with the slow pace of regional integration in Southeast Asia. Singapore has sought to achieve its free trade goals through bilateral agreements, hoping that its example would be followed by other ASEAN members. Following the conclusion of the Singapore-Japan Economic Partnership Agreement in 2002, an imitation effect has indeed been observed. Malaysia, which initially accused Singapore of undermining ASEAN, abandoned its opposition and negotiated its own FTAs (Teofilo *et al*, 2003).

19. It is said that Peter Mandelson, the EU Commissioner who replaced Lamy, changed Lamy's strategy, which would explain the EU's willingness to consider an FTA with ASEAN. At the same time, EU sources openly admit that the failure of the 2003 and 2005 WTO Ministerial Conferences forced the EU to rethink its strategy (Rommel, 2005). Regrettably, there has been much less willingness on the EU part to admit that this failure was in large part due to the EU's own refusal to make concessions to the developing countries.

20. In April 2005, the sixth consultation of ASEAN Economic Ministers and the EU Trade Commissioner, held in Vietnam, established a Vision Group to examine the feasibility of an FTA and other initiatives. The Vision Group was given a one-year deadline to complete its work. In July 2005, terms of reference of the Vision Group and of the impact studies were agreed upon. Further meetings were held in Brussels (10-11 November, 2005), Bangkok (24-25 January, 2006), Kuala Lumpur (25-27 March, 2006) and Hanoi (10 April, 2006).

21. The Vision Group's working methods have been quite opaque. It has

not even proved possible to identify the Group's members, let alone their qualifications. It goes without saying that records of their meetings have not been made public. Even more remarkable is the fact that the qualitative and quantitative impact studies are not accessible to the public. All we know is that the Quantitative Study was carried out by the French think tank, Centre d'etudes prospectives et d'informations internationales, Center for International Prospective Studies and Information), while the qualitative studies were undertaken by another French think tank, the Institut français des relations internationales (IFRI, French Institute for International Relations) and the University of Limerick, in Ireland (ASEAN-EU Vision Group, 2006). In this respect, the process suffers by comparison with that which led to the adoption of the proposal for a China-ASEAN FTA: all the country studies commissioned for this purpose are publicly available.

22. It is also worth pointing out the obvious: that no think tank from Southeast Asia did independent evaluations or at least worked together with the European think tanks named above. The fact that the EU alone bore the costs of the studies was probably the decisive factor in the selection of exclusively European think tanks.

23. Press reports indicate that the ASEAN-EU Economic Partnership, one of whose components was an FTA, was adopted at the ASEAN-EU Economic Ministers' Retreat, held in Manila on 17 May 2006. Again, there are no publicly accessible records of the discussions between the ASEAN and EU at the time. Indeed, it is fair to say that the meeting's outcome was more widely reported in neighboring Southeast Asian countries than in the host country itself (Gabriel, 2006).

24. At ASEM 6 in Helsinki, the President of the European Commission informed European journalists that the EU was considering negotiations for a free trade agreement with ASEAN, starting in 2007 (Ricard, 2006). A month later, the EU plan was confirmed, and Korea was added to the list of negotiating partners (European Commission, 2006).

The Rationale for an ASEAN-EU FTA

25. An analysis of the rationale of the FTA must precede the examination of its scope: if the rationale is not convincing, there will be little need to discuss the scope. Any analysis must rely not only on the ASEAN-EU Vision Group Report, but also on the European Commission's own publications.

26. The rationales seem to be both negative and positive, although they are not explicitly characterized as such.

27. The negative rationale is allegedly associated with the risk that ASEAN-EU relations might suffer from the conclusion of FTAs by both organizations with other countries or organizations: "ASEAN and the EU will have to act promptly – if the partnership is delayed or postponed to the distant future, it may be overshadowed by other regional and bilateral initiatives."[24] The implication is that if the EU concluded FTAs with other developing countries or regions, ASEAN goods entering Europe would have to pay higher tariffs

than the goods originating from the countries with which the EU has an FTA. In this respect, the Vision Group cited the EU's ongoing negotiations with Mercosur and the Gulf Cooperation Council. The specific risk is that "both may unintentionally penalize each other by trading on MFN basis only."

28. These arguments are misleading, to say the least. First of all, it is not only the tariff rate that determines the competitiveness of a product on the European market. The African, Caribbean and Pacific (ACP) countries have enjoyed, for more than thirty years now, duty-free access for their industrial goods entering Europe and much larger reductions of tariffs on agricultural products exported to Europe, yet they have not been as successful in increasing their exports to the EU as many ASEAN members. It is doubtful if ACP exports will be any more competitive than ASEAN products once free trade is established between the ACP and the EU. These circumstances probably explain why the ongoing FTA negotiations with the EU were not mentioned by the Vision-Group.

29. The ASEAN countries that could conceivably encounter the most difficulties arising from competition with the ACP countries are the least developed countries, which export agricultural products. But all least developed countries already enjoy duty-free access to the EU under the "Everything but Arms" Initiative (EBA) of the EU. Moreover, in agriculture, the EU's Common Agricultural Policy (CAP) constitutes the major obstacle to market access. Hence, if the goal is market access for the products of least developed countries, the better approach would be to reform the CAP.

30. Second, as regards Mercosur, these countries, like the ASEAN countries (with the exception of Singapore and Myanmar) are subject only to the Generalized System of Preferences (GSP) and thus have less favorable access to the EU market than the ACP countries. In the past, the Mercosur countries' exports have been concentrated in agricultural rather than industrial products, and in the last decade, they have consistently had trade deficits with the EU. In other words, they were less competitive than many ASEAN countries in EU markets. In the event of a Mercosur-EU FTA, the chances that Mercosur will be more competitive than ASEAN countries in exporting industrial products to the EU are questionable. If Mercosur companies are overwhelmed in their domestic markets by imports of industrial goods from Europe, there will be very few Mercosur companies that can export to Europe.

31. At any rate, the Mercosur-EU negotiations failed in October 2004, after nearly ten years of discussions. From the Mercosur perspective, the main reason for the failure lay in the EU's persistent refusal to grant concessions on Mercosur agricultural exports to Europe. Any progress on the negotiations seems to be subject to the resumption of the WTO negotiations. In other words, it may take a long time before the threat to ASEAN exports from Mercosur exports materializes, assuming it ever does.

32. The reference to the MFN (Most-Favored-Nation) tariff rate, i.e., the tariff applied to goods coming from all sources, raises another implicit threat. At present, Southeast Asian exports to Europe are not subject to the MFN rate

but to GSP rates. On the other hand, since the ASEAN members do not grant tariff preferences to the EU, European products enter their markets under the MFN rate. Consequently, it is already the case that ASEAN countries apply MFN rates to the EU. The Vision Group seems to be anticipating the possibility that if ASEAN-EU FTA negotiations do not succeed, the EU will withdraw GSP privileges from ASEAN and apply the MFN rate.

33. The positive rationale for the FTA is said to be the ability to attract foreign direct investment, The EU-25 (now 27) were said to be the largest sources of FDI to ASEAN, but European FDI to the latter has declined in favor of China and Hong Kong. A more "stable and predictable framework" could attract European firms once more to Southeast Asia.

34. It is true that there has been some diversion of FDI away from ASEAN in favor of China, and that ASEAN countries are concerned about this trend. Nevertheless, the argument that an FTA will attract FDI to ASEAN is not convincing.

35. To begin with, the statement that the EU is the largest source of FDI is a statistical artifact. Since statistics for 25 countries are aggregated, it is almost inevitable that the sum will be larger than the corresponding figures for Japan and the US. In reality, only a handful of EU members invest in Southeast Asia, with Germany, the UK, and the Netherlands being the major sources. Japan is still the primary country of origin of FDI for most Southeast Asian countries.

36. Second, while China's growth rate has been a powerful incentive for European companies to invest there, much of European investment is what economists call market-seeking. Their aim is to produce for the local market, and not to export (this second type is called resource-seeking). If an increase in export capacity through such means as joint ventures or transfer of technology is one reason for attracting FDI, then market-seeking FDI will not be helpful in achieving it. Survey shows that most European companies prefer to export to Southeast Asia, rather than to invest there. Those that wish to invest do so in order to sell to the local market, in which case they will be competing with domestic firms. An FTA, if it succeeded in attracting FDI, would not attract the type of FDI desired by ASEAN members.

37. Third, it is European firms specialized in services (e.g., banking, insurance, telecommunications, education) that wish to invest in Southeast Asia. Again, FDI in services does not produce tradable goods, i.e., goods that can be exported. It will therefore not have any direct impact on exports to Europe. At most, FDI in services could improve production conditions and indirectly enhance the competitiveness of locally-produced goods. Even then, this outcome is not certain if the cost of services increases substantially and/ or the quality of the services actually declines.

38. An EU official in Bangkok is reported to have given a supplementary reason for free trade: an FTA would lower the costs of raw materials imported (presumably from Europe) into Thailand and in this manner lower costs of production.

39. There are of course many types of inputs, so that it becomes difficult

to make general statements. Several considerations should be kept in mind. First, one reason why inputs from Europe may not be imported is that they are expensive. In this connection, the European Commission proudly refers to European companies' "ability to sell products at premium prices." Second, if inputs from Japan compete with European inputs, and the tariffs on both are reduced as a result of the respective FTAs, the prices of the goods in relation to each other may well change very little. The only change will be due to the abolition of the tariffs. Third, if European inputs are not as efficiently produced as Japanese inputs and the abolition of tariffs on the former leads to an increase in Southeast Asian imports from Europe, free trade will in effect divert trade from the more efficient producer to the less efficient producer. Economists call this effect "trade diversion", which is generally considered undesirable, even from the point of view of liberal economics.

40. The secrecy surrounding the work of the ASEAN-EU Vision Group appears not to have bothered the European Commission and the EU member states, an attitude that is difficult to reconcile with the EU's claims to promote democracy, human rights and the rule of law in the Third World.

41. Even with the little information that has been made available to the public, it is possible to raise fundamental challenges to the rationale behind the proposed ASEAN-EU FTA.

42. Unfortunately, the experience with the ACP countries and Mercosur demonstrates that the European Commission is impervious to any arguments marshaled by civil society against FTAs.

43. We should not forget that ASEAN is officially in favor of the launch of ASEAN-EU FTA negotiations. That said, given the haste and the secrecy in which the Vision Group's work was carried out, it is plausible to assume that a number of ASEAN members have not weighed all of the consequences of an FTA. If this were indeed the case, they may lend a more willing ear to civil society arguments than the EU.

44. Should negotiations push through, then the EU, which probably feels that circumstances compelled it to accept the idea of an FTA, can be expected to adopt a tough attitude and to be less than generous with concessions. In that case, ASEAN should be ready, as Mercosur was, to break off negotiations rather than to end up with an unsatisfactory agreement.

Looking Beyond AFTA: Prospects and Challenges for Inter-Regional Trade

The world trading environment has witnessed the proliferation of regional trading arrangements during the last decade. This development was accompanied by the perceived threat that this may bring to the rules-based multilateral trading system. The ASEAN for one have not only reaffirmed their commitment to move forward beyond the ASEAN Free Trade Area and towards higher level of economic integration but also are looking at enhanced interaction and closer linkages with other regional groupings. This paper examines the prospects and challenges for expanding AFTA for inter-regional trade by first identifying the elements and principles that should govern such expansion for it to contribute towards realizing global-scale liberalization. Areas for inter-regional linkage are also identified highlighting the possible issues and conflicts that might arise considering the differing objectives and scope that AFTA has with the other trade blocs which it might want to develop an inter-regional linkage. Some probable arrangements for linking/expanding AFTA with other groupings or non-ASEAN countries are then explored, particularly those involving CER, the East Asian countries and the Andean Community.

At the 1999 informal summit meeting in Manila, ASEAN leaders reaffirmed their commitment to have ASEAN move forward beyond the ASEAN Free Trade Area (AFTA) and towards higher levels of economic integration as it enters the new millennium. They reiterated the goal of accelerating and deepening of their commitments in trade, investment and industrial cooperation. The meeting confirmed the Statement of Bold Measures and the Hanoi Plan of Action adopted at the 1998 Hanoi Summit. These included the acceleration of AFTA, the further liberalization of trade in services, improvement of the region's investment climate, and stronger financial and macroeconomic coordination. At the same time, ASEAN took steps towards "enhanced interaction and closer linkages" with their Eastern Asian neighbors. Spurred by the Asian financial crisis and the institutional evolution of the Asia-Europe Meeting (ASEM) arrangement, consideration for "ASEAN plus Three" in trade, financial, investment and development cooperation began to take shape between the Association and China, Japan, and South Korea.

Members of the ASEAN have also taken steps the expansion of inter-regional trade cooperation. The prospect of closer economic linkages between ASEAN and Australia-New Zealand Closer Economic Relation (AFTA-CER) has been under discussion as early as 1993. Lately, there have been proposals to broaden economic exchange between ASEAN and the Andean Community. Individual members have also considered membership in extra-regional groupings as for instance Singapore's aspiration to join the North American Free Trade Area (NAFTA).

Motivations for Expansion

The ASEAN Free Trade Area (AFTA) was established in 1992 with the objective of increasing ASEAN's competitive edge as a production base for the world market (ASEAN Secretariat, 1993). The mechanism for achieving this is through the Common Effective Preferential Tariff (CEPT) Scheme where intra-regional tariffs will be reduced to 0-5 percent within a 15-year time period beginning in 1993.

Over the years, however, AFTA has taken significant leaps towards its goal. First, the deadline has been continuously accelerated from the original date of 2008 to 2003 and finally to 2002 (with later implementation dates for its newer members: Vietnam, Burma, Laos and Cambodia). Since the latest decision to accelerate was made in 1998 when the region underwent its worst ever financial and economic crisis, it showed the outside world that ASEAN was not slowing down on its intra-regional liberalization commitments but is even bent on maintaining its commitment to regional economic integration.

Second, the coverage of the CEPT has been widened by including into the scheme products that were originally excluded (e.g. unprocessed agricultural products). Third, AFTA has also widened its scope beyond the CEPT scheme by including other measures to complement and supplement the removal of tariffs and other border barriers. These initiatives include harmonization of standards, reciprocal recognition of tests and certification of products and removal of barriers to foreign investments, among others (ASEAN Secretariat, 1993). Finally and the most important, AFTA's original goal of 0-5 percent ending tariff rates was deepened by targeting a zero ending tariff rates on all products by 2010 for the original six members, ahead of the original schedule of 2015; and by 2015 for the four new members, ahead of the original date of 2018 (APEC Secretariat, 2000).

As AFTA is coming close to attaining its original objective, questions arose as to what is next for AFTA. The new wave of economic integration has moved beyond the regional level to become inter-regional and even hemispheric (e.g. EU-MERCOSUR, ANDEAN-MERCOSUR, EU-Chile, EU-Mexico) (Onguglo and Cernat, 2000).

Furthermore, while regional trading arrangements are generally classified either as free trade areas, customs unions, common markets or economic unions, the new regional trading arrangements (RTAs) contain elements of more than one of these forms making integration deeper (Krueger, 1999). The increasing trend towards this type of regionalism creates pressures for inclusion for non-members and AFTA is not exempted.

The motivations for the rise of regionalism have been greatly discussed in Baldwin (1997) and Krueger (1999). Some of these include geopolitical considerations as in the case of EU's Single Market, the rise of US protectionism in the 1980s for the case of the US-Canada FTA, the possible trade diversionary effects of a US-Mexico FTA for the case of the NAFTA and the desire to achieve more bargaining power in dealing with North America for the case of MERCOSUR. Proximately, the experience of the Asian financial crisis, China's impending entry into the WTO, and discussions on setting up an FTA throughout the American continent and across the Atlantic has spurred similar discussions on inter-regional trade arrangements from within the Asian region. Except possibly for trade diversionary effect the same cannot be said of any possible inter-regional expansion of AFTA. In the first place, AFTA is not a regional trade bloc as the CEPT Scheme encourages not just intra-ASEAN trade liberalization but also liberalization on an MFN basis1. Given this external orientation of AFTA, any 1 The CEPT has a provision that allows the members to enjoy CEPT concession even if they reduce their tariffs to 0-5 percent on an MFN basis (ASEAN Secretariat, 1995).

The expansion for inter-regional arrangement is a further step of overcoming barriers to trade beyond what could be achieved within the multilateral framework of the WTO. This is particularly true for specific sectors of particular export interest to the ASEAN like textiles and clothing, and in other areas like services. Likewise, trade facilitation, particularly in the areas of custom procedures and harmonization or mutual recognition of standards and other importing country regulations, has been increasingly taking center stage in recent years. The diverse standards and technical regulations among developed countries along with the corresponding testing procedures for compliance limits market access and raises production and testing costs for the ASEAN.

ASEAN also needs to continuously improve its competitive strength for its exports and its attractiveness to foreign direct investment. Compared with other RTAs, AFTA is small to carry any weight in influencing the flow of international trade and investment. Moreover, the proliferation of RTAs has brought forth many new competitors to the ASEAN, both for its export markets and for the increasingly scarce foreign investment that has been its engine of growth. The potential competitors include the Andean Community and MERCOSUR in Latin America, the emerging economies in Central and Eastern Europe which are being slowly integrated with the EU through bilateral free trade agreements, and China in Northeast Asia. Likewise, the changing nature and dynamism of the RTAs by going beyond the traditional border barriers greatly affects non-members. For instance, rules of origin and standards (covering technical, sanitary and phytosanitary, and environmental) have become essential features of the new RTAs, both of which make it harder for non-members to trade with members of an RTA. On the whole, the revolution in information and communication technology and transportation has been facilitating the rapid integration of the world. These developments have given birth to global problems that require deeper inter-regional cooperation. The growth of transnational crime and environmental concerns are some of issues that increasingly challenge national authorities. The Asian financial crisis has also made clear the need to strengthen institutions and improve governance, not only domestically, but across the region as well. All these require deeper inter-regional cooperation and strengthening of ties to undertake common efforts to address these emerging concerns.

Appreciably, efforts at expanding AFTA by fostering greater ties with other regions are complex and difficult. This is due primarily to differences in economic situations, institutional and legal framework, and even political relationships between AFTA and its prospective partner region/s. This is further complicated by the initiatives of Singapore, which on its own contracted free trade arrangements with a number of countries outside the region. Malaysia has severely criticized Singapore and warned that such moves could weaken AFTA.

The challenge of setting up inter-regional trade arrangements can be overcome by building on the strengths of AFTA and its potential regional partners and focusing on their common interests. To be sure, market imperatives and pressures from international specialization will be the driving force behind inter-regional cooperation. But this will entail the development of common principles and norms as well as the creation of formal institutions or mechanisms. The expansion of trade and investment will only proceed if member-states are guided by a framework of rules and procedures. This will require for ASEAN and its partner region to agree on a common approach to trade negotiations.

IV. EU-ASEAN Trade facing Free-Trade Negotiations

The political and commercial relations of the European Union (EU) with non-member states in its closer neighbourhood, as well as in other parts of the world, have become an increasingly crucial issue at a time when the Single Internal Market project is about to mature, and when the slower growth of the US economy and the stumbling US Dollar towards the Euro in 2007 have put Europe's role in the global economy more in the limelight than in earlier years. The external commercial relations of the EU have shifted gradually from being westbound to being eastbound during the last three decades. The trade turnover (exports + imports) with ASEAN+3 (ASEAN, China (incl. Hong Kong), Japan and Korea) accounted for 24 per cent of EU-27 total extra-regional a significant increase since 1977 when the share was 6 per cent for the then nine members of the European Community (EC).

The main reason for this notable geographical shift is the soaring foreign trade with China, but it is equally of importance to point at the efforts of the EU to sustain its traditional political and commercial linkages with the ten Southeast Asian nations constituting the Association of Southeast Asian Nations (ASEAN), historically closely linked with Europe in a common colonial past and today balancing its external trade relations between America, Europe and its own neighbours in the East Asian region. When it comes to trade policy preferences, both ASEAN and the EU are characterized by an ambivalence between on the one hand an active support to the multilateral process within the World Trade Organization (WTO), and, on the other, an even more pronounced endeavour to support and to enforce intraregional trade relations, but also to explore opportunities to promote interregional trade agreements. Furthermore, separate states within ASEAN may in parallel aim at speeding up the process of liberalizations by closing bilateral trade agreements with other individual states or entire trade blocs.

The Global political Environment of EU-ASEAN Trade

The WTO today embraces 153 member states, and should be seen as the most powerful arena for common rules governing international trade in all sectors of industry. The original signatories of the European Economic Community (EEC) as well as those Western European states that later joined the EC/EU, were among the inaugural contracting parties of the General Agreement on Tariffs and Trade (GATT) in 1948 or were incorporated into the agreement shortly thereafter. The centrally planned economies of Eastern Europe applied for membership in the EU as well as in the GATT/WTO soon after the collapse of the Soviet-led Council of Mutual Economic Assistance (CMEA). The intricate balance between multilateral and regional/bilateral cooperation is as sensitive today as it was in the 1970s, although the number of bilateral agreements that challenged the dominance of the multilateral trade order was limited at that time.

The Common Commercial Policy within the EEC, operationalised through the implementation of the customs union, can be seen as the most notable practical application of Article XXIV within the GATT treaty, regulating the opportunities for regional trade cooperation to coexist with the GATT rounds. Thirty years ago, the Tokyo Round of Multilateral Trade Negotiations (MTNs) within the GATT (MTN VII) was entering its final phase. This process was later successfully brought to an end in 1979, six years after its formal start. The likewise successful conclusion in 1993 of the Uruguay Round (MTN VIII) represented an even higher ambition in the long-term mission to liberalize world trade. Despite the subsequent launching of the WTO, the DDA, the latest MTN, is already nearly four years delayed in relation to the original deadline that was commonly decided in 2001. During the last seven years political leaders have repeated the 'mantra' of optimism regarding the opportunity to achieve a final deal in the DDA despite very little visible progress in reality.

V. U.S.-Southern African Customs Union FTA

On April 18, 2006, the United States abandoned work on an FTA with the Southern African Customs Union (SACU). Instead, the United States announced that it would begin a new work program on trade and investment issues. The talks had begun in November 2002, when the USTR notified Congress of the intent to negotiate an FTA with the five nations of SACU.28. The first round of talks began in Johannesburg, South Africa, on June 3, 2003. SACU is a customs union composed of South Africa, Botswana, Lesotho, Namibia, and Swaziland. The negotiations were hampered by the reluctance of SACU to negotiate on the full range of issues that have been addressed in other bilateral and regional FTAs that the United States has signed.

At one point, SACU countries envisioned a two-stage negotiating process, with a market access agreement serving as an early harvest. Other issues of concern to the United States such as government procurement, investment, and intellectual property rights would be put off in a follow-up agreement. Such a strategy would have represented a departure from U.S. negotiating practices. While all the SACU states are eligible for the tariff preferences under the Africa Growth and Opportunity Act (Title I, P.L. 106-200), the negotiation of an FTA would have "locked-in" and potentially expanded such tariff advantages (http://italy.usembassy.gov/pdf/other/RL33463.pdf).

Developing Countries and the Trade Negotiation Process

Global economic governance depends on frequent negotiations among national governments and non-state players. These negotiations determine how financial crises, environmental stresses, and trade conflicts are managed and who receives the gains and bears the costs, with powerful consequences for local communities around the world. Yet social science still does not understand the process of negotiation, as distinct from the issues on the table, well enough. Developing countries have become far more active in multilateral and bilateral trade negotiations in recent years, yet negotiation processes has not kept up (http://www.ruig-gian.org/research/outputs/output.php?ID =124). What happens inside these negotiations between delegations and what difference does it make? What determines the outcomes? Do strategies of developing country negotiators make any difference, considering the power disparities they face? Is it possible to generalize about this complex international process?

At one level these are social-scientific questions, analogous to other questions about the behavior of markets and politics that social scientists attempt to answer. At another level, the answers could have practical significance as well. We often read about a shortage of communication between practitioners of international relations and academics, at least political scientists. Our group of political scientists wishes humbly to take up that challenge. It is widely agreed that many, especially in least developed countries, still need substantial improvements in their negotiation capacity, presumably including the capacity to understand how the process works. One of our goals is to add to the body of empirically grounded scholarship on the economic negotiation process that is available to support the world of practice. Thus this book is written for interested readers in both worlds.

Its unifying theme is that the content of developing countries' international trade agreements varies with the process of negotiation that produces them. This section summarizes how we develop this theme. By *the international negotiation process* we mean a sequence of actions in which two or more governments address demands and proposals to each other for the ostensible purpose of reaching an agreement and changing the behavior of at least one party. The central feature is the behavior of official negotiators and mediators. But trade negotiations may also involve more than government officials; they also interact with markets, constituents, and sometimes international officials, mediators and non-state actors.

The negotiation process intervenes between other causal conditions and the outcomes. Those other conditions those are largely or partly exogenous to the process—such as technological change, market trends, power structures, international rules. The terms "negotiation" and "bargaining" are used interchangeably here. This process is more general than trade; it also observed when governments bargain over military-security matters, human rights issues, financial flows, and environmental problems. Some generalizations that apply to trade negotiations in particular are almost certainly valid more generally as well.

In complex episodes like the Uruguay round and the Doha round, dozens of governments seek to reach multilateral agreements to regulate market access and write rules for the world trading system. In the second type, two or a few governments attempt to negotiate settlements to disputes taking place in the shadow of these rules. When WTO members file legal complaints attempting to achieve fuller compliance, they often engage in settlement negotiations with the defending states simultaneously. In fact most disputes brought legally under the GATT and WTO has been settled by negotiation before the adjudication process has run its full course.

After 1990 developing country participation in dispute settlement talks increased, and their participation in multilateral trade negotiations exploded. During and after the Uruguay round (1986-1994) more developing countries shifted their policies toward reliance on international markets for development. After establishment of the World Trade Organization, more countries established or reinforced their missions in Geneva. Most notably in 1999, during preparations for the WTO's Seattle ministerial conference, developing countries voiced their concerns and injected dozens of formal proposals into the negotiation process. This participation explosion drew in many smaller trading countries that had been largely passive or not signatories at all prior to 1994. Many increased their investment in training their officials for international commercial negotiations, with the help of UNCTAD, the WTO and regional organizations. Many formed or joined bargaining coalitions to defend common negotiating positions through direct coordination. Almost every member state sent its minister to Seattle and again to Doha in 2001 and Cancún in 2003. These events and developing countries' role in them became front-page news worldwide.

Newer organizations are now part of the negotiator's context as well. The South Centre and AITIC are intergovernmental organizations created to support developing countries in trade negotiations. Non-governmental organizations have become quite active not only in public protests but also behind the scenes in some cases, supplying applied analysis and proposals to developing country delegations. Meanwhile, developing countries were targeted as defendants in far more legal disputes under the WTO than under the GATT. From 1995 through 2000, they were defendants in 81 cases—amounting to 37 percent of all disputes—which was dramatically higher than the 8 percent of disputes that had targeted developing countries during the GATT period.

The Association of Southeast Asian States (ASEAN) and the South American countries of the Mercado Común Del Sur (MERCOSUR) launched free trade areas in the early 1990s. The Andean Pact and the Central American Common Market were reactivated during that time. The Caribbean Community and Common Market (CARICOM) have existed since 1973. Western hemisphere states began to negotiate a Free Trade Area of the Americas in 1994. In 1997 the South Asian Association for Regional Cooperation agreed to make itself into a free trade area. The African, Caribbean, and Pacific Countries engaged in continuing talks with the European Union. African states have negotiated a variety of sub-regional and region-wide trade and monetary pacts since the 1960s. They launched the continent-wide African Economic Community in 1991 and the African Union in 2002.

After the Agreement on the Trade-Related Aspects of Intellectual Property Rights (TRIPS) came into operation in 1995 developing countries have found themselves in a process of continual negotiation over intellectual property rights and access to medicines. These negotiations have taken place in the World Trade Organization and in the context of free trade agreements. The only real win for developing countries has been the Doha Declaration on the TRIPS Agreement and Public Health in 2001. Developing countries will do better if they adopt a networked governance approach to negotiation rather than continuing to rely on traditional coalition formation (http://www.springerlink.com/content/k7878861m11h5m15/).

Economic cooperation among developing countries has been a key aspect of their development strategy for years. The Group of 77, since 1964, has provided the institutional umbrella under which various other forms of economic and trade cooperation among developing countries have been evolved and concretized. The need for cooperation and solidarity among developing countries is becoming even more pressing, particularly in trade negotiations at the multilateral and regional levels as these negotiations become continuous, involve multiple players, and extend into the national policy space domain. In this setting, developing countries are confronted with difficult challenges of transforming and using trade as an engine of promoting growth, development and poverty reduction. Some critical elements of a development strategy for developing countries will include the strengthening of trade negotiation capacity, strengthening regional integration and improved networking among integration organizations, and enhancing South-South trade, especially in commodities (UNCTAD, 2004).

In addition to WTO negotiations, efforts to negotiate regional trade agreements have accelerated in recent years (see discussion in Section II). Developing countries have been negotiating and concluding agreements with both developed and developing countries. Emerging from such negotiations is a widening array of regional trade agreements, some 300 of them, with a significant bearing on the development prospects of developing countries and on the multilateral trading system. Some 40 per cent of world trade takes place within the regional trade agreements that are in force today, and this share is projected to grow.

Recent *new-generation* regional trade agreements cover not only trade in goods, but also *behind-the-border* regulatory areas. Some regional trade agreements cover more of these areas than the WTO, and extend more deeply into them. Often referred to as 'WTO-plus' agreements, they extend beyond multilateral disciplines and liberalization commitments in areas such as services, investment, competition policy, intellectual property rights and environment. Negotiations have been launched for large-scale, plurilateral agreements that would transform economic relationships based on pre-existing unilateral preferences into relationships based on strict reciprocity, as with the

Free Trade Area of the Americas (FTAA) and ACP-EU negotiations for economic partnership agreements. These negotiations will have implications for multilateral trade negotiations as the negotiations of North-South regional trade agreements tend to involve deeper market access and higher regulatory standards than negotiations at the multilateral level. Hence capacity building must enable negotiators to foresee and assess the extent of the policy and systemic impacts of a growing number of regional trade agreements.

UNCTAD's role in trade negotiations capacity building for Developing Nations

By virtue of its accumulated expertise, and its mandates from Bangkok (UNCTAD X) and São Paulo (UNCTAD XI), UNCTAD continues to be in a unique position to assist developing countries and their regional groupings in trade and trade negotiations through research and analysis, intergovernmental consensus building and technical cooperation. Given the extended scope, complexity, structure and process of Doha Round negotiations, UNCTAD's capacity building activities could be increased to meet the needs of the *Geneva process* and *national process*, as well as intergovernmental consensus building more generally. In addition, there may be a need as negotiations on the July Package accelerate to design a set of informal seminars for Geneva-based negotiators on specific Doha Round 6 These include services by AITIC and the negotiating issues, as well as on effective negotiating strategies and networking options. Such seminars would also allow for informal exchange and improved networking among developing country negotiators and thus their sharing of information on the outcomes of various consultations associated with the Geneva Process. The Box 1 summarizes some illustrative Trading Arrangements through inter-regional negotiations across developing countries in the World.

Box 1: Regional Trading Arrangements of Developing Countries

In Africa, some 14 regional trade agreements are in force, including the Arab Maghreb Union (UMA) in North Africa and in sub-Saharan Africa, the following Central African Economic and Monetary Community (CEMAC), Common Market for Eastern and Southern Africa (COMESA), East African Community (EAC), Indian Ocean Commission (IOC), Economic Community of Central African States (ECCAS), Economic Community of West African States (ECOWAS), West African Economic and Monetary Union (UEMOA), Southern African Customs Union (SACU) and Southern African Development Community (SADC). These sub-regional groupings are expected to constitute a continental scale African Common Market under the auspices of the African Union by 2008. In the Asia-Pacific region, some 10 groupings are in force, including Association of South-East Asian Nations (ASEAN), South Asian Association for Regional Cooperation (SAARC),

Economic Cooperation Organization (ECO) in continental Asia and Melanesian Spearhead Group (MSG), Pacific Island Countries Trade Agreement (PICTA/PACER) in the Pacific, and the Bangkok Agreement. In the Americas, Southern Common Market (MERCOSUR), the Andean Community, Caribbean Community (CARICOM) and Central American Common Market (CACM) operate alongside several plurilateral economic cooperation agreements. In the Middle East, the Gulf Cooperation Council (GCC) plans to establish an economic union by 2010. Negotiations for the Greater Arab Free Trade Area (GAFTA) were launched with a target date of 2008. Four Mediterranean-Basin countries (Egypt, Jordan, Morocco and Tunisia) have signed the Agadir Agreement as a stepping stone towards a Euro-Mediterranean FTA to be established by 2010.

South-South Trade and Regional Integration

New trade geography is emerging in international trade with three interlinked determinants, namely the increasing role and importance of developing countries to drive trade and growth, South-South trade and economic cooperation, and the changing context of North-South interdependence. This emerging new trade geography, however, needs to be treated with caution in order to avoid unrealistic expectations in terms of its scope and impact, particularly given that many countries, including African countries, LDCs and SIDS, do not appear to participate significantly in this trend. Developing countries face a considerable challenge in sustaining, maximizing and exploiting the opportunities emerging in the new trade geography, and in particular in mainstreaming into this dynamism the participation of those developing countries that remain marginalized from international trade.

Developing country Governments, their regional integration groupings, and their economic operators need to consult, coordinate and cooperate closely and actively on South-South trade, investment and economic cooperation initiatives to devise strategies and actions to advance mutual trade and investment. Such cooperation needs to be conducted on the basis of mutuality of advantage for all parties to maximize the development gains. Approaches that engage countries and their economic operators in mutually advantageous relationships, in which all participants gain, have higher chances of being sustained and strengthened. The challenge is to develop and implement a strategic approach and positive agenda for South-South trade and economic cooperation. The annex to this paragraph provides herein an 11-point Positive Agenda for South-South economic and trade cooperation that was discussed by UNCTAD's Trade and Development Board at it 51st session.

A Positive Agenda for South-South Trade (Annexure)

1. Increasing focus on South-South cooperation

Governments and economies operators in the South need to place more deliberate focus and build on the new dynamism in South-South trade and economic cooperation. Developing countries are already assimilating and actively integrating South-South trade, investment and economic cooperation strategies into their development policies and plans. Success stories need to be replicated more widely and across different regions. These efforts need to be continued and strengthened, particularly with respect to cooperation at the interregional level, which remains the weaker link in South-South trade. It also requires the full engagement of the economic operators of the South and for them to integrate South-South business opportunities into their business plans (This agenda is outlined in UNCTAD document on "Follow-up to UNCTAD XI: New developments in international economic relations—The new geography of international economic relations" (TD/B/51/6).

2. Boosting trade in new and dynamic sector

New complementarities can be exploited to assist developing countries to enter into and build export capacities in dynamic and new sectors in commodities, manufactures and services. Developing countries have become major players in international markets for some of these sectors – they account for 30 per cent of world exports of the 20 most dynamic product groups. Additional work is needed to support South-South economic cooperation to identify opportunities for new – and further develop existing – Southern supply chains in new and dynamic sectors. This will require, *inter alia,* the identification of specific sectors and products, and their actual and potential markets; policy options and practical actions for translating opportunities into actual export activities and higher domestic value added; sharing of experiences and lessons learnt; and partnerships and twining of economic operators.

3. Strengthening regional cooperation and integration

Consolidating and strengthening the South's processes of regional trade and economic integration among developing countries so as to maximize their full potential is a major challenge. The potential for such cooperation remains to be fully exploited.

4. Expanding the potential for inter-regional trade

The time now, in the backdrop of rising South-South trade, appears ripe for a paradigm shift to promote South-South interregional trade and investment flows including through trade liberalization. The Global System of Trade Preferences among Developing Countries (GSTP) provides a promising avenue for developing countries to increase and expand their interregional trade.

5. *Cooperating in commodities trade*

With growing South-South trade in commodities, cooperation among commodity producers become important to meet consumption needs in the South in respect of basic commodities including food and fuel and to ensure sufficient supplies of production inputs in related Southern supply chains. By enabling Southern commodity producers to achieve sustainable management of their commodity production and trade and increase their participation in supply and value chains, including on a regional basis, South-South cooperation could substantially increase returns to producers. In addition to the well-known coordination that has been achieved by oil-producing developing countries, recent enhanced cooperation between a number developing countries producing, for example, rice and rubber has also resulted in better prices and returns for their producers.

6. *Expanding trade in services*

Exploiting complementarities in South-South services trade can offer important trade and investment opportunities. Services have gained prominence in the economies of developing countries and now account for about 50 per cent of their aggregate GDP and 15 per cent of their total exports. Efficient services are also important for economic competitiveness and advancing human and social welfare. South-South trade in services in all four modes of GATS is on the rise and has substantial possibilities. Most of this trade is currently conducted at the regional level; increasingly it is being facilitated by the incorporation of disciplines to liberalize services trade within regional trade agreements. Further building up South-South trade in services requires closer cooperation at the bilateral, regional and interregional levels in services sectors with high growth potential and that can also impact positively on social welfare. These include education services, health services, professional services, construction services, computer and related services, tourism services and energy services.

7. *Cooperating on trade and environment*

Environmental measures – especially in Northern markets but also in Southern markets – affecting exports of developing countries have become increasing stringent, frequent and complex. As a result, these may undermine gains from tariff liberalization by acting as disguised barriers to trade, and inhibiting effective market entry. Addressing such barriers becomes important in facilitating trade and assuring market entry for exports of developing countries into each other's markets. Several practical South-South initiatives could be implemented to address these concerns, such as sub-regional early warning systems, regional cooperation in standards development and conformity assessment, and the integration of processes to advance harmonization and recognition of equivalency within South-South regional and interregional trade arrangements in order to facilitate related South-South trade.

8. Ensuring market entry

South-South exports, as is the case with South-North trade, must respond to requirements such as technical regulations and sanitary and phyto-sanitary measures. These will need to be addressed, including through sharing of information, setting up of mutual recognition agreements, and coordination and harmonization within regional integration arrangements. Cooperation within the South in dealing with such market entry issues, including restrictive rules of origin, will be important in facilitating market access openings derived from mutual tariff liberalization.

9. Cooperating on competition law and policy

Cooperation in competition law and policy can complement national development strategies and ensure that the gains from trade liberalization expand South-South trade, growth and development. In agriculture, industry, services and technology sectors, developing countries need to calibrate competition policy to help build supply capacity and competitiveness and ensure both efficiency gains for the economy and welfare gains for the population. Several regional groupings of developing countries have adopted common regional competition policies, as well as establishing regional consultation forums on the control of cross-border anti-competitive practices.

10. Enhancing trade-related and reducing transaction costs

Trade-related infrastructure: Much of the trade that would naturally take place between developing countries fails to materialize due to insufficient trade-related infrastructure. Historically, significant progress has been made in building trade-related infrastructure for North-South and South-North trade, but relatively little effort and investment has been focused on the development of such infrastructure for South-South trade. Resolving these deficiencies is a fundamental requirement for sustained growth in South-South trade and investment. Resources are needed to build infrastructure and create a virtuous circle whereby the existence of good-quality infrastructure encourages trade and, in turn, increased trade encourages further generation, upgrading and development of trade-supporting infrastructure. Such a virtuous circle will facilitate trade, expand trade-support infrastructure, and reduce transaction costs for the products (and services) of developing countries that are more competitive and attractive to consumers in the South as much as the North.

Facilitating trade: In trading with each other and also with the rest of the world, developing countries confront major problems of trade facilitation relating to excessive trade documentation, insignificant use of information technology, lack of transparency and of clear import/export requirements, inadequate procedures, and lack of modernized institutions relating to customs clearance. In addition, difficulties in obtaining visas, especially business visas, to facilitate South-South business contacts significantly hinder the development of South-South trade and investment. Thus, addressing trade facilitation issues can contribute significantly to reducing inefficiencies in such areas as customs, including through simplification, rationalization and harmonization of procedures, greater transparency, and the elimination or minimization of avoidable administrative and procedural delays and costs incurred in international goods and services transactions, including streamlining and easing procedures for business visas.

Financing trade: One of the crucial bottlenecks in South-South cooperation relates to the lack of adequate and organized finance for South-South trade and investment. Building the required trade and financial institutions and channels should be given high priority, including through enhanced cooperation among the South's trade finance institutions. More support could be given to the expansion of the capacity of Southern banking systems, especially export-import banks, to provide normal, structured and concessional trade finance for South-South trade. Creating an enabling environment for accessing trade finance for South-South trade would in turn facilitate greater South-South investment in productive activities.

Enabling information flows: Promoting access to and effective use of, ICTs in developing countries can foster trade, including South-South trade. ICTs are expanding the possibilities of developing economies to participate in international markets. In addition, ICTs enable trade in other sectors by enhancing market access and broadening the customer base, facilitating customs, transport and logistics. Most importantly, ICTs play a critical role in facilitating networking between economic actors in the South.

11. *Increasing awareness of opportunities for South-South trade*

Trade promotion and marketing activities among developing countries, both regionally and inter-regionally, can be used effectively to raise awareness of business opportunities and promote trade and investment activities. In this direction, trade fairs, buyer/seller meets, market surveys and specific sectoral initiatives/expositions could be actively used by developing countries and their regional organizations. Creating direct, cost-efficient marketing and distribution links, channels and networks between Southern traders could give a significant boost to South-South trade. Improved information flows should accelerate progress in developing more direct marketing channels, including by stimulating entrepreneurial efforts to capture new trade opportunities.

Country-Specific Strategies for Global Business Negotiation

Each country in the world is characterized by its culture, values, religious beliefs, traditions and life-styles. This aspect assumes great significance in trade transactions and cross-country or inter and intra-regional cooperation or business negotiations. In this section, some country-specific strategies as well as styles for business negotiations are described on a selected basis for illustration.

Negotiation Style in the Netherlands

Stereotypes

Stereotypes are simplifications and generalizations of the world. Many of them are partly true. A few common stereotypes of Dutch people would be the following: Cloggies, tulip-eaters, Coffee shop-addicts, abortionists, tolerant, liberal and stingy. Most of all the Dutch are labeled as liberal because of their government policies which are seen as controversial by a lot of people. Examples of these kinds of laws are the legalization of marihuana and the freedom of abortion and euthanasia. As a country we get a critics as well as compliments for the way we deal with these kinds of problems in society. The Dutch are also seen as very tolerant to other people and different cultures. In my opinion this is one of the stereotypes we like to life up to and we would label ourselves tolerant but it's only partly true. Behind this facade of tolerance there is a lot of intolerance hidden, for example towards foreign people living in our country. On the other hand the stereotype of the Dutch on wooden shoes in fields of tulips and windmills exist. Although this stereotype is more pleasant than the first one it's not closer to the true nature of the Dutch people.

In governmental issues the Dutch have a history of consensus. People are always trying to a find a solution that brings the goals and wishes of the different people as close together as possible. I think this element of our culture can be found in back in out negotiation style. Another major stereotype of the Dutch is their stinginess. We are very concerned about the price of goods and don't like to spend anymore money than strictly necessary. This old stereotype can be traced back to the period of great wealth due to our good trade position in the golden century. The Dutch have a history of trade which of course is accompanied by negotiation. This stereotype is again partly true and that this element can be traced back to the negotiation style used.

Hofstede

Geert Hofstede is an expert in the field of national cultures, organizational cultures and interactions between cultures. Hofstede identified five different dimensions of national influences. *Power distance,* the degree to which differences in power levels exist. Higher scores characterize countries with high rates of political violence while lower scores are associated with countries which aim for equal rights. The score of the Netherlands on these dimensions is 38 (Scores are based on a 0-120 scale) which is a low score. This means that the differences in power levels are relatively low and there is an aim for equal positions and rights.

Individualism vs. Collectivism, the degree to which people are integrated into groups.

Individualists have loose ties with other individualist. People are looking after themselves and close family. Collectivism is characterized by societies in which people are integrated in strong, cohesive groups. The Netherlands scores very high on this dimension (80) and is in this study of 63 countries. This means that the Dutch are very individualistic orientated.

Masculinity vs. Femininity, concerns the value placed on traditional male or female values. Masculine values are competitiveness, assertiveness, ambitions and the accumulations of material possessions and wealth. Feminine values are concerned with relationships and quality of life. The Netherlands scores very low on this dimension and holds a very low position. This means the Dutch attach more value to the more female values as quality of life and relationships.

Uncertainty avoidance is the degree to which a society tries to minimize uncertainty. Cultures that score high tend to attach a lot of value to rules and lasting relationships. With a score of 53 the Netherlands are positioned low compared to most countries. This means that the Netherlands are positioned between uncertainty avoidance with rules and laws and on they other hand are not afraid of taking some risks.

Long vs. short terms orientation, describes the orientations of time and the concerns with long term planning and short term orientations. Some characteristics of the opposing sides are: Persistence, thrift and having sense of shame (long-term orientations) and personal steadiness and stability, protecting your face, respect of tradition (short term orientations). A score of 44 is relatively low meaning the Netherlands is more short term orientated.

The Dutch Culture

General

In the Dutch culture family plays a great role and is seen as the foundations of the social structure, families tend to be small and relatively few woman work fulltime outside the house. The Dutch are disciplined, conservative and pay attention to details. Appearances are important to them and they place high value on cleanliness and neatness. The Dutch are very private people and dislike displays of wealth as they run counter to their egalitarian beliefs. The do not draw attention to their accomplishments of their material possessions and do not value accoutrement of success.

Dutch hold strong egalitarian beliefs and them a highly tolerant of individual differences. This egalitarian view is carried out over the raising of children, social programs and the workplace. Every person is allowed to give his opinion and in most cases this opinion is valued. Moreover the boss will, although he/she is the final decision maker, ask for input from the workers and strive for consensus. Respect is of high value to the Dutch. When involved with outsiders the Dutch tend to be reserved and formal. They do not like to display their possessions neither emotions. As already said the Dutch are private people and they don't like to be asked personal questions. In many cases they will refuse to answer. More important business and personal life are strictly separated.

Business

Because the Dutch have a long history of international trade they are familiar with doing business with foreigners. They attach a lot of value to clarifying the benefits that you could offer to their business and how you would benefit of this relationship. Also in business the Dutch tend to be reserved and formal and they do not appreciate touching and showing emotions. The Dutch value their space and it's advisable to keep some distance.

Another important point is that the Dutch are very direct in their communication. They like people to say what they mean. People coming from less direct cultures, for example Asian cultures, can experience their communication as rude. The Dutch value the opinions of other people and ideas and thoughts are discussed very openly. The Dutch attach a lot of value to your word, making a claim which you cannot make true will mark you as unreliable. It's important to be honest.

Business meeting etiquettes

The Dutch value punctuality, unlike some other cultures being on time is taken extremely serious. By coming late people will think you will always be late and unable to make deadlines. Cancelling a meeting is not a problem but make sure that this is done in time. Cancelling last minute can seriously damage the relationship. Because of the Dutch way of being very direct in their communication they spend very little time on pleasantries in negotiations and meetings. Furthermore because of their need of privacy they will keep meetings rather formal. During the meeting maintaining direct eye contact while speaking is seen as a way of showing respect.

The Dutch Culture and Negotiation

From this brief description of the Dutch culture and the Dutch people we can derive some elements important to negotiation. First of all the egalitarian belief is important. The Dutch value equalness, respect and consensus. One can also see this in the score on power distance in the framework of Hofstede. The low score on power distance means that we strive for a low distance in power levels. For negotiation this would mean that the Dutch are likely to be interested in the opinion, interests and argument of their negotiation partner. Moreover their will be a strive for consensus. Goal in the negotiation will be to arrive at a solution that satisfies both partners. Showing respect for each other is also seen as very important as the Dutch like to be treated with respect as they will treat their partner with respect.

Another important aspect of the Dutch culture is their need for privacy. The Dutch don't like to be asked personal questions and they prefer to keep business and personal life separated. Overall they tend to be reserved and formal when meeting strangers. For negotiations this means that it's not wishful to ask a Dutch negotiation partner for example how his wife is doing. In some cultures it would be seen as very impolite or even rude not to address personal questions to your negotiation partner. This stressed they need for knowledge of the culture of your negotiation partner. Because the Dutch like to keep meetings formal and direct in negotiation the will come down to business quickly. And due to their direct way of communicating they will not engage in small talk or they will keep this to a minimum.

As talked about the Dutch don't like to show their emotions. Because of this it's important to come up with rational arguments instead of emotional ones. Also important in negotiation is the fact that the Dutch pay a lot of attention to details. They will take their time to asses your proposal and they want to understand the agreement. As said they are very interested in the benefits to both partners. Using background information's, statistics and facts will help to make everything clear and will be valued.

Furthermore, to talk about the consensus orientation of the Dutch there is a need for consensus the Dutch will tend to take into account all the people that might be affected by the decision. This process of making an analysis of the consequences for all the stakeholders of a decision can slow down the negotiation process. It's advisable not to put pressure on the process because the Dutch will not appreciate such behaviour. It is also important to know that a decision in any form is a decision in the Netherlands. It can take some time to come to a decision but once the decision is made it will not be change. Moreover, contracts are taken very seriously.

The Harvard Principles

A brief description of the Harvard principles is given here in order to be able to analyze the use of these principles in the Dutch negotiation style. The Harvard concept exists of four basic principles:

- *Separating the people from the problem.* We all enter the negotiation process as people and people always have certain emotions. These emotions can influence the process tremendously and can cause problems in the negotiation. It's very important to distinguish between people (emotions) and issues (objective needs). There are four different areas of concern in this process: emotions, perceptions, personality and communication.
- *Concentrate on interest not positions.* It's important to clarify the interests of both parties since people act according to these interests. Learning about the interests of your negotiation partner can help in solving the problem.
- *Invent options for mutual gains.* When the interests are discovered this offers possibilities to find solutions that will be capable of satisfying the interests of both sides to the greatest extend. This creative process can increase the possibilities of reaching a final agreement.
- *Insist on using objective criteria.* Negotiations can turn into debates, which is not a good development for the negotiations. One of the reasons this can happen is because of both sides using different standards. To solve this problem it can be useful to discuss the different criteria and develop a shared set of criteria.

These criteria can help to reach results which are satisfactory for both parties in the negotiation process. Managing the relationship between the parties is of great importance in this framework.

The Dutch Negotiation Style and the Harvard Principles

After describing the Dutch culture and the Dutch negotiation style let us now analyze as to what degree the Harvard principles are applicable in the Netherlands.

The first principle stated that in a negotiation one should try to separate people from the problem. This principle is very well represented in the Dutch style of negotiation. The Dutch don't like to show their emotions and in business showing emotions is not common and not appreciated. On the other hand the Dutch tend to be open to opinions and be respectful. If emotions are so high that are affecting the negotiation it's possible to address them. Moreover the Dutch are very direct in their communication. They dislike small talk and like to come to the issue, the problem as quickly as possible. This also helps to separate people from business.

The second principle states to focus on interests, not positions. This principle is also well represented in the Dutch negotiation style because of the Dutch concern with the benefits to both parties. They want to know what their benefits will be and they want to see they benefits to the other party. Revealing these benefits means also revealing the interests. Again also the direct communication influences this process. The Dutch like people to say what they want and what they mean. The Dutch also value relationships; this is supported by their low score on masculine on the Hofstede research. For the development of these relationships is of great importance to acknowledge the various interests involved in a negotiation. Correlating with the third principle, invent options for mutual gains, is their orientation towards consensus. It's important to the Dutch to strive for solutions that benefit everybody involved. This means to the Dutch are likely to be open to developing new solutions. This will enhance the chances of coming to final agreements.

Putting everything together the most important things to know when entering into negotiation with a Dutch person are in my opinion the following:

Privacy, the Dutch very much values their privacy and they dislike people trying to enter their personal space. Business is business and is kept separated from personal life.

Direct communication, I think this element of the Dutch culture is very important because it can cause communication problems in cross-cultural communications. For example to Asian people this direct way of communicating can seem blunt but for the Dutch is just the way they communicate.

Consensus orientation, the Dutch are consensus orientated and are very willing to come to a solution that offers the most satisfaction to all parties. Negotiating with a Dutch person can be seen as working together to find a good solution. This offers a good basis for long term relationships and it should be used.

Tolerance and respect, Dutch people are tolerant to foreigners and they have a history of international trade. They do want to be treated and respected in the same way and this is highly valued.

Punctuality, the value attached to punctuality should not be underestimated. Although it might be very common and accepted in other cultures, for example the Spanish culture, being late will give you a bad image.

Negotiating with Germans

Geert Hofstede's Cultural Dimension

"Culture is more often a source of conflict than of synergy. Cultural differences are a nuisance at best and often a disaster." Prof. Geert Hofstede, Emeritus Professor, Maastricht University. (http://www.geert-hofstede.com/)

People from different cultures vary a lot. So of course this is also valid for the business world and with that for negotiations between people with different cultural backgrounds. We cannot just go to a different country and try to negotiate with our opponent as we are used to back home. It is necessary to take into consideration cultural differences.

Enter: Geert Hofstede's research. Dr. Geert Hofstede (picture on the right) conducted a study that was trying to find answers to the question of how culture can influence values in the workplace. For this study he gathered data from over 100,000 individuals that came from forty different countries. This data collection and analyze took place between 1967 and 1973.

The results of the analysis, and later additions, gave Hofstede the information for his now so famous model, http://www.colostate.edu/Depts/Speech/rccs/theor which looks at follows: it distinguishes between four primary dimensions to differentiate cultures, which were followed by a fifth dimension after another analysis as explained in short in 5 dimensions.

- *Power Distance Index (PDI):* the degree of (in-) equality between people from one country. High score: there are inequalities of power and wealth. "These societies are more likely to follow a caste system that does not allow significant upward mobility of its citizens." (http://www.cyborlink.com/besite/hofstede.htm) The opposite is true for a low ranking.
- *Individualism (IDV):* do people in a country place importance on the individual or collective achievement? High: individuality and individual rights are of greater importance within the society. "Individuals in these societies may tend to form a larger number of looser relationships." (http://www.geert-hofstede.com/) Low: Here the collective achievement is desired: families are important; and concerning business, it is common that one person is responsible not only for his own actions but also for the actions of their colleagues.

- *Masculinity (MAS):* Does a society still have the old picture of the man being the one working for the family, having control and of course the power? High: there is rather a lot gender differentiation in the country, men are believed to be the head of the family and have the say, they control women. Low: Man and females are treated equally, so both have the same rights and power.
- *Uncertainty Avoidance Index (UAI):* This point deals with how people in a certain country handle unstructured situations, what is their level of tolerance for uncertainty and ambiguity. High: low tolerance. "The country is rather rule-oriented and institutes laws, rules, regulations, and controls to be able to reduce the amount of uncertainty."(http://www.geert-hofstede.com/)

  Low: people in a country with a low score for UAI do not worry that much about uncertainty; they can handle different opinions and have the heart to take on risk. In addition they don't adhere to rules and regulations as much as people in a country with a relatively high score.
- *Long-Term Orientation (LTO):* "long-term devotion to traditional, forward thinking values" (http://www.geert-hofstede.com/). *High*: People in this country like to stick to traditions and pursue long-term goals; they always look in the future. *Low:* the focus here is on short-term achievements and change is welcomed.

Germany's Scores

Power Distance 35
Individualism 67
Uncertainty Avoidance 65
Masculinity 66
Long-term Orientation 31

Having a look at Germany's scores, one can see that they, or we, put great importance on *individualism, masculinity, and uncertainty avoidance.* On the opposite, power distance and long-term orientation have only low scores. This shows that Germans believe people should be treated as equals. In addition to that Germans are able to change and adapt rapidly. For negotiating this could mean: Considering the low score of power distance one could say that Germans will accept the other person as an equal person and not try to be the leader of the negotiation. The high score of uncertainty avoidance could indicate that Germans like to be very clear about what they want, how they want to say it and how the negotiation is structured. They like to be very organized and be on time. The relatively high score for Masculinity indicates that it is still common that men are the ones caring for the rest of the family, they are the ones working. So for negotiations this implies that one will more often meet on men than women. Concerning the Individualism score, it could imply that Germans "are more sensitive to their own public "face." (http://www.executiveplanet.com/business-etiquette/Germany.html)

Before the negotiation Germans will inform and prepare themselves properly, which they also expect from their negotiation partners. Unlike many other European countries, Germans will not spend the whole first meeting on chatting and getting to know the other person; they will take some time to get to know important things about the other person, but want to get to the core of the negotiation quite soon. They have their set agenda, which they do not like to exceed too much or often. Additionally, Germans are private people that don't like to talk to much about their personal "business"/life if possible. It is not that they do not like to talk or get to know the other person at all, it will just take its time, and Germans have to defrost as we would say in Germany!

When talking to Germans, you should keep in mind to call them with their academic title if known to you, like: "Dr. Derichs". These you will always find on their contact cards. In difference to people from for example the USA, Germans and European people in general write their first name in front of their last name, so: "Rebecca Derichs" instead of "Derichs, Rebecca".

During the negotiation, Germans will not hesitate to ask questions to clarify what hasn't been fully understood, because they want to prevent complications from the early beginning to keep the negotiation as efficient as possible. Furthermore, they will openly address shortcomings of your products, arguments, if they see them and have no problem with saying "no" if that is what they think. But if you flip the coin and criticise Germans, they might react quite sensitive, since it is not easy for them to deal with criticism. In addition to that they like to base their arguments on facts, figures, numbers, and use a lot of examples to make their point most clear to their opponent. This also leads to the conclusion that Germans tend to try to keep feelings and relationships out of the discussion. Germans also tend to adhere to things that proved to work good in the past, which means that they are not as flexible or spontaneous as some other countries. "The bigger and older the institution, the more slow-moving internal management will tend to be (...) why change something that has proven itself through time?" (http://www.executiveplanet.com/businessetiquette/Germany.html)

The Four Harvard Negotiation Principles (HNPs)

- *Separate the people from the problem*
- *Focus on interests, not positions* ("The purpose of a negotiation is to realize your interests, not to defend your position.")
- *Invent options for mutual gain*
- *Insist on using "objective" criteria* ("Measure the result of your negotiation against mutually agreed objective criteria.")

Comparison HNPs with Negotiation Style in Germany

- *Separate the people from the problem*

As explained earlier, Germans try to separate the people from the problem through clarifying the goal of the negotiation in the beginning and not getting too personal. In addition to that, Germans like to hold on to what has proven to be good in the past, which goes in line, with trying to pursue long-term commitment, talked about in the HNPs.

- *Focus on interests, not positions*

This point also fits to the German negotiation style, since Germans like to express what they want right in the beginning, as well as clarify their goals. The say directly what they think, so their interests should be quite obvious in a negotiation.

- *Invent options for mutual gain*

Germans like to be perfectly prepared before entering a negotiation, which includes having worked out alternatives, to be able to react on everything the other person might suggest.

- *Insist on using "objective" criteria*

When there are people from two different countries, they of course have different ways to approach a negotiation. To achieve a common ground for the discussion, they should talk about criteria before they start negotiating. I think this will work out well with Germans, since they like to have a well structured negotiation and be sure about what will follow next. The only problem could be, that they worked out the structure of the negotiation before and don't like to deviate from their way to do it. But I think, you can talk about everything and find a solution that is best for both.

To conclude, it is always good to prepare well before a negotiation with people from another country. For this it can always be of help to consider Geert Hofstede's research, since it gives you insight in the character from people all over the world, which is important for negotiations. Of course this cannot be applied to all people in a society, but for me it is a good tool to start your preparation with. And preparation is what is especially important before talking to Germans.

Negotiation Strategy in the Czech Republic

In the study published in 1990, American Professor C.A. Nelson advised the companies how to negotiate with then Czechoslovak partners. He recommended keeping the time arranged for the business meeting, to avoid debates about politics and to bring the conversation round to the topics concerning sports. He suggested to exchange small presents, but not to exaggerate it in order not to embarrass the partners. Such instructions tend to be too much simplified though.

Much more realistic was the approach of the Austrian Chamber of Commerce, published in 1997 advising the Austrian businessmen how to deal with the Czech side. "*The Czech Republic is the state with high technical and scientific potential. The Czechs are mostly non-believers (highest level of believers is in the Southern Moravia and in the Southern Bohemia). It is necessary to bear in mind that after 40 years of the reign of the communist party the whole social system is absolutely changed and it will take a lot of time until the country adjusts to the new structures. Particularly branches lacking experience with market economy structures are lagging behind Western Europe. Mother language is Czech. Czech, German and English are usual languages used during business negotiations. The crucial advantage for direct investments are both stable political scene and rather low wage level. In addition, there is quite a high education level as well as employee motivation. However, not everything is running smoothly all the time. It happens that partners do not fulfill deliveries, are not able to pay or cancel orders. Working moral and quality standards do not correspond fully to our expectations. Giving presents is sometimes tricky especially according to relatively low wage rate. There is almost no difference between Austria and the Czech Republic as for politeness, accuracy and equal rights of men and women."*

Czech Cultural Standards

"Relationship orientation"

This typical Czech standard describes the fact that the Czechs prefer relationship aspect to material one during mutual communication. This means that negotiators perceive persons and their interactions usually stronger than material side of negotiation. Smooth communication, positive atmosphere, mutual sympathies and understanding, wide range of conversational topics including personal interests and problems as well as informal communicational style are not only necessary introduction into a lot of business negotiations, but also important social value which may help achieve goals. Warm-up phase means for the Czech side obvious and essential introduction into the negotiation procedure which can not be taken as waste of time. It is not possible to neglect emotions although in comparison with many cultures (e.g. Roman) the Czechs are quite restraint and do not show emotions dramatically. However, compared to German culture the Czechs are very explosive.

People are searching for personal relationships, are appreciating mutual understanding, but they are easily vulnerable. Therefore the Czechs struggle for creating as pleasant atmosphere as possible as this is a very important value for both sides. Once are the good relationship built, they tend to keep and take care of them.

"Underestimating of structures—tendency to improvisation"

The Czechs are skeptical against structures and they like to get round of them by improvisation. They regard flexibility and resourcefulness as their typical qualities. Not only are they proud of them but they are also appreciating them on the partners' side. They are convinced that successful negotiation full of inventive and meaningful options is based on such procedure. Whereas some nations prefer to set a strict plan for negotiation procedure as it helps to manage time and material stuff, the Czechs consider it as personal limitation. They feel that the plan organizes persons not the procedure. That is why they often tend to disregard it, take it easy, moreover they sometimes ignore it. Rules and regulations are often regarded as stupid and meaningless. Who follows them is considered to be a fool who is not Negotiation strategy in The Czech Republic able to use his or her own brain as the intelligence consists in the way to get round them. Structures set from outside are typically refused.

The Czechs are able to use improvisation during the negotiation procedure; moreover they feel it as strengthening of self-confidence and expression of freedom and sovereignty. Suspicion and doubts are typical against everything which is not entrenched in their minds and is seemed to be new. First of all they would probably examine such a new situation, change it slightly and then decide if it is acceptable or not. *"We don't want to be ripped off"*, they explain. They regard themselves as to be in a weaker position towards strangers and therefore have to be very careful. Czech negotiators need to believe that the decisions they make are free and without any interference. At the same time they want to show their dignity and intelligence.

Negative perception of structure comprises the following:

- Resourcefulness to be free
- Creativity and improvisation
- Lower quality requirements
- Indifference towards sticking to them

Improvisation is for the Czechs a symbol of the highest professional skills. This is demonstrated by the ability to manage unfavorable, complex, unstructured and unpredictable situations. Improvisation is considered to be the most efficient competitive advantage in comparison with other European cultures especially the German one. This cultural standard appears mostly in unclear and uncertain situations which may lead up to a conflict. However, improvisation is not to be taken equally to desire to change or something like dynamism as the Czechs are on the whole rather conservative people. Desirable goal is to be achieved by many ways and every problem has its solution. The only thing needed is to find and carry out this solution. Sometimes it is necessary to change the given goal a bit or find some alternative so far unknown method in order to achieve the goal. These are the most frequent comments so typical for the Czechs.

"Unless it works how it should maybe it will work in some another way."
"It seems not to work, but we will try it."

Negotiation Strategy in the Czech Republic

In the Czech Republic the term "quality" is often interpreted as the ability to perform quite well. When the goal is satisfactorily achieved and the result of the negotiation is to be applied the task was successfully fulfilled. Completely perfect solution is regarded as unnecessary protraction hampering decision-making process. The Czech culture is characterized by the ability to learn and adapt to new circumstances quickly. The Czechs are able to learn from their mistakes quite immediately if they consider them as individually useful.

To take everything easy is sometimes a source of conflict with other nations especially the Germans as they regard it as indifference whereas for the Czechs it means not making mountains out of the molehills.With respect to improvisation it is useful to mention the feature of Josef Švejk. The main protagonist of the world famous novel written by Jaroslav Haš ek represents such attitudes towards problems and their solutions which are taken as typical Czech. Searching for alternatives, manifested obedience, strong efforts to avoid direct conflict, sarcasm, black humour even in the most serious case is typical for the Czech character.

"Simultaneousness"

Simultaneousness means that the Czechs are doing a lot of business at the same time; in any case they focus on the only one. They like doing that whereas they are changing priorities during negotiation according to their subjective importance and believe to use their improvisational skills appropriately. They do not want to miss any chance and keep their eyes open. They are not very goal-seeking unless there is a pressure. They prefer to deal with a lot of ideas more than being under pressure as for expected results and terms.

"Human-oriented control"

This principle means that the Czechs tend to offend against general rules in order to keep moral obligations and mutual relationships. It contradicts rules-oriented control which is typical for e.g. Germany. That means that the German way of thinking is strongly rules oriented which stems from the fact that rules and agreements must be kept irrespective of situations and persons. The Czechs emphasize particular situation and specific personal relationships and subsequently comfortable feeling which results from it. Friendship is binding and the Czechs Negotiation strategy in The Czech Republic prefers it to abstract rules. The basic motive for human-oriented control which the Czechs are applying is the same as in the previous cultural standard "Underestimating of structures"—keeping own sovereignty.

"Diffusion"

Cultures are divided into specific and diffused. This stands for level of restraint during negotiation with the others. It is important to recognize if we get to know each other in certain "specific" spheres of life and get in touch only with particular aspects of personalities or if we keep in touch with our partners fully including entire character so called in a "diffused" way. The former means that the individual spheres of life and personal aspects are relatively solid and separate, the latter that they are on the contrary highly porous.

The Czechs show obvious signs of diffusion. In their interactions we can observe diffusion of the personal aspects "sensitivity—rationality" as well as diffusion of particular spheres of their lives "working life—privacy", "role in society—personality" and "formal-informal structures"—in all social positions.

Lack of transparency is considered to be one of the fitting characteristics of the Czech negotiators. Even after long-lasting personal contexts and mutual cooperation partners do not know about the Czechs' way of thinking and do not know what to expect from them. Cultural standard of diffusion seems to be one of the key reasons.

"Strong Communicational Context"

This term stands for different proportion of that what is expressed explicitly, verbally and unambiguously related to the whole message or information. If the proportion of verbally unstated information is high then we speak about strong communicational context and vice versa. The outstanding feature of Czech negotiators is the strong communicational context.

They apply such a communicational style which includes:

(a) a lot of indirect information;
(b) is more implicit, which means that it is necessary to understand additional nonverbal signals needed to be precisely interpreted, extracted out of the context, however they are important for understanding the whole message.

Negotiation Strategy in The Czech Republic

That is why the Czechs are convinced to negotiate more diplomatically as they do not need to convey everything they want or need. According to nonverbal communication there are a lot of aspects which are worth taking notice of. Body language, face-play, emotions, eloquent silence, eye-contact but also timing of the negotiation, different social status or common friends expresses much without words.

Czech verbal communication includes a lot of hints, allusions, ambiguity, and links to a broader context, remote causes and possible consequences. At the same time the facts are expressed in great details with a lot of words in which it is easy to get lost. The Czechs are proud of their communicational style and the communication which is led entirely in a direct, brief and material way is considered to be less sophisticated.

The Czech negotiation strategy results from strong communicational context. It is based on careful, indirect, step-by-step revealing of interests. Counterpart's reaction is assessed gradually; the Czechs prefer rather defensive tactics. Czech negotiators wait on partners' mistake; they try to stagger them, refer to strong and weak points and leave the negotiation outstanding as long as possible. Direct conflict or confrontation with the Czech side is seldom. That is because it is regarded as communicational disturbance and failure of cooperation.

"Avoiding conflicts"

The Czechs claim that they do not like or even are not able to use hard style of negotiation and try to avoid it as much as possible. Facing pressure seems to be very difficult for the Czech side. If it is not possible to leave the topic and find an alternative way, disappointment and ensuing resignation prevail. However they still hope in changing minds of the counterpart, which is highly improbable. The Czechs do not enter such conflicts which are lost in advance and comply with temporary loss or they simply leave the battlefield. Whereas the Czech interpretation of such situation would be: "the wiser one steps aside", the polish would definitely regard such position as cowardice. Whenever it is possible the Czechs try to avoid conflict rather than to run into it.

What happens when the conflict is inevitable?

They fear to call the situation "conflict". The Czechs do not take into account that there is a conflict as long as possible. Contextual signals are used frequently, explicit conversation leading to the gist of the problem is tried to be extended and when it comes to it Negotiation strategy in The Czech Republic the conflict tends to be simplified as the initial tiny problem can become more serious. If the pressure is unbearable and the open conflict is inevitable there is a danger of "explosion". Explosion can happen "in silence". Respective person leaves the negotiation suddenly and without any explanation. On the other hand sometimes explosion can be very loud and can lead to the end of the relationship.

Next phase of conflict depends on the characters of each negotiator. Either is the tension calmed down and everything is forgiven, or the negotiators lose their temper and the cooperation is over. One of the most obvious effects which can complicate mutual communication and cooperation is a low level of social skills in term of dealing with negative information. During mutual communication every negative information play decisive role in potential disturbing of positive social climate, personal relationships, even future cooperation. Therefore it is necessary to minimize the amount of negative information as well as its factual and sensitive strength. Whole range of disagreements, problems or conflicts can be solved in an informal way. Coffee break, restaurants or just informal conversation can make our hard job easier and more pleasant.

"Unsteady self-confidence"

So far as the self-confidence of the Czechs is concerned, they succumb to big disparities. On one hand they are extremely modest and underestimate themselves deliberately, on the other hand they tend to overestimate themselves and exaggerate. That means that some Czechs have too much self-confidence and some of them hardly any, but adequate one is scarce.

The Czechs feel that they are not able to stand the competition, that they are too weak, with lack of power. It is accompanied by embarrassing feelings and concerns which may even decrease the current low self-confidence. This plays decisive role in a cautious communication. Communicational scheme usually starts with a lot of excuses for petty shortcomings and concerns not to tell something which may demonstrate own overestimating.

The Czech side regards such an introduction as politeness expecting the same from the counterpart. They think that the partner would disagree with intensely a bit exaggerated excuses. However it happens rarely and the Czechs unknowingly and unnecessarily grade Negotiation strategy in The Czech Republic down own negotiation position. The thing is that the counterpart hardly ever softens such excuses.

Another extreme situation is excessive self-confidence. Usually it is not convincing and makes stupid impression as the style is sometimes only blindly copied from foreign handbooks. The problem is the fact that the above mentioned extremes can be seen just at one person. Of course, we can list some other weak points in the Czech nature:

- Envy
- Lack of ability and willingness to appreciate the others who are able to earn more money by their own effort
- Lack of national pride with respect to the history, personalities, art, however overestimating of the sport performances
- Ability to adapt to negative situations, come to terms with them
- Depreciation of the significance of entrepreneur and entrepreneurship
- Unnecessary searching for someone who could be taken as an example, however arrogant manners, where we are "world champions"

To the group of the middle and east European countries belong Czech Republic, Poland, Slovakia, Hungary, Russia and other former members of the Soviet Union as well as countries in the southeastern Europe e.g. Romania, Bulgaria and the countries of the former Yugoslavia.

The partners and especially those, who had recent business experience within these countries, regard the negotiations in these counties as quite difficult, the entrepreneurial environment as variable, but offering a lot of new opportunities. The main cultural factors influencing the negotiations are apart from the above mentioned:

- Group orientation (explained as the result of the former political system),
- preference of the team negotiating,
- relatively large sense for time and punctuality, Negotiation strategy in The Czech Republic,
- limited competence and unwillingness to accept personal responsibility,
- uncertainty in the division of roles and decision process,
- considerable bureaucracy and corruption practices.

Based on above, we can say that business ethics in Central Europe (if we ignore partial differences) is not much diverse from the ethics of the western

European countries). However the countries differ in the ethnic composition, religion and its importance in the society, traditions, mentality and the habits not just between each other but also inside of each of them, between particular ethnical and religious groups. Better readiness, punctuality, faster progress and direct style of negotiation can be expected rather in the central European and Baltic countries, lower sense for time, more important introductory phase and ornate speech style mainly in the southern Europe. As the negotiation language can be used one of the world languages, negotiating in the local language is for sure an advantage.

Russian Negotiation Style

Although Russia is geographically close to Europe, there are much more cultural differences than one might expect. One of the most difficult tasks for a foreign managers doing business in Russia or with Russians is overcoming this "cultural gap". A lot of perspective deals failed only because during the negotiations the partners did not pay attention to these differences. There are a lot of articles in Europe and US telling about the "mysterious Russian soul". What are the peculiarities of doing business with Russians? In which dimensions the Russian negotiating style differs from western and the one proposed by Harvard concept? How to be a success in your negotiations? It is difficult to answer these questions without having a look at historical and cultural background.

Overview of the Russian negotiation style

Influence of the historical heritage

Submission vs. autonomy: One of the historical features of Russians is passiveness –lack of autonomy. Up to 19th century all Russian peasants belonged to the owners of the land. During the Soviet times all the important decisions were made by the top authorities and supported by the army and KGB. The employees didn't have any autonomy as all the decisions came from above. This historical heritage is still influencing Russian managers and employees, who are often afraid of taking on responsibility and sometimes cannot make even simple decisions without asking the permission of the boss. This decision-making style might be perceived as slow and non-flexible by Western partners.

Secrecy vs. openness: During its long history Russia was under foreign attack and intervention many times. In 20th century USSR authorities cultivated the hostile attitude towards western countries, which unfortunately cannot be extirpated very quickly. This can explain the distrust towards foreigners and unwillingness of Russian businessmen to disclose the information to their partners. The total KGB control and the violence done by the authorities forced people to be more closed and secret. The businessmen prefer not to disclose their wages, the companies' financial structure is not transparent, which may result in illegal activities.

Attitude towards law and contracts: For many decades Russian laws were the enemies of capitalism and market economy and it was very difficult to establish the new legal system quickly. Even now after 15 years of changes it is very far from being perfect. In the West the partners rely on the legal environment in which business is performed, whereas in Russia people are unsure that the law can protect them.

Peculiarities of the Russian Negotiation Style

We decided to present the Russian negotiation style from the viewpoint of a foreigner, namely a western negotiator. As a typical example of the western style (which goes along well with the Harvard one) we choose an American style. Conducting negotiations in Russia can be complex and challenging. Russians are tough negotiators and require time to build trust. Russians often spend a long time working out a larger picture. Once the grand plan is in place, they move to specifics. Russian negotiators favor the "chess" approach – several moves are planned ahead, which requires time and results in very little initial progress. In contrast, Americans tend to move from specifics to a bigger picture, favoring a linear approach. The goal is to open with sequential moves to advance quickly in early stages and obtain tangible results. These key American-Russian differences in conceptualizing and planning negotiations are also reflected in the approaches to time and relationship-building during negotiating.

Cross Cultural Comparison within Hofstede's framework

As we mentioned before the negotiation style and the style of doing business in general is influenced by the culture. In order to characterize Russian culture we decided to use the cultural dimensions framework of Hofstede:

Hofstede has identified following five dimensions of culture in his world-famous study of national influences:

1. Power Distance
2. Uncertainty Avoidance
3. Individualism—Collectivism
4. (Masculinity—Femininity)
5. (Long-Term Orientation—Short-Term Orientation)

For each country an index can be found according to Hofstede, and thus a cross country comparison can be performed. The following figures can be found in academic literature ("Doing Business in Russia: Cross-Cultural Focus" Prof. Irina Pshenichnikova http://www.jyu.fi/economics/opiskelu/kurssimat/YJOCL78Lecture22005.ppt#11) Kwintessential: Language and Culture Specialists:(http://www.kwintessential.co.uk/intercultural/play/cards.php).

Russia

Power Distance: 90
Individualism: 50
Uncertainty Avoidance: 90
Masculinity: 40

As for the orientation in time, from our own experience and background, we would say the Russian negotiators are rather short-term oriented, which is probably caused by the great instability of the environment.

Austria

Power Distance 11
Individualism 55
Uncertainty Avoidance 70
Masculinity 79

U.S.A.

Power Distance 40
Individualism 91
Uncertainty Avoidance 46
Masculinity 62

The power distance is very high (90) compared to Austria (11) which is very low also compared to the U.S.A. (40). A high power distance means how much the unequal distribution of wealth and power is accepted and common in a society. Since in Russia money, power and hierarchies play a vital role, the high power distance can be observed during business negotiations and in everyday life. Individualism is low compared to the USA. In individualistic societies like in the USA decisions tend to be made by an individual himself. Motivation, acceptance of the individuality of others, responsibility is the most important factors influencing the behaviour. In more collectivistic societies words like shared responsibility, harmony and obeying are in the foreground. A high power distance in Russia yields a lower individualism since the individual is part of a strong hierarchy and thus enjoys less freedom of decision-making in business. Uncertainty avoidance means the degree describes the degree of the insecurity in the society because of restructuring or contradictory situation. Here the number is very high (90).

Life in Russia after the break-up of the USSR was and is still an adventure (banking crisis; sporadic legal protection; immense sudden distribution of wealth). This is why people in Russia strive for a more stable life and the uncertainty avoidance is high.

Harvard principles and the Russian negotiation style

The Harvard concept describes the negotiation process, the way how it is mostly conducted in the Western countries, however negotiation works a bit differently in Russia and we would like to point out these differences and the possible causes of this differences:

The four basic concepts of the Harvard process are:

1. Separate people form the problem
2. Focus on interest and not positions
3. Invent options for a mutual gain
4. Use objective criteria.

1. *Separate the People from the problem*

In the Western World (US; Europe) people try to focus mostly on the process of the negotiation than on the person with whom they are negotiating. In Russia it is generally the case that the business is more people oriented then process oriented. The reason for this phenomenon is that after the collapse of the Soviet Union many small individual businesses were built up. Often it is not an agent who was doing negotiation on behalf of the owner, but it was the owner himself who was negotiating for his own interest and for his own business.

Moreover business is very risky. A lot of dishonest businessmen were trying to make money and, as we know, the Russian legal system is still quite complicated and corrupted and in order to sue a company not only legal means would be involved, but also bribes would have to be paid which would be very expensive. This explains why Russian businessmen take a lot of time to build up a network of relations and going business is not separated from the person you are dealing with. You might be invited to the home of a businessman, you have dinner together, you get acquainted with his family, etc. This is why also often emotions are mixed up in the negotiation.

2. *Focus on interest, not positions*

The skilful western managers would probably follow this smart rule. Positions is disclosed information, interests lie deeper and the partners need some skills and a wish to arrive to a win-win solution in order to disclose each others interests and "play an open game". As for Russian negotiators in general we would say they tend to focus on positions rather than interests. That comes from the lack of skills and the experience of doing business with the foreign partners, as well as from the perception of the concessions as signs of weakness. Some Russians may even see it as an exiting game – to make the partner agree on their conditions and see it a confirmation of their negotiation skills and tough character. Power-based position-oriented negotiation may often be a case.

3. *Invent options for mutual gain*

Mutual gain makes sense for the Russians, big importance is put on the reciprocity: "If you give me this, I will give you this" or "I get half, you get half". Thus the Russians are very creative in developing options in order to find joint solutions. If they have built up a good, profitable business then they will try to close the deal by inventing options.

Insist on using objective criteria

In negotiating a price an objective standard could be used such as the: market price; expert opinion; comparison or the BATNA. The court appellation or the law clause might not work as a good criteria (due to the weakness of the legal system), but the appellation to the customs, tradition, common practice or even moral might often work well. As for using a fair procedure, such as meeting in a neutral place or asking a third party for an advice, this can also be applied, though the final solution is not expected to be that much "neutral", as "suiting both".

Doing Business & Negotiating in Russia as a Foreigner

One should be aware that there are differences between written law and law in reality. Therefore personal Relationship with customs, local government, and bureaucracy are part of business success. A business agreement is mostly a paper for the court. Usual number is 20% legal business, 80% unofficial business for small and middle sized business. Having formal partners is far not that important as having informal ones. One should also be prepared to the level of corruption. Russia has the 126th place among 157 counties according to the "Transparency International" index. An average amount of a kickback has recently risen from 10000$ to 135000$ one time since 2013.

Russians often use techniques which are perceived in the West as "Manipulation Techniques". They buy fancy dinners, invite you to the ballet or offer small gifts. They impress with status symbols like expensive watches, suits, cars or offices.

"Nowie Russkie" New Russian is a term denoting the newly rich business class in post-Soviet Russia. Having a modest education and social background, New Russians are perceived as arrogant; lavish consumption with poor taste. Money and status symbols are prominently displayed by the New Russian, in particular jewelry and luxury cars.

If doing Business with the "New Russians" the "Manipulation Techniques" shown above are used very frequently and you are expected to give something back in return during the negotiation. Still nowadays many Russian businessmen are aware of the negotiation procedures in different cultures because of the process of globalization and the increase of international business. They often adjust their behaviour in accordance with their expectations.

As a foreigner, one should realize that "Final Offers" are often not the end of the negotiations and that often times the outcome will be more beneficial and attractive if you can hold out. It is extremely difficult to do business in Russia without help from a local. To help with this, gifts, money or other items can be a good idea when doing business in Russia.

To conclude, it may not seem so easy to build up partnership with a

Russian businessman due to the peculiar negotiating style and business environment. It is challenging – even for Russians! Good news is that gradually more and more Russians get westernized business education and the experience of dealing with the foreign partners. Some of them learn fast. Besides, if a foreign manager has enough knowledge concerning this specific business culture and make an effort to adapt, he/she will ultimately find it not that hard. After all, the Russians like win-win solutions (although they don't show it) and are creative at looking for options to satisfy both sides!

French Negotiation Style

The word "negotiation" is rooted in the Latin *negotium,* meaning "not leisure" (which means that what is not leisure is business). In Old French, "negociacion" meant "dealing with people." Both definitions, though archaic, are right on the mark because the fact is that all dealings between people (whether social or business) constitute negotiation. This means that everyone has to negotiate in its everyday life. In our globalizing world, it is important to understand other cultures to take the most out of our international relations. Moreover, France is one of the pillars of the European Union and number one worldwide in the tourism sector, therefore a meaningful partner on the global trade scene. It seems very important that France's business partners understand the way the French negotiate to obtain more easily what they want, and in a friendlier way.

The French Culture and Values

France is a modern and very diverse country, and one can only admit the deep influence that France's culture has had on western countries for the last hundred of years, especially in art, literature and philosophy. The French are proud of their history and their prominent culture is influenced by a mix of cultural and historical differences.

One of the characteristics of the French culture is the centralization. France has a long and notable history of centralization reflected in its geography, transportation system, Government and business. France is organized pretty much around Paris. In business, centralization is reflected in the concentrated authority. It is especially true in SMEs, where the personality of the manager/ founder strongly influences the life of the company, because he/she has difficulties decentralizing power.

To be successful in business in France, it is necessary to understand the culture. Culture has indeed an impact on the values, which in turn affect the attitude, which eventually influences behaviours. Let's see, through the model of Geert Hofstede (1970's), which is the French values regarding business. We use this model here to make our analysis understandable, since it has become a well-known standard.

Power distance: France is getting more moderate. As Hofstede studied France for his model, it was the only country scoring high on power distance. Nowadays, the hierarchy is usually to be respected. Even though employees can bypass their bosses, it is not often the case, and they often have to ask for their bosses assent before taking a decision.

Individualism Vs Collectivism: the French love uniqueness and freedom of opinion both in society and in business. The individualism is therefore a very important cultural characteristic. Achievement VS Nurturing: the French place more interest in quality of life (nurturing) than on their career (achievement). It's obvious in the way they defend their rights concerning their 5-week paid holidays and other social advantages and benefits. Uncertainty avoidance: the French pay a lot of attention to rules and regulations. Moreover, the French don't like ambiguity and they try to reduce them by establishing formal rules in order to avoid ideas and behaviours they don't desire.

Long term Vs Short-term orientation: France seems more short-term oriented: the French look more in the past and try to keep their social system the way it is, even though it will need reforms pretty soon. However, companies try to be more long-term oriented, through commitment to sustainable development and other future-oriented actions.

Having seen what the French culture consists in concerning business, one would like to see to what the typical French negotiator looks like. According to our culture, and also to some comments made by other countries such as the USA, Sweden and Finland, a French person while negotiating has the following characteristics:

- Intellectual style: the French are very intellectual and have a high level of culture. They also are very creative and political. The problem, as seen by other countries, is that it makes them arrogant and they feel intellectually superior to their negotiating partner.
- Nationalistic and self-centered: Frenchmen always try to find a solution for France. Most of the time, they give the impression to be fighting for France during a negotiation. This is because they are proud of their country, its history and what it nowadays represents (see previous part on culture).
- Non-verbal communication: the body language is used a lot through the gestures and the facial expressions while talking.
- Verbal communication: most people prefer speaking French, because they don't feel comfortable with English or have a feeling of inferiority when speaking English with their counterpart. If there is a real language problem, it's good to let the Frenchman speak French and the counterpart speaks English or another language and has someone who understands the subject translates. In addition, it is very important to start the negotiation by trying to know the counterpart and not by getting to the business right away. It also is important to keep in touch afterwards through e-mails, phone calls etc. Furthermore, when a Frenchman says "yes", you can usually trust it. But when he says "no", it often means that the negotiation should go on, and not stop right at that time.

- Formality: it appears in different aspects of one's behaviour. First, the French are formal in the way of talking: they don't use the "tu", the informal you, and they usually expect the same behaviour in return. Moreover, it is important to be correctly dressed while negotiating with Frenchmen. It is a sign of respect.
- Bargaining techniques: the French don't bargain more than any other western country and they like to discuss the price just because they like to discuss every little detail while negotiating. Here we find the high uncertainty avoidance developed in the previous part.
- Attitude to female negotiators: they don't make any difference between men and women. The person across the table is judged for what he/she represents and not whether it's a man or a woman.
- Type of decision: the hierarchical organization of French companies has a high influence on decision-making. If the Frenchman is high in the hierarchy, he will have a lot of independence to make decisions. However, a person lower in the hierarchy will have to ask his superior for agreement on the decision to take, and the superior will take the final decision. We see here the problem of power centralization in the hands of a few executives, and the power distance.
- Personal relations: French people do not like to talk a lot about private life, but they like when the other person shows interest in the French culture, and why not speak French! Business lunches are not as common as they used to be. As we have seen, the French culture has a great influence on their negotiation characteristics, especially because of national pride.

How culture influences 10 Negotiation Factors

According to a survey made by Salacuse in 1998 entitled "Ten ways that culture affects negotiating style: some survey results", there are ten negotiation factors that can be influenced by one's culture. Let us here try to relate these factors to the French culture to see what its influence is on negotiation.

1. **Negotiating goals**: the contract seems to be more important than the relationship, even though keeping in touch is a good thing after the negotiation.
2. **Attitudes to the negotiating process**: a win-win situation seems to be wanted by French negotiators.
3. **Personal styles**: as we've seen on the previous part, the French are formal and considers it as a sign of respect.
4. **Styles of communication**: indirect, because of the use of complex sentences while speaking. That's why the French feel uncomfortable speaking English, because they can't use as many language ellipses and images as they do in French. Moreover they use the non-verbal communication a lot.
5. **Time sensitivity**: fairly low, because most of the French are always late.

6. **Emotionalism**: neither high nor low, because the French don't show their emotions too obviously but don't keep everything to themselves either.
7. **Agreement form**: the French prefer specific form of agreement because they like to go over details while negotiating, so they'd rather have a detailed contract with all the possibilities. The important part in the negotiation is the deal and not the relationship.
8. **Agreement building process**: they prefer a top-down agreement, which means to start agreeing in general principles and then go over the details.
9. **Negotiating team organization**: even though the French are fairly individualist and seek often a solution "a la française", they still want a negotiating team based on consensus.
10. **Risk taking:** in this survey, French are said to be fairly high risk takers, probably because of their creativity and also their feeling of intellectual superiority. But this is not the feeling we have.

The French always like to discuss every little detail during the negotiation, which considerably reduces uncertainty and, of course, the intensity of the risk taken. So we could say that French are risk takers but in an environment they know fairly well. These ten factors are really influenced by the French culture and should be taken into consideration while negotiating, as well as the typical French negotiator portrait.

Cross-Cultural Negotiation Capability for Foreign Investment-The Legal Dimension

Social and economic forces are challenging the way people do business around the world and interact with others. Globalization is making our world smaller and cross-cultural situations are at the core. International trade and foreign investment constitute part of this fast-growing development of international relationships. Regardless of specific legal systems, law firms and international lawyers help clients to find new markets and must help them with cross-cultural negotiations because many issues involved in international transactions contain cultural challenges.

The various Governments around the world need and want to receive as much fresh capitals and foreign investments as possible to improve the conditions of their economies and ultimately the living conditions of their national population. As international and foreign investment increases in developing countries, economic development and conflicting situations become more interrelated with environmental issues. Local, regional and national governments, business people and investors, local communities and population in general deal with the challenge of balancing environmental protection on one plate and economic activity and development on the other (Luis E. Ore, http://www.wiserearth.org/uploads/file/893b8cdf7a2c0bedbdc08364a9e0c8e0/Cross_Cutural_Negotiation_Capability_for_Foreing_Investors%5B1%5D_sep_2008%20PDF.pdf).

A legal framework is crucial to protect foreign investments. Beyond legal systems and right-based approaches to deal making and dispute resolution, shareholders of foreign investments and professionals in charge of negotiating and designing deals as well as professionals in charge of the implementation of investments and projects many times tend to overlook or generalize cultural factors. Overlooking or generalizing cultural factors when managing negotiations and relationships with potential local strategic partners or local communities and other stakeholders might determine the success or failure of the endeavor.

Besides governmental issues and regulation compliance surrounding all aspects of foreign investment, foreign investors have to deal with local parties whether they are potential strategic partners or local communities where the projects and facilities will be placed. Intercultural and cross-cultural awareness among international business and foreign investors is increasing dramatically but sometimes simplistic approaches to dealing with cross-cultural differences can prevent parties from reaching shared understanding, creating value on the negotiating table or generating lasting agreements.

International Business Negotiation: A Case for Nigeria

The most populous country in Africa and the sixth largest exporter of oil in the world, Nigeria's most common description is as the African country with "incredible potential"—yet, its leadership has not yet been able to ever solve the problems that keep its over 100 million citizens living in poverty. The Nigerian economy is nearly entirely dependent on oil exports. Irrepressible corruption and fraud throughout the bloated civil service prevent the growth of other industries.

Though Nigeria has been a member of the WTO since its inception, some Nigerian government officials question the ability of its weak, oil-dependent economy to continue to participate in the organization's agenda for trade liberalization. National chairman of the Peoples Democratic Party (PDP) Audu Ogbeh has said that "membership of the WTO is not helping matters. Everything is being imported into the country," and has also convened meetings to call for reconsideration of Nigeria's WTO membership.

On the other hand, supporters of Nigerian Minister of Finance Malam Adamu Ciroma maintain that opting out of participation in organizations like the WTO, IMF or World Bank would be detrimental to Nigerian development; the country must instead learn to protect its interests within the context of such modern necessities. Throughout the controversy, Nigeria has stayed active in global trade negotiations, participating in the 2003 WTO meeting in Cancun as an active member of the newly unified G20 negotiating block.

The G-20 Negotiating Group

At the WTO Cancun meeting, Nigeria became of member of the newly coalesced G20 trade block of articulate developing countries led by India, Brazil, China, and South Africa. The group came together over their insistence that they could not consider further lowering their import tariffs until developed countries, particularly the US and EU, committed to significantly lowering their subsidies of domestic agriculture production and export. Reluctance to lower import tariffs is very strong in Nigeria, where the Manufacturers Association of Nigeria (MAN) has argued that maintaining tariffs are essential if stimulatory policies for small and medium business are to succeed. The G20's rejection of the investment issues pushed in the negotiations by developed countries and its insistence on prioritizing agriculture instead has shifted the course of the Doha Development Round.

Oil and Gas

Ranking tenth in the world in oil and gas reserves, Nigeria is Africa's largest oil producer and the sixth biggest exporter in the world. Its daily output is about 2 million barrels, from which the country derives over 90 percent of its earnings. The government, however, has set out a plan to increase daily production and reserves, encouraging new operations of private refineries. The goal of the policies is for Nigeria to begin to export refined oil with greater value-added and to stop importation of refined products, which has hampered plans to eliminate government subsidy in the sector. Nigeria maintains OPEC membership, and it agreed to a regional gas project in early 2003 that will enable the piping of natural gas to five cities in Ghana, Togo and Benin.

Restoring a Tarnished Image

Despite prolonged efforts by both government and private sector to lure tourists to the country, Nigeria remains a destination limited almost only to business travelers linked with oil, gas, and consulting services in other sectors. Some trace the paucity of international and domestic tourist activity to over-priced, poor-quality hotel rooms and the high cost of living in the country, which earned Lagos a ranking on the list of the 10 most expensive cities in the world.

Addressing another problem of ill repute—the high levels of production and sale of counterfeit drugs—Nigeria's National Agency for Food and Drug Administration and Control (NAFDAC) received accolades for its recent program that required all drugs sold in the country to be registered by December 2003 and that prosecutes sellers of unregistered drugs. Counterfeit, expired and substandard drugs on the Nigerian market have poisoned buyers, ruined legitimate manufacturers and distributors, and further tarnished the country's image as drugs originated in or merely passing through its territory have been intermittently banned in some West African nations.

The widespread circulation of spam email messages from fictitious Nigerians in search of international partners willing to provide startup money in exchange for a cut of the profits from multi-million dollar money laundering schemes propagates Nigeria's reputation as a hotspot of financial advance-fee frauds. Rampant bribery demands among the civil service also deter the interest of would-be international investors in Nigeria. In an unlucky exposé that highlights the extent of the problem, the Economist recently published a report from its Nigerian correspondent after she was deported from the country for failing to pay a bribe to information ministry officials.

Regionalism

As of March 2004, the Economic Community of West African States (ECOWAS) plans to achieve a single customs union by 2007 to promote trade and commerce among the 16 states in the sub-region under a West African Monetary Union. The International Monetary Fund (IMF) has advised the other nations against cooperating with Nigeria in this project, citing government problems with corruption and uncontrolled spending. However, the EU has pledged to support this integration effort with up to $10 million euros in loans. A significant level of trade already occurs in the sub-region, and addressing current transport and immigration problems in a unified manner would likely increase business activity.

Nigeria and NEPAD

Nigerian President Olusegun Obasanjo has made the New Partnership for Africa's Development's (NEPAD) continent-wide millennial development plan a priority of his administration, including by pursuing policies that will make Nigeria business-friendly and facilitating domestic production and its competitiveness against imports. Nigeria is responsible for specific aspects of the NEPAD including economic governance, the banking sector and financial institutions, debt relief for Africa, ODA (Official Development Assistance), as well as corruption and money laundering on the continent. Though the President has paid much attention to NEPAD in speeches, significant policy changes regarding business facilitation have yet to be accomplished.

Over the last two years, despite debate over what level of participation Nigeria should maintain in both regional integration and WTO matters, the country has developed political relationships with G20 partners, and increased economic ties with neighbors, including Uganda and the Gambia, with whom Nigeria signed trade agreements in 2003. It seems likely that Nigeria will remain fully engaged in both global and regional trade deals, with a priority of gaining credibility in the international system.

It must be acknowledged that before any significant benefits from world trade can be gained, the domestic economy of Nigeria will have to diversify away from over-dependence on oil exports. In order for economic growth to happen in other industries, physical infrastructure must be greatly ameliorated, and corruption, financial fraud, regulatory barriers, and the threat of violent crime must be checked. There is potential for progress in the efforts of President Olusegun Obasanjo, who tried to cut domestic gas subsidies in October in an attempt to free up the market and reduce corruption generated by the huge subsidy program. He also has plans to reduce the size of the civil service, speed up privatization, and invest in agriculture and infrastructure. However, the entrenched corruption and inefficiencies of the state, as well as the strength of the money laundering industry, are immense obstacles to be overcome before any more of Nigeria's great potential can be realized.

Energy in International Trade Agreements

Most relevant are the rules established by the United States for Canada under the existing North American Free Trade Agreement (NAFTA). NAFTA is widely considered to be the "state of the art" in trade deals because it goes more deeply into restricting government powers than any other agreement to date. As Maude Barlow, explains in an IFG Special Report "The Free Trade Area of the Americas," NAFTA removed Canada's control over its vast energy resources by the following measures:

- Established rights of foreign companies to invest in the energy sector;
- stripped Canada's National Energy Board of its powers and dismantled the "vital-supply safeguard" that required Canada to maintain a twenty-five year surplus of natural gas (the US maintained its 25 year reserve for national security purposes);
- imposed a system of "proportional sharing" that guaranteed Canadian energy;
- supplies to the US, in perpetuity;
- lifted requirements for export applicants to file an impact assessment;
- banned export taxes (a major source of government revenue Exports: $39.4 billion (f.o.b., 1993 est.) petroleum and petroleum products 92% The petroleum sector accounts for roughly 75% of KSA budget revenues. (www.geographic.org)
- banned preferential pricing for domestic customers.

As a result, Canada's exports to the US more than quadrupled in a decade while oil exports doubled. Now, President, USA is preparing to deepen access to Mexico's energy resources via expanded NAFTA talks. The US has also introduced this energy policy framework throughout the hemisphere, covering Venezuela, Colombia, and Ecuador, via the so-called Free Trade Area of the Americas (FTAA). Building acceptance of this agenda in regional trade fora is important for introducing the topic, and similar agenda, at the global level in the WTO.

Energy and WTO's New Expansion Format

WTO's could penetrate the energy sector by either creatively expanding existing agreements, or by introducing new subject areas for negotiation. Below are three negotiating themes (Services, Investment, and Competition) currently in the WTO, in which new rules over energy and oil could expand to remove the ability of citizen's to use their governments to control the oil and gas industry.

Services

"The US has called upon WTO members to open markets eligible for private participation in the entire range of energy services, from exploration to the final customer. The energy service proposal would ensure non-discriminatory access to foreign provider energy services. Equally important, the US proposal suggests that WTO members consider how to create a "pro-competitive regulatory environment for energy services, so that opaque or discriminatory regulatory practices do not undermine their commitments to open their domestic markets to foreign service providers...The National Energy Policy Document (NEPD) group recommends that the President direct the Secretaries of Commerce, Energy, and the US Trade Representative, to support a sectoral initiative to expand investment and trade in energy-related goods and services that will enhance exploration, production, and refining, as well as the development of new technologies." http://www.bushenergy.com/energyplan.asp

The General Agreement on Trade in Services, or GATS, is an existing accord in the WTO which is mandated to restrict government actions in a broad range of "services" via WTO-enforced trade sanctions. The WTO's current work plan calls for an expansion of GATS, and negotiators in Geneva have been proposing which sectors might be covered in an expanded set of rules. According to a March 2000 proposal submitted to WTO Services negotiations: "oil and gas services include a wide range of services, such as: drilling services; derrick erection; repair and dismantling services; services necessary for oil or gas extraction such as well casing; cementing, pumping and plugging wells; as well as specialized fire extinguishing services...In addition to services incidental to mining, different related oil and gas services may be included in real estate services, rental/leasing services, technical testing and analysis services, services incidental to energy distribution, related scientific and technical consulting services, and construction and related engineering services".

Typical obstacles to trade in energy services include:

- restrictions for the entry and stay of energy services managers, professionals and experts;

- restrictions for the entry of the equipment and tools needed to provide the service;
- arbitrary business and licensing requirements; and
- absence of transparence of regulatory framework." (COMMUNICATION FROM CANADA, Initial Negotiating Proposal on Oil and Gas Services, S/CSS/W/58, (01-1413),14 March 2001, WTO Council for Trade in Services, Special Session)

It is clear from proposals such as the one above that nearly everything related to oil and gas is on the negotiating table in Geneva. One of the world's largest oil services firms, Halliburton Energy Services (formerly operated by US Vice President Richard Cheney) describes itself as, "Capabilities range from initial evaluation of producing formations to drilling, completion, production enhancement and well maintenance." WTO talks on Services raise a number of questions about how Saudi Arabia would maintain current restrictions on foreign participation in the nation's oil and petro-economy.

Investment

"The NEPD group recommends that the President direct the Secretaries of State, Commerce, and Energy to use our membership in WTO to implement a system of clear, open, and transparent rules and procedures governing foreign investment, to level the playing field for US companies overseas and to reduce barriers to trade and investment." (http://www.whitehouse.gov/energy/Chapter8.pdf, www.bushenergy.com).

WTO currently has a narrow range of rules on investment, known as Trade Related Investment Measures, or TRIMs. A proposed expansion of WTO investment rules is an integral part of the WTO's new Work Programme established during the November 2001 Ministerial in Doha, Qatar. Among other things, the new WTO investment agenda aims to:

- establish the right of foreigners to invest in any sector;
- establish the right of foreign investors to receive the same treatment as domestic companies, so-called National Treatment (which WTO currently applies only to goods an services, not investments) Any preferential terms of business or any benefit offered to domestic companies, i.e., preferential tax breaks or interest free loans, would also have to be made available to foreign investors. Other restrictions, such as limits on joint ventures, foreign ownership, or residency requirements, would likely be banned;
- establish rights for foreign investors in the event of privatizing state-owned assets, whereby they would be offered terms no less preferable than those offered to domestic investors;
- ban measures that conditions foreign investment to certain outcomes, such as retaining a portion of profits to be reinvested domestically, or operating for a minimum period of time.

Under the new WTO investment rules, authorities charged with regulating foreign investment could become politically irrelevant.

An important question to ask in considering these issues is, for instance, how might major foreign investors gain new leverage over the country's control of its own energy supplies when new WTO investment rules are applied?

Competition

WTO's competition agenda would eliminate government practices that protect national monopolies, both state owned and private. To promote competition, disciplines on what governments can and can not do, including with state-owned businesses, are intended to break up national industries that restrict competition. China's entry into the WTO scaled back the way in which its state-owned petro, trading, and financial services companies could operate. Mexico's state-owned oil company, PEMEX, managed to maintain significant barriers to US energy companies upon its entry to NAFTA. But now President, USA appears ready to widen access in one round of negotiations to deepen NAFTA.

CHAPTER 5

Strategic and Geo-Political Dimensions of Global Business Negotiation

Global Negotiation is a process of understanding and influencing others in various political, legal, social and cultural environments. If an organization needs to negotiate more effectively in a multicultural context, then negotiation services become essential to help succeed in a diverse and competitive global environment. All organizations are exposed to the negotiation process but few strategically and consciously plan and develop the requisite level and varieties of skills to cope and eventually succeed in a multicultural business environment. Hence, learning more about corporate culture and functional style as well as best practices along with that of counterparts' during the process can improve the outcome of all of organization's negotiation processes. This includes the ability to illuminate the preparation and strategy analytics, business and emotional intelligence, and the appropriate strategic fit of the corporate style of management with any given global negotiation situation (http://www.thunderbird.edu/executive_education/consulting_network/business_consulting_solutions/global_negotiations.htm). Strategic negotiation is about the implementation of the strategic choices already made by the organization, by different people. It is an operational activity which implements the necessary decisions that are made as a result of the plans aiming to take it to the organization's planning horizon (Scott, 2005).

Fundamentally, negotiation strategies reflect combinations of tactical behaviors. Individual behaviors are tactical and their combinations are strategic because they are enacted to move the individual or dyad closer to goal attainment. Depending on their outcome goals, negotiators' initial strategic approach may be integrative, supporting the cooperative goal of maximizing own and others' outcomes, or distributive, supporting the individualistic goal of maximizing own outcomes (Lewicki, Saunders & Minton, 1999; Pruitt, 1981; Putnam, 1990; Walton & McKersie, 1965). Although many negotiations are mixed-motive, requiring negotiators to blend integration and distribution, one can argue that one of these approaches is dominant at any given point in time.

Negotiations start with the actions taken by individuals. These actions reflect individual goals at the beginning of negotiations. They are represented by the specific tactics that negotiators choose, for example to make demands, to attack the other party or to share information. These tactics aggregate over time to signal negotiators' dominant strategic approach, which can be either integrative or distributive. Negotiation processes can be analyzed at the level of either tactics or strategic approaches, one may limit this for the present purpose to the strategic level. Despite starting with the actions of individuals, negotiation processes are defined by the interplay of actions between two negotiators. This is because negotiators monitor progress towards their goals. In the absence of goal discrepancies, negotiators make strategic choices that maintain the negotiation process. When discrepancies arise between where negotiators are and where they want to be, they take corrective action by shifting the strategic focus of the negotiation (Brett, Northcraft, & Pinkley, 1999).

The emergent aspects of negotiations are thus best understood by focusing on how strategies aggregate over time (Mara Olekalns, Emergent Negotiations: Stability and Shifts in Negotiation Dynamics, https://littlehurt.tepper.cmu.edu/gsiadoc/WP/2004-E17.pdf).

Global Mindset – Strategic, Psychological and Social

Strategic intelligence (SI) has mostly been used in military settings, but its worth goes well beyond that limited role. It has become invaluable for improving any organization's strategic decision-making process (http://www.routledgebusiness.com/books/Strategic-Intelligence-isbn 9780849398681). Rigorous strategic planning can bolster a negotiator's chances of success. However, leadership in negotiation also requires an understanding of, and an ability to practice critical emotional and behavioral skills. Such capabilities may sound "soft," but there is a strong relationship between negotiators who are aware of their own emotions and behaviors with whether they can successfully influence others in a negotiation. The emotional skill of empathy, for example, is a significant source of leverage because a negotiator has the ability to understand the emotional and behavioral make-up of other negotiators. This competency and skill to treat people according to their emotional reactions and motivations allows negotiators to build rapport and trust—two factors that, not surprisingly, are also important in developing and retaining clients, customers and employees through a service and consulting orientation. With a global mindset (GMS) negotiators are able to influence others who have a diverse world views. The power of GMS, along with BI and ESI, makes for a unique set of capabilities that many negotiators do not have.

Insight and skills around potential cultural preferences and differences are important frameworks for the appropriate behavioral demands in global negotiation. Assessment tools such as the Cultural Orientations Indicator (COI) generate insight about targeted behavioral changes which can impact negotiations. This tool creates an efficient learning and skill building around the key differences in cultural preferences and practices across national, organizational and or individual boundaries. This assessment tool is fundamental to the confidence and optimism needed in the most difficult and competitive negotiation situations. As the economic downturn demands more of negotiation skill, the search for increased leverage and cross-cultural social skills will become an essential quest. Strategic negotiation skills and adaptation competences are tested more than ever during a decline in global economic activity..

Social Engagement: Plan for Multicultural Complexities

Social engagement skills or emotional and social intelligence (ESI) are required in addition to strategic planning if negotiators ever wish to elevate their prospects of success in an increasingly diverse economic environment. A good plan is only as good as the ability to style switch, influence and collaborate with others in a multicultural negotiation. Today's complex markets have created progressively more demand for rigorous insight and cross-cultural social skills in order to problem solve creatively and create sustainable agreements. A successful organizational or individual negotiation plan can only be achieved when there is an integrated approach of analytical, psychological and social insights and skills. Most accredited negotiation programs focus either on strategic planning *or* behavioral skills in one-to-three day sessions. However, Thunderbird's negotiation program combines preeminent frameworks from the research fields of business, cultural, social and emotional intelligence—including the latest developments in neuroscience.

The Thunderbird International School of Management, in their Executive training programmes has developed a training Module encompassing, among other things, a broad framework that have been tested through practical application by working with hundreds of executives and companies, as summed up below in Fig 1. The Business Group strives to consult with companies to develop plans and processes that provide negotiators with clarity on their strategic planning and cross-cultural practices that are pertinent in today's global context (http://knowledgenetwork.thunderbird.edu/research/2009/03/04/negotiation/).

Understanding Emotional and Social Intelligence

Emotion in Negotiation

Much emotion research has been devoted to the study of its relationship with cognition. According to psychologist Klaus Scherer (2003), the dichotomous approach that views cognition as "an antagonist to emotion" and that sees emotion "as an impediment to the proper functioning" of cognition and rational thought has its roots in Plato and Aristotle's philosophical musing. In modern psychology, the debate over the primacy of cognition over emotion has and continues to draw a great deal of attention. On one side, cognition is championed as a necessary condition of emotion. In this tradition, appraisal

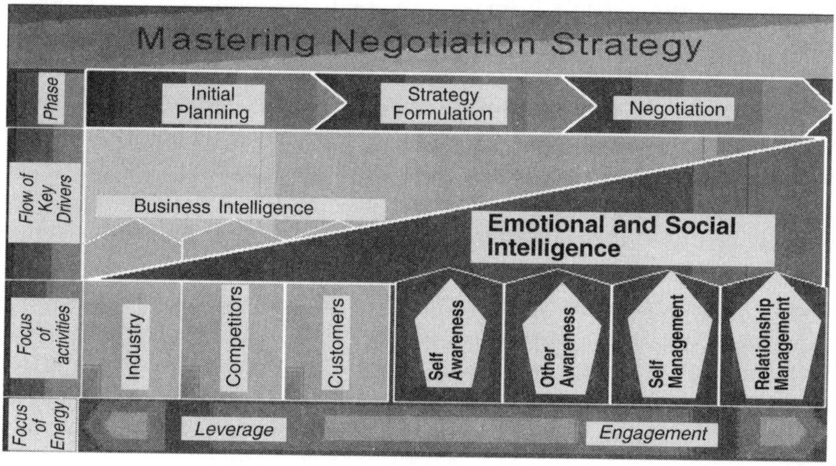

Fig. 1: Mastering Negotiation Strategy with focus on Business, Emotional and Social Intelligence

theories trace the elicitation of emotions to "subjective evaluations of the significance of events to the well-being of the person concerned. On the other side of the debate, Robert Zajonc, a major proponent of the independence of emotion, argues that emotion and cognition are distinct and separate processes and that experience of emotion is possible without cognitive input i.e., cognitive evaluations. These disparate perspectives, while promoting and deepening our understanding of the mechanism of the cognition-emotion interactions, unnecessarily cast cognition and emotion in opposition and preclude one in the smooth functioning of the other. In recent years, however, more efforts have been made to "integrate rather than oppose the two"—to incorporate affect in rational decision-making and cognitive appraisal in emotional reactions.

The study of emotion and negotiation is characterized by a social functionalist approach that posits that emotion is informative, evocative, and serves as an incentive in social interactions and causes social consequences. For example, positive emotion can signal cooperativeness and trustworthiness, elicit cooperation, trust, and concession from others, and promise rewards for others. Negative emotion, on the other hand, impresses the other party as aggressive, competitive, and reckless, elicits compliance from the other party, and signals punishment or negative consequences for the non-complying opponent (Thompson et al, 2001). Perhaps because positive emotion shares an undertone of cooperativeness with principled, integrative bargaining, it has received relatively more scholarly attention. On the other hand, negative emotions such as anger, frustration, and depression seem to violate the rational principle of integrative bargaining, which might be the reason that negative affect has not been studied as much. Then, in what is now a classic study of ultimatum games, Madan Pillutla and Keith Murnighan (1996) brought negative emotion back to the study of negotiator behavior. Bargainers would reject economically beneficial offers, the authors found, out of anger and spite caused by their perception of unfairness in their opponents' offers, rather than on the basis of rational economic consideration. This study has been a wonderful antidote to the purely rational and emotion-free approach to negotiation: negotiator behavior is not always guided or determined by rational analyses of utility. However imperfect and irrational negative emotions might be, they actually led bargainers to "revolt," despite knowledge of potential economic damage associated with such outbursts of feelings.

The execution of a successful negotiation strategy also requires an understanding of social engagement rules and preferences. How to negotiate becomes just as critical as what to negotiate. Successful social engagement requires negotiators to have a strong sense of self and an understanding of their own value preferences about how to build trust and get agreement. Skilled negotiators are aware of their own cultural profiles, psychological and behavioral biases about fairness, how to build trust, and how to win. Confident and successful negotiators have the ability to accomplish their own goals, along with assisting others to achieve the same by fostering social resonance among negotiators. Awareness of one's own and others' emotions, and how to manage social relationships and interaction are critical for the execution of a negotiation strategy. If a problem-solving negotiation strategy is required, a negotiator must have the strategic knowledge, cultural sensitivity, optimism, resiliency and ability to connect and generate positive energy among diverse negotiators (LI, Michael E. Roloff, 2006).

Negotiators with both the strategic knowledge of the negotiation *and* the required social and psychological competencies can achieve significant results despite any economic downturn. These qualities of a global mindset serve as a foundation for collaboration and adaptation required even more than ever in an uncertain market. Negotiators with global mindset have the social and psychological awareness and ability to approach a negotiation not solely from their own perspective, but they also have the willingness and curiosity about others' goals, interests and beliefs about negotiation and trust building. Preparation, reflection and practice about emotional and social competencies such as listening, patience, empathy and optimism also enhance the strategic leverage for a negotiator.

Negotiation is indeed a fascinating site where we can observe the intertwining of cognition, emotion, and culture in shaping social behaviors. Strategic emotion, in particular, is the tactical display of emotions that calls for the negotiator's cognitive evaluation and planning, emotional regulation and presentation, and cultural sensitivity. Even the individual traits we addressed have both cognitive and emotional elements in them. Empirical work on strategic emotion and the emotional strategist is needed to advance our knowledge of negotiation and strategy. We conclude this chapter with a look at one of our recent efforts in this direction. In a study on how negotiators enact positive and negative emotional strategies, we found that strategic negative negotiators (i.e., those instructed to adopt a negative emotional strategy) not only increased their negative display during the negotiation, as instructed, but also significantly increased their positive display (Li, &. Roloff, 2004). Eventually, these strategists outperformed their targets and their strategic positive counterparts (i.e., negotiators instructed to employ a positive emotional strategy). A plausible interpretation is that, in order to maximize the effect of strategic negative emotions, these strategists decided to also maintain a seemingly contradictory positive display, either in an effort to counteract the negative relational impact of negative emotions or to induce more cooperative behaviors by means of a contrast strategy of positive display. Past research on negotiation has touched on this "dual display" phenomenon. In a study of role-differentiation as a negotiation team tactic, Brodt and Tuchinsky reported that the bad-cop/good-cop routine was more successful than just the good-cop/good-cop or the bad-cop/bad-cop arrangement. In the latter case, pressuring by two "bad cops" actually backfired (Brodt and Tuchinsky, 2000). Hilty and Carnevale addressed a similar tactic—what they called the "black-hat/white-hat" strategy—in an earlier study and found that strategy shifts played an important role in negotiation, such that when a new strategy was presented, participants made more and bigger concessions (Hilty, and Carnevale, 1993).

Interestingly enough, two people were not necessary for executing this dual strategy. In fact, one person playing both the good and the bad cop, so long as the transformation is coherent and table, is sufficient in producing the intended influence on the opponent. That participants in our study adopted this dual contrast strategy strongly suggests that strategic emotion is a highly complex behavior that is simultaneously cognitive and affective. Existing research on the highly nuanced interpersonal effects of dual play strategy invites direct empirical exploration of whether the combination of negative and positive emotional strategies is more effective than either strategy alone in its influence on individual outcomes. If emotional strategies, especially dual strategies, are complex and subtle processes that require much evaluation, planning, and execution, individual traits like self-monitoring could have a vital part in this process, because it represents negotiators' capacity for such cognitive and behavioral tasks. It is possible that high self-monitoring negotiators can accurately judge how much positive versus negative emotional display is needed and how to maintain the balance between the two; they may also be superior than low self-monitors at administering the right "dose" of the needed emotions. If this explanation can be tested in future research, it will offer valuable information on the dynamics of strategic emotion in negotiation and communication in general.

Collaborative Negotiation Strategy

In collaborative negotiation, the approach is to treat the relationship as an important and valuable element for effective and result-oriented negotiation (http://changingminds.org/disciplines/negotiation/styles/collaborative_negotiation.htm#col). There is also a philosophical dimension to the approach to negotiation pursued by many organizations. Some organizations are renowned for their collaborative approach to doing business whilst others have a reputation for a mercenary approach to conducting business. Some players in the retail sector have reputations of dealing ruthlessly with suppliers—they rationalize the approach by arguing that it is in the interest of the consumer. Whilst one would tend to agree that this approach is short sighted and probably not sustainable in the long run, it would be naïve not to recognize the fact that, at least commercially speaking, a lot of organizations have little interest in collaborative or compromising type negotiations within certain departments (http://www.articlealley.com/article_202390_15.html).

Organizations and individuals should recognize that collaborative negotiation demands the investment of significant resources. In order for us to be truly collaborative, we have to spend much time getting to know each other. In a commercial context, this plainly does not make sense in some cases. Consider the purchase of a pure commodity such as paper for a small or medium sized organization—if there are no value added services presented or required, it would be sub optimal to pursue a collaborative relationship with the provider of such a commodity. It would make more sense to pursue a competitive approach to the procurement of paper than a collaborative or even compromising approach.

The following are generally considered to be some of the cardinal principles that can be applied in a Collaborative negotiation process:

Win-win

The competitive approach to negotiation assumes a fixed pie, zero-sum, win-lose situation. In collaborative negotiation, it is assumed that the pie can be enlarged by finding things of value to both parties, thus creating a win-win situation where both parties can leave the table feeling that they have gained something of value.

Fair process

As humans we have a deep need for fairness, and when this does not happen, *even if we emerge as winners* from a competitive negotiation, the result is not truly satisfying. The most comfortable result from a negotiation happens when our needs are met, including the need for fairness.

Joint problem-solving

The collaborative approach to negotiation seeks to convert individual wants into a single problem and to bring both parties together to work on solving this problem. By converting individual positions and wants into separated problems, the people can be freed up from jealous and personal attachment to their requirements so they can then take a more objective and equitable position from which they can act in a more collaborative way.

Collaborative strategy

Being collaborative does *not* mean being weak and giving in. On the contrary, a collaborative approach seeks to gain the best possible solution.

Transparency and trust

Whilst you may not give away all of your information, deceptive practices need to be curtailed if trust is to be gained. A simple way of eliminating suspicion is to be open and transparent, giving information before it is requested.

When the other person is competitive

The biggest dilemma occurs when the other person is acting competitively, and will try to take advantage of your collaborative approach (possibly seeing it as a weakness).

The approach with aggressive others is to be assertive and adult rather than fall into the fight-or-flight reaction, for example naming attempts at deception and showing your strength whilst offering an olive branch. A critical preparation for this is to have your fall-back alternative to a negotiated agreement ready, and to show that you are prepared to use it. Customarily, the results of any negotiation can be designated into one of the proceeding groups (Jan Potgieter: http://www.dhhs.tas.gov.au/__data/assets/pdf_file/0004/35374/Collaborative_Negotiation_Strategy.pdf):

- Lose/Lose (all parties lose)
- Win/Lose (I win and you lose)
- Lose/Win (I lose and you win)
- Win/Win (we both win, but this could also be described as compromise)
- Win More/Win More (we maximize our shared resources by being collaborative)

A win/win viewpoint is the only practical means to achieve a measure of competitive advantage in the marketplace, it is equally important that this approach is applied in a sensible manner in today's global marketplace. All negotiated agreements in a way are mutually equitable and ought to be tackled on a consistent basis. It would be like suggesting that a particular nation's culture and beliefs defines our meaning of culture and that only the standards of this specific culture should be used in connecting with people throughout the world, regardless of their respective backgrounds.

There is another aspect of commercial negotiations that is equally vital—the old economic quandary of 'guns or butter'. The 'guns or butter' story reveals that when resources are limited, organizations and individuals must make hard choices. If they want to have more butter, then they have to sacrifice some guns and vice versa. In reality, resources can only be shared as they relate to their strategic importance qt that specific moment. Any negotiations that are of strategic importance to the organization will likely prompt us to take a collaborative or compromising approach. Likewise, when we believe that certain negotiations will have a limited impact or no impact at all on our strategic objectives, we might decide to become competitive in our approach or even to completely steer clear of the negotiation.

There is also an ideological component to negotiations that has been adopted by many organizations. Some organizations are well known for their collaborative style to doing business while there are those that have a reputation for being mercenary in their business approach. Some members of the retail sector are renowned for being ruthless with suppliers—they defend this approach by claiming that it is in the best interest of the consumer. Many organizations do not possess a clear organizational negotiation strategy & process which exposes them to the perils associated with a huge disparity in the results of their negotiated agreements. Organizations and individuals should realize that collaborative negotiation requires the investment of significant resources. To be truly collaborative, we have to spend a lot of time getting to know each other. Partnering doesn't happen overnight—partnerships require significant investments of time and money, so choose your partners wisely. In a commercial context, this obviously does not make sense in some cases.

How then do we determine which negotiation strategy to follow? Within a commercial perspective, the following negotiation strategy options are conceived to be open to us:

1. Steer clear of negotiation altogether.
2. Aggressively achieve our goals through competitive negotiation.
3. Satisfy the needs of our counterparty to the exclusion of our own needs by being accommodating in our negotiations.
4. Compromising by realizing some of our needs and some of the needs of our counterparty.
5. Satisfy all our needs and all the needs of our counterparty by taking a collaborative negotiation approach.

The negotiation strategy that is appropriate will be established by how you answer the following two questions:

- How strong are my alternatives to this specific negotiation?
- How vital is a long-term relationship in the context of this negotiation? It follows that in many instances, buyers would either follow an approach where they avoid negotiation or become competitive, while sellers would like to be either compromising or collaborative as shown in the following illustration (Fig. 2).
- How should this situation be handled strategically?

A vital component of the negotiation preparation process should be focused

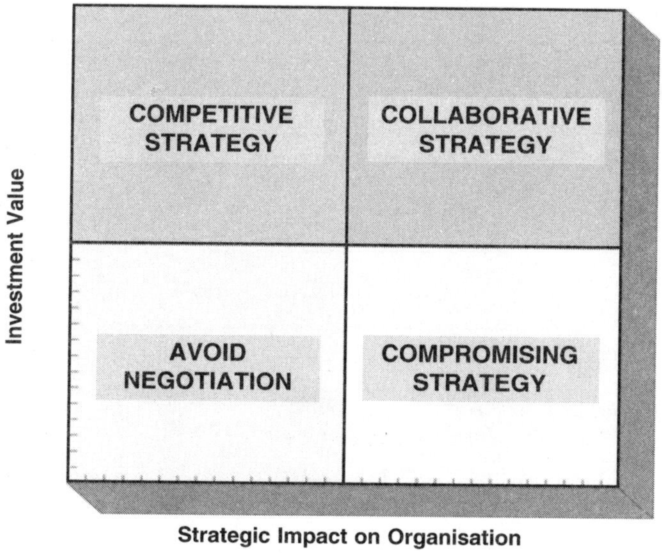

Fig. 2: Buyer Side of Negotiation Model

on trying to understand the needs, interests and objectives of your counterparties. This will help you to identify the likely negotiation strategy that your counterparties will adopt. If your counterparty is avoiding a negotiation, you can be certain that your organization is not being seen as offering any competitive advantage to your counterparty's organization. In the first instance, your challenge would be to reconsider the way that your products and services are packaged. The objective should be to add to the strategic business objectives of your counterparty by identifying those components that meets their strategic needs. If you find yourself at the wrong end of a competitive negotiation, you should familiarize yourself with the negotiation tactics they might use against you, as you will most certainly be faced with a tactical approach. Unless you understand negotiation tactics, it will be difficult for you to gain the most value that you will be derive from the negotiation because your counterparty will have no sincere interest to satisfy any of your needs or interests. Strategic Negotiations entails the following essential features (Fig 3: http://www.brianbabcock.com/strategic-negotiation.shtml):

1. If necessary, change the rules of the game.
2. Prepare your strategy, tactics & negotiations communications
3. Understand your "BATNA"—test theirs.
4. Negotiate with results and relationship in mind; create an enduring agreement.
5. Remain "principled" with commitment in all of the above.

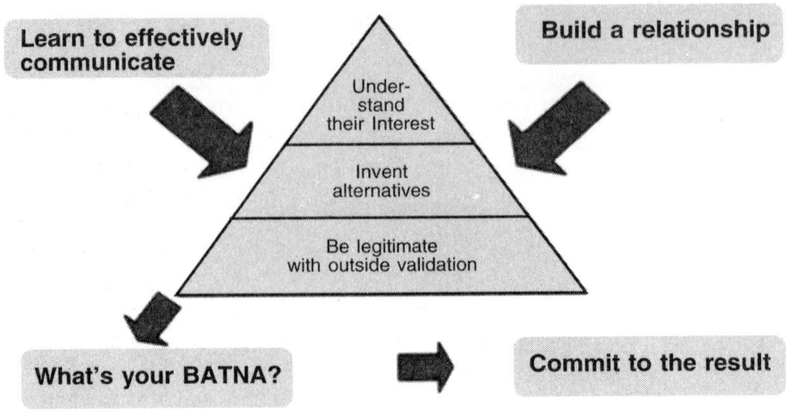

Fig.3: Pyramidal Strategic Negotiation Model

Strategic Negotiation is about the middle- to long-term strategic context in which the tactical skill sets of negotiation are applied. Strategy is about what you want to happen; tactics are about making it happen. Hence, there are few overlaps between this book and the typical book on negotiation skills. Competence in negotiation is properly a complement to competence in strategy, but they do not substitute for each other.

Strategic Negotiation can perhaps be better understood by developing some kind of Strategic Negotiation Process Model. The foundations of such Process Model rely on knowledge-based information and primarily they cover the kinds of content with which every strategic negotiator has to be familiar. A set of tools is introduced that are used in strategic negotiation processes, particularly in the analysis and diagnosis of the negotiation problem in its strategic context. The strategic process is essentially a practical exercise that applies the strategic process model to business problems, mainly through the implementation of the steps necessary for the achievement of the organization's business plan, identified, analyzed and negotiated using the Negotiation Agenda method. The scale and context of complex negotiations require strategic awareness because the interests of the parties are more complex, the options more numerous and the outcomes more critical than at the tactical level. Strategic interests drive proposals and bargains and, beyond a low level of complexity, there are many more significant off-table events, which require coordination with the events happening across the table, than in simple two-person bargaining. *Strategic Negotiation* is about higher-level judgement and discussion of the interests, issues and positions, and the attendant options. Strategic negotiation is not an exact science like physics or introduction mathematics.

Strategic Leadership and Decision-Making

Decision-making-and the strategic leadership of decision-making teams-is a process which moves an individual or a group toward common goals. However, people are not alike in their values and beliefs; there are huge differences among people within a single organization, and even greater differences between people in different organizations. Strategic leaders must know how to operate across such boundaries that mark differences in expectations and perspectives, and competing values and goals. It is one thing to influence a group essentially in agreement; it is quite a different thing to influence a group with goals in conflict with those that one wants to pursue.

Positional Negotiation

Positional negotiation is essentially *adversarial*. The negotiators see the process as "win-lose," in which any gains by the opponent are losses by the home team. A classic example of this type of negotiation is contract negotiations in the automobile industry. A union tactic in recent years has been to identify one of the "big three" manufacturers, one particularly vulnerable to the effects of a strike. This company is then targeted for hard negotiations around some key issue. When neither side yields on the issue, a strike ensues and persists until some agreement is reached or one side collapses under the cost of the strike. There are definite winners and losers in this type of negotiation.

Positional negotiation can be illustrated on a more personal basis by the bargaining that accompanies the purchase of a new car. The salesman has a sticker price to begin with. The customer has a desired purchase price. Each wants to come as close to his own figure as possible. The salesman's commission is based on the profit margin achieved, directly from the customer's pocket. The customer wants the lowest possible profit margin, directly from the salesman's commission. Each gains at the other's expense. It is true zero-sum and adversarial. These are examples of "hard" positional negotiation. The negotiators are demanding and unyielding. Positional negotiation can also be "soft." A "soft" bargainer is quite willing to make concessions to "keep the ball rolling." The two negotiators start at different positions in a bargaining range and compromise toward the middle. In "soft" bargaining, agreements are reached quickly. However, "soft" bargainers run a great risk if they happen to encounter a "hard" bargainer. Furthermore, "hard" and "soft" bargaining is zero-sum in nature. Both aim at splitting the pie in order to get what they want. In positional negotiation, each side stakes out its position, and simultaneously (a) attacks the other position and (b) defends its own.

The problem of positional negotiation is that an opponent may become an enemy by a demeaning personal attack. Fisher and Ury and Colosi consider this a big mistake. They think the goal of every effective negotiator is to get the opponent onto their turf-essentially onto their side of the bargaining table-so viewpoints will be similar. If the negotiation is successful, each negotiator will believe that the agreement is a good one. So, if you are a negotiator, your former opponent is going to be advocating a bit of your arguments to his/her boss, and you will be doing the same thing for him/her with your boss.

Principled Negotiations

Principled negotiation has a great deal in common with the process of *Consensus Team Decision-Making.* First of all there are four conditions which are essential if a principled negotiation is to have a successful outcome.

- Mutual trust.
- A positive relationship.
- Shared interests (goals or objectives).
- Satisfactory zone of possible agreement.

Mutual trust comes from experience, either within the negotiation process or from previous contact. If it does not already exist, it must be built. A negotiator can be trusted when experience shows that person (a) is dependable and will do what he/she promises to do, and (b) does not create surprises. Surprises can take many forms: a sudden demand "out of the blue," a sudden opponent's threat, or an unexpected shift in position. In this sense, trust is a kind of conclusion about the credibility of the other side. Clearly, one of the objectives of a negotiator is to establish his/her credibility in the eyes of the other negotiator.

As a negotiator, your goal is to have more influence on the other side than they have on you. Your goals and objectives must be seen to gain merit while the goals and objectives of the other side lose merit. This means your presentation of "facts" and other evidence must be convincing. You must also create some doubt in the mind of the other negotiator about the validity of his/her position. In essence, you will be influencing that person's belief system, about both your position and his/hers. A positive relationship with the other negotiator is essential if you are to have this kind of influence. This sounds difficult, especially in view of the fact that negotiation has the potential for conflict. However, experienced negotiators emphasize that it is both possible and required.

A positive relationship makes possible the development of common ground; in principled negotiation the common ground can include similar goals and objectives. Instead of negotiating against each other, the negotiators form a team and negotiate "against" the problem. They now have shared interests.

Finally, a Zone of Possible Agreement (ZOPA) must exist. As a negotiator, you must know what your zone is. This may appear to apply more to positional than to principled bargaining because a ZOPA is the least favorable agreement you would accept, and the most favorable one you believe the other negotiator would accept. However, with a bigger pie, the ZOPA shifts for both in the positive direction.

A negotiator must also have a Best Alternative To a Negotiated Agreement (BATNA). As part of the preparations prior to beginning negotiations, each negotiator must decide at what point it is best to cease negotiating and to be satisfied. Although the BATNA may change slightly as negotiations proceed, a negotiator will use the BATNA agreed upon by his team as a touchstone throughout the negotiation process. With a BATNA a negotiator never feels cornered or under pressure to yield to pressure from the other side—the predetermined goal has defined the point at which negotiations are no longer profitable and may be ended.

Negotiators rarely have the authority to make final decisions. They are sent as representatives of those who do have that authority, who are the "closers." As "closers," they have a significant advantage. They are protected from the possibility that in a weak moment they will accept an impossibly poor agreement. In addition, if principled negotiation has not been possible, there may be times when the negotiator has no easy reply to a hard bargaining opponent. It may be useful to end a session with the need to go back and discuss options with your "closer." By the same token, a negotiator would never want to enter negotiations without detailed instructions from the "closer" as to what options are satisfactory and what options are not; i.e., the Zone of Possible Agreement and the Best Alternative to a Negotiated Agreement.

Principled Negotiation Process

Once you have established the necessary conditions for negotiations, what is the advantage of principled negotiations? As with Consensus Team Decision-Making, there is a process for principled negotiations. Each of these steps is discussed in detail below:

Principled Negotiation Requirements

- People: Separate the people from the problem
- Interests: Focus on interests, not positions
- Options: Generate several before deciding what to do

Separate the People from the Problem

A common failing when there is a difference of opinion or goals is to attack the opposing person while attacking the opposing position, especially if the attack is demeaning. It will unfailingly have negative outcomes in both decision-making and bargaining. Experienced leaders and experienced negotiators separate the people from the problem. Some of the ways Fisher and Ury suggest are:

- *Relationships:* Bargaining, even principled bargaining, may involve strong comments about the substantive issues. It is only human nature that these, on occasion, are taken as personal attacks, generating emotions that block communication. A good relationship can be a vaccine against communication blockages. But the relationship needs to be built early in the game, just as a vaccine works best before exposure to the disease. Some negotiators do this by chatting in a friendly way during the breaks. On more consequential issues, negotiators may ask for and get a "book" on the other side, that includes background and interests, to facilitate building a good relationship.

- *Perceptions:* In the heat of battle, it is easy to view the opponent as a personal enemy, as opposed to someone who is just doing a job. Effective negotiators must get inside the heads of their opponents so they can see the issues as they do. From inside the opponent's frame of reference, many things become clear: why a given position is held so fiercely, where the vulnerabilities are, where there are doubts, and where there may be blind spots.

The primary goal of principled negotiation is to achieve rational outcomes in the best interest of both parties. However, sometimes this just doesn't work, and positional bargaining is the only option. Then it becomes imperative to know the issues well from your opponent's perspective while denying that advantage in turn. In that way, you can control your opponent's perceptions better than your opponent can control yours.

Perceptions come in many ways. Colosi makes a point of the importance of body language and tone as communications channels that give information, sometimes information of crucial value, to the other side. Fisher and Ury emphasize such things as acting inconsistently with expectations. For example, they believe an important part of the peace process between Israel and Egypt was that Sadat upset Israeli-and Arab—expectations by flying to Jerusalem in November 1977. "Holding the door" for your enemy is inconsistent with the perception of being an enemy; so do it.

- *Emotion:* The heat of battle is truly felt by all. And while a principled negotiator would not launch invective toward the other side, the other side might not be so principled. Experienced negotiators have long since learned how to manage their emotions. A part of this is understanding that there are going to be emotions. Skillful strategic leaders—and skillful negotiators—can turn anger on and can turn it off for effect, while at the same time avoiding the blow and counterblow that gets out of control. This is not always easy, especially when the other side is trying to destabilize your side by personal attack.

If under personal attack, promise—don't threaten: You might say, "These are personal attacks which are not relevant to the substantive issue, and for that reason they are unfair. If they continue, I am going to leave and return tomorrow. Perhaps we can make more substantive progress then." The essence of promise versus threat is that the statement takes the form of what the speaker will do as opposed to what will be done to the other party.

- *Communication:* The essence of communication is the transmission of meaning. Fisher and Ury think much communication in positional bargaining fails because meaning is not clearly transmitted. Where the bargaining is positional, Colosi adds that one may want to be judicious about the direction of communication. If the bargaining is positional, the negotiator who gets "inside the other negotiator's head" has a competitive advantage. The mandate is for active listening, getting the other person to talk more—and thus reveal more. Listening with interest to what the other negotiator has to say pays dividends, you are getting valuable information about his/her position and intentions, without giving away your own.

These are only a few of the many ways to build a positive relationship. Your image as a negotiator must be that of someone who is credible, reliable, trustworthy, and principled. In many negotiations, this image can be used as a tool to move toward negotiating on the merits of the case, rather than on the relative hard-headedness of the negotiators.

Interests

If a positive relationship can be established with the other negotiator, the only remaining ingredient for principled negotiation is finding shared interests that can serve as the common ground for generating creative options. (Remember that the defining characteristic of principled negotiation is making a bigger pie.) Interests are a key issue because interests are the factors underlying the decisions.

Fisher and Ury provide an example of how an understanding of the underlying interests may lead to a win-win solution, a bigger pie. In the Camp David negotiations between Israel and Egypt in 1978, the positions seemed to be non-negotiable. Israel occupied the Sinai and was not about to cede it back to Egypt. Egypt wanted it back and was not about to sign a peace agreement with Israel until that happened. Examination of the underlying interests, however, was revealing. Israel did not really want the Sinai; what it wanted was security. And Egypt did not really want to threaten Israel's security; what it wanted was the land back. So the solution to the problem (not the negotiated middle ground between two positions) was to return the Sinai to Egypt, on the condition that it be de-militarized. Once the interests were properly framed, the solution was relatively easy.

There is one final reason for an in-depth understanding of both sets of interests. Sometimes principled negotiation is not possible and harder positional bargaining must be used. When that is the case, it pays to know if there are divisions in the enemy camp. Colosi points out that there probably will be "stabilizers" who would bargain "soft," and "de-stabilizers" who would bargain very "hard" indeed, and might scuttle the negotiations if they could. A thorough understanding of the other side's case is essential for the exploitation of their differences.

Options

It is here that negotiators have the best opportunity to expand the pie. It is also here that principled negotiation begins to look a lot like Consensus Team Decision-Making. There are three strong points of similarity. The first is that neither can go forward without common ground. In CTDM, it is shared goals and objectives; here it is mutual interests. The second is that a divergent, or creative, thinking phase is required. The third is that creativity can be squelched, and by much the same thing: premature evaluation and/or early closure. Fortunately, many of the tools that work for CTDM also work here.

The primary obstacle to expansion of the pie is that convergent thinking takes place too early in the process. For example, taking a narrow view of what is possible, or focusing upon obstacles rather than on possibilities. As in CTDM, these obstacles can be avoided by leadership that keeps options open and deliberately challenges tendencies toward closure. To make this happen, the negotiator must concentrate on actually leading the process, as opposed to being a participant in it. Here we see another similarity to the CTDM process, where one or more interested parties must monitor a process while they are also participating in it.

As long as options are kept open, many avenues for creative ideas may appear. One of the more interesting examples given by Fisher and Ury concerns dovetailed interests for mutual gain. These may result when the participants have different beliefs about possible outcomes and are willing to "bet" on their beliefs: An aging baseball player wants a salary increase and is confident he can perform well in the coming season. His manager does not agree. The player offers to bet on his belief. The manager agrees and a deal is struck. Each gets what he wants in the negotiation.

Negotiations within Negotiation

One aspect of negotiations seldom addressed is that of the negotiations which take place on each side of the table, in contrast to those which take place across the negotiating table. In reality, the most difficult aspect of the negotiation process can be reaching consensus with your ratifier or your team members. Experienced negotiators prepare relentlessly and set aside time and energy for these "internal" negotiations. The effective management of your relationship with your organizational hierarchy may be the most important issue to ensure success.

When Principles don't work

Sometimes, even with the best of intentions and skill, a principled negotiator cannot bring the other side around. Sometimes, the other side simply won't play fair and use bullying, psychological warfare, or deliberate deception tactics. And, on occasion, there may be no evidence of dirty tricks but the issues are so monumental that trust is unthinkable. SALT negotiations is an example. There was ample evidence that both sides had a shared interest in negotiating a downsizing of the nuclear arsenal, both to lessen the global threat and to reduce its maintenance cost. But the potential consequences of possible deception in implementation made trust impossible. The talks could not bear fruit until both sides could agree on methods for inspection compliance.

The point is that trust doesn't exist in negotiation until it is established by credible actions. Even then agreements must be backed up by iron-clad ways of verifying compliance. Rose-colored glasses seem to be the favorite apparel of ex-negotiators who were taken to the cleaners by their previous opponents. Any negotiator must remember that he/she is entering a contest. There is a mandate for ethical behavior in this contest, and there are gains if it is principled. However, there are no judges or referees in this contest, and the assumption that an opponent will be playing by your ethical and principled rules is unwarranted. Trust may be a conclusion but trust may never be an assumption.

One of the essential elements of negotiation is knowing if there are viable alternatives. Again, this is like strategic leadership. When strategic goals are being nailed down, a good strategist envisions options and asks about the downside of each. Creative vision is necessary to identify the options, but it must be paired with analytic rigor in the evaluation phase.

What happens if they simply won't agree? With a BATNA (Best Alternative to a Negotiated Agreement), the question is already answered. Without a BATNA, a negotiator doesn't know how important the negotiations are, and will be vulnerable to pressure from the other side—and that pressure will come. With a BATNA, the pressure switches to the other side, unless they also have prepared one. So the first element in preparation strategy is to develop the best BATNA possible. That doesn't mean just knowing that there is an alternative. It means searching for a good one, and even working hard to improve it. Negotiation may not be necessary if a good BATNA can be developed ((http://www.au.af.mil/au/awc/awcgate/ndu/strat-ldr-dm/pt3ch13.html).

Strategic Effectiveness of Negotiators

Some of the common characteristics of effective negotiators are having objective skills, patience tranquil and a good knowledge about party with whom the proposed negotiation is to be made. In the international arena, an effective negotiator would try to have a complete knowledge about the history of the country in which he is going to negotiate. An effective negotiator would be objective in the sense that he would not criticize the system, political structure and form of government of the country in which he is negotiating. He would also keep himself updated with the cultural dimensions of the country in which he proposes to negotiate. It is very important for a negotiator to understand that cultural dimensions play an important role in the process of negotiations. It is often seen that people belonging to 'low context cultures' would have lower negotiation skills than those belonging to 'high context cultures'. Finally an effective negotiator would set apart all aggressions, exertions and emotions during the process of negotiations.

Technical Ability	Social Skills
Achievement	Ascription
Scientific Skills	Status
Legal training	Personal Attributes
General Knowledge	Kinship
Language fluency	Social class

To quote a specific example, *Google's Strategic Negotiators* spearhead the acquisition and allocation of Google's global networking infrastructure. Strategic negotiators must interact closely with outside vendors to design, develop, and deliver highly innovative contracts for fiber, collocation, peering, voice, and data services across the world. The position o *Google's Strategic Negotiator, for instance,* requires substantial knowledge of global networks, in-depth technical expertise, and strategic analysis skills in addition to rock-solid negotiation, collaboration, and delivery capabilities. One needs to track record that matches our philsophy of leading by innovation, have a detailed understanding of both the technological and the commercial sides of networking infrastructure, and have the ability to deliver against aggressive deadlines with a driving passion for cost reduction and highly scalable solutions (http://www.google.com/support/jobs/bin/answer.py?answer =162304). Google's strategic negotiators are generally dynamic personalities who can work successfully across diverse geographies, circumstances, expectations, environments, cultures, paradigms, and technologies.

Mastering Negotiation in an Economic Downturn: Focus on Skills

Professors Karen S. Walch and Paul C. Kinsinger of Thunderbird School of Global Management in a paper titled 'Mastering Negotiation in an Economic Downturn' have highlighted the significance of negotiation in a competitive environment under the glo0bal economic recession which was experienced in recent times globally (http://www.thunderbird.edu/executive_education/consulting_network/business_consulting_solutions/2b344d2b-cf44-44f6-aa53-879f0396d6c5.htm). Strategic negotiation skills and adaptation competences are tested more than ever when there is a decline in global economic activity. Currently, many global MBA candidates attend courses and multinational companies consult with Thunderbird about how to strengthen negotiation skills for all levels of management in an uncertain and flagging world economy. When it comes to transforming challenges into opportunities, there are two critical areas of expertise required according to Thunderbird Global Management Group:

1. Knowledge concerning strategic leverage
2. Social engagement practices in a cross-cultural context

Strategic leverage in an uncertain climate requires a robust understanding of global business intelligence (BI), often a less visible component of a successful negotiation strategy. Many experienced negotiators would recognize this as the "preparatory" phase of a negotiation when they undertake their "due diligence" to uncover the fundamental needs and goals of their counterparts (a process that often provides useful insight into one's own goals as well).

Of course, very few negotiators would ever pursue negotiation without knowing something about the background and interests of the other players. However, in a rapidly changing and declining economic market, the impulse to bypass rigorous BI preparation is seductive. Although it is tempting, the pursuit of a negotiation planned on the 'back of an envelope' without a systematic challenge of key assumptions or 'lore' about what has worked in the past should be avoided. Quality information increases negotiation leverage.

Social engagement skills or emotional and social intelligence (ESI) are required in addition to strategic planning if negotiators ever wish to elevate their prospects of success in an increasingly diverse economic environment. A good plan is only as good as the ability to style switch, influence, and collaborate with others in a multicultural negotiation. Today's complex markets have created progressively more demand for rigorous insight and cross-cultural social skills in order to creatively problem solve and create sustainable agreements. A successful organizational or individual negotiation plan can only be achieved when there is an integrated approach of analytical, psychological, and social insights and skills.

Most accredited negotiation programs focus either on strategic planning or on behavioral skills in one-to-three day sessions. However, Thunderbird's negotiation program combines preeminent frameworks from the research fields of business, cultural, social and emotional intelligence—including the latest developments in neuroscience. The frameworks have been tested through practical application by working consultatively with hundreds of executives and companies. We strive to consult with companies to develop plans and processes which provide their negotiators with clarity on their strategic planning and cross-cultural practices that are pertinent in today's global context.

Political Dimension of Global Negotiation

The adoption of international norms of antitrust enforcement has so far eluded the international community. With a few exceptions, antitrust harmonization has come, where it has come at all, through the coincidental and unilateral decisions of individual states. Not only key substantive differences, but also important procedural ones characterize the disparate enforcement regimes. And there are at least 80 separate jurisdictions that are active in enforcing competition laws against actions both within and without their borders. Harmonization is arguably desirable for its perceived efficiency effects, and the debate over harmonization or internationalization rightly centers around the prospects for adopting a workable worldwide antitrust standard that would reduce the burdensome costs of legal uncertainty occasioned by divergent local standards. But while many states—including particularly the European Union—have advocated in favor of the internationalization of antitrust laws, most notably under the auspices of the WTO, the United States has steadfastly resisted a multilateral solution. Existing efforts to describe or explain the lack of international harmonization have generally focused on the direct economic effects of, and the narrow political difficulties of, the harmonization of competition laws through certain international mechanisms, such as the WTO and the OECD..

The United States has an interest in obtaining credible long-term commitments from other states—particularly developing states—to the dominant norms of global economic and political liberalization. First, to the extent that adherence to the tenets of economic liberalization preferred by the United States is costly, adherence to those standards conveys a measure of long-term commitment. By crafting institutions in which the other parties are made to alter their domestic political structures as a condition of agreement, the dominant state receives a credible commitment from the other state of its willingness to adhere to the terms of the specific agreement under negotiation.

The fact that the international agreement is institutionalized into domestic political structures has the effect of increasing the likelihood of enforcement as domestic political incentives are brought more directly in line with the international commitment. Second, and as a consequence of this process, the United States may initiate a process of internalization, whereby the adaptations made create a lock-in effect which helps to further the processes of market liberalization and democratization that the United States believes are essential for the maintenance of its preferred international order. By facilitating domestic normative change in other states, the dominant state will gain a stronger level of compliance with international agreements along with a more stable commitment to its vision of international order. This in turn helps the dominant state identify potential allies, as those states likely to be challengers would be unlikely to accede to institutions that remake their domestic political structures according to the vision of a hegemony.

Being able to separate budding friends from probable foes is a critical task of international security, and, as a consequence, nations derive political benefits from international agreements in a way that transcend the substance of the agreements themselves (http://www.allacademic.com/meta/p_mla_apa_research_citation/0/7/0/3/2/p70322_index.html).

Political Impact on Global Negotiations

Negotiators have a general understanding of their own local political environment. They are raised in a business milieu that clearly distinguishes who the key players are, and who has to be pitched about a proposal. They learn the roles that each level of government may bring to the table, and its impact on the negotiations. When negotiators take their proposals abroad and negotiate with a foreign power, they may not fully realize the impact that different political systems will affect the manner in how the negotiation should be conducted. The scope of the impact by the governments of individual nations will vary in the degree in the amount of influence they may have on international negotiations (http://www.negotiations.com/case/political-impact/).

A major U.S. defence contractor, Raytheon found out for themselves several years ago just how differently this impact can have on their negotiations. Their first initial foray into international negotiations occurred in Europe. Raytheon was attempting to put together a consortium of European companies to produce a NATO weapons system. They had thoroughly researched all the possible contenders and compiled a list of those companies that they believed were best able to handle the contract they were trying to put together.

Raytheon then contacted those companies and started negotiations. Talks became suddenly stalled in their tracks when, much to Raytheon's dismay, the governments of several European nations abruptly advised Raytheon to cease negotiations with the firms within their respective countries. These European governments said it was not up to Raytheon to decide who they would conduct business with in their respective countries. They would decide which companies could be contacted, and that Raytheon had no choice in the matter if they expected to fulfill the contract.

Raytheon realized that it had no choice in the matter. Accepting the political reality of the situation, they terminated talks with the companies that they had initially chosen. They then entered into talks with the consortium of companies chosen by the respective NATO members instead, and successfully completed the weapons system contract.

Several years later, the U.S. government convinced Raytheon to develop a similar weapons system for Japan. Having learned their lesson with the European consortium, they immediately initiated their talks with the Japanese government instead of going to individual companies like they did in the NATO situation. They sat back and waited for the Japanese government to tell them which companies to use in their weapons system project.

The Japanese government remained curiously quiet. Some time elapsed before a senior executive from Raytheon had a conversation in private with the Japanese deputy minister of defence. The deputy minister advised the Raytheon executive that it was up to the U.S. company to make the decision about which companies to use, and not the Japanese government. It turned out that since two of Japan's main electronics firms were considered as possible contenders; the Japanese government did want to anger either of these companies by choosing one over the other on behalf the American firm. The reason was because both of these companies wielded some considerable political clout with the Japanese government.

Competitive Conflict Escalation

Competition is clearly a healthy means to increase sales for any business. It is essential because it provides a stimulus for our company or organization to prosper and grow. However, does this mean that a company should compete at all costs? The answer is no! There comes a point when excessive competition may cause serious harm when the losses exceed the gains. Sounds like simple commonsense, doesn't it? Yet, there are many examples of escalated competition that are unsound. Even the big players can be drawn in this irrational escalation.

Back in1981, American Airlines introduced the first frequent-flyer program. It was truly a unique marketing plan. Anyone who flew regularly could redeem their travel miles for rewards. Taking American Airlines' lead, all their competitors jumped on the bandwagon and provided a similar frequent-flyers program. To get a leg up on American's initial advantage, several competitors enhanced what they offered by doubling the air miles. They also offered points for car rentals, hotel accommodations and other innovative tactics.

The airlines continued this escalating competition through the early 1980's as each airline tried to outdo their competitors. In 1987, Delta Airlines offered triple miles to any passenger who charged their tickets on their American Express card for all of the year of 1988. Analysts took a hard look what this would actually mean as a cost to the airline industry. They estimated that the airlines combined would end up owing their passengers somewhere between $1.5 and $3 *BILLION* dollars in *free trips*. Whew! This was not small change to say the least.

The airlines industry was in quite a quandary now. How could the industry get out of this marketing war that had spiraled so out of control? It finally occurred to them that somebody had to step forward and draw a line, but nobody did at first. The total airline debt continued to increase with estimates placing it as high as $12 billion dollars towards the end of the 1980's. The airline companies couldn't stop competing and had to keep matching whichever one of them raised the stakes. and clear. They also announced the cancellation of their rebate programs.

The same thing had happened in the U.S. auto industry who engaged in rebate programs. The other players quickly escalated their rebate offers to potential customers accordingly. It actually reached a point where the major car manufacturers were selling every single car at a loss. Finally, the CEO of Chrysler, Lee Iacocca held a press announcement. He stated that Chrysler would not renew its rebate program when it expired at the end of the year if the other companies followed suit. He also stated that if they didn't, he would match or exceed their rebate programs otherwise. Iacocca drew a line in the sand and sent out a strong message to his competitors. The other manufacturers got the message loud.

Creative Problem-Solving in Negotiations

All too often, negotiators can become tied up and bound as they commit to taking a competitive approach to their negotiation. As a result, they don't allow themselves to be flexible nor consider a creative approach to derive more value from the negotiations. On the other hand, a common error committed by those who believe they are taking *the win-win approach* to their talks is to overcompensate their need to find agreement by making unwise compromises. A compromise invariably means that both resources and money will likely be left on the table, unclaimed by either party.

Here is how two west coast energy producers, Southern California Edison Co. and Bonneville Power Administration created a joint partnership through creative problem solving whereby each party met their objectives. In 1991, the two parties conceived of a way to help the Columbia River salmon in the Pacific Northwest, while improving the polluted air of southern California, and they managed this feat without spending any money in the process!

Here is a précis of this very unique and imaginative problem solving that illustrates the powerful benefits of the create process at work. During the summer months, Bonneville Power would increase the flow of water into the Columbia River. This would automatically increase the amount of hydroelectric power generated by California Edison. The increased flow of water allowed the young salmon to swim through the channels more easily. It also increased their survival rate because a weaker current made them more prey to becoming lost or more vulnerable to being devoured by predators.

Later, in the fall and winter months, California Edison returned the power back to Bonneville Power Administration that it had borrowed during the preceding summer months. As a result, Bonneville had very little need to run its coal-fired and oil plants during the summer months.

This was truly a win-win agreement. The exchange of power, roughly equivalent to about 100,000 households improved the migration of the salmon, thereby increasing their survival rates and expanding the fish population. Additionally, air pollution was reduced significantly as Bonneville didn't have to resort to smog producing plants during the stifling and oft smoggy summer months that normally occur. What kind of impact? It's been estimated the saving was about equivalent to taking about 5,000 cars off the highways.

Political economy is a particularly useful approach to studying the process of trade negotiations or the design of international trade institutions. A Stockholm workshop on 'Political Economy of Trade Negotiations', held at the Institute for International Economic Studies on 1/2 October, brought together leading researchers in this field.. The workshop formed part of CEPR's (Centre for Economic Policy Research) research initiative on 'Market Integration, Regionalism and the Global Economy', supported by the Ford Foundation. The papers presented in the conference considered two main areas: the impact of regional integration on multilateral free trade and the effects of lobbying on trade policies in political equilibrium (http://www.cepr.org/PUBS/bulletin/meets/2209.htm).

Multinational Corporations in Global Governance

International regimes are a critical element of global governance. Regime theory has been widely criticized for its state centered approach, and increasing attention has been paid to domestic political factors and non-state actors, especially non-governmental organizations (NGOs). Very few, however, have examined regimes from the perspective of multinational corporations (MNCs), despite their critical influence in the international political economy. Drawing on international business and international political economy literatures, this paper outlines an approach to analyzing regimes from the perspective of MNCs. In doing so, we build upon the work of Raymond Vernon, whose Product Life Cycle theory of trade and investment moved the conceptual spotlight from nations to corporate strategy. In this tradition, we seek to understand the formation and content of regimes of international governance in terms of the interests and strategies of MNCs.

The increasing internationalization of production and markets over the last several decades, however uneven and incomplete, has been accompanied by the emergence of various forms of supranational/global governance, both at regional and international levels. From regional trade agreements to international environmental treaties, we are witnessing the emergence of multilateral institutions and sources of authority that increasingly influence the operations of multinational corporations (MNCs). Even in the absence of a supranational authority, negotiations among governments, firms and NGOs are leading to the establishment of regimes—rules, norms, codes of conduct, and standards—that constrain, facilitate, and shape MNCs' market behaviors.

In recent debates, three arguments have frequently been made, often implicitly, concerning the power and preferences of MNCs in relation to institutions of global governance. The first argument is that the power of MNCs to shape outcomes has increased in relation to governments and other societal actors (the decline of the Westphalian state hypothesis). The second is that MNCs prefer to see regulatory authority shift away from national governments and toward supranational institutions, and that this shift has, indeed, been underway (the decline of the regulatory state hypothesis). The third is that, as part of the MNC agenda, supranational regimes facilitate the lowering of regulatory standards across jurisdictions, particularly in the areas of labor, environment, health and safety (the race-to-the bottom hypothesis).

A Negotiation approach to understanding International Governance

MNCs do not always succeed in securing the regimes they desire. This section examines how outcomes of negotiations over regime formation among MNCs, governments, and NGOs depend on the relative power of the actors and idiosyncrasies of the bargaining process. In the obsolescing bargaining model of the 1970s, MNCs wanted to maximize their share of financial gain, by keeping taxes and royalties paid to the host country low, and by gaining access to subsidies for capital investment and infrastructure development. In addition, MNCs were seen as desiring a predictable and stable environment, and autonomy from "arbitrary" governmental interventions in areas such as currency conversion, profit repatriation and local content requirements. These goals have not disappeared in the new bargaining over international governance structures. Indeed, the effort to establish the MAI and broaden the WTO to include services (GATS), intellectual property rights (TRIPS), and trade-related aspects of foreign investment (TRIMS), can be understood, at least in part, as an attempt to incorporate some of these objectives into a new set of ground-rules for MNC–host country bargaining. Rather than bargain with states deal-by-deal, however, some of the new multilateral trade and investment regimes institutionalize MNC positions by greatly reducing the ability of states to impose performance requirements, discriminate between domestic and foreign investors, or otherwise reduce the value of an investment.

Building upon the obsolescing bargaining model, it was suggest that the complexity and dynamic nature of bargaining processes, with multiple actors attempting to exert leverage through various sources of power, leads to somewhat indeterminate outcomes. The bargaining model of MNC–host country relations focused primarily on bilateral regulatory regimes with domestic locus of authority. This model was developed in the context of the polarized debate in the 1970s between those who saw foreign direct investment (FDI) as a manifestation of the growing power of multinational corporations and fundamentally antithetical to host country interests and those who argued that the power of MNCs had been exaggerated and their economic benefits ignored. The bargaining model represented a pragmatic approach in which the benefits of FDI to the host country would be contingent on the specific contractual arrangements of each deal. MNCs and host countries would bargain over the distribution of benefits from each instance of FDI, and the bargaining power of each side was determined by the possession of rare or unique assets.

MNCs, for example, might offer certain technological and marketing capabilities, while host countries could control access to natural resources and local markets. Over a period of time, the shifting balance of power between the MNC and the host country would tend to make the original bargain obsolete, leading to some renegotiation of terms. In the three decades since Vernon laid the groundwork for the bargaining model, evolving global political and economic conditions require its revision. As Vernon himself later recognized, conflict over the potential value of FDI to host countries has by and large disappeared. Whether through conviction or coercion, developing countries have increasingly opened their economies to trade and inward investment. In part, this trend reflects the broader ideological shift towards open markets and deregulation. As tools of governance, market-enabling regimes had become as important as regulatory regimes.

During the 1980s, scholars shifted their attention from concerns about MNC power toward the efficiency gains available in the internalized structure of the MNC. Intellectual and political challenges to the role of MNCs waned as the institutional bases for such perspectives weakened. In the new atmosphere, collaborative dimensions of state–MNC relations have received more attention than conflict. In the 1990s, however, the increased visibility of NGOs opposing unfettered globalization has renewed debates over the power of MNCs vis-à-vis other actors. NGOs have successfully added non-economic issues such as environmental standards to bargaining agendas that traditionally have focused on MNC–state distributional concerns. Thus, dyadic bargaining between states and MNCs has developed into multiparty bargaining among NGOs, governments and firms. A confluence of issues, from genetically modified organisms to sweatshops, has mobilized a new generation of activists and generated pressure for new modes of international governance that accord a more significant role to civil society. Governments and MNCs have increasingly granted NGOs a seat at the negotiating table, and consequently the strategies and tactics of NGOs influence the bargaining process over governance structures and processes.

The revised bargaining model presented here reflects the emergence of a new, broader, terrain of contestation, one that relates to the very structures and processes of international governance. It seeks to examine both regulatory and market-enabling regimes. Eden has discussed the multifaceted nature of globalization and has identified three components in particular: the convergence of production, financial, and technological structures, the synchronization of national economies, and the interpenetration of flows of trade, investment, and technology. Concurrent with this economic globalization, though less noted in the literature, is the growth of governance structures at regional and international levels that provide an institutional context of rules and norms for the global economy. Just as MNCs have been major agents of economic interdependence, they are interested and important actors in constructing the edifice of the new global polity. In doing so, they negotiate and bargain with a range of other actors, including home and host governments, NGOs, and existing international and supra-national organizations.

Despite the effort within regime theory to focus attention on the institutions of governance rather than governments, regime theory has been much criticized for its state-centered perspective, and for its functionalist emphasis on reducing transaction costs and solving collective action problems. Only recently have scholars begun to take non-state actors more seriously as important agents in the processes of international governance. Peter Haas has pointed to the importance of "epistemic communities" of scientists as key agents in shaping environmental regimes, while some have looked more broadly to the role of global civil society and business.

If *Regime theory* has been too state-centered, then *the neo-Gramscian historical materialist* perspective in IR has placed too much emphasis on the power of capital in the global polity. In the process of forging a transnational hegemonic bloc dominated by MNCs, in alliance with internationally oriented state and NGO elites, national states are viewed as passively adapting to accommodate the demands of the new global economy. Robinson argues that national states are converted "into transmission belts and filtering devices for the imposition of the transnational agenda." Although Gramsci's concept of hegemony represents a negotiated consensus reflecting a historically specific balance of social forces, the rendition in the IR literature tends to be a top-down account in which national and global governance structures are determined by the economic needs of MNCs.

The Centre for Global Negotiations was created in 2001 and incorporated as a 501(c)3 non-profit organization in 2003. Its purpose is to inform and educate the public, media, business, and governments about the interdependence of global development issues and the need to discuss these issues together for the co-management of the international economy. The CGN has created a comprehensive update of the 1980 Brandt Commission Report (www.brandt21forum.info), worked closely with the Commission for Africa to develop an agenda for the 2005 G8 Summit, and is now an active partner in the Coalition for the Global Commons (http://enewschannels.com/2008/03/07/enc2733_053940.php).

Global Business Negotiations: A Sectoral Review

If we happen to scan global business scene, we find that negotiations do take place in most of emerging sectors of the vastly differentiated and transforming global economy; viz. joint ventures, oil and gas, energy, infrastructure, environment, airlines, defense deal etc. This can also form an integral part of the negotiation processes linked to economic regions, across countries, or companies. In many instances, this can also be a part of the growth as well as competitive strategy; especially of the MNCs. The following paragraphs provide some selected exposure to the readers about some illustrative cases of business negotiations at the International levels, the modalities in which negotiation processes were conducted together with issues addressed and resolved through negotiations etc. to help learning lessons therefrom.

1. Negotiations in International Joint Ventures

There was a time when business formation was relatively simple but now the law and related regulations, including taxation liabilities, intrude to the point that without legal expertise it is unlikely that the essentially simple decision of two parties agreeing to cooperate for some purpose would be achievable without high-level legal, taxation and accounting advice and guidance (it certainly would be extremely inadvisable for you to attempt it on your own). The business plan could envisage that a product is to be taken to a wider market beyond the initial jurisdiction within three years. That strategic decision creates an agenda for future negotiations. New opportunities bring their rewards, but also their burdens. What appears to be a logical development from a strong domestic market for an organization's products, in turn produces a host of questions that complicate what starts out as a straightforward decision. Among these questions is that of how the organization is going to give effect to the decision to market beyond current boundaries. One answer could be to form a joint venture (JV) with another company already located in the target market. This is where strategic negotiators ought to have some exposure to what is involved in a JV and what to look out for.

Why a joint venture?

To take a simple point: any decision to form a JV between two separate companies is bound to raise high-level policy concerns among regulators about the reduction in competition implied in this decision:

- Why don't the two entities remain separate and compete?
- Are the gains to the public good from their JV such that they should override considerations of a reduction in competition?

No firm answers can be given without detailed consideration of the circumstances. One such consideration operating in favour of a JV might be one between two separate companies domiciled in separate markets which combine to pursue a worthwhile or necessary project that neither could do on its own. Joint ventures in R&D also are looked on favourably, except, perhaps, in drug medication where the major drug companies are strong enough to conduct independent projects without recourse to partners from among their rivals. Many smaller companies specializing in fine chemicals are sub-contracted by organic growth strategies the main drug research firms to mass-produce their products, but these are covered by normal commercial contracts and not JV agreements.

Full-scale JVs face regulatory interventions or at least close scrutiny by the competition authorities. This led to experiments with various forms of alliances among passenger airline firms around the world. These are subject to approval by national authorities, and some notable attempts to form code-sharing alliances were frustrated by being linked to separate issues, such as the degree of freedom accorded to non-US airlines for open-sky routing across the USA, or to the vexed and continuing problem of the redistribution of landing slots at Heathrow, London. The takeover of KLM, the Dutch national carrier, by Air France was dressed up as an alliance to deter intervention by the European competition authorities, though the takeover was backed by each country's government.

Joint ventures are useful vehicles for separate businesses to cooperate in the supply of products or services to markets. Cooperation between organizations within the same country, and sometimes among organizations formed under different laws in different countries, is not unusual, despite the difficulties in forming them and their less-than-startling performance.

The nature of a JV varies from arms-length licences through franchises to a formal legal entity ('NewCo'), jointly owned and operated by the partners. The range of intermediate structures for marketing products and services is extensive and necessarily I have reduced them to a few. You could consider almost any relationship between two organizations that cooperates in an arrangement as intermediate suppliers as a kind of JV – the outputs of one company are inputs into another company's outputs. In the normal course of business our suppliers are in a kind of JV with us to deliver added value to final customers. However, the JVs we are concerned with are of the kind where there is a relationship with independent organizations (an existing entity, or a NewCo, jointly owned or not) that delivers added value product to final customers (Kennedy-http://www.ashgate.com/pdf/SamplePages/Strategic_Negotiation_Ch6.pdf)

During the negotiations of an international joint venture the common interest between the partners is the joint venture itself. Conflict will arise when partners seek to each maximize their own stake in the venture. International negotiations are some of the most complex of all bargaining situations. Cross border negotiations add cultural dimensions to the classic one-on-one bargaining. These cross-cultural dimensions include varying expectations, perspectives, motives, and priorities that individually or collectively can derail even simple negotiations. Negotiations involve two or more parties trying to find a mutually acceptable solution to a problem. Negotiations normally include bargaining that implies a competitive exchange between parties, but may also be win-win situations where both parties pursue mutually beneficial avenues [Pruitt & Rubin, 1986]. It should be noted that international negotiations are not restricted to two private organizations; rather, in many countries government agencies often take a prominent place at the bargaining table. For example, in China international joint ventures are exclusively tripartite, including the foreign company, the domestic firm, and a government agency.

Turning to the many models of negotiations, one may find that most fall into two categories: either distributive or integrative. Distributive negotiations involve a zero sum game in which the parties involved in the negotiations are competing to maximize their share of the outcomes. In a zero sum game the amount of the outcomes is fixed, therefore whatever one party wins, the other party must lose. A more collaborative model is found in integrative negotiations where parties involved in the negotiations seek to increase the pool of outcomes. Therefore each party maximizes their individual benefits through the division of the collective results; it is a win-win situation (Lewicki *et al.*, 1994).

International Joint Ventures

A joint venture is considered to be international if at least one of the parents has its headquarters outside the joint venture's country of operation. They are also considered international if the joint venture itself has a significant level of operation in a number of countries. The issue of control in international joint ventures often speaks to the great difficulties facing the potential partners. The fact that the venture is jointly owned/managed means that issues of who controls what, and who controls when, remain at the heart of the arrangement.

Whenever there are two or more owners and/or two or more managers, questions of control become paramount. Moreover, with those control issues comes the issue of conflict. The criticism most often levelled at international joint ventures is the concern over control of the venture. The loss or dilution of managerial control by joint venture partners seems to strike fear in their collective hearts. Killing (1982) argues that parties to the joint venture need to find a balance of power and control amongst all players. Joint venture partners need to determine the level of control they require to feel at ease in the partnership. They also need to determine how much control is needed to accomplish the joint venture firm's goals. Finally, joint venture partners have to decide how they will acquire the control they require.

Joint Venture and Corporate Governance—A Case of CalPERS

CalPERS is the nation's largest public pension fund. Headquartered in Sacramento, CalPERS provides retirement and health benefit services to nearly 1.5 million public servants and more than 2,500 public employers. The System also operates eight Regional Offices located in Walnut Creek, Glendale, Orange County, Fresno, Sacramento, San Bernardino, San Diego, and San Jose.

CalPERS is led by a 13-member Board of Administration (http://www.mckinseyquarterly.com/Governance/Boards/Governing_joint_ventures_1586). The CalPERS Board of Administration is guided by the Board's Investment Committee, management, and more than 210 Investment Office staff who carry out the daily activities of the investment program. The Corporation's goal is to efficiently and effectively manage investments to achieve the highest possible return at an acceptable level of risk. In doing so, CalPERS has generated strong long-term returns (http://www.calpers-governance.org/docs-sof/marketinitiatives/2009-04-01-corp-governance-pub20-final-glossy.pdf). Shareowners have a direct interest in the returns, risks, and governance of all wholly and partly-owned assets that make up public companies. To date, the focus of CalPERS efforts on governance, and that of regulators and investors, has been on wholly-owned business units, subsidiaries, and affiliates of public companies. CalPERS believes that ensuring the effective governance of material equity joint ventures – a key asset class with well documented and unique performance challenges where there has been historically less transparency than for similar-sized wholly owned businesses – is also an essential part of effective corporate governance (http://www.calpers-governance.org/docs-sof/marketinitiatives/2009-03-26-joint-venture-governance-guidelines.pdf).

To enhance investor confidence and to raise performance, CalPERS believes that companies need to raise the level of transparency, accountability, and discipline in the governance of their material joint ventures. As a minimum, any joint venture accounting for 10 percent or more of a publicly-traded parent company's total assets, invested capital, costs or revenues –or that is expected to account for 10 percent of the profit and loss of the corporation – should be viewed as material, as should smaller joint ventures that are strategically important, or that carry disproportionate risks. We believe that companies may wish to adopt a more inclusive standard for materiality, and, for instance, draw the line at joint ventures at or above $500 million in annual revenues or invested capital. For this class of joint ventures, CalPERS believes that the Company Board – i.e., the Board of parent companies that have ownership interests in joint ventures – should ensure the adoption of certain practices related to these joint ventures:

1. Corporate-Level Joint Venture Governance Practices

For any publicly-held company with one or more material joint ventures, that parent company should:

1.1 Require that the Audit Committee of the Company Board annually review the governance integrity and compliance policies of the company's material joint ventures Designate a Corporate Board member to be responsible for ensuring that the Company's corporate-level strategic business review process includes the Company's material joint ventures, and this review process holds joint ventures to similar performance standards to one another and to similar-sized business units.

1.3 Adopt and make available to the public a set of Joint Venture Governance Guidelines for the Company's material joint ventures (such as those in Appendix I, co-authored by CalPERS and Water Street Partners) which define a set of minimum expectations for overseeing such ventures.

1.4 Designate a Corporate Board member to be responsible for ensuring, on an annual basis, that the Company's material joint ventures are subject to a review of their adherence to these Joint Venture Governance Guidelines, and that the results of the review are discussed and approved by the Corporate Board.

2. Public Disclosure and Transparency

For any material joint venture that has at least one public company shareholder, that parent company should disclose to its public investors:

2.1 The name, business scope and objectives, and current financial impact of each material joint venture of the Company.

2.2 A list of the Lead Director of the Joint Venture Board of Directors of each material joint venture.

2.3 Whether each material joint venture is complying with the guidelines outlined in Appendix I; to the extent that the venture is not meeting any of these governance standards, provide an explanation for why such governance standards are not being met.

Good governance matters to joint ventures—and joint ventures matter to many public companies and, therefore, their public shareowners. Today there are more that 1000 joint ventures (JVs) with more than $1 billion in annual revenues or invested capital. The 8 largest publicly listed oil and gas companies and 6 metals and mining majors have more than $500 billion in assets in major joint ventures. More broadly, many public companies hold a dozen or more material JVs in their portfolios, and depend on JVs for 10-20 percent of total corporate revenues, assets, or income, using joint ventures as a key tool to access technology and innovation, gain scale and reduce costs, share risk, and build new businesses. In such industries as conventional petroleum, alternative energy, chemicals, basic materials, and aerospace, joint ventures account for upwards of 30-50 percent of many company's economic activity. Likewise, joint ventures are widely used in China, India, Russia, Korea, Latin America, and the Middle East.

More than 10 years ago, CalPERS established a set of governance principles for public companies at the corporate level with the underlying tenet that fully accountable corporate governance structures produce, over the long term, the best returns to shareowners. We believe a similar level of scrutiny and focus should be extended to the largest joint ventures of public companies, and that shareowners will benefit by the application of more consistent standards of governance. These JV Governance Guidelines, co-authored by CalPERS and Water Street Partners, are an effort to promote such attention and, in time, drive improved performance and reduced risk within a large but relatively less-transparent asset class.

Joint Venture Governance Challenge

The governance of these joint ventures introduces unique challenges. These challenges are an outgrowth of the way the corporate-parent shareholders inter-relate to the venture, most notably: shared oversight and control; significant economic and business flows between the shareholders and JV for various services, inputs or outputs; differing appetites for growth, investment, and cash returns from the shareholders (i.e., corporate parents); and changes in shareholder strategies and reactions to new market conditions that put pressure on the JV. To understand why joint ventures are different, consider how the governance of joint ventures compare to that of public companies:

Board composition and decision-making

- Public Company Governance: Non-executive/independent Board members constitute a majority of the Board, and the Board is an agent for independent shareowners, who are aligned around the basic desire to maximize overall shareowner returns
- JV Governance: In JVs, there are typically no independent Board members from outside the JV and the parent companies; Board members represent parent companies which often have differing objectives, investment and risk preferences, and receive asymmetric benefits from the venture Resource flows from the shareholders:
- Public Company Governance: The company does not depend on

shareowners for operational inputs into the business — or, if the company does, those transactions are conducted on a true arms-length basis, and subject to legal and governance protections against conflicts of interest

- JV Governance: Commercial relationships are not always easily conducted at arms-length market prices, and conflicts of interest cannot be completely avoided.

Using the petroleum and basic materials industries as proxies, it is possible to estimate the amount of "value restoration" associated with improved JV good governance. For the top 8 petroleum companies and the top 6 basic and mining companies, material joint ventures today account for $72 billion in annual earnings (on a $503 billion asset base). Calculations by Water Street Partners indicate that, conservatively, there is $5-13 billion in improved annual earnings available collectively to these 14 companies. At current trading multiples, this represents roughly $50-130 billion in added market capitalization that could be created through better JV governance and enhanced performance in just these 14 companies. When we extrapolate to other companies in the petroleum and mining industries – and to other industries such as telecom, chemicals, aerospace and defense, industrial manufacturing, and high-tech—there is, at minimum, $15-36 billion in value restoration available from the improved governance and shareholder relationship of material joint ventures.

Joint Venture Governance Guidelines

CalPERS and Water Street Partners recommend that the Boards of material joint ventures adopt the following guidelines, and put into place practices to support them:

A. Board Mandate and Structure

1. The Joint Venture Board of Directors is the primary means for governing the joint venture, and the JV CEO reports directly and only to the JV Board. Shareholder input to the JV CEO and JV CFO should be channeled through the Board (and not communicated in an uncoordinated manner to JV management).
2. The JV Board has an explicit charter and delegation of authority framework that defines its role in relation to JV Management, JV Board Committees, and the Boards and Management of the Parent Companies. This charter and framework specifically spells out where venture management has the power to act on its own and where the parents (individually or through the JV Board) will have control, influence or close involvement. The framework also identifies decisions that require separate approval by the Parent Company Boards or Parent Company Management – where approval by the JV Board is not sufficient. The scope of the framework should include matters to fiscal authority,

operations, personnel. decisions, and strategy (such as changes to the venture's product, pricing or market positioning). The Board periodically reassesses this delegation of authority framework, and takes measures to adjust approval levels based on JV performance and business conditions.

3. The JV Board is responsible for performing the roles of a traditional Corporate Board, including: (i) setting strategy and direction; (ii) approving major capital investments; (iii) ensuring strong performance management and managing financial risk; (iv) protecting shareholder and public interests, including legal, safety, ethics and environmental considerations; and (v) overseeing CEO and top-management hiring, evaluation, compensation and succession planning. In addition, the JV Board is responsible for JV-specific roles, including:

   3a. Securing needed resources and organizational commitments from the corporate parents, on a timely basis. This includes facilitating staff rotations as needed between the JV and parent companies 3b. Overseeing the negotiation of major commercial agreements between JV and parent, and shielding the JV CEO and management team from negotiating with parent stakeholders on issues where parent interests are misaligned 3c. Periodically assessing the need for major change in the venture strategy, scope, ownership/financial structure and operating model within the strategic confines defined by the parent company – much as a corporation would challenge the strategy, structure, and, if needed, continued corporate ownership of a business unit

4. The Board has established and maintains an active Audit Committee, which meets more than once a year, and is responsible for reporting and oversight of compliance, financial statement integrity, and overall risk management.21 At least one Board member has significant financial expertise and is the chair of the Audit Committee.
5. The Board has established and maintains an active Compensation Committee, which meets regularly and is responsible for: (i) approving the compensation and incentive framework for the venture's top management team, including developing an annual Performance Contract for the JV CEO; (ii) nominating, evaluating, and determining compensation for the CEO; (iii) overseeing succession planning for the JV CEO and other members of venture top management; and (iv) assisting the JV CEO in ensuring access to skills and people, as needed, from the parent companies.
6. The JV Board conducts an annual audit of the joint venture's governance performance, which would include compliance with these governance guidelines and a view of the overall health of the governance system. Related to this:

   6a. The JV Board has designated at least one Board member (likely a Lead Director, as described in section B.4) to lead such a review and discussion 6b. The review involves a level of rigor and seriousness similar to other major reviews, and includes a set of criteria against which the shareholders agree to evaluate the venture, a summary of performance, and a discussion of opportunities to improve how the shareholders relate to each other and the venture.

B. Board Composition and Individual Roles

1. Absent compelling, unusual circumstances, the JV Board should range from 4 to 10 members. If outside that range, the number of members should be justified.
2. The JV Board has established—and at least annually updates—a set of skills it seeks from Director candidates. Minimally, these skills, across the Board, should include general Management experience, finance expertise, experience in the JV industry and with the geographic markets in which the JV operates, and prior experience with other JVs. In selecting members of the Board, the parent companies explicitly account for the desired mix of skills and personal dynamics within the Board overall.
3. Each shareholder has appointed to the JV Board at least one representative who is a senior executive of the parent company, and who is able to truly represent the interests of the parent company and command internal resources to support the venture. The following test is to be used to determine if such authority level exists: that Board member has the proven authority to: (i) sign-off on the JV's annual budget and operating plan, within limits consistent with the parent company strategy, budget, and operating plan; (ii) approve the JV's material supply or service contracts; and (iii) approve the JV CEO's annual performance 4. Each parent has designated a Lead Director. The Lead Director is a senior executive of the parent company who:

   4a. Spends at least 20 days per year in an active non-executive capacity overseeing and supporting the venture 24

   4b. Performs the following roles: (i) coordinates other Directors from his or her parent company, i.e., ensure opinions heard, consistent voice presented to JV and partner; (ii) accesses resources from inside the parent company in support of the JV; (iii) works with the other Lead Director(s) and JV CEO between Board meetings to resolve issues that do not require full Board approval; (iv) shields the JV from excessive parent company information requests and bureaucracy (e.g., duplicative reporting requirements, slow capex approval processes); and (v) supports the parent executive team and parent board in ensuring that the JV is meeting governance, compliance, risk management and transparency requirements; and, ideally, (vi) explains the JV's strategy, performance, risks and prospects at corporate-level reviews in the parent company.

5. Each Lead Director has an element of his or her annual performance review and short-term variable compensation tied to the performance of the joint venture, and his or her performance as the Lead Director. In no circumstances does the JV account for less than 10 percent of his or her total performance review and short-term variable compensation calculation.
6. The JV Board has designated a Chairperson (who may be the Lead Director from one parent company) to be additionally responsible for: (i) managing the overall Board agenda (including syndication prior to Board meetings of key issues and decisions); and (ii) overseeing the quality, quantity and timeliness of the flow of information to the Board from venture management; and, (iii) unless assigned to another Board member or committee, ensuring the integrity of the governance system, including being responsible for an annual assessment and discussion about governance performance, underlying health, and potential changes to the governance, scope or structure venture to improve its performance.
7. No member of the Joint Venture Management Team is a member of the JV Board.
8. The JV Board ensures that it has a strong independent perspective, preferably by the inclusion of an Independent Director, with stature in the industry. An Independent Director would not be expected to hold a swing vote in Board decisions, and may be a non-voting member of the Board. To additionally promote independence, the Board should: (i) endorse the principle that Board members and full-time venture staff (including *secondees*) are first and foremost to promote the interests of the venture as a whole (rather than the singular interests of one shareholder), and (ii) periodically invite independent outsiders (e.g., industry experts, customers) to Board meetings to share their perspectives and challenge the Board. To function effectively, an Independent Director needs to have a professional stature and personality that allows him or her to raise issues to and influence the shareholders.

C. Board Processes and Evaluation

1. Working with executives in the parent companies if need be, the JV Board establishes and periodically updates a set of guiding principles defining the parents' shared philosophy toward the venture. These principles include statements regarding the desired level of independence from the parents, whether the venture is to be run as a business or an operating asset, and the evolution path and, if possible, planned endgame of the venture. The Board has established

performance criteria for itself as a collective body, and periodically reviews its performance against these criteria.

3. The Board has established performance criteria for its individual Board members, including individual behavioral expectations. Minimally, these criteria address the level of Board member attendance, preparedness, participation, and candor. To be re-nominated, directors must satisfactorily perform based on the established criteria; re-nomination on any other basis is neither expected nor guaranteed.
4. Each director has an attendance rate of at least 75 percent at Board meetings and 75 percent of Board Committee meetings of which they are members, and the Board has established a minimum standard to that effect.

2. *Emissions Reduction Negotiations: Emerging Issues*

Representatives of 188 nations met in Poznan, Poland this December as part of the United Nations Framework Convention on Climate Change (UNFCCC). This meeting will mark the midpoint of their negotiations on a new treaty to replace the Kyoto Protocol, which began last year in Indonesia with the announcement of the Bali Action Plan.

The principal goal of the Poznan meeting was to outline an ambitious schedule of talks that will culminate in Copenhagen in 2009 with agreement to a global emissions pact to take effect in 2012. The Poznan climate conference is the 14th Conference of the Parties (COP-14) to the Framework Convention, and the 4th Meeting of the Parties to the Kyoto Protocol (http://www.pewtrusts.org/uploadedFiles/wwwpewtrustsorg/Reports/Global_warming/UN_Negotiations_08.pdf).

Having ratified the Framework Convention on September 8, 1992, the United States is a full party to that treaty. Its concurrence is required for decisions to be adopted by conferences of the parties, which proceed by consensus, not by majority vote. When matters specific to the Kyoto Protocol are under discussion, the United States may participate as an observer, but its concurrence in decisions is not required since it has signed but not ratified the agreement.

The Bali Action Plan—2007

The Bali conference launched formal negotiations on a new, post-2012, international global warming agreement and set a firm deadline for its adoption in December 2009, when the 15th Conference of the Parties will meet in Copenhagen, Denmark. The outline of those negotiations is contained in the Bali Action Plan, approved in a dramatic conclusion to the talks on December 15, 2007.

One of the most important developments in Bali was the fact that developing countries came to the table willing to discuss emission reductions of their own. The Bali Action Plan opens discussion on "measurable, verifiable and reportable" emission reduction actions that may be undertaken by developing countries. While the developing countries stepped up and brought this new position to Bali, the United States maintained its long-held rejection of binding numerical commitments for emission reduction targets and renewed its obstructionist behavior of previous climate change talks.

In exchange for their willingness to consider making reduction commitments, the developing countries wanted assurance from developed nations that they would provide them with assistance in acquiring cleaner technologies. On the final day of the conference, India proposed that the same language used to describe mitigation actions, "measurable, verifiable and reportable," also be applied to technology transfer and financing assistance from developed countries. The meeting almost ended without an agreement to launch negotiations when the U.S. stood to oppose this concession. However, when its traditional cast of allies, including Canada, Japan, and Australia (who ratified Kyoto on the second day of the talks), refused to join this position and the U.S. was faced with the possibility of being solely responsible for the breakdown of the negotiations, the U.S. withdrew its opposition and the language was adopted.

Key Issues and Progress to-date in the Negotiations

In three separate negotiation sessions this year, the parties explored the key issues in the Bali Action Plan and came to a clearer common understanding of the goals of the five building blocks which include the "shared vision? for long term action, mitigation, adaption, technology and finance. However, few countries have issued concrete proposals that would implement any of those aspects of a new agreement. Countries were strongly encouraged in the August 2008 meeting in Accra, Ghana to submit those proposals for discussion in Poland and the Chair of the 'Ad hoc Working Group on Long Term Cooperation (AWG-LCA)' was directed to assemble those proposals into a document that could ultimately become draft negotiating text.

- *Mitigation/Emission Reductions*: The purpose of the next year of negotiations is to determine the new term of emissions reductions. Guided by the 2007 Fourth Assessment Report of the Intergovernmental Panel on Climate Change (IPCC), the Ad Hoc Working Group on Further Commitments for Annex I Parties (AWG on Article 3.9) under the Kyoto protocol had approved language in the meetings prior to the Bali conference suggesting that the next round of emission reductions by developed counties should be in the range of 25-40% below 1990 levels. The IPCC scenarios suggest that global emissions should peak in 10-15 years and decline to "well below half" of 2000 levels by 2020 in order to keep average global temperature increases around 2 degrees Celsius. The U.S. blocked the inclusion of numerical guidelines in the final text, resulting in emission reduction goals only being referenced in a footnote of the Bali Action Plan. Nonetheless, the negotiators are still mindful of the need to outline medium and long term emissions goals that are consistent with the recommendations of the worlds leading scientists.

Talks in 2008 have not made much progress on mitigation or their "shared vision" for the long term goal. At the G8, Heads of State agreed to work toward reducing emissions by 50% by 2050, a goal that is not binding on the UNFCCC. The European Union announced its Climate and Energy plan in January of 2008, which included mandatory targets for reducing greenhouse gas emissions by 20% below 1990 levels by 2020. The E.U. also announced that it would be willing to reduce emissions by 30% below 1990 if other industrialized countries made the same commitment. No developed countries have yet indicated their willingness to meet the E.U. challenge, nor even indicated the levels of reductions they might consider. Developing countries continue to indicate a willingness to take actions to reduce emissions that are "measurable, reportable, and verifiable," but have insisted that agreement must be reached first on the financing available for adaptation and technology before they are able to indicate what kind of mitigation efforts might be possible in their countries in the following manner:

- *Reducing Emissions from Deforestation*: Since the Montreal talks in 2005, the UNFCCC has been considering options for developing countries that would incentivize forest conservation, thereby avoiding emissions from deforestation activities. Reducing deforestation does not qualify as a Clean Development Mechanism (CDM) project, which is currently the only structured way for developing countries to get credit for emission reduction activities under the Kyoto Protocol. The Bali Action Plan encourages tropical forest countries to undertake demonstration projects and establishes a new committee to consider "policy approaches and positive incentives" for reducing emissions from deforestation. Last year, the negotiations have centered on whether the incentives to reduce emissions from deforestation and degradation (REDD) will come in the form of carbon credits or direct financial assistance and whether or not sub-national projects will qualify.
- *Adaptation:* The United Nations Development Program estimated that the adaptation needs of developing countries to cope with the impacts of global warming will cost more than $80 billion up to 2015, making adaptation a key issue for many developing countries. The Bali Action Plan provides a solid basis for creating the necessary adaptation assistance, calling for better access to more assistance for both adaptation and emissions reduction activities in developing countries. In Bali, negotiators also reached agreement on implementation of the Adaptation Fund that was created under the Kyoto Protocol, setting up the Global Environment Facility (GEF), as the day-to-day implementing body for the fund and creating an executive board comprised of a majority of developing countries to oversee the expenditures from the fund.

Talks on adaptation over the last year have centered on the need for coordination among UN agencies and other multilateral bodies; how to implement National Adaptation Plans (NAPA)s; long term, stable funding options; development and improvement of regional cooperation to disseminate expertise and promote refined implementation; risk assessment and insurance options for vulnerable countries; and a mechanism to transfer technology that helps to develop, implement and enhance a country's technological capacity to implement their national adaptation plans.

- *Technology and Finance*: The key to reducing emissions globally lies in the accelerated deployment of clean technologies. The UNFCCC secretariat earlier this year issued a paper on financing of mitigation and adaptation as a way to shift the focus of the discussion. The developing countries came to Bali determined to get a commitment to make progress on this issue, which they demonstrated just minutes after the ceremonial opening by requesting that technology be added to the UNFCCC committee on implementation (the Subsidiary Body on Implementation). In addition to adding the words "measurable, verifiable and reportable," to the technology and adaptation language in the final deal, the Bali decision reconstitutes an „experts group? with a 5-year mandate to establish a strategy for overcoming the barriers to technology transfer.

Consistent with the pace of the rest of the negotiations, progress on technology and finance has been slow. However, at the last meeting in Accra, the G77 put forth a proposal on technology and finance that is under consideration by delegates. The G77 set out some guiding principles, starting with the position that the technology mechanism operate under the authority and guidance of the UFCCC and should aim to achieve:

- Accessibility, affordability, appropriateness and adaptability of technologies required by developing countries for enhanced action on mitigation and adaptation;
- Provision of full costs and full incremental costs;
- Adequacy and predictability of funds for technology transfer;
- Removal of barriers for technology development and transfer.

Financing for both technology and adaptation will likely be as difficult a question for negotiators as the emission reduction levels. Several proposals for financing have been proposed but none have yet seemed to have achieved the kind of support needed to advance the discussions in any significant way.

- *U.S. Participation*: Throughout the talks, proposals were offered to establish a separate negotiating track to determine the emission reduction goals for non-Kyoto countries, (U.S., Kazakhstan, Belarus and Lichtenstein). None of the proposals prevailed. Over the next two years parallel negotiations will take place on developing country commitments under the UNFCCC, and under a more detailed process

> that has been set up under the Kyoto protocol. The Bali Action Plan language guiding the UNFCCC discussion was clearly designed to create a space for eventual U.S. re-entry, establishing that the U.S. would have to agree to: "Measurable, reportable and verifiable nationally appropriate mitigation commitments or actions, including quantified emission limitation and reduction objectives," consistent with those of developed country Parties under Kyoto but also "taking into account differences in their national circumstances."

The U.S. fully participated in the UN negotiations in 2008, but has not put forth specific proposals on any of the major building blocks. President-elect Barak Obama supports mandatory caps in the U.S. and has called on all major emitting nations to join in the solution, stating "developing nations like China and Brazil must not be far behind? in making their own binding commitments. This statement is a shift from the current U.S. position that emerging economies, like China and India, must take on the same commitments as the U.S. as a pre-condition of our approval of the agreement, but it makes clear that developing countries will have to play a much larger role in emissions reduction than under the current Kyoto regime.

Stepping up International Action on Climate Change: The Road to Copenhagen

Climate change is today widely recognized as one of mankind's greatest challenges in the 21st century. If left unchecked, climate change can seriously harm economies, societies and eco-systems all around the world, especially in developing countries. Climate change is not restricted to national boundaries. Fighting it therefore only makes sense through concerted action on the international level. To this end the international community adopted the United Nations Framework Convention on Climate Change (UNFCC) at the historical Earth Summit in 1992 in Rio de Janeiro.

In December 1997, an agreement was reached to add the Kyoto Protocol to the Convention. The Kyoto Protocol includes binding emission reduction targets for developed countries for the period 2008-12.

The year 2007 brought again new momentum. In spring the Intergovernmental Panel of Climate Change (IPCC), the leading body to review climate change science, published its Fourth Assessment Report. The report gave a clear signal that climate change is happening and accelerating, that much of it is caused by the continued and increasing emissions of greenhouse gases from human activities and that it can have severe impacts.

The IPPC report injected a new sense of urgency into the UN climate change negotiations. At the Climate Change Conference in Bali in December all Parties to the UNFCCC—both developed and developing countries—agreed to step up their efforts to combat climate change and to this end adopted a number of decisions, which together made up the Bali Road Map. They agreed to advance ongoing work on key issues including technology, adaptation and reducing emissions from deforestation. Furthermore, Parties decided to launch formal negotiations on a deal on long-term cooperative action. These negotiations are set to be concluded by the end of 2009 at the Climate Change Conference in Copenhagen. The aim is that the Copenhagen deal would enter into force no later than by the end of 2012 when the first commitment period of the Kyoto Protocol expires.

This fact sheet consists of two parts. The first part provides an overview of the mechanics of the UN climate change negotiations and explains what the negotiating process leading up to Copenhagen looks like. The second part zooms in on the main issues in these negotiations; curbing emissions of green house gases (mitigation), dealing with the impacts of climate change (adaptation), finance and technology.

UN Climate Change Negotiations

Regular meetings

Negotiations on the Convention and its Kyoto Protocol take place at a number of occasions throughout the year and culminate at the end of each year in the "UN Climate Change Conference". These yearly Climate Change Conferences have over the years grown in size and are attended by thousands of participants, including government representatives, participants from business and industry, environmental organizations and the media. The next Climate Change Conference will take place from 1-12 December in Poznan, Poland.

It is at the UN Climate Change Conference where the so-called Conference of Parties (COP) meet. This is the supreme body and highest decision-making authority of the Convention and includes all 192 countries that have signed and ratified the UNFCCC.

The supreme body of the Kyoto Protocol also meets at the Climate Change Conference every year. This body is referred to as the CMP (Conference of the Parties serving as the Meeting of the Parties to the Kyoto Protocol) and is the association of those Parties to the Convention that have also signed and ratified the Kyoto Protocol.

To prepare for the major decisions made at the UN Climate Change Conferences, smaller UNFCCC meetings called "UN Climate Change Talks" are held. Under the Convention two permanent subsidiary bodies exist: the "Subsidiary Body for Scientific and Technological Advice" (SBSTA) and the "Subsidiary Body for Implementation" (SBI). These bodies meet twice a year (in June and December) and give advice to the COP. Each has a specific mandate. As its name suggests, the SBSTA's task is to provide the COP with advice on scientific, technological and methodological matters. The SBI gives advice on all matters concerning the implementation of the Convention.

Extra meetings

With the decision in Bali to launch formal negotiations on a new climate change deal, extra meetings are scheduled in the run up to Copenhagen. Between now and the clinching of the Copenhagen deal, a total of seven UNFCCC meetings will take place. At each of the extra meetings, there are two working groups gathering which are of particular interest in the negotiations on a Copenhagen deal. They are the "Ad-hoc Working Group on Long-term Cooperative Action under the Convention (AWG-LCA)" and the "Ad-hoc Working Group on further commitments for Annex I Parties under the Kyoto Protocol (AWG-KP)."

The "Ad-hoc Working Group on Long-term Cooperative Action under the Convention" (AWG-LCA) is established exclusively to conduct negotiations on a Copenhagen deal. The group was established at the Climate Change Conference in Bali and assembles all192 Parties to the UN Climate Change Convention. The group met for the first time at the Bangkok Climate Change United Nations Framework Convention on Climate Change.

Talks last April where it adopted its work programme for 2008. In 2008, it would have met three more times: at the Bonn Climate Change Talks (2-12 June, 2008), in Accra (21-27 August, 2008) and in Poznan (1-12 December). In 2009, at least four other meetings will take place. The group decided to address at each of these the following five building blocks of a deal on stronger international action on climate change: a shared vision (including a long-term global goal for emission reductions) and enhanced action in the areas of mitigation, adaptation, technology and finance. In addition, each session will pay attention to specific subjects under these elements. For example, during the Bonn session there will be workshops on adaptation, technology and finance. In Accra, a workshop was planned on reducing emissions from deforestation and sectoral action. The other group that is of particular interest to get to an agreed outcome in Copenhagen, is the working group under the Kyoto Protocol. Parties to the Kyoto Protocol initiated a process in 2005 in Montreal to consider further commitments of industrialized countries under the Kyoto Protocol for the period beyond 2012. The negotiations on further commitments of developed countries are also set to conclude in 2009.

Background to the Copenhagen Convention

In order to take account of the reservations expressed by developing countries, as well as the fact that the United States (the largest emitter of greenhouse gases) has not ratified the Kyoto Protocol, the negotiations leading up to Copenhagen will be held in two separate negotiating groups, both ending in 2009.

One group, the Ad-Hoc Working Group on Further Commitments (AWG KP), was founded in 2006 and will hold negotiations on future emissions reduction obligations for industrialized countries that have ratified the Kyoto Protocol. It was agreed at the Bali Conference that the reductions corridor for industrialized countries put forward by the International Panel on Climate Change, 25-40 per cent by 2020 compared to 1990 levels, would be used as the basis for further deliberations. They also agreed on the fact that emissions trading, the Clean Development Mechanism and joint implementation will be used from 2012.

The other group, the Ad-Hoc Working Group on Long-term Cooperative Action (AWG LCA) will hold negotiations on emissions reduction contributions by non-Kyoto industrialized countries, the United States in particular, as well as on what developing countries can contribute to future climate protection regimes. This group was set up during the Bali Conference and will be dealing with the following issues that will be the cornerstones of the Copenhagen Convention: a long-term, global emissions reduction target, verifiable and comparable reductions targets for industrialized countries, reduction measures to be taken by developing countries, technical and financial support to be given to developing countries both when reducing emissions and when adapting to climate change.

Encouraging for both of these groups was the recent commitment at the *G8 Summit in L'Aguila Italy* in early July that global warming must not exceed 2 degrees Celsius. The leaders' committed to reducing emissions by 80 percent by 2050 compared to 1990 levels. This is a tall order but the heads of state hope that in their respective nations, the population will also demonstrate the political will to achieve these critical goals.

Main Issues on the Road to Copenhagen

Mitigation

In accordance with the UNFCCC, all Parties are required to undertake efforts to stabilize greenhouse gas concentrations in the atmosphere at a level that will prevent dangerous human interference with the climate system. According to the principle of 'common but differentiated responsibilities and capabilities', the commitments for developed countries are different than those for developing countries.

To avoid the most dramatic impacts of climate change, the Intergovernmental Panel on Climate Change (IPCC) has indicated in its most ambitious scenario that the increase of worldwide emissions need to be halted within the next 10 to 15 years and be dramatically cut back by 50% in 2050 compared to 1990 levels. Currently, the Kyoto Protocol includes emission reduction targets for industrialized countries (Annex I countries) for the period 2008-2012, the so-called first commitment period of the Kyoto Protocol. All these national targets together amount to a worldwide cut of around 5% from 1990 levels.

To monitor the progress made towards meeting the goals of the UNFCCC, all Parties have to periodically maintain national inventories to report on their emissions of greenhouse gases. Developed countries are required to do this every year. Furthermore, all Parties give a general description of the steps taken or envisaged by them to implement the Convention through national reports. The required contents of these reports are different for developed countries and developing countries (non-Annex I countries) but usually contain information on national circumstances, trends in GHG emissions, policies and measures (developed countries) or national and regional programmes (developing countries). Developing countries can get assistance in drawing up their national reports.

Work in progress

In 2005 the AWG-KP was established to discuss further commitments for Annex I countries under the Kyoto Protocol. At the Climate Change Talks in Vienna in August 2007, the AWG-KP concluded that these discussions should be guided by a range of a total cut by developed countries in between 25% and 40% in 2020. This range is based on the most ambitious scenario presented by the IPCC so far to keep the global temperature rise in between 2.0-2.4 degree Celsius. In 2008 the AWG-KP will focus its work on an analysis of the possible tools and the rules available to developed countries to reach reduction commitments. It is important to first come to an agreement on the tools and rules, because the way in which countries can reach targets will determine for an important part their level of ambition when discussing new emission reduction targets for the period after 2012. The tools under analysis include:

- emission trading and the so-called project based mechanisms (such as the Clean Development Mechanism that allows developed countries to meet part of their emission reduction target by investing in emission reduction projects in developing countries);
- land use, land-use change and forestry;
- greenhouse gases, sectors and source categories to be covered;
- possible approaches for targeting emissions from specific sectors (for example energy intensive industries, such as the steel, aluminium, cement and paper and pulp sector)

One of the main outcomes of the meeting of the group at the Bangkok Climate Change Talks was the agreement that the use of emission trading, the Clean Development and Joint Implementation should be continued. Furthermore, the group also agreed to continue the use of forest and land use-related activities as a means to achiever emission reductions. In Bonn discussions will continue. The AWG-KP is expected to get to an agreement on the 'rulebook' at its session in Climate Change Talks in Accra in August. In 2009 the working group will continue working on identifying possible emission reduction targets for developed countries. This work should lead to an agreed outcome in Copenhagen in 2009.

The aim of the UN climate change convention, which will be held in Copenhagen in December 2009, is to conclude negotiations on a wide-ranging, post-December 2012 climate protection convention. That was what the international community agreed at the Bali Conference on Climate Change in 2007 when it adopted what has become known as the Bali Roadmap. The convention will come into force in 2013, following directly from the first commitment period in the Kyoto Protocol.

3. *Iran's Foreign Policy and the Iran-Pakistan-India Gas Pipeline*

Shortly after the revolution in 1979, Iran somewhat irrationally distanced itself from the international community. Partly because of revolutionary fervor, Iran initially made itself vulnerable. The American hostage crisis and the eight-year war with Iraq exposed Iran to economic hardship and international isolation.

Post-revolutionary Iran has sought to overcome its weakness by using economic and political resources to create an international coalition aimed at counteracting pressure imposed by the West. To achieve this goal, Iran has played different cards, including strengthening ties with Middle Eastern groups such as Hizbullah and Hamas; keeping a window of dialogue open or trying to avoid confrontation with the European Union with the aim of challenging the US embargo and political pressure; engaging in military-industrial cooperation with Russia and China in order to create a friendlier environment at the UN Security Council while advancing its nuclear agenda; and pursuing a policy of *détente* with the GCC states, with the broader objective of reducing US influence in the Persian Gulf (http://www.payvand.com/news/09/feb/1203.html)

In addition to these efforts, Iran has sought to build a pipeline to transfer Iranian natural gas to the Indian subcontinent — though bringing this project to fruition has proven elusive. Natural gas reserves were discovered in Iran's South Pars field ten years after the revolution. Soon after this discovery, the governments of Iran, Pakistan, and India increased their efforts to realize a natural gas pipeline project that will serve the twin purpose of increasing Iran's gas exports and meeting high energy demand in South-Asian countries. The Iran-Pakistan-India (IPI) gas pipeline, also called the "Peace Pipeline," has special significance for both economic and political reasons. Not only would this project greatly benefit energy-deficient countries such as India and Pakistan, but it also has the potential to affect the nature of the relations among them and to contribute to greater regional stability.

Iran, which has the world's second largest proven natural gas reserves after Russia, has been eager to exploit this resource not only as source of revenue, but also as leverage for political gains. India, with an increasing need for energy as its population quickly approaches 1.3 billion, is the biggest potential customer. Pakistan, which refuses to establish normal trading ties with India, also can benefit greatly from the pipeline by earning hundreds of millions of dollars in transit fees and other annual royalties from both Iran and India. Were this pipeline to be constructed, Pakistan's role between Iran and India would be very similar to that of Ukraine between Russia and the European Union.

The United States has been opposed to the gas pipeline project, citing various security concerns. Washington is fearful that a situation might emerge where these countries would directly or indirectly confront the United States and other Western countries for the control of energy bases. In addition, emerging strategic relations between Iran and India could lead to cooperation in the nuclear sphere, or at a minimum provide the revenue that could be used to further Iran's alleged nuclear weapons program and its support for terrorism. In addition, this project could help to shape an environment in which Iran might be able to perpetuate its poor human rights record.

Until recently, Iran faced two main challenges in bringing this project to fruition. The first challenge is the historic conflict between India and Pakistan over Muslim Kashmir, in which Iran has taken the pragmatic stance of non-intervention. Regarding the Kashmir conflict, it is worth noting that Iran has had similar experiences with its northern neighbors, maintaining a more or less neutral position on the Chechens' conflict with Russia, basically because of the strategically significant gains that this posture promised to yield. Similarly, Iran's position on the Armenia-Azerbaijan conflict over Nagorno-Karabakh was driven by strategic concerns, which ruled out taking a pro-Azeri position, rather than by religious ideology.

The second and more important challenge was and still is the American perception—with which most Western states appear to agree—that Iran should not be allowed to make long-term commitments on its strategic resources with non-Western countries. It is important to mention that these Western concerns are not limited to Iran; there is a general concern that the revenues generated by Pakistan also could be further used to support terrorist activities, depending on who channels the funding. The Pakistani involvement in the terrorist attacks in Mumbai in November 2008 confirms that this concern is not baseless.

The focal issue for Iran is to push the pipeline project into an operational phase. However, Iran faces several obstacles and uncertainties. First, although the United States recognizes the growing energy needs of India and Pakistan, it has repeatedly expressed concerns over international participation in energy projects with Iran. Second, it is not clear which countries/companies will eventually become involved in the implementation of the project. China, Russia, Japan, and even some European countries have expressed interest in the project's long-term potential. Obviously, Russian involvement in the pipeline project, in addition to their involvement in Caspian Sea projects, could complicate the situation further by reducing US companies' participation in the region.

The *Iran–Pakistan–India gas pipeline*, also known as the *IPI pipeline* or the *Peace pipeline*, is a proposed 2,775-kilometre (1,724 mi) pipeline to deliver natural gas from Iran to Pakistan and India. In April 2008 Iran expressed interest in the People's Republic of China's participation in the project. The project is expected to greatly benefit India and Pakistan, which do not have sufficient Natural gas to meet their increasing domestic demand for energy. India is predicted to require 146 billion cubic meters (bcm) of gas per annum by 2025, up from 33 bcm per annum in 2005 (http://en.wikipedia.org/wiki/Iran%E2%80%93Pakistan%E2%80%93India_gas_pipeline).

The project was conceptualized in 1989 by Rajendra K. Pachauri in partnership with Ali Shams Ardekani, former Deputy Foreign Minister of Iran. Dr Pachauri proposed the plan to both Iranian and Indian governments in 1990. The Government of Iran responded positively to the proposal. At the annual conference of the International Association of Energy Economics, 1990, Dr Ardekani backed Dr Pachauri's proposal. The deal reached a setback on July 16, 2006, when Iran demanded a price of US$7.20 per million British thermal unit (US$6.80/GJ) of gas against India's offer of US$4.20 per million British thermal unit ($4.00/GJ). The Indian spokesperson stated that the price offered by Iran was more than 50% above the prevailing market price in India.[2] India and Pakistan finally agreed in February 2007 to pay Iran US$4.93 per million British thermal units (US$4.67/GJ) but some details relating to price adjustment remained open to further negotiation.[3] The long-stalled talks made a breakthrough in April 2008 when Iranian President Mahmoud Ahmadinejad made whistle-stop visits to Pakistan and India.

India, Asia's third-largest economy, can produce only half the gas it needs to generate electricity, causing blackouts and curbing economic growth. The Indian government has called for trilateral talks on the project in July 2008. The 2008 Pakistani general election has created a new Petroleum ministry in Pakistan which would be invited for the talks.

Since the discovery of natural gas reserves in Iran's South Pars fields in 1988, the Iranian government began increasing efforts to promote higher gas exports abroad. The prospects for profit are especially high in South Asian countries like India and Pakistan, where natural gas reserves are low and energy demand exceeds energy supply. In 1995, Pakistan and Iran signed a preliminary agreement for construction of a natural gas pipeline linking the Iranian South Pars natural gas field in the Persian Gulf with Karachi, Pakistan's main industrial port located at the Arabian Sea. Iran later proposed an extension of the pipeline from Pakistan into India. Not only would Pakistan benefit from Iranian natural gas exports, but Pakistani territory would be used as a transit route to export natural gas to India. Initially, the Indian government was reluctant to enter into any agreement with Pakistan due to the historically tense relationship between the two neighbors. As an alternative, India suggested the development of a deep sea pipeline where no threat to security of resources could exist. At present, in 2000, Indian, Iranian, and Pakistani government officials continue to negotiate the possible routes, modes of transport, and geopolitics of the Iran to India natural gas pipeline. These negotiations indicate a significant shift in inter and intra-regional politics between the states. The potential for economic and developmental gain from natural gas will force India, Iran, and Pakistan to reassess their roles and policies in regional conflicts, like Kashmir, Afghanistan, and national security issues. Furthermore, potential economic collaboration and gain will also lead to a possible transformation of social and political discourse between the countries, perhaps even leading to mediation and resolution of regional conflicts.

The Peace Pipeline: Implications for Conflict Resolution, Foreign Policy and Regionalism

The exportation of natural gas from Iran to India through Pakistan is a venture which may change the face of regional politics in South Asia. It is a study in how economic collaboration possesses the power to engender as well as transform social and political discourse between countries. The Indian government speculated whether Pakistan could guarantee security for the flow of natural gas in the pipeline. Furthermore, Pakistan's collaboration with Iran may foster conflict resolution as well. In the past, Iranian and Pakistani foreign policies have disagreed on the issues of Afghanistan and Shi'a-Sunni conflicts in the region. Thus, trade and the larger experience of economic globalization possesses the ability to exist as mediators in conflicts in the region and between regions (http://www1.american.edu/TED/iranpipeline.htm). Natural gas trade between India, Iran, and Pakistan challenges the geopolitical, historical, and strategic realities of the three countries and the general regions of the Mideast and Asia. In this way, the relationship between the pipeline venture and globalization is multidisciplinary. It is not characterized solely by economic factors, even though the current economic realities in Iran, India, and Pakistan do foreshadow the future necessity of economic collaboration. The realities of this case study are representative of the notion that multidisciplinary globalization is changing the face of regional politics and altering the social and political landscape of regions.

Negotiations in Pipeline Project

Holding approximately 9 percent of the world's total reserves, Iran is OPEC's second largest producer of oil (Iran Background Information). Along with oil reserves, Iran contains the world's second largest natural gas reserves "at an estimated 812 trillion cubic feet (Tcf)". While Iranian natural gas consumption is high, the country desperately needs to promote export markets for gas due to its faltering economy and to meet the demands of modernization. To meet these demands, Iran has targeted emerging regional markets like South Asia for natural gas exports. Iran has proposed the export of natural gas from Iran to India since 1993. Alongside this proposal was the plan to export natural gas to Pakistan as well. The Iranian government proposed the construction of a pipeline from its South Pars fields in the Persian Gulf to Pakistan's major cities of Karachi and Multan and then further onto Delhi, India.

India has considered various proposals for international pipeline connections with other countries. One such scheme is the Iran-Pakistan-India (IPI) Pipeline, which has been under discussion since 1994. The plan calls for a roughly 1,700-mile, 5.4-Bcf/d pipeline to run from the South Pars fields in Iran to the Indian state of Gujarat. While Iran is keen to export its abundant natural gas resources and India is in search of projects to meet its growing domestic demand, a variety of economic and political issues have delayed a project agreement. Indian officials have made it clear that any import pipeline crossing Pakistan would need to be accompanied by a security guarantee from officials in Islamabad. Apart from security concerns, natural gas pricing disputes have also held up an agreement. Both Indian and Pakistani officials refused Iran's proposed price of $8.00 per million Btu (MMBtu), stating that they would not pay more than $4.25/MMBtu. Due to the uncertainties involving this pipeline, the Indian government's 11th Five Year plan does not project any gas supply from this route or the following two discussed pipelines.

Turkmenistan-Afghanistan-Pakistan-India Pipeline

India has worked to join onto the Turkmenistan-Afghanistan-Pakistan Pipeline (TAP or Trans-Afghan Pipeline). With the inclusion of India, the project consists of a planned 1,050-mile pipeline originating in Turkmenistan's Dauletabad natural gas fields and transporting the fuel to markets in Afghanistan, Pakistan, and India. In 2008, all parties agreed to induct India as a full member into the project, thereby renaming the pipeline TAPI. TAPI will have a capacity of 3.2 Bcf/d and work is expected to commence in 2010, with supplies scheduled to flow in 2015. Concerns about the project have included the security of the route, which would traverse unstable regions in Afghanistan and Pakistan. Furthermore, a review of the TAPI project raised doubts about whether Turkmen natural gas supplies are adequate to meet proposed export commitments.

Globalization and Regional Cooperation

Because of the demand for energy in South Asia, both Pakistan and India must reevaluate their positions on the Iran-India pipeline project. They must view the project as the emergence of an economic globalization by which regional cooperation could save them from a common future crisis. Historically, "as the globalization process began to gather speed, states quickly realized that their neighbors, who often had similar economies to their own, faced many became one way of attempting to come to grips with these common problems". In the context of South Asia, this economic globalization thus plays an influential role in forming and transforming regional politics and relations. The Pakistani and Indian governments must realize that their situations fall on common ground. Only once this happens can regional politics and relations significantly transform.

4. *Indo-US Nuclear Deal*

The *Indo-U.S. civilian nuclear agreement*, known also as the Indo-U.S. nuclear deal, refers to a bilateral accord on civil nuclear cooperation between the United States of America and the Republic of India. The framework for this agreement was a July 18, 2005 joint statement by Indian Prime Minister Manmohan Singh and then U.S. President George W. Bush, under which India agreed to separate its civil and military nuclear facilities and place all its civil nuclear facilities under International Atomic Energy Agency (IAEA) safeguards and, in exchange, the United States agreed to work toward *full* civil nuclear cooperation with India. This U.S.-India deal took more than three years to come to fruition as it had to go through several complex stages, including amendment of U.S. domestic law, a civil-military nuclear *Separation Plan* in India, an India-IAEA safeguards (inspections) agreement and the grant of an exemption for India by the Nuclear Suppliers Group, an export-control cartel that had been formed mainly in response to India's first nuclear test in 1974. In its final shape, the deal places under permanent safeguards those nuclear facilities that India has identified as "civil" and permits broad civil nuclear cooperation, while excluding the transfer of "sensitive" equipment and technologies, including civil enrichment and reprocessing items even under IAEA safeguards. On August 18, 2008 the IAEA Board of Governors approved and on February 2, 2009, India signed an India-specific safeguards agreement with the IAEA. Once India brings this agreement into force, inspections will begin in a phased manner on the 35 civilian nuclear installations India has identified in its Separation Plan (http://en.wikipedia.org/wiki/Indo-US_civilian_nuclear_agreement)

Following are the key aspects of the Indo-US civil nuclear deal (http://www.financialexpress.com/news/highlights-of-indous-nuclear-deal/208405):

- The agreement not to hinder or interfere with India's nuclear programme for military purposes.
- US will help India negotiate with the IAEA for an India-specific fuel supply agreement.
- Washington will support New Delhi develop strategic reserves of nuclear fuel to guard against future disruption of supply.
- In case of disruption, US and India will jointly convene a group of friendly supplier countries to include nations like Russia, France and the UK to pursue such measures to restore fuel supply.
- Both the countries agree to facilitate nuclear trade between themselves in the interest of respective industries and consumers.
- India and the US agree to transfer nuclear material, non-nuclear material, equipment and components.
- Any special fissionable material transferred under the agreement shall be low enriched uranium.
- Low enriched uranium can be transferred for use as fuel in reactor experiments and in reactors for conversion or fabrication.
- The ambit of the deal include research, development, design, construction, operation, maintenance and use of nuclear reactors, reactor experiments and decommissioning.
- The US will have the right to seek return of nuclear fuel and technology but it will compensate for the costs incurred as a consequence of such removal.
- India can develop strategic reserve of nuclear fuel to guard against any disruption of supply over the lifetime of its reactors.
- Agreement provides for consultations on the circumstances, including changed security environment, before termination of the nuclear cooperation.

- Provision for one-year notice period before termination of the agreement.
- The US to engage Nuclear Suppliers Group to help India obtain full access to the international fuel market, including reliable, uninterrupted and continual access to fuel supplies from firms in several nations.
- The US will have the right to seek return of nuclear fuel and technology.
- In case of return, Washington will compensate New Delhi promptly for the "fair market value thereof" and the costs incurred as a consequence of such removal.
- Both the countries to set up a Joint Committee for implementation of the civil nuclear agreement and development of further cooperation in this field.
- The agreement grants prior consent to reprocess spent fuel.
- Sensitive nuclear technology, nuclear facilities and major critical components can be transferred after amendment to the agreement.
- India will establish a new national facility dedicated to reprocessing safeguarded nuclear material under IAEA safeguards.

NSG Amendments to its Guidelines

In the earlier plenary, the NSG members had decided that they would work on the amendments to NSG Guidelines only after the US had modified its domestic laws to enable US-India civil nuclear commerce. Therefore, at present, there is no NSG draft of any amendment to its guidelines other than the one circulated by the US in March 2006. According to the US draft "Participating governments may transfer trigger list items and/or related technology to the safeguarded civil nuclear facilities in India (a State not party, and never having been a party, to the NPT) as long as the participating government intending to make the transfer is satisfied that India continues to fully meet all of the aforementioned nonproliferation and safeguards commitments, and all other requirements of the NSG Guidelines"—conditions far less severe than the US laws. India would have had no problem with such a formulation. However, while not part of the amendment to US laws, the conferees had suggested that the "United States must ensure that any decision that the NSG makes regarding granting an exemption for nuclear commerce does not disadvantage US industry by setting less strict conditions for countries trading with India than those embodied in the conditions and requirements of this Act (http://blogs.ibibo.com/DHARA39/abc-of-indo-us-nuclear-deal)."

At this moment there is no clue—at least in the public domain—as to the direction in which the NSG amendments may go. But an amendment to the NSG Guidelines along the US draft—or as close to it as possible—would pose no problem to India. Therefore it is to be hoped that both the US government and other governments interested in Indian participation in future global nonproliferation efforts would not succumb to some of the background suggestions of the US Congress. Much depends on the attitude the US and others take at the NSG plenary. It is to be hoped that India would exert its influence on NSG members to convey its discomfort with the US conditions for civil nuclear trade and have the amendment to NSG Guidelines suitably formulated.

India-specific IAEA safeguards and additional protocol

The additional protocol need not even be concluded before the various amendments to US laws and NSG Guidelines are put in place. Much has been made by some critics that Sec. 110 of the US bill defines the term "additional protocol" as being one based on a Model Additional Protocol as set forth in INFCIRC 540. INFCIRC 540, as it stands, is applicable to non-nuclear weapon states. However, all additional protocols, even those with the nuclear weapon states, are based on INFCIRC 540. In fact, the additional protocol is identical to INFCIRC except for the qualifying articles restricting applicability to only those facilities declared by the US as not being of national security significance. The additional protocol that India will have with the IAEA too would be based on INFCIRC 540 but, as in the case of US, be made applicable only to facilities declared as civil by India. In any case this is yet to be negotiated and the additional protocol would have to be approved by the IAEA Board of Governors and not the US Congress.

As for the India specific IAEA safeguards, these are still under negotiation. These negotiations are likely to be long and hard. A number of issues not hitherto faced by IAEA in its safeguards negotiations have to be settled to the satisfaction of both India and the Board of Governors. These would include an assurance on fuel supplies. So far the IAEA had never faced the issue of fuel supply assurances in its safeguards agreements with various countries. The India specific safeguards agreement would be the first of its kind. Given that the director general of IAEA had welcomed the India-US nuclear agreement, there is no reason to doubt that the Indian and IAEA negotiators would be able to draft an agreement that would address both Indian and international concerns. India will have to negotiate both the safeguards agreement and the additional protocol taking into account all potential future scenarios. It is not unreasonable to expect that the Indian negotiators will take fully into account various national security concerns that may have been expressed by the various organs of the Indian state. As such it is pointless to speculate how such an agreement will affect India's national security.

5. Production Sharing Contract (PSC) and Mode of Negotiations

(a) A case of Bangladesh

Production Sharing Contract (PSC) is an agreement between the parties to a well and a host country regarding the percentage of production each party will receive after the participating parties have recovered a specified amount of costs and expenses (http://www.glossary.oilfield.slb.com/Display.cfm?Term=production%20sharing%20contract).

Production Sharing Contract (PSC) —a special agreement between the government of Bangladesh and foreign contractors signed mainly for petroleum exploration and development in the country. Under the Bangladesh Petroleum Act 1974, the government owns all mineral resources including petroleum within the territory, continental shelf and economic zone of the country and has the exclusive right and authority to explore, develop, exploit, process, refine and market petroleum resources. The government has also the exclusive right under the act to enter into petroleum agreements with any person for the purpose of any petroleum operations. On behalf of the government, the PETROBANGLA exercises the rights and powers to explore, develop, process and market petroleum and also to enter into petroleum agreements with any person/company for these purposes.

In 1973, following a comprehensive policy review, the government started setting up a new legal framework to encourage rapid exploration and development of natural gas and oil and to safeguard the national interest. The government also took initiative for development of national capacity in the oil and gas sector with assistance by international companies. The idea came from the experience of significant success achieved under production sharing contracts (PSC) of Indonesia, Malaysia, Egypt, China, India and some other countries with international oil companies.

In 1974, the government of Bangladesh invited bids from international oil companies for exploration and development of petroleum in the territory of the country under established criteria and ground rules. The bids submitted were evaluated on a 40-points grading, ten points for each of the four criteria including financial capability, technical capacity, experience, and work programme. A selected number of qualified companies were invited to negotiate on the basis of the model PSC and finally, seven contracts were concluded for offshore exploration and development. The companies with which the PSC was signed were Atlantic Richfield, Union Oil of California (later renamed as UNOCAL) and Ashland of the USA, Superior Oil Company of Canada, Deminex and Ina-Napthaline of Europe, and a Japanese company. UNOCAL discovered an offshore gas reservoir at Kutubdia but under some economic considerations, the company did not start its exploitation.

The foreign companies soon started loosing interest in PSC since they found Bangladesh to have large reserve of gas and not of petroleum. In 1981, Shell Oil signed a PSC for onshore areas. In the mean time Petrobangla developed capability for exploration and development of oil and gas resources and in 1989, established the Bangladesh Petroleum Exploration Company (BAPEX) for exploration of petroleum in the country. Petrobangla made the first discovery of oil in the Bangladesh territory in 1986 at Haripur, Sylhet. There were different offers from reputed international oil companies for development of the oil field and one of them was Scimitar, a company incorporated in British Virgin Islands in June 1987 with an authorized capital of only $50,000. The technical experts of Petrobangla suggested not to award the contract to Scimitar but the suggestion was ignored and in December 1987, the government signed a PSC with the company. Scimitar was not able to start work by the stipulated dates. It repeatedly sought extensions, which were granted and meanwhile, it explored the whole world to raise necessary funds.

Production Sharing Contract: Terms of Reference

The international scenario for gas development underwent major changes since the end of the nineteen eighties. A review of the policy and legal framework carried out under the World Bank's Petroleum Exploration Promotion Programme in 1987 pointed out that there were bright prospects for gas exploration. A new model PSC was formulated in 1988 to encourage exploration for gas and to ensure that the price for gas would have parity with the market price for fuel oil. It was further revised in 1993 commensurate with government policy changes and new incentives to the investors for petroleum exploration. Some more changes in the model PSC were made in 1997 (http://banglapedia.search.com.bd/HT/P_0290.htm).

Production Sharing Contract norms

In most contractual systems, the facilities put in place by the contractor within the host government domain become the property of the state either the moment they are landed in the country or upon startup or commissioning. Sometimes, the title to the assets or facilities does not pass to the government until the attendant costs have been recovered. Contractual systems are divided into *service contracts* and *production sharing contracts*. The difference between them depends on whether or not the contractor receives compensation in *cash* or in *kind* (crude).

Basic features of production sharing contracts are (http://www.beg.utexas.edu/energyecon/new-era/case_studies/Fiscal_Terms_for_Upstream_Projects.pdf):

- The title of the hydrocarbons remains with the state.
- The State maintains management control and the contractor is responsible for the execution of petroleum operations in accordance to the terms of the contract.
- The contractor is required to submit annual work programs and budgets for scrutiny and approval the State Company.
- The contract is based on production sharing and not profit-sharing basis.
- The contractor provides all financing and technology required for the operations and bore the risks.
- During the term of the contract, after allowance for up to a specified percentage of annual production for recovery of costs, the remaining production is split between the contractor and State.
- Equipment purchased and imported by the contractor become property of the State. Service company equipment and leased equipment are exempt.

Bangladesh signed a PSC in May 1994 with Cairn Energy and Holland Sea Search, a British-Dutch joint venture for exploration of oil and gas in block 16. The joint venture signed another PSC for block 15 in June next year. These two blocks cover partly Chittagong onshore and adjacent offshore areas. In January 1997, Hallibarton Energy of United States joined the Cairn-Holland Sea Search in the Sangu gas field portion of Block 16. Shell Oil purchased Cairn's PSC rights in these two blocks in mid-1999. In 1995, Occidental signed PSCs for blocks 12, 13 and 14 in the Sylhet area (Surma basin) but transferred its PSC rights to UNOCAL in 1999. A low profile US joint venture Rexwood-Oakland signed PSC in January 1997 with Petrobangla for blocks 17 and 18 located in Cox's Bazar-Teknaf region with 80% offshore exploration areas. Rexwood later merged with Oakland. The United Meridian Corporation (UMC) was another small US oil company that signed PSC in late 1996 for oil and gas exploration and development in block 22 in the Chittagong Hill Tracts area. Later, the UMC transferred its rights to a US company Ocean Energy.

The PSCs resulted in new discoveries of gas fields in the Surma basin by Occidental-Unocal (Bibiana and Maulavibazaar) and at Sangu (offshore). They also generated new gas production and supply of over 200 million cubic feet of gas per day to national gas grid. The additions accounted for one fifth of the country's daily consumption. By 1997, both Cairn and Occidental signed gas purchase and sales agreement with Petrobangla for the sale and delivery of the gas into the national gas distribution systems operated by Petrobangla. Enthusiasm of both government and private investors in the gas sector was so great between 1996 and 1997 that during the period, Bangladesh attracted attention of top international investors in petroleum sector. In this backdrop the government following exploration promotion meetings in London and Huston in February-March 1997, issued a worldwide invitation to bidders in April 1997 (Second round gas bidding). International oil companies were invited to submit bids by 15 July 1997 on the basis of the model PSC updated in 1997 for remaining 15 blocks.

The number of companies showing interest in response to the invitation for bids was 23, some of which were less known and perhaps appeared in the exploration scene for the first time. Companies like Tallow Oil Plc., Hondo Oil and Gas, South Asia Oil and Gas, Nico Resources, Triton and Pangea, Maersk Oil were the new entries. Texaco, Shell, Mobil, Chevron, Unocal and Enron are known names in the international petroleum exploration business. Available information indicates that there was no bid for blocks 1, 2 and 23. Of the remaining 12 blocks, number 9 attracted the largest number of bidders, followed by block 10, 11, 6, 5 and 7 (onshore) and there was more than two bids for each of the offshore blocks 19, 20 and 21. No block was kept reserved for the national company BAPEX. Negotiations were in process in 2001 for blocks 5 and 10 (with Shell Oil and Cairn), block 8 (with Pangea) and for blocks 19, 20 (with Maersk Oil) and two PSC were concluded, one with Unocal for block 7 and the other with Chevron-Texaco-Tullow for block 9. In this second round bidding, however, different percent of shares by the name of carried over interests for BAPEX were considered.

In their proposals the companies were to indicate their competitive bids in respect of six items: (a) cost recovery ratio, (b) profit of oil/gas sharing ratio, (c) work programme, (d) performance guarantee in support of work programme, (e) discovery bonus, and (f) production bonus. Arthur Andersen, an international firm of chartered accountants was appointed as consultant to assist the government in evaluation of the bids. A large number of international oil companies came up with proposals for petroleum exploration in Bangladesh during that period. However, subsequent global oil crunch and uncertainty in government decisions caused a decline in the enthusiasm of the private investors. The whole process was further complicated by the issue of gas export to India through pipelines raised by the World Bank in 1995 on the ground that when PSC operators would start selling gas to Bangladesh in large quantity, the country would face a Balance of Payment crisis. Almost simultaneously, the international oil companies initially having no agenda to export gas also started arguing that there was no ready gas market in the country and therefore investment would no longer be attractive. The idea created a controversy as to whether the gas reserves in Bangladesh are sufficient enough to justify pipeline export or, the country itself has a market potential to use its reserves for domestic consumption and industrial purposes.

Key provisions of the present model PSC includes following:

Contact area: Block size ranges from 1,650 to 13,500 sq km. Two blocks can be in one contract if geologically justified and in offshore, more than two blocks are allowed to include in one PSC. Separate work programme is necessary for each block.

Term of exploration: seven years (basic period of three years plus two extensions of two years each).

Production: For each area 25 years from the contract effective date for an oil field and 30 years for a gas field, subject to an extension of five years on mutually agreed terms.

Relinquishments: 25% of contract area at the end of the third year and an additional 25% at the end of the fifth contract year are to be relinquished. All areas which are not declared production areas are to be relinquished at the end of the seventh contract year. First relinquishment will be waived if the contractor has completed an exploratory well within three years of the initial exploration period.

Repatriation of profit: Repatriation of all the profit as per PSC provision will be allowed.

Production sharing: Petrobangla and the contractor shall allocate any petroleum from the contract area between themselves in tranches according to total average daily production over the contract period in a mutually agreeable terms separately before and after the cost recovery period.

Cost recovery: Biddable up to 40% for oil and 50% for gas.

Valuation of gas: The pricing for associated gas would be on a cost plus basis, while for non associated gas it will be 75% of the international price of high sulfur fuel oil with negotiated discounts. To encourage exploration in offshore areas associated or non-associated gas from such fields will be priced at 25% higher than the gas from onshore areas.

Tax and duty: No duty will be levied on machinery, equipment and consumables imported for petroleum operations during the exploration, development and production stage. Companies will be free of all corporate tax and such other taxes as are determined under the terms of PSC.

Deductible costs: Operating costs, exploration costs and other capital costs.

Other payments to government: Discovery and production bonuses biddable and applicable as specified in the agreement, not cost recoverable.

Annual contract service fee: Negotiable, but not less than US$ 50,000 per block. This cost is recoverable.

Annual training fee: US$100,000, not recoverable.

Export of gas: Contractor may export natural gas (contractor—cost recovery and profit gas; Petrobangla—profit gas) in the form of liquefied natural gas subject to negotiation with government. Petrobangla will compensate contractor for relinquishment of rights for required volume of discovered and apprised natural gas located west of Padma-Jamuna rivers up to a maximum 1 TCF. The required volume represents the minimum volume estimated to be economically recoverable for domestic use.

Domestic consumption: Contractor shall provide pro rata up to 25% of his profit oil at 15% discount and remaining, if required at full fair market price in convertible currency.

Partnerships in oil and gas production-sharing contracts

In countries with large or potentially large oil and gas deposits, the resource and its extraction tend to become vital cornerstones of the economy. However, uncertainties involved in finding commercial quantities of oil and gas and the intensive capital required for undertaking exploration and production result in significant business risks. The petroleum fiscal systems in many developing countries are now opting for production-sharing contracts (PSC) as a new model of agreement for the exploration and production of oil and gas resources.

This project is based on the principal-agent theory to foster understanding of partnership between the host government and its foreign contractor in the realm of PSC. The theory highlights the importance of moral hazard and adverse-selection problems. To avoid these uncertainties and asymmetric information, the principal (national oil company) needs to design an incentive contract that induces the agent (International Oil Company—IOC)) to undertake actions that will maximize the principal's welfare. Under a PSC, the state has to offer contract terms that are attractive enough for the IOC to enter into an agreement. At the same time, the terms must allow the state to receive maximum economic returns from the venture (http://www.emeraldinsight.com/Insight/viewContentItem.do;jsessionid=748C389CEA72EB607C280DA192282119?contentType=Article&hdAction=lnkhtml&contentId=868037).

Production Sharing Contract (PSC) - Cases

(b) A Case of Trinidad & Tobago

A Production Sharing Contract (PSC) is an agreement between a contractor and a host government whereby the contractor bears all exploration risks, development and production costs in return for a stipulated share of the production resulting from this effort. The use of PSCs in Trinidad and Tobago began in 1974. As a result of a World Bank study conducted in 1991, a model PSC was developed. This improved some of the terms and conditions obtained under an Exploration and Production licence, such as the encouragement of immediate work on the blocks, definite periods for exploration and guidelines for relinquishments. It also added flexibility to the method of sharing economic rent between the contractors and the Government. This model contract was successfully utilized in the Competitive Bid Round 1995-98. Recent allocation of areas for exploration and production was undertaken through a three-phased Competitive Bid Round.

In January 1998, the Ministry of Energy & Energy Industries, Trinidad & Tobago concluded negotiations of the terms and conditions of the contracts for four(4) of the nine (9) Deep Water blocks for which bids were invited. By mid February 1998, the Minister signed contracts for Blocks 25(a),25(b), 26 & 27, the southern most of the original 9 blocks offered. The contracts which were signed attracted a total signature bonus of approximately TT$550 million, a geophysical work program exceeding TT$350 million and a drilling program with an expenditure of over TT$1.0 billion. During 1995-2002, a total of 15 Production Sharing Contacts were successfully negotiated and signed for acreage in the East Coast, North Coast and South Coast Marine Areas (http://www.energy.gov.tt/applicationloader.asp?app=articles&id=817).

(c) A Case of Cheveron Corporation

Cheveron Corporation's main Chinese subsidiary signs 30-year production sharing contract with China National Petroleum Corporation (CNPC) for development of Chuandongbei natural gas area in China. Chevron will take over the role of operator and will hold a 49 percent participating interest and CNCP will hold a 51 percent interest in the project. The Chuandongbei gas development area—which includes the Tieshanpo, Dukouhe-Qilibei and Luojiazhai gas fields—covers nearly 2,000 square kilometres in the Sichuan province and has an estimated resource base of 5 trillion cubic feet of natural gas (http://www.energydigital.com/Chevron—CNPC-to-sign-product-sharing-contract-to-develop-Chuandongbei-gas-project_4391.aspx).

(d) The Krishna-Godavari (KG) Basin Negotiation issue

As the name implies, this refers to the area broadly enclosed by the deltaic basins of the two major rivers in Andhra Pradesh Krishna and Godavari. It includes part of the Bay of Bengal into which these rivers drain. The area has been identified as one of India's biggest oil and gas fields, several times the size of Bombay High. Onland, the KG basin has an area of about 28,000 sq km, while the offshore area is estimated at 21,000 sq km till a depth of 200m and another 18,000 sq km between 200m and 3000m (http://journal.shankarananth.com/?p=167).

How is Reliance Industries involved in the KG basin?

Under the government's New Exploration and Licensing Policy (NELP), various blocks in identified oil and gas fields were offered to private operators on lease for exploration and production. RIL won the bids for 12 such blocks in the KG basin in 2000. Under the NELP, private operators sign a production sharing contract (PSC) with the government, which sets out the terms and conditions under which they operate their lease, including the share of revenues that would accrue to the government. The PSC for block D6, which is at the heart of the current controversy, was signed between RIL, the government and Niko, which is partnering RIL, in April 2000.

How is the Anil Ambani group involved?

When the Reliance group was still a unified entity with both brothers sharing management responsibilities, RIL had announced in 2003 that group company Reliance Energy Ltd (REL) would be setting up a gas-based power plant at Dadri in western Uttar Pradesh for which gas would supplied from RIL's KG basin production. In 2005, however, the group broke up with each brother acquiring control of different business areas. While the oil and gas business went to elder brother Mukesh, Anil had control of the power business. As part of the division of the group, RIL was demerged and Reliance Natural Resources LTD (RNRL) was formed to act as a conduit for the gas from the KG basin to REL. All RIL shareholders were made RNRL shareholders, except that Mukesh's holding in the parent company was substituted by Anil in the new firm. Thus, RNRL was part of the Anil Dhirubhai Ambani group (ADAG).

An MOU between RNRL and RIL

In 2005, RNRL and RIL signed a memorandum of understanding (MoU) on the terms under which gas would be supplied for the Dadri project. This MoU specified that the price at which the gas would be supplied would be the same as the price at which RIL would supply gas to an NTPC project. NTPC had invited global bids for supply of gas in 2003 and RIL finally won the bid and was issued a letter of intent by NTPC in June 2004. The price quoted by RIL in its bid was $2.34 per mmbtu (million metric British thermal units). So what's the dispute about? RIL argues that the $2.34 per unit price is not applicable to its deal with RNRL for various reasons. First, gas prices had since the 2005 MOU risen sharply.

Second, it has not concluded a deal with NTPC on that price, since it had some issues pertaining to damages it would have to pay in case of failure to supply the agreed quantity of gas. Hence, it says, there is no NTPC price to be followed as per the MOU with RNRL. Third, it says under the PSC signed with the government, the government has the final say on the price at which it can sell gas to third parties and in fact can even dictate to whom the gas should be sold.

RNRL contests each of these claims. It argues that international gas prices have historically been much higher than Indian prices and so that can't be a benchmark. Further, the bid price for the NTPC project must be followed under the MOU irrespective of whether or not RIL and NTPC have finalized their deal. Finally, it maintains that the government only has the right under the PSC to fix the price at which gas will be valued for the purpose of determining the government's share of revenues from the project. RIL, it insists, is free to sell its share of the gas at whatever price it decides.

Where did the price of $4.2 per unit come from?

In May 2007, RIL invited bids from various gas users like power and fertilizer companies and on that basis arrived at a price of $4.2 per, which was then approved by the petroleum ministry as a market-determined price. RNRL alleges that this was an eyewash and an orchestrated auction between small time users and that the ministry has been partisan towards RIL in the whole issue.

How did the Government get involved?

When, after sustained pressure from RNRL, RIL sought approval of the government for the price of $2.34 per unit, the government refused. It said the price was not market determined and in any case gas was a national asset and its allocation could not be decided by some private agreement between two brothers. ADAG points out that the ministry's stance in the matter which suits RIL's current position—has been a feature since Murli Deora became the petroleum minister in 2006.

How are courts involved?

Following RIL's refusal to supply gas at the terms specified in the MOU with RNRL, the Anil group company went to the Bombay HC seeking an order to RIL to follow the terms of the MOU. The Bombay HC finally in June this year passed an order that RIL must renegotiate a deal with RNRL that would make suitable arrangements for supply of gas. It also added that the basis for such an arrangement must be the scheme of demerger agreed between the brothers in 2005. RNRL has now gone to the Supreme Court seeking a direction from the apex court that the HC order on renegotiation should be set aside and RIL should be asked to supply gas under the terms of the MoU.

5. (e) Contract Renegotiation with the Chilean Government

Although starting a contract renegotiation at a disadvantage, with a weak BATNA, US company Kennecott managed to enhance and turn things around with an offer the Chilean government couldn't refuse. Here is a Case (http://www.negotiations.com/case/contract-renegotiation/).

In the 1960's Kennecott, a U.S. company, was about to enter into renegotiation over its contract with the government of Chile concerning its El Teniente copper mine. At the time, Chile's BATNA appeared overwhelmingly strong as the government was possessed of a strong pro sovereignty stance towards foreign management of its natural resources. Can we take some lessons for our mortgage renegotiations? The government of Chile was politically positioned to establish their own tough financial terms or had the option of declining to renegotiate by simply ejecting Kennecott from their involvement altogether by expropriating the mine. Chile had its own experts who could manage and operate the mine, perform the processing, and could readily market this very useful natural resource. Simply put, Kennecott found itself in the position of either acceding to the contract renegotiation terms dictated by the Chilean government or have the mine snatched out from under them.

Realising that their own BATNA was weak, Kennecott executives came up with a very creative solution which ultimately weakened Chile's position while leveraging their own BATNA more favourably by creating value for both sides.

The proposal made by Kennecott entailed the following six point strategy thereby changing the rules of the game:

1. The deal consisted of Kennecott offering to sell a majority equity interest in the mining operation to the Chilean government.
2. Realising that Chile would not particularly care to divest the funds of the sale into U.S. banks, Kennecott offered to use the funds, combined with an outside loan, to finance the mine's expansion. This allowed Chile to preserve its nationalistic interests and have greater financial

gain from future profits. They were able to renegotiate and establish a partnership which was mutually acceptable to both parties.

3. Next, Kennecott then persuaded the Chilean government to guarantee the loan and have this guarantee subject to the law of the state of New York.
4. Then, as many of the company's mining assets as possible were insured with U.S. backed guarantees, against the potential expropriation threat.
5. Kennecott then negotiated that the copper output derived from the expansion would be sold exclusively to clients in Europe and North America.
6. Lastly, the rights to collect from these new contracts would be sold to a consortium of financial institutions based in Japan, the United States and Europe.

This allowed for a greater diversity in the customer base and additional partners. In future contract renegotiations, this would result in a much larger multi party negotiation then just Kennecott having to renegotiate on its own. Many of these outside interests would also be engaged in other unrelated negotiations with the Chilean government, thereby reducing Chile's leverage in any future contract renegotiations. Mortgage re-negotiators won't have as much flexibility to change the negotiation game when they renegotiate their contracts.

Lastly, because of the insurance guarantees obtained by Kennecott, even if the renegotiations collapsed, Kennecott had succeeded in protecting a good portion of its interests should Chile opt to go ahead and appropriate the copper mine. Additionally, the company could also call in its other partners to act as allies.

In the end, some years later, the mine was eventually expropriated by Chile, but Kennecott was in a far much better position than it had initially been before it initially started to renegotiate the contract. Kennecott enhanced its BATNA by making an offer the Chileans couldn't refuse, while taking steps to protect their interests should negotiations collapse.

6. International Airline Alliances: Code-Sharing Contract

(a) An analysis of 'code-sharing' impact on airlines and consumers

Code Sharing and Negotiation in International Airlines

From January 1992 to June 1995, the number of code-sharing alliances between US and foreign airlines more than tripled, increasing from 19 to 65. Code-sharing alliances can generate large gains for airline partners in terms of added passengers and revenues. Besides the overall scope of a code-sharing arrangement, a critical ingredient for successful alliances to be the degree of integration achieved by the airlines in operations and marketing. In addition, it has been observed that the gains achieved through alliances are largely zero-sum in that they come at the expense of competing airlines. However, it is likely that at least some of the gains come from new traffic stimulated by increased competition among alliances and between alliances and other airlines (Timothy F Hannegan and Francis P Mulvey-http://www.sciencedirect.com/science?_ob=ArticleURL&_udi=B6VGP-3YBB08D-J&_user=10&_rdoc=1&_fmt=&_orig=search&_ sort=d&_docanchor=&view =c&_ searchStrId =987929139&_rerunOrigin=google&_acct=C000050221&_ version=1&_urlVersion=0&_userid=10&md5=c102cbfa79912c0b10216dafac375710).

Economics of International Code-Sharing: An Analysis of Airline Alliances

International airline alliances allow airlines to coordinate their operations in providing international service. The above study conducted by Timothy F Hannegan and Francis P Mulvey analyzes the effect of such alliances on traffic levels, fares, and welfare. In the model, the benefits of alliances arise because cooperative pricing of trips by the partners puts downward pressure on fares in the interline city-pair markets (these are markets where travel on both carriers is necessary). The loss of competition in the inter-hub market, which connects the hub cites of the partners, generates a countervailing effect, tending to raise the fare in that market. While the presence of economies of traffic density complicates these impacts by generating cost links across markets, simulation analysis shows that the above tendencies typically prevail. Welfare analysis shows that both consumer and total surplus typically rise following formation of an alliance despite the harm to inter-hub passengers, suggesting that the positive effects of alliances may outweigh any negative impacts.

Code sharing or Code-share is an aviation business term which was first coined in 1989 (first flights operated in 1990) by Qantas Airways and American Airlines (*Financial Review*, November 21, 1989). Air Malta started to share capacity with Alitalia on flights between Catania and Malta. The flight was operated with Alitalia equipment and crew, however it carried a flight number for one of the airlines, enabling both airlines to sell seats on the same flight as a connecting flight creating what is now known as an interline agreement. Whilst maintaining competition, to an extent, it eliminated destructive competition which makes thin routes unfeasible (Jan K. Brueckner-http://en.wikipedia.org/wiki/Codeshare_agreement).

In the early 1980s, Air Malta made a similar agreement with Tunisavia, a Tunisian airline, and equipment and crew shared with them on flights to/from Tunis. In 1990 the Australian airline, Qantas Airways and the U.S.'s American Airlines combined services between an array of U.S. domestic cities and Australian cities creating the first Code-share arrangement as we now know it. The code share was part of a "cooperative services" agreement between two carriers before the various airline alliances were formed in the 1990s. It refers to a practice where a flight operated by an airline is jointly marketed as a flight for one or more other airlines. Most major airlines today have code sharing partnerships with other airlines and code sharing is a key feature of the major airline alliances.

The term "code" refers to the identifier used in flight schedule, generally the 2-character IATA airline designator code and flight number. Thus, XX123, flight 123 operated by the airline XX, might also be sold by airline YY as YY456 and by ZZ as ZZ9876. Under a code sharing agreement, participating airlines can present a common flight number for several reasons, including:

- Connecting flights—This provides clearer routing for the customer, allowing a customer to book travel from point A to C through point B under one carrier's code, instead of a customer booking from point A to B under one code, and from point B to C under another code. This is not only a superficial addition as cooperating airlines also strive to synchronize their schedules and coordinate luggage handling, which makes transfers between connecting flights less time-consuming.
- Flights from both airlines that fly the same route—This provides an apparent increase in the frequency of service on the route by one airline.
- Perceived service to unserved markets—This provides a method for carriers who do not operate their own aircraft on a given route to gain exposure in the market through display of their flight numbers.

Under a code sharing agreement, the airline that actually operates the flight (the one providing the plane, the crew and the ground handling services) is called the *operating carrier*. The company or companies that sell tickets for that flight but do not actually operate it are called *marketing carriers* or validating carriers

Competitive Concerns

In Global Distribution Systems, such as Amadeus, Galileo, Worldspan, or Sabre, this results in the same flight details, except for the flight number, being excessively displayed on computer screens, forcing other airlines flights to be displayed on following pages where they may be missed by passengers searching for required flights.

Much competition in the airline industry revolves around ticket sales (also known as "seat booking") strategies (revenue management, variable pricing and Geo-marketing). Most passengers and travel agents have a preference for flights which provide a direct connection. Code sharing gives this impression. Computer reservations systems (CRS) also often do not discriminate between direct flights and code sharing flights and present both before options that involve several isolate stretches run by different companies.

Code-sharing Partners

US Code-sharing Partners

Aero California (Mexico), Air Liberte (France), Air Pacific (Fiji), Asiana (Korea), British Midland (Belgium, Germany, Netherlands, United Kingdom), Canadian, China Airlines (Taiwan), China Eastern (Mainland China), Gulf Air (Bahrain, Oman, Qatar, United Arab Emirates), Iberia (Spain), LOT Polish

(Poland), Qantas (Australia, New Zealand), Singapore Airlines, South African Airways, TACA Group (Central America), TAM-Brazil.

CONTINENTAL AIRLINES: CODE-SHARING PARTNERS

Air France, Alitalia (Italy), British Midland, CSA Czech Airlines, Transavia (Netherlands), Virgin Atlantic (United Kingdom), ACES; (Colombia), Air Aruba, Aserca (Venezuela), COPA (Panama), VASP (Brazil), Avant (Chile), Air China, EVA Air (Taiwan), China Airlines

DELTA AIR LINES—ALLIANCES

Austrian Airlines, Swissair, Sabena (Belgium).Code-sharing partners:Aer Lingus (Ireland), AeroMexico, AeroPostal (Venezuela), AirFrance, Air Jamaica, Korean Air, MALEV (Hungary), TAP Air (Portugal), Trans Brasil

NORTHWEST AIRLINES-ALLIANCES

KLM Royal Dutch Airlines (Netherlands), Air China, Japan Air System, Malaysia Airlines, Kenya Airways, Braathens (Norway)

CODE-SHARING PARTNERS

KLM (Europe, Middle East, Africa, India); Air China (trans-Pacific), Eurowings (Germany), Martinair (Netherlands), Pacific Island Aviation (Micronesia)

TWA AIRLINES-ALLIANCES

Icelandair (frequent flier only)

Code-sharing partners: Royal Jordanian Airline, Kuwait Airways, Royal Air Maroc (Morocco)

US AIRWAYS

Code-sharing partners

Deutsche BA (Germany)

UNITED AIRLINES-ALLIANCES

Air Canada, Lufthansa German Airlines, Scandinavian Airlines System, Thai Airways International, Varig Brazilian Airlines

Code-sharing partners:

Aeromar (Mexico), Air Canada, Air New Zealand, Ansett, Australia, Cayman Airways, Saudi Arabian Airlines, Aeromexico, Air-India, ALM Antillean Airlines, British Midland, Emirates Airlines, Mexicana Airlines

6. (b) Code-share Partners of Singapore Airlines

One of the closest forms of Singapore International airlines (SIA's) cooperation with partner airlines is through code-sharing where SIA places it's flight numbers on partners' services. Thus, the passengers get to enjoy the convenience of enhanced frequency and greater choice of destinations as one SIA product offering. Certain restrictions and entitlements are subjected to the rules of the operating carrier.

For the specific terms and conditions of any Singapore Airlines code-share partners (as indicated below) sold on singaporeair.com, may be visited in the operating carrier's website directly (http://www.singaporeair.com/saa/en_UK/content/company_info/partners/codeshare_partners.jsp#Header1):

- Air Canada
- Air New Zealand
- All Nippon Airways
- Asiana Airlines
- EGYPTAIR
- LOT Polish Airlines
- Lufthansa
- Malaysia Airlines
- SilkAir
- South African Airways
- Swiss International Air Lines
- Turkish Airlines
- US Airways
- Virgin Atlantic Airways

Flights to/from USA operated by Code-share Partners of Singapore Airlines

Singapore Airlines code-shares on Air Canada, All Nippon Airways, US Airways and Virgin Atlantic to/from various US cities. A Singapore Airlines code-share flight will have a four-digit SQ flight number although the flight is operated by another airline. When a passenger travels on a code-share flight, he/she will be informed of the airline operating your flight. It is however to be noted that applicable restrictions and entitlements are subject to the rules of the operating carrier. It is therefore important to familiarize oneself with the operating carrier's terms and conditions, including but not limited to those regarding:

- Flights to/from USA operated by Code-share Partners of Singapore Airlines
- Check-in time limits
- Unaccompanied minors
- Carriage of Animals
- Baggage acceptance, allowance, and liability
- Refusal to Transport

7. *Negotiating International Strategic Alliances: Building Lasting Agreements*

Negotiating Strategic Alliances

When seeking distribution agreements, joint ventures or merger/ acquisitions, organizations may think about engaging in negotiations to establish strategic alliances to achieve their organizational goals. People seek negotiating with others to be better off and to create value. The challenge organizations face deals with the way we approach negotiations. If we see it as an exchange of concessions, we might leave value on the negotiating table.

But, if we see negotiations as continuous talks, an ongoing dialogue to reach a shared understanding of the parties' interests and jointly design a negotiation process, we might reach mutually beneficial outcomes and lasting agreements (Luis E. Ore, http://www.mediate.com/acrcommercial/docs/Negotiating %20Int'l%20Strategic%20Alliances %20Ore%20Article%20IF%20Aug09.pdf).

Strategic alliances mainly involve organizations and how the effects of their negotiations will affect organizational members, who will have to implement any reached agreement. Organizational members have diverse interests; personal and organizational interests. When planning to engage in any strategic alliance negotiation, organizational members are likely to assume they have to reach an agreement on some instructions that reflects a position on what the negotiator or negotiating team will demand or the minimum they will accept to commit. Beyond this positional bargaining approach, engaging in internal negotiations with an interest-based approach can lead to more flexible and manageable instructions and mandates to negotiate strategic alliances with others.

Organizations need to decide who should be involved in the internal negotiation process as stakeholders and identify who can support or block the successful implementation of an agreement. It is important to get the insights of organizational members who are closer to the action and the ones who will be in charge of implementing any reached agreement. When involving others during this process, everyone needs to have a positive working assumption beyond blame games and finger pointing. Negotiating parties need to be able to work together with a collaborative mindset, not with an either/or mindset but with a both/and mindset, which will enable them to share information, explain reasoning behind ideas, and do joint problem solve looking forward. Including a 7-Elements framework analysis for negotiation planning (Interests, Legitimacy, Relationship, BATNA, Options, Commitments, and Communication) will help negotiators or negotiating teams clearly identify interests, the priority of those interests and possible tradeoffs. It will generate a wide range of options to explore with the other negotiating parties and help with selection of agreeable standards of fairness and precedents that can persuade both parties beyond a simplistic contest of will. To facilitate the internal process, parties can use a "Single-Text-Procedure", an agreement-building strategy by which stakeholders—organizational members with interests at stake—engage in constructive dialogue over a starting proposal, which they intend to improve as opposed to tearing it down. This strategic tool can also facilitate external negotiations and good-faith efforts to jointly explore interests and create potential options to address those interests with the other party (Fisher, 1999).

A jointly designed negotiation process can facilitate the use of experts, fact-finders, taskforce committees, small group discussions, and others who can contribute the needed information to help executives make informed decisions. A jointly designed negotiation process with some ground rules or rules of engagement regarding how to act and what expected behavior to have, how to interpret data and resolve disagreements about information, how to manage time, and what decision-making processes will be used during negotiations, will help to develop a positive working relationship. Negotiators need to be unconditionally constructive in order to foster a positive working relationship that: (1) creates a positive environment to develop effective communication; (2) understands and recognizes the interests of diverse stakeholders; (3) explores persuasive criteria of fairness; (4) generates creative options; and (5) educates each other about their alternatives. An unconditional constructive strategy includes: (1) balancing emotions with reason; (2) trying to understand the other party; (3) consulting them before deciding; (4) being reliable; (5) being open to persuasion and trying to persuade them; (6) accepting them as worthy of our consideration; and (7) being open to learning from them. (Fisher,1988).

Going Abroad with International Strategic Alliances

Understanding cultural factors that influence how people approach negotiations can help understand the logics that motivate their actions and behaviors. People's actions reflect people's thinking and belief systems. Another challenge we all face is the way we differently think about the other negotiating parties. When interacting with others, people assume and attribute intentions. The way people attribute meaning to their actions and interactions is a factor to be considered too. In general, lack of understanding of cross-cultural differences is one factor to be considered when dealing with international negotiations.

Beyond international, cross-cultural challenges and stereotyping national cultural differences (for example, tendencies to be goal-oriented vs. relationship-oriented or direct vs. indirect communication styles or linear-thinking vs. circular-thinking processing styles) negotiators find diverse organizational cultures around the globe. Whether it is formal or informal, organizations have a belief system regarding how they communicate, engage in negotiations, and share information. But also, they value and approach differently decision-making processes, hierarchical/horizontal, high/low power distance, different hiring practices and profits distribution, the importance of seniority, etc. The fact is that we all filter information differently and have selective perceptions based on our own interests, beliefs and past experience, and make conclusions based on such reasoning. Negotiating parties can bridge cultural differences and engage in mutual-gains negotiation to foster a new organizational culture, which will govern the relations among organizational members.

Even though parties can engage in good-faith efforts, negotiate with an interest-based approach, and be strategically mindful about organizational cultural differences, sometimes challenging situations will occur and parties may find it difficult to follow through and fulfill their commitments. Beyond mediation and arbitration clauses to resolve potential difficulties, negotiating parties can build into their agreements mechanisms to respond to any potential challenges and constructively face whatever might go wrong. It may be wise to design mechanisms for people to reconvene and fix the agreement if and when the unexpected happens. (L. Susskind & J. Cruikshank, Breaking Robert's Rules: The New Way to Run Your Meetings, Build Consensus, and Get Results, 2006, New York: Oxford University Press, Inc.) For instance, 4 negotiating parties of strategic alliances can agree to have a team of stakeholders getting together quarterly to assess how the implementation and relationship are working. Parties can design a collaborative internal procedure, a conflict management system, and integrate interest-based mechanisms and other ADR processes to resolve their differences before getting into adversarial blame games or right-based approaches.

To sum-up, when negotiating strategic alliances, a mutual-gains negotiation approach will not only model and foster a positive strategic alliance working relationship, but it will contribute to building wise, implementable, lasting agreements and organizational effectiveness, and ultimately contribute to the growth and development of organizations and communities. The approach must engage relevant stakeholders during internal and external negotiations, use agreement-building strategies with a deal-implementer mindset beyond a simple deal-maker mindset, consider organizational cultural challenges, and jointly design a collaborative process.

Recent Policy Reforms and Issues under Consideration

Economic reforms are taking place in India in a number of Services sector such as Financial Services, Telecom Services, Air Transport Services, Education Services, Health Services, Postal Services, Professional Services. Brief details of some of the recent developments in this regard are indicated below:

Financial Services	- RBI road map for liberalizing presence of foreign banks in India. - Reforms undertaken by IRDA: Foreign equity upto 26% permitted in Insurance sector
Telecom Services	- FDI limit raised to 74% in recent policy reforms
Postal Services	- Amendment to the Indian Postal Act proposed with the objective to regulate Courier Services
Air Transport	- Private sector participation in Delhi and Mumbai airports sectors/areas, excluding those sectors/areas in which India is a requesting member and therefore a deemed recipient.

All Members, including India, are expected to respond to the plurilateral requests and bilateral requests placed on them by making improved Offers in the second round. Presently the negotiations are suspended. The Second Revised Offers by the Member countries will be submitted once the negotiations are resumed.

8. *Global Negotiation under CTBT*

The Comprehensive Test Ban Treaty (CTBT), which opened for signature in 1996, is intended to prohibit all nuclear weapon test explosions. The CTBT has achieved near universal adherence, however, Article XIV of the Treaty requires ratification by 44 named states, before the Treaty can enter into force (http://www.acronym.org.uk/ctbt/index.htm).

The book of Rebecca Johnson (http://www.acronym.org.uk/dd/dd91/91ctbt.htm) on "Unfinished Business", published by the United Nations Institute for Disarmament Research (UNIDIR) in May 2009, tells the story of how the CTBT was fought for, opposed and finally negotiated. It considers how a decade of political and institutional obstacles have prevented the CTBT from entering into full legal effect, including the Indian and Pakistani nuclear tests of May 1998, the US failure to ratify the treaty in 1999, and the October 9, 2006 nuclear test by North Korea.

The book focuses on the test ban treaty as it was negotiated in the immediate post-cold-war period, and contains lessons of contemporary relevance for diplomats and non-governmental organizations (NGOs) seeking to bring further disarmament treaties to fruition. Whether aiming to put a nuclear weapons convention onto governments' agendas, or pave the way to negotiate space security agreements, or finally get the deadlocked CD to carry out its mandate to negotiate a fissile materials treaty, this history of the CTBT negotiations contains useful insights and theoretical perspectives on how to foster positive-sum solutions that integrate different national and international needs and interests.

Unfinished Business focuses on the multilateral processes and actors that brought the CTBT to the United Nations on 24 September 1996, where it was signed by the leaders of the major nuclear-weapon states and more than half the world. The major remaining political challenge is to enable entry into force by convincing the remaining states to sign and ratify the treaty. The book briefly discusses the CTBTO's advances in setting up the International Monitoring System (IMS) and developing procedures for carrying out on-site inspections (OSI), most recently through exercises such as IFE08 (an Integrated Field Exercise, coordinated by the CTBTO at the former Soviet Semipalatinsk test site, in Kazakhstan in September 2008).

As early as 1954, India and Japan, as well as civil society campaigners, had put the concept of a comprehensive treaty banning all nuclear testing onto the political agenda. *Unfinished Business* briefly summarizes how efforts to achieve this total test ban failed and how US President Kennedy, Soviet General-Secretary Krushchev and UK Prime Minister Macmillan decided to agree a

Partial Test Ban Treaty (PTBT) in 1963. France and China refused to sign and continued to test in the atmosphere for some years after, but despite these violations and years of political setbacks, many states and NGOs continued to hold up the demand for a truly comprehensive test ban as a necessary and achievable objective. Now a growing number of NGOs and governments are mobilizing around the objective of a comprehensive treaty to abolish nuclear weapons, generally referred to as a nuclear weapons convention (NWC), after the biological and chemical weapons conventions.

Anyone who participated in the Conference on Disarmament (CD) when it negotiated the Comprehensive Test Ban Treaty (CTBT) from January 1994 to September 1996 would agree that the work was hard and long, but few would have wanted to be anywhere else. The CD was developed at a time when national security was regarded as paramount, and every government got to determine its own definition of national security, whether this included developing tens of thousands of nuclear weapons, pursuing armed conflict for oil, minerals or territory, or even torturing and executing civilians with dissident views. In the past 30 years such notions of the sovereign right of governments to pursue their own determinations of national security have come under question, particularly if they undermine international peace, security and human rights or cause indiscriminate harm to civilians.

Like other international institutions, the CD needs to be restructured as a forum where processes of challenge and change can take place, and where governments are encouraged—and also persuaded—to reframe their understandings of national security to become consistent with—or at least responsive towards—international and human security imperatives.

This does not mean that the CD rules should enable treaty decisions to be imposed by riding roughshod over governments' concerns. This may be the spectre raised by objectors to CD reform, but it is not what anyone is suggesting. However, the present system, where the consensus rule is invoked to prevent the CD getting started is untenable. By denying all states the opportunity to participate in the process of reaching convergence, which is what negotiations should be about, the current system rides roughshod over the security needs and objectives of the vast majority of states and peoples. The CD has almost used up the international community's patience. Without reform this forum will not survive much longer.

The point here is not that national security and interests should be subsumed in favour of others' interests—few states would agree to that. The point is to create a process whereby actual security interests can be given priority over the special interests of the few that have vested military or economic interests in maintaining an insecure status quo. As practiced in the CD, the consensus rule gives a carte blanche to a single reluctant government to impose its narrow determination of particular national interests on everyone else and block developments that could greatly enhance its country's actual security, as well as improving the security of others.

The argument for CD reform is based on modern understandings of how national interests are formed and shaped. Far from being fixed and necessarily competitive, as outdated realist theories would have us believe, perceptions of national security are the product of a number of changing factors. From global heating and climate change to weapons of mass destruction and terrorism, our 21st century security threats are trans-boundary and global. In today's world, the concept of national security has no meaning in a vacuum. It makes sense only in relation to international and regional security. Nor can governments be assumed to have a sacrosanct monopoly on defining and protecting their countries' security, as poor governance is itself a cause of great 'national' insecurity for many people.

As the CTBT experience demonstrated, through the process of negotiations, many governments come to change or recast their perceptions of their state's interests and security. The process of negotiations demonstrates the benefits of cooperative security and the interdependence of national, regional and international security. Negotiations should not be aimed at over-riding national security considerations but to facilitate governments to reshape their understanding of national security and to come to the understanding that however large or small, powerful or independent a country is, harmonizing with the security needs and interests of the wider international community will enhance rather than diminish its own security environment.

Unfinished Business considers the differences between integrative negotiations—the strategies and tactics for reaching positive sum convergence—and traditional, distributive negotiating approaches, which assume that if there are winners there must also be losers. Though the CTBT negotiations contained examples and elements of both distributive and integrative convergence, it became clear that better and more sustainable decisions arose through integrative convergence than through the concealing, obstructing and manipulative tactics traditionally employed by zero sum practitioners.

Different kinds of lessons can be drawn from the CTBT negotiations. According to Johnson (http://www.acronym.org.uk/dd/dd91/91ctbt.htm) those that may be particularly useful for the CD in its efforts to make progress on a *fissban* is highlighted below:

> *Start without preconditions—states' objectives and dynamics can be shaped by factors that emerge through the process of negotiations, thereby facilitating progressive solutions that were previously ruled out.*

There are parallels between the CTBT and the fissban in the emphasis some states put on whether the primary objective should be non-proliferation or disarmament. States that seek to specify certain outcomes or delineate the parameters of negotiations before allowing negotiations to go ahead are nearly always masking their real policy preference, which is to have no negotiations at all. Once there is basic agreement to negotiate, the mandate should be broad enough to accommodate different perspectives on what the final treaty should encompass. It is a mistake to create too narrow a mandate or to try to pre-negotiate agreements on controversial issues. The process of negotiations at its best can reveal or create new solutions to contested issues.

Unfinished Business details how this worked for the CTBT on the issue of scope, which was as deeply contested as the current argument over stocks in the fissban. A core interest shared by the P-5 nuclear-weapon states was to preserve their nuclear weapon programmes while curbing the options of others. As the negotiations convened in January 1994, all the state negotiators, including the nonaligned, believed that the P-5 would refuse to agree to a test ban treaty unless they could retain some nuclear testing options. However, though the P-5 shared the aim of keeping open some testing options under the rubric of "activities not prohibited", they couldn't agree on what these should be—a low threshold, exceptions for safety tests or the right to conduct "peaceful nuclear explosions". They conducted their scope negotiations in their own mini-lateral forum, away from the multilateral CD, but failed to reach agreement because their asymmetrical technological capabilities, political distrust and rivalries impeded their collective attempts to agree on even a maximum threshold for conducting low-yield hydro-nuclear experiments.

Multilateralism does not require participation by all states, but it needs to be representative to be credible. If states have directly participated in the negotiations, they are more likely to have a sense of ownership regarding the outcome, making universal implementation more likely. Due to the differences among governments, multilateralism must have structures and mechanisms for addressing asymmetries in a fair and cost-effective manner. The institutionalization of differential obligations in the nuclear non-proliferation regime gives rise to special challenges in negotiating nuclear weapons treaties, but these are not insurmountable as long as the interests of all states in building peace and security in a world free of nuclear weapons is recognized.

9. *Cross-Border Negotiations for Water Resource Security: A Mediterranean Case*

Water has been recognized as a key natural resource for environmental security, socioeconomic development and human well-being. In the Mediterranean area, sustainable water resources management is a major issue, given the semi-arid climate, the variability of hydrological characteristics and the fragile socio-economic conditions. The majority of the population around the Mediterranean lives in trans-boundary river basins. Sharing water and securing social and political stability in these regions present several technical and cooperative challenges.

Nowadays, the concept of human security on a global scale may be extended from its traditional meaning of worldwide political and military security to also embrace the idea that every citizen should be able to benefit from sustainable socio-economic development From amongst different natural resources, water has been recognized as the key environmental resource for social security, economic growth and prosperity. Human security can therefore be seen to be related to environmental preservation (water, ecosystems and biodiversity) and to socio-economic stability and sustainable development. The concept of sustainable management of water resources was first mentioned in Stockholm in 1972, during the United Nations World Conference, and then at the Rio summit in 1992 with Agenda 21.

Historically speaking, internationally shared water resources in trans-boundary river catchments have always been of importance. Rivers and lakes have often been used to determine frontiers between countries (e.g. the Rhine between France and Germany, the Rio Grande between the USA and Mexico and the Evros/Meric between Greece and Turkey). There have been numerous conflicts but also cases of cooperation over trans-boundary water resources. In many cases, one or several countries may occupy parts of the upstream or downstream area of the river catchments (Linkov, (2004). This makes the issue of water sharing even more complicated (e.g. the Nile between Egypt and the Sudan, the Middle East conflict over the Jordan River and the Danube between many European countries).

On a global scale, the importance of trans-boundary water resources is far from negligible: according to reports submitted to the UN, about 50% of the world's landmass (excluding Antarctica) is located in internationally shared water catchments. About 40% of the world's population lives in internationally shared water catchments, extending over more than 200 international river basins. In the Mediterranean, trans-boundary water resources are extremely important. In SEE, 90% of the area lies in international basins. The Nile basin is shared by 10 countries from deepest Africa to Egypt. In North Africa and in the Middle East, trans-boundary aquifers are very important.

Main Issues in Trans-boundary Water Resources Management (TWRM)

TWRM involves addressing not only physical and technical issues but should also take into consideration social actors, institutions and administrative procedures. According to LeMarquant (1990), five foreign-policy factors influence international water situations:

(1) international posture of each country,
(2) international law,
(3) linkage between water and other issues,
(4) mutual commitment (reciprocity), and
(5) national sovereignty.

The main objective of effective TWRM is to satisfy the demands of all riparian countries, given the possibilities and limitations of water supply. This balance between supply and demand should take into consideration both water quantity and quality aspects and the protection of the environment. Water quantity and quality problems are very much inter-related and should be studied in an integrated framework. According to Frey (1984), in order to understand the origin of serious conflicts over international water systems, three main factors should be considered:

(1) the importance of water (both in quantity and quality),
(2) the relative power of the actors, and
(3) the respective riparian position of the countries.

The Engineering Approach

This approach has been developed mainly by engineers and management experts. Depending on the number of objectives and decision-makers and their combination, models may be formulated as *optimization, multi-objective trade-off* computerized codes or on the basis of the *team and game theories*. Most of these models are based on the fundamental notion of Pareto optimality and are predictive in the sense that they suggest a quantitative "optimal" situation, which should be to terminate a conflict by finding an equitable resolution between the countries involved. Recent advances and related theoretical developments in this area can be found in the literature, including the application of the fuzzy set theory. However, the success in practice of this kind of *engineering* or *rational modelling* is mainly dependent on the interested actors' and countries' acceptance of the model assumptions, which rely on a set of prescribed objectives, and the relative weights or preferences between conflicting goals. In the real world this is not usually the case, and therefore, there is a need to develop better, easier-to-use, interactive and reliable predictive models for TWRM (Ganulis, 2004).

The Institutional Approach

This approach is used mainly by law experts and political analysts, who focus on describing the anatomy of a given situation of conflict or cooperation. They determine the function of different parameters and factors influencing the behaviour of each country, such as the political perception of the importance of water, the international image and status of the country and also social and institutional issues. Such models, including the behaviour of institutional structures, international negotiation strategies, alternative dispute resolutions and political models are very useful. They are mainly prescriptive and not predictive. They do not necessarily give a quantitative output (such as costs and benefits), but are extremely important for understanding the processes and analyzing the origin and evolution of conflicts or cooperation. Many alternative negotiation strategies are available to modify a complex framework of TWRM issues. Decision makers and those who may negotiate on their behalf have a choice of six universal negotiation strategies:

(1) "Win-Win" solutions or Positive sum benefits
(2) "Lose-Lose" solutions or Negative sum benefits
(3) "Win-Lose" negotiations or Zero-sum benefits
(4) Unilateral creation of new facts
(5) Conflict and threats of violence
(6) No action, causing opportunity costs from neglect and/or delayed decisions.

The choice of a particular negotiation technique is always subject to political considerations and controversy. Preferences depend on the balance of power among trans-boundary stakeholders and the cost of concessions. The more powerful and wealthy stakeholders can resort to the creation of facts with minimal risk of counteraction by weaker and impoverished neighbours. They also can afford to make gestures of friendship through "Win-Lose" agreements in the interest of enhancing regional stability (Eaton and Eaton, 1996).

It may be mathematically proven that "Win-Win" agreements result in positive benefits for both parties and consist of the best trade-off between alternative solutions. The so-called "Prisoner's Dilemma", well known in the literature, gives insight to the fact that failure to reach an agreement between interested parties may increase benefits to each individual party but will decrease the total benefits. This is because when each party acts independently it will tend to over-use the resource.

Cooperation schemes may provide better net benefits to both parties. However, "Win-Win" solutions may not always be sufficient when considering cases where natural water resources are limited. In these cases regional networks of water stakeholders can play a very important role. By combining the expertise and state-of-the-art knowledge of different scientific communities and disciplines, such as engineering, economics and environmental and social sciences, regional partnerships may contribute to the development of new methods and models in order to more efficiently resolve conflicts and controversial issues in TWRM (Ganulis, 2004).

Conflicts in sharing trans-boundary water resources are usually due to the fact that countries use either different attributes or different goals to evaluate impacts from alternative strategies The methodology used by Ganulis (2004) in his study on 'Water Resource Management and Environmental Security in Mediterranean Trans-boundary River Basins' is based on a combination of Integrated Risk Analysis and MCDA techniques adapted to conflict resolution. Trade-offs according to the findings of the study are made either at the level of countries' different appreciation of individual attributes, or at the level of countries' different goals. The methodology is easy to use and the results obtained are fair, transparent and simple to communicate to decision makers; as also universally applicable to all cross-border Water Resource Management projects/issues/disputes for ensuring a greater long-term environmental security.

Almost 40 percent of the world's population lives in more than 200 river basins that are shared by more than two countries. Twenty-two countries around the world are heavily dependent upon the flow of water originating in other upstream nations for a large part of their supply. Shared watercourses need to be managed to resolve issues before they develop into conflicts, manage the resources for all users and riparian countries, maintain shared ecosystems, and improve water productivity in agriculture.

USAID is participating in a wide range of trans-boundary-related activities targeted at improving water resources management, consistent with the principles of Integrated Water Resources Management (IWRM). These activities include regional frameworks for cooperation in selected river basins, increasing stakeholder awareness of river basin management issues, and strengthening the capacity of relevant regional river basin institutions. USAID is advancing the adoption of IWRM practices in a number of trans-boundary rivers, including conducting major activities in Central Asia, the South Caucasus, and Southern Africa. These efforts emphasize the application of sound science and the active participation of stakeholders, and include (http://www.usaid.gov/our_work/environment/water/transboundary_wrm.html):

- Promotion of water demand management, negotiation, and conflict management;
- Stakeholder-based decision-making to manage competing water demands;
- Improved Sanitation
- Institutional strengthening and capacity-building;
- Training programs for monitoring, analysis, and planning of water resources management;
- Harmonization of national laws with the management of the shared water course;
- Coastal Resources Management; and
- Regional information collection, management, analysis, exchange and application to decision-making.

Trans-boundary waters have the potential to stimulate cooperation rather than conflict. Ultimately, shared watercourses have a chance of influencing regional politics in the direction of increased co-operation to lay a foundation for social and political stability, sustainable economic prosperity and poverty alleviation. A dialogue on water and its role in social and economic development provides a means for building trust among the parties in a region, with the aim of managing shared waters in an efficient, equitable and sustainable manner. In 2006, a Trans-boundary Water Management programme, supported by the Swedish International Development Cooperation Agency (Sida), was initiated by Ramboll Natura and the Stockholm International Water Institute (SIWI) (Capacity Building Programmes for Effective Trans-boundary Water Management: http://www.worldwatercongress2008.org/resource/authors/abs690_article.pdf). This programme aims at strengthening the capacities of the individuals and organizations involved in trans-boundary water management in developing countries globally. Over a six month period modules on topics such as negotiation tactics, stakeholder participation, hydro-politics, environmental water requirements and benefit sharing are presented by international experts. A wide range of trans-boundary water management practitioners, mainly government officials, who have first-hand experience of managing shared waters and negotiating agreements around them, interact with participants through panel discussions and site visits. In addition to these inputs, the participants engage in intensive peer-to-peer knowledge exchange, sharing their wealth of experience with each other. The programme has also been implemented in specific locations and basins – the Middle East and Northern Africa (MENA) region and Lake Victoria basin, respectively. The programme has now embarked on its third intake of participants, each group comprising about 30 mid-career professionals from a variety of sectors – government, NGOs, private sector, academia and the media. In essence, organizational capacity building is aimed for through strengthening the skills of the individual and linking those skills to their job situation. One of the mechanisms used is an Individual Project, an analysis of a real-world issue currently being dealt with by the participants' organization. Over time a type of "alumni network" is developing—demand driven by the participants themselves. This has allowed them to interact with course participants form previous years and from other regions—thus further institutionalizing the learning experience.

London Water Research Group conducted the Fourth International Workshop on Hydro-Hegemony on 31 May/1 June 2008 with the thematic focus on 'Understanding and Challenging Water and Power Asymmetry'.

As a prelude to the Workshop, the following observation of Ban Ki-Moon is relevant (http://www2.lse.ac.uk/geographyAndEnvironment/CEPG/LWRG/HH4%20-%20UpdatedProgramme%20-23Apr08.pdf):

> Darfur is an environmental crisis – a conflict that grew at least in part from desertification, ecological degradation and a scarcity of resources, foremost among them water.
>
> —*Ban Ki-Moon: What I Saw in Darfur. The Washington Post, 14 Sept 2007.*

Environmental determinism endures as the widespread sense of insecurity related to the environment and water continues to spread. Attribution of the roots of political conflicts to water is either useful securitization, or disingenuous de-politicization. If Darfur was heavily forested and as awash in water as it is in unexplored oil, after all, would we expect to see peaceful relations between the government and rebel groups?

The dominant paradigm in the global water community emphasizes, on the other hand, that collectively we are moving away from water conflict and towards water 'cooperation'. The 2006 UN World Water Development Report states that we can discern "a shift from confrontation to cooperation, from monologue to dialogue and from dissent to consensus". But considering the number of highly asymmetric water conflicts that continue to contribute to regional insecurity, can we safely assume that all's quiet on the waterfront?

These opposing views play out in a world replete with various intensities of co-existing water conflict and cooperation at the sub-national, international, trans-national and global levels. Water policy-makers and analysts are obliged to confront our incomplete understanding of the forces that influence water and security at each level. We need to scrutinize power asymmetry and its effects as policy and funding are directed towards increasing 'security' by reducing uncertainty (LSE,2008).

10. Build-Operate-Transfer (BOT) Type Procurement in Mega-Projects

Lessons are drawn from the recent resurgence in public-private partnerships for the procurement of large scale infrastructure, with a focus on Asian mega-projects. BOT (build-operate-transfer)-type win-win cooperation aligns well with the paradigm shift that has repeatedly been called for in addressing construction industry shortfalls. However, the many volatile variables involved and the limited experience in dealing with the special risks encountered highlights the need for decision support frameworks to evaluate and select the optimal from among: (1) potential BOT-type projects; (2) prospective franchisees; and (3) innovative project financing packages. Such frameworks should include appropriate success criteria and indicators for their evaluation. Benchmarking of good practices would establish reasonable ranges of values for such indicators. Identification of critical success factors, classifications of common risks, and comparisons of recent experiences on BOT-type projects lead to recommendations for the development of a "BOT body of knowledge" with related guidelines and toolkits. These would assist both public and private sector decision makers considering BOT-type modalities to attain multiple win-win-win targets that benefit their respective interests, as well as those of the general public end users (http://scitation.aip.org/getabs/servlet/GetabsServlet?prog=normal&id =JCEMD4000128000002000093000001&idtype=cvips&gifs=yes).

The terms of concession including tariff and concession period are often discussed intensively during negotiations of build-operate-transfer (BOT) contracts. Based on prior studies on negotiation terms and risk of BOT contracts, incorporates risk attributes of the BOT project into the formulation of a contractual-negotiation model. The proposed model by Lieu and Chih-Pin Huang, (2008) allows the government and the sponsor to reach a consensus on the terms should the financial return as well as the risk of the project be determined. The pro forma cash flow of a BOT project is developed and used to generate the probability distribution of net present values (NPV) from the owner's viewpoint by using Monte Carlo simulation. High- and low-risk scenarios are obtained to determine whether the contractual-negotiation models vary in accordance with risk levels. Results show that, given the expected NPV, the sponsor should be offered more favorable concessional terms for projects with high risk than that with low risk. Hence it was suggested by Lieu and Chih-Pin Huang that the government and industry practitioners embody the risk attributes of the project in the automated contractual-negotiation model (Fen May Lieu and Chih-Pin Huang, 2008). One of the issues to successfully apply the BOT project is that must have an adequate procurement strategy or procedure. Differently with traditional projects, procurement procedures for BOT projects will be influenced by a variety of factors, including the host country's existing legislation governing public procurement of construction work, internationally accepted rules for public procurement, the business environment, the overall infrastructure policy and the nature of the particular BOT project (UNIDO, 1996; TO Nam Toan, Kazumasa OZAWA, http://management.kochi-tech.ac.jp/PDF/SOCIAL_MANAGEMENT_INFRA/SESSION_B4/smsri_28_Toan.pdf).

In the mid-1980s, many Asian countries turned to privatization of infrastructure to overcome problems which threatened to constrain economic growth. Getting private sector management and capital into transport, power, water and sewage, and telecommunications services, was seen as a way of obtaining and maintaining infrastructure more quickly and more cheaply than traditional, state-led methods. Various privatization methods such as corporations, public flotation and straightforward sell-offs of state-owned enterprises, became a popular option in Asian countries. One important approach for building new infrastructure facilities was the Build-Operate-Transfer (BOT) concept (Handley, 1997).

In order to formulate an efficient procurement framework for BOT projects, several researches (Zhang 2004, 2005; Kumarawamy and Zhang, 2001) as well as guidelines (UNIDO 1996, WB 1998) indicate that the competitive tendering system is suitable method to improve the efficiency of procurement systems of BOT projects. The experiences of Asian countries indicate that they develop the procurement systems of BOT projects based on the trial-and-error exercises (Kumaraswamy *et al.* 2002). This suggests the usefulness of learning from the successful "trials" so as to minimize any further "errors" in developing the future procurement systems of BOT projects.

Infrastructure mega projects involve several complex clusters of inter-related and interacting activities. Establishing suitably integrated management support systems for construction clients should be useful in targeting best value with reduced rework and wastages. The management of large projects is usually quite complicated and therefore challenging for many construction clients (http://www.itcon.org/data/works/att/2006_15.content.06065.pdf). The necessity for information and communication technologies (ICT) enabled management support systems is increasingly evident (Love *et al.* 2000; McCaffer and Hassan, 2002). However, general observations of several existing decision support aids and management support systems in various client organizations indicated that many of those systems targeted only narrowly focused independent sets of objectives (Kumaraswamy et al., 2004). They are therefore mostly discrete or non-connected.

An ongoing Hong Kong based research initiative aims to develop a more holistic framework and sample working modules of a knowledge-based and integrated Management Support System (MSS) that will empower the formulation of more effective and efficient infrastructure project procurement and operational/ delivery systems. The main objectives of this MSS research are (i) to build rich knowledge-bases of best practices, founded on sound principles, in optimizing selected infrastructure procurement and operational/

delivery sub-systems, in the context of both client priorities and project contextual conditions; (ii) to develop these knowledge-bases further, e.g. by incorporating and extrapolating both paradigmatic/ theoretical frameworks, as well as recent and potential innovations in particular scenarios; and (iii) to design an MSS framework and develop prototype working modules of this MSS that would draw on these knowledge-bases in providing appropriate advice on the selection, development and integration of procurement and operational sub-systems for a particular infrastructure construction project (http://www.itcon.org/data/works/att/2006_15.content.06065.pdf).

The various approaches chosen for developing the pilot modules of the MSS include: (i) Delphic strategies for mapping and prioritizing client-specific requirements and project-based needs; (ii) bespoke decision-making constructs and group decision arrangements; (iii) hybrid decision logic strategies of both data driven forward chaining and goal driven backward chaining; and (iv) reusable system modelling and integrated system designing with object oriented programming concepts. Some of these approaches have been used already, while others are being used or will be applied in due course on relevant modules.

The envisaged MSS is structured under the following four broad clusters: (i) integrated procurement system, (ii) collaborative delivery system, (iii) inter-organizational learning system, and (iv) synergistic technological system. The present initiative as a broad framework under the proposed study focuses on the development of procurement related subsystems and operational/project delivery related subsystems; i.e., on the first two broad clusters; while the third and fourth are expected to be dealt with later. The procurement subsystems include work packaging, payment modalities, contract conditions and selection methodologies. The operational/delivery subsystems include time management, cost management, quality management, performance appraisal, safety management, risk management, value management, claims and dispute management, human resources management, and information and communications management.

Although China, Russia and India may be rich in natural resources, their need for construction materials and knowledge from the global marketplace illustrates their current level of maturity, which the World Economic Forum defines as "Efficiency Driven". Their current macro economic performance highlights the commencement of their journey towards becoming "Innovation Driven" economies—the level of maturity said to be held by Western economies. However, these three economies (together with the Middle East) face competition for materials from international "mega projects" in locations around the globe. The Olympics in the UK, South Africa's staging of the World Cup Football, and skyscrapers and other infrastructure across our lands are all driving demand for the construction factors of production leading to some of the price inflation headlined in the news from Dubai. All of the foregoing points reinforce the need to be more creative in procurement and being able to reach further into global markets to deliver viable options or solutions into our local markets.

Davis Langdon's 'International Procurement Group' has been set up to help us tackle this challenge head on and the Group has now published their first series of articles to raise awareness of some of the issues being faced and how we are responding to them (http://www.davislangdon.com/upload/images/publications/USA/International%20Procurement%20Series%202_All%20Articles.pdf)

Geopolitics in Global Trade

Since the World Trade Organization (WTO) was first created in 1995, trade issues have ceased to be technical. Instead, they have become highly political, not only because trade issues have changed but also because the geopolitical context in which these exchanges take place has been altered (Zaki Laidi, http://www.laidi.com/comment/summer2008.pdf). The creation of the WTO in 1995 in the wake of the General Agreement on Tariff and Trade (GATT), which was set up after World War II, was a direct response to three fundamental changes in the world order. The first was the exponential growth in world trade. Between 1980 and 2005, the volume of trade quadrupled, while during the same period world gross national product (GNP) barely doubled. Trade has thus become the most powerful agent of globalization. This considerable increase was only made possible due to a significant reduction in tariff protection in southern countries, which dropped from an average 30 percent in 1985 to 10 percent some 20 years later.

The second change is more qualitative in nature. It has to do with the extension of the range of products subject to trade liberalization. For rich countries whose economies now rely on the creation of added value in the service sector, the issue is how to protect intangible products generated by these services with guarantees of intellectual property. Simply put, free trade no longer involves simply abandoning customs and tariff protection but requires scrupulous respect for the rules of intellectual property that so often accompanies broader trading relationships. In exchange for this extension of the perimeter of trade liberalization, developing countries have obtained the inclusion of agriculture in the sphere of liberalization. This quid pro quo arrangement only seems logical. Each party wants to extend trade liberalization to the areas where it has a real comparative advantage. Rich countries take services; developing countries take agriculture. Yet even if the agricultural sector only represents 8 percent of world trade, its debut on the agenda has carried a heavy weight.

The third change has to do with the massive increase of developing countries now in the WTO system. This prefigured the advent of multipolar global governance and the reconfiguration of international relations in the twenty-first century. The WTO now has 153 member states; this transformation did not happen overnight.

In the first phase, developing countries that were not members of GATT and that joined the WTO did so with caution. They feared that a binding liberal agenda would be imposed on them in areas where rich countries had offensive interests (e.g., liberalization of services and setting up strong patent protection regimes) but less certain in areas where the interests of developed countries were more defensive (e.g., agriculture, social norms). These contradictions, which were scarcely discussed and thus not smoothed out when the WTO was created, burst out in the open at the summit in Seattle in 1999, where a new round of trade negotiations was supposed to be launched. Developing countries felt terribly uncomfortable in an institution without clear procedural rules and in which developed countries seemed to want to maintain the informal procedures inherited from GATT, like the famous "Green Rooms," which are sort of closed sessions for informed negotiators.

The budding anti-globalist movement amplified this North-South collision and harnessed it to its advantage, taking advantage of the stalled negotiations to put forward new demands, such as the consideration of environmental questions and a refusal to see the world held hostage by the merchant class. Tapping into this current, the most radical non-governmental organizations (NGOs) demanded that the WTO simply be dismantled, claiming it was simply created to represent multinational corporations. But, paradoxically, most of the NGOs' demands regarding environmental matters, social rights, and better representation in WTO World Policy Journal: Yet, far from leading to the premature death of a new institution, the Seattle conference actually prefigured a considerable change in the role of trade in global governance. This change was two-fold. It marked the end of the Euro-American duopoly on trade liberalization, which China's entrance into the WTO one year later spectacularly amplified. Furthermore, it accented the reality that trade liberalization interacts increasingly with a huge number of social concerns (e.g., environment, health care, civil rights) and that non-governmental organizations and non-state social actors can no longer be ignored.

In a climactic fashion, the creation of the WTO demonstrated a major aspect of globalization—that trade liberalization in a globalized world no longer refers simply to competition between economies, but between social systems. A host of new factors now comprise world competition, including protectionist tariff systems, education, economic infrastructure and administration, and tax systems. Moreover, the WTO system demonstrated convincingly that lowering tariffs was no longer enough to harmonize trade competition. In WTO vocabulary, liberalization issues no longer include only "products" (downstream) but also "processes" (upstream). The system must be equally concerned, for instance, with how much the Chinese will pay in customs duties for toys entering Europe or the United States, as well as ensuring that these toys were not manufactured by prisoners and that they meet health and environmental standards in the consumer countries.

WTO and Global Governance

So while the WTO is not only the institution in charge of overseeing trade liberalization, it has become the body that is supposed to settle global governance conflicts. The change in issues related to trade liberalization was brought to light in the Doha Round negotiations in November 2001. During this summit, rich countries sought to erase the memory of the Seattle disaster while the southern developing countries, invigorated by China's entrance, for the first time sought to reprogram the WTO to their advantage. They succeeded in exploiting a factor rarely taken into account: at the WTO, there is no Security Council or supreme body—all nations have the right of veto, so all parties must agree in order to launch a negotiating round. Developing countries, despite their diversity, have realized that the WTO'S one-country, one-vote nature represents a considerable political asset. As a result, the Doha Round was launched with a broad agenda designed to take into account the diversity of objectives and expectations among the vastly expanded membership of the original WTO. Indeed, Doha was even baptized the "development round" at the request of southern countries. Its agenda, which debuted in 2001 and remains open, includes no fewer than 21 subjects, ranging from agriculture, industry, services, and intellectual property to rules of origin, anti-dumping regulations, trade facilitation, environmental protections, basic social issues, special and differential treatment for the least-advanced countries, and fisheries—among a host of others. It has become easier to inventory subjects not listed on the WTO agenda than to count all those that appear on it.

This entire complex infrastructure exists within a geopolitical framework of new political coalitions among states and new political demands for trade liberalization. Basically, the geopolitics of the WTO is now built on four major pillars: the United States, the European Union, the G-20 and the G-90. The G-20 bloc encompasses most of the emerging countries in Asia and Latin America that want to break up the EU-U.S. duopoly at the WTO. Most of these G-20 nations export agricultural products and feel disadvantaged either by the closed doors of certain European agricultural markets or by the unfair competition represented by domestic subsidies for American farmers. The G-20 coalesced in 2004 during the Cancun summit. The members derailed the conference to show the United States and the European Union that they could no longer resist the demands of developing countries to change agricultural protections. Brazil and India dominate the G-20. However, these two countries do not necessarily share the same interests: Brazil, for example, has much more defensive positions than India. But both are united by a simple goal—not to yield ground on the protection of domestic industry and agriculture unless they are rewarded by an end to agricultural export subsidies, the opening of European agricultural markets, and the opening of service markets to qualified Indian workers.

China must also be added to this equation, though it had not, until the July session in Geneva, generally acted overtly. In part, Beijing wants to avoid scaring off developing countries that are afraid of its power, while it avoids campaigning for more trade liberalization on the multilateral level. Beijing believes it paid a high enough price in this area when China joined the WTO.

The birth of the G-20, which neither the United States nor the European Union saw coming, and whose importance they immediately underestimated (probably because they thought its members' interests were too diverse to suggest any possible joint negotiating positions), has created a de facto multi-polarity in WTO governance. Yet, surprisingly, opposition to the creation of the G-20 did not come from the North but from other southern countries which banded together to form the G-90. This bloc was formed at the Cancun Conference as an umbrella alliance of emerging and least-developed countries—those nations classified by the United Nations as having the lowest socioeconomic development indicators.

Although much larger and much more diverse, the formation of the G-90 suggested the existence of a group of lesser-developed countries that were worried about the effects of trade liberalization and troubled by the potential loss of preferential access to American and especially European markets. The EU-U.S. duopoly came under fire, and the bloc of southern countries fragmented: emerging countries on one side and less advanced countries on the other. The G-90 therefore has a more defensive agenda than the G-20, which seeks better access to markets in northern countries—even if that means undermining G-90 interests.

Multi-polarity at the WTO

The result of this entire system is four basic, though often fluid, coalitions that fluctuate depending on the subject. First, there is the United States plus the European Union versus the G-20. In this case, the priorities for the first two are to open the industrial and service markets of emerging nations, while the G-20 seeks agricultural liberalization in the EU and the United States. In other cases, the United States and the G-20 are pitted against the EU on the issue of access to agricultural markets protected by customs or sanitary barriers. A third set of issues—elimination of agricultural export subsidies—pits the United States and the EU against the G-20 and G-90. And finally, the EU, G-20, and G-90 may line up against the United States in efforts to dismantle market-distorting domestic support for agricultural products, especially cotton. From this analysis, it's clear that American and Europeans frequently have congruent interests, but may not always be able to articulate them. The G-20 and the G-90 have fundamentally opposite interests, but Third World solidarity prevents them from admitting it. Lastly, China scares everyone. Thus, Beijing it seems, is pleased with the status quo. Still, and perhaps most fundamental, it would be utterly misleading to assume that the lack of results in the Doha Round of negotiations has in any way prevented world trade from moving ahead.

The multipolar geopolitics of the WTO largely flows from the global redistribution of wealth in favor of emerging powers, even if the weight of the United States and the European Union remains considerable. But this reality is also accompanied by increased expectations that trade liberalization will provide more and more societal benefits. In fact, within the WTO there are three major visions of trade liberalization. Naturally, these visions are not airtight and not necessarily mutually exclusive. But they reflect the preferences and the priorities of the main groups of countries.

The first, the so-called market access strategy adopted by Brazil, the EU, and the United States, is a managed trade vision that sees the WTO as the privileged instrument to obtain better market access through a reduction in tariff and non-tariff barriers. In this sense, free trade refers to the strong priority given to opening up one's competitors' markets. In a way, all countries except for those of the G-90, which have a very defensive attitude, share this priority. The United States and the European Union are seeking to obtain access to emerging countries that have the strongest potential for economic growth. This is a priority for the United States and Japan, which have seen dwindling export market shares since the middle of the 1990s, and for Europe, which has better preserved its market share of world trade, but must hedge against future trends that appear substantially less favorable.

In fact, European exports are high in countries where demand is static, and lower in those where it is growing rapidly. On this level, the EU is at a greater disadvantage than the United States and Japan. This weakness is important to note, as it has a very strong social and political impact. Indeed, in recent years, globalization is the yardstick by which European citizens judge and assess the legitimacy of a united Europe. But Euro-barometer surveys continually indicate that Europe does not offer its citizens assess the legitimacy of a united Europe. But Euro-barometer surveys continually indicate that Europe does not offer its citizens enough protection against globalization. In concrete terms, this means that Europe is expected to use trade to create more wealth in Europe, and in particular more jobs. This demand, which was notably expressed during the French debate on the European Constitutional Treaty in 2005, led the European Commission to reorient its trade policy after 2006. Significantly, the commission report entitled "Global Europe: Competing in the World" is subtitled "A Contribution to the EU's Growth and Jobs Strategy." The concern has become all the more acute since one of the major social benefits of globalization—the deflationary effect that kept down costs of imported products and thus compensated for low growth in wages—is starting to dwindle.

Certainly, EU commitment to multi-lateralism has been clearly reaffirmed. But emphasis is presently on access to emerging markets with a strong potential (namely, growing middle classes with rising consumer power). This shift has been confirmed by an increase in bilateral free trade agreements (FTAs) with countries that have high market potential or restrain penetration of European products due to import restrictions. This reorientation is all the more striking since it occurs after the freeze on free trade agreements from 2000 to 2004 in favor of a very pronounced multilateral engagement. Europe had also to renegotiate its preferential agreements with the least-developed countries to comply with WTO regulations which prohibit discrimination on a regional basis. But this move created a bilateral tension between the European

Commission and African states. Some of these states believe that European Trade Commissioner Peter Mandelson is not really interested in Africa—his major concern is emerging countries and large markets.

The second vision, which I call the regulatory approach, is based on a concept of liberalization, which in turn breaks down into two dimensions. First is the instrumental dimension that seeks to frame trade with rules regarding competition, investment, and trade facilitation. Facilitation, for instance, includes such realities as the two weeks (on average) that it takes to unload a container in India versus six days in Organization for Economic Co-operation and Development (OECD) countries. These types of issues had been high on the European Union's agenda until the Cancun Conference in 2003 and 2004, where Europe felt the full hostility toward its regulatory approach. Second, and more broadly, there's the more ambitious dimension that amounts to positioning trade as part of a broader social framework. In this sense, environmental, health, and social protection issues need to be fully taken into account. This was at the heart of Pascal Lamy's political agenda when he was European Trade Commissioner. Lamy is now, of course, spearheading the entire Doha Round as head of the WTO. European concern over genetically modified foods and fears of foot-and-mouth disease have moved trade into a new realm, linking market access to environmental, health, and societal requirements.

This vision is shared by such countries as Japan and South Korea, as well as the United States. But Europe has gone the farthest in defining this regulatory strategy—one imposed by the rise of European demands for social, environmental, and health safeguards. Europe seeks to apply enlightened social norms to trade relations, and thus has every interest in encouraging its partners to align, so as not to find itself at a comparative disadvantage or caught up in a race to the bottom. This debate has been rekindled today by the issue of climate change and over taxing products that come from countries that do not respect the Kyoto Protocol. This European exceptionalism is all the more marked since it is strongly resisted by most developing countries. They see it as a new form of imperialism—wanting to impose European norms on others—or the expression of a neo-Machiavellianism that wields protectionism through Western standards. The paradox is that, within Europe, many politicians argue that, on the contrary, Europe is too open and not protected enough. That is the main argument of the French President Nicolas Sarkozy, who regularly attacks the European Commission for not protecting Europeans against Globalization.

Developmentalism

The third vision is a developmentalist vision held largely by the least-developed countries. Until Doha, this was entirely absent from the global discussions. Since then, it has constantly been reinforced, at least on the level of discourse. For even if the G-90 countries are economically weak, they are strong in number. Moreover, they have the support of many western NGOs that have made them aware of the unfairness of world trade rules. In the case of cotton protections and subsidies, for instance, Oxfam has helped African countries make their case against the United States at the WTO. While these countries do not have the heft to obstruct the world dynamics of trade liberalization, they can certainly slow down the entire process. In a multilateral system where opting out is not allowed, they strive to obtain special, differentiated treatment in order to prepare their markets for the harsh realities of global competition. Therefore, their position is very defensive. They have to be convinced that more opening will harsh realities of global competition. Therefore, their position is very defensive. They have to be convinced that more opening will bring more development.

The deadlock of multilateral negotiations at the WTO reflects the difficulty and complexity of this tripartite struggle. The European Union and Brazil may each prioritize access to their respective markets. But that doesn't mean they have the same interpretation of what market access means or implies in terms of concessions. With respect to agriculture, for instance, Europeans will never be able to go as far as the Brazilians want them to go, even if rising agricultural product prices are likely to encourage Europe to yield more ground. These divergences very often become extraordinarily technical matters that are impenetrable to non-specialists in world trade. But that is not where the root of the problem lies. The fundamental problem lies in the fact that trade liberalization has made considerable progress in the world over the past 20 years. Furthermore, and contrary to what common sense would dictate, two-thirds of the tariff reductions in developing countries are the result of unilateral choices rather than multilateral negotiations. But due to the social and political costs—in countries both rich and poor—that further steps towards liberalization will require, the political will is very weak at this point.

Simply put, trade issues have become too political to submit to purely market demands. Therefore trade negotiations will be always difficult and unpopular for one major reason: the benefits of trade are rarely immediate and visible whereas the costs are viscerally and instantly felt. For the Doha Round to succeed, its negotiators must paint a coherent and positive picture of a future that may be quite opaque for the moment.

11. *Geopolitical Consequences of Inadequate Action on Climate Change*

There have been a few attempts to describe some of the geopolitical ramifications of the impacts of climate change. These studies suggest that climate change may heighten the risk of violent conflict between countries, and stimulate large scale movements of 'climate refugees', and these effects are seen to be more pronounced in developing countries (Brauch 2002; Dupont and Pearman 2006; Homer-Dixon 1999; McNeill 2003; Myers 1997; Schwartz and Randall 2003; van Ireland *et al.* 1996).

The most dramatic of these assessments is a report commissioned by the US Department of Defense that argues that climate change could 'potentially destabilize the geopolitical environment, leading to skirmishes, battles, and even war due to resource constraints' (Schwartz and Randall 2003,). It identifies shortages of food, water and disrupted access to energy as being key impacts that might trigger war, and talks in terms of 'carrying capacity', 'ancient enmities' and 'struggles for access'. This and other geopolitical scenarios are to varying degrees informed by the same neo-Malthusian assumptions about the response of social systems to resource scarcity that inform the larger literature on environmental security. These assumptions are for the most part the product of ideology more than they are of evidence about conflict (Barnett, 2001; Dalby 2002; Gleditsch, 1998; Hartmann, 2001). They are even more difficult to sustain when applied to the case of climate change given that the outcomes of climate change on biophysical systems are still somewhat uncertain, and the response of social systems to these changes is highly uncertain.

Predictions of international conflicts arising from climate change are premature. More careful analyses suggest that conflict between countries is unlikely, but that the effects of climate change on migration may increase the risk of civil conflicts between groups under certain circumstances (Barnett 2003; Nordås and Gleditsch 2007; Salehyan, 2005). Based on a review of expected climate impacts, of research on the causes and consequences of social vulnerability to climate change, and of the links between livelihoods and civil conflict, Barnett and Adger (2007) suggest that climate change may increase the risk of violent civil conflicts by undermining the livelihoods of people and groups that are dependent on natural resources, and undermining the capacity of states to provide the opportunities and services that help people to sustain their livelihoods and that help to maintain and build peace. They suggest that in combination these two processes may increase the risk of civil conflict, but that risk does not mean predetermined outcomes.

As is the case with the study of environmental security more generally, the focus on the risk of violent conflict reflects the security interests of those Western countries that are both militarily powerful and least vulnerable to environmental change (Barnett, 2001; Dalby, 2002). However, the most pressing security risks posed by climate change do not concern violent outcomes but the human insecurity associated with the risk of lost livelihoods, homes, health and life itself. The 2007 report from the IPCC describes a wide range of likely climate impacts that will undermine human security, including an increase in drought-affected areas, affecting, for example, up to 250 million people in Africa; decreasing flows in rivers that supply water to millions in Latin America and a billion people in Asia; declining crop productivity in low latitudes, including a 50% decline in yields in some parts of Africa and 30% decline in yields in some parts of Central and South Asia; millions of people exposed to flooding in the densely populated and economically productive mega deltas of Asia; increases in malnutrition in low-income societies; increased deaths, diseases and injuries associated with extreme events such as droughts, floods, heat-waves, fires and storms; decreasing yields of fish from most of the world's freshwater and coastal fisheries; loss of lands and homes and possibly islands in many of the small island states in the South Pacific, Caribbean, Indian and Atlantic oceans (IPCC, 2007).

The solutions to these problems rest in two broad strategies. The first is to reduce emissions of greenhouse gases to stabilize concentrations of gases in the atmosphere such that dangerous outcomes are avoided. This is called 'mitigation' in climate policy. The second is actions to enable people, places and systems to avoid or adjust to the adverse effects of climate change. This is called adaptation in climate policy. Because of existing concentrations of greenhouse gases in the atmosphere some degree of climate change is now inevitable, and so some degree of adaptation needs to take place to avoid damaging outcomes on the people, places and sectors most at risk. The two strategies are both called for in the UNFCCC and the Kyoto Protocol.

The politics involved in the UNFCCC and the Kyoto Protocol has largely concerned the issue of reducing emissions of greenhouse gases. However, since COP-8 in 2002 negotiations on the ways and means of implementing adaptation have become more intense. There is now a Least Developed Country (LDC) Fund that is beginning to assist the LDCs to plan adaptation activities, a Special Climate Change Fund that can also potentially assist countries in adaptation, and there exists in principle if not yet in practice an Adaptation Fund that is intended to finance adaptation projects in the most vulnerable countries.

There are no clear rules about how decisions are to be made under the UNFCCC. Decisions are theoretically not possible without the consent of all Parties. This means that objections to a decision are frequently vetoes. This potentially gives a lot of power to dissenting Parties. However, there are examples where the objections of small groups have been overridden in final agreements (Oberthür and Ott, 1999). Yet, it remains unclear how many objections make for a veto, and much seems to depend on which Party is making the objection. Parties such as the EU and the USA, which are influential because of the scale of their emissions, the size and capacities of their delegations, and their influence in other arenas of global politics, tend to have considerably more power in negotiations than other countries.

One implication of the near-veto power of any Party, and the de facto power of powerful Parties, is that coalition building is essential for reaching decisions in climate negotiations. The community of climate negotiators is relatively small, and negotiators have become well known to each other through long and intense meetings over the years. Relations among these negotiators are cordial outside of negotiation sessions, and this familiarity is an important reason why climate change negotiations progress. Villagrasa (2002) argues with a good reason that women have played a key role in coalition building in the climate negotiations in ways that defy the rule of 'might'. This gendered perspective on the micro-politics of the climate regime stands in stark contrast to the majority of economic analysis of outcomes, which assumes instead that all outcomes are the product of rational calculations in the national interest. Indeed, much of the analysis of global environmental governance remains trapped in such rational actor theories of environmental regimes. These theories struggle to explain the determinants of the outcomes of the environmental agreements they study, and they do not provide a way to understand the more complex and pluralistic institutions that comprise the larger milieu of global environmental governance (Conca, 2006).

The Geopolitics of Climate Governance

The positions of various countries in the climate regime are nevertheless largely the product of a 'two-level game' in which national leaders seek to maximize the domestic political benefits of action or inaction on the basis of their reading of domestic interests, and seek to minimize the negative effects of international factors on this domestic game (Paterson 1996; Putnam 1988). This interlocking internal-external dynamic is important to understand in the case of a given country's position on climate change. For example, most Europeans are supportive of action to address climate change and there is a reinforcing cycle of information through the public, government, media and many industry groups that makes a proactive international position on climate change domestically acceptable. In the USA and Australia, in contrast, media skepticism on climate change's causes, consequences and solutions has been high, and the opposition of fossil fuel and heavy industry groups to the Kyoto Protocol has been strong and influential (Newell, 2000).

The geopolitics of the UNFCCC cannot be explained merely as a matter of the differences between the 'North' and the 'South'. There are vast differences in the positions of countries within both groups. For example, the collective position of the Alliance of Small Island States (AOSIS) group, which is comprised of 44 of the world's small island states, has more in common with that of the collective position of the EU (27 member countries) than it does with the collective position of the 11 Organization of Petroleum Exporting Countries (OPEC), and within the North there are large differences between the EU and the USA – so much so that the EU has been described as a 'protagonist' to the USA on the issue (Vogler and Bretherton, 2006).

The main actors in the climate regime discussed in the remainder of this article are the EU, the USA, the G77 and China (actually comprised of 130 countries), its subgroups of OPEC, the AOSIS, business groups and NGOs. Other kinds of actors have also been influential in the climate regime, and these notably include the LDC group (50 countries within the G77), United Nations agencies, research institutions and the IPCC. Much has been written about the reasons for the positions of these various countries and groups, the strategies they use, and their influence in the regime (e.g. Bang *et al.* 2005; Grubb et al. 1999; Gupta 1997; Newell 2000; Oberthür and Ott 1999; Paterson, 1996).

The EU is most often characterized as a leader in climate politics because of its early and consistent advocacy for reducing greenhouse gas emissions. Four reasons are offered for this: European electorates, businesses, scientists and the media are for the most part supportive of emissions control; the costs of reducing emissions in Europe are lower than in most other developed countries, in part because under the Kyoto Protocol EU countries are allowed to pool their emissions and then reallocate them; the EU has recognized the value of the new markets for clean energy technologies; and the costs of inaction on climate change may be high in some sectors (such as alpine tourism), places (such as the Netherlands) and ecological processes (such as the North Atlantic current that helps keep Europe temperate) (Grubb *et al.* 1999; Hovi *et al.* 2003; IPCC, 2007; Newell, 2000). Europe's leadership on climate change has become stronger because the USA stated its intention to not ratify the Kyoto Protocol in 2001. This created an opportunity for Europe to pursue its ambitions towards global leadership, and such leadership was necessary given that the USA had near-veto power over the Protocol (Bang et al. 2005; Vogler and Bretherton, 2006). Most analysts argue that the future of the climate change regime rests with Europe, and that countries are unlikely to make further or new commitments to reduce emissions if the EU countries cannot meet their existing Kyoto targets.

The position of the USA on climate change has varied over time; however, two constants have been its opposition to limits on emissions from the USA without imposing similar limits on major developing countries, and a strong preference for flexible and market approaches to emissions reductions. This position stems from a belief that the costs of implementing the Kyoto targets would be relatively greater in the USA than in Europe and other Annex B countries, the strong lobbying by oil- and energy-intensive companies on policymakers, and their funding and heavy public promotion of studies that question the need to act to reduce emissions.

The financial and political power of these companies has limited the influence of researchers and environmental NGOs on public opinion and policy in the USA. Since the late 1990s, alternative voices have begun to lobby in Washington and to influence public opinion on climate change. Many companies, some states and numerous cities have announced emissions reductions targets, and faith-based groups and a larger number of NGOs have become increasingly active in lobbying and raising awareness of climate change. There is also a confluence of interest in renewable energy technologies between those seeking solutions to climate change and those seeking solutions to problems arising from dependence on imports of fossil fuels for reasons of energy and national security (Busby, 2006). For these reasons, climate change and energy are increasingly significant issues in the USA, and their significance in the Democratic victory in the 2006 Congressional Elections suggests that presidential and congressional opposition to binding emissions reductions targets may be politically untenable in the future. In the lead-up to the Kyoto Protocol, the G77-China group adopted the position that the developed countries should be the only countries to commit to emissions targets in the first instance.

Although developing countries were not asked to accept binding emissions targets under the Kyoto Protocol, in other respects they remain dissatisfied with the agreement, feeling that the equity-based principles that should have informed the allocation of emissions targets were abandoned in favour of what was effectively 'global horse trading' on targets (Najam *et al.* 2003). Their demands for commitments from developed countries for the development of clean energy and for assistance for adaptation have since been marginalized by the focus of efforts to bring the Kyoto Protocol into force. They also maintain deep concerns about the three adaptation funds, believing that they are underfunded, and lacking confidence in the Global Environmental Facility's management of the Special Climate Change Fund and the LDC Fund. The strong desire to maintain unity within the G77-China group means that the interests of many countries get watered down, ignored or overridden. For example, the OPEC group opposes emissions reductions, while the AOSIS group depends on them for their survival, yet OPEC has far more influence in the position of G77 in climate negotiations.

Developing countries are still very coy about accepting emissions targets, although there is increasing pressure for the large emitters – in particular China and India – to commit to targets under a successor agreement to the Kyoto Protocol. Both countries continue to accede to the common position of G77, and neither countries are particularly willing to talk about future commitments. However, both may gain from international assistance to help them reduce emissions as this can have significant co-benefits in terms of reducing energy costs through improved efficiency, and decreasing the costs of air pollution, which the World Bank (1997) estimates costs China 7% of gross domestic product (Boudria *et al.*, 2002). Both countries are concerned about the impacts of climate change, particularly on their rapidly developing coastal regions, both have adopted targets for the share of electricity to be generated by renewable sources (10% in India, 20% in China), and both have imposed stringent emissions standards on imported vehicles. Indian NGOs have been prominent in the climate negotiations, and research from India and China on climate change has been influential in understanding the impacts of climate change in those countries. There have been in recent years some signs that China is slightly more willing to talk about emissions targets, probably because of the co-benefits of clean energy technologies, and possibly as a means to distinguish itself from the USA in world affairs. Should China accept an emissions target under a post-Kyoto agreement this would significantly enhance the environmental effectiveness of the agreement, increase the pressure on the USA to join, and demonstrate to other developing countries that constraining emissions need not constrain growth.

China and India, along with the USA, Japan, Australia and South Korea, have formed a new multilateral initiative that seeks reductions in greenhouse gas emissions. Officially announced in July 2005, the Asia–Pacific Partnership on Clean Development and Climate (AP6) seeks 'to develop, deploy and transfer cleaner, more efficient technologies and to meet national pollution reduction, energy security and climate change concerns, consistent with the principles of the UNFCCC.' The group accounts for over 40% of global greenhouse gas emissions, close to half of world production, and 45% of the world's population. The AP6 does not set binding emission reduction targets as the Kyoto Protocol does, it includes some technologies that are much opposed in the United Nations climate regime such as carbon capture and storage, and civilian nuclear power, and it is poorly funded. It seems to most observers of climate geopolitics to be an attempt by Australia and the USA to create an alternative climate regime that competes with the UNFCCC for legitimacy, and as such it has not been well received by countries outside of the partnership.

The OPEC group are the most vociferously opposed to efforts to reduce greenhouse gas emissions. Its members are to varying degrees dependent on the sale of oil for revenue, and because oil consumption is responsible for a quarter of greenhouse gas emissions efforts to reduce emissions may reduce oil export revenues. OPEC have used the power of objection in the UNFCCC process frequently and largely effectively, including to delay progress on the implementation of funding for adaptation, which they have opposed until there is a parallel process to compensate them for potential losses in oil revenue (Barnett et al. 2004). Their frequent objections and obstruction in the UNFCCC process have alienated them from most other countries on the issue of climate change, although they still receive tacit support from the larger G77-China group because they are very influential within that group (since 1988, five of the ten presidents of the G77 came from OPEC member countries). On the basis of available evidence OPEC has nothing to fear from the Kyoto Protocol – as even their own modelling shows (Barnett *et al.*, 2004). The group is heavily influenced by Saudi Arabia, and Saudi Arabia appears to be heavily influenced by the same oil companies that effectively lobby the US government.

The interests of the AOSIS group are diametrically opposed to those of OPEC. The AOSIS countries are all highly vulnerable to the impacts of climate change. As such, they seek strong emission-reduction commitments and assistance for adaptation to the adverse effects of climate change. AOSIS has been influential in climate negotiations in part because it commands roughly 20% of votes in the United Nations System, and in part because it has exercised strong moral pressure on countries (Shibuya 1996). It can claim some success in the ultimate form of the Kyoto Protocol as its call for a 20% reduction in emissions set a moral standard that helped prevent a weaker Protocol from emerging. In the early days of climate negotiations, oil- and energy-intensive businesses opposed to reductions dominated the 'business' lobby in climate negotiations, and these companies continue to influence the policies of the USA and oil-exporting countries (Newell 2000). However, in more recent times, some large energy companies such as BP, and numerous local energy providers have embraced the potential for renewable energy sources and do not oppose, or are encouraging, measures to reduce greenhouse emissions from energy sources. The rising costs of insuring against hydro climatic disasters has seen insurance companies from around the world engage in lobbying, awareness-raising, coalition building for environmental NGOs, and the development of standards, tools and instruments for responding to climate change (Jagers and Stripple, 2003). They offer a 'business case' for strong action to reduce emissions that contrasts markedly with that of the oil companies. The insurance industry has been influential in EU climate policy, but less so in the USA and the developing world.

Environmental NGOs have and continue to play an important role in the development of the UNFCCC and the Kyoto Protocol. In the lead-up to Rio, they were actively involved in highlighting the need for a climate change convention, and they had some influence in the development of the convention itself. They have maintained a watching brief on the negotiations ever since, publicly criticizing those they perceive as acting in bad faith, and identifying existing and potential problems with policies and measures proposed in the convention. Where states are favourable to influence from NGOs they have had some influence on policy. However, where states are unfavourable – as in the USA – the efficacy of NGOs is marginal (Newell, 2000). The value of NGOs is in their ability to set norms that guide the regime, the way they maintain pressure for change and expose those that resist change, and their ability to connect the domestic and international politics that inform state action (Newell, 2000). While they do not have voting or veto power within the UNFCCC, they nevertheless do have power, and they offer an alternative site of climate governance that challenges the assumed hegemony of states in climate geopolitics.

The Hidden Agenda of International Negotiations

The only reason someone is negotiating with you is that you have a value which he wants. The more you can make that value visible, and make the negotiation pivot around it, the stronger your position will be. Almost every day at work, we are faced with some type of negotiation. Not only must we negotiate for our salary, perks, benefits, title, office space and support staff, but daily issues involving our duties, the need for increased manpower, authority over projects, flexibility with clients, arrangements, communication or sharing of the workload with co-workers; all require a form of negotiation, which, if we fail to recognize, we will, in all probability, fail to win.

Beneath the surface of all negotiations are "hidden agendas and masked assumptions", most of which are unfavorable to women. Women, generally, are expected to acquiesce, keep the peace, not make waves, and be the first to make concessions. Women need to learn not to buy into this self-defeating set of expectations. There are reasons women take home only seventy four cents for every dollar of men's take-home pay, and one of those reasons is that women accept the terms they are first offered and fail to negotiate for more, not only more salary, but more support, better hours, more flexibility, better travel conditions and office space.

In "The Shadow Negotiation," authors Deborah Kolb, Ph.D., and Judith Williams, Ph.D. point out that the results of failing to bargain hard and smart

" accumulate over time, widening a gap that is no longer measured in money alone." This gap can result in a woman not being given the resources or authority to allow her to succeed, and in being passed over for plum assignments, where she will gain visibility and recognition. The effects of acquiescing, rather than holding your opposition's feet to the fire, can snowball, not only becoming increasingly negative, as time goes by, but sending your career on a downward trajectory as well (http://www.advancingwomen.com/workplace/hidden_agendas_negotiate.html). Negotiating well is therefore really a matter of learning some basic techniques, bringing to bear all your observations and insights about the other parties, speaking up for yourself, and practicing every day, in every negotiation, no matter how small.

There has been a significant increase in international negotiations in the last two decades. In an increasingly Globalized world, more and more businesses are conducting business across borders. Negotiations preceded all international business transactions; sale of a product, formation of a joint venture, merger or acquisitions of companies abroad, or the licensing of the technology to or from a foreign firm. Negotiations are inevitable when a required outcome is impossible to obtain unilaterally without incurring unacceptable political, legal, or economic consequences. As a result, International negotiations are of significant importance to get an acceptable multinational business agreement.

The impact of international trade on U.S. economy has been well understood. The international trade affects all parts of the economy, with two-way trade in goods and services amounting to more than $81.6 trillion or nearly 25 percent of the U.S. GDP (Binnendijk, 1997). As a result, behavioral guidelines for effective cross-cultural negotiations have gained new importance. This paper explores the basic understanding cultural implications on cross-cultural negotiations. It has been observed that people tend to form a simplistic stereotypes for other cultures (Adler, 2000). While these stereotypes has its benefits when used carefully, there are several hidden challenges in cross-cultural challenges. This paper will examine some of the hidden dangers to cross-cultural negotiations arising from differences in governance and decision-making across cultures and explore means to overcome such barriers

Cultural Stereotypes

To succeed in these international negotiations, one needs to know how to communicate with and influence members of other cultures. In the last two decades, enormous research has been conducted on international negotiation styles. Several documents on negotiating with Chinese(Adler, 1992), Brazilians(Graham, 1986), Russians (Beliaev, 1985), Middle-eastern Arabs (Al-Ghamdi, 1999), Japanese (Blaker, 1977), Mexicans (Weiss, 1994) etc. have been published. In addition, Hofstede's studies (Hofstede, 1980) and classification of cultures based on: Uncertainty avoidance, Individualism—Collectivism, Masculine—Feminine, Power distance and Confucian dynamism. All these research and documents have created a stereotyping of negotiation styles of various cultures. Stereotyping a county or a culture can be useful or harmful depending on how it is used. For example, table-1 shows some of the typical stereotypes developed from various studies (Glenn, 1997).

However most people forget that stereotypes can be helpful or harmful depending how its used. Effective stereotyping allows people to a fast method to understand a new culture and act appropriately. To be useful, knowledge from a known stereotype should be used as a first best guess, when it is accurate and when it is descriptive rather than evaluative. However, most stereotypes carried in people's minds are inaccurate perceptions which are selectively learned and held rigidly (Ratiu, 1983).

Hidden Challenges

Cultural difference can disrupt international negotiations. But in the recent past, firms and organizations have invested in cross-cultural training for their executives and negotiators. Negotiators have learnt the do's and don't of a foreign culture and have become quite skillful at handling cultural etiquette. Obedience to these rules is not enough in International negotiations. The hidden challenges, such as knowing the important players, the negotiation process and negotiation approach to build consensus and shaping expectations, play a key role in having a successful negotiations.

Cultural differences can influence business negotiations in significant and unexpected ways, as many a hapless deal maker has learned. In some cases, it's a matter of ignorance or blatant disrespect, as with the American salesman who presented a potential Saudi Arabian client with a multimillion-dollar proposal in a pigskin binder, considered vile in many Muslim cultures. He was unceremoniously tossed out and his company blacklisted from working with Saudi businesses. But the differences can be much more subtle, arising from deep-seated cultural tendencies that influence how people interact—everything from how people view the role of the individual versus the group to their attitudes, say, about the importance of time or relationships. In response to these challenges, a great body of literature has emerged to help executives navigate differences not only in protocol and deportment but in deeper cultural tendencies as well (James K. Sebeneus: The Hidden Challenge of Cross-Border Negotiations-HBS, http://hbr.harvardbusiness.org/2002/03/the-hidden-challenge-of-cross-border-negotiations/ar/1)

Know the Players

The real purpose of the negotiation is to influence the organization, not just the negotiators. In international negotiations, an unfamiliar territory, it is difficult to know exactly who is involved and what roles they play. In all negotiations, there will be two sets of decision makers, formal decision makers and informal decision makers. Not all formal decision makers will be at the negotiating table and even experts sometimes fail to identify them as seen in the following examples.

Table 1: Some of the Typical Stereotypes

	US & Canada	Arabs	Russians
Primary Negotiating style & process	Factual appeals made to logic	Effective appeals made to emotions	Axiomatic appeals made to ideals
Conflict: Arguments countered with..	Objective facts	Subjective Feelings	Asserted Ideals
Making Concessions ?	Small Concessions made early to establish a relationships	Concessions made throughout the bargaining process	Few if any concessions are made. Concessions are seen as sign of weakness
? Response to counterparts concessions	Usually reciprocate counterpart's concession	Almost always reciprocate	Almost never reciprocate
Relationship ?	Short term	Long Term	No continuing relationships
Authority	Broad	Broad	Limited
Initial Position ?	Moderate	Extreme	Extreme
Deadline	Very important	Casual	Ignored

Source: Glen-1997—International Journal of Inter cultural Relations, 1997.

Formal decision makers

Consider a merger negotiation in United States, The key players will include the two firms, SEC, Department of Justice, the federal trade commission, European Union Trade commission and others. Similarly, while negotiating abroad there will be other important players. These other players may not be obvious to you. So one needs to take extra time to know who the players are.

For example, Consider GE's merger negotiation with Honeywell in 2002. GE suffered a humiliating defeat in part because GE's management underestimated the nature and seriousness of European Union's concerns about competitiveness and their potential to block the merger (Sebenius, 2002).

Knowing the key players also means to understand each player's role—who takes which decision. Not knowing the role of all the players can be a costly mistake—As discovered by Pirelli. Italian tyre maker Pirelli had gained control of the majority shares in Germany's Continental Gummiwerke. It even had approval from Deutsche bank and Gerald Schroder.

In a U.S. transaction, having majority shares is enough to acquire a company. But not in Germany. According to Germany's corporate governance rules, management board, shareholders, a supervisory board and labor have to agree for the merger or acquisition or any major decision. In addition, the labor union elects members to the supervisory board, which in turn elects the management board. The management board has powers to prevent any single shareholder from taking control over the company irrespective of the percentage of shares owned by that shareholder.

Pirelli failed to get a buy-in from labor and management board, thus it could not complete the acquisition even though it controlled majority of the shares.

These examples show the need to understand the deeply entrenched business structures while dealing with organizations abroad. Cultural and legal assumptions can sometimes make it difficult to recognize the other key decision makers.

Informal Decision Makers

These are really the "hidden" decision-makers in any negotiations, particularly in International negotiations. The informal decision makers may not have the legal right to affect the current negotiations but they wield enormous influence over the business. For example, *keiretsu* network in Japan, *Guanxi* (personal connections) in China, *Mafia* in Russia, etc. In addition, competitors from home country and in foreign country can influence the outcome of a negotiation. In many countries, the informal decision makers may have a greater influence than the actual parties making the deal. Outsiders need to understand who these players are and how to influence them.

For example, In 1994, Both Ford and GM were bidding to build an automobile factory in China. Ford appointed Jim Paulson as president of Ford in China. Paulson, an excellent engineer and had worked in several foreign countries. GM on other hand had appointed Shirley Young, a Shangai born executive, daughter of former Chinese ambassador to U.S. Even though Ford was ahead in the bidding phase, Young was able to secure the contract to GM in 1997. GM had won this negotiation primarily through good *Guanxi* brought in by Shirley Young. While Ford got bogged down in intellectual property right regulations in China (Graham *et al*, 2003).

In international negotiations, there will be a great gap between the laws on the books and the actual situation on the field. Frequently negotiators often underestimate the power of informal influences because they have the legal ability to enforce the contract. Successful international negotiations begin with identifying the key players who have formal and informal influence over the decision process. Develop a strategy to address their interests to reach a mutually agreeable negotiated settlement.

12. Ethical Dimension for negotiation in Food and Agriculture

Ethical Guidelines for Trade

An ethical discernment in the context of international trade must be based upon the principle of the inalienable value of the human person, source of all human rights and every social order. The human being must always be an end and not a means, a subject and not an object, not a commodity of trade. When placed at the service of human development, the international trade system works for people—persons and communities. Trade should benefit people, not just markets and economies. Economic freedom is only one element of human freedom and the economy is only one dimension of the whole of human activity. Economic life cannot be absolutized. Economic activities must be pursued within a broader context of human development, the promotion of human rights and especially overarching policies and targets aimed at eliminating poverty.

History demonstrates that ensuring some amount of free exchange of goods and services is indispensable for development and peace. However, neither free trade nor any set of rules are fair by themselves. Free trade can only be called such when it conforms to the demands of social justice and it is fair inasmuch as it allows developed and developing countries to benefit in the same way from the participation in the global trading system and enables them to foster the human development of each and all of its citizens. The prevailing of national interests in current trade negotiations, despite all the declarations of respect for the development targets of the poor countries, does not serve the idea of a "family of nations", which is by nature a community based on mutual trust, mutual support and sincere respect. In an authentic family the strong do not dominate; instead the weaker members because of their very weakness, are all the more welcomed and served.

Further, the concept of a "family of nations" calls forth an international collective responsibility for development and for the universal common good. This implies the obligation of the richer countries to tackle and remedy the shortcomings and less favorable conditions of poor countries as if these were internal problems of their own. Trade policy must be organized in such a way as to not be harmful to poor countries but as a contributory factor to their sustainable economic development. The amount and range of concessions should be proportional to the development level of countries, and not the contrary. In trade relations, the good of people cannot be finally achieved against the good of another people.

Ethics is concerned with norms of conduct, whether for persons, states, organizations, or other kinds of actors. In relation to public policy, ethical issues are problematic questions about what action should be taken by governmental agencies in particular kinds of situations relating to the public interest. The globalization of food and agriculture means that decisions made in one place are likely to have widespread impacts. Thus, there are not only separate national food and agriculture systems, but also a global system with its own dynamics. This global system needs to be studied, and it needs to be managed through appropriate measures of global governance.

A core ethical principle in public policymaking is that those who are likely to be affected by particular policies should have an opportunity to participate in their formulation. Meaningful participation is also a key element of good governance. Thus, to move toward good governance with regard to global issues relating to food and agriculture, it would be useful to create regularized institutional arrangements for carrying out dialogues among the concerned parties, with a view to formulating appropriate normative guidelines for dealing with these issues.

Agriculture remains a key sector of the world economy today. It accounts for 4 percent of world GDP and 9 percent of global merchandise exports, with developing countries responsible for about 60 percent and 40 percent of these figures, respectively. More precisely, agriculture provides for 12 percent of developing countries' GDP, more than 50 percent of their total employment, and 13 percent of their merchandise exports. While it has declined in relative importance in developed countries, the sector remains a key source of exports and significantly shapes domestic political agendas.

The social dimension of agriculture is as important as its economic dimension. Progress in poverty reduction and the fight against hunger hinge on successful rural and agricultural development policies, as well as trade reforms. Although the number of people living on less than US$1 a day declined from 40 to 21 percent of the population in developing countries between 1990 and 2001, there were still 1.1 billion poor people in 2001. About 70 percent of these poor lived in rural areas, relying heavily on agricultural activities for their livelihood. Moreover, despite sufficient food supplies worldwide, 840 million people were chronically undernourished in 2000 and 95 percent of them lived in developing countries.

Trade in food and agricultural raw materials amounted to US$552 billion in 2001, equivalent to 45 percent of total agricultural GDP. Yet, agricultural markets are affected by widespread distortions and market imperfections. The "disarray" observed in agricultural markets in the 1970s and 1980s has persisted up to now, with:

- High level of domestic support to agriculture, particularly to producers in member countries of the Organization for Economic Cooperation and Development (OECD);
- Secular declining trend and high volatility of agricultural prices; and
- Misallocation of resources and efficiency losses.

GATT rules have been largely ineffective in disciplining key aspects of agricultural trade, even after the Uruguay Round Agreement on Agriculture (URAA) in late 1994. However, the success of bringing agricultural policies into trade negotiations under the URAA, coupled with commitments to reduce export subsidies, domestic support and import duties on agricultural products, has created a negotiating framework conducive to future progress. Yet, developing countries have made significant progress in reducing, if not reversing, the negative protection of their agricultural sectors. Adjustment in OECD countries remains an issue. OECD support still accounted for nearly

50 percent of the total value of agricultural production in 2001, and prices received by OECD farmers were on average 31 percent above world prices in 2002 (Xavier Maret-http://assets.panda.org/downloads/ntoasummary.pdf).

In 2000, FAO Director-General Jacques Diouf established an independent Panel of Eminent Experts on Ethics in Food and Agriculture. Its mandate is to examine key ethical issues in food and agriculture, and to help raise the level of public awareness and debate. The panel, meeting for the first time at FAO headquarters in Rome in September 2000, agreed to focus initially on issues related to biotechnologies and genetically modified organisms. In the following year it released its study on *Ethical Issues in Food and Agriculture* (FAO Ethics 2001 a), and also its study on *Genetically Modified Organisms, Consumers, Food Safety, and the Environment* (FAO Ethics 2001b).

At its second meeting, held in Rome in March 2002, the panel decided to request an overview study on the ethical dimensions of the globalization of food and agriculture. This is that study. It was agreed that it would be framed as follows:

> The approach is to be based on the premise that ethical issues are about decisions for action relating to the public interest that are difficult to make. They may be difficult because they are about uncertainties within particular parties (dilemmas) or differences in preferences between parties (conflicts). The ultimate task is to find agreed principles to guide action relating to the ethical issue at hand.

There are many excellent analyses of the ethical issues relating to the globalization of food and agriculture (Dommen, 2002; FAO, 2002). However, so long as these views remain entrapped in documents, they are not very useful. There is a need for active and respectful engagement to creatively formulate new positions that transcend the contradictory positions held in the separate analyses.

The basic tool for dealing with ethical issues is meaningful participation by interested parties in formulating the principles that will guide policymaking. There may at times be sensible limits to participation. Criminals don't get to draft criminal codes. The need for dialogue in dealing with ethical issues converges with the need for open participation in good governance. The World Bank defines governance as "the manner in which power is exercised in the management of a country's economic and social resources for development (World Bank, 1992)." The principle tool of good governance is broad participation, based on open processes for arriving at agreed normative frameworks.

Procedures for the formulation of principles of the sort suggested here can be facilitated by the relevant governing agencies at any level. They already do that to some extent. For example, the Committee on General Principles of the Codex Alimentarius Commission is working on a *Code of Ethics for International Trade in Foods* (Codex, 2003), and discussions are being carried out through FAO on a proposed *Code of Conduct on Biotechnology as it Relates to Genetic Resources for Food and Agriculture* (Biocode, 2003). However, these are not regularized, broadly participatory, multi-party dialogues of the sort envisioned here.

FAO's ethics panel said, "It might be advisable to develop a code of conduct for economic globalization to avoid some of the negative consequences and to ensure a better and more equitable sharing of benefits for all (FAO Ethics, 2003)." While that is an intriguing idea, there are too many ethical dimensions to the globalization of food and agriculture to allow them all to be addressed adequately in a single code. Many codes are needed, and they should be elaborated and updated on a regular basis.

There is a need for a regular institutionalized process through which such codes can be designed and periodically refined. When the focus is on ethical issues that arise from globalization, processes that are global in scope are required. International agencies, acting on behalf of the international community, could facilitate these processes for arriving at relevant principles.

The United Nations System Standing Committee on Nutrition would be an appropriate venue for this work. SCN is the UN's designated body for coordination with respect to food and nutrition issues. It is comprised mainly of representatives of UN agencies concerned with food and nutrition, bilateral donors, and civil society. A new SCN Working Group on the Globalization of Food and Agriculture could be created to address the ethical issues. It could carry out this work in a systematic way, based on a carefully designed and agreed procedure for structuring the dialogue about the issues.

Alternatively, the Intergovernmental Working Group that is formulating voluntary guidelines on implementation of the right to food could be extended and adapted to address other issues, or a new body using similar procedures could be created. No matter which agency takes the lead, some institutional arrangement should be established to facilitate the systematic and sustained global dialogue that is needed to deal with the many ethical issues relating to the globalization of food and agriculture. That arrangement could provide the beginnings of the democratic global governance that is needed to address the issues.

13. Web-based Global Business Negotiation

Access to, and the ability to use computer and communication technologies varies widely between countries. It is often lack of proficiency rather than access that creates the barriers between developed and developing countries. The InterNeg Web site and its online systems INSPIRE and INSS, aim at overcoming these barriers by educating people around the world about decision and negotiation analysis and providing them with an opportunity to use decision support techniques. The systems allow one to conduct simulated negotiations with people from different cultures and solve realistic managerial decision problems (http://www.iiasa.ac.at/Admin/PUB/Documents/IR-98-049.pdf).

Policy makers and managers in developing countries face numerous new challenges in such diverse fields as labor management, international affairs, business relationships, and environmental regulations. Governments, judiciary, business and other organizations, and the public are breaking new grounds in decision processes related to the environment, ecology and policy making (Zartman, 1994). In most cases these decisions can only be made through negotiations which are one of the most common processes for making decisions and resolving conflicts at every organizational level. The old colonialist tradition was that it was up to the nobles and representatives of the rich and well educated to initiate interaction and to negotiate (Mumford, 1996). This tradition was based on the naive and a short-sighted assumption that those educated in Western universities were more competent to make decisions. Furthermore, it was assumed that the North (or West) knew more or was superior in all areas pertaining to governance, development, organization and business. The results of this tradition were also visible in negotiation behaviour, i.e., the assumption that there was no need for negotiations because one side knew what was good for the other. The second half of the twentieth century clearly showed how naive this approach was and how wrong its underlying assumptions were. It also showed that the past divisions and assumptions were inadequate and that business, educational, and other links now flow in all directions and not just from the developed to developing countries. These links are established by people and organizations from different cultures who have to negotiate among themselves.

There are similarities to every negotiations and also significant differences that recently have attracted more interest with the globalization of markets (Hofstede 1989; Adler 1993; Faure and Rubin 1993). With the increasing economic and political roles of developing countries studies were undertaken on similarities and differences between developing and developed countries in the process, context and form of negotiations (Graham 1993; Druckman *et al.*, 1976; Stone, 1989; Pechter, 1992). Cultural implications impact attitudes towards contracts, value for formality, and status in human relations in both the developing and developed countries (Swierczek, 1990). Pechter (1992), having analyzed more than fifty real life negotiations amongst Western and developing countries, states that the ethic of trust in most Asian countries is alloyed with an appreciation of shrewdness. While compromise is considered an appropriate outcome of negotiation in the Western world, it may often be considered defeat in Asian countries. These differences have significant implications for designing training programs that stress effective mediation. They also have to be considered in the construction of tools (including software) to provide with understanding of the valuation of the decision alternatives, assessment of concessions made by both sides, and the utility of a compromise in some situations.

Graham (1985, 1993), in his studies of negotiation styles of business people in various countries, observed that the Japanese offered more extreme initial offers, used the word "no" less frequently, were silent longer and used aggressive tactics only in later stages of negotiation. Brazilians' behavior in negotiation was characterized by more extreme first offers (even more extreme than those made by the Japanese), fewer promises and commitments, more commands, and longer interactions than exhibited by Americans in their negotiations.

The existing organizational and institutional structures in a developing country often do not provide support for negotiation efforts. In a developing country, the negotiators seldom have a past bargaining relationship or a history that establishes channels of communication. This may be a reason behind a less structured setting for resolving disputes and informal dispute settlement practices (Ghauri, 1988).

With an increase of international trade and shifting manufacturing from developed to developing countries there is an increased pressure on managers to engage in negotiations. This leads to growing interest in studying negotiation theory and practice, and cultural similarities and differences in decision-making. Studies have revealed that most developing countries lack negotiators capable of translating their own and their organizations principles and general goals into concrete bargaining proposals, and systems for widespread and efficient training of decision makers (Stubbs, 1984; Schermerhorn *et. al*, 1985; Ghauri, 1988). To bargain effectively, one must not only have the ability to articulate interests and bargaining positions, but also the skill to interpret and transmit bargaining communications to other negotiators. Similarly, one must now learn the opponent's mindset rooted in their national and organizational cultures.

While the abilities to understand and effectively communicate with counterparts from different cultures are critical to negotiations, they are also a known weakness. Feliciano (1990) states that developing countries do not have a long history of negotiations with other countries or with foreign corporations; and this situation has not changed significantly till today. "They generally lack cadres of experienced negotiators in their foreign offices, in their ministries of finance and of trade and industry, in their boards of investment, in their agencies charged with coordination and implementation of development work, and in their private sector." (Feliciano 1990, p. xxi). Language, customs and time zones also act as barriers to effective communication between the developing and developed worlds (Xing, 1995).

Negotiators from developing countries often rely, "more or less consciously, on confused, romantic notions of 'special' or 'historic relations' or shared 'fundamental interests', and feel grievously disappointed when such counterparts refuse to sacrifice their own interests and defer to the former's claims." (Feliciano,1990). They may also rely on the cultural differences and ignore the processual and analytical aspects that are similar to any negotiations. The concept of process in negotiation and negotiation analysis are complex issues that are being taught at universities and executive development courses. Training in negotiations at the university level was first introduced in the United States, and later spread to other parts of the world. In developing countries there are educational organizations with highly developed infrastructure. In most of them, however, the infrastructure is underdeveloped. Furthermore, the available infrastructure is often poorly utilized due to a lack of highly skilled instructors and missing elements (e.g., up-to-date teaching materials). These are some of the reasons that teaching negotiations to managers has been fraught with many problems.

The traditional tools for teaching negotiations are cases, experiments and simulations. These tools are often culture-specific, require highly skilled instructors, and organizational support. Their focus is often on the development of communication skills, situation assessment and evaluation. If they are used in conjunction with formal problem solving techniques and information and decision support tools, their effectiveness is greatly enhanced. This is the case in undergraduate and graduate management programs where negotiation courses are offered.

Rapid changes in communication patterns and an exponentially increasing number of new organizations that are engaged in electronic commerce and negotiations require changes in the traditional approach to teaching negotiations. One trend is to increase the cultural content and the other to enhance the analytical and technological aspects. Developing and sustaining programs that allow for teaching behavioral and organizational aspects of negotiation together with decision and negotiation analysis and computer-based support have been undertaken at American and European universities. These programs can be fully or partially offered via the Web and thus they have a very significant potential to alleviate some of the key difficulties that many instructors and students in developing countries face. The new trend in which negotiation analysis and negotiation support is being recognized as a significant component in negotiation teaching and training is the underlying concept behind the InterNeg project, the Web site and its Web-based support systems.

The Web and Negotiation Teaching and Training: A Case of INSPIRE

Technology is a critical resource that can eliminate some of the problems related to teaching and training of communication and negotiation in developing countries. Some of these technologies, being system independent (in terms of operation and maintenance), allow users from remote parts of the world to communicate and to use previously inaccessible resources. Widespread use of computer networks, especially Web-based systems, indicate that the information access barrier between the developing and developed worlds could be overcome.

The principal feature of the World Wide Web is that it provides people at different locations and time zones a communication medium that is rich in functionality, and gives them the ability to use previously inaccessible computational resources. While the Web's greatest use currently is as a powerful source and means for dissemination of information, it is increasingly being used as a means for remote execution and control of complete software systems, thus adding another dimension to the value it delivers. In education, its ability to access and run remote programs and databases allows users to extend classroom and laboratory boundaries across geographical and time zones. It thus allows instructors and students to retrieve and use resources from remote sites. This flexibility can nullify the effects of inequality between developing and developed country managers, policy makers and citizens by enhancing their ability to communicate, negotiate and participate in business and other activities.

These technologies allow rich communication amongst the actors in a negotiation, by virtue of computation-intensive techniques and visualization of data. The users can review the negotiation process and its dynamics. Language and other barriers shrink or disappear since these technologies allow extreme customization. User-specific front ends can be built which can be connected to the common core of the system, thus increasing participation while retaining functionality. The cost of duplicating a technological solution is another major factor that determines whether a particular solution can reach a larger population. Web browsers allow for portability and thus increase the access of the users in remote countries to training and real-life negotiations with minimal computing resources. These tools and systems are accessible to everyone, lay people and experts alike, and enable them to interact more directly with persons from different cultures, thus immensely reducing the effect of distances.

The flexibility of Web-based systems enables customization of the case material to reflect regional specifics. It is also easier to bring about a discipline based orientation in teaching and training sessions. The systems can be tailored to reflect, say, behavioral, decision theoretic or any other focus to suit the teaching and training needs. This is very useful for management teaching and training where different modules are combined to reflect a particular focus of the course. Web pages are very good at representing context, and independent Web pages may be assembled by a dispatching system that determines which page to present, based on a given situation. The InterNeg Web site and its Web-based system INSPIRE have been constructed to exploit these technologies and their use in teaching. They aim to provide people around the world with analytical knowledge and decision support techniques within the domain of negotiations. The INSPIRE system allows to analyze and solve real-like decision problems and conduct negotiations by people from different cultures.

The INSPIRE system is the first Web-based negotiation support system. It is based on analytical models rooted in decision and negotiation analysis (Kersten 1985; Kersten and Szapiro 1986; Rangaswamy and Shell 1994). Developed in the context of a cross-cultural study of decision-making and negotiation, the system has been primarily used to conduct and study negotiation via the World Wide Web as well as in teaching information systems, management science, international management and English as a second language.

Although INSPIRE has been implemented as an application accessible remotely over the Web, it is conceptualized as a client-side software assisting a negotiator, much like a traditional desktop application belonging to the negotiator, and communicating over the Internet with a similar "copy" of the software belonging to the other negotiator. The intention is to convey that INSPIRE does not act autonomously like a third party arbitrator; rather each "copy" acts entirely in support of a given negotiator. INSPIRE supports asynchronous negotiations, thus ameliorating the time zone problem. To facilitate this type of negotiations the system saves the state resulting from each user's actions in a form that can be retrieved when the counterpart logs on some time later (Kersten and Noronha, 1997). INSPIRE views negotiation as a process involving three stages: pre-negotiation, conduct of negotiation and post-settlement. The first stage involves understanding of the negotiation problem, issues and options and preference elicitation through hybrid conjoint analysis. This allows one to obtain a rating for every possible offer. The second stage involves support for offer construction and counter offer evaluation, and finally, the last stage involves computation of possible offers that dominate the most recent compromise and re-negotiation. Details of the methodology and the system's architecture can be found in Kersten and Noronha, (1998) and at http://interneg.org/.

The system can be used to conduct multiple bilateral negotiations. The most commonly used case involves trade negotiations between two companies: Itex, a producer of bicycle parts and Cypress Cycles, which builds bicycles. To reflect the dynamics of negotiation in developing countries, we have developed cases about negotiations for international technology transfer and for the sustainable development of natural resources.

The increasing number of international negotiations involving multiple languages has triggered a growing reliance on computer-based multilingual support. Whereas empirical studies on negotiation support systems (NSS) have shown that NSS generally improve negotiation performance, very few NSS exist that cater for multilingual negotiations. With multilingual support, international negotiators of different language backgrounds are expected to address communication barriers and problems. This study involves the development of an NSS prototype with multilingual support as well as a laboratory experiment to examine the efficacy of such support on six important negotiation outcome variables (individual outcome, joint outcome, equality of outcome, time to settlement, satisfaction with process and satisfaction with outcome). Findings suggested significant effects of NSS support on individual outcome and joint outcome. Multilingual support helped to improve equality of outcome (under qualified conditions), but the time taken was significantly longer. The paper underlines the possibility and significance of computer-based multilingual support to address diverse linguistic groups in global negotiation context (http://portal.acm.org/citation.cfm?id=1451125).

Enhancing Decision and Negotiation Support in Enterprise Networks Through Semantic Web Technologies

The SEWASIE project within the Semantic Web Action Line of the European IST Programme focuses on the question how to assist networks of small and medium enterprises (so-called Integrated Economies) in enhancing their intra- and inter-organizational information management capabilities. While the project also includes novel techniques for semantic enrichment, query management, and presentation techniques in multi-lingual information acquisition from the web, this paper addresses the question how to further exploit the acquired information; firstly, by linking it into more established decision support environments based on OLAP technologies; secondly, by using it as a basis to engage in negotiations concerning inter-organizational cooperation across European countries (schoop@cs.rwth-aachen.de).

Small and Medium Enterprises (SMEs). SMEs are often organized in industrial districts, i.e. sectarian and regional clusters, for social and historical reasons. In times of globalization this structure causes severe vulnerability. In order to compete in a global market it is thus vital for European enterprises to form strategic alliances. Even in a regional context, many studies show the need for cooperation competence development as a prerequisite of success, and a number of analysis and support techniques have been developed. At a European level, many additional issues arise, of which we focus on the information and communication aspects. In particular, these include finding the right partner who brings in suitable products, methods, partnerships, or customer networks – or to be found by customers and potential strategic partners to prepare for business interactions leading to a deal. Cooperation also requires significant additional capabilities of financial information management, using not only internal accounting data but also external information sources to retain financial stability in a rapidly changing world. Last not least, it requires trustworthy and cost-effective means of entering into actual business, usually via a negotiation process (http://www.sewasie.org/documents/xsw2002.pdf).

The European SEWASIE project investigated the applicability of Semantic Web and Agent Systems in such Integrated Economies. Generally speaking, SEWASIE strives for methods and tools that provide sophisticated and integrated retrieval, brokering, and communication services for business-related information based on semantic web technology. These methods will be demonstrated in the context of a large network of small and medium enterprises surrounding the fashion industry in Northern Italy.

Starting from carefully managed *domain ontologies*, the first step in constructing a distributed network of *intelligent information sources* is to semantically enrich the data sources by intelligent agents. Furthermore, the SEWASIE project will develop a *query management component* that is able to detect which data sources are able to provide answers to a query. In addition, the query manager will combine the results from different sources and present to the user an integrated and reconciled representation of the answer via a *user interface*. A specific focus will be a user-friendly and application effective interaction environment, not only for the end users, but also for the information administrators who manage domain ontologies exploiting description logic technologies.

As in other Semantic Web approaches (e.g. [DM+01, MS+01]), XML technologies such as RDF, XML Schema, or XML Query will play a central role in the SEWASIE project. These standards will be mainly used to describe and exchange data in the distributed network of agents and data sources. However, in the user interface, the corporation will focus on an understandable and meaningful representation of the data that encapsulates the technical complexity of the core of the system. On the other hand, data sources that provide data in XML format are rare. Therefore, the system must be able to access heterogeneous sources that may have many different physical access methods and different logical representations of data.

However, as indicated above, acquiring and representing information in this manner is not enough to gain a business advantage from the usage of Semantic Web technologies. On the one hand, the external information collected via the web must be integrated with company-internal information, re-targeted and personalized to the right people within a participating organization. On the other hand, these people might not only need this information for company-internal analysis and decision-making but often wish to use it in a seamless manner to engage in communication and negotiation with other companies. This value-adding process of (internal) decision support (via a *brokering agent*) and (external) negotiation support (via a *negotiation agent*) beyond the information search task is the focus of the present paper. Altogether, the resulting system aims at helping European SMEs to find the right strategic information at the right time in a multinational environment; provide advanced and novel services for monitoring and linking information in the context of risk management and competitor analysis; and provide ontology-based communication mechanisms for negotiation in multi-language environments.

Structured Web-Based Negotiation

A business interaction in a B2B network of SMEs usually follows a three-phase pattern. Starting with a search for business partners, contract conditions are negotiated before the contracted task is executed and monitored for contract fulfillment. A semantic search engine using business ontologies enables efficient search using the ontological structures. Most approaches are not concerned with the communication about these structures with the aim of knowledge sharing and knowledge transfer. approach will be concerned with structured web-based communication exemplified for electronic negotiations in e-commerce. The search and negotiation phase of a business transaction will be combined through the continued usage of search results and ontologies in the communication/ negotiation phase. A typical scenario would be a fashion designer configuring a vision of fabrics, colouring, and production technologies from a multitude of highly specialized potential and actual suppliers, each with their specific capabilities, reputations, idiosyncrasies, interests and business conditions.

A negotiation support tool will be developed using speecn act elements and deontic logics in addition to ontologies for structured messages exchange (in XML) between human agents. Communication agents are also integrated for use in the early phases of electronic commerce. The negotiation process will be structured as follows. The early phases of a negotiation will be conducted by intelligent software agents. Based on the search results that will provide information about the desired services or products and the related provider or information about possible customers, these agents will find out details about potential partners, ask for references, ask for preliminary quotations, contact the companies etc. Thus, the informal part of any negotiation can be conducted by such agents after which a human negotiator then takes over and is efficiently supported by the communication tool.

The next step is that of serious negotiations performed by human agents. Based on the reaction of the business partners, complex negotiations will be conducted directly between representatives of the related companies, supported by an integrated system of structured message exchange and efficient document management. Each interaction is performed via a structured message that then leads to a document representing a contract version. The structure is based on speech act terms and deontic logic to ensure unambiguous interactions. For example, each message has a message type that specifies the illocution of the exchange to make it clear to all partners involved how a particular utterance is meant, e.g. as a mere request or as a formal offer. Communication problems are also due to problematic message contents. In order to avoid such problems, the novelty of ontology-based negotiations will be developed. The propositional content of each message is linked to the business ontology, i.e. the user can use the ontological terms and relations for the message content. On the other hand, the message exchange enables an extension of already defined ontological elements to account for the fact that each negotiation is different and that there are many contexts that require specific contractual terms.

Therefore, the message exchange is semi-structured by providing a message structure (e.g. illocution, negotiation protocol, the related obligations) and a propositional content that can use the business ontologisms for communicating while enabling user-driven extensions to the propositional structures. By aiming for semi-structured message content, the communication partners are, on the one hand, able to refer to shared ontologies and thus to be able to express themselves in an unambiguous way and to avoid many terminological problems while, on the other hand, the problems associated with rigorous forms and templates in human interaction are avoided. Reasoning mechanisms will be developed that are able to reason about the structure (e.g. a directive commits the recipient to the action specified), content (e.g. this offer is unsatisfactory in the current context due to a lack of resources), and interrelations of negotiations.

References

A cuff, Frank L. (1997), How to Negotiate Anything with Anyone Anywhere around the World, New York: American Management Association.

Adair *et al.* Negotiating Behavior When Cultures Collide: The United States and Japan. *Journal of Applied Psychology,* Vol. 86(3), June 2001

Agency for International Trade Information and Cooperation (AITIC): http://www.acici.org/aitic/index.html

Agreement on Agriculture- AoA (2003), World Trade Organization, *The Uruguay Round Reform Program for Trade in Agriculture* (Geneva: WTO, 2003).

Adler, Nancy (1997), *International Dimensions of Organizational Behavior (3rd Ed.),* Cincinnati, OH: South-Western College Publishing, 1997, p. 217.

Andrew Elek-Crisis & Reinventing WTO Negotiation- http://www.eastasiaforum.org/2009/04/15/the-crisis-and-reinventing-wto-negotiations

A Note by the UNCTAD Secretariat: http://commerce.nic.in/wto_counsel_paper.htm

Anonymous (1983), *Negotiating with the Americans,* Disseminated by James T. Felicita, Head of contract systems for NASA Systems Division, Hughes Aircraft Co. March 1983

AAhad M. Osman-Gani & Joo-Senf Tan. "Influence of Culture on Negotiation Styles of Asian Managers" Thunderbird International Business Review, December 2002

Adair *et al.* Negotiating Behavior When Cultures Collide: The United States and Japan, *Journal of Applied Psychology.* Vol. 86(3), June 2001.

Adler, N.J. (1993). "Do Cultures Vary?" in: Societal Culture and Management, T.D.

Adler, N.J. and J.L. Graham (1989), "Cross Cultural Interaction: The International Comparison Fallacy?", *Journal of International Business Studies,* 20 (3), 515-537.

Adler, Nancy (1997), International Dimensions of Organizational Behavior (3rd Ed.,) Cincinnati, OH: South-Western College Publishing, 1997, p. 217.

Adler, Nancy J. "International Dimensions of Organization Behavior" South-Western, 2000.

Adler, Nancy J. and Graham, John L., "Strategy Implementation: A comparison of face-to-face negotiations in the People's Republic of China," *Strategic Management Journal,* Vol. 13, No. 7, 1992, pp. 449-466.

Alfredo C. Robles, Jr. (2005), "The Asia-Europe Meeting (ASEM): The Theory and Practice of Inter-regionalism", 2005, pp. 271-81 (Unpublished manuscript, De La Salle University).

Al-Ghamdi, Salem M. (1999), "Success and Failure in Saudi-American Negotiations: American Views," *International Negotiation,* Vol. 4 no.1 1999, pp.23-36

Armstrong, Robert W. and Sweeney, Jill (1994), "Industry Type, Culture, Mode of Entry and Perceptions of International Marketing Ethics Problems: A Cross-Cultural Comparison", *Journal of Business Ethics*, 13(10), 1994, 775-785.

Article 10 of TRIPS- http://www.wto.org/english/tratop_e/trips_e/t_agm3_e.htm

Arun Kottoli: http://arunkottolli.blogspot.com/2007/01/how-to-avoid-pitfalls-in-cross.htm

ASEAN-EU Vision Group (2006), "Report of the ASEAN-EU Vision Group: Transregional Partnership for Shared and Sustainable Prosperity," Hà Nôi, Viêt Nam, 10 May 2006, §§3.1-3.3, pp. 7-8.

Asia-Europe Vision Group Report, 1999: http://www.mofa.go.jp/POLICY/economy/asem/asem2/vision.html

Aslam, Malik Amin *et. al.* (2001), Greenhouse Gas Market Perspectives: Trade and Investment Implications of the Climate Change Regime. UNCTAD/DITC/TED/Misc.9 (Geneva: United Nations, July 2001), http://www.unctad.org/ghg/Publications/Manual_draft.PDF

Aspect of Transparency under GATS: http://www.wto.org/gatt_docs/English/SULPDF/92020181.pdf

Bagozzi, Richard P (1995), "Reflections on Relationship Marketing in Consumer Markets", *Journal of the Academy of Marketing Science*, 23(4), 1995, 272-277

Baier, S.L, and J.H. Bergstrand (2005), "Do Free Trade Agreements Actually Increase Member's International Trade," Federal Reserve Bank of Atlanta Working Paper 2005–3

Banas, J.T. & Parks, J.M (2002), "Lambs among Lions? The Impact of Ethical Ideology on Negotiation Behaviors and Outcomes," International Negotiation, 7, 2002, 235-260.

Bang, G., Heggelund, G., and Vevatne, J. (2005), Shifting strategies in the climate negotiations. FNI

Barnett, J. (2001), The meaning of environmental security. London: Zed Books.

Barnet, J. (2003), Security and climate change. Global Environmental Change 13 (1), pp. 7-17.

Barnett, J., Dessai, S., and Webber, M (2004), Will OPEC lose from the Kyoto Protocol? Energy Policy 32 (18), pp. 2077–2088.

Barnett, J., and Adger, N. (2007), Climate change, human security and violent conflict, Political Geography 26 (6): 639–655.

Bartels, Robert (1967), "A Model for Ethics in Marketing", *Journal of Marketing*, 31(1), 1967, 20-26.

Basic Provisions of Trade agreement: http://www.nlc.org/assets/3f3c00db0d8c42bcbb28c3dc5794fdd3/ipissuepapertrade041406.pdf

Baysan, T., A. Panagariya, and N. Pitigala, 2006, "Preferential Trading in South Asia," World Bank Policy Research Working Paper No. 3813 (Washington: World Bank).

Beliaev, E (1985), "Understanding Cultural Environment: U.S.A- U.S.S.R. Trade Negotiation," *California Management Review*, Vol. 27 no. 2 1985, pp.100-112

Bergsten, C.F. (1997). 'Open Regionalism.' In: Bergsten, C.F. (ed.), Whither APEC? - The progress to Date and Agenda for the Future, Washington, D.C., Institute for International Economics.

Bilaterals http://www.bilaterals.org/

Binnendijk, H. (1997), National Negotiating Styles. Center for the Study of Foreign Affairs, Foreign Service Institute, U.S. Department of State, Washington, D.C., 1997.

Biocode (2003), Food and Agriculture Organization of the United Nations, *Draft Code of Conduct on Biotechnology as it Relates to Genetic Resources for Food and Agriculture* (Rome: FAO, 2003). http://www.fao.org/ag/cgrfalbiocode.htm

Blaker, M *Japanese International Negotiating Style* New York: Columbia University Press 1977

Blanchard, K., and Peale, N. V (1988), The Power of Ethical Management, New York: William Morrow and Company, Inc., 1988.

Boudria, J., et al. (2002), The potential contribution of renewable energy in air pollution abatement in China and India. *Energy Policy* 30 (5), pp. 409–424.

Brauch, H. (2002), Climate change, environmental stress and conflict. In: Federal Ministry for the Environment, Nature Conservation and Nuclear Safety (eds) Climate change and conflict. Can climate change impacts increase conflict potentials? What is the relevance of this issue for the international process on climate change? Berlin, Germany

Brod, S.E.t and M. Tuchinsky (2000),Working together but in opposition: An examination of the "goodcop/bad-cop" negotiating team tactic. Organizational Behavior and Human Decision Processes,(2000), *81*, 155-177.

Federal Ministry for the Environment, Nature Conservation and Nuclear Safety, pp. 9-112.

Brett, J.F., Northcraft, G.B., & Pinkley, R.L. (1999), Stairways to heaven: An interlocking self-regulation model of negotiation, *Academy of Management Review, 24*, 452-471

Brett *et al.* From Adair *et al.* (2001),Negotiating Behavior When Cultures Collide: The United States and Japan. *Journal of Applied Psychology,* Vol. 86(3), June 2001

Brodt, S.E.t and M. Tuchinsky (2000), Working together but in opposition: An examination of the "goodcop/bad-cop" negotiating team tactic. Organizational Behavior and Human Decision Processes, (2000), *81*, 155-177.

Busby, J. (2006), Climate change and collective action: troubles in the transition to a post-oil Economy, St. Antony's International Review 2 (1), pp. 35–55

Byrne, J.A (1988), "Businesses Are Signing Up for Ethics 101," Business Week, February 15, 1988, pp. 56-57.

Byrne, Gabriel J. and Bradley, Frank (2007), "Culture's Influence on Leadership Efficiency: How Personal and National Cultures Affect Leadership Style", *Journal of Business Research*, 60(2), 2007, 168-175.

CalPERS- http://www.mckinseyquarterly.com/Governance/Boards/Governing_joint_ventures_1586// http://www.calpers-governance.org/docs-sof/marketinitiatives/2009-03-26-joint-venture-governance-guidelines.pdf

Cao, L. (ed.) (2001), Business English for Negotiation. Foreign Language Teaching and Research Press

Carnevale, P.J. (1995), "Property, Culture and Negotiation", in R.M. Kramer and D.M

Cassell, E.J (1989), "Ethics in Medical Education," *Journal of Continuing Education in the Health Professions*, 9, No. 4 (1989): 225-228.

Centre for Economic Policy Research (CEPR): http://www.cepr.org/PUBS/bulletin/meets/2209.htm

Centre for Global Negotiations -http://enewschannels.com/2008/03/07/enc2733_053940.php

Centre for Socio-Economic Development (CSEND)-http://www.csend.org

Charnovitz, S. (2002) 'Improving the Agreement on Sanitary and Phytosanitary

Standards', in G. Christie, P. Maria Joseph, Kwon, Ik-Whan G., Stoeberl, Philip A. and Baumhart, Raymond (2003), "A Cross-Cultural Comparison of Ethical Attitudes of Business Managers: India, Korea and the United States", *Journal of Business Ethics*, 46, 2003, 263-287.

Codex (2003), Codex Alimentarius Commission, *Proposed Draft Revised Code of Ethics for International Trade in Foods*, (Rome: Joint FAO/WHO Food Standards Programme, Codex. Committee on General Principles, April 2003). http://www.fao.org/docrep/meeting/005/x7e/x7e0b.htm

Conca, K. (2006). Governing water: contentious transnational politics and global institution building. Cambridge, MA: MIT Press.

D. Keltner and A.M. Kring (1998), Emotion, Social Function, and Psychopathology. *Review of General Psychology*, (1998), 2, 320-342.

Dahl, Stephan (2004), "Intercultural Research, the Current State of Knowledge" in Middlesex University", Discussion Series, 2004

Dalby, S. (2002), Environmental security, Minneapolis, MN: University of Minnesota Press.

David A. Lax and James K. Sebenius (1991), "Interests: The Measure of Negotiation." In *Negotiation Theory and Practice*, eds. J. William Breslin and Jeffrey Z. Rubin, (Cambridge: The Program on Negotiation at Harvard Law School, 1991), 165

Davis Langdon's 'International Procurement Group'-International Procurement: http://www.davislangdon.com/upload/images/publications/USA/International%20Procurement%20Series%202_All%20Articles.pdf

Deborah Kolb and Judith Williams - "The Shadow Negotiation", http://www.advancingwomen.com/workplace/hidden_agendas_negotiate.html

Dennis Lock: The Gower handbook of management; Gower Publishing Company & P.D.V. Marsh-Gower's Contract Negotiation Handbook (3 rd Edition):

Deresky, H. (1996). International Management: Managing across borders and cultures: http://www.toodoc.com/International-Management-Managing-Across-Borders-and-Cultures-pdf.html

DilploFoundation -http://www.diplomacy.edu/

Diplomacy in Negotiation: http://www.commercialdiplomacy.org/manuals/trade_negotiations.htm

Dominique Burlone: http://www.apeccp.org.tw/doc/Canada/Policy/1b.htm

Dommen, Caroline (2002), "Raising Human Rights Concerns in the World Trade Organization: Actors, Processes and Possible Strategies," *Human Rights Quarterly*, Vol. 24 (2002), pp. 1-50.

Deresky, H. (1996), *International Management: Managing across borders and cultures*

Druckman, D., A.A. Benton, F.Ali, and Bagur, J.S. (1976), "Cultural Differences in Bargaining Behaviour: India, Argentina, and the United States", *Journal of Conflict Resolution*, 20(3), 413-452.

Dupont, A., and Pearman, G. (2006), Heating up the planet: climate change and security. Lowy Institute Paper 12, Double Bay, NSW: The Lowy Institute.

Earthscan van Ireland, E., *et al.* (1996). Climate change: socio-economic impacts and violent conflict. Report No. 410 200 006. Wageningen, The Netherlands: Dutch National Research Programme on Global Air Pollution and Climate Change.

Eaton J.W. and D.J. Eaton (1996) Negotiation Strategies in Trans-boundary Water Disputes In:

Trans-boundary Water Resources Management: Institutional and Engineering Approaches, pp. 37-45, NATO ASI Series, Springer-Verlag, Heidelberg, Germany.

Ecologist (1993), "Cakes and Caviar: The Dunkel Draft and Third World Agriculture," The Ecologist, Vol. 23, No. 6 (November-December 1993), p. 220.

Economic Diplomacy: http://textus.diplomacy.edu/textusBin/BViewers/oview/EconomicDiplomacy/oview.asp

Economic Negotiation Network: http://www-rcf.usc.edu/~enn/

Elahee, M. and Brooks, C.M. (2004), "Trust and negotiation tactics: perceptions about business-to-business negatiations in Mexico", *The Journal of Business and Industrial Marketing*, 19(6), 2004, 397-404.

European Commission Doc SEC (2006), 1230 (4 October 2006), Commission Staff Working Document, Annex to the Communication from the Commission to the Council, the European Parliament, the European Economic and Social Committee and the Committee of the Regions, "Global Europe: Competing in the World: A Contribution to the EU's Growth and Jobs, Strategy," pp. 14, 16

European Commission Doc. COM (2003), 399/4, "Communication from the Commission, A New Partnership with Southeast Asia"

FAO (2000), Food and Agriculture Organization of the United Nations, Commodities and Trade Division, *Agriculture Trade and Food Security: Issues and Options in the WTO Negotiations, Country Case Studies* (Rome FAO, 2000). http://www.fao.org/DOCREP/003/X8731e/x8731e00.htm

FAO (2002a), Food and Agriculture Organization of the United Nations, *The State of Food Insecurity in the World* (Rome: FAO, 2002). http://www.fao.org/docrep/005/y7352e/y7352e00.htm

FAO (2002b), Food and Agriculture Organization of the United Nations, *FAQ Papers on Selected Issues Relating to the WTO Negotiations on Agriculture,* (Rome: FAO, 2002).

FAO (2002c), Food and Agriculture Organization of the United Nations, Summary of Proceedings: Measurement and Assessment of Food Deprivation and under nutrition: *International Scientific Symposium, Rome, 26-28 June 2002*. (Rome: FAO, 2002). http://www.fao.org/docrep/005/y4250E/y4250E00.htm

FAO - Regionalism & Food Security- http://www.fao.org/docrep/004/y4793e/y4793e09.htm

FAO Ethics (2001), Food and Agriculture Organization of the United Nations, *Genetically Modified Organisms, Consumers, Food Safety and the Environment*, (Rome: FAO Ethics Series 2, 2001)

Faure, G. O. and J. Z. Rubin (1993), "Culture and Negotiation", *Negotiation Journal*, 9(4), 380-381.

Feliciano, F.P. (1990), "Foreword: Process and Culture in Development Negotiations: The management of Consent", in R.B. Sunshine, Negotiating for International Development, Dordrecht: Martinus Nijhoff Publishers.

Fen May Lieu and Chih-Pin Huang (2008), Automated Approach to Negotiations of BOT Contracts with the Consideration of Project Risk; J. Constr. Engrg. and Mgmt. Volume 134, Issue 1, pp. 18-24, 2008

Feridhanusetyawan, T., (2005), "Preferential Trade Agreements in the Asia-Pacific Region," IMF Working Paper No. 05/149 (Washington: IMF).

Ferrell, O.C., Gresham, L. and Fraedrich, J. (1989), "A Synthesis of Ethical Decision Models for Marketing", *Journal of Macro-marketing*, 9(2), 1989, 55-64

Financial Review-November 21, 1989

Fisher and Ury (1981) in Chapter 1 of *Getting to Yes*, Roger Fisher and William Ury, *Getting to Yes: Negotiating Agreement Without Giving In*. (New York: Penguin Books, 1981), 5.

Fisher, R. and Ury (1981), *Getting to Yes* Boston: Houghton Miffin, and New York: Penguin, 1981

Fisher, R. (1999), Negotiating Inside Out, in J.W. Breslin & J.Z. Rubin (Eds.), Negotiation Theory and Practice, 1999, pp. 71-79.

Fisher, R. and S. Brown (1988), Getting Together: Building Relationships As We Negotiate, 1988, New York: Penguin Books.

Fisher, M.M., and Raper, R. F (1990),"Withdrawing and Withholding Treatment in Intensive Care, Part 1, Social and Ethical Dimensions," *Medical Journal of Australia* 153 (August 20, 1990): 217-219.

Fisher, Roger, and Ury, William, with Bruce Patton (1991), Getting to Yes: Negotiating Agreement Without Giving In, 2nd ed. Boston: Houghton Mifflin.

Flory, J.H. and Kitcher, P. (2004), Global health and the scientific research Agenda, Fillos Public Aff- 2004, Winter; 32 (1):36-65.

Ford, John B., LaTour, M.S., Vitell, S.J. and French, W.A (1997), "Moral Judgment and Market Negotiation: A Comparison of Chinese and American Managers", *Journal of International Marketing*, 5(2), 1997, 57-76.

Francis, J.N.P. (1991), "When in Rome? The effects of Cultural Adaptation on Intercultural Business Negotiations", *Journal of International Business Studies*, 22, 403-428.

Frey, F.W. (1984) Middle East water: the potential for conflict or cooperation. In Naff T. and Matson, R.C. (eds.) *Water in the Middle East*, pp. 180-198, Westview Press, Boulder, Co

Ganulis, J (2004), Water Resource Management and Environmental Security in Mediterranean Trans-boundary River Basins, UNESCO Chair for Water,Laboratory of Hydraulics, Department of Civil Engineering,Aristotle University of Thessaloniki, 54124 Thessaloniki, GREECE (In: Linkov, I. ed. (2004) "The Role of Risk Assessment in Environmental Security and Emergency Preparedness in the Mediterranean Region." Kluewer, Amsterdam.).

Gerry & Elizabeth Wilson: The University of Calgary-Communication & culture- http://jmm.aaa.net.au/articles/85.htm

Gower's handbook of management; Dennis Lock, Gower Publishing Company, 3 rd Edition, 2001

G. Loewenstein and J. S. Lerner (2003),The role of affect in decision making, In R. J. Davidson (Ed), Handbook of affective sciences (pp. 619-642), Cary, NC: Oxford University Press, 2003.

Ghauri, P.N. (1988), "Negotiating with Firms in Developing Countries: Two Case Studies", *Industrial Marketing Management*, 17(1), 49-53.

Ghauri, P. and Usunier, J-C. (1996), International Business Negotiations, Great Britain, Redwood Books Ltd

Ghauri, P.N. (1996). Introduction, Pp. 3-20 in P.N. Ghauri & J.C. Usunier (Eds.), Global Business Negotiation, Elsevier Publication, The Netherlands.

Ghoshal, Sumantra, Piramal, Gita and Budhiraja, Sudeep (2001), "World Class in India" *Peguin Books India Ltd*, 2001

Gleditsch, N.P. (1998), Armed conflict and the environment: a critique of the literature. Journal, International Peace Research Institute, Oslo (PRIO) & Norwegian University of Science and Technology, Trondheim: http://jpr.sagepub.com/cgi/content/abstract/35/3/381

Global Trade Negotiations Homepage http://www.cid.harvard.edu/cidtrade/

Graham, J. L. (1985), "The Influence of Culture on the Process of Business Negotiations: An Exploratory Study", *Journal of International Business Studies*, 16(1), 81-96

Graham, John L (1986), "Across the Negotiating Table from the Japanese," International Business Review, Autumn, 1986, PP.58-70

Graham, Sano, and March (1994), Negotiating Behaviors in Ten Foreign Cultures. *Management Science*, Vol. 40(1), January 1994.

Graham, John L and Lam, Mark N (2003), "The Chinese Negotiation" *Harvard Business Review*, October 2003

Grubb, M., Vrolijk, C., and Brack, D. (1999), The Kyoto protocol: a guide and assessment. London: Royal Institute of International Affairs and Earthscan

Google's Strategic Negotiation: http://www.google.com/support/jobs/bin/answer.py?answer=162304

Gulbro, R., & Herbig, P. (1995) Differences in cross-cultural negotiation behavior between industrial product and consumer product firms, *Journal of Business & Industrial*, Gulf Publishing Company. 1991.

Gupta, J. (1997), The climate change convention and developing countries: from conflict to consensus? : http://www.flipkart.com/climate-change-convention-developing-countries/0792345770-y6w3fkakob

Handley, P.(1997), BOT Privatization in Asia: Distorted goals and process, *Working Paper No.82*, National Library of Australia.

Hartmann, B. (2001). Will the circle be unbroken? A critique of the project on environment, population, and security, In: Peluso, N. and Watts, M. (eds) Violent environments. London: Cornell University Press, pp. 39–62.

Harvard Business Essentials 'Negotiation' Harvard Business School Press, (2003), USA.

Harvard Business School (2003) Negotiation, HBS Press, 2003, USA

Hendon, Donald, Hendon, R.A. and Herbig, P. (1996), Cross-Cultural Business Negotiations, Westpost, CT: Quorum.

Hertsgaard, Mark (2001). "Bush and Global Warming," *The Nation* 10 Dec 2001: 5-6.

Hilaire, Alvin and Yongzheng Yang (2003), The United States and the New Regionalism/Bilateralism, IMF Working Paper, Oct. 2003, 8 Maxey/ Macor 11

Hilty, JJ and P. Carnevale (1993), "Black-hat/White-hat" strategy in bilateral negotiation, Organizational Behavior and Human Decision Processes, (1993), *55*, 444–469.

Hofstede, G. (1980), Culture's Consequences, Sage Publications, London, UK.

Hofstede, Geert, Culture's Consequences: International Differences in Work-Related Values, Beverly Hills, CA: Sage, 1980.

Hofstede, Geert, "Motivation, Leadership, and Organization: Do American Theories Apply Abroad?" *Organizational Dynamics* Summer 1980.

Hofstede, G. (1989), "Cultural Predictors of Negotiation Styles", in Mauter-Markhof, Process of International Negotiations, Westview Press, 193-201.

Hofstede, G. (1991) Cultures and Organizations: Software of Mind. McGraw-Hill

Hofstede, Geert. Cultures' Consequences, Comparing Values, Behaviors, Institutions, and Organizations across Nations, Thousand Oaks, CA: Sage Publications, 2001.

Hofstede, Geert: Culture is more often a source of conflict than of synergy. Cultural differences are a nuisance at best and often a disaster." Maastricht University. (http://www.geert-hofstede.com/

Holden, Nigel (2002), Cross-cultural Management: A Knowledge Management Approach, Harlow: Prentice Hall – Financial Times, 2002.

Homer-Dixon, T. (1999), Environmental scarcity and violence, Princeton, NJ: Princeton University Press.

Horrocks, I. (2000), The Semantic Web: The Roles of XML and RDF, IEEE Internet Computing, 4(5), pp. 63-74, 2000.

Hovi, J., Skodvin, T., and Andresen, S (2003), The persistence of the Kyoto Protocol: why other annex I countries move on without the United States. Global Environmental Politics 3 (4), pp. 1–23.

Hunt, S.D. and Vitell, S.J. (1986), "A General Theory of Marketing Ethics", *Journal of Macro-marketing*, 6(1), 1986, 5-16

Indo-US civil nuclear deal: http://www.financialexpress.com/news/highlights-of-indous-nuclear-deal/208405

ICTSD: http://ictsd.net/i/publications/11451/

International Centre for Trade and Sustainable Development (ICTSD): http://www.ictsd.org/issarea/dsu/index.htm

International Monetary Fund, World Economic Outlook Database, April 2007

Institute for Trade and Commercial Diplomacy (ITCD):

http://www.commercialdiplomacy.org/index.html

Intercultural Communication Presentation, European Career Orientation available at http://eco.ittralee.ie/personal/presentation.php; Internet

Ilona Nurmela- http://www.juridica.ee/juridica_en.php?document=en/articles/2006/2/101530.SUM.php

IPCC- International Panel on Climate Change, 2007

Irina Pshenichnikova: Doing Business in Russia: Cross-Cultural Focus"

http://www.jyu.fi/economics/opiskelu/kurssimat/YJOCL78Lecture22005.ppt#11

Jeffrey J. Schott, 2004: http://www.cato.org/pubs/journal/cj19n3/cj19n3-5.pdf

Jagers, S., and Stripple, J. (2003), Climate Governance Beyond the State. Global Governance 9 (3),

James K. Sebeneus: The Hidden Challenge of Cross-Border Negotiations-HBS- http://hbr.harvardbusiness.org/2002/03/the-hidden-challenge-of-cross-border-negotiations/ar/1

Jan K. Brueckner-http://en.wikipedia.org/wiki/Codeshare_agreement

Jan Potgieter: http://www.dhhs.tas.gov.au/__data/assets/pdf_file/0004/35374/Collaborative_Negotiation_Strategy.pdf

Japan Services Network, Mission to Geneva: http://www.keidanren.or.jp/english/policy/2000/066.html

John Burton, "EU-Asia Trade Pact in Prospect," The Financial Times, 17 May 2006.

Jeffrey J. Schott, 2004: http://www.cato.org/pubs/journal/cj19n3/cj19n3-5.pdf

John S. Odell (1999) The Negotiation Process and International Economic Organizations, Prepared for delivery at the 1999 Annual Meeting of the American Political Science Association, Atlanta Marriott Marquis and Atlanta Hilton and Towers, September 2-5, 1999. Copyright by the American Political Science Association.

John V. Mitchell (2008), Energy and Environmental Program, Royal Institute of International Affairs, London SW1Y4LE, England; e-mail: john@jvmitchell.demon.co.uk

Kamath: http://www.indianmba.com/Faculty_Column/FC535/fc535.html

Kennedy- http://www.ashgate.com/pdf/SamplePages/Strategic_Negotiation_Ch6.pdf

Kent, George (2002), "Food Trade and Food Rights", *United Nations Chronicle,* Vol. XXXIX, Issue 1 (2002).

K.R. Scherer (2003), Introduction: Cognitive components of emotion, In R.J. Davidson (Ed), Handbook of affective sciences (pp. 563-571), Cary, NC: Oxford University Press, 2003.

Kersten, G.E. (1985), "NEGO – Group Decision Support System", Information and Management, 8(5), 237-246.

Kersten, G.E. and T. Szapiro (1986), "Generalized Approach to Modeling Negotiations", *European Journal of Operational Research,* 26 (1), 142-149.

Kersten, G.E. and S.J. Noronha (1997), "Supporting International Negotiations with a WWW-based System", Interim Report, IR-97-053, IIASA, Austria

Kersten, G.E. and S.J. Noronha (1998), "Negotiations via the World Wide Web: A Cross-cultural Study of Decision Making", Group Decision and Negotiations (to appear).

Kimmel, Paul. Cultural Perspectives on International Negotiations, *Journal of Social Issues,* 50, (1), 1994, PP. 179-196

Kirrane, D.E (1990), "Managing Values: A Systematic Approach to Business Ethics." *Training and Development Journal,* 44, No. 11 (November 1990): 53-60.

Killing, J. (1982), "How to make a global joint venture work," Harvard Business Review, May.

Kimmel, Paul (1994), Cultural Perspectives on International Negotiations, *Journal of Social Issues,* 50, (1), 1994, PP. 179-196

Kirkman, Bradley L., Lowe, Kevin B. and Gibson, Cristina B. (2006), "A Quarter Century of Culture's Consequences: A Review of Empirical Research Incorporating Hofstede's Cultural Values Framework", *Journal of International Business Studies,* 37(3), 2006, 285-320.

Kumarawamy, M.M and Zhang, X.Q, (2001), Governmental Role in BOT-led Infrastructure Development, International *Journal of Project Management,* 19:195-205

Kumaraswamy, M.M., Anvuur, A. and Rahman, M.M. (2005) 'Balancing Contractual and Relational Approaches for PPP success and sustainability', Conference on Public Private Partnerships –Opportunities and Challenges, Feb. 22, 2005, Hong Kong, CICID, The University of Hong Kong and HKIE Civil Divisions, 105-114.

Kwintessential: Language and Culture Specialists: http://www.kwintessential.co.uk/intercultural/play/cards.php

Kolb, D.A. (1974), "Management and the learning process", in Organizational psychology: A book of readings, edited by D.A. Kolb, I.M. Rubin, and J. McIntyre, Englewood Cliffs, N. J.: Prentice Hall.

Lankard, B.A (1987), Practice Ethical Behavior, Connections, School and Work Transitions, Columbus: The National Center for Research in Vocational Education, The Ohio State University, 1987. (ED 288 981)

Lax, D.A. and Sebenius, J.K (1986), The Manager as Negotiator: Bargaining for Cooperation and Competitive Gain, The Free Press: New York, 1986.

LeBaron, Michelle (2003), Bridging Cultural Conflicts: A New Approach for a Changing World. San Francisco: Jossey Bass, 2003.

LeBaron, Michelle (2003), "Culture-Based Negotiation Styles," Beyond Intractability. Eds. Guy Burgess and Heidi Burgess, Conflict Research Consortium, University of Colorado, Boulder, Posted: July 2003: http://www.beyondintractability.org/essay/culture_negotiation/

Le Marquant, D. G. (1990) International Development of the Senegal River. *Water International*, 15 (4): 223-230

Lederach, John Paul (1995), Preparing for Peace, Syracuse, NY: Syracuse University Press, 1995, p. 43.

Leigh Thompson (2001),, 'The Heart and Mind of the Negotiator-2nd Edition', Prentice Hall Business Publishing, (2001)

Lewicki, R. and Litterer, J. (1985), *Negotiation*, Homewood, Illinois: Irwin.

Lewicki, R.J. (1986), "Challenges of Teaching Negotiation", *Negotiation Journal*, **2**(1), 15-27.

Lewicki, Roy J, David Saunders and John Minton, "Zone of Potential Agreement," In *Negotiation, 3rd Edition*. Burr Ridge, IL: Irwin-McGraw Hill, 1999. Pages: 71-74.

Lewicki, R.J, Saunders, D.M., and Minton, J.W. (1999), Negotiation (3rd Ed), McGraw-Hill International Edition.

Lewicki, R. J. Litterer, J. Minton and D. Saunders (1994), Negotiations, Boston, MA: Irwin.

Lewicki, R.J., Litterer, J.A., Minton, J.W. & Saunders, D.M (1994), Negotiation (2nd ed.). Burr Ridge, IL: Richard Irwin. Read Chap. 5: "Negotiation planning and strategy", 1994.

Lewicki, R.J. and Robinson, R.J (1998), "Ethical and Unethical Bargaining Tactics: An Empirical Study," *Journal of Business Ethics*, 17, 1998, 665-692.

Li, S. and M.E. Roloff (2004), Strategic negative emotion in negotiation. Paper presented at the International Association for Conflict Management Conference in Pittsburgh, PA, 2004.

Linkov, I. ed. (2004), "The Role of Risk Assessment in Environmental Security and Emergency Preparedness in the Mediterranean Region," Kluewer, Amsterdam

Lodon School of Economics (2008), Understanding and Challenging Water and Power asymmetry Weekend of 31 May/1 June 2008, Vera Anstey Room, Old Building, London School of Economics and Political Science (LSE)

Love, P.E.D. Irani. Z., Li, H. Tse, R.Y.C and Cheng, E.W.L. (2000), An Empirical Analysis of IT/IS Evaluation in Construction, *International Journal of Construction Information Technology*, 8(2), 21-38.

Luis E. Ore- http://www.wiserearth.org/uploads/file/893b8cdf7a2c0bedbdc08364a9e0c8e0/Cross_Cutural_Negotiation_Capability_for_Foreing_Investors%5B1%5D_sep_2008%20PDF.pdf

Luis E. Ore- http://www.mediate.com/acrcommercial/docs/Negotiating%20Int'l%20Strategic%20Alliances%20Ore%20Article%20IF%20Aug09.pdf

Lynne R. Christen: http://www.quazell.com/library/011401.html

Mac Hart: http://drmalcolmhart.com/userfiles/254960/file/Your_Blind_Spots_Know_Thyself.doc

MacLaren,D: (http://rspas.anu.edu.au/economics/publish/papers/aciar/aciar_2002_mclaren.pdf

M.M. Pillutla and J.K. Murnighan (1996), Unfairness, anger, and spite: Emotional rejections of ultimatum offers. Organizational Behavior and Human Decision Processes, (1996), *68*, 208-224.

MacLeod Roderick (1997), "China Inc: How to do Business with Chinese" *Harper & Row*, 1997

McCaffer, R. and Hassan, T.M. (2002), Changes in large scale infrastructure arising from ICT Developments, *Journal of Building and Construction Management*, 7(1), 1-8.

Madeley, John (2000), *Hungry for Trade: How the Poor Pay for Free Trade* (London: Zed Books, 2000).

Madeley, John (2001), *Food for All: Can Hunger Be Halved?* (London: Panos Institute, 2001).

Mara Olekalns -Emergent Negotiations: Stability and Shifts in Negotiation Dynamics -https://littlehurt.tepper.cmu.edu/gsiadoc/WP/2004-E17.pdf

Mark Kenczyk http://www.negotiationtraining.com/images/Cross-Cultural_Negotiations.doc

Mattoo & Subramanium, 2009- http://www.voxeu.org/index.php?q=node/3367

Max, H. Bazerman, Margaret A Neale (1992), 'Negotiating Rationally', The Free Press - MacMillian, (1992)

Michael, LI; E. Rollof (2006), Strategic Emotion in Negotiation: Cognition, Emotion, and Culture, In G. Riva, M.T. Anguera, B.K. Wiederhold and F. Mantovani (Eds.) From Communication to Presence: Cognition, Emotions and Culture towards the Ultimate Communicative Experience (Ch.8). Festschrift in honor of Luigi Anolli IOS Press, Amsterdam, 2006, (c) All rights reserved – http://www.emergingcommunication.com

Michalle Le Barron-http://www.beyondintractability.org/essay/culture_negotiation

Michal Zieba-Cross cultural negotiation- http://www.calumcoburn.co.uk/articles/cross-cultural-negotiation/

Michael Watkins and Susan Rosegrant (2001), *Breakthrough International Negotiation: How Great Negotiators Transformed the World's Toughest Post-Cold War Conflicts* (San Francisco: Jossey-Bass Publishers, 2001), 26-28.

Miller, P.F., and Coady, W.T (1986), Vocational Ethics: Toward the Development of an Enabling Work Ethic. Springfield: Illinois Department of Adult, Vocational, and Technical Education, 1986. (ED 288 062)

Mooradian, Todd A. and Scott, Swan, K(2006), "Personality-and-Culture: The Case of National Extraversion and Word-of-Mouth", *Journal of Business Research*, 59(6), 2006, 778-785.

Moran, Roberts T. and Stripp, WG., Successful International Business Negotiations, Houston:

Morton Deutsch (1995), eds., B.B. Bunker and Morton Deutsch (San Francisco, Jossey-Bass Inc. Publishers, 1995), 261

Morton Deutsch (2000), "Justice and Conflict" In 'The Handbook of Conflict Resolution: Theory and Practice', ed. M. Deutsch and P.T. Coleman (San Francisco, Jossey-Bass Inc. Publishers, 2000), 43.

Mueller, F. (2003), Is the General Agreement on Tariffs and Trade Article XIX "Unforeseen

Mumford, K. (1996), "Arbitration and ACAS in Britain: A Historical Perspective", Joint Working Parties: A Case Study of the ACAS Approach to Improving Industrial

Relations- British *Journal of Industrial Relations*, http://www.emeraldinsight.com/Insight/viewKeyReadings.do;jsessionid=AA5056B1F30358CB831B8DEF22E27AD5?contentId= 1704488&articleTitle= Joint%20Working %20Parties ::%20A%20Case%20Study%20of%20the%20ACAS%20Approach%20to%20Improving %20Industrial%20Relations

Myers, N. (1997), Environmental refugees. *Population and Environment* 19 (2), pp. 167–182.

Nadejda Stahovski- http://www.sociology.org/content/vol004.003/romanian.html

Najam, A., Huq, S., and Sokona, Y (2003), Climate negotiations beyond Kyoto: developing countries concerns and interests. *Climate Policy* 3 (3), pp. 221–231.

Nakanishi, Masayuki and Kenneth M Johnson (1993), Implications of Self-Disclosure on Conversational Logics, Perceived Communication, Communication Competence, and Social Attraction: A Comparison of Japanese and American Cultures

Neale, M.A and Bazerman, M.H., (1991), "Cognition and Rationality in Negotiation: Negotiation and Cooperation, Coverdale, 2002

Newell, P. (2000), Climate for change: non-state actors and the global politics of the greenhouse. Agricultural & Forest Meteorology, Volume 150, Issue 1, Pages 1-134 (15

Nordhaus, Robert R., Kyle W. Danish, Richard H. Rosenzweig, and Britt Speyer Fleming (2000), "International Emissions Trading Rules as a Compliance Tool: What Is Necessary, Effective, and Workable?" Environmental Law Reporter, October 2000

Novinger, Tracy (2001), Intercultural Communication: A Practical Guide. Austin, TX: University of Texas Press, 2001, p. 121, quoting from Baldrige, Letitia. Letitia Baldrige's New Complete Guide to Executive Manners, New York: Macmillan, 1993, p. 121.

NRDC- The Evolution of International Environmental Governance: http://www.nrdc.org/international/fgovernance.asp

Oberthür, S., and Ott, H. (1999), The Kyoto Protocol: international climate policy for the 21st century. Berlin, Germany: Springer.

Offiong, Daniel A (1997), Conflict Resolution among the Ibibio of Nigeria. *Journal of Anthropological Research*, 53, 4, Winter- 1997, pp. 423-442.

Oliver, Jim R. (1996). "A Machine Learning Approach to Automated Negotiation and Prospects for Electronic Commerce." http://opim.wharton.upenn.edu/-oliver27/papers/jmis.ps. July 31, 1996.

Paterson, M (1996), Global warming and global politics. London: Routledge

Paul Gabriel (2006), "EU to Make Stronger Presence in South-East Asia," The Star (Kuala Lumpur), 6 August 2006

Pechter, K. (1992), "Can we make a Deal?" International Business, 5(3), 46-50

Perdikis, N., W.A. Kerr, and J.E. Hobbs (2001), Reforming the WTO to Defuse Potential Trade Conflicts in Genetically Modified Goods, *The World Economy*, 24(3): 379-398.

Peter Rittgen (2007): Supporting Inter-Business Collaboration via Contract negotiation and enactment http://www.aifb.uni-karlsruhe.de/Forschungsgruppen/BIK/wi2007/papers/wi-2007-1-041.pdf

Philippe Ricard (2006), "L'Union européenne veut placer l'Asie au coeur de sa politique commerciale," [The EU wishes to put Asia at the heart of its trade policy] Le Monde (Paris), 12 September 2006; Paul Falzon, "L'UE ouvre la voie aux accords bilatéraux avec l'Asie," [The EU paves the way for bilateral agreements with Asia] Le Monde (Paris), 13 September 2006.

Prestwich, Roger (2007), Cross-Cultural Negotiating: A Japanese-American Case Study from Higher Education, International Negotiation, Volume 12, Number 1, 2007 , pp. 29-55(27)

Processes of International Negotiation Network (PIN): http://www.iiasa.ac.at/Research/PIN/index.html?sb=1

Production Sharing Contract (PSC): http://www.glossary.oilfield.slb.com/Display.cfm?Term=production%20sharing%20contract

Pruitt, D.G. (1981). *Negotiation Behavior*, New York: Academic Press.

Pruitt, D.G. (1986), Trends in the Study of Negotiation and Mediation, *Negotiation Journal*, 2(3), 237-244.

Putnam, L.L. (1990), Reframing integrative and distributive bargaining: A process Perspective, Research on Negotiation in Organizations, 2, 3-30.

Pye, Lucian W (1992). Chinese Negotiating Style-Commercial Approaches and Cultural Principles, New York: Quorum Books.

Ramcharran, H. (1999), Trade liberalization in services: An analysis of the obstacles and the opportunities for trade expansion by U.S. law firms: http://findarticles.com/p/articles/mi_qa3674/is_199904/ai_n8849050/

Rangaswamy, A. and Shell, G.R, (1994), "Using Computers to Realize Joint Gains in Negotiations: Towards an Electronic Bargaining Table", Computer Assisted Negotiation and Mediation Symposium, Harvard Law School, Cambridge MA.

Ratiu, Indre (1983), "Thinking Internationally: A comparison of How International Executives Learn," International studies of Management and Organization, Vol. 13, pp. 139-150, 1983

Rebecca Johnson (http://www.acronym.org.uk/dd/dd91/91ctbt.htm) on "Unfinished Business", published by the United Nations Institute for Disarmament Research (UNIDIR) in May 2009.

Robert T. Buttram, Robert Folger, and B.H. Sheppard, "Equity, Equality and Need: Three Faces of Social Justice," In Conflict, Cooperation, and Justice: http://www.beyondintractability.org/essay/procedural_justice/

Roger Fisher and William Ury, *Getting to Yes* (New York: Penguin Books, 1983)

Robinson, R.J., Lewicki, R.J. and Donahue, E.M., "Extending and Testing A Five-Factor Model of Ethical and Unethical Bargaining Tactics: Introducing the SINS Scale", *Journal of Organization Behavior*, 21(6), 2000, 649-664.

Roger Fisher and William Ury, *Getting to Yes* (New York: Penguin Books, 1983).

Ross, L., & Stillinger, C. (1991), Barriers to Conflict Resolution, *Negotiation Journal*, 1991, 8, 389-404.

Salacuse, J.W. (1991), Making Global Deals: What Every Executive Should Know About Negotiating Abroad. Random House

Salacuse, J.W. (1998), 'Ten Ways that Culture Affects Negotiating Style: Some Survey Results', *Negotiation Journal*, 14(3) pp.221-240.

Salacuse, Jeswal (2004), The Global Negotiator : Making, Managing and Mending Deals Around the World, Palgrave MacMillan, 2004

Schermerhorn, J.R. Jr.; Bussson, R.S, Elsaid, H and Wilson, H.K. (1985), "Managing the Inter-organizational Context of Management Development in a Developing Country: A Case Study", *Leadership and Organizational Development Journal*, 6(1), 27-32.

Schott, J.J. (ed.) (1998), Launching New Global Trade Talks: An Action Agenda. Washington: Institute for International Economics.

Scott 2005, Strategic Planning, Edinburgh Business School, p. 7/2

Schwartz, P., and Randall, D. (2003), An abrupt climate change scenario and its implications for United States national security, San Francisco: Global Business Network. [Online], retrieved on April 8 2007 from http://www.gbn.com/ArticleDisplayServlet.srv?aid=26231

Sebenius, James K. (2002), "The hidden challenges of cross-border negotiations" *Harvard Business Review*, March 2002

Shibuya, E. (1996). Roaring mice against the tide: the South Pacific islands and agenda-building on global warming. Pacific Affairs, 69 (4), pp. 541–555.

Shubik, M. (1971), "The Dollar Auction Game: A Paradox in Non-cooperative Behavior and Escalation", *Journal of Conflict Resolution*, 15, 109-111.

Sonnesyn, S.E. (1991), Ed. "Four by Four," *Training and Development Journal*, 45, no. 3 (March 1991): 29-37.

Steve Minter-2009: http://www.industryweek.com/articles/are_you_cued_in_to_cultural_intelligence_20200.aspx

Stone, R. (1989), "Negotiating in Asia", Practicing Manager, 9(2), 26-29

Stubbs, R. (1984). "The International Natural Rubber Agreement: Its Negotiation and Operation", *Journal of World Trade Laws*, 18(1), 16-31.

Sunshine, R.B. (1990), Negotiating for International Development, Dordrecht: Martinus Nijhoff Publisher.

Swierczeck, F.W. (1990), "Culture and Negotiation in the Asian Context: Key Issues in the Marketing of Technology", *Journal of Managerial Psychology*, 5(5), 17-24.

Teofilo C. Daquila and Le Huu Huy, "Singapore and ASEAN in the Global Economy: The Case of Free Trade Agreements," Asian Survey, 43:6 (November-December 2003), pp. 911-914.

The Economist, October 15, 2005.

Thierry Rommel (2005), Head of the EU mission to Malaysia, in Riyadi Suparno, "EU, ASEAN View FTA to Boost Trade," The Jakarta Post, 15 July 2005.

Thomas, David, C and Kerr (2004), Inkson's Cultural Intelligence: People Skills for Global Business, San Francisco, Berrett-Koehler Publishers, Inc. 2004

Thomas Noble-http://library.findlaw.com/2001/Jan/1/130785.html

Thomas Noble of Law Offices of Thomas Noble, P.C.: http://library.findlaw.com/2001/Jan/1/130785.html

Thompson, B. L. "Ethics Training Enters the Real World," Training 27, no. 10 (October 1990): 82-94.

Thompson, B.L. (1991), "Negotiation Training: Win-Win a What?" *Training*, 28(6), 31-35.

Thompson, L; V.H. Medvec, V. Seiden and S. Kopelman (2001), Poker face, smiley face, and rant'n'rave: Myths and realities about emotion in negotiation. In M. A. Hogg & R. S.

Tindale (Eds.), *Blackwell Handbook of Social Psychology: Group Processes* (pp. 139-163). Malden, MA: Blackwell Publishers, 2001.

Teofilo C. Daquila and Le Huu Huy, "Singapore and ASEAN in the Global Economy: The Case of Free Trade Agreements," Asian Survey, 43:6 (November-December 2003), pp. 911-914.

Timothy F Hannegan and Francis P Mulvey- http://www.sciencedirect.com/science?_ob=ArticleURL&_udi=B6VGP-3YBB08D-J&_user=10&_rdoc=1&_fmt=&_orig=search&_sort=d&_docanchor=&view=c&_searchStrId=987929139&_rerunOrigin=google&_acct=C000050221&_version=1&_urlVersion=0&_userid=10&md5=c102cbfa79912c0b10216dafac375710

TO Nam Toan, Kazumasa OZAWA- http://management.kochi-tech.ac.jp/PDF/SOCIAL_MANAGEMENT_INFRA/SESSION_B4/smsri_28_Toan.pdf

UNCTAD, Trade Negotiations and Commercial Diplomacy Branch (TNCDB): http://www.unctad.org/Templates/StartPage.asp?intItemID=1917&lang=1

United Nations (2006), "LDCs List" Available via the Internet: http://www.un.org/. World Bank, 2004, Global Economic Prospects 2005: Trade, Regionalism and Development (Washington: World Bank).

UNIDO (1996),Guidelines for infrastructure development through Build-Operate-Transfer (BOT) Projects, UNIDO, Vienna, 309p.

Villagrasa, D. (2002). Kyoto Protocol negotiations: reflections on the role of women: http://www.popline.org/docs/1556/173135.html

Viner, J. (1950), The Customs Union Issue (New York: Carnegie Endowment for International Peace).

Vitell, Scott J., Nwachukwu, S. and Barnes, J(1993), "The Effects of Culture on Ethical Decision Making: An Application of Hofstede's Typology", *Journal of Business Ethics*, 12, 1993, 753-760.

Volkema, R.J. and Fleury, M.T.L., "Alternative Negotiating Conditions and the Choice of Negotiation Tactics: A Cross-cultural Comparison", *Journal of Business Ethics*, 36(4), 2002, 381-398.

Volkema, R.J (2004), "Demographic, Cultural, and Economic Predictors of Perceived Ethicality of Negotiation Behavior: A Nine-Country Analysis", *Journal of Business Research*, 57(1), 2004, 69-78.

Volkema, R.J., Fleck, D., and Hofmeister-Toth, A (2004), "Ethicality in Negotiation: An Analysis of Attitudes, Intentions, and Outcomes", International Negotiation, 9(2), 2004, 315-339.

Vogler, J., and Bretherton, C (2006), The European Union as a protagonist to the United States on climate change. International Studies Perspectives 7 (1), pp. 1–22. Vol. 17, No. 1, pp. 3-26.

Walker, D.E. and Walker, T (2000), Doing Business Internationally: The Guide to Cross-cultural Success (2nd Ed.) McGraw-Hill

Wathne, K.H. and Heide, J.B. (2000), "Opportunism in Interfirm Relationships: Forms, Outcomes, and Solutions", *Journal of Marketing*, 64(4), 2000, 36-51.

Walton, R.E. and McKersie, R.B. (1965), *A Behavioral Theory of Labor Negotiations*. Ithaca, NY: ILR Press.

Watkins, Michael and Susan Rosegrant (2001), Breakthrough International Negotiation: How Great Negotiators Transformed the World's Toughest Post-Cold War Conflicts (San Francisco: Jossey-Bass, 2001), 31.

Watkins, Michael, Susan Rosegrant and Shimon Peres (2001), "BATNAs and ZOPA," In Breakthrough International Negotiation: How Great Negotiators Transformed the World's Toughest Post-Cold War Conflicts. San Francisco: Jossey-Bass Publishers, 2001. Pages: 26-35.

Weiss, Stephen E (1994), "Negotiating with Romans - Part-1," *MIT* - Solan Management Review, Winter, 1994

Weiss-Wik, S, (1983), "Enhancing Negotiators' Successfulness", *Journal of Conflict Resolution*, **27**(4), 706-739.

Weldon, Elizabeth and Karen A. Jehn (1995), Examining Cross-Cultural Differences in Conflict Management Behavior: A Strategy for Future Research, The *International Journal of Conflict Management*, 1995, 6, (4) October, pp. 387-403.

Williamson, O.E (1985), The Economic Institutions of Capitalism, The Free Press: New York, 1985.

Winham, G.R and H.E. Bovis (1979), "Distribution of Benefits in Negotiation", *Journal of Conflict Resolution*, 23(3), 408-424.

Wiseman, Richard L. and Jolene Koester (1993), Intercultural Communication Competence, Newbury Park, CA: Sage Publications, 1993, p. 207.

Woranuj Maneerungsee (2006), "'Vision Group' Says ASEAN and EU Regions Would Benefit from Pact," *The Bangkok Post*, 6 September 2006.

World Bank (1998), Concession for infrastructure: A guide to their design and award, World Bank Technical paper No.339, 194p.

World Trade Law net's Dispute Settlement Commentary (DSC): http://www.worldtradelaw.net/

Xavier Maret-http://assets.panda.org/downloads/ntoasummary.pdf

Xing, F, (1995), "The Chinese Cultural System: Implications for Cross-cultural Management", *SAM Advanced Management Journal*, 60(1), 29-33.

Zhang, X.Q., M.M. Kumaraswamy, 2001. Hong Kong experience in Managing BOT projects, *Journal of Construction Engineering and Management, ASCE*, 127(2):154-162.

Zhang, X.Q., M.M. Kumaraswamy, W. Zheng, and E.Palaneeswaran, (2002), Concessionaire selection for Build-Operate-Transfer tunnel projects in Hong Kong, *Journal of Construction Engineering and Management, ASCE*, 128(2): 155-163.

Zhang, X.Q., 2004. Concessionaire selection: methods and criteria, *Journal of Construction Engineering and Management ASCE*, 130(2):235-244.

Zhang, X.Q., (2005), Paving the way for Public-Private Partnerships in infrastructure development, *Journal of Construction Engineering and Management ASCE*, 131(1):71-80.

Zaki Laidi -http://www.laidi.com/comment/summer2008.pdf

Zartman, I.W. (Ed.), (1994), International Multilateral Negotiation, San Frasico: Jossey-Bass.

ZOPA: http://en.wikipedia.org/wiki/Zopa. **Wertheim: http://iiasa.ac.at/Research/DAS/interneg/training/conflict_overview.html**

Websites

http://www.commercialdiplomacy.org/manuals/trade_negotiations.htm

http://www.indianmba.com/Faculty_Column/FC178/fc178.html

http://www.laynetworks.com/TYPES-OF-NEGOTIATION-IN-ORGANIZATIONS.html

http://www.negotiations.com/articles/negotiation-types/

http://www.negotiationgenius.com/4.htm

http://www.champtrainer.com/content/files/whitepapers/the_psychology_of_negotiation.pdf

http://www.negotiationgenius.com/4.html

http://changingminds.org/disciplines/negotiation/styles/styles.htm

http://en.wikipedia.org/wiki/Negotiation

http://www.beyondintractability.org/essay/zopa/

http://www.negotiations.com/articles/negotiator-agreement/

http://www.springerlink.com/content/j5763734w5rjj752

http://www.calumcoburn.co.uk/articles/cross-cultural-negotiation

http://www.associatedcontent.com/article/12134/characteristics_of_culture_and_their.html?cat=

http://www.routledge-ny.com/textbooks/0415311330/resources/case/06.pdf

http://oncampus.malone.edu/documents/Characteristics_of_Culture.pdf

http://oncampus.malone.edu/documents/Characteristics_of_Culture.pdf

http://en.wikipedia.org/wiki/Technology_and_society

http://www.geocities.com/Athens/Delphi/9158/kwulectureccn8.html

http://www.geocities.com/Athens/Delphi/9158/kwulectureccn8.html

http://www2.iath.virginia.edu/time/research/cultural.html

http://www.indianmba.com/Faculty_Column/FC178/fc178.html

http://www.iveybusinessjournal.com/view_article.asp?intArticle_ID=544

http://workabroadtravel.suite101.com/article.cfm/hofstedes_five_dimensions_of_culture

http://www3.interscience.wiley.com/journal/119547388/abstract?CRETRY=1&SRETRY=0

http://arunkottolli.blogspot.com/2007/01/how-to-avoid-pitfalls-in-cross.html

http://www-rcf.usc.edu/~odell/APSA99.DOC

http://www.moneyinstructor.com/art/freetrade.asp

http://www.depdag.go.id/files/publikasi/berita_menteri_perdagangan/data/keynoteaddress-wto_forumfeb2.doc

http://www.nlc.org/assets/3f3c00db0d8c42bcbb28c3dc5794fdd3/ipissuepapertrade041406.pdf).

http://www.wto.org/gatt_docs/English/SULPDF/92020181.pdf

http://henryckliu.com/page9.html

http://www.wto.org/english/tratop_e/trips_e/t_agm3_e.htm

http://en.wikipedia.org/wiki/Agreement_on_Trade_Related_Investment_Measures

http://jobfunctions.bnet.com/abstract.aspx?docid=321594

http://www.aifb.uni-karlsruhe.de/Forschungsgruppen/BIK/wi2007/papers/wi-2007-1-041.pdf

http://www.springerlink.com/content/2bed0u8tt8a89pg5

http://www1.american.edu/TED/kyoto-emissions.htm

http://www.businessdictionary.com/definition/free-trade-agreement.html

http://www.petersoninstitute.org/publications/papers/paper.cfm?ResearchID=1173

http://www.bangkoklogistics.com/international-business/Three-Barriers-To-International-Trade.html

http://www.dfat.gov.au/media/speeches/department/990428_mtn_challenge.html

http://www.dfat.gov.au/media/speeches/department/990428_mtn_challenge.html.

http://www.dfat.gov.au/media/speeches/department/990428_mtn_challenge.html

http://www.cid.harvard.edu/cidtrade/Papers/das2003.pdf
http://www.witsa.org/papers/WTOCancun03.pdf
http://www.export.gov/fta/
http://trade.ec.europa.eu/doclib/docs/2008/may/tradoc_138792.pdf
http://italy.usembassy.gov/pdf/other/RL33463.pdf
http://www.ruig-gian.org/research/outputs/output.php?ID=124
http://www.springerlink.com/content/k7878861m11h5m15/
http://www.geert-hofstede.com/
http://www.executiveplanet.com/business-etiquette/Germany.html
http://www.executiveplanet.com/businessetiquette/Germany.html
http://www.whitehouse.gov/energy/Chapter8.pdf, www.bushenergy.com
http://www.thunderbird.edu/executive_education/consulting_network/business_consulting_solutions/global_negotiations.htm
http://knowledgenetwork.thunderbird.edu/research/2009/03/04/negotiation
http://changingminds.org/disciplines/negotiation/styles/collaborative_negotiation.htm#col
http://www.articlealley.com/article_202390_15.html
http://www.brianbabcock.com/strategic-negotiation.shtml
http://www.au.af.mil/au/awc/awcgate/ndu/strat-ldr-dm/pt3ch13.html
http://www.google.com/support/jobs/bin/answer.py?answer=162304
http://www.thunderbird.edu/executive_education/consulting_network/business_consulting_solutions/2b344d2b-cf44-44f6-aa53-879f0396d6c5.htm
http://www.allacademic.com/meta/p_mla_apa_research_citation/0/7/0/3/2/p70322_index.html
http://www.negotiations.com/case/political-impact/
http://www.cepr.org/PUBS/bulletin/meets/2209.htm
http://enewschannels.com/2008/03/07/enc2733_053940.php
http://www.mckinseyquarterly.com/Governance/Boards/Governing_joint_ventures_1586
http://www.calpers-governance.org/docs-sof/marketinitiatives/2009-03-26-joint-venture-governance-guidelines.pdf
http://en.wikipedia.org/wiki/Iran%E2%80%93Pakistan%E2%80%93India_gas_pipeline
http://www.financialexpress.com/news/highlights-of-indous-nuclear-deal/208405
http://blogs.ibibo.com/DHARA39/abc-of-indo-us-nuclear-deal
http://banglapedia.search.com.bd/HT/P_0290.htm
http://www.beg.utexas.edu/energyecon/new-era/case_studies/Fiscal_Terms_for_Upstream_Projects.pdf
http://www.emeraldinsight.com/Insight/viewContentItem.do;jsessionid=748C389CEA72EB607C280DA192282119?contentType=Article&hdAction=lnkhtml&contentId=868037
http://www.energy.gov.tt/applicationloader.asp?app=articles&id=817
http://www.energydigital.com/Chevron—CNPC-to-sign-product-sharing-contract-to-develop-Chuandongbei-gas-project_4391.aspx
http://journal.shankarananth.com/?p=167

http://www.negotiations.com/case/contract-renegotiation/
http://www.advancingwomen.com/workplace/hidden_agendas_negotiate.html
http://www.iiasa.ac.at/Admin/PUB/Documents/IR-98-049.pdf
http://portal.acm.org/citation.cfm?id=1451125
schoop@cs.rwth-aachen.de
http://www.sewasie.org/documents/xsw2002.pdf
http://www.acronym.org.uk/ctbt/index.htm
http://www.usaid.gov/our_work/environment/water/transboundary_wrm.html
http://www.worldwatercongress2008.org/resource/authors/abs690_article.pdf
http://www.itcon.org/data/works/att/2006_15.content.06065.pdf

Index

D